". . . a valuable reference book which ought to find a place in every Catholic publication office."—*Catholic Journalist*

". . . a masterful compendium which proves that it is possible to be both scholarly and popular."—*U.S. Catholic*

". . . it is remarkable how the most significant facts are recorded here, even those of a legendary character. This makes the volume ideal for ready reference."—*National Catholic Register*

"DICTIONARY OF SAINTS has used all the latest critical investigations into the lives of the saints . . . We have here a fascinating company of men and women who devoted their lives to Christ in widely varied ways . . . not only a careful and thoughtful presentation of all the saints you would want to know about, but it is delightful reading to dip into."—*America*

"The author is careful to separate legend from history, but includes as legend most of the popular stories about the saints . . . a 'dictionary of saints' is a sine qua non of a church library's reference collection. This one suits the purpose admirably . . . [and] is heartily commended to the pious amateur."—*Church & Synagogue Libraries*

". . . comprehensive . . . abounds with interesting tidbits."—*Christianity Today*

"This readable, up-to-date one-volume compendium . . . gives more about more saints than similar dictionaries."—*Library Journal*

". . . as a reference and resource book this volume contains all the saints the ordinary person will ever seek information about . . . no matter where you start reading in it, it is interesting and hard to put down. That's a compliment to both the saints and the author of the book."—*Spiritual Book News*

POCKET DICTIONARY OF SAINTS

BY JOHN J. DELANEY

Abridged Edition

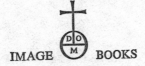

IMAGE BOOKS

A Division of Doubleday & Company, Inc.
Garden City, New York
1983

This abridged Image Book edition published March 1983 by special arrangement with the author and Doubleday & Company, Inc.

ISBN: 0-385-18274-0
Library of Congress Catalog Card Number 79–7783
Copyright © 1980, 1983 by John J. Delaney

To
The two wonderful women in my life
My mother
and
My beloved Ann

CONTENTS

INTRODUCTION

This version of *Dictionary of Saints* has been prepared to provide biographical information about the lives, activities, and spirituality of a group of saints selected from the larger volume in a handy, convenient-sized volume. It is the hope of the author that the reader will find in these pages those saints and *beati* of interest to him or her. The selection is that of the author but in choosing the saints to be included I tried to include as broad a selection as possible to appeal to all tastes. All the biographies included are full and unabridged as they appear in the complete *Dictionary of Saints*. For a more comprehensive collection I refer the reader to that volume.

A word about the saints selected for inclusion in this volume. Among them are saints that some may have felt had been disowned by the Church a few years ago, such as St. Ursula, St. Philomena, St. Barbara, and St. Catherine, when they were dropped from the liturgical calendar. But such is not the case. The Vatican weekly *L'Osservatore Della Domenica* explained it this way: "Generally the removal of a name from the calendar does not mean passing judgment on the nonexistence of a saint or lack of holiness. Many have been removed because all that remains certain about them is their names, and this would say too little to the faithful in comparison with many others. Other feasts were removed because they lacked universal significance." In short, the Church did not rule out the legitimacy of any saint's claim to sainthood in the reorganization of the liturgical year and calendar for the Roman Rite as approved by Pope Paul VI in his 1969 *motu proprio Paschalis mysterii*. It merely relegated to another category (not included in the revised calendar) saints who had formerly been included. The key words of *L'Osservatore*'s remark above is that some saints have been removed "because all that remains *certain* about them is their names . . ." (italics mine).

For much of our knowledge of many saints is not known with any degree of certainty. It is based on legend, myth, tradition, distorted biographies, hearsay—what have you. But as modern scholars know, much that is legendary and mythical is a method—often very practical—of passing to future generation a fact or a truth. Often the core of truth is so embellished and exaggerated over the centuries that it is obscured. But the basic fact or truth is there, often requiring decades of scholarly research to sift aside the accretions of centuries to reveal the truth. And so it is with saints' lives and activities. The human tendency to exaggerate, especially about our greats, is applied to the saints as well as to other people and aspects of history; so one must be careful not to dismiss accounts that seem incredible, for buried therein may be a rich and rewarding lode of truth.

And so much of the information about the lives and activities of the saints included in this volume is based on sources that can by no stretch of the imagination be considered "certain." But in many cases these legends, myths, traditions, and untrustworthy sources are the only sources of information. Consequently I have not hesitated to use such material, but where I have done so I have been careful to point out that the sources are unreliable and the material is often legendary. But I emphasize the core of truth and fact in practically any myth or legend, so such material cannot be arbitrarily discarded in a book of this nature. That myth and legend are often fact in different garb is not sufficiently appreciated though legend, myth, and rumor are frequently integral parts of portraits of even modern and contemporary great figures, despite the modern insistence on factual approaches. The answer, of course, is that though we accept and understand our own myths, we tend to discount those of other eras because the forms they take are often unfamiliar to us. Information from such sources is valid material for reconstructing the lives of long gone people but must be used with care and understanding.

Which brings us to a consideration of the nature of sainthood and how it is achieved. We are all familiar with the modern process of beatification and canonization. Intensive investigation is conducted of the life, holiness, activities, writings, and miracles of the person proposed for canonization, extending over years, decades, even centuries before the infallible papal declaration is made during the elaborate canonization ritual in St. Peter's in Rome, when the Pope declares that a person who died a martyr and/or practiced Christian virtue to a heroic degree is now in heaven and worthy of honor and imitation by the faithful. But this process is a comparatively recent development in the history of the Church. The first official canonization by a Pope was of St. Ulrich by Pope John XV in 993; the process of canonization was not reserved to the Holy See until 1171 by Pope Alexander III; and the present process dates back to 1588, when Pope Sixtus V established the Sacred Congregation of Rites principally to handle cases for beatification and canonization, now handled by the Congregation for the Causes of Saints.

In the early days of Christianity, cults developed around certain holy individuals, which grew until the person was acclaimed a saint. Practically all martyrs in early Christianity were considered saints, though public official honor required the authorization of the local bishop. Many of the claims of these early saints have been investigated officially by the Church in modern times and their cults have been approved or sanctioned; in other such cases the claim has been disallowed. But many of these early saints' claims to sainthood rest on veneration accorded them from earliest times with no records or documents to substantiate their claims surviving. These are accepted by the Church for the recognition given them by their early bishops and contemporaries, but their cults are restricted to local areas. In all probability many of these saints would be unable to withstand the scrutiny given candidates for canonization today, but as I have earlier pointed out, different eras have different methods, and though the methods of making a saint in the past differed from our own criteria it would be eminently unfair to arbitrarily dismiss these earlier saints from veneration by the faithful who desire to pay tribute to them.

All persons recognized as saints by these various means are enrolled in the Canon of the Saints and his or her name is inserted in the Roman Martyrology or official catalogue proposed for the veneration of the Universal Church.

And so included in the present work is a wide variety of saints and *beati*, some canonized or beatified by our modern method but far more by the less demanding criteria of the past. All are worthy of inclusion.

Now for a word on how to use this volume. All entries are

saints unless it is indicated that they are Blessed (Bl.) or Venerable (Ven.), titles given to those persons along the way to canonization who do not necessarily become saints but are worthy of veneration. The names are arranged alphabetically; when there are more than one saint with the same name they are arranged chronologically under that name. Saints with surnames and/or descriptive appellations attached to their names are arranged alphabetically under the saints' names, with the names with no surname or descriptive appellation listed first (and arranged chronologically) followed by the saints' names with surnames and descriptive appellations following arranged alphabetically according to surname.

The numerals after a saint's name are ignored in arranging the order of listing. Also a surname, identifying appellation, and identifying place name are treated alike and arranged in alphabetical order so that John of Avila precedes John the Baptist—the "of" and the "the" being ignored in the alphabetical arrangement.

The dates after each entry are the birth and death dates of the saint. Where there is only one date, preceded by d., it is the date of death. Where c. precedes a date, it indicates there is an uncertainty about that date and that this is the most plausible date without absolute certainty.

There are numerous cross references throughout and they all fall into one of two categories: 1. The cross reference is the name of a person described in another person's entry. In this case the name of the saint will be followed by the date of birth. For example:

OCTAVIUS (d. c. 287). *See* Maurice.

2. The cross reference is merely another name of the saint referred to. For example:

MAUD. *See* Matilda.

In some cases there will be several identical names of persons to whom the reference is made. In such cases the name referred to will have the date of death after it to facilitate tracking it down. For example:

EOGHAN. *See* Eugene (d. c. 618).

For saints in modern times the entry will be found under the surname. For example, Elizabeth Ann Seton will be listed under Seton, Elizabeth Ann; Thomas More will be listed under More, Thomas. Since the time when alphabetizing under surnames became common practice varies, some latitude is taken with names from the thirteenth and fourteenth centuries. In such case the name will be found listed under its most common usages; in some cases, to facilitate finding the name, there will be a dual listing. For example, most people know Bernadette of Lourdes but are not aware that her family name was Soubirous. The main entry is under Soubirous, but there is also a cross reference to Bernadette of Lourdes.

And finally, the date after an entry is the feast date of the saint, which usually, though not always, is the date of his or her death. Where there is no feast date at the end of the entry, there will be a death date in the body of the entry, and this is the feast day.

Though designed to be used for readily accessible and easy-to-use reference, it is the fervent hope of the author that it will be used for more than mere reference and will lead the peruser to further study and a deeper understanding of the saints and an awareness of the riches God has bestowed on mankind in his saints.

POCKET DICTIONARY OF SAINTS

"The Church has always believed that the apostles and Christ's martyrs, who gave the supreme witness of faith and charity by the shedding of their blood, are closely united with us in Christ; she has always venerated them with the Blessed Virgin Mary and the holy angels, with a special love, and has asked piously for the help of their intercession. Soon there were added to these others who had chosen to imitate more closely the virginity and poverty of Christ, and still others whom the outstanding practice of the Christian virtues and the wonderful graces of God recommended to the pious devotion and imitation of the faithful.

"Exactly as Christian communion between men on their earthly pilgrimage brings us closer to Christ, so our community with the saints joins us to Christ, from whom as from its fountain and head issues all graces and the life of the People of God itself. It is most fitting, therefore, that we love those friends and co-heirs of Jesus Christ who are also our brothers and outstanding benefactors, and that we give due thanks to God for them, humbly invoking them, and having recourse to their prayers, their aid and help in obtaining from God through his son, Jesus Christ, Our Lord, our only Redeemer and Savior, the benefits we need. Every authentic witness of love, indeed, offered by us to those who are in heaven tends to and terminates in Christ, 'the crown of all the saints,' and through him in God who is wonderful in his saints, and is glorified in them."

Dogmatic Constitution on the Church, No. 50

A

ABBO OF FLEURY (c. 945–1004). Born near Orléans, France, he studied at Paris, Rheims, and Orléans, and settled at the monastery of Fleury-sur-Loire. In about 986 he became director of the monastery school in Ramsey, Huntingdonshire, England, but returned to Fleury two years later to resume his studies. He was elected abbot in a disputed election, which was not finally accepted until quite some time later through the help of Gerbert, who later became Pope Sylvester II in 999. Abbo fought for monastic independence of bishops, was mediator between the Pope and the King of France, was active in settling disputes in various monasteries, and was murdered while attempting to settle a dispute among the monks at La Réole in Gascony. He was widely known as a scholar in astronomy, mathematics, and philosophy, wrote a life of St. Edmund, and edited a collection of canons. November 13.

ABDECHALAS (d. 341). *See* Simeon Barsabae.

ABDULLAH IBN KAHN. *See* Aretas.

ABEL, BL. THOMAS (c. 1497–1540). After receiving his doctorate in divinity from Oxford, he was ordained, and became chaplain to Catherine of Aragon, wife of Henry VIII. Sent with a letter from Catherine to Emperor Charles V to secure the brief of Pope Julius II permitting Henry to marry Catherine, he told the Emperor the Queen had been coerced into writing the letter and returned to England without the brief. Henry evidently suspected what he had done and harassed him and when he published *Invicta Veritas*, opposing university support of Henry's efforts to end his marriage to Catherine, he was imprisoned in the Tower of London in 1532. Released, he was again arrested, supposedly for his implication in the Holy Maid of Kent affair in 1533, and after six years' imprisonment he was briefly released on parole by the warden. He was again brought back to prison, and the warden was sent to the Tower. Abel was attainted of high treason in 1540 for denying the ecclesiastical supremacy of the King and hanged, drawn, and quartered at Smithfield on July 30 with B. B. Edward Powell and Richard Fetherston. He was one of the fifty-four English martyrs beatified in 1886 by Pope Leo XIII. July 30.

ABIBUS (d. 297). *See* Hipparchus.

ABRAHAM OF KRATIA (474–c. 558). Born in Emesa, Syria, he became a monk but was forced to flee to Constantinople because of raids on the community to which he belonged. He became procurator of a monastery there and when he was twenty-six he became abbot of the monastery in Kratia. After a decade as abbot he decided to leave the monastery and went to Palestine, to seek solitude for a life of contemplation. He was forced to return by his bishop, and shortly after his return was made bishop of Kratia. He served in this office for thirteen years when he again fled to Palestine in quest of solitude and spent the rest of his life in a monastery there. December 6.

ACUTIUS (d. c. 305). *See* Januarius.

ADALBERT OF MAGDEBURG (d. 981). A monk of St. Maximin Benedictine monastery in Trèves, he was sent by Emperor Otto the Great to convert the Russian subjects of Princess Olga at her request after she became a Christian in Constantinople at 70. When Olga's son Svyatoslav, a pagan, took the crown from her in 961, the missionaries were forced to flee, and some were killed near Kiev. Adalbert escaped, spent four years at the imperial court in Mainz, and then was made abbot of Weissenburg abbey, where he became known for his patronage of learning. He was named first archbishop of Magdeburg, Saxony, at Otto's insistence in 962, with jurisdiction over Slavs. He spent the rest of his life trying to spread Christianity among the Wends and reforming religious groups in his diocese. He died on a visit to Merseburg. June 20.

ADALHARD (753–827). Grandson of Charles Martel and son of Bernard, King Pipin's brother, and also known as Adelard, he probably studied under Alcuin, and became a monk at Corbie, Picardy, in 773. Though he preferred the life of the monastery, he was brought to the court by his cousin Charlemagne, and became one of his advisers. He was chief minister to Charlemagne's oldest son, Pepin, and when Pepin died in 810 was named tutor of Pepin's son Benard. Adalhard was exiled to an island off the coast of Aquitaine when accused of supporting a revolt against Emperor Louis the Debonair. After five years Louis decided he was innocent and recalled him to the court in 821, but he was soon after again banished, this time to Corbie, where his reputation for holiness, austerity, and concern for the poor and the sick soon spread. He established another monastery, Corvey in Paderborn, and made both monasteries centers of learning and teaching, not only in Latin but also in the vernacular of German and French. He died at Corbie. January 2.

ADAMNAN (c. 624–704). Born in Drumhome, Donegal, Ireland, he became a monk at the monastery there and later at Iona, of which he became ninth abbot in 679. He gave sanctuary to Aldfrid when the crown of Northumbria was in dispute after the death of Aldfrid's father, King Oswy. In 686, when Aldfrid had ascended the throne, Adamnan visited him to secure the release of Irish prisoners. Two years later Adamnan visited several English monasteries and was induced by St. Ceolfrid to adopt the Roman calendar for Easter. Adamnan worked ceaselessly thereafter with much success to get Irish monks and monasteries to replace their Celtic practices with those of Rome. His success in convincing the Council of Birr that women should be exempt from wars and that women and children should not be taken prisoners or slaughtered caused the agreement to be called Adamnan's law. A scholar noted for his piety, he wrote a life of St. Columba, one of the most important biographies of the early Middle Ages. He also wrote *De locis sanctis,* a description of the East told to him by a Frank bishop, Arculf, whose ship was driven ashore near Iona on the way back from Jerusalem. Adamnan is thought by some in Ireland to be the same as St. Eunan, though this is uncertain. He died at Iona on September 23.

ADAUCTUS (d. c. 304). *See* Felix.

ADDAI (d. c. 180). According to legend, as a result of correspondence between the Oesrvene King Abgar the Black and Christ in which Abgar asked the Lord to cure him of an incurable disease, and Christ promised to send one of his disciples to Abgar, the apostle Thomas sent Addai, one of the seventy-two disciples, to Abgar's court at Edessa, Mesopotamia. Addai cured Abgar and converted him and his people to Christianity. Among the converts was Aggai, the royal jeweler, whom Addai consecrated bishop and named his successor; Aggai later suffered martyrdom for his missionary activities. Addai also sent his disciple Mari as a missionary to Nisibis, Nineveh, and along the Tigris. Mari built churches and monasteries, destroyed pagan temples, and made many converts until his death near Seleucia-Ctesiphon. All that is known with any degree of certainty is that Addai was probably a missioner around Edessa toward the end of the second century and that Addai and Mari have been venerated as the holy apostles of Syria and Persia since earliest times. August 5.

ADELARD. *See* Adalhard.

ADEODATUS I. *See* Deusdedit.

ADILIA. *See* Odilia.

ADJUTOR (d. 1131). A Norman knight and lord of Vernon-sur-Seine, he went on the First Crusade in 1095, was captured by the Moslems, but escaped from prison, and on his return to France became a monk at the abbey of Tiron. He led the life of a recluse there the last years of his life and died at Tiron on April 30.

ADRIAN (d. c. 304). According to legend he was a pagan officer at the imperial court of Nicomedia. Impressed by the courage of a group of Christians who were being tortured, he declared himself a Christian and was imprisoned with them and suffered excruciating tortures before he was put to death. His young wife, Natalia, who was present at his death (she had bribed her way into the prison), comforted him in his agony, recovered one of his severed hands, and took it to Argyropolis near Constantinople, where she fled to escape the importunities of an imperial official of Nicomedia who wanted to marry her. She died there peacefully on December 1. Adrian is the patron of soldiers and butchers. September 8.

ADRIAN (d. 710). Born in Africa, he became abbot of the monastery at Nerida, near Naples, declined an appointment as archbishop of Canterbury, but accompanied St. Theodore to England when the latter was appointed archbishop. Theodore appointed him abbot of SS. Peter and Paul monastery (later changed to St. Augustine's) in Canterbury, and during his thirty-nine years' abbacy the monastery became renowned as a center of learning. He died on January 9 in Canterbury, and his tomb soon became famous for the miracles wrought there.

ADRIAN III (d. 885). Little is known of Adrian or his pontificate and why he is venerated as a saint, though it is known he worked to mitigate the rigors of a famine in Rome. Of Roman descent, he was elected Pope probably on May 17, 884, opposed the aristocratic faction in Rome led by Formosus, bishop of Porto, had George of the Aventine, a member of the Formosan group and notorious for several murders he committed, tried, condemned, and blinded, and had a widow of one of the opposing nobility whipped naked through the streets of Rome. He died either in early September or on July 8 near Modena while on the way to a diet in Worms, Germany, at the invitation of Emperor Charles the Fat, probably to settle the question of Charles' succession. July 8.

ADVENTOR (d. c. 287). *See* Maurice.

AEDH MAC BRICC (d. 589). The lives of this saint are full of extraordinary tales of miracles of healing, transit through the air, and other marvels. The son of Breece of the

Hy Neill, he worked on his father's farm, was dissuaded by Bishop Illathan of Rathlíhen, Offay, from kidnaping a girl from his brothers' household when they refused him his inheritance on his father's death, and remained with the bishop. He founded a monastery at Cill-áir in Westmreath and eventually became a bishop. He is reputed to have cured St. Brigid of a headache, so is often called on to cure headaches. November 10.

AEGIDIUS. A variation of Giles.

AELRED (1110–67). Born in Hexham, England, and also known as Ethelred, he became master of the household in the court of King David of Scotland, beloved for his piety, gentleness, and spirituality. Desiring a more austere life than he could lead at the court, he left Scotland when twenty-four and became a Cistercian monk at Rievaulx, Yorkshire, England. He was made abbot of a new Cistercian monastery in Revesby, Lincolnshire, in 1142, and five years later returned to Rievaulx as abbot. Famed for his preaching and asceticism, he traveled widely in England and Scotland and was considered a saint in his own lifetime. He wrote on the spiritual life in *On Spiritual Friendship* and composed numerous sermons and prayers. He died at Rievaulx on January 12. February 3.

AENGUS MACNISSE. *See* Macanisius.

AGABUS (1st century). A Jewish-Christian prophet from Jerusalem, he came to Antioch, and predicted a famine throughout the Roman Empire (Acts 11:28–29), which actually occurred in 49 during the reign of Emperor Claudius. He is probably the same Agabus who predicted Paul's imprisonment in Jerusalem (Acts 21:10ff.). According to tradition, he died a martyr at Antioch. February 13.

AGAPE (d. 304). Agape and her sisters Chionia and Irene, Christians of Thessalonica, Macedonia, were convicted of possessing texts of the scriptures despite a decree issued in 303 by Emperor Diocletian naming such possessions a crime punishable by death. When they further refused to offer sacrifice to pagan gods the governor, Dulcitius, had Agape and Chionia burned alive. When Irene still refused to recant, Dulcitius ordered her sent to a house of prostitution. There, when

she was unmolested after being exposed naked and chained
she was put to death either by burning or by an arrow
through her throat. April 3.

AGAPITUS (d. 258). *See* Sixtus II.

AGAPITUS I (d. 536). A Roman, son of a priest named
Gordian who had been murdered, Agapitus was archdeacon
of the Roman clergy and an old man when elected Pope on
May 13, 535. He died in Constantinople on April 22 after an
eleven-month reign while on a mission for Ostrogoth King
Theodahad to convince Justinian to call off a threatened invasion of Italy. Agapitus was unsuccessful, but while there
he convinced Justinian to remove Patriarch Anthimus, a monophysite, and replace him with Mennas, whom Agapitus consecrated.

AGATHA (date unknown). According to untrustworthy
legend she was born either in Palermo or Catania, Sicily, of a
wealthy family and early dedicated herself to God and a life
of chastity. During one of the Emperor's persecutions, Quin-
tian, a consul who desired her, used the persecutions as a pre-
text to possess her. When she refused he subjected her to all
kinds of indignities and tortures, sending her to a house of
prostitution, racking her, cutting off her breasts, and then
rolling her over red-hot coals until she died. She is often
depicted in art holding a pair of pincers or bearing her breasts
on a plate; later these were mistaken by some to be bread and
led to the practice of blessing bread on St. Agatha's day. She
is the patron of nurses. February 5.

AGATHO (d. 681). A Sicilian, probably from Palermo, he
was married for twenty years and successful in financial matters when he became a monk at St. Hermes monastery in
Palermo (he may be the Agatho referred to in a letter from
Gregory the Great authorizing the abbot to accept him if his
wife entered a convent). He succeeded Donus as Pope on
June 27, 678. He settled a dispute between Bishop Wilfrid of
York and Archbishop Theodore of Canterbury, but the most
important event of his pontificate was the Council of Constantinople, November 680–September 681, to which Agatho
sent legates and a letter that condemned the monothelite heresy and expounded traditional Catholic belief in two wills in

Christ, one divine, one human. Most bishops there, led by Patriarch George of Constantinople, accepted, saying, "Peter has spoken by Agatho." The monothelite heresy was condemned and Constantinople was reunited to Rome in what is now named the Sixth General Council of the Church. By the time its decrees reached Rome, Agatho had died. January 10.

AGATHUS. *See* Acacius (d. c. 303).

AGGAI (d. c. 180). *See* Addai.

AGILBERT (d. c. 685). A Frank who had studied under abbot Ado at Jouarre monastery in Ireland and was a bishop, he was invited by King Coenwalh of the West Saxons to remain in Wessex as bishop. He was active in missionary activities, ordained St. Wilfrid, and with him was a leader in the group seeking to replace the Celtic customs with Roman at the synod of Whitby. He resigned his see when Coenwalh divided his diocese and returned to France, where he became bishop of Paris in 668. Coenwalh later invited him back but he refused and sent his nephew Eleutherius in his place. October 11.

AGNES (d. c. 304). Of a wealthy Roman family and noted for her beauty, she early resolved to live a life of purity, consecrating her virginity to God. She was denounced as a Christian to the governor during Diocletian's persecution by unsuccessful suitors and though only thirteen refused to be intimidated by the governor's display of instruments of torture. Infuriated, he sent her to a house of prostitution in Rome, where she successfully retained her purity by her saintly bearing, and in one instance by a miracle. When returned to the governor he ordered her beheaded, which was done. (Some authorities believe she was stabbed in the throat.) Although much of her story is unreliable, there is no doubt that Agnes suffered martyrdom and was buried on the Via Nomentana, where a cemetery was named after her. Over the centuries she has become the great Christian symbol of virginal innocence, usually represented in art by a lamb (*agnus*–Agnes). January 21.

AGNES OF ASSISI (c. 1197–1253). Born in Assisi, the younger sister of St. Clare, she joined Clare when fifteen at the Benedictine convent of Sant' Angelo di Panzo, determined to follow her sister's life of poverty and penance, resisted her relatives' attempts to force her to return home, and was given the habit by St. Francis and sent to San Damiano with Clare, thus founding the Poor Clares. She was made abbess of the Poor Clares convent at Monticelli near Florence by Francis in 1219, established convents at Mantua, Venice, and Padua, and supported her sister's struggle for poverty in their order. Agnes was with Clare at her death and died three months later, on November 16, reportedly as predicted by Clare. Many miracles have been reported at her tomb in Santa Chiara church in Assisi.

AGRICOLA (c. 497–580). Son of a Gallo-Roman senator and also known as Arègle, he was made bishop of Chalon-sur-Saône, France, in 532. He was a friend of St. Gregory of Tours, lived a simple, austere life devoted to the spirituality of his people, and in the forty-eight years of his bishopric attended several Church councils and enlarged and beautified many of the churches of his diocese. He died in his see city, March 17.

AIDAN (d. 626). Information about the life of Aidan is entirely from legendary sources. Also known as Maedoc, he was born in Connaught, Ireland, had portents attached to his birth and childhood, and after a stay at Leinster, went to St. David monastery in Wales to study Scripture. He remained there for several years, reputedly repelling several Saxon raids by miracles, and then returned to Ireland, built a monastery at Ferns, Wexford, and eventually was consecrated bishop there. His miracles are legendary and reveal him as a man of great kindness to animals and to his fellow man. He is represented in art by a stag, reputedly because he once made a stag invisible to save it from hounds. January 31.

AIDAN OF LINDISFARNE (d. 651). Born in Ireland, he may have studied under St. Senan before becoming a monk at Iona. At the request of King Oswald of Northumbria, Aidan went to Lindisfarne as bishop and was known throughout the kingdom for his knowledge of the Bible, his learning, his eloquent preaching, his holiness, his distaste for pomp, his kindness to the poor, and the miracles attributed to him. He founded a monastery at Lindisfarne that became known as the English Iona and was a center of learning and missionary activity for all of northern England. He died at the royal castle at Bamburgh. August 31.

AILBHE (d. c. 526). That he was a preacher in Ireland is probably true, but all else about him is known only through legend and myth. Among them is the legend that he was abandoned as an infant, suckled and raised by a wolf, and that years later, while he and some companions were hunting, an aged female wolf ran to him for protection. One story says he was baptized by a priest while a boy in northern Ireland; another that he was baptized and raised in a British settlement in Ireland, and then went to Rome, where he was consecrated a bishop. He undoubtedly was a most effective missionary and may have received a grant from King Aengus of Munster of the Aran Islands for St. Enda, who founded a monastery at Killeaney Inishmore. He is also reputed to have been the first bishop of Emly and the author of a monastic rule. Also known as Ailbe and Albeus, he may have died in 526 or 531 or 541. September 12.

ALACOQUE, MARGARET MARY (1647–90). Daughter of Claude Alacoque and Philiberte Lamyn, she was born on July 22, at L'Hautecour, Burgundy, France, was sent to the Poor Clares' school at Charolles on the death of her father, a notary, when she was eight. She was bedridden for five years with rheumatic fever until she was fifteen and early developed a devotion to the Blessed Sacrament. She refused marriage, and in 1671 she entered the Visitation convent at Paray-le-Monial and was professed the next year. From the time she was twenty, she experienced visions of Christ, and on December 27, 1673, she began a series of revelations that were to continue over the next year and a half. In them Christ informed her she was his chosen instrument to spread devotion to his Sacred Heart, instructed her in a devotion that was to become known as the Nine Fridays and the Holy Hour, and asked that the feast of the Sacred Heart be established. Rebuffed by her superior, Mother de Saumaise, in her efforts to follow the instructions she had received in the visions, she eventually won her over but was unable to convince a group of theologians of the validity of her apparitions, nor was she any more successful with many of the members of her community. She received the support of Bl. Claud La Colombière,

the community's confessor for a time, who declared that the
visions were genuine. In 1683 opposition in the community
ended when Mother Melin was elected superior and named
Margaret Mary her assistant. She later became novice mistress, saw the convent observe the feast of the Sacred Heart
privately beginning in 1686, and two years later a chapel was
built at Paray-le-Monial to honor the Sacred Heart; soon ob-
servation of the feast of the Sacred Heart spread to other
Visitandine convents. Margaret Mary died at Paray-le-Monial
on October 17, and was canonized in 1920. She, St. John
Eudes, and Bl. Claud La Colombière are called the "saints of
the Sacred Heart"; the devotion was officially recognized and
approved by Pope Clement XIII in 1765, seventy-five years
after her death.

ALBAN (d. 304). Probably the first martyr of Britain, his
life story is based on unverifiable legend. According to it, he
was a leading citizen of Verulamium (now St. Albans),
Hertfordshire, England, who hid a priest during the persecution of Diocletian. Alban was so impressed by the priest, he
was converted to Christianity, changed clothes with the priest,
and was mistakenly arrested as the priest because he was
wearing his clothes. When he refused to worship the pagan
gods, he was tortured, ordered to be executed, reportedly performed several miracles on the way to the execution grounds,
and was beheaded. June 22.

ALBERIC (d. 1109). A hermit near Châtillon-sur-Seine,
France, he and fellow hermits built a monastery at Molesmes
with Robert as abbot and Alberic as prior. The monastery
flourished, but new monks ignored the strict rule; Robert left
and Alberic was imprisoned. He left too, returned, was unsuccessful in reforming the monastery, and in 1098 twenty-
one monks left and established a new monastery at Cîteaux
with Robert as abbot, Alberic as prior, and Stephen Harding
as subprior—thus establishing the Cistercians with the three
as cofounders. Robert returned to Molesmes soon after and
Alberic was elected abbot. He restored the primitive Benedictine rule and added new austerities to it, thus putting his
stamp on the Cistercian observance, though his successor,
Stephen Harding, was mainly responsible for the charac-
teristics associated with the Cistercians. Alberic died at
Cîteaux on January 26.

ALBERT THE GREAT (c. 1206–80). Eldest son of the count of Bollstädt, he was born in the family castle at Lauingen, Swabia, Germany, studied at the University of Padua, and in 1223 became a Dominican there despite family opposition. He was teaching at Cologne in 1228 and later taught at Hildesheim, Freiburg-im-Breisgau, Regensburg, and Strasbourg. By the time of his return to Cologne, he had a widespread reputation for his learning and intellect. He went to teach and study at the University of Paris, where he received his doctorate in 1245, and he was named regent of the newly established *studia generalia* at Cologne in 1248. Among his students at Paris and Cologne was Thomas Aquinas, whose genius he early perceived and proclaimed; Aquinas was to be his close friend and comrade in intellect until his death in 1274. Albert was named provincial of his order in 1254, went to Rome in 1256 to defend the mendicant orders against attacks by William of St. Armour (who was condemned later in the year by Pope Alexander IV), and while there served as personal theologian to the Pope. Albert resigned his provincialate in 1257 to devote himself to study, and in 1259 with Peter of Tarentasia and Thomas Aquinas drew up a new study curriculum for the Dominicans. Against his wishes, he was appointed bishop of Regensburg in 1260 but resigned two years later to resume teaching at Cologne. He was active in the Council of Lyons in 1274, working for the reunion of the Greek Church with Rome. He fiercely and brilliantly defended Aquinas and his position against Bishop Stephen Tempier of Paris and a group of theologians at the university there in 1277. In 1278 a memory lapse progressed into two years of ailing health and mind, which led to his death in Cologne on November 15. He was canonized and declared a Doctor of the Church by Pope Pius XI in 1931. Albert was one of the great intellects of the medieval Church. He was one of the first and among the greatest of natural scientists. His knowledge of biology, chemistry, physics, astronomy, geography (one of his treatises proved the earth to be round) was so encyclopedic, he was often accused of magic. He wrote profusely on logic, metaphysics, mathematics, the Bible, and theology. He pioneered the Scholastic method, so brilliantly developed by his pupil and disciple, Thomas Aquinas, by applying Aristotelian methods to revealed doctrine. A keen student of Arabic learning and culture, his and

Aquinas' adaptation of Aristotelian principles to systematic theology and their attempts to reconcile Aristotelianism to Christianity caused bitter opposition among many of their fellow theologians. His brilliance and erudition caused him to be called "the Universal Doctor" by his contemporaries. Among his many works are *Summa theologiae, De unitate intellectus contra Averrem, De vegetabilibus,* and *Summa de creaturis.*

ALBERTA (3rd century). *See* Faith.

ALBERTUS MAGNUS. *See* Albert the Great.

ALBEUS. *See* Ailbhe.

ALCUIN (c. 735–804). Probably born in York, England, he studied under St. Egbert, was a disciple of Bede at the York cathedral school, and in 767 became its head. Under his direction it became a well-known center of learning. He was invited by Charlemagne to set up a school at his court in Aachen in 781 and became Charlemagne's adviser. He was appointed abbot of St. Martin's abbey at Tours in 796 by Charlemagne and later of abbeys at Ferrières, Troyes, and Cormery; it is not certain if Alcuin was ever ordained beyond the diaconate, though some scholars believed he did become a priest in his later years. Under his direction the school at Aachen became one of the greatest centers of learning in Europe. He was the moving force and spirit in the Carolingian renaissance and made the Frankish court the center of European culture and scholarship. He fought illiteracy throughout the kingdom, instituted a system of elementary education, and established a higher educational system based on the study of the seven liberal arts, the trivium and the quadrivium, which was the basis of the curriculum for medieval Europe. He encouraged the use of ancient texts, was an outstanding theologian, and fought the heresy of Adoptionism, which was condemned at the Synod of Frankfurt in 794, and exerted an influence on the Roman liturgy that endured for centuries. He wrote biblical commentaries and verse and was the author of hundreds of letters, many still extant, and a widely used rhetoric text, *Compendia.* He died at St. Martin's in Tours, where he had developed one of his most famous schools, on May 19. Though his cult has never been formally confirmed, he is often referred to as Blessed; he may also have been a Benedictine.

ALDHELM (c. 639–709). Related to King Ine of the West Saxons, he was born in Wessex, England, studied at Malmesbury, probably became a Benedictine monk at Canterbury (though this may have been earlier), and studied there under St. Adrian. He then returned to Malmesbury as director of the school there and about 683 became abbot. He was adviser to Ine, was known for his scholarship and spirituality, advanced education in all of Wessex, founded several monasteries, and was active in supplanting the Celtic liturgical customs with those of Rome. He was appointed bishop of Sherborne in 705 and died on a visitation to Doulting. He wrote Latin poems and a treatise on virginity, composed ballads and songs in English and Latin, and is considered the first English scholar of distinction. May 25.

ALEXANDER (d. c. 113). Tradition has him tortured and executed on the Via Nomentana near Rome with two priests, Eventius and Theodulus, who after a lengthy imprisonment were burned and then beheaded during Hadrian's persecution. Although called Pope Alexander in the Roman Martyrology, it is believed this is an erroneous listing. May 3.

ALEXANDER (d. c. 165). *See* Felicity.

ALEXANDER (d. c. 284). *See* Thalelaeus.

ALEXANDER (d. c. 287). *See* Maurice.

ALEXANDER (d. c. 290). *See* Victor of Marseilles.

ALEXANDER (c. 250–328). Named bishop of Alexandria in 313, he was an implacable opponent of Arianism. When his mild censures failed to bring Arius back to orthodoxy, Alexander excommunicated him at a meeting of his clergy about 321; the excommunication was confirmed by a bishops' council at Alexandria. Alexander is reputed to have drawn up the Acts of the first General Council of Nicaea in 325, where Arianism was formally condemned. He died at Alexandria. February 26.

ALEXANDER (c. 244–340). Elected patriarch of Constantinople in 317, when he was seventy-three, he was known for his wisdom and his holiness. He attended the Council of Nicaea in 325 and was active in his opposition to Arius and Arianism. In 336, Arius came to Constantinople with an order from the Emperor that he be received into the Church there. Reportedly Alexander prayed that either he or Arius be removed; the day before the scheduled reception, Arius died. August 28.

ALEXANDER OF JERUSALEM (d. 251). A native of Cappadocia, he studied at Alexandria, where Origen was a fellow student, and was named bishop of his native city. He was imprisoned for his faith during Severus' persecution but was released and then went on pilgrimage to Jerusalem, where he was made coadjutor in 212—the first known instance of a coadjutor and of a bishop translated from one see to another. He gave refuge to the exiled Origen and participated in Origen's ordination, for which he was censured by Bishop Demetrius of Alexandria. He founded a library and school at Jerusalem, was imprisoned at Caesarea during Decius' persecution, and died in prison there. March 18.

ALEXIS (5th century). An unknown biographer who refers to him only as the "Man of God" states he was the son of a wealthy Roman senator, was known for his charity even as a child, and to please his parents married a wealthy Roman girl. They parted by mutual consent on their wedding day and he went to Syria, where he spent seventeen years in abject poverty and great holiness in a shack adjoining a church dedicated to Mary in Edessa. When a statue of Mary spoke revealing him to the people of Edessa as the "Man of God," he returned to Rome where his father, not recognizing the bedraggled beggar as his son, gave him a job and a place to live under a staircase in his home. Unrecognized by all, he lived there for seventeen years, humbly, uncomplainingly, and patiently; his identity was revealed only at his death, when his autobiography was found. His story spread to the West in the ninth and tenth centuries but was undoubtedly a pious myth. At best, scholars believe he may have lived, died, and was buried in Edessa and was not the man whose bones were found in St. Boniface church in Rome in 1217 and was believed to be those of Alexis, as the "Man of God" came to be called. July 17.

ALIPIUS. *See* Alypius.

ALMACHIUS (d. c. 400). An Eastern ascetic who was stoned to death in Rome when he tried to stop a contest between gladiators in the arena, his death, according to Theodoret, caused Emperor Honorius to abolish gladiatorial contests. He is also known as Telemachus. January 1.

ALMOND, JOHN (1577–1612). Born at Allerton, near Liverpool, England, he spent his boyhood in Ireland, and then studied at the English college in Rheims, where he was ordained in 1598, and in Rome. He was sent on the English mission in 1602 and ministered to the Catholics of England for a decade until he was arrested and imprisoned for a time in 1608. He was again arrested in 1612, and when he refused to take the Oath of Supremacy, he was convicted of treason for being a priest and hanged, drawn, and quartered at Tyburn on December 5. He was canonized as one of the Forty Martyrs of England and Wales by Pope Paul VI in 1970.

ALOYSIUS GONZAGA. *See* Gonzaga, Aloysius.

ALPHEGE (c. 954–1012). Also known as Elphege, he became a Benedictine monk at Deerhurst monastery, Gloucestershire, England, when a young man but left to become a hermit at Bath. He was appointed abbot of the monastery there and enforced a strict rule. Over his objections he was appointed bishop of Winchester in 984, eliminated poverty in his diocese through his aid to the poor, and continued to live a life of great austerity. In 1006 he was appointed archbishop of Canterbury, receiving the pallium from Pope John XVIII in Rome. When the Danes and Earl Edric besieged Canterbury, he refused to leave. When the city fell he was imprisoned for exhorting the pillaging Danes to desist from their murdering and looting. When an epidemic broke out he was released to minister to the ill, but when he refused to pay a ransom of three thousand gold crowns for his permanent release, he was taken to Greenwich and put to death. Danish King Canute brought his body to Canterbury in 1023 from London, where it had been buried. April 19.

ALPHONSUS MARY LIGUORI. *See* Liguori, Alphonsus Mary.

ALTMAN (c. 1020–91). Born at Paderborn, Westphalia, he studied at Paris, was ordained, became canon head of the cathedral school at Paderborn, then provost of the chapter at Aachen and chaplain to Emperor Henry III. Altman went on a pilgrimage to the Holy Land in 1064, was captured with thousands of his fellow pilgrims by the Saracens in Palestine, but eventually reached Jerusalem when they were released through the intercession of a friendly emir. By the time the pilgrimage reached home half the party had died of sickness, hardships, and attacks by the Saracens. He was named bishop of Passau on his return in 1065 through the good offices of dowager Empress Agnes. He put into effect plans to reform the diocese, improve education, and help the poor; he founded an Augustinian abbey at Göttweig, and he reformed several others. When he attempted to enforce Pope Gregory VII's renewal of the decrees forbidding simony and married clergy, most of his clergy refused to obey. The next year his support of Gregory's decree forbidding lay investiture added Emperor Henry to the list of his enemies, and he was driven from his see. He went to Rome, was appointed apostolic delegate to Germany by Gregory, and was again driven from his see when he returned there in 1081. He spent the rest of his life in the abbey of Göttweig, Austria, still working to reform his see. His cult was confirmed by Pope Leo XIII. August 8.

ALYPIUS (c. 360–430). Born at Tagaste, North Africa, he was a close friend of St. Augustine from their childhoods, and studied under him at Carthage, becoming a Manichaean with him until his father forbade him to associate with Augustine. Alypius went to Rome to study law, rejoined Augustine when he came to Rome, accompanied him to Milan, and was baptized with Augustine there in 387. Alypius was with Augustine at Cassiciacum and returned to Africa with him in 388. They lived in a community established by Augustine dedicated to prayer and penance at Tagaste for three years, and then they went to Hippo, where they were both ordained. After a pilgrimage to Palestine, Alypius became bishop of Tagaste about 393, served for more than three decades, and was the confidant and aide of Augustine for the rest of his life. He is prominently featured in the dialogues Augustine wrote at Cassiciacum. His name is also spelled Alipius. August 18.

AMADOUR (no date). Also known as Amator, fanciful legend has him a servant in the household of the Holy Family. He married St. Veronica, was driven from Palestine by a persecution of Christians, and went to Gaul, where he evangelized the area around Bordeaux. He went to Rome, where he witnessed the deaths of Peter and Paul, and then returned to Gaul, where he continued his missionary activities and founded several monasteries. When Veronica died he became a hermit at Quercy, where he built a shrine to our Lady. A shrine at Quercy called Rocamadour did in fact become a great sanctuary. August 20.

AMAND (c. 584–c. 679). Born at Nantes, Lower Poitou, France, he became a monk about 604 at a monastery on the island of Yeu, was ordained at Tours, and then lived as a hermit for fifteen years at Bourges. On his return from a pilgrimage to Rome, he was consecrated a missionary bishop in 629, with no see, and devoted himself to missionary activities in Flanders, Carinthia, and probably Germany. He was banished for censuring King Dagobert I, was recalled, and then despite initial difficulties, was highly successful in evangelizing the area around Ghent. He founded numerous monasteries in Belgium, may have been chosen bishop of Maestricht, but after three years resigned to return to missionary work. He spent the last years of his life as abbot of Elnon, where he died. February 6.

AMATOR. *See* Amadour.

AMATUS (d. c. 630). Born in Grenoble, France, of a Gallo-Roman family, and also known as Amé, he was taken as a child to St. Maurice abbey at Agaunum, where he spent the next thirty years. He became a Benedictine monk there and during his last few years at the abbey, he lived as a hermit. In 614, at the instigation of St. Eustace, he became a monk at the monastery of Luxeuil. He was responsible for the conversion of Romaric, a Merovingian nobleman, who gave his belongings to the poor, became a monk at Luxeuil, and in about 620 founded a double monastery at Habendum (later

renamed Remiremont) with Amatus its first abbot. Amatus
spent the last years of his life there and died there. September 13.

AMBROSE (c. 340–97). Born in Trier, Germany, son of
Ambrose, the praetorian prefect of Gaul, he was taken back
to Rome when a child on the death of his father. He became
a lawyer there noted for his oratory and learning. His success
led Ancius Probus, praetorian prefect of Italy, to name him
his assessor, and Emperor Valentinian appointed him governor of Liguria and Aemilia with his capital at Milan about
372, a position he filled with great ability and justice. In 374
the death of Auxentius, bishop of Milan and an Arian, threw
the city into turmoil as Arians and Catholics fought to have
their candidate made bishop. When Ambrose, nominally a
Christian but not yet baptized, went to the cathedral to attempt to quiet the seething passions, he was unanimously
elected bishop by all parties. Despite his refusal to accept the
office, he was forced to do so when the Emperor confirmed
the election. He was baptized and on December 7, 374, was
consecrated bishop. He gave away all his possessions, began a
study of theology, the Bible, and the great Christian writers
under his former tutor, Simplician, and began to live a life of
great austerity. He soon became the most eloquent preacher
of his day and the most formidable Catholic opponent of
Arianism in the West. He became an adviser to Emperor
Gratian and in 379 persuaded him to outlaw Arianism in the
West. In 383, when Emperor Gratian was killed in battle by
Maximus, Ambrose persuaded Maximus not to attempt to extend his domain into Italy against the new young Emperor
Valentinian II. Ambrose was successful in defeating an attempt by Quintus Aurelius Symmachus to restore the cult of
the goddess of victory in Rome, and in 385 successfully
resisted Valentinian's order to turn over several churches in
Milan to a group headed by Valentinian's mother, Empress
Justina, a secret Arian. In 386, Ambrose flatly refused to
obey an imperial edict that practically proscribed Catholic
gatherings and forbade any opposition to turning churches
over to Arians. When the conflict between Catholics and
Arians deepened, Maximus invaded Italy despite Ambrose's
pleas. Valentinian and Justina fled and sought the aid of Eastern Emperor Theodosius I, who defeated Maximus and had
him executed in Pannonia and restored Valentinian to the

throne; Theodosius now controlled both Eastern and Western empires. At Milan, Theodosius convinced Valentinian to denounce Arianism and recognize Ambrose, but himself soon came into conflict with Ambrose when Ambrose denounced his order to the bishop of Kallinikum, Mesopotamia, to rebuild a Jewish synagogue destroyed by the Christians there, an order he rescinded. In 390, the two clashed again when Theodosius' troops massacred some seven thousand people in Thessalonica in reprisal for the murder of the governor, Butheric, and several of his officers. Ambrose denounced the Emperor for his action and refused him the sacraments until he performed a severe public penance—which Theodosius did. In 393, Valentinian II was murdered in Gaul by Arbogastes, whose envoy, Eugenius, had attempted to restore paganism. Ambrose denounced the murder, and the defeat and execution of Arbogastes at Aquileia by Theodosius finally ended paganism in the Empire. When Theodosius died a few months after his victory, it was in the arms of Ambrose, who preached his funeral oration. Ambrose died two years later, in Milan, on April 4. Ambrose was one of the great figures of early Christianity, and more than any other man he was responsible for the rise of Christianity in the West as the Roman Empire was dying. A fierce defender of the independence of the Church against the secular authority, he wrote profusely on the Bible, theology, asceticism, mainly based on his sermons, and numerous homilies, psalms, and hymns written in iambic dimeter that became the standard for Western hymnody. He brought St. Augustine, who revered him, back to his Catholic faith, baptizing him in 387, and was considered by his contemporaries as the exemplar par excellence of what a bishop should be—holy, learned, courageous, patient, and immovable when necessary for the faith—a worthy Doctor of the Church. His best-known works are *De officiis ministrorum*, a treatise on Christian ethics especially directed to the clergy, *De virginibus*, written for his sister St. Marcellina, and *De fide*, written against the Arians for Gratian. December 7.

AMÉ. *See* Amatus.

AMIDEI, BARTHOLOMEW (d. 1276). *See* Monaldo, Buonfiglio.

AMMON (d. 250). During the trial of a group of Egyptian Christians during Decius' persecution, five of the soldiers guarding the prisoners, Ammon, Zeno, Ptolemy, Ingenes, and Theophilus, exhorted a Christian wavering under torture to stand fast in his faith. When the judge saw what they were doing he had them added to the prisoners and then had them all beheaded. December 20.

ANACLETUS. *See* Cletus.

ANANIAS (1st century). The disciple who was commanded by the Lord to seek out Saul, he brought Saul's eyesight back by laying hands on him and then baptized him (Acts 9:10–19), bringing to Christianity one of its greatest missionaries, Paul. According to tradition, Ananias worked as a missionary in Damascus and Eleutheropolis, and suffered martyrdom. January 25.

ANANIAS (d. 341). *See* Simeon Barsabae.

ANASTASIA (d. c. 65). *See* Basilissa.

ANASTASIA (d. c. 304). Possibly a native of Sirmium, Pannonia, she was martyred during Diocletian's persecution of Christians there. According to legendary sources she was the daughter of Praetextatus, a noble Roman, and married Publius, a pagan. On the death of Publius while he was on a mission to Persia, she went to Aquileia to minister to the Christians suffering persecution during Diocletian's persecution, was herself arrested as a Christian, and was burned to death on the island of Palmaria after a ship she was on with a group of pagan prisoners was miraculously rescued by St. Theodota. She has been venerated in Rome since the fifth century, but aside from that fact all else about her is probably pious fiction. December 25.

ANASTASIUS I (d. 404). Born in Rome, the son of Maximus, he was elected Pope on November 27, 399. His pontificate was marked by his condemnation of Origen, his urging the African bishops to continue their opposition to Donatism, and his personal holiness and poverty. He died in Rome. December 19.

ANASTASIUS (d. c. 1040). The first archbishop of Hungary, he was probably a Croat or a Czech from Bohemia named Radla who became a monk at Brevno taking the name Anastasius (or Astrik or Astericus). He engaged in missionary work among the Magyars, was in the service of the wife of Duke Géza in 997, and was named first abbot of St. Martin's in Pannonhalma, the first monastery in Hungary, which Géza founded. When St. Stephen succeeded his father Géza as duke, Anastasius set up a hierarchy, renewed his evangelization work among the Magyars, to which he devoted the rest of his life, and was appointed archbishop of the Hungarian Church with his see probably at Kalocsa. A visit to Pope Sylvester II in Rome probably was responsible for Stephen receiving papal recognition as King of the Hungarians and his crowning by Emperor Otto III in 1001 with a crown sent by the Pope to him through Anastasius. He worked closely with Stephen the rest of his life and died two years after him. November 12.

ANDRÉ, BROTHER. *See* Bessette, Bl. André.

ANDREW (1st century). The son of John, a fisherman, and brother of Simon Peter, he was a native of Bethsaida, Galilee, and a fisherman. He became a disciple of John the Baptist, and when he met Jesus at Jesus' baptism by the Baptist, Andrew was called to be Christ's first disciple and then brought Peter to Jesus. For a time, they followed him intermittently, but when the Savior returned to Galilee, he called them from their fishing, saying he would make them fishers of men. After Jesus' death, he is reputed to have preached in Scythia and Greece, and later a dubious tradition has him going to Byzantium, where he appointed Stachys bishop. Where and how he died are uncertain, but a very old tradition has him crucified at Patras, Acaia, on an X-shaped cross. He is the patron saint of Russia, though the tradition he preached there is unfounded, and of Scotland, where another tradition says some of his relics were brought in the fourth century in consequence of a dream to St. Rule, who was custodian of Andrew's relics. Reportedly an angel guided Rule to a place called St. Andrew's, and he became its first bishop and evangelized the Scots in the area for three decades. November 30.

ANDREW AVELLINO. *See* Avellino, Andrew.

ANDREW OF CRETE (c. 660–c. 740). Born in Damascus, he became a monk at St. Sabas in Jerusalem when fifteen, was sent to Constantinople by Patriarch Theodore of Jerusalem to accept the decrees of the Council of Constantinople in 685, and stayed on there as head of an orphanage and of an old men's home. He was named archbishop of Gortyna, Crete, and in 712 attended a synod invoked by Phillipicus Bardanes, a monothelite, who had seized the imperial crown and denounced the decisions of the Council of Constantinople. When Anastasius II defeated Bardanes, Pope Constantine accepted the explanation of Andrew's patriarch that he had attended under duress. Also surnamed "of Jerusalem," Andrew was known as a forceful preacher, wrote many hymns, and is believed to have inaugurated a form of hymnody known as *kanon* in the Byzantine liturgy. July 4.

ANDREW OF JERUSALEM. *See* Andrew of Crete.

ANDREW THE TRIBUNE (d. c. 300). A tribune in the army of Galerius sent by Emperor Diocletian against the Persians, he called upon Christ in a battle, and when the army was victorious, he and some of his men decided to become Christians. Discharged by their superior, Antiochus, on Galerius' orders, they were baptized by Bishop Peter of Caesarea, and then arrested by Seleucus, military governor of Cilicia. He had them executed in the Taurus Mountains in Cilicia for their faith. The story is untrustworthy, but Andrew is known in the East as "the Great Martyr." August 19.

ANDRONICUS (d. 304). *See* Tarachus.

ANGELO, BL. (1669–1739). Born at Acri, Italy, he was refused admission to the Capuchins twice but was accepted on his third attempt in 1690, and was ordained. Unsuccessful in his first sermons, he eventually became a famous preacher after a tremendous success when he preached in Naples during Lent in 1711. For the rest of his life, he preached missions in Calabria and Naples, converting thousands and performing many miracles of healing. He was reputed to have had the gifts of prophecy and bilocation, experienced visions and ecstasies and was a sought-after confessor with the ability to see into men's souls. He died in the friary at Acri on October 30, and was beatified in 1825.

ANGILBERT (c. 740–814). Nicknamed "Homer" because of his Latin verses, he was raised at the court of Charlemagne and studied under Alcuin. He married Charlemagne's daughter, Bertha (some scholars believe it was an affair rather than a marriage), but turned to the religious life when his prayers for a successful resistance to a Danish invasion were answered when a storm scattered the Danish fleet. Bertha entered a convent and he became a monk, spending the last years of his life at Centula, of which he was abbot and where he established a library. He also introduced continuous chanting in the abbey, using his three hundred monks in relays to do so. He was a close friend and confidant of Charlemagne, was his court chaplain and privy councilor, undertook several diplomatic missions for the Emperor, and was one of the executors of the Emperor's will. February 18.

ANIANUS (1st century). The apocryphal Acts of Mark have him a shoemaker in Alexandria who became second bishop of the city. Other sources have him a noble who was named bishop by Mark, whom he succeeded. April 25.

ANICETUS (d. c. 166). A Syrian from Emesa, he became Pope about 155 and actively opposed Marcionism and Gnosticism. His pontificate saw the appearance of the controversy between East and West over the date of Easter. St. Polycarp, a disciple of John, is reported to have visited him in Rome about the dispute, which was to accelerate and grow more heated over the following centuries. April 17.

ANNA (1st century). Daughter of Phanuel and a prophetess, she was a widow of eighty-nine, living in the Temple, when the child was presented at the Temple, whereupon she prophesied he was the redeemer of Israel (Luke 2:36–38). September 1.

ANNE (1st century B.C.). According to the apocryphal *Protevangelium of James,* she was the wife of Joachim, both of whom were desolate because of their childlessness. One day while Anne was praying, an angel appeared to her and told her she would have a child, and Anne promised to dedicate the child to God. The child was Mary, mother of Jesus. Other unreliable legends have her born in Nazareth, the daughter of Akar, a nomad. She married Joachim when about twenty and gave birth to Mary when she was forty. Joachim died just after the birth of Christ. All of the above is from untrustworthy sources, and we know nothing with certainty about the grandmother of Jesus, not even her name. July 26.

ANSELM (c. 1033–1109). Born at Aosta, Italy, he was refused entrance to a monastery when he was fifteen because of his father's disapproval, and led a worldly life. He left home in 1056 to study in Burgundy and in 1059 became a disciple and friend of Lanfranc at Bec in Normandy. Anselm became a monk there about 1060 and three years later succeeded Lanfranc as prior when Lanfranc was elected abbot of St. Stephen's in Caen. Anselm was named abbot of Bec in 1078, a position that required him to visit England to inspect abbey property there. In 1092, the English clergy elected Anselm archbishop of Canterbury which position had been vacant since the death of Lanfranc, who had been archbishop since 1070, three years earlier. Anselm refused to compromise the spiritual independence of the archdiocese in consequence, of which King William II (William Rufus) refused his approval. Anselm did not leave Bec until 1093, and almost on his arrival came into bitter dispute with King William. The King refused to permit the calling of needed synods and demanded an exorbitant payment from Anselm as the price of his nomination to the see, and Anselm refused to pay it. Though some recalcitrant bishops backed William, the barons upheld Anselm. In 1097, he went to Rome, where Pope Urban I refused William's demand that he depose Anselm, whereupon William threatened to exile Anselm and confiscated diocesan properties. The Pope supported Anselm, refused his offer to resign, and ordered William to permit Anselm to return to England and to return all confiscated property to him. In 1098, at Urban's request, Anselm attended the Council of Bari and ably defended the *Filioque* of the Creed in the East-West controversy on the procession of the Holy Spirit. Anselm returned to England on the death of William in 1100 but again encountered difficulties with William's successor, Henry II, when Anselm refused the demands of the new King for lay investiture. In 1103, Anselm again went to Rome, and Pope Paschal II supported his refusal of lay inves-

titure of bishops to Henry. Once again Anselm was threatened with exile and confiscation of Church revenues, but a
reconciliation was effected when Henry renounced his right to
the investiture of bishops and abbots, and Anselm in turn
agreed they could pay homage to the King for their temporal
possessions. The reconciliation endured for the rest of Anselm's life, and in 1108, Henry appointed him regent while he
was in Normandy. In 1102, at a council in Westminster, Anselm vigorously denounced the slave trade. Though preoccu-
pied for many years with defending Church rights against English kings, Anselm was a pre-eminent theologian and has
been called "the Father of Scholasticism." He believed revelation and reason could be harmonized and was the first to incorporate successfully the rationalism of Aristotelian dialec-
tics into theology. He was the author of *Monologium*, on the
existence of God, and *Proslogium*, which deduces God's existence from man's notion of a perfect being, which influenced
the great thinkers of later ages, among them Duns Scotus,
Descartes and Hegel. Anselm's *Cur Deus homo?* was the outstanding theological treatise on the Incarnation in the Middle
Ages. Among his other writings are *De fide Trinitatis, De
conceptu virginali, De veritate, Liber apologeticus pro in-
sipiente*, letters, prayers, and meditations. He died at Canterbury on April 21, and was named a Doctor of the Church in
1720.

ANSELM (1036–86). Born at Mantua, Italy, he was named
bishop of Lucca in 1073 by his uncle Pope Alexander II, who
had just vacated the see. Anselm immediately became embroiled in a dispute about imperial investiture and refused to
accept the symbols of his office from Emperor Henry IV. Anselm eventually did, but then retired to the Cluniac monastery
at Polirone and became a Benedictine monk. Recalled by
Pope Gregory VII, he soon became involved with his canons
over their lack of observance of an austere life. When they
were placed under an interdict by the Pope and excommunicated, they revolted, were supported by the Emperor, and in
1079, drove Anselm from his see. He retired to Canossa, became spiritual director of Countess Matilda, reformed the
monks and canons in the territory she controlled, and was a
firm supporter of Pope Gregory's struggle to end lay investiture. After Gregory's death Pope Victor III appointed him
apostolic visitor to administer several dioceses in Lombardy

vacant because of the investiture struggle. He died in Mantua, held in high regard for his holiness, austerity, biblical knowledge, and learning. March 18.

ANSGAR (c. 801–65). Born of a noble family near Amiens, he became a monk at Old Corbie monastery in Picardy and later at New Corbie in Westphalia. He accompanied King Harold to Denmark when the exiled King returned to his native land and engaged in missionary work there; Ansgar's success caused King Björn of Sweden to invite him to that country, and he built the first Christian church in Sweden. He became abbot of New Corbie and first archbishop of Hamburg about 831, and Pope Gregory IV appointed him legate to the Scandinavian countries. He labored at his missionary works for the next fourteen years but saw all he had accomplished destroyed when invading pagan Northmen in 845 destroyed Hamburg and overran the Scandinavian countries, which lapsed into paganism. He was appointed first archbishop of Bremen about 848, and the see was united with that of Hamburg by Pope Nicholas I. Ansgar again returned to Denmark and Sweden in 854 and resumed his missionary activities, converting Erik, King of Jutland. Ansgar's success was due to his great preaching ability, the austerity and holiness of his life, and the miracles he is reputed to have performed. Though called "the Apostle of the North" and the first Christian missionary in Scandinavia, the whole area lapsed into paganism again after his death at Bremen on February 3. His name is also spelled Anskar.

ANSKAR. *See* Ansgar.

ANTELLA, BENEDICT DELL' (1203–68). *See* Monaldo, Buonfiglio.

ANTHELM (1107–78). Born in the castle of Chignin near Chambéry, Savoy, he became a secular priest but joined the Carthusians about 1137. He was sent to the Grande Chartreuse, was elected seventh abbot in 1139, rebuilt its physical facilities, and established it as the mother house of the order. He called the first general chapter of the Carthusians, united the charter houses (previously under the jurisdiction of local bishops), and had Bl. John the Spaniard draw up a constitution for women wishing to live under the Carthusian rule.

He resigned his abbacy in 1152 to live as a hermit but served as prior of Portes in 1154–56. On his return to Grande Chartreuse, he was active in rallying support for Pope Alexander III against antipope Victor IV, who had the backing of Emperor Frederick Barbarossa. Over his objections, Anthelm was named bishop of Belley in 1163. He instituted widespread reforms in the see, restored a celibate clergy, punished wrongdoers, and excommunicated Count Humbert III of Maurienne when one of his priests was killed on a mission to free a priest imprisoned by Humbert. Anthelm retired to Portes to protest the lifting of the excommunication by Pope Alexander but remained on good terms with the Pope, who later asked him to go as papal legate to England to settle the conflict between Henry II and Thomas Becket; unfortunately, he was unable to go. His last years were spent working with lepers and the poor. He died on June 26, and while he lay dying was visited by Humbert seeking his forgiveness.

ANTHERUS (d. 236). A Greek, the son of one Romulus, he was elected Pope on November 21, 235, but ruled only forty-three days when he died on January 3, probably a martyr. During his short tenure, he ordered copies of the trials of the martyrs to be collected and kept in the episcopal archives.

ANTHONY. See Antony.

ANTHONY OF PADUA (1195–1231). Born in Lisbon, Portugal, Ferdinand de Bulhoes was the son of a knight at the court of King Alfonso II of Portugal. He studied as a youth under the priests of the Lisbon cathedral, joined the Canons Regular of St. Augustine at their house near the city when fifteen, and in 1212 was transferred to the priory at Coimbra because he found the visits of friends too disturbing, and was ordained in 1219 or 1220. He transferred to the Franciscans in 1221, taking the name Anthony, went to Morocco to preach to the Moors but was forced to return because of illness, and arrived back in time to participate in a general chapter of his order at Assisi in 1221. He was assigned to the hospice of San Paoli near Forli and at an ordination there delivered a sermon that was to launch him on his career as a preacher. He was assigned to preaching all over Italy and was sensationally successful. His sermons, noted for their eloquence, fire, and persuasiveness, attracted huge crowds everywhere he preached. He was appointed the first lector in theology for the Franciscans, became minister provincial of Emilia or Romagna, was envoy from the 1226 general chapter to Pope Gregory IX, and secured the Pope's release from his official duties to devote himself to preaching. His success as a convertmaker and confessor was phenomenal. He settled in Padua after 1226 and his bold and brilliant preaching, attacking corruption and wrongdoing wherever he saw them, and completely reformed the city. He worked to abolish debtors' prisons, helped the poor, and worked ceaselessly and untiringly with heretics. In 1231, exhausted and plagued with dropsy, he went to Camposanpiero for a brief respite but died on the way back to Padua in a Poor Clare convent at Arcella just outside Padua on June 13 at the age of thirty-six. He was canonized the following year and declared a Doctor of the Church by Pope Pius XII in 1946. Stories of the miracles Anthony wrought and of his preaching prowess are legendary, and he was undoubtedly one of the greatest preachers of all times. His contemporaries called him "Hammer of the Heretics" and "Living Ark of the Covenant," and he is known as the "Wonder Worker" for the miracles he wrought. He is the patron of the poor (alms given for his intercession are called St. Anthony's bread) and oppressed and he is widely invoked for the return of lost articles. His depiction in art with the Infant Jesus on his arm is because of an episode in which a visitor reported this happening.

ANTIDE THOURET, JOAN (1765–1826). Born on November 27 at Sancey-le-Long, France, daughter of a tanner, she became head of her father's household on the death of her mother when she was sixteen; in 1787, she joined the Sisters of Charity of St. Vincent de Paul in Paris. When religious orders in France were abolished by the revolutionary government in 1793, she had not yet been professed and returned to Sancey. She opened a school for children there, aided the poor and sick, and hid priests from the persecution of the revolutionaries. Denounced for this latter activity, she was forced to flee and went to Switzerland in 1796, accompanied the Sisters of Christian Retreat to Germany, but then returned to Switzerland. She was invited to open a school at Besançon and did so in 1799 with four sisters. The community grew, she was placed in charge of the municipal female asylum at Belleveaux, and in 1807 her rule was approved by

Archbishop Le Coz of Besançon. The group spread to Switzerland, Savoy, and Naples, and in 1818, Pope Pius VII gave it his approval with the name Daughters of Charity under the protection of St. Vincent de Paul. When Archbishop de Pressigny of Besançon refused to accept a provision of the Holy See's approbatory brief that future convents of the congregation were to be subject to local bishops and not to the archbishop of Besançon, as had been the situation up to that time, and even forbade members of the community in France to communicate with others outside of France, a schism developed; even Joan was refused admission to the mother house in Besançon. She spent the last years of her life founding convents in Italy, years saddened by her inability to solve the split in her community. She died on August 24, and was canonized in 1934. August 25.

ANTIPAS (d. c. 90). Called by St. John "my faithful witness" (Acts 2:13), he was bishop of Perganum in Asia Minor and was burned to death for his faith during Diocletian's persecution. April 11.

ANTONINUS (3rd century). A soldier in the Theban Legion, he was executed for his Christianity near Piacenza, Italy. Reputedly, some of his blood, kept in a vial, liquefies and bubbles, much as does that of St. Januarius. September 30.

ANTONY (251–356). Born at Koman, near Memphis, Upper Egypt, of well-to-do Christian parents, he distributed their inheritance on their death about 269, placed his sister in a convent, and in 272 became a hermit in a tomb in a cemetery near Koman. He lived a life of prayer, penance, and the strictest austerity, ate only bread and water once a day, and engaged in struggles with the devil and temptations that are legendary. About 285, in quest of greater solitude, he left this hermitage and took up residence in an old fort atop Mount Pispir (now Der el Memun), living in complete solitude and seeing no one, eating only what was thrown to him over the wall of the fort. After twenty years, in 305, he emerged to organize at Fayum the colony of ascetics that had grown around his retreat into a loosely organized monastery with a rule, though each monk lived in solitude except for worship. It was the first Christian monastery. In 311, at the height of

Emperor Maximin's persecution, he went to Alexandria to give encouragement to the Christians being persecuted there. He returned when the persecution subsided and organized another monastery at Pispir but again retired, this time to Mount Kolzim near the Red Sea, with a disciple, Macarius. About 355, Antony again went to Alexandria to join those combating Arianism, working with his close friend St. Athanasius, whose *Vita Antonii* is the chief source of information about Antony. On his return, he retired to a cave on Mount Kolzim, where he received visitors and dispensed advice until his death there on January 17. Antony was the founder of Christian monasticism and was famous all over the civilized world for his holiness, asceticism, and wisdom, and was consulted by people from all walks of life, from Emperor Constantine to the humblest monk. January 17.

ANTONY OF HOORNAER (d. 1572). *See* Pieck, Nicholas.

ANTONY PECHERSKY (983–1073). Born at Lubech, Ukraine, he became a hermit but decided he needed to be educated for that life and went to Mount Athos, where he became a hermit attached to the monastery of Esphigmenou. After several years there, he returned to Russia and built a hermitage at Kiev on the Dnieper River. His wisdom and holiness attracted others seeking the eremitical life, and from these beginnings grew the Caves of Kiev (Kiev-Pecherskaya Laura), the first Russian monastery established by Russian monks for Russians, on land granted him by Prince Syaslav. Antony established another monastery at Chernigov but returned to his cave at the Pecherskaya Laura and lived there the rest of his life. With Theodosius Pechersky, he is considered the father of Russian monasticism. July 10.

ANTONY OF WEERT (d. 1572). *See* Pieck, Nicholas.

APHRAATES (d. c. 345). Of a pagan family, he was born in Syria on the Persian border, was converted to Christianity, and became a hermit at Edessa in Mesopotamia, living in the greatest austerity. He then moved to a hermitage next to a monastery in Antioch and attracted great numbers of visitors drawn by his holiness and reported miracles. He publicly opposed the Arians, who tried to have him exiled, but Emperor

Valens refused to do so, reportedly because he thought the death of one of his attendants who had threatened to murder Aphraates was retribution for his threat. Some scholars consider him to be the same as the bishop of the monastery of Mar Mattai near Mosul, Mesopotamia, and the author of *Demonstrations,* twenty-three treatises written between 336 and 345, the oldest extant document of the Church in Syria, which give a survey of the Christian faith, who may have suffered persecution at the hands of King Sapor the Great and was known as "the Persian Sage." April 7.

APOLLINARIS (d. c. 179). Bishop of Hierapolis, Phrygia, Claudius Apollinaris was famed for his teaching and his writings, none of which have survived. In them he attacked various heretics, particularly the Encratites and the Montanists. He was called "the Apologist" for an apologia of Christianity he directed to Emperor Marcus Aurelius. In it Apollinaris described a miracle that had brought victory to the Emperor in Germany when his army was surrounded by Quadi in Moravia and threatened with annihilation—a miracle ascribed by Apollinaris to the prayers of the 12th Legion, which was mainly Christian. The apologia resulted in an imperial edict forbidding the denunciation of Christians for their religion. He is also known as Apollinaris the Apologist. January 8.

APOLLINARIS THE APOLOGIST. *See* Apollinaris (d. c. 179).

APOLLONIA (d. 249). During the reign of Emperor Philip, mobs at Alexandria ranged the streets torturing and killing Christians. Among their victims was Apollonia, an old deaconess, who was tortured when she would not renounce her Christianity and when given a moment's respite leaped voluntarily into the fire the mob had built and was threatening to throw her into. She is represented in art by a gold tooth or pincer, since her teeth were pulled out during her torture. In the same mob action, Metras, an old man, was tortured and stoned to death; Quinta was scourged and stoned to death when she refused to sacrifice to pagan gods; and Serapion was tortured and thrown from the roof of his home to his death. Apollonia is the patron of dentists. February 9.

APOLLONIUS THE APOLOGIST (d. c. 185). A Roman

senator, he became a Christian and was denounced by one of his slaves to Perennis, the praetorian prefect, for his Christianity. Though the slave was put to death as an informer, Perennis demanded that Apollonius renounce his Christianity. When the senator refused, the case was remanded to the Senate, where a remarkable dialogue took place between Perennis and Apollonius in which Apollonius defended his religion. Despite his eloquent defense, Apollonius was sentenced to death and beheaded. April 18.

APPHIA (1st century). *See* Philemon.

AQUILA (1st century). A Jewish tentmaker, he and his wife Prisca (or Priscilla) were forced to leave Rome when Emperor Claudius forbade Jews to live there. They went to Corinth, where St. Paul lived with them during his stay there and may have converted them to Christianity. They accompanied Paul to Ephesus and remained there; Paul stayed with them on his third missionary journey. They then returned to Rome, where their house was also used as a church and then went back to Ephesus. They suffered martyrdom in Asia Minor, according to the Roman Martyrology, but a tradition has them martyred in Rome. July 8.

AQUINAS. *See* Thomas Aquinas.

ARAGHT. *See* Attracta.

ARCHIPPUS (1st century). Traditionally considered the first bishop of Colossae, he was admonished by St. Paul, "Remember the service that the Lord wants you to do and try to carry it out." (Col. 4:17). March 20.

ARÈGLE. *See* Agricola (d. 280).

ARETAS (d. 523). Chief of the Beno Harith community of Hadran in southwestern Arabia and also known as Abdullah Ibn Kahn, he and 340 of the townspeople were massacred after they had been offered and accepted amnesty from the band of Jews under Dhu Nowas (Dunaan), a convert to Judaism who had led a revolt against the Aksumite Ethiopians. The massacre horrified the entire civilized world and was denounced by Mohammed in the Koran. October 24.

ARNOUL. Another form of Arnulf.

ARNULF (d. c. 643). Of noble parents, he was a member of the court of King Theodebert II of Austrasia, a valiant warrior, and a valued adviser. He married the noble Doda (the marriage of his son Ansegisel to Begga, daughter of Pepin of Landen, produced the Carolingian line of Kings of France), and when Doda became a nun, despite his desire to retire to the monastery of Lérins, he was made bishop of Metz about 610. He played a prominent role in affairs of state, was one of those instrumental in making Clotaire of Neustria king of Austrasia, was chief counselor to Dagobert, son of King Clotaire, when the King appointed him King of Austrasia, and then, about 626, Arnulf resigned his bishopric to retire to a hermitage (later Remiremont monastery), where he died. July 18.

ARROWSMITH, EDMUND (1585–1628). Son of a farmer, he was born at Haydock, England, baptized Brian, but always used his confirmation name of Edmund. The family was constantly harassed for its adherence to Catholicism, and in 1605 Edmund left England and went to Douai to study for the priesthood. He was ordained in 1612 and sent on the English mission the following year. He ministered to the Catholics of Lancashire without incident until about 1622, when he was arrested and questioned by the Protestant bishop of Chester. He was released when King James ordered all arrested priests be freed, joined the Jesuits in 1624, and in 1628 was arrested when betrayed by a young man he had censured for an incestuous marriage. He was convicted of being a Catholic priest, sentenced to death, and hanged, drawn, and quartered at Lancaster on August 28. He was canonized as one of the Forty Martyrs of England and Wales by Pope Paul VI in 1970.

ARS, CURÉ D'. *See* Vianney, John Baptist.

ARSACIUS (d. 358). A Persian in the Roman army, he was persecuted for his Christianity during the reign of Emperor Licinius but was then released. Arsacius became a hermit on a tower in Nicomedia, was known for his miracles and the gift of prevision, and was killed on August 24 in an earthquake he had predicted. August 16.

ARSENIUS (c. 355–c. 450). At the recommendation of Pope St. Damasus, Emperor Theodosius the Great appointed the Roman deacon Arsenius tutor of his children. He served at the court for a decade, and about 395 he left Constantinople to live with the monks at Alexandria. On the death of Theodosius, he retired to the wilderness of Skete, was tutored in eremitical customs by St. John the Dwarf, and lived in the greatest austerity, refusing the legacy left him by a relative who was a senator, preferring the life of a solitary to the life of luxury he could have enjoyed with the legacy. Forced to leave Skete about 434 because of barbarian raids, he spent the next ten years on the rock of Troë in Memphis, spent some time on the island of Canopus near Alexandria, but then returned to Troë, where he died. He is often surnamed "the Great." July 19.

ASTERICUS. *See* Anastasius (d. c. 1040).

ASTERIUS (d. c. 284). *See* Thalelaeus.

ASTRIK. *See* Anastasius (d. c. 1040).

ATHANASIUS (c. 297–373). Probably born of Christian parents at Alexandria, he was well educated, especially in Scripture and theology, was ordained a deacon, and became secretary to Bishop Alexander of his native city about 318. Athanasius was present with his bishop at the Council of Nicaea, which condemned Arianism and excommunicated Arius. Athanasius was elected bishop of Alexandria on Alexander's death about 327 and in addition to his rule as bishop of the city became the spiritual head of the desert hermits and of Ethiopia. He was immediately confronted with a revival of Arianism in Egypt and its rapid growth throughout the Mediterranean world and the continued schism of the Meletians who supported the Arians. In 330, Eusebius of Nicomedia, a supporter of Arius, persuaded Emperor Constantine to direct Athanasius to admit Arius to communion. When Athanasius flatly refused, Eusebius incited the Meletians to use every means to discredit Athanasius; they charged him with various crimes, and when he was cleared at a trial before Constantine they accused him of murdering Arsenius, a Meletian bishop everyone knew was alive and in hiding. Aware of this, Athanasius refused the summons of the Meletians to attend a synod

to answer the preposterous charge but was obliged to attend a
council at Tyre in 335 when summoned by the Emperor. The
council was completely dominated by his enemies and presided over by the Arian who had usurped the bishopric of
Antioch. Athanasius was found guilty, and though the Emperor, after an interview with Athanasius, repudiated the
findings of the Council, he later reversed himself, and Athanasius in 336 was banished to Trier in Germany. When Constantine died in 337 and his Empire was divided among his
sons, Constantine II, Constans, and Constantius, Constantine
recalled him to his see in 338. Eusebius then denounced him
to Constantius (Alexandria was in Constantius' portion of
the Empire) for sedition and succeeded in having Athanasius
again deposed at a synod at Antioch and an Arian bishop intruded into his see. A letter from this synod asking Pope St.
Julius to confirm its actions was followed by another one
from the orthodox bishops of Egypt supporting Athanasius, a
copy of which was also sent to the bishops in the West. When
Gregory, a Cappadocian, was installed as archbishop supplanting Athanasius, riots broke out in Alexandria. Athanasius
then went to Rome to attend a synod suggested to Pope
Julian I to hear the case; when none of the Eusebians showed
up for the synod, it proceeded with its deliberations and completely vindicated Athanasius, a decision that was confirmed
by the Council of Sardinia. It was while he was in Rome that
Athanasius established close contact with the bishops of the
West who supported him in his struggles. He was unable to
return until Gregory died in 345, and Constantius, at the urging of his brother Constans, the Western Emperor, unwillingly restored Athanasius to his see. But when Constans
was assassinated in 350, Constantius, now Emperor of both
East and West, moved to exterminate orthodoxy and deal
with Athanasius once and for all. Constantius caused packed
councils at Arles in 353 and at Milan in 355 to condemn
Athanasius and exiled Pope Liberius to Thrace, where he
forced him to agree to the censures. Arianism was now in
control, but Athanasius continued to resist until one night soldiers broke into his church, killing and wounding many in the
congregation. He fled to the desert and was protected there by
the monks for the next six years while an Arian bishop,
George of Cappadocia, occupied his see. It was during these
years that he wrote many of his great theological works.
When Constantius died in 361, George was murdered soon

after, to be briefly succeeded by Pistus. When the new Emperor, Julian the Apostate, revoked all of his predecessor's banishments of bishops, Athanasius returned to Alexandria. Soon, however, he came into conflict with the new Emperor when he opposed his plans to paganize the Empire and was again forced to flee to the desert. When Julian was killed in 363, Athanasius was brought back by Emperor Jovian, but on his death after only an eight-month reign Athanasius was forced into hiding for the fifth time when the new Emperor, Valens, banished all orthodox bishops in 365. He revoked the order four months later, and Athanasius, after seventeen years of on-and-off exile, returned to his see and spent the last seven years of his life in Alexandria helping build the new Nicene party whose support secured the triumph of orthodoxy over Arianism at the General Council of Constantinople in 381. He died in Alexandria on May 2. Athanasius is one of the great figures of Christianity. A Doctor of the Church and called "the champion of orthodoxy," he resolutely opposed one of the greatest threats Christianity ever faced—Arianism—and persevered in the face of trials and difficulties that at times seemed insuperable in a struggle that was eventually won. A friend of the monks Pacholius and Serapion and St. Antony, whose biography he wrote, he aided the ascetic movement in Egypt and was the first to introduce knowledge of monasticism to the West. Through it all, he guided his flock and found time to write treatises on Catholic doctrine that illuminated the areas in which he wrote. Among his outstanding works are *Contra gentes* and *De incarnatione verbi Dei*, defenses of the Incarnation and redemption written early in his life (318–23), and the major treatises he produced in exile: *Apologia to Constantius, Defense of Flight, Letter to the Monks,* and *History of the Arians.* He did not write the Athanasian Creed, but it was drawn from his writings, probably by some unknown cleric.

ATHANASIUS THE ATHONITE (c. 920–c. 1000). Son of an Antiochene and baptized Abraham, he was born at Trebizond, studied at Constantinople, and became a monk, taking the name Athanasius, at St. Michael's monastery at Kymina, Bithynia, a *laura* (a group of monasteries where the monks lived individual lives around their church). To avoid being named abbot of St. Michael's he went to Mount Athos in Greece. There an old friend from Constantinople,

Nicephorus Phocas, asked his help in preparing an expedition against the Saracens. On its successful completion, Athanasius returned to Mount Athos and with money given him by a grateful Phocas began the first monastery on Athos in 961. When Nicephorus Phocas became Emperor, Athanasius fled to Cyprus to avoid being called to the court, but the Emperor found him, reassured him, and gave him money to continue his work on Athos. Athanasius encountered great opposition from hermits living on Mount Athos long before he had arrived there as he attempted to install the *laura* system there. He escaped two murder attempts, and resistance ended only when Emperor John Tzimisces forbade any opposition to Athanasius. In time he became superior over fifty-eight communities of monks and hermits on the Mount. Thousands of monks still live and pray there today; it is now and has been for centuries the center of Eastern Orthodox monasticism and not in communion with Rome. Athanasius and five of his monks were killed when the arch of a church on which they were working collapsed. July 5.

ATTALAS (d. 627). Born in Burgundy, he studied under Bishop Aregius of Gap, became a monk at Lérins, but then went to Luxeuil under St. Columban in search of a stricter rule. Attalas accompanied Columban when the Irish monk missionaries in France were exiled by King Theodoric of Austrasia when Columban denounced him for his concubines. Eventually they founded a monastery at Bobbio, between Milan and Genoa in Italy, on land granted them by King Agilulf of the Lombards. When Columban died a year later in 615, Attalas became abbot. Despite some opposition to the rigor and severity of his rule, Bobbio under his abbacy became one of the great monastic centers of northern Italy. Like Columban, he was a vigorous opponent of Arianism, and was known for the miracles he performed. He died at Bobbio and was buried there in the tomb with Columban. March 10.

ATTRACTA (6th century). Also known as Araght, legend has her the daughter of a noble Irish family who, when refused permission by her father to become a nun, fled to St. Patrick at Coolavin and received the veil from him. She founded a hospice on Lough Gara, which endured for a thousand years as Killaraght. The legends also attribute spectacular miracles to her. In reality, she probably lived a century after Patrick. August 11.

AUBERT (d. c. 725). The bishop of Avranches, France, he built Mont St. Michel early in the eighth century in response to an order from St. Michael he received in a vision. September 10.

AUBIERGE. *See* Ethelburga (d. c. 664).

AUDOENUS. *See* Ouen.

AUDOMARUS. *See* Omer.

AUDREY. *See* Etheldreda.

AUGUSTINE (354–430). Born at Tagaste, northern Africa, son of Patricius, a pagan Roman official, and Monica, a Christian, he received a Christian upbringing and in 370 went to the university at Carthage to study rhetoric with a view to becoming a lawyer. He gave up law to devote himself to literary pursuits and gradually abandoned his Christian faith, taking a mistress with whom he lived fifteen years and who bore him a son, Adeodatus, in 372. He became keenly interested in philosophy and about 373 he embraced Manichaeism. After teaching at Tagaste and Carthage for the next decade, he went to Rome in 383 and opened a school of rhetoric but became discouraged with his students' attitudes, and in 384 he accepted the chair of rhetoric at Milan. There, impressed by the sermons of Ambrose, bishop of Milan, and of his tutor, Simplicianus, he returned to his Christian faith and was baptized on Easter Eve in 387. With his mother, brother, and several others, he lived a community life of prayer and meditation. Later in 387, he started back to Africa, and on the way, Monica died at Ostia. The following year he founded a sort of monastery at Tagaste, and in 389 Adeodatus died. In 391, he was seized by the populace of Hippo and ordained there. He established a religious community and though continuing to live a monastic life, began to preach; he met with phenomenal success. In 395, he was made coadjutor to Bishop Valerius of Hippo and succeeded to the see on Valerius' death the following year. He became the dominant figure in African Church affairs and was the leader in the bitter fights against Manichaeism, Donatism, and Pelagianism. He died at Hippo during Genseric's siege of the city on August 28. Augustine's towering intellect molded the thought of Western Christianity to such an extent that his ideas dominated the thinking of the Western world for a thousand years after his death. He wrote profusely, expositing and defending the faith, and to this day many of his two hundred treatises, some three hundred letters, and nearly four hundred sermons are of major import in theology and philosophy. Among his best-known works are his *Confessions,* one of the great spiritual classics of all times; *City of God,* a magnificent exposition of a Christian philosophy of history; *De Trinitate; De doctrina christiana; Enchiridion;* and his treatises against the Manichaeans and the Pelagians. Called Doctor of Grace, he is one of the greatest of the Fathers and Doctors of the Church, and with the possible exception of Thomas Aquinas, the greatest single intellect the Catholic Church has ever produced. August 28.

AUGUSTINE OF CANTERBURY (d. 604). A Roman, and prior of St. Andrew's monastery in Rome, he was sent with some forty of his monks by Pope St. Gregory the Great to evangelize the English in 596. Although the group desired to turn back, Gregory refused them permission to do so and they landed on the isle of Thanet in England in 597. They were favorably received by King Ethelbert of Kent, who was baptized the year of their arrival. Augustine then went to France to be consecrated bishop and on his return was highly successful, making thousands of converts. He built a church and Benedictine monastery at Canterbury on land given him by the King but was unsuccessful in his attempts to convince the bishops observing the Celtic rites in Britain to adopt the discipline and practices of Rome; they also refused to recognize him as their metropolitan. He spent the rest of his life working in Kent and established sees at London and Rochester. He died on May 26, the first archbishop of Canterbury and "the Apostle of the English." He was sometimes called Austin. May 27.

AUSTIN. *See* Augustine of Canterbury.

AUXENTIUS (d. 473). The son of Addas, a Persian, he was an equestrian guard of Emperor Theodosius who left the

guard to become a hermit in the desolate area around Mount
Oxia near Constantinople. He later cleared himself of charges
of Eutychianism before Emperor Marcion and resumed his
eremitical life on Mount Skopa near Chalcedon, where he attracted numerous disciples by his austerity and holiness. He
also attracted a group of women who formed a community of
nuns at the foot of the mountain. He died in his hermitage on
Skopa on February 14.

AVELLINO, ANDREW (1521–1608). Born at Cas-
tronuovo, Italy, he was baptized Lorenzo, studied civil and
canon law in Naples, received his doctorate, and was ordained. After a period as a canon lawyer, he turned to pastoral work and in 1556 was assigned the task of reforming Sant'
Arcangelo convent in Baiano, where he was almost killed by
those opposing his reforms. He left Baiano and joined the
Theatines in Naples, taking the name Andrew. He eventually
became superior of the Naples house and was known for his
efforts to improve the quality of priests. In 1570, he was sent
to Lombardy at the request of St. Charles Borromeo, founded
houses at Milan and Piacenza, and was most successful in reforming the area in spite of great resistance. He returned to
Naples in 1582 and spent the rest of his life ministering to the
spiritual needs of his people, converting many and combating
Protestantism. He is credited with many miracles, and blood
taken from his body after his death was reported to bubble
like that of St. Januarius, also in Naples. An investigation of
the matter by Msgr. Pamphili (later Pope Innocent X) gave
no credence to the report. Andrew Avellino died in Naples on
November 10.

B

BACCHUS (d. 303). *See* Sergius.

BAIRRE. *See* Finbar.

BALTHASAR (1st century). It is related (in Matt. 2:1–2) that wise men came from the East to worship the Infant Jesus. They were queried by Herod as to the child's whereabouts, found the child, "did him homage," and "offered him gifts of gold and frankincense and myrrh." Warned in a dream, they returned to their own country by a different route so they did not have to report to Herod where Jesus could be found. Ancient tradition calls them "magi" and says there were three of them, named Balthasar, Caspar, and Melchior. Modern scholars believe they were astrologers from Babylonia or Arabia. July 23.

✗ **BARAT, MADELEINE SOPHIE** (1779–1865). Born at Joigny, Burgundy, France, on December 12, the daughter of a cooper, she was educated by her older brother Louis, who later became a priest and who imposed the strictest discipline and penances on her. On his recommendation, Fr. Varin, who planned to form an institute of women to teach girls, a female counterpart of the Jesuits, received her and three companions into the religious life in 1800, thus founding the Society of the Sacred Heart of Jesus. They founded their first convent and school at Amiens the following year, and in 1802 Madeleine, though the youngest member of the group, now grown to twenty-three, was appointed superior; she was to rule for sixty-three years. The Society spread throughout France, absorbed a community of Visitation nuns at Grenoble in 1804 (among whom was Bl. Philippine Duchesne, who was to bring the Society to the United States in 1818), and received formal approval from Pope Leo XII in 1826. In 1830 the Society's novitiate at Poitiers was closed by the revolution, and Madeleine founded a new novitiate in Switzerland. By the time of her death in Paris on May 21, she had opened more than one hundred houses and schools in twelve countries. She was canonized in 1925. May 25.

BARBARA (4th century). Although one of the most popular saints of the Middle Ages, scholars doubt if there ever really was a virgin martyr named Barbara. An elaborate legend has her the daughter of a pagan *paynim* Dioscorus in the time of Emperor Maximian who resisted her father's demands that she marry. She lived in a tower, and during the absence of her father had three windows built into a bathhouse he was having constructed (she did this to explain the Trinity), but was miraculously spared the wrath of her father when he returned and found what she had done. However, he took her before a judge, who had her tortured. Not satisfied with this punishment, her father took her up a mountain, killed her, and was then destroyed by fire from heaven as he came down from the mountain. The site of her martyrdom was variously described as at Antioch, Heliopolis, Nicomedia, and Rome. She is one of the Fourteen Holy Helpers and is the patroness of architects and builders. December 4.

BARBERI, BL. DOMINIC (1792–1849). Born near Viterbo, Italy, on June 22, he joined the Passionists in 1814, taking the name Dominic of the Mother of God, and was ordained in 1818. He taught for ten years, served in several posts of his order, and in time became provincial. He founded the first Passionist retreat in Belgium, in Ere, in 1840, and in 1842 he established the Passionists in England at Aston Hall, Staffordshire. He was known for his asceticism and learning, published sermons, theological, and ascetical works, founded two other Passionist houses in England, and received several members of the Oxford movement into the Church, notably John Henry Newman. Barberi died at Reading, England, on August 27, and was beatified in 1964.

BARLOW, AMBROSE (1585–1641). The fourth of fourteen children of Sir Alexander Barlow and christened Edward, he was born in Barlow Hall, Manchester, England, and brought up a Protestant. He was converted to Catholicism, went to Douai in 1614, studied there and at Valladolid, Spain, then joined the Benedictines at St. Gregory's in Douai, taking the name Ambrose, in 1615. He was ordained in 1617 and then returned to England, where he engaged in pastoral work in Lancashire. He was arrested four times in the next two and a half decades but each time was released. However, when priests, in 1641, were ordered from England or be labeled traitors and suffer the consequences of that state, he stayed on and was arrested on Easter of that year. When he refused to discontinue his priestly duties if released he was condemned to be executed. He refused to allow his friends to intercede for him and was hanged, disemboweled, and quartered in Lancaster on September 10, a week after he had been named prior of Canterbury. He was canonized by Pope Paul VI in 1970 as one of the Forty Martyrs of England and Wales.

BARNABAS (1st century). All we know of Barnabas is to be found in the New Testament. A Jew, born in Cyprus and named Joseph, he sold his property, gave the proceeds to the apostles, who gave him the name Barnabas, and lived in common with the earliest converts to Christianity in Jerusalem. He persuaded the community there to accept Paul as a disciple, was sent to Antioch, Syria, to look into the community there (Acts 11:22ff.), and brought Paul there from Tarsus. With Paul he brought Antioch's donation to the Jerusalem community during a famine, and returned to Antioch with John Mark, his cousin. The three went on a missionary journey to Cyprus, Perga (whence John Mark returned to Jerusalem), and Antioch in Pisidia, where they were so violently opposed by the Jews that they decided to preach to the pagans. They then went to Iconium and Lystra in Lycaonia, where they were first acclaimed gods and then stoned out of the city, and then returned to Antioch in Syria. When a dispute arose regarding the observance of the Jewish rites, Paul and Barnabas went to Jerusalem, where at a council it was decided pagans did not have to be circumcised to be baptized. On their return to Antioch, Barnabas wanted to take John Mark on another visitation to the cities where they had

preached, but Paul objected because of John Mark's desertion
of them in Perga. Paul and Barnabas parted, and Barnabas
returned to Cyprus with Mark; nothing further is heard of
him, though it is believed his rift with Paul was ultimately
healed. Tradition has Barnabas preaching in Alexandria and
Rome, the founder of the Cypriote Church, the bishop of
Milan (which he was not), and has him stoned to death at
Salamis about 61. The apochryphal *Epistle of Barnabas* was
long attributed to him, but modern scholarship now attributes
it to a Christian in Alexandria between 70 and 100; the *Gospel of Barnabas* is probably by an Italian Christian who became a Mohammedan; and the *Acts of Barnabas* once attributed to John Mark are now known to have been written in
the fifth century. June 11.

BARR. *See* Finbar (d. 633).

BARSABAS (4th century). A pious fiction with no foundation in fact according to which he was an abbot in Persia and
was arrested with twelve of his monks during the persecution
of King Sapor II. They were all cruelly tortured and then
beheaded. A passing Mazdean, impressed by their fortitude
and constancy under torture, joined them and was executed
with them. December 11.

BARTHOLOMEW (1st century). All that is known of him
with certainty is that he is mentioned in the synoptic gospels
and Acts as one of the twelve apostles. His name, a pat-
ronymic, means "son of Tolomai," and scholars believe he is
the same as Nathanael mentioned in John, who says he is
from Cana and that Jesus called him an "Israelite . . . incapable of deceit." The Roman Martyrology says he preached
in India and Greater Armenia, where he was flayed and
beheaded by King Astyages. Tradition has the place as Aban-
opolis on the west coast of the Caspian Sea and that he also
preached in Mesopotamia, Persia, and Egypt. The Gospel of
Bartholomew is apochryphal and was condemned in the decree of Pseudo-Gelasius. August 24.

BASIL (d. 370). He and St. Emmelia were the parents of
SS. Basil, Gregory of Nyssa, and Macrina the Younger. They
were exiled for their Christianity during the persecution of

Galerius Maximinus but were later allowed to return to Caesarea, Cappadocia, where they lived the rest of their lives.
May 30.

BASIL (329–79). One of ten children of St. Basil the Elder
and St. Emmelia, he was born in Caesarea, Cappadocia, Asia
Minor, and was educated by his father and his grandmother,
St. Macrina the Elder. He took advanced studies at Constantinople and Athens, where Gregory Nazianzen and the future
Emperor Julian the Apostate were classmates. On the completion of his studies, Basil taught rhetoric at Caesarea and then
decided to pursue the religious life. He was baptized, visited
monasteries in Palestine, Syria, and Egypt, and in 358 settled
as a hermit by the Iris River in Pontus. He attracted numerous disciples, whom he organized into the first monastery
in Asia Minor. He was ordained in 363 at Caesarea but returned to Pontus because of a disagreement with Archbishop
Eusebius. Basil remained there until 365, when his friend
Gregory requested his assistance in combating Arianism in
Nazianzus. He returned to Caesarea, was reconciled to Eusebius, and in 370, on Eusebius' death, was elected archbishop
of Caesarea and consequently metropolitan of some fifty
suffragen bishops, despite the opposition of Arian Emperor
Valens. When Valens launched his persecution of the Orthodox, he demanded that Basil submit to his demands; Basil refused, and in the confrontation of wills that followed, Valens
capitulated and left Caesarea. Basil was soon faced with another struggle when Bishop Anthimus of Tyana claimed to be
metropolitan of New Cappadocia when Cappadocia was divided, politically, into two provinces; Basil was forced to submit to the partition of his see into two dioceses. He was active
in helping the sick and the poor, built a hospice and a huge
complex to minister to the ill, and attracted huge throngs with
his preaching. He became the leader of the Orthodox in the
East in the continuing struggle against Arianism, though not
too successful in securing aid from Rome and the West
against the heresy that threatened to destroy the Church in
the East. He died at Caesarea on January 1 (when his feast
is celebrated in the East), a few months after Valens died on
the battlefield, and the accession of Gratian to the throne
halted the spread of Arianism. Basil was one of the giants of
the early Church. He was responsible for the victory of

Nicene orthodoxy over Arianism in the Byzantine East, and the denunciation of Arianism at the Council of Constantinople in 381–82 was in large measure due to his efforts. The organization and rule he devised at Pontus became the basis of monastic life in the East (as was so of Benedict in the West) and remains so to the present day. Basil fought simony, aided the victims of drought and famine, strove for a better clergy, insisted on a rigid clerical discipline, fearlessly denounced evil wherever he detected it, and excommunicated those involved in the widespread prostitution traffic in Cappadocia. He was learned, accomplished in statesmanship, a man of great personal holiness, and one of the great orators of Christianity. His doctrinal writings and his four hundred letters (many still extant) had tremendous influence. Among his outstanding treatises are *On the Holy Spirit*, the three *Books against Eunomius*, and with Gregory Nazianzen, he compiled a selection of passages from Origen, *Philocalia*. He is a Doctor of the Church and patriarch of Eastern monks. January 2.

BASILISSA (d. c. 65). Questionable legend has her and Anastasia noble Romans who were converted by and became disciples of St. Peter and St. Paul. When they recovered and buried the bodies of the two saints after their executions, they were imprisoned for doing so, tortured, and then beheaded by order of Emperor Nero when they acknowledged their Christianity. April 15.

BATHILDIS (d. 680). Born in Britain, she was brought as a slave to the household of the mayor of the palace under King Clovis II in France. Evidently of great ability, she advanced herself and in 649 married Clovis, bearing him three sons, each of whom became King: Clotaire III, Childeric II, and Thierry III. On the death of Clovis in 655, she became regent and ruled capably and wisely. She ransomed many captives, helped promote religion in the realm, and endowed and founded numerous monasteries, including St. Denis, Corbie, and Chelles, where she retired about 665. She died there on January 30, and was canonized by Pope Nicholas I.

BAYA. *See* Brigid (5th century).

BAYLON, PASCHAL (1540–92). Born at Torrehermosa,

Aragon, he was a shepherd in his youth, taught himself to read and write. He was refused admission to the Franciscans, but a few years later, in 1564, he became a Franciscan lay brother of the Alcantarine reform. He served most of his life as porter at different friaries in Spain known for his mortifications, charities, and devotion to the sick and the poor. He had an intense devotion to the Eucharist, which he successfully defended against a Calvinist minister in France, and was reputed to have possessed supernatural gifts. He died at the friary at Villareal, was canonized in 1690, and was declared the patron of Eucharistic confraternities and congresses in 1897. May 17.

✕ **BEDE THE VENERABLE** (c. 672–735). Born near St. Peter and St. Paul monastery at Wearmouth-Jarrow, England, he was sent there when three and educated by Abbots Benedict Biscop and Ceolfrid. He became a monk at the monastery, was ordained when thirty, and except for a few brief visits elsewhere spent all of his life in the monastery, devoting himself to the study of Scripture and to teaching and writing. He is considered one of the most learned men of his time and a major influence on English literature. His writings are a veritable summary of the learning of his time and include commentaries on the Pentateuch and various other books of the Bible, theological and scientific treatises, historical works, and biographies. His best-known work is *Historia ecclesiastica,* a history of the English Church and people, which he completed in 731. It is an account of Christianity in England up to 729 and is a primary source of early English history. Called "the Venerable" to acknowledge his wisdom and learning, the title was formalized at the Council of Aachen in 853. He was a careful scholar and distinguished stylist, the "father" of English history, the first to date events *anno Domini* (A.D.), and in 1899 was declared the only English Doctor of the Church. He died at Wearmouth-Jarrow on May 25.

BEE. *See* Bega.

BEGA (7th century). According to legend she was the daughter of an Irish King, fled on the day of her marriage to a son of the King of Norway, and was miraculously transported to Cumberland. She lived as a hermitess for a while but on the advice of St. Oswald, she received the veil from St. Aidan and founded St. Bee's (Copeland) monastery. As abbess, she was venerated for her aid to the poor and the oppressed. September 6.

BEGGA (d. 693). Daughter of Pepin of Landen, mayor of the palace, and St. Itta, she married Ansegilius, son of St. Arnulf of Metz, and their son was Pepin of Herstal, founder of the Carolingian dynasty of rulers of France. On the death of her husband in 691, she built a church and convent at Andenne on the Meuse River and died there. December 17.

BELLARMINE, ROBERT FRANCIS ROMULUS (1542–1621). Born at Montepulciano, Tuscany, Italy, on October 4, he joined the Jesuits, despite his father's opposition, in 1560. He studied at Florence and Mondovi and then at Padua and Louvain and was ordained at Ghent in 1570. He was appointed a professor at Louvain, the first Jesuit to become a professor at Louvain, lectured on Thomas Aquinas' *Summa,* counteracted Baius' teaching, and gained a reputation for his learning and brilliant preaching. He studied Scripture and the Church Fathers and learned Hebrew for his studies. In 1576, he was recalled to Rome, where he occupied the chair of controversial theology at the newly founded Roman College for eleven years. It was during this period that he prepared his monumental *Disputationes de controversiis Christianae Fidei adversus hujus temporis Haereticos,* a study of the Catholic faith to refute the Protestant *Centuries of Magdeburg.* He was sent on an unsuccessful mission to Paris in 1589, enduring the eight-month siege of Paris by Henry of Navarre. In 1592, he was the leader in preparing the Clementine revised version of the Vulgate for which he wrote an Introduction, was named rector of the Roman College in 1592, and in 1594 became provincial of the Naples province of the Jesuits. He became Pope Clement VIII's theologian in 1597, prepared two catechisms that were still in use in modern times, and in 1599 was created a cardinal by Clement. He was appointed archbishop of Capua in 1602 but was recalled to Rome three years later by the newly elected Pope Paul V. Bellarmine soon became the most effective spokesman and apologist of the Church in the later years of the Counter Reformation, noted, in his opposition to the Protestants, for his reasoning and rational argumentation rather than for rhetoric and dogmatic assertions. He was the great champion of the papacy, brilliantly defending the interdict placed on Venice against Fra Paoli Sarpi. Bellarmine overwhelmed King James I of England, who had written two books defending his theory of supremacy in the controversy that developed when Archpriest Blackwell took an Oath of Allegiance to the King that denied papal jurisdiction in temporal matters. Bellarmine incurred further royal opposition with his *De potestate papae,* denying the divine right of kings, which was publicly burned by the Paris *parlement.* However, he alienated Pope Sixtus V when he declared Popes had only indirect jurisdiction over secular rulers; Sixtus threatened to put the first volume of *Disputationes de controversiis* on the Index but died before doing so. Bellarmine's position became basic Catholic teaching on the subject. He became embroiled in the controversy over his friend Galileo, who accepted his admonition in 1610 that it would be wise to advance his findings as hypotheses rather than as fully proved theories. In the last decade of his life, his writings were on spiritual matters, among them *Art of Dying Well* and a commentary on the Psalms. He retired to St. Andrew's novitiate in Rome the last days of his life and died there on September 17. He was canonized in 1930 and declared a Doctor of the Church in 1931.

BENEDICT (c. 480–c̄. 547). Born in Nursia, Italy, he was educated in Rome, was repelled by the vices of the city and in about 500 fled to Enfide, thirty miles away. He decided to live the life of a hermit and settled at mountainous Subiaco, where he lived in a cave for three years, fed by a monk named Romanus. Despite Benedict's desire for solitude, his holiness and austerities became known and he was asked to be their abbot by a community of monks at Vicovaro. He accepted, but when the monks resisted his strict rule and tried to poison him, he returned to Subiaco and soon attracted great numbers of disciples. He organized them into twelve monasteries under individual priors he appointed, made manual work part of the program, and soon Subiaco became a center of spirituality and learning. He left suddenly, reportedly because of the efforts of a neighboring priest, Florentius, to undermine his work, and in about 525 settled at Monte Cassino. He destroyed a pagan temple to Apollo on its crest, brought the people of the neighboring area back to Christianity, and in about 530 began to build the monastery that was to be the birthplace of Western monasticism. Soon disciples again flocked to him as his reputation for holiness, wisdom, and miracles spread far and wide. He organized the monks into a single monastic community and wrote his famous rule prescribing common sense, a life of moderate asceticism, prayer, study, and work, and community life under one superior. It stressed obedience, stability, zeal, and had the Divine Office as the center of monastic life; it was to affect spiritual and monastic life in the West for centuries to come. While ruling his monks (most of whom, including Benedict, were not ordained), he counseled rulers and Popes, ministered to the poor and destitute about him, and tried to repair the ravages of the Lombard Totila's invasion. He died at Monte Cassino on March 21 and was named patron protector of Europe by Pope Paul VI in 1964. July 11.

BENEDICT II (d. 685). Born in Rome, and active in Church affairs since his youth, he was an expert in Scripture and sacred music. Elected to succeed St. Leo II as Pope in 683, his consecration was delayed almost a year until June 26, 684, awaiting the Emperor's confirmation. During his pontificate he secured a decree from Emperor Constantine the Bearded permitting the exarch of Ravenna to confirm papal elections, thus eliminating the long delays. Benedict was highly regarded by Constantine, who sent him locks of his sons' hair, thus making them the Pope's spiritual sons. Benedict was successful in bringing back to orthodoxy Macarius, ex-patriarch of Antioch, from his Monothelitism, and restored several Roman churches. He died on May 8 in Rome.

BENEDICT XI, BL. (1240–1304). Born in Treviso, Italy, Nicholas Boccasini was educated there and at Venice, where he joined the Dominicans when he was fourteen. He became a professor and taught at Venice and Bologna, served as Dominican prior general of Lombardy, and in 1296 was elected master general of the Order. He was made a cardinal in 1298 and bishop of Ostia and served as papal legate to Hungary to try to settle a civil war there. He was one of only two cardinals who supported Pope Boniface VIII against the infamous charges of Philip the Fair of France and was in favor of Boniface's unpromulgated decree excommunicating Philip. It was Benedict who rallied papal forces and rescued

Boniface from Anagni, where he had been imprisoned by William Nogaret, Philip's councilor. Benedict was elected Pope on October 22, 1303, made an uneasy peace with Philip, worked to reconcile warring factions in Europe and the Church and to increase spirituality, but died suddenly in Perugia on July 7 only eight months after his election. Some scholars believe he may have been poisoned. He was beatified in 1736.

BENEDICT OF ANIANE (c. 750–821). Son of Aigulf of Maguelone, he was cup-bearer to King Pepin and Charlemagne and served in the army in Lombardy. He left the army and became a Benedictine at St. Seine, near Dijon, France, in 773. He refused the abbacy there and in 779 returned to Languedoc, where he had lived as a hermit on his estate, attracted numerous disciples, and built a monastery and a church. Supported by Emperor Louis the Pious, who built a monastery for him at Inde, near Aachen, he became director of all the monasteries in the Empire and instituted widespread reforms, though because of opposition they were not as drastic as he wanted. In 817, his *Capitulare monasticum,* a systemization of the Benedictine rule was approved by the Council of Aachen as the rule for all monks in the Empire. He also compiled the *Codex regularum,* a collection of all monastic regulations, and *Concordia regularum,* showing the resemblance of Benedict's rule to those of other monastic leaders. He is considered the restorer of Western monasticism and is often called the "second Benedict." February 11.

BENEDICT BISCOP (c. 628–90). Of noble parents and a courtier at the court of King Oswy of Northumbria, his real name was Biscop Baducing. He went on pilgrimage to Rome in 653 and on his return decided to devote himself to biblical studies and spiritual matters. On the way back from a second trip to Rome, he became a monk at Lérins in 666 and remained there for two years. On a third trip to Rome, Pope St. Vitalian in 669 assigned him to accompany St. Theodore, the new archbishop of Canterbury, and St. Aidan back to England. Theodore appointed him abbot of SS. Peter and Paul monastery at Canterbury, and two years later he was back in Rome collecting relics, religious articles, paintings, and manuscripts. In 674 he founded a monastery at the mouth of the Wear River and it became Wearmouth, dedicated to St. Peter

and built of stone, with a lead roof and glass windows, all unknown in the buildings in England of that time, by artisans he
brought over from France. He built a second monastery six
miles away on the Tyne River in 682, dedicated it to St. Paul,
and called it Jarrow. He made a fifth trip to Rome and
brought back more treasures and Abbot John of St. Martin's
there, the archcantor of St. Peter's and a musical expert, to
teach the monks of Wearmouth and Jarrow how to sing the
Divine Offices and Gregorian Chant. Under his direction the
two monasteries became outstanding centers of learning and
Roman liturgical practices, and their collection of books,
manuscripts, and religious art was unequaled in all of England. Paralyzed and bedridden the last three years of his life,
Benedict died on January 12. His life was written by Bede,
the famous English historian, who had been entrusted to his
care at the age of seven.

BENEDICT THE BLACK. *See* Benedict the Moor.

BENEDICT THE MOOR (1526–89). Born a slave near
Messina, Italy, he was freed by his master and became
a solitary, eventually settling with other hermits at Mon-
tepellegrino. He was made superior of the community, but
when he was about thirty-eight, Pope Pius IV disbanded communities of solitaries and he became a Franciscan lay brother
and the cook at St. Mary's convent near Palermo. He was appointed, against his will, superior of the convent when it
opted for the reform, though he could neither read nor write.
After serving as superior, he became novicemaster but asked
to be relieved of this post and returned to his former position
of cook. His holiness, reputation for miracles, and his fame as
a confessor brought hordes of visitors to see the obscure and
humble cook. He died at the convent, was canonized in 1807,
and is the patron of blacks in the United States. The surname
"the Moor" is a misnomer originating from the Italian *il
moro* (the black). April 4.

BENEN (d. 467). Son of Sechnan, a chieftain in Meath,
Ireland, who had been converted by St. Patrick, he was very
attached to Patrick as a boy. He later became his disciple and
companion, and eventually his confidant and right-hand man,
and in time succeeded him as chief bishop of Ireland. He is
credited with evangelizing Clare, Kerry, and Connaught, and

reportedly headed a monastery at Drumlease, built by Patrick, for some twenty years. He is also known as Benignus. November 9.

BENET BISCOP. *See* Benedict Biscop.

BENIGNUS. *See* Benen.

BENJAMIN (d. c. 421). A deacon, he was imprisoned for preaching Christianity during the persecution of Yezdigerd of Persia and his son Varanes. Benjamin was released at the intercession of the Emperor in Constantinople, who promised he would stop preaching. As soon as he was released he again began preaching, was arrested and tortured, and then was impaled when he refused to agree to stop his preaching if released again. March 31.

BENNO (d. 940). Of a noble Swabian family, he became a canon at Strasbourg and in 906 a hermit on Mount Etzel in the canton of Schwyz, Switzerland. He occupied the hermitage in which St. Meinrad had lived, restored a shrine to Mary, and soon attracted disciples. In 927, he was named bishop of Metz by German King Henry I the Fowler in opposition to a locally elected candidate; two years later he was blinded by the enemies his reforms and the method of his appointment had made. He resigned his see and returned to Mount Etzel, where he was joined in 934 by Eberhard, provost of Strasbourg cathedral, and Benno's hermitage was developed into a monastery that in time became the famous Einsiedeln monastery. He died on August 3 and has long been venerated, though his cult has never been formally recognized.

BERCHMANS, JOHN (1599–1621). Eldest son of a shoemaker, he was born at Diest, Brabant, early wanted to be a priest, and when thirteen became a servant in the household of one of the cathedral canons at Malines, John Froymont. In 1615, he entered the newly founded Jesuit college at Malines, and the following year became a Jesuit novice. He was sent to Rome in 1618 to continue his studies, and was known for his diligence and piety, impressing all with his holiness and stress on perfection in little things. He died there on August 13. Many miracles were attributed to him after his death, and he was canonized in 1888. He is the patron of altar boys. November 26.

BERNADETTE OF LOURDES. *See* Soubirous, Marie Bernarde.

BERNARD (c. 778–842). Born in the Lyonnais, France, of a distinguished family and a member of Charlemagne's court, he married and about 800 founded the monastery of Ambronay. He later became a monk there and in time abbot. He was appointed archbishop of Vienne in 810, founded the abbey of Romans about 837 and became a most influential prelate. He died there and was buried on January 23, noted for his saintliness and insistence on strict ecclesiastical discipline. His name is sometimes spelled Barnard.

BERNARD (1090–1153). Son of Tescelin Sorrel and Aleth, daughter of the lord of Montbard, he was born at Fontaines les Dijon, the family castle near Dijon, Burgundy, the third son of seven children. He was sent to study at Châtillon and after a frivolous youth decided, on the death of his mother, to pursue a religious life. In 1112, he persuaded thirty-one of his friends and relatives (including four of his brothers) to go with him to Cîteaux, which had been founded in 1098, the first Cistercian monastery, which observed a strict interpretation of the Benedictine rule. They were welcomed by the abbot, St. Stephen Harding. In 1115 Bernard was sent with twelve monks to found a Cistercian house at Langres, with Bernard as abbot. Though there were initial difficulties because of Bernard's strict discipline and austerities, his holiness soon attracted scores of disciples. The name was changed from the Vallée d'Absinthe to Clairvaux and was to become the mother house of some sixty-eight Cistercian monasteries established by its monks. Bernard soon became involved in matters outside the monastery as his reputation for learning and wisdom spread, and he soon was one of the most powerful influences in Europe, consulted by rulers and Popes. He supported the legitimacy of Pope Innocent II's election in 1130 against the claims of antipope Anacletus II and successfully led the struggle that led to Innocent's acceptance as Pope. Bernard was the leader in convincing the Lombards to accept Lothaire II as Emperor. In 1140 Bernard began preaching in public and was soon regarded with awe for the miracles attributed to him and for the eloquence of his preaching, for which he was acclaimed as the greatest preacher of his times. He was the leader in the attacks on Abelard questioning his rationalism and extreme exaltation of human reason and opposed it with his own certitude of faith and reliance on traditional authority. He was instrumental in having Abelard condemned at the Council of Sens and forcing him into retirement. In 1142, Bernard arbitrated the disputed succession to the see of York in England, and in the same year he saw the abbot of the Cistercian Tre Fontane monastery in Rome, whom he had brought to Clairvaux as a postulant, Peter Bernard Paganelli, elected Pope as Eugene III. In 1145 the papal legate asked him to go to Languedoc in southern France to combat the Albigensian heresy, and his preaching was most successful, though not enduring. In 1146 he helped stop a series of *pogroms* in the Rhineland, and in the same year, at Eugene's request, he preached a crusade against the Turks, who had captured Edessa on Christmas in 1144. He roused all of Europe to the Second Crusade, headed by Emperor Conrad III and Louis VII of France, which was to end in disaster—a fate he blamed on the wickedness and lack of dedication of the crusaders. In 1153 Bernard left Clairvaux to effect a peace between the duke of Lorraine and the inhabitants of Metz, which had been attacked by the duke. He was stricken on his return and died at Clairvaux on August 20. Bernard is considered the second founder of the Cistercians, and from the time at twenty-five when he became abbot of Clairvaux he soon became the dominant influence in the religious and political sphere of Western Europe. His influence during the last forty years of his life was enormous and he was prominently involved in practically every major event of those years. His mystical writing, especially *De Diligendo Deo,* one of the outstanding medieval mystical works, formed the mysticism of the Middle Ages, and his other writings, his more than three hundred sermons, his treatise *De consideratione,* written for Pope Eugene's guidance, some five hundred known letters, his reflections on Scripture, and his deep devotion to Mary and the Infant Jesus all had a profound effect on Catholic spirituality. Called the Mellifluous Doctor, he was canonized in 1174, was formally declared a Doctor of the Church in 1830, and is considered the last of the Fathers of the Church. August 20.

BERNARD OF MENTHON. *See* Bernard of Montjoux.

BERNARD OF MONTJOUX (c. 996–1081). Probably born in Italy, he became a priest, was made vicar general of Aosta, and spent more than four decades doing missionary work in the Alps. He built schools and churches in the diocese but is especially remembered for two Alpine hospices he built to aid lost travelers in the mountain passes named Great and Little Bernard after him. The men who ran them in time became Augustinian canons regular and built a monastery. The order continued into the twentieth century. He was proclaimed the patron saint of Alpinists and mountain climbers by Pope Pius XI in 1923. He is sometimes fallaciously referred to as Bernard of Menthon and the son of Count Richard of Menthon, which he was not. May 28.

BERNARDINO OF SIENA (1380–1444). Son of the governor of Massa Marittima, Italy, where he was born Bernardino degli Albizzeschi, was orphaned at seven, and was raised by an aunt. He joined a confraternity of our Lady when seventeen, ran the hospital at Siena during a plague in 1400, joined the Franciscans, and was professed in the nearby convent of Colombaio in 1403. He was ordained the following year and then lived as a solitary at Colombaio for the next twelve years. In 1417 he began to preach at Milan, and in a short time his eloquence and fiery sermons attacted attention. He preached missions all over Italy and attracted great crowds as he preached devotion to the Holy Name and denounced the evils of the times. He declined the bishopric of Siena in 1427 after Pope Martin V had cleared him of all charges made against him by his enemies, later declined the sees of Ferrara and Urbino, and was elected vicar general of the Friars of the Strict Observance in 1430. He rejuvenated and reformed the order, increasing its numbers from three hundred to over four thousand, and was really its second founder. He resigned as vicar general in 1442 to return to his preaching and missions and died at Aquila while on a mission trip on May 20. He was canonized in 1450.

✱ **BERTHA** (d. c. 840). Related to the Dukes of Lorraine, she owned extensive properties on the Rhine, married a pagan, and when he was killed in battle, devoted herself to raising her son Rupert as a Christian. She founded several hospices for the poor, and after a visit to Rome, they gave away their possessions and became hermits near Bingen (Rupertsberg), Germany. He died when twenty and she spent the remaining twenty-five years of her life there. May 15.

BERTHOLD (d. c. 1195). Born at Limoges, France, he studied at Paris and was ordained there. He went on the Crusades with Aymeric, a relative, and was in Antioch during its siege by the Saracens, during which he had a vision of Christ denouncing the evilgoing ways of the Christian soldiers and labored to reform them. He organized and became superior of a group of hermits on Mount Carmel, and is thus considered by some to be the founder of the Carmelites, and ruled for forty-five years. March 29.

BERTINUS (d. 700). With St. Mommolinus and St. Bertrand, all natives of Coutances, France, he was a monk at Luxeuil when he was sent with them to assist St. Omer, bishop of Therouanne, in evangelizing the Morini around Pas-de-Calais. They built a monastery at what is now St. Mommolin with Mommolinus as abbot, and another one at Sithiu, of which Mommolinus also became abbot. When Mommolinus was appointed bishop of Noyon about 661, Bertinus became abbot of Sithiu and built it into one of the great monastic centers of France (it was later renamed St. Bertin's) and evangelized the whole area. A church he built with St. Omer near Sithiu in 663 afterward became the cathedral of the see of St. Omer. September 5.

BERTOUL. *See* Bertulf.

BERTRAN (or BERTRAND), LOUIS (1526–81). Born at Valencia, Spain, he joined the Dominicans when eighteen, and was ordained in 1547. He served as master of novices for some thirty years of his life, became an outstanding preacher, and in 1557 he met and encouraged St. Teresa of Avila in her proposed reform of the Carmelites. In 1557 he did heroic work in the plague that ravaged Valencia, and in 1562 he went to Colombia as a missionary. He traveled throughout the Caribbean area, converting thousands and trying to secure better treatment for the Indians. He became known for his prophecies, miracles, and gift of tongues. He returned to Valencia in 1569 and spent the rest of his life as prior of several houses and in training preachers. He died on October 9, and was canonized in 1581.

BERTULF (d. 640). A pagan, he was converted to Christianity by his relative St. Arnulf of Metz and became a monk at Luxeuil about 620. After several years there, he went to Bobbio in Italy, and in 627 became abbot. He later was involved in a dispute with Bishop Probus of Tortona, who claimed jurisdiction over Bobbio, but Pope Honorius I made the abbey exempt from episcopal control and directly subject to the Holy See, the first such recorded exemption. Bertulf was reputed to have performed miracles and was held in high regard for his holiness and the austerity of his rule. August 19.

BESSETTE, BL. ANDRÉ (1845–1937). Born in a small village near Montreal, Canada, he worked in mills and on farms in New England during his youth and then returned to Montreal where he joined the Congregation of Holy Cross in 1870. He spent the next sixty-seven years of his life as a lay brother serving in such menial positions as porter and gardener and gaining a reputation for miraculous cures that drew millions of pilgrims to Montreal to see him. Devoted to St. Joseph from his childhood he spent his life fostering devotion to him and building St. Joseph's Oratory in Montreal. By the time of his death it had become one of the most popular shrines in North America. He was beatified by Pope John Paul II in 1982.

BETTELIN (8th century). A hermit and a disciple of St. Guthlac in Croyland, England, his fictitious legend has him the son of a Stafford ruler who fell in love with a princess while on a visit to Ireland. On their return to England she died a terrible death; while he was gone for a midwife when the pangs of childbirth overtook her in a forest, she was torn to pieces by ravenous wolves, whereupon he became a hermit. Later legend has him leaving his hermitage to drive off invaders with an angel's assistance. He then spent the rest of his days in his cell, where he died. September 9.

BEUZEC. *See* Budoc.

BIANCHI, FRANCIS XAVIER (1743–1815). Born at Arpino, Italy, he studied at Naples, was tonsured at fourteen, and despite his father's objections, joined the Congregation of Clerks Regular of St. Paul (the Barnabites). He was ordained in 1767, served as president of two colleges, and became famous for his gift of prophecy and the miracles credited to him (he is reported to have stopped the flow of lava from the erupting Vesuvius in 1805). In ill health, he was left alone at his college when his order was expelled from Naples, and he died there on January 31. He was canonized in 1951.

BIBIANA (4th century). Though the church of St. Bibiana in Rome dates from the fifth century, attesting to the veneration early paid her, her legend is untrustworthy. According to it she was the daughter of the ex-prefect, Flavian, who had been tortured for his faith and banished to Acquapendente during the persecution of Julian the Apostate. After Flavian's death, his wife, Dafrosa, was beheaded and Bibiana and her sister, Demetria, were deprived of all their possessions and then were arrested. Demetria dropped dead on her arrest, and Bibiana was scourged to death. She is also known as Viviana. December 2.

BICCHIER, BL. EMILY (1238–1314). Born at Vercelli, she refused her father's plans for her to marry and convinced him to build a convent—the first of Dominican regular tertiaries—of which she became abbess when twenty. She was noted for her frequent communions (uncommon in those days), her ecstasies and visions, and the miracles attributed to her. She died on May 3, and her cult was approved in 1769. August 19.

BICHIER DES ANGES, ELIZABETH (1773–1838). Born in the Chateau des Anges at Le Blanc, France, daughter of Antony Bichier, lord of the manor, she was christened Joan Elizabeth Mary Lucy but always used Elizabeth. She was educated in a convent in nearby Poitiers and when her father died fought successfully to save her family's property from confiscation by the National Assembly. She moved to Bethines, a suburb of Poitiers, with her mother in 1796 and devoted herself to keeping religion alive in the village against the atheism and constitutional priests of the revolutionary regime. In 1797, she met and became friends with Abbe Fournet (St. Andrew Fournet), who drew up a rule for her to follow as she dedicated her life to teaching and to the care of the sick and needy. When her mother died in 1804, she went as a novice to the Carmelite convent in Poitiers and then to the Society of Providence to prepare herself to be a member of a community of nuns Abbe Fournet proposed to establish. When Elizabeth returned she was put in charge of a group of women he had formed into a community to teach children and to care for the sick and aged. The group took vows in 1807 and had its rule approved by the bishop of Poitiers in 1816. The congregation, the Daughters of the Cross, spread despite several jurisdictional disputes and by 1830 had some sixty convents all over France. At Elizabeth's encouragement, Michael Garicoits, the spiritual director of the Basque house at Igon, founded the Priests of the Sacred Heart of Betherran; at Abbe Fournet's death in 1834, he became his replacement. Elizabeth died on August 26, and was canonized in 1947.

BILFRID (d. c. 758). A monk hermit at Lindisfarne off the coast of Northumberland in northern England, he was an expert goldsmith and bound with gold, silver, and gems the famous St. Cuthbert's copy of the Gospels of Lindisfarne. March 6.

BILLIART, JULIA (1751–1816). Of a well-to-do farming family, she was born on July 12 at Cuvilly, Picardy, France, and christened Marie Rose Julia. She early evinced an interest in religion and helping the sick and the poor. She was paralyzed by a mysterious illness and was forced into hiding when her opposition to constitutional priests and her aid to fugitive priests became known to the revolutionary authorities. She stayed for a time at Amiens with a friend, Frances Blin Bourdon, viscountess of Gezaincourt, who joined her and accompanied her to Bettencourt where, with a group of women, they conducted catechetical classes for the villagers. There she met Fr. Joseph Varin, and when she returned to Amiens, she began, under his direction, the Institute of Notre Dame, devoted to the spiritual education of poor children, the training of religious teachers, and the Christian education of girls. They opened an orphanage and in 1804, during the course of a mission in Amiens, Fr. EnFantin, after a novena, ordered Julia to walk and she did—after having been an invalid for twenty-two years. The order flourished but trouble developed when Fr. Varin was transferred and his successor as confessor to the Sisters of Notre Dame became antagonistic to the Sisters, as did the bishop of Amiens, who forced Julia to leave Amiens in 1809. She moved the mother house to Namur, and though she was later exonerated in the affair, she kept the Institute's mother house there. During the rest of her life she worked to expand her Institute, and at her death at Namur on April 8, fifteen convents had been established. She was canonized by Pope Paul VI in 1969.

BIRGITTA. *See* Bridget.

BLAISE (d. c. 316). That he was bishop of Sebastea, Armenia, and was martyred by order of Governor Agricolaus of Cappadocia and Lower Armenia during Licinius' persecution is all we know with certainty of Blaise. According to unreliable legend, he was of wealthy Christian parents and was made a bishop in his youth. He became a hermit when persecutions of the Christians began, was brought to Agricolaus by hunters who observed him curing sick and wounded wild animals, and was imprisoned, then tortured and beheaded by the governor for his faith. The blessing of throats on his feast day is attributed to his healing of a young boy who was choking to death from a fish bone in his throat; the two candles used in the ceremony are derived from the candles brought to Blaise in prison by the boy's mother. His name is also spelled Blase. February 3.

BLASE. *See* Blaise.

BOBOLA, ANDREW (1591–1657). Of an aristocratic Polish family, he was born in Sandomir, Poland, joined the Jesuits in 1611 at Vilna, Lithuania, and was ordained in 1622. He engaged in parish work in Vilna, and in 1630 was made superior of the Jesuit house in Bobrinsk, where he became known for his work during a plague there. Beginning in 1636, he spent the next twenty years in successful missionary work, especially among the Orthodox, a success that gained him much opposition and hatred among those opposed to his religion. Because of Cossack, Russian, and Tartar raids on Poland, the Jesuits were forced into hiding; he accepted a house in Pinsk from Prince Radziwell in 1652 and made it into a center for fugitive Jesuits. Five years later he was captured during a Cossack attack on Pinsk, tortured, and after refusing to disown his faith was subjected to further merciless torture and then beheaded at Janow on May 10. He was canonized in 1938. May 16.

BOISIL (d. 664). Trained under St. Aidan, he became a monk at Melrose, Northumbria, was ordained, and became abbot. He was a biblical scholar, and was famed for his preaching, his gift of prophecy, his holiness, and his aid to the poor. He died of a plague that wracked the country. He is also known as Boswell. February 23.

BONAVENTURE (1221–74). Giovanni di Fidanza was born in Bagnorea, Italy, son of Giovanni di Fidanza and Maria la Ritella, and according to an untrustworthy legend, received the name Bonaventure from St. Francis of Assisi, who cured him of a childhood illness. He became a Franciscan in 1238 (or 1243) and studied at Paris under Alexander of Hales, whose disciple he became. He taught theology and Scripture at Paris, 1248–55. His teaching was interrupted because of the opposition of the secular professors to the new mendicants. He was involved in the controversy defending the mendicant orders against the attacks, headed by William of Saint-Armour and his book *The Perils of the Last Times*, and wrote *Concerning the Poverty of Christ* in refutation. In 1256 Pope Alexander IV denounced Saint-Armour and ordered the attackers of the mendicant orders to desist. When the mendicant orders were re-established at Paris, Bonaventure received his doctorate in theology, with Thomas Aquinas, in 1257. Earlier the same year Bonaventure had been elected minister general of the Friars Minor and labored to reconcile the dissident factions in the Order, pursuing a policy of moderation but condemning the policies of the extremist groups. At a general chapter of the Order at Narbonne in 1260, he promulgated a set of constitutions on the rule, which had a profound and lasting impact on the Order. He refused the archbishopric of York in 1265, and in 1271 he helped secure the election of Pope Gregory X. In 1273, he was appointed cardinal-bishop of Albano, and the following year Gregory appointed him to draw up the agenda for the fourteenth General Council at Lyons to discuss reunion of the Eastern churches with Rome. Bonaventure was a leading figure in the success of the Council that effected reunion, but he died at Lyons on July 15 while the Council was still in session.

Bonaventure was an outstanding philosopher and theologian and one of the great minds of medieval times. Known as "the Seraphic Doctor," he wrote numerous treatises, notably his *Commentary on the Sentences of Peter Lombard*, the theological tracts *Breviloquium, Itinerarium mentis in Deum*, and *De reductione artium ad theologium*, the spiritual works *Perfection of Life, Soliloquy*, and *The Threefold Way*, biblical commentaries, some five hundred sermons, and the official Franciscan biography of St. Francis. Bonaventure was canonized in 1482 and declared a Doctor of the Church in 1588. July 15.

BONIFACE I (d. 422). A Roman priest, he was elected Pope in 418 when an old man, the day after a group of dissidents had seized the Lateran and elected Eulalius Pope. Emperor Honorius called two councils, decided in favor of Boniface, and ousted Eulalius and his faction. Boniface continued his predecessor's opposition to Pelagianism, persuaded Emperor Theodosius II to return Illyricum to Western jurisdiction, and supported Augustine, who dedicated several treatises against Pelagianism to him. He died on September 4.

BONIFACE IV (d. 615). Son of a doctor named John, he was born at Valeria, Italy, may have been a student under Gregory the Great, was possibly a Benedictine monk in Rome, and became a *dispensator* when he entered papal service. He was elected Pope in 608, was responsible for converting the Roman temple of the gods, the Pantheon in Rome, into a Christian church, and had correspondence with Columba, who chided him for some of his theological stances while expressing devotion and loyalty to him. May 8.

BONIFACE (c. 680–754). Probably born at Crediton, Devonshire, England, and baptized Winfrid, he was sent to a monastery school near Exeter when seven, then to the Benedictine Nursling abbey in Winchester when fourteen, where he studied under Winbert and became director of the school. He was ordained about 715, was a successful teacher and preacher, but decided he wanted to be a missionary to Friesland. Unsuccessful in a first attempt in 716, he went to Pope Gregory II in Rome in 718 and was sent by the Pope to evangelize the pagans in Germany. He changed his name to Boniface, was a missionary under St. Willibrord in Friesland for three years, and then preached successfully in Hesse. In 722 he was recalled to Rome and was consecrated regionary bishop for Germany, secured a pledge of protection from Charles Martel, and on his return to Germany, preached in Hesse. He won instant success with a huge gathering of pagans at Geismar by demolishing the Oak of Thor, an object of pagan worship, without harm to himself. He then went to Thuringia, established a monastery at Ohrdruf, and was successful in securing English monks as missionaries to Germany. In 731, he was made metropolitan of Germany beyond the Rhine, authorized to create new sees, went to Bavaria as papal legate, and established a hierarchy and several new sees in the area. He founded several monasteries, Reichenau (724), Murbach (728) and Fritzlar (734), and in 735, he and St. Sturmi founded Fulda, which in the years to come became a great monastic center for northern Europe. He reformed the Frankish church, which Charles Martel had plundered, with five synods called after Charles' death in 741 by his sons, Carloman and Pepin, over which he presided between 741 and 747. In 747 his metropolitan see was established at Mainz and he was named primate of Germany by Pope St. Zachary. He was also appointed apostolic delegate for Germany and Gaul, and crowned Pepin sole ruler of Gaul at Soissons when Pepin's brother Carloman entered a monastery. Boniface resigned his see in 754 to spend the last years of his life reconverting the Frieslanders, who had lapsed into their pagan customs after the death of St. Willibrord. He was preparing for the confirmation of some of his converts at Dokkum, Friesland (northern Netherlands), when he and a group of his followers were attacked by a band of pagans and murdered on June 5. Called "the Apostle of Germany," his feast day was extended to the universal Church by Pope Pius IX in 1874. June 5.

BONIFACE (974–1009). Of a noble Saxon family, he was born at Querfurt, Germany, and baptized Bruno. He studied at Magdeburg, joined the court of Otto III, was made court chaplain, and accompanied the Emperor to Rome in 998. There he became a Camaldolese monk with the name Boniface about 1000. The following year he entered a monastery at Pereum founded by Otto. When two of its monks, Benedict and John, and three companions (the Five Martyred Brothers whose story he wrote) were martyred in 1003 at

Kazimierz, near Gniezno, he went as a missionary to Germany. He was appointed missionary archbishop, preached to the Magyars with considerable success, and then went to Kiev to preach to the Pechenegs. He eventually worked to evangelize the Prussians, and on February 14, he and eighteen companions were massacred on the Russian border near Braunsberg, Poland. He is also known as Bruno of Querfurt and is often called "the Second Apostle of the Prussians." June 19.

BONIFACE OF SAVOY, BL. (d. 1270). Son of Thomas, count of Savoy, he entered the Grande Chartreuse as a youth, became a Carthusian, and was made prior of Mantua. He served seven years as administrator of the diocese of Belley in 1234–41 and then of Valence. He was elected archbishop of Canterbury in 1241 through the influence of his niece, Eleanor, wife of King Henry III of England, but did not go to his see until 1244. His attempts to reform the see and effect economies in the heavily indebted see met with strenuous opposition, particularly from the suffragans of the various sees he attempted to visit. He excommunicated the bishop of London and the clergy of St. Bartholomew's, and while an appeal to Rome upheld his visitation rights he was forced to rescind his excommunications, and his visitations had restrictions placed on them. He acted as regent for Henry while the King was out of the country, accompanied him on a diplomatic mission to France, and successfully negotiated a peaceful solution to difficulties over the succession in his native Savoy. He died on the way to a crusade with Edward I at the castle of Sainte-Hélène des Millières in Savoy. Boniface's cult was confirmed in 1838. July 14.

BORGIA, FRANCIS (1510–72). Son of the Duke of Gandia of the Spanish branch of the Borgia family and Juana of Aragon, daughter of the illegitimate son of King Ferdinand V of Aragon, he was born at Gandia, near Valencia, Spain. He was educated by his uncle, the archbishop of Saragossa, and in 1528 was made a member of the court of Charles V, and marquis of Lombay. He married Eleanor de Castro in 1529, served as Charles' adviser for ten years, and in 1539 was appointed viceroy of Catalonia by the Emperor. He succeeded to the dukedom of Gandia on the death of his father in 1543. He served as master of the household of Prince Philip and then retired from public life to his estate when Philip's engagement to the princess of Portugal was broken. When his wife died in 1546, leaving him with eight children, he decided to pursue the religious life that had beckoned him all his life, and in 1548 he decided to join the Jesuits. He went to Rome in 1550, returned to Spain the next year to turn over his inheritance to his son Charles, and was ordained later in the year. He preached in Spain and Portugal, attracting huge crowds to his sermons, and in 1554 was appointed commissary general of the Jesuits in Spain by St. Ignatius. In this position Francis founded numerous monasteries, colleges, and foundations, and ministered to the dowager Queen and the abdicated Charles V. In 1561, Francis was summoned to Rome and in 1565 was elected father general of the Jesuits. During the seven years of his generalate, he expanded the Society, was one of the leaders in combating the Reformation, encouraged Jesuit participation in foreign missionary work, was one of those responsible for the founding of Gregorian University, built Sant' Andrea, and began the Gésu, all in Rome, established the Polish province, built colleges in France, and opened American missions. In 1567, he revised the rules of the Society, and in 1571 accompanied Cardinal Bonelli on a tour through Spain that drew huge crowds to see and hear him. He returned to Rome exhausted from the trip and died there two days later, shortly after midnight September 30. So successful was he in revitalizing and reinvigorating the Jesuits that he is often called their second founder. He was canonized in 1671. October 10.

BORIS (d. 1015). Son of Vladimir of Kiev, and baptized Romanus, he learned of the plans of his brother Svyatopolk to defraud him and another brother Gleb (baptized David) of their inheritance on the death of their father while returning from a military expedition. He refused to claim his legacy by force, as urged by his officers, saying that as a Christian he could not raise his sword against his older brother. He retired to a lonely spot with one of his followers to pray. The next morning a group of Svyatopolk's followers found him and sworded him to death while he prayed for them. Gleb, invited to Kiev by Svyatopolk, was stabbed to death, reportedly by his own cook, when his brother's men boarded his boat on the Dnieper River near Smolensk. Five years later another brother, Yaroslav, buried their bodies in St. Basil's church at Vyshgorod; miracles reported at their graves made it a popular pilgrimage place. Boris is the patron of Moscow, and their cult was confirmed in 1724. July 24.

BORROMEO, CHARLES (1538–84). Son of Count Gilbert Borromeo and Margaret Medici, sister of Pope Pius IV, he was born at the family castle of Arona on Lake Maggiore, Italy, on October 2. He received the clerical tonsure when twelve and was sent to the Benedictine abbey of SS. Gratian and Felinus at Arona for his education. He continued his studies at Milan, went to Pavia in 1552 to study civil and canon law under Alciati, and received his doctorate in 1559. In the same year his uncle was elected Pope Pius IV and the following year named him his Secretary of State and created him a cardinal and administrator of the see of Milan. He served as Pius' legate on numerous diplomatic missions, and in 1562 was instrumental in having Pius reconvene the Council of Trent, which had been suspended in 1552. Charles played a leading role in guiding it and in fashioning the decrees of the third and last group of sessions. He refused the headship of the Borromeo family on the death of Count Frederick Borromeo, was ordained a priest in 1563, and was consecrated bishop of Milan the same year. Before being allowed to take possession of his see, he oversaw the catechism, missal, and breviary called for by the Council of Trent. When he finally did arrive at Trent (which had been without a resident bishop for eighty years) in 1566, he instituted radical reforms, despite great opposition, with such effectiveness that it became a model see. He put into effect measures to improve the morals and manners of clergy and laity, raised the effectiveness of the diocesan operation, established seminaries for the education of the clergy, founded a Confraternity of Christian Doctrine for the religious instruction of children, and encouraged the Jesuits in his see. He increased assistance to the poor and the needy, was most generous in his help to the English college at Douai, and during his bishopric held eleven diocesan synods and six provincial councils. He founded a society of secular priests, Oblates of St. Ambrose (now Oblates of St. Charles) in 1578, and was active in preaching, resisting the inroads of Protestantism, and bringing back lapsed Catholics to the Church. He encountered opposition from many sources in his efforts to reform people and institutions. In 1567, he aroused the enmity of the Milan Senate over episcopal jurisdiction when he imprisoned several layper-

sons for their evil lives; when the episcopal sheriff was driven
from the city by civil officials, he excommunicated them and
was eventually upheld by King Philip II and the Pope. Again
his episcopal rights were challenged by the canons of Santa
Maria della Scala, and he was barred from entering the
church, but Philip and the Pope again upheld his position,
though the Senate supported the canons. He was wounded by
an assassin, Jerome Donati Farina, a Humiliati priest, in 1569
in a plot on his life by the Humiliati to end his insistence on
the Order's reform. He helped mitigate the famine that struck
Milan in 1570 by securing food for the poor and feeding
some three thousand people a day for months. Another
conflict with the Senate over his ecclesiastical rights led to the
removal of the governor, Luis de Requesens, whom Charles
had excommunicated, by Philip, who upheld the claims of the
archbishop. When plague struck Milan in 1576 Charles mobi-
lized the clergy and religious to aid the stricken after the governor and other officials had fled the city, personally ministered to the afflicted, and ran up huge debts to care for the
thousands of sick, dying, and the dead who littered the streets
until the plague finally abated early in 1578. He met and
aided many of the young priests sent on the English mission
at a gathering in Milan in 1580, and in 1583 was apostolic
visitor to Switzerland, where he preached against the Protestants and fought an outbreak of alleged witchcraft and sorcery. He died at Milan on the night of November 3–4, and
was canonized in 1610. He was one of the towering figures of
the Catholic Reformation, a patron of learning and the arts,
and though he achieved a position of great power, he used it
with humility, personal sanctity, and unselfishness to reform
the Church of the evils and abuses so prevalent among the
clergy and nobles of the times. November 4.

BOSA (d. 705). A Benedictine monk at Whitby, England,
he became bishop of Deira in 678, with his see at York, when
St. Wilfrid was driven out by King Egfrid when he refused to
accept the division of his see of York. Wilfrid returned in
686, but Bosa took over the diocese in 691 when Wilfrid was
again exiled following a quarrel with King Aldfrid; Bosa
ruled it with great holiness and ability until his death.
March 9.

BOSCO, JOHN (1815–88). Born at Becchi, Piedmont,

Italy, of poor parents, he lost his father when two, entered the seminary at Chieri when sixteen, continued his studies at Turin, and was ordained. He began his work with neglected boys at Turin at the encouragement of Fr. Joseph Cafasso, was appointed chaplain of St. Philomena's Hospice for girls there in 1844, and housed his boys in an old building on the grounds of the Hospice. When they became too unruly he was ordered to give up his care of the boys or resign as chaplain. He resigned and with his mother opened a refuge for the boys. He began workshops and schools, built a church for the boys, and by 1856 he was housing 150 boys and had another 500 in oratories with 10 priests. He was immensely successful with the boys, using a minimum of restraint and discipline, lots of love, keeping careful watch over their development, and encouraging them personally and through religion. The work expanded and he paid for it by preaching, writing popular books, and from charitable donations. His need for dependable assistants led him to found the Society of St. Francis de Sales (the Salesians), which received general approval from Pope Pius IX in 1859, though formal approval was not obtained until 1884. By the time of his death, some sixty-four Salesian foundations had been made in Europe and the Americas, and there were almost 800 Salesian priests. In 1872, he founded the Daughters of Our Lady, Help of Christians, to care for poor and neglected girls, and followed this with a third order called Salesian co-operators. He died in Turin on January 31, and was canonized in 1934. January 31.

BOSTE, JOHN (c. 1544–94). Born at Dufton, Westmorland, England, he studied at Queen's College, Oxford, and was a fellow there. He became a Catholic in 1576, went to Rheims in 1580, and was ordained there the following year. He was sent on the English mission, ministered to the Catholics of northern England, and became the object of an intensive manhunt. He was betrayed by a Francis Ecclesfield near Durham, and taken to London, where he was crippled for the rest of his life by the racking he was subjected to. Sent back to Durham, he was condemned to death for his priesthood and hanged, drawn, and quartered at Dryburn, near Durham, on July 24. He was canonized by Pope Paul VI in 1970 as one of the Forty Martyrs of England and Wales.

BOSWELL. *See* Boisil.

BRÉBEUF, JOHN DE (1593–1649). Born on March 25, at Condé-sur-Vire, Normandy, France, he attended the university at nearby Caen, was a farmer on his parents' farm, and in 1617 joined the Jesuits at Rouen. Ordained in 1622 after tuberculosis had almost ended his aspirations to the priesthood, he was sent to Canada at his request in 1625 and labored among the Huron Indians there for the next twenty-four years despite great opposition from the Huguenots, trading company officials, and renegade Indians. His stay there was interrupted when the English captured Quebec in 1629 and ousted the Jesuits. He returned to France, was treasurer at the college in Eu, and then returned to the missions in 1633, when the English returned Canada to the French. When smallpox killed thousands of Indians in 1637, the missionaries were blamed by the medicine men of the tribes for the disaster, but Brébeuf stayed with the Indians until 1640, when he went to Quebec. He remained there for four years and then returned to the Indians. He was captured by Iroquois Indians, the bitter enemies of the French and Hurons, on March 16 at Ste. Marie, near Georgian Bay, and was cruelly tortured for hours until he died. Known for his holiness and courage, he was responsible for some seven thousand conversions among the Indians, and composed a dictionary and catechism in Huron. He was canonized in 1930. October 19.

BRENDAN (c. 484–c. 577). Though one of the most popular of the Irish saints and certainly a real person, much of what we know of him is legendary. Son of Findlugh, he was probably born near Tralee, Kerry, Ireland, and was placed as an infant in the care of St. Ita. When six he was sent to St. Jarlath's monastic school in Tuam for his education, and was ordained by Bishop St. Erc in 512. He founded numerous monasteries in Ireland, the most famous of which was Clonfert, which he founded about 559 and which was a center of missionary activity for centuries. Some three thousand monks lived, studied, and prayed there under his direction. He made missionary journeys to England, Ireland, and Scotland, established several sees in Ireland, and became famed for his voyages, particularly a seven-year journey to the Land of Promise, which he described in his epic saga *Navigatio Sancti Brendani Abbatis*. It was tremendously popular in the Middle Ages and was translated into most European languages.

Though scholars long doubted the voyage to the Promised Land he described in the *Navigatio* in the middle of the sixth century could have been to North America, as was sometimes claimed, some modern scholars now believe he may have done just that. In 1976–77, Tim Severin, an expert on exploration, following the instructions in the *Navigatio*, built a hide-covered *curragh* and then sailed it from Ireland to Newfoundland via Iceland and Greenland, demonstrating the accuracy of its directions and descriptions of the places Brendan mentioned in his epic. Brendan probably died while visiting his sister Brig, abbess of a community of nuns at Enach Duin (Annaghdown). He is the patron of sailors. May 16.

BRIANT, ALEXANDER (d. 1581). Born in Somerset, England, he studied at Oxford, where he returned to the Church, and then went to France to study at Douai. He was ordained in 1578 and returned to England the following year. He was active in Somerset but came to London in 1581, where he was arrested at the home of Fr. Robert Persons. He was mercilessly tortured for a month in a futile effort to get him to reveal the whereabouts of Persons, and then was tried with other Catholics on the trumped-up charge of plotting in Rome a rebellion in England. He was found guilty and executed at Tyburn on December 1 with SS. Edmund Campion and Ralph Sherwin. They were all canonized as among the Martyrs of England and Wales by Pope Paul VI in 1970.

BRICE (d. 444). Raised by St. Martin of Tours at Marmoutier and also known as Britius, he became a vain, overly ambitious cleric, holding Martin in great contempt. Despite Brice's attitude, Martin was most patient with him, and in time, in great remorse, he asked Martin's forgiveness for his attitude toward him. He succeeded Martin as bishop of Tours in 397 but reverted to his old ways, neglected his duties, was several times accused of laxness and immorality, and though cleared of the latter charge was exiled from his see. He went to Rome and in the seven years of his exile there repented and completely changed his lifestyle. When the administrator of his see in his absence died, he returned and ruled with such humility, holiness, and ability he was venerated as a saint by the time of his death. November 13.

BRIDE. *See* Brigid (c. 450–525).

BRIDGET. *See* Brigid.

BRIDGET (1303–73). Daughter of Birger Persson, governor of Upland, Sweden, and a wealthy landowner, and his second wife Ingeborg Bengtsdotter, she was born on June 14, and was raised by her aunt at Aspenas when her mother died when Bridget was twelve. She early experienced visions, was married when only fourteen to Ulf Gudmarsson when he was eighteen, and they had eight children, one of whom was St. Catherine of Sweden. In 1335, Bridget became lady-in-waiting to Blanche of Namur, who had just married King Magnus II of Sweden. After Bridget's eldest daughter made a bad marriage and her youngest son died about 1340, she made a pilgrimage to the shrine of St. Olaf at Trondhjem, Norway. On her return she left the court and went on pilgrimage to Compostela with her husband. He became ill at Arras but recovered, as she had been assured in a vision of St. Denis. Her husband died in 1344 at the Cistercian monastery of Alvastra, and she spent the next four years there living a life of great austerity and experiencing numerous visions and revelations, which her confessor assured her were authentic and which were all recorded by Prior Peter of Alvastra. As the result of a revelation, she denounced the King and Queen for their frivolous lives, and when Bridget founded a monastery at Vadstena in 1344, Magnus endowed it. It marked the beginning of the Order of the Most Holy Trinity (the Brigettines), and Vadstena became the intellectual center of fifteenth-century Sweden. She refused to support King Magnus' crusade against the pagan Letts and Estonians, terming it a marauding expedition, and then wrote to Pope Clement VI at Avignon, telling him a vision demanded that he return the papacy to Rome and that he mediate peace between England and France. In disfavor with the court for her outspokenness, she went to Rome in 1349 and impressed the whole city with her austerity, holiness, concern for the poor and pilgrims, and her unceasing efforts to get the Pope to return to Rome. She reformed monasteries around Rome and became famous for her prophecies and denunciations of those in high office, including Pope Urban V, who returned to Rome briefly in 1370 when he approved her constitution for the Brigettines. She continued her efforts to get the Pope back to Rome when Urban's successor, Gregory XI, remained at Avignon. The last years of her life were marred

by the unsavory romance that developed between her son
Charles and Queen Joanna I of Naples, both married, while
he was on the way to the Holy Land on a pilgrimage with his
mother and a group of others. It ended abruptly when he died
of a fever a few weeks later. On her way back in 1372, she
stopped off at Cyprus to denounce the royal family for its evil
ways. She died shortly after her arrival in Rome on July 23.
She was canonized in 1391, and is the patron saint of Sweden. Throughout her life Bridget experienced remarkable visions and revelations, which she wrote about in her *Revelations*. After her death the Council of Trent ordered a critical
examination of the revelations to be made by John Torque-
mada, who later became a cardinal; he approved them for
reading by the faithful. She is also known as Birgitta. July 23.

BRIGID (5th century). Also known as Britt, according to
legend, she and her sister Maura were Scottish princesses
from Northumbria who were murdered by pagan outlaws at
Balagny-sur-Thérain, Picardy, while on their way home from
a pilgrimage to Rome. They were buried there and a cult
grew up around them, abetted by reports of numerous miracles at their grave. They were enshrined at Nogent-les-Vierges
in 1185. July 13. They are believed to be the same as Maura
and Britt, two solitaries at Ariacum (St. Maure), who also
died in the fifth century and whose remains were miraculously revealed to St. Euphronius according to St. Martin of
Tours. A chapel was built, and a cult grew up around them in
Touraine, where their feast is observed on January 28. Still another legend links Brigid and Maura with St. Baya, a recluse
in Scotland, and her pupil Maura, who attracted disciples and
became their abbess. Their feast is celebrated on November 2.

BRIGID (c. 450–525). Probably born at Faughart near
Dundalk, Louth, Ireland, her parents were baptized by St. Pat-
rick, with whom she developed a close friendship. According
to legend, her father was Dubhthach, an Irish chieftain of
Leinster, and her mother, Brocca, was a slave at his court.
Even as a young girl she evinced an interest for a religious
life and took the veil in her youth from St. Macaille at
Croghan and probably was professed by St. Mel of Armagh,
who is believed to have conferred abbatial authority on her.
She settled with seven of her virgins at the foot of Croghan
Hill for a time and about 468 followed Mel to Meath. About

470 she founded a double monastery at Cill-Dara (Kildare) and was abbess of the convent, the first in Ireland. The foundation developed into a center of learning and spirituality, and around it grew up the cathedral city of Kildare. She founded a school of art at Kildare and its illuminated manuscripts became famous, notably the Book of Kildare, which was praised as one of the finest of all illuminated Irish manuscripts before its disappearance three centuries ago. Brigid was one of the most remarkable women of her times, and despite the numerous legendary, extravagant, and even fantastic miracles attributed to her there is no doubt that her extraordinary spirituality, boundless charity, and compassion for those in distress were real. She died at Kildare on February 1. The Mary of the Gael, she is buried at Downpatrick with St. Columba and St. Patrick, with whom she is the patron of Ireland. Her name is sometimes Bridget and Bride.

BRITES. *See* Silva, Bl. Beatrice da.

BRITT (5th century). *See* Brigid.

BRUNO (c. 1030–1101). Born in Cologne of the prominent Hartenfaust family, he studied at the cathedral school at Rheims, and on his return to Cologne about 1055 was ordained and became a canon at St. Cunibert's. He returned to Rheims in 1056 as professor of theology, became head of the school the following year, and remained there until 1074, when he was appointed chancellor of Rheims by its archbishop, Manasses. Bruno was forced to flee Rheims when he and several other priests denounced Manasses in 1076 as unfit for the office of papal legate. Bruno later returned to Cologne but went back to Rheims in 1080 when Manasses was deposed, and though the people of Rheims wanted to make Bruno archbishop, he decided to pursue an eremitical life. He became a hermit under Abbot St. Robert of Molesmes (who later founded Citeaux) but then moved on to Grenoble with six companions in 1084. They were assigned a place for their hermitages in a desolate mountainous Alpine area called La Grande Chartreuse by Bishop St. Hugh of Grenoble, whose confessor Bruno became. They built an oratory and individual cells, roughly followed the rule of St. Benedict, and thus began the Carthusian Order. They embraced a life of poverty, manual work, prayer, and transcribing manuscripts, though as yet they had no written rule. The fame of the group and their founder spread, and in 1090 Bruno was brought to Rome, against his wishes, by Pope Urban II (whom he had taught at Rheims) as papal adviser in the reformation of the clergy. Bruno persuaded Urban to allow him to resume his eremitical state, founded St. Mary's at La Torre in Calabria, declined the Pope's offer of the archbishopric of Reggio, became a close friend of Count Robert of Sicily, and remained there until his death on October 6. He wrote several commentaries on the Psalms and on St. Paul's epistles. He was never formally canonized because of the Carthusians' aversion to public honors, but Pope Leo X granted the Carthusians permission to celebrate his feast in 1514, and his name was placed on the Roman calendar in 1623. October 6.

BRUNO (1049–1123). Born at Solero, Piedmont, of a noble family, he studied at Bologna, and became a canon at Siena in 1079. He defended Church teaching on the Blessed Sacrament against Berengarius at a council in Rome, and in 1080 was appointed bishop of Segni. An outstanding Scripture scholar, he opposed simony and lay investiture, worked with St. Gregory to reform the Church, and incurred the enmity of Count Ainulf, a follower of Emperor Henry IV, who imprisoned him for three months. In 1095, he resigned his see to become a monk at Monte Cassino, but because of the objections of the people of Segni, he was forced to withdraw his resignation, though he remained at Monte Cassino. He was elected abbot in 1107 but was ordered to resign the abbacy and return to his see by Pope Paschal II when he rebuked the Pontiff for concessions in ecclesiastical matters he had made to Emperor-elect Henry V. Bruno was canonized in 1183. July 18.

BRUNO THE GREAT (925–65). Youngest son of Emperor Henry the Fowler and St. Matilda, he was sent to the cathedral school of Utrecht when four, joined the imperial court when fourteen, and in 940 became personal secretary to Emperor Otto I, his brother. He was ordained in 950, became Otto's chancellor, and in 953 was appointed archbishop of Cologne. He founded the abbey of St. Pantaleon there, insisted on high ecclesiastical standards, reformed monasteries, and encouraged learning. He was made duke of Lorraine by Otto when the Emperor deposed Duke Conrad the

Red for leading a rebellion, played a leading role in imperial as well as ecclesiastical affairs, and helped settle numerous political disputes. He was coregent of the Empire when Otto went to Rome to be crowned. Bruno died at Rheims on October 11, and his cult was confirmed in 1870.

BRUNO OF QUERFURT. *See* Boniface (974–1009).

BUDEUX. *See* Budoc.

BUDOC (6th–7th centuries). Unreliable legend has him the son of the King of Goëllo (Tréguier), Brittany, and Azenor, daughter of the ruler of Brest. Budoc was supposed to have been born at sea under incredible circumstances (his mother had been exiled and cast into the sea in a cask, where he was born, attended by St. Brigid). He was raised and educated at a monastery near Waterford, Ireland, became its abbot and was elected bishop, and then returned to Brittany, where he became bishop of Dol, succeeding St. Maglorius, and ruled for twenty-six years. Another tradition in England has him an Irish hermit who immigrated to Britain and settled at Budock near Falmouth. His name is also spelled Budeux and Beuzec. December 9.

BUONAGIUNTA, JOHN (1206–57). *See* Monaldo, Buonfiglio.

BURGUNDOFARA (d. 657). Daughter of Count Agneric, courtier of King Theodebert II, she refused her father's demands that she marry and became abbess of a convent she convinced him to build, and ruled for thirty-seven years. Named Evoriacum, the convent was renamed for her after her death, and in time became the famous Benedictine abbey of Faremoutiers. She is also known as Fare. April 3.

C

CABRINI, FRANCES XAVIER (1850–1917). The youngest of thirteen children of Augustine Cabrini, a farmer, and Stella Oldini, she was born on July 15 at Sant' Angelo Lodigiano, Italy, and christened Maria Francesca. She was destined to be a schoolteacher but when orphaned at eighteen, she decided to follow a religious life. She was refused by two communities, but in 1874 she was invited by Msgr. Serrati to take over a badly managed orphanage, House of Providence, at Codogno. Fierce opposition by its foundress, Antonia Tondini, eventually led to its closing by the bishop of Todi, who then invited Frances to found an institution. With seven followers, she moved into an abandoned Franciscan friary at Codogno and founded the Missionary Sisters of the Sacred Heart, devoted to the education of girls. The institute received the approval of the bishop in 1880 and soon spread to Grumello, Milan, and Rome. In 1889, Frances went to New York at the invitation of Archbishop Corrigan to work with Italian immigrants. During the next twenty-seven years, in the face of great obstacles, she traveled extensively and the congregation spread all over the United States (in 1892, it opened its first hospital, Columbus, in New York), Italy, South and Central America, and England. Its constitutions received final approval from the Holy See in 1907 (first approval had been in 1887), and by the time of her death in Chicago on December 22 there were more than fifty hospitals, schools, orphanages, convents, and other foundations in existence. She became an American citizen in 1909. She was canonized by Pope Pius XII in 1946, the first American citizen to be so honored, and was named patroness of immigrants by Pius in 1950. November 13.

CADFAN (6th century). A missionary from Letavia (probably in Brittany but possibly in southeastern Wales) to Wales, he founded monasteries at Towyn in Merioneth and Llangadfan in Montgomeryshire, and later a monastic center on the island of Bardsey, where he was first abbot and which developed into a great center of monasticism. He probably died at Bardsey. November 1.

CADOC (d. c. 575). A Welshman and son of St. Gundleus and St. Gwladys, he was educated by St. Tatheus, an Irishman, at Caerwent. He became a monk, founded a monastery at Llancarfan, near Cardiff, which became famous, studied for three years in Ireland and then at Brednock, and founded a church at Llanspyddid. He returned to Llancarfan as abbot, visited Brittany, Cornwall, and Scotland, made pilgrimages to Rome and Jerusalem, and probably died at Llansannor near Llancarfan. Some authorities believe he was killed near Weedon fighting invading Saxons. September 25.

CADWALLADER. *See* Caedwalla.

CAECILIA. A variant of Cecilia.

CAEDMON (d. c. 680). A laborer, perhaps a herdsman, at Whitby monastery, England, he is said to have received the gift of composing verses in praise of God in a vision. He became a lay brother there and studied Scripture, which he turned into verses, the first Anglo-Saxon writer of religious poetry. Though only one of his hymns, said to have been composed in a dream, survives, he is called "the Father of English Sacred Poetry." February 11.

CAEDWALLA (c. 659–89). He became the King of the West Saxons in 685 or 686, subjugated Sussex, made Surrey and Kent dependencies, and conquered the Isle of Wight, whose pagan inhabitants he annihilated. Under him Wessex became a powerful kingdom, but in 688, he resigned his throne and went to Rome. He was baptized there on Easter Eve, April 10, by Pope Sergius I, taking the name Peter, died a few days later, and was buried in St. Peter's on April 20. Still to be seen on his tomb in St. Peter's is his metrical epi-

taph, ordered by Sergius, preserved on the original stone. His
name is sometimes spelled Cadwallader. November 12.

CAESARIUS OF ARLES (470–543). Of a Gallo-Roman
family, he was born at Châlons, Burgundy, decided to pursue
an ecclesiastical career, entered the monastery at Lérins when
eighteen, and as cellarer incurred the enmity of some of the
monks. Illness caused him to leave, but while recuperating at
Arles he came to the attention of his Uncle Eonus, the bishop
there, who had him transferred from Lérins to his see, and
ordained him. After three years spent in reforming a nearby
monastery, he was elected, against his wishes, to succeed his
uncle as bishop of Arles in 503. Caesarius put into effect
numerous reforms, fought Arianism, ordered the Divine
Office to be sung in Arles' churches every day of the week,
and preached frequently and successfully. He founded a convent at Arles, with his sister Caesaria as abbess, wrote a rule
for its nuns, and presided over several synods as metropolitan. In 505, he was banished to Bordeaux by King Alaric
II of the Visigoths in the mistaken belief he was trying to
make Arles part of the Burgundian kingdom where he had
been born, but was recalled when Alaric discovered the falsity
of the accuser's charge. Caesarius aided the victims of the
siege of Arles by the Burgundian King and was again arrested
when Theodoric the Ostrogoth seized Arles; again all charges
against him were dropped at a meeting with Theodoric at
Ravenna in 513. Caesarius then traveled to Rome, was made
apostolic delegate in Gaul, and received the pallium from
Pope St. Symmachus, reportedly the first instance in which it
was granted to any Western European bishop. After the
Franks captured Arles in 536, Caesarius spent most of his
time at St. John's convent, where he died on August 27. At
the time of his death, he had ruled his see for forty years and
was the most famous bishop in Gaul, noted for his holiness,
charity, and ability. He was largely responsible for the condemnation of semi-Pelagianism at the Council of Orange in
529 and published an adaptation of Roman law, largely based
on the Theodosian code, *Breviarium Alarici,* which became
the civil code of Gaul. Several of his sermons have survived.

CAESARIUS OF NAZIANZEN (c. 329–69). Son of Gregory
the Elder, bishop of Nazianzen and brother of St. Gregory
Nazianzen, he studied philosophy and medicine at Alex-

andria and Constantinople and became a famous physician.
He was named physician to Emperor Julian the Apostate,
rebuffed the Emperor's efforts to get him to abjure his religion
though he was as yet only a catechumen, and resigned his position. He was later physician to Emperor Jovian, treasurer
for Emperor Valens, and in 368 was baptized, after he had
narrowly escaped death in an earthquake at Nicaea in Bithynia. His fortune was left to the poor on his death. February 25.

CAINNECH. See Canice.

CAIUS (d. 296). Nothing is known of him except from
unreliable tradition, which has him a Dalmatian and a relative of Emperor Diocletian. He became Pope in 283, decreed
bishops must be priests before consecration, and when Diocletian's persecution of Christians began, fled to a cave, where
he lived for eight years until his death. How unreliable the
tradition about him as a source of factual information may
be judged from the fact that Diocletian's persecution did not
begin until six or seven years after his death on April 22.

CAJETAN (1480–1547). Son of Count Caspar of Thiene
and Mary di Porto, he was born in Vicenza, Italy, and was
two when his father was killed fighting for the Venetians
against King Ferdinand of Naples. He was raised by his
mother, studied at the University of Padua, and received his
doctorates in civil and in canon law. He became a senator in
Vicenza and in 1506, went to Rome, where Pope Julius II
made him a protonotary, and he revived the Confraternity of
Divine Love, consisting of devout priests. He resigned the position of protonotary on Julius' death in 1513, was ordained
in 1516, and returned to Vicenza. He joined the Oratory of
St. Jerome there, worked with the poor and the sick, particularly the incurable, founded a similar oratory at Verona, and
in 1520 went to Venice, where he continued his work with
the needy. In 1523, he went to Rome and with John Peter
Caraffa, later to be Pope Paul IV, Paul Consiglieri and Boniface da Colle founded an institute of clergy devoted to reforming the Church, preaching to the people, aiding the sick,
and improving the state of the clergy, which was at a very
low ebb. The institute was approved by Pope Clement VII,

with Caraffa, bishop of Chieti, as provost general in 1524. Called the Theatines (Theate is the Latin for Chiete), the institute was to consist of regular clergy living in community, bound by vows, and engaged in pastoral work. Not too successful at first, it barely survived the destruction of its house in Rome when Charles V sacked the city in 1527. In 1530, Cajetan was elected superior, but Caraffa was reelected in 1533, and Cajetan then went to Verona and later to Naples, where he fought widespread opposition to the reforms of the bishops there and the heretical teachings so prevalent. Later, with Bl. John Marinoni, he founded the *montes pietatis* to help extend loans to the poor and combat usury. He died in Naples on August 7, and was canonized in 1671. Also known as Gaetano, Cajetan was one of the great Catholic reformers; many of the reforms of the Council of Trent were anticipated by Cajetan and put into effect by him long before that council was convened. August 7.

CALASANZ, JOSEPH (1556–1648). Youngest son of Pedro Calasanz, he was born at his father's castle near Peralta de la Sal, Aragon, Spain, on September 11. He studied at Estadilla, the University of Lérida (where he received his doctorate in law), Valencia, and Alcalá, and was ordained in 1583, despite his father's wish that he be a soldier. He was appointed vicar general of Trempe by the bishop of Urgel, who then sent him to revive religion and reform the clergy in a desolate section of his see in the Pyrenees. Successful, he was appointed vicar general of the whole diocese on his return but resigned in 1592 and went to Rome. He became attached to the household of Ascanio Cardinal Colonna, distinguished himself with his heroic work in the plague of 1595, and labored to improve the education of needy children. With two priests he opened a free school in 1597 and became supervisor of a community of teachers that developed to take care of the tremendous increase in the number of students at the school. An investigation of complaints about the school was so favorable that Pope Clement VIII took it under his protection, as did Pope Paul V. Other schools were opened, and in 1621 the community was recognized as a religious order, the Clerks Regular of Religious Schools, with Joseph as superior general. The last years of his life were saddened by internal dissension when a Fr. Mario Sozzi accused him of incapacity and became general; when Sozzi died in 1643, his successor, Fr. Cherubini, followed his direction. The order was torn apart by their actions, and in 1645 a commission appointed by the Pope restored Joseph to the generalate. But dissension continued, and in 1646 Pope Innocent X in effect dissolved the congregation by making it a society of secular priests subject to local bishops. Fr. Cherubini, assigned the task of drawing up a new constitution, was convicted of maladministering Nazarene College, of which he was rector, and forced to resign; repentant, he was reconciled to Joseph in 1648 on his deathbed. Joseph died a few months later in Rome on August 25, and was canonized in 1767. His foundation was reformed in 1656, restored as a religious order in 1669, and is in existence today, popularly known as the Piarists or Scolopi. He is also referred to as Joseph Calasanctius.

CALIXTUS. *See* Callistus.

CALLISTUS I (d. c. 222). A Roman from the Trastevere section of Rome, son of one Domitius, he was a slave of Carpophorus, who put him in charge of a bank. He lost the bank's money, fled, was caught at Porto and sentenced to a punishment reserved for slaves—the dreaded hand mill. Released at the request of the creditors, he was again arrested for fighting in a synagogue, presumably trying to recover some of the money, and sentenced to the mines in Sardinia. He was again released with other prisoners at the request of Emperor Commodus' mistress, Marcia, and about 199 was made a deacon and director of the Christian cemetery on the Via Appia (now St. Callistus cemetery) by Pope Zephyrinus and became the friend and adviser of the Pope. He was elected to succeed Zephyrinus as Pope in 217 and was denounced by his bitter enemy, St. Hippolytus, a candidate for the papal throne, who set himself up as an antipope and who wrote the unfriendly account of him that is the source of most of our information about him. Hippolytus condemned him of leniency to the Monarchian heretics, though Callistus had condemned their leader Sabelius, and for such actions as forgiving repentant murderers and adulterers, permitting multimarried men to become priests, recognizing the marriages of free women and slaves, and refusing to depose repentant bishops who had committed mortal sins. It is believed Callistus was killed in an uprising, and is so considered to be a martyr. October 14.

CAMILLUS DE LELLIS. *See* Lellis, Camillus de.

CAMPION, EDMUND (c. 1540–81). Born in London, son of a bookseller, he was raised a Catholic, given a scholarship to St. John's College, Oxford, when fifteen, and became a fellow when only seventeen. His brilliance attracted the attention of such leading personages as the Earl of Leicester, Robert Cecil, and even Queen Elizabeth. He took the Oath of Supremacy acknowledging Elizabeth head of the Church in England and became an Anglican deacon in 1564. Doubts about Protestantism increasingly beset him, and in 1569 he went to Ireland, where further study convinced him he had been in error, and he returned to Catholicism. Forced to flee the persecution unleashed on Catholics by the excommunication of Elizabeth by Pope Pius V, he went to Douai, France, where he studied theology, joined the Jesuits, and then went to Brno, Bohemia, the following year for his novitiate. He taught at the college at Prague and in 1578 was ordained there. He and Fr. Robert Persons were the first Jesuits chosen for the English mission and were sent to England in 1580. His activities among the Catholics, the distribution of his *Decem rationes* at the university church in Oxford, and the premature publication of his famous *Brag* (which he had written to present his case if he was captured) made him the object of one of the most intensive manhunts in English history. He was betrayed at Lyford, near Oxford, imprisoned in the Tower of London, and when he refused to apostatize when offered rich inducements to do so, was tortured and then hanged, drawn, and quartered at Tyburn on December 1 on the technical charge of treason but in reality because of his priesthood. He was canonized by Pope Paul VI in 1970 as one of the Forty English and Welsh Martyrs.

CANDIDA (no date). Long venerated in Rome, her remains were enshrined in St. Praxedes church there by Pope St. Paschal I in the ninth century. She was one of a group of martyrs executed for their faith on the Ostian Way.

CANDIDUS (d. c. 287). *See* Maurice.

CANICE (c. 515-99). All we know about him is from unreliable legend, according to which he was born at Glengiven, Ireland, became a monk under St. Cadoc at Llancarfan, Wales, and was ordained there. After a trip to Rome, he studied under St. Finnian at Clonard, Ireland, accompanied SS. Kieran, Columba, and Comgall to St. Mobhi at Glasnevin, preached for a time in Ireland, and then went to Scotland. A close friend of Columba's whom he accompanied on a visit to King Brude of the Picts, he was a most successful missionary, built a monastery at Aghaboe, Ireland, and probably one at Kilkenny. He is also known as Kenneth and Cainnech. October 11.

CANISIUS, PETER (1521-97). Born at Nijmegen, Netherlands, on May 8, son of the nine-times-elected burgomaster there, he received his master's from Cologne University, studied canon law at Louvain, and then, inspired by a retreat given by Bl. Peter Fabre at Mainz, joined the Jesuits in 1543. Peter gave his inheritance to the poor, was ordained in 1546, and became noted for his preaching. He attended two sessions of the Council of Trent, was sent to teach at the Jesuits' first school at Messina by St. Ignatius, and then was sent in 1549 to Ingolstadt at the request of Duke William IV of Bavaria to combat Protestantism and revive Catholicism there. He served as rector and then as vice chancellor of the university, effected a religious revival among the people, and in 1552 was sent on a similar mission in Vienna at the request of King Ferdinand. He was most successful, administering the diocese for a year, but refused to consider an appointment to head the see. In 1555, he published the first edition of his *Catechism*, which was to be enormously successful, with hundreds of printings in some fifteen languages. He was sent to Prague in 1556 to help found a new college and while there was appointed provincial of a new province, consisting of southern Germany, Bohemia, and Austria. He traveled all over Germany, lecturing, preaching, debating with Protestants, founding colleges, and restoring Catholicism in the cities in which he preached, and was responsible for the spread of Jesuit influence to Poland. He was in Augsburg, 1559-65, was instrumental in having the Reichstag restore public schools, and when his term as provincial expired, he taught at the Jesuit college at Dillengen, Bavaria. He was court chaplain at Innsbruck and helped heal a rift between the Emperor and Pope

Pius IV, was selected to promulgate the decrees of the Council of Trent in Germany, and in 1580 founded a college at Fribourg that became the University of Fribourg; his preaching at Fribourg was a major factor in keeping Fribourg Catholic. He suffered a stroke in 1591 but continued dictating his writing until his death at Fribourg on December 21. He was a prolific writer, edited the works of St. Cyril of Alexandria and St. Leo the Great, an edition of St. Jerome's letters, a martyrology, a revision of the breviary, and a *Manual of Catholics,* among other works. Often called "the Second Apostle of Germany," after St. Boniface, it was due mainly to Peter's efforts that the Counter-Reformation was successful in southern Germany. He was canonized in 1925, when he was declared a Doctor of the Church. December 21.

CANUTE (c. 1086). Illegitimate son of King Sweyn Estrithson of Denmark, nephew of King Canute who had reigned over England, he was unsuccessful in an attempt to claim that crown in 1075 but became King of Denmark as Canute IV, succeeding his brother Harold in 1081. He married Adela, sister of Count Roberts of Flanders, aided the clergy and missionaries, built many churches, and in 1085 prepared to invade England when he reasserted his claim to that country. His heavy taxes and disputes with the *jarls* (the nobles) led to a rebellion headed by his brother Olaf, which forced him to abandon the invasion and flee to the island of Funen. He was tracked down by the insurgents and he, his brother Benedict, and seventeen followers were slain on July 19 in the church of St. Alban in Odense, where he had taken refuge. Reportedly numerous miracles occurred at his tomb, and together with the fact that he was kneeling at the altar of the church after confession when he was slain caused Pope Paschal II to authorize his cult at the request of King Eric III of Denmark in 1101. January 19. His name is also spelled Knute.

CANUTE LAVARD (d. 1131). Son of King Eric the Good of Denmark, he spent part of his youth at the Saxon court, and when he came of age he was made duke of southern Jutland. He fought Viking raids, brought peace and order to his territory, and aided the missionary activities of St. Vicelin. In 1129, Emperor Lothair III recognized him as King of the Western Wends, a move strongly opposed by his uncle, King

Nils of Denmark, and which two years later, on January 7, led to Canute's murder near Ringsted by Magnus Nielssen and Henry Skadelaar, his cousins. He was canonized in 1169. He is also known as Knud.

CARACCIOLO, FRANCIS (1563–1608). Of noble parents, he was born on October 13 at Villa Santa Maria, Abruzzi, Italy, and was christened Ascenio. In fulfillment of a vow to devote his life to God if he was cured of a serious ailment thought to be leprosy when he was twenty-two, he studied at Naples and was ordained. He joined the *Bianchi della Giustizia*, a confraternity devoted to caring for prisoners, and in 1588, he, Fr. John Augustine Adorno, and twelve companions founded the Minor Clerks Regular, devoted to missionary work and to ministering to the sick in hospitals and to prisoners. When Pope Sixtus V approved the foundation in 1588, Adorno was named superior, and Ascanio took the name Francis. They established a house in Naples and then went to Spain, where they were refused permission to found a house by the royal court; they were shipwrecked on the way home. The foundation flourished and soon spread all over Italy, and it was asked to take over Santa Maria Maggiore in Naples. On the death of Adorno, Francis was named superior. On visits to Spain he was more successful than on his previous visit and made foundations at Madrid, Valladolid, and Alcala in 1595 and 1598. He was granted leave to resign as superior after seven years, became prior of Santa Maria Maggiore and master of novices. He died on June 1 at Agnone, where he had gone to establish a new foundation. Miracles were attributed to him, and he was reputed to have had the gifts of ecstasies and prophecy. He was canonized in 1807. June 4.

CARANNOG. *See* Carantoc.

CARANTAC. *See* Carantoc.

CARANTOC (6th century). A Welshman, also known as Carannog, he founded a church at Llangrannog, Wales, spent some time in Ireland, and on his return founded a monastery at Cernach (it may have been at Carhampton in Somerset, Crantock in Cornwall, or even possibly in Ireland), of which he was abbot. He is known to have visited Brittany but then returned to Cernach, where he died. He is sometimes identified with a Welsh prince, Carantac, who worked with St. Patrick in the evangelization of Ireland. May 16.

CARTHACH (d. 637). Born at Castlemaine, Kerry, Ireland, and probably named Cuda, he was a swineherd who became a disciple of St. Carthach the Elder, taking his name, who ordained him. About 590, he became a hermit at Kiltulagh and then at Bangor under St. Comgall. After visiting several monasteries, Carthach settled for a time at Rahan in Offaly, and then in 595 founded a monastery there and ruled over eight hundred monks, two of whom, Britons, tried to drown him, as they felt the time had arrived for the monastery to have a new abbot. He wrote a rule in metrical verse, a later version of which is still extant. He also was probably a bishop at Fircall. After forty years, he and his monks were driven from the monastery by Blathmac, a local ruler. He founded a new monastery at Lismore and spent the last years of his life as a hermit in a nearby cave, where he died on May 14. He is also known as Carthage and Mochuda. His cult was confirmed in 1903.

CARTHAGE. *See* Carthach.

CARVALHO, BL. VINCENT (d. 1632). Born at Alfama, near Lisbon, Portugal, he joined the Augustinians at Lisbon and was sent as a missionary to Mexico in 1621; sent to Japan in 1623, he suffered martyrdom there at Nagasaki by being burned to death. He was beatified in 1867 as one of the Martyrs of Japan. September 3.

CASANOVA, LEONARD (1676–1751). Born at Porto Maurizio, Italy, and baptized Paul Jerome, he was sent to the Jesuit Roman College when he was thirteen. His uncle Augustine, with whom he was living, wanted him to become a physician, and when he refused, disowned him. He joined the Franciscans of the Strict Observance at Ponticelli in 1697, taking the name Leonard, continued his studies at the Observant St. Bonaventure's in Rome, and was ordained there in 1703. He went to St. Francesco del Monte monastery in Florence in 1709 and from there preached all over Tuscany with tremendous effect. He became guardian of San Francesco, founded a retreat for religious at nearby Incontro, and spent six years conducting missions around Rome. He was named guardian at St. Bonaventure's in 1736 but was released from this position the following year to continue his missions, which were now attracting huge crowds. He was an ardent promoter of the Stations of the Cross devotion (reputedly setting up almost six hundred Stations throughout Italy), and devotion to the Blessed Sacrament, the Sacred Heart, and Mary. He served for a time as spiritual director of Clementina Sobieska, wife of the claimant of the English throne, King James III, and in 1744 was sent to Corsica by Pope Benedict XIV to preach and to restore peace there but was unsuccessful, since the Corsicans felt he was more a political tool of the Genoese who ruled the island than a missionary. He returned to Rome from a discouraging missionary tour in 1751 completely exhausted and died at St. Bonaventure the night he arrived, November 26; he had been engaged in the most arduous missionary work for forty-three years. Canonized in 1867, he is the patron of parish missions.

CASAS, PHILIP DE LAS (1571–97). Born on May 1 in Mexico City of Spanish parents, he later joined the Franciscans at Puebla but left the order in 1589. He became a merchant and went to the Philippines. While there he regretted his decision and in 1593 rejoined the Franciscans in Manila. He was on his way back to Mexico City in 1596 to be ordained when his ship was driven off course to Japan. He was arrested late in 1596 and crucified the following year with twenty-five other Christians at Nagasaki on February 5 during the persecution of Christians unleashed by the *Taikó*, Toyotomi Hideyoshi. They were all canonized in 1862 as the Martyrs of Japan of 1597. He is also known as Philip of Jesus. February 6.

CASIMIR OF POLAND (1458–84). Third of the thirteen children of King Casimir IV of Poland and Elizabeth of Austria, daughter of Emperor II of Germany, he was born at the royal palace in Cracow on October 3, was taught by Fr. John Dlugosz, and from childhood was attracted to a life of holiness, austerity, and charity. Convinced the cause was unjust, he refused to lead an army against King Matthias Corvinus of Hungary in 1471 to seize the Hungarian throne, as his father and the Hungarian nobility demanded. Though confined to the castle of Dobzki, Casimir resisted all efforts to make him

change his mind. He also resisted his father's efforts to have
him marry and devoted himself to study and prayer. He
served as viceroy while his father was out of Poland,
1479–83, and died on March 4 at the court of Grodno while
on a visit to Lithuania. Many miracles were reported at his
tomb at Vilna, and he was canonized by Pope Adrian VI
in 1522. He is the patron saint of Poland and Lithuania.
March 4.

CASPAR (1st century). *See* Balthasar.

CASPAR DEL BUFALO. *See* Del Bufalo, Caspar.

CASSIAN. *See* John Cassian.

CASSIAN OF TANGIERS (d. c. 298). An official recorder
(court stenographer) at the trial of St. Marcellus the Centurion before Deputy Prefect Aurelius Agricolan at Tangiers,
he denounced the unjust death penalty imposed on Marcellus,
became a Christian, and was imprisoned. Shortly after, he
was put to death. He is the patron of stenographers. December 3.

CASTILLO, BL. JUAN DE (d. 1628). *See* Gonzalez, Bl.
Roque.

CASTORIUS (d. c. 306). He, Claudius, Nicostratus, and
Symphorian are called "the Four Crowned Martyrs" who
were tortured and executed in Pannonia, Hungary, during the
reign of Emperor Diocletian. According to legend, they were
employed as carvers at the imperial quarries at Sirmium
(Mitrovica, Yugoslavia) and impressed Diocletian with their
art, as did another carver, Simplicius. Diocletian commissioned them to do several carvings, which they did to his sat-
isfaction, but they then refused to carve a statue of Aesculapius, as they were Christians. The Emperor accepted their
beliefs, but when they refused to sacrifice to the gods, they
were imprisoned. When Diocletian's officer Lampadius, who
was trying to convince them to sacrifice to the gods, suddenly
died, his relatives accused the five of his death; to placate the
relatives, the Emperor had them executed. Another story has
four unnamed *corniculari* beaten to death in Rome with

leaden whips when they refused to offer sacrifice to Aesculapius of all his troops by Diocletian. They were buried on the Via Lavicana and were later given their names by Pope Miltiades. Probably they were the four Pannonian martyrs (not counting Simplicius) whose remains were translated to Rome and buried in the Four Crowned Ones basilica there. A further complication is the confusion of their story with that of the group of martyrs associated with St. Carpophorus in the Roman Martyrology under November 8.

CATHAL (d. c. 685). Born in Munster, Ireland, he became a pupil and later, noted for his great learning, taught at Lismore. He became headmaster but resigned to go on pilgrimage to Jerusalem. On his way home he was elected bishop of Taranto, Italy, and served there with great distinction and holiness. He is also known as Cataldus and Catald. May 10.

CATHERINE (d. c. 310). Venerated in the East since the tenth century, nothing of any certainty is known of her. Her unreliable legend has her born in Alexandria of a patrician family and converted to Christianity by a vision. She denounced Emperor Maxentius in person for his persecution of the Christians, and when fifty pagan philosophers were converted by her arguments, he had them burned to death. When she refused his bribe of a royal marriage if she would apostatize, he had her imprisoned. On his return home from a camp inspection, he found that his wife, an officer, and two hundred soldiers of her guard had been converted. He had them all put to death. He then condemned Catherine to death on a spiked wheel, and when the wheel miraculously broke, he had her beheaded. Supposedly her body was brought to the monastery of Mount Sinai, where it reputedly still is. Catherine is one of the Fourteen Holy Helpers, was one of the voices heard by Joan of Arc, and is the patroness of philosophers, maidens, and preachers. November 25.

CATHERINE OF BOLOGNA. *See* Vigri, Catherine de'.

CATHERINE OF GENOA (1447–1510). Daughter of James Fieschi and Francesca di Negro, she was born in Genoa, their fifth and last child. She early evinced an interest in the religious life, but when her father died, she was married when sixteen to Julian Adorno. He was shiftless, unfaithful, and a spendthrift, and after ten years of marriage his extravagance reduced them to poverty. Julian then reformed his life, became a Franciscan tertiary, and they agreed to live a continent life together. Catherine began to live a most unusual and intensive spiritual life while they devoted themselves to working in the Pammetone hospital, and six years later, in 1479, they went to live in the hospital, of which she was made director in 1490. She almost died of a plague that wiped out three quarters of the inhabitants in 1493, recovered, but was obliged to resign her position in 1496 because of ill health, though she and her husband continued to live in the hospital. Julian died the following year, and about 1499, Catherine met Don Cattaneo Marabotto, who became her spiritual director. Catherine experienced many mystical episodes and suffered from bad health the last years of her life before her death in Genoa on September 14. Her *Dialogue Between the Soul and the Body* and *Treatise on Purgatory* are outstanding documents in the field of mysticism. She was canonized in 1737. September 15.

CATHERINE LABOURÉ. *See* Labouré, Catherine.

CATHERINE OF SIENA (1347–80). Born on March 25 at Siena, Italy, daughter of a dyer and the youngest of twenty-five children, she began to have the mystical experiences she was to have all her life when she was only six. She resisted all efforts of her parents to have her marry and devoted herself to prayer and fasting. She became a Dominican tertiary when she was sixteen and increasingly experienced visions of Christ, Mary, and the saints, interspersed with diabolical visions and periods of spiritual aridity. She ministered to the ill in hospitals, devoting herself to caring for patients with particularly distressing illnesses like leprosy and advanced cancer cases. Her supernatural gifts attracted ardent supporters, but many believed she was a faker and caused her to be brought before a chapter general of the Dominicans in Florence, where the accusations were dismissed. At this time, Bl. Raymond of Capua was appointed her confessor, in time became her disciple, and later was her biographer. On her return to Siena, she devoted herself to caring for those stricken by a plague that devastated the city, ministered to condemned prisoners, and was acclaimed for her holiness, aid to the spiritually troubled, and abilities as a peacemaker. She whole-

heartedly supported Pope Gregory XI's call for a crusade
against the Turks, and while on a visit to Pisa in 1375 (a
visit that brought on a religious revival in that city) received
the stigmata, invisible during her lifetime but clearly apparent
at the time of her death. She was unsuccessful in attempting
to mediate between Florence and Pope Gregory, but her
meeting with the Pontiff in Avignon and her urging led him
to return the papacy to Rome in 1376. At his request, she
again returned to Florence, and this time she was successful
in reconciling Florence· and the Holy See. On her return to
Siena, she devoted herself to recording her mystical experiences, which were published as the *Dialogue* of St. Catherine.
On Gregory's death in 1378, the Great Schism began when
Urban VI's election as Pope was contested by a group of dissident cardinals, who elected Robert of Geneva antipope
Clement VII at Fondi and set up a papal court at Avignon.
Catherine worked unceasingly to secure support for Urban
and end the schism, though never hesitating to censure Urban
for some of his actions. He welcomed her criticisms and
brought her to Rome, where she continued her efforts to gain
support for him. She suffered a paralytic stroke on April 21
and died in Rome a few days later, on April 29. Catherine
was one of the greatest of Christian mystics. In addition to
her *Dialogue,* some four hundred of her letters to people in
every class of society are still extant. She was canonized in
1461, made patroness of Italy in 1939, and was declared a Doctor of the Church by Pope Paul VI in 1970. April 29.

CATHERINE OF SWEDEN (c. 1331–81). Fourth of eight
children of St. Bridget of Sweden, Catherine Ulfsdotter was
born at Ulfasa, Sweden, and when about fourteen was married to Eggard von Kürnen but convinced him to join her in a
vow of chastity. In 1350, she visited her mother in Rome and
was persuaded by her to stay there with her. Catherine was
widowed later the same year, as prophesied by her mother,
repeatedly refused marriage to persistent suitors, and spent
the next twenty-five years as her mother's constant companion. When Bridget died, Catherine returned to Sweden to
Vadstena, which Bridget had founded, with her body and
devoted herself to organizing the Bridgettines her mother had
founded. She spent five years, 1375–80, and finally secured a
new papal approval of the congregation from Pope Urban VI.
She was in failing health when she returned to Vadstena, and

she died there on March 24. In 1484, Pope Innocent VIII gave permission to venerate her as a saint.

CATHERINE OF VADSTENA. *See* Catherine of Sweden.

CEADDA. *See* Chad.

CEALLACH. *See* Celsus of Armagh.

CECILIA (date unknown). Of a patrician family and also known as Cecily, she was born in Rome and raised a Christian. She was married against her will to Valerian (or Valerius) and convinced him to respect her virginity and become a Christian. She also converted his brother Tiburtius. Valerian (feast day, April 14) and Tiburtius devoted themselves to charitable works until apprehended burying the bodies of martyred Christians. They were arraigned before the prefect, Almachius, and when they refused to sacrifice to the gods, were scourged and beheaded at Pagus Triopius, near Rome, together with Maximus (April 14), who had been so impressed by their witness to Christ that he became a Christian. Cecilia buried the three and in turn was arrested. She debated with Almachius and when he was unable to shake her faith, sentenced her to death. When her sentence of death by suffocation was miraculously prevented, a soldier was assigned to behead her. He bungled the job and she lay dying for three days before expiring on September 16. Though veneration of Cecilia has been for centuries one of the most popular cults in the Church, her story has been constructed from legends, many of which are untrustworthy, so that even the date of her death is uncertain and is estimated as having occurred anywhere from 177 to the fourth century (the Roman Martyrology says Tiburtius and the others suffered martyrdom under Emperor Alexander, who ruled 222–35). She is the patroness of music and musicians, since supposedly at her wedding she did not hear the nuptial music and sounds of merriment but sat apart, singing to God in her heart. November 22.

CECILY. *See* Cecilia.

CEDD (d. 664). A native of Northumbria, England, and brother of St. Chad, with whom he was raised, he became a monk at Lindisfarne and in 653 was sent with three other priests to evangelize the Middle Angles when their King Peada became a Christian. Cedd left to preach in Essex when King Sigebert of the East Angles was converted, was consecrated bishop of the East Saxons by St. Finan at Lindisfarne in 654, and spent the rest of his life with the Saxons. He founded monasteries at Bradwell, Tilbury, and Lastingham, built several churches, attended the Synod of Whitby in 664, where he accepted the Roman observances, and died of the plague at Lastingham, Yorkshire, on October 26.

CELESTINE I (d. 432). Born in Campania, Italy, he became a deacon in Rome, and was elected Pope on September 20, 422. He was a stanch supporter of St. Germanus of Auxerre in the fight against Pelagianism, and a friend of St. Augustine, with whom he corresponded. An unyielding foe of Nestorianism, he held a council in Rome in 430 that condemned the heresy and threatened Nestorius with excommunication if he did not desist from his heretical teaching and in 431 sent three legates to the General Council of Ephesus, which formally condemned Nestorianism. He wrote a treatise against semi-Pelagianism and sent Palladius to Ireland to evangelize the Irish; some scholars believed he may have sent Patrick, but this is unlikely. He died on July 27. April 6.

CELESTINE V (1210–96). Born at Isernia in the Abruzzi, Italy, the eleventh of twelve children of peasant parents, Peter di Morone became a hermit when twenty, left his cell to study for the priesthood, and was ordained in Rome. He became a Benedictine at Faizola in 1246 and was permitted to return to his eremitical life on Monte Morone near Sulmona, attracting great crowds. After five years he retired with two companions to Monte Majella in quest of greater solitude but was persuaded to return to Monte Morone, where he organized the hermits into a community and eventually a monastery, with a strict rule, and he was elected abbot. In 1274, he received approval of his order of monks, the Celestines. When the papacy, after the death of Pope Nicholas IV, remained vacant for two years because of political bickering, Peter reputedly threatened the cardinals with the wrath of God if they did not elect a new Pope at once, whereupon at Perugia, they elected the eighty-four-year-old Peter as Pope on July 5, 1294. Despite his grievous misgivings, he was installed as Pope Celestine V on August 29 and immediately became a prey of the scheming King Charles of Naples, who took advantage of his otherworldliness, inexperience, and naïveté. Heartbroken at what was taking place and overwhelmed by the burden of the office he had not sought and was incapable of filling, he abdicated on December 13, 1294, and returned to his monastery. Cardinal Gaetani was elected Pope Boniface VIII to succeed him, and fearful that the great popularity of his holy predecessor might lead some plotters to attempt to put him back on the papal throne and cause a further split in Christendom, Boniface imprisoned Celestine in the castle of Fumone, near Anagni, where he died ten months later, on May 19. He was canonized by Pope Clement V.

CELSUS OF ARMAGH (1079–1129). A layman named Ceallach mac Aedha, he succeeded to the bishopric of Armagh (it was a hereditary see) in 1105 when he was twenty-six, was consecrated bishop, put into effect many reforms in his diocese, and ruled well and effectively. He mediated between warring Irish factions, was a friend of St. Malachy, and ended the hereditary succession to his see by naming Malachy as his successor on his deathbed. He died on April 1 at Ardpatrick, Munster. April 7.

CEOLFRID (642–716). Probably born in Northumbria, England, he became a monk at Gilling monastery when eighteen and then at St. Wilfrid's monastery at Ripon, where he was ordained. He served as master of novices at Ripon and then was appointed prior of St. Peter's at Wearmouth by St. Benedict Biscop. His strictness with the monks caused such hostility that he returned to Ripon. He accompanied Benedict to Rome in 678, and when Benedict founded St. Paul monastery at Jarrow, six miles from Wearmouth, in 685, he made Ceolfrid deputy abbot. Shortly after, a plague wiped out all the monks at Jarrow except Ceolfrid and a young student. When Benedict died in 690, Ceolfrid was elected abbot, ruled with great ability the next quarter century, and developed the twin monasteries into great centers of learning, building up the libraries and becoming a noted biblical scholar. In 716, he resigned because of the infirmities of old age and set out for Rome, where he wanted to die, but died on the way at Langres, Champagne, on September 25. One of his pupils was

Bede, the great English historian, who wrote of him in his *Historia Abbatum.*

CEOLWULF (d. c. 764). A king in Northumbria, England, he resigned in 738 after reigning eight years and became a monk at Lindisfarne. He was highly venerated and Bede dedicated his *Ecclesiastical History* to "the Most Glorious King Ceolwulf." January 15.

CERNEUF. *See* Serenus the Gardener.

CHABANEL, NOEL (1613–49). Born on February 2 near Mende, France, he joined the Jesuits in 1630 and in 1643 was sent as a missionary to the Huron Indians in New France. He became assistant to Fr. Charles Garnier at the Indian village of Etarita in 1649 and was murdered on December 8 by an apostate Indian while returning from a visit to neighboring Ste. Marie. He was canonized in 1930 by Pope Pius XI as one of the Martyrs of North America. September 26.

CHAD (d. 672). Born in Northumbria, England, and also known as Ceadda, he and his brother Cedd studied under St. Aidan at Lindisfarne, became monks there, and when Aidan died, Chad spent several years with St. Egbert at Rathmelsigi in Ireland. Chad went back to England as abbot of Lastingham abbey in Yorkshire which Cedd had founded, and the following year, Chad was appointed bishop of York by King Oswy. Meanwhile, Oswy's son King Alcfrid had appointed Wilfrid bishop of York, and when Theodore, the new archbishop of Canterbury, arrived in England in 669 and visited Northumbria, he accused Chad of an improper consecration. Impressed by Chad's humble acceptance of his verdict, Theodore regularized his consecration and had him appointed bishop of Mercia by Oswy. He established his see at Lichfield, founded Bardney abbey, and built a retreat house near the church at Lichfield. He died at Lichfield. March 2.

CHAMPAGNAT, BL. MARCELLINUS (1789–1840). Born at Le Rosey, Loire, France, on May 20, the son of a miller, he studied at Lyons seminary, was ordained in 1816, and was sent to La Valla as a curate. Interested in founding a new teaching order for boys since his seminary days, he founded the teaching congregation of the Little Brothers of

Mary (the Marist Brothers) in 1817, which received formal approval from Rome in 1836. He published *Guide des Écoles,* which became the basis for Marist teaching in 1853, and died at Notre Dame de l'Hermitage on June 6. He was beatified in 1955.

CHANEL, PETER MARY (1803–41). Born at Cluet, near Belley, France, he was a shepherd in his youth, studied under the parish priest at Cras, and was ordained in 1827. He served as parish priest at Crozet, joined the Marists in 1831, and was a professor at their seminary in Belley for the next five years. In 1836, he was sent as a missionary to the New Hebrides in the Pacific Ocean, worked with some success on the island of Futuna, and was murdered there on April 28 by order of the chief when he found that his son wanted to be baptized. Peter was canonized by Pope Pius XII in 1954—the first Marist martyr and the first martyr of Oceania. April 28.

CHANTAL, JANE FRANCES DE (1572–1641). Daughter of the president of the Burgundy parliament, Benigne Frémyot, she was born on January 28 in Dijon, France. She married Baron Christopher de Chantal when she was twenty, and the couple had seven children by the time he died in a hunting accident in 1601. She was deeply affected by St. Francis de Sales when she heard him preach in 1604, recognized him from a vision she had had, and convinced him to become her spiritual director. She desired to enter the Carmelites but he convinced her not to do so and in 1607 explained to her his concept of a new congregation he wished to found. After making provision for her children and putting her affairs in order, she, Mary Favre, Charlotte de Bréchard, and a servant, Anne Coste, were clothed by Francis in 1610 in a house on the shores of Lake Annecy, and the Congregation of the Visitation was founded for young girls and widows desirous of following a religious life but unable to follow the severe ascetic life that was customary in the religious houses of that time. Despite numerous difficulties, the order spread all over France, and in the following three decades more than sixty houses were founded. During the last years of her life, Jane experienced periods of spiritual aridity and more than once suffered the torments of the dark night of the soul. She died at Moulins on December 13 on her return from a trip to Paris to visit Queen Anne. Jane was buried at

Annecy near St. Francis de Sales, and was canonized in 1767. It was for her and her nuns that St. Francis wrote his great spiritual classic *On the Love of God*. December 12.

CHARITY (2nd century). According to an Eastern allegory explaining the cult of Divine Wisdom, Faith, Hope, and Charity were the daughters of Wisdom (known as Sophia in the Roman Martyrology on September 30), a widow in Rome. The daughters suffered martyrdom during Hadrian's persecution of Christians: Faith, twelve, was scourged, and when unharmed when boiling pitch was poured on her, was beheaded; Hope, ten, and Charity, nine, were also beheaded after emerging, unscathed, from a furnace; and Wisdom died three days later while praying at their graves. August 1.

CHARLES BORROMEO. *See* Borromeo, Charles.

CHARLES OF SEZZE. *See* Marchioni, John Charles.

CHASTAN, BL. JAMES HONORÉ. *See* Imbert, Bl. Laurence.

CHIONIA (d. 304). *See* Agape.

CHRISTIANA. *See* Nino.

CHRISTINA THE ASTONISHING (1150–1224). Born at Brusthem, near Liège, Belgium, she was orphaned at three, had an epileptic fit when she was about twenty-one, and seemed to have died when suddenly she soared to the roof of the church where Mass was being said for her. When the priest ordered her to come down, she did so, and said she had been to hell, purgatory, and heaven and then was allowed to return to earth to pray for the suffering souls in purgatory. This is just one of the incredible events that supposedly took place during her lifetime. She could not tolerate the odor of human beings and resorted to such extraordinary means to escape human contact as climbing trees, soaring to the rafters of churches, and hiding in ovens. She lived a life of poverty and was thought to be insane by many but venerated by others. She spent the last years of her life in St. Catherine convent at Saint-Trond, where she died on July 24.

CHRISTOPHER (d. c. 251). According to tradition he died at Lycia, and many legends have grown up around his name. According to one he was an ugly giant who made his living carrying people across a river. He tried to find someone more powerful than himself and decided this could only be Christ, since the devil feared the Savior. One day one of his passengers was a small child who grew so heavy as they crossed the river he feared they would be drowned. The child then revealed that he was Christ, and the heaviness was caused by the weight of the world he was carrying on his shoulders. Christopher means Christ-bearer, and because of this legend he is the patron of travelers and in modern times particularly of motorists. July 25.

CHRODEGANG OF METZ (712–66). Born at Hesbaye, Brabant, near Liège, and a relative of Pepin, Chrodegang was probably educated at St. Trond abbey, and became Charles Martel's secretary and referendary. In 742, though a layman, he became bishop of Metz. He served as ambassador to Pope Stephen III for Pepin, mayor of the palace, and was very much involved in the coronation of Pepin as King of the Franks, the first Carolingian King, in 751, and Pepin's defense of the papacy and Rome against the Lombards and his restoration of the exarchate of Ravenna, which he had won from the Lombards, to the Holy See. Chrodegang put into effect many ecclesiastical reforms in his see, and in large measure, through a code of rules he wrote for his canons, he was responsible for the establishment and spreading of the canon regular movement. He was active in founding and restoring churches and monasteries, including the abbey of Gorze, Italy, introduced the Roman liturgy and Gregorian Chant in his see, and established a choir school at Metz, which became famous all over Europe. He died at Metz on March 6.

CHROMATIUS OF AQUILEIA (d. c. 407). A native of Aquileia, he became a priest, participated in 381 in the Synod of Aquileia, which denounced Arianism, and in 388 was elected bishop of Aquileia. He was a friend of St. Jerome, who dedicated several books to him, encouraged Rufinus, whom he had baptized, to translate Eusebius' *Ecclesiastical History*, and helped finance Jerome's translation of the Bible. Chromatius was unsuccessful in attempts to reconcile Jerome and Rufinus, was a supporter of Chrysostom, was widely regarded as an outstanding scholar and prelate, and wrote several scriptural commentaries. December 2.

CIARAN. *See* Kieran of Saighir.

CLARE (1194–1253). Born at Assisi, Italy, on July 11, the daughter of the noble Faverone Offreduccio and Ortolanadi Fiumi, she refused to marry when she was twelve and was so impressed by a Lenten sermon of St. Francis in 1212 that she ran away from her home in Assisi on Palm Sunday and received the habit from Francis at the Portiuncula. Since Francis did not yet have a convent for women, he placed her in the Benedictine convent of St. Paul near Bastia. She resisted the forcible efforts by her family to remove her and bring her home and was moved by Francis to Sant' Angelo di Panzo convent, where she was soon joined by her sister, Agnes, fifteen, who also received the habit from Francis. Her father sent twelve armed men to bring Agnes back, but Clare's prayers rendered her so heavy they were unable to budge her and she remained. In 1215, Clare moved to a house adjoining the church of St. Damiano, was made superior by Francis, and ruled the convent for forty years. The Poor Clares were thus founded, and Clare was soon after joined by her mother, another sister, Beatrice, three members of the famous Ubaldini family of Florence, and others. They adopted a rigid rule, practiced great mortifications and austerities, and took a vow of strict poverty—a vow that was to cause future difficulties. Clare obtained from Pope Innocent III a privilege guaranteeing their absolute poverty, and when Pope Gregory IX in 1228 tried to get the order to accept the ownership and income of land and buildings and offered to absolve Clare from her vow of absolute poverty, she was so convincing in a personal meeting with him that he granted the convents of San Damiano, Perugia, and Florence the *privilegium paupertatis*. Other houses did accept the mitigation, which was the beginning of the two observances among the Poor Clares; when a formal modification of the rule was granted by Pope Urban IV in 1263 to these houses, they became known as Urbanists. In 1247, Pope Innocent IV again sanctioned the holding of property, and Clare's response was to draw up a rule based on that of Francis, enjoining absolute poverty; Innocent approved it two days before her death. The order flourished and spread to other parts of Italy and to

France and Germany, and Clare's influence became such that she was consulted by Popes, cardinals, and bishops. She was credited with many miracles, and in 1241 her prayers were credited with saving Assisi from the besieging soldiers of Emperor Frederick II. She, next to St. Francis, was most responsible for the growth and spread of the Franciscans. She died at Assisi on August 11, and was canonized two years later, in 1255. She is the patroness of television. August 11.

CLARET, ANTHONY MARY (1807–70). Son of a weaver, he was born on December 23 in Sallent, Spain, and became a weaver himself. He entered the seminary at Vich in 1829 and was ordained in 1835. Ill health caused him to leave a Jesuit novitiate in Rome and he returned to pastoral work at Sallent in 1837 and spent the next decade preaching missions and retreats in Catalonia. He went to the Canary Islands and after fifteen months there (1848–49) with Bishop Codina, Anthony returned to Vich and founded the Missionary Sons of the Immaculate Heart of Mary (the Claretians), dedicated to preaching missions. He was appointed archbishop of Santiago, Cuba, in 1850, and incurred bitter enemies in his efforts to reform the see (he was wounded in an assassination attempt against his life at Holguín in 1856). He returned to Spain in 1857, became confessor of Queen Isabella II, and was deeply occupied with the missionary activities of his congregation. He resigned his see in 1858, was appointed Director of the Escorial, and actively encouraged literature, the arts, and the sciences. He followed Isabella to France when a revolution drove her from the throne in 1868, and after attending Vatican Council I (1869–70), he retired to Prades, France, but was forced to flee to a Cistercian monastery near Narbonne when the Spanish ambassador demanded his arrest. He died there on October 24. Anthony Claret was a leading figure in the revival of Catholicism in Spain, preached over 25,000 sermons, and published some 144 books and pamphlets during his lifetime. He was canonized in 1950.

CLAUDIA (1st century). Mother of Linus, who became the second Pope, tradition has her the daughter of British King Caractacus, who was sent to Rome with his family in chains when he was defeated by Aulus Plautius. Released by Emperor Claudius, one of his daughters took the name Claudia, remained in Rome, was baptized, and is the Claudia mentioned in St. Paul's second letter to Timothy. Another tradition has her the daughter of Cogidubnus, a British ally of Claudius, who took the Emperor's name. Martial mentions a British lady, Claudia Rufina, and says she was married to his friend Aulus Pudens, a Roman senator. Another tradition has this senator the Pudens also mentioned in St. Paul's second letter to Timothy. August 7.

CLAUDIUS (d. c. 306). *See* Castorius.

CLAVER, PETER (1580–1654). Born at Verdu, near Barcelona, Spain, he studied at the University of Barcelona and joined the Jesuits when he was twenty. He studied further at Montesione College at Palma, Majorca, was greatly influenced by St. Alphonsus Rodriguez, whom he met there, and decided he wanted to work in the New World. After further study at Barcelona, he was sent as a missionary to New Granada in 1610 and was ordained at Cartagena in present-day Colombia in 1615. Cartagena was an important center of the slave trade, and Peter joined Fr. Alfonse de Sandovel in trying to alleviate the horrible conditions of the slaves who poured into the city. He worked in the yards where the slaves were penned after being disembarked from the trip from West Africa, ministering to them with food and medicine, instructing them in the faith, and baptizing them, reportedly making some three hundred thousand converts in the forty years he labored among the slaves. He pleaded with the owners to improve their lot and visited plantations around Cartagena, usually lodging in the slaves' quarters to make sure the few laws for the protection of the slaves were enforced. He ministered to the lepers in St. Lazarus Hospital and to condemned prisoners and was always available as a confessor. He preached in the main plaza of the city, practiced great austerities, and became known as one blessed with supernatural gifts—prophecy, the power to perform miracles, and the ability to read men's minds. He was stricken with a plague that beset Cartagena in 1650 and never recovered from it. Despite his illness, he carried on his work on a much-reduced scale, lived in his cell pretty much neglected by all, and died there on September 8. He was canonized in 1888 and named patron of all missionary activities to Negroes by Pope Leo XIII in 1896. September 9.

CLEMENT I (d. c. 99). All that is known with certainty about Clement is that he was a Roman and suffered martyrdom away from Rome. According to tradition he was probably a freed man in the imperial household and was baptized by St. Peter. He succeeded Cletus as Pope in 91, was exiled to the Crimea by Emperor Trajan, and labored so zealously preaching the faith among the prisoners working in the mines there that he was condemned to death and thrown into the sea with an anchor around his neck. It is also agreed by scholars that he was the author of a letter to the Corinthians in which he rebuked them for a schism that had broken out in their church. The letter is of particular historical importance as one of the outstanding documents of the early Church and significant as an instance of the bishop of Rome intervening authoritatively as the pre-eminent authority in the affairs of another apostolic church to settle a dispute as early as the first century. November 23.

CLEMENT MARY HOFBAUER. *See* Hofbauer, Clement Mary.

CLEMENT OF OKHRIDA (d. 916). Probably of Slavic descent and from southern Macedonia, he became a bishop during the reign of Khan Simeon, the first Slav to become a bishop. Clement founded a monastery at Okhrida near Velitsa, Bulgaria, which became his primatial see and of which he is considered the founder and first bishop. He was so successful in his missionary work with the Bulgars that he is one of the Seven Apostles of Bulgaria. He died at Okhrida on July 17.

CLEOPHAS (1st century). He was one of the two disciples to whom Jesus appeared on the road to Emmaus after he had risen (Luke 24:13–35). Some scholars believe he is the same as Clopas, the father of one of the women named Mary at the foot of the cross, and perhaps the same as Alphaeus, father of St. James the Less. September 25.

CLETUS (d. c. 91). All that is known about him is that he was a Roman elected Pope in 76 as the second successor of St. Peter and that he suffered martyrdom probably in Rome during the persecution of the Christians by Emperor Diocletian. He is also known by the Greek version of his name, Anacletus. April 26.

CLITHEROW, MARGARET (c. 1555–86). Daughter of Thomas Middleton, a wealthy candlemaker, she was born at York, England, married John Clitherow, a well-to-do butcher, in 1571, and was converted to Catholicism two or three years later. Her husband was fined repeatedly because Margaret did not attend Protestant services. She was once imprisoned for two years; on her release she set up a Catholic school for children and arranged to have Mass said in her home or in a house she rented. Her home became one of the most important hiding places for fugitive priests in England. In 1584, she was confined to her home for a year and a half, apparently for sending her eldest son to Douai in France to be educated. She was arrested in 1586, and when a search of her house revealed a secret hiding place with a missal and vessels used in saying Mass, she was accused and found guilty of hiding priests, a capital offense. She was executed at York by being pressed to death under an eight-hundred-pound weight on March 25, and was canonized in 1970 by Pope Paul VI as one of the Forty Martyrs of England and Wales.

CLOTILDA (c. 474–545). Daughter of King Chilperic of Burgundy, she was born at Lyons, France, and married Clovis, King of the Franks, in 492 or 493. She converted him to Christianity on Christmas Day in 496 after he had won a seemingly lost battle by appealing to "Clotilda's God." Clovis died in 511, and the rest of her life was spent mourning the fratricidal feuds of her three sons, Clodimir, Childebert, and Clotaire, over their inheritance. Anguished at the murder of two of Clodimir's children by Clotaire, she left Paris for Tours and spent the rest of her life helping the sick and the poor. June 3.

COEMGEN. *See* Kevin.

COLETTE (1381–1447). Daughter of a carpenter named De Boilet at Corbie abbey in Picardy, France, she was born on January 13, christened Nicolette, and called Colette. Orphaned at seventeen, she distributed her inheritance to the poor, became a Franciscan tertiary, and lived at Corbie as a solitary. She soon became well known for her holiness and spiritual wisdom, but left her cell in 1406 in response to a dream directing her to reform the Poor Clares. She received the Poor Clares habit from Peter de Luna, whom the French recognized as Pope under the name of Benedict XIII, with orders to reform the Order and appointing her superior of all convents she reformed. Despite great opposition, she persisted in her efforts, founded seventeen convents with the reformed rule, and reformed several older convents. She was renowned for her sanctity, ecstasies, and visions of the Passion, and prophesied her own death in her convent at Ghent. A branch of the Poor Clares is still known as the Colettines. She was canonized in 1807. February 7.

COLLERT. *See* Gerard Sagredo.

COLM. *See* Columba.

COLMAN (d. c. 689). *See* Kilian.

COLMAN OF CLOYNE (530–606). Born in Munster, Ireland, son of Lenin, he became a poet and later royal bard at Cashel. He was baptized by St. Brendan when fifty with the name Colman. He was ordained, was reputed to be St. Columba's teacher, and became the first bishop of Cloyne, of which he is patron, in eastern Cork. November 24.

COLMAN OF LANN ELO (c. 555–611). Of a Meath family, he was born at Glenelly, Tyrone, Ireland, was deeply influenced by his uncle, St. Columba, and in about 590 built a monastery at Offaly called Lann Elo (Lynally). He also founded and became first abbot of Muckamore and later was bishop of Connor. He is probably the author of *Aibgitir in Chrabaid* (*Alphabet of Devotion*) and is also known as Colman Macusailni. He died at Lynally on September 26.

COLMAN OF LINDISFARNE (c. 605–76). Born in Connacht, Ireland, he became a monk at Iona under St. Columba and was appointed third bishop of Lindisfarne. At the Synod of Whitby in 663 or 664, he was the chief defender of the Celtic ecclesiastical practices against St. Wilfrid and St. Agilbert. When King Oswy ruled for Wilfrid and the Roman practices, Colman resigned his bishopric and with a group of

Irish and English monks from Lindisfarne founded a monastery on the Isle of Inishbofin off the coast of Connacht, where they continued their practice of the Celtic rites. When dissension broke out between the Irish and the English monks, he founded another monastery at Mayo and was abbot of both monasteries. February 18.

COLMAN MACUSAILNI. *See* Colman of Lann Elo.

COLMCILLE. *See* Columba.

COLOMBINI, BL. JOHN (1304–67). Born at Siena, Italy, he became a successful businessman and married Biagia Cerretani. He changed his worldly lifestyle after reading a book of saints' lives, donated much of his wealth to the poor, and converted his home into a hospital. Sometime later, after providing for his wife, he embraced a life of poverty and penance and devoted himself to ministering to the sick poor in hospitals. He was banished from Siena when he began to attract members of wealthy families as followers and then visited other Italian cities, where his disciples gained the name Gesuati (Jesuats) because of their devotion to the name of Jesus. After an investigation into charges that they were perpetuating the errors of the Fraticelli, Pope Urban V approved the Jesuats as a congregation with the name the Apostolic Clerics of St. Jerome, an institute of lay brothers dedicated to a life of great austerity and to caring for the sick. Soon after, John was taken ill at Lake Bolsena and died on the way back to Siena. He was beatified by Pope Clement IX. July 31.

COLUMBA (c. 521–97). Also known as Colm, Colum, and Colmcille, he was probably born at Gartan, Donegal, Ireland, the son of Fedhlimidh (or Phelim) and Eithne, both of royal descent. He was baptized one of the names listed above and educated at Moville, where he became a deacon. He then studied at Leinster and continued his studies at Clonard, where he was probably ordained, and then went to Glasnevin under St. Mobhi. When plague caused Glasnevin to be disbanded in 543, he returned to Ulster and spent the next decade and a half preaching and founding monasteries all over Ireland, among them Derry, Durrow, and Kells. He became involved in a dispute with St. Finnian when he copied the first copy of St. Jerome's psalter (owned by Finnian) to reach Ireland, and Finnian claimed his copy; King Diarmaid ruled Columba's copy must go to Finnian. Columba again crossed swords with Diarmaid, this time literally, when Curnan of Connaught, a kinsman who had sought sanctuary with Columba, was murdered by Diarmaid's men. In the family feud that ensued between Diarmaid's men and Columba's clan, some three thousand men were killed at the Battle of Cuil Dremne. A synod at Telltown held Columba responsible and censured him. In remorse, Columba decided to leave Ireland and do penance for the deaths by converting a like number of pagans. In 563, with twelve relatives, he went to Iona off the coast of Scotland and built on that island a monastery that grew into the greatest monastery in Christendom. He devoted himself to evangelizing the Picts of Scotland, converted King Brude at Inverness, and in time evangelized all of Pictland. He attended the Synod of Drumceat in Meath, Ireland, in 575, where he successfully fought to exempt women from military service, visited Ireland again in 585, and is believed responsible for the Battle of Cuil Feda near Clonard in 587. In the meanwhile, Iona had become famous all over Europe, and his holiness, austerity, and reputation for miracles attracted all manner of visitors to the monastery, where he died on June 9. Columba's influence on Western Christianity was enormous. Monks from Iona went all over Europe, and the monastic rule he developed was practiced widely on the Continent until the Rule of St. Benedict became almost universal. Columba's practices dominated the churches of Scotland, Ireland, and Northumbria though, in time, the Celtic practices he introduced came into conflict with the Roman practices, which eventually supplanted them. June 9.

COLUMBAN or COLUMBANUS (c. 540–615). Born in West Leinster, Ireland, sometime between 540 and 550, he decided, when a youth, to dedicate himself to God despite his mother's opposition. He lived for a time on Cluain Inis, an island in Lough Erne, with a monk named Sinell, and then became a monk at Bangor. With twelve other monks he was sent as a missionary to Gaul about 585. He built his first monastery at Annegray about 590, and it was so successful that he followed with two more, at Luxeuil and Fontes (Fontaines). Soon his followers spread all over Europe, building monasteries in France, Germany, Switzerland, and

Italy. He aroused much opposition, especially from the Frankish bishops, by the Celtic usages he installed in his monasteries and for refusing to acknowledge bishops' jurisdiction
over them. He defended his practices in letters to the Holy
See and refused to attend a Gallican synod at Châlons in 603
when summoned to explain his Celtic usages. In 610 King
Theodoric II of Burgundy, angered by Columban's denunciation of his refusal to marriage and his practice of keeping
concubines, ordered all Irish monks banished from his realm.
Columban was shipwrecked on the way to Ireland but was
offered refuge by King Theodebert II of Neustria at Metz and
began to evangelize the Alemanni in the area around Bregenz
on Lake Constance. Though successful, he was again
banished in 612, when Burgundy warred against and conquered Neustria; Theodoric now ruled over the area in which
Columban was working. Columban decided to flee his old ad-
versary and crossed the Alps to Italy, where he was welcomed
to Milan by Arian King Agilulf of the Lombards. Columban
founded a monastery at Bobbio, between Milan and Genoa,
which became one of the great monasteries of its time—a
center of culture, learning, and spirituality. He died there on
November 23. Columban wrote his Monastic Rule, sermons,
poetry, and treatises against Arianism. November 23.

COMGALL (c. 517–603). Born in Ulster, Ireland, he studied under St. Fintan at Cluain Eidnech Monastery, was ordained, and with several companions became a hermit in
Lough Erne. The rule he imposed was so severe that seven of
them died. He left the island and founded a monastery at
Bangor, where he taught St. Columban. In time, it became the
most famous monastery in Ireland, and Comgall is reported
to have ruled over some eight thousand monks there and in
houses founded from Bangor. He also accompanied St. Columba on a missionary trip to Inverness and founded a monastery at Land of Heth. Comgall died at Bangor after years of
suffering brought on by his austerities. May 11.

COMPIÈGNE, MARTYRS OF (d. 1794). At the outbreak
of the French Revolution in 1789, a group of twenty-one Discalced Carmelite nuns were living in a monastery at Compiègne, France, that had been founded in 1641. In 1790 the
revolutionary authorities ordered the monastery closed and
the nuns dispersed. In 1794, sixteen of the twenty-one nuns

were accused of violating the law by living as a religious community (they dressed in secular attire but continued their religious life). They were arrested on June 22 and imprisoned in the former Visitation convent in Compiègne. Though they had taken the oath of Liberté-Égalité in 1790, they now formally retracted their oaths and resumed the practice of their religious exercises. On July 12, they were sent to Paris and five days later, after a travesty of a trial, they were convicted of being counter-revolutionists living as religious under obedience to their superiors and conspiring against the people. They were all guillotined on July 17, and were beatified in 1906 as the Martyrs of Compiègne. The nuns who suffered martyrdom were: Marie Claude Brard (Sister Euphrasia of the Immaculate Conception); Madeleine Brideau (Sister St. Louis), the sub-prior; Marie Croissy (Sister Henrietta of Jesus), grandniece of Colbert; Marie Dufour (Sister St. Martha); Marie Hanisset (Sister Thérèse of the Heart of Mary); Marie Meunier (Sister Constance), a novice; Rose de Neufville (Sister Julie of Jesus); Annette Pebras (Sister Mary Henrietta of Providence); Marie Anne Piedcourt (Sister Jesus Crucified); Madeleine Lidoine (Mother Thérèse of St. Augustine), the prioress; Angélique Roussel (Sister Marie of the Holy Spirit); Catherine Soiron and Thérèse Soiron, both extern sisters, natives of Compiègne and blood sisters; Anne Mary Thouret (Sister Charlotte of the Resurrection); Marie Trezelle (Sister Thérèse of St. Ignatius); and Elizabeth Vérolot (Sister St. Francis).

CONAN (7th century). That he actually lived is probably true; all else is uncertain. He was probably from Scotland or Ireland, may have taught St. Fiacre during Fiacre's childhood, went from Scotland to the Isle of Man, where he finished the evangelization of the people of that island begun by St. Patrick, and was probably consecrated a bishop. January 26.

CONRAD (d. 975). Of the famous Guelph family and son of Count Henry of Altdorf, he was educated at the cathedral school of Constance and was ordained. He was made provost of the cathedral and in 934 was elected bishop of Constance. He gave his share of his inheritance to the Church and to the poor and built and renovated many churches in his see. He accompanied Emperor Otto I to Italy in 962, though he concentrated on ecclesiastical matters and avoided secular affairs during the forty-two years he was bishop. He was canonized in 1123. November 26.

CONSTANTINE (6th century). King of Cornwall, unreliable tradition has him married to the daughter of the King of Brittany who on her death ceded his throne to his son and became a monk at St. Mochuda Monastery at Rahan, Ireland. He performed menial tasks at the monastery, then studied for the priesthood and was ordained. He went as a missionary to Scotland under St. Columba and then St. Kentigern, preached in Galloway, and became abbot of a monastery at Govan. In old age, on his way to Kintyre, he was attacked by pirates who cut off his right arm, and he bled to death. He is regarded as Scotland's first martyr. March 11.

CONSTANTINE (d. 1321). *See* Theodore (d. 1299).

CORBINIAN (670–725). Born at Châtres, France, and baptized Waldegiso (his mother changed it to Corbinian), he lived as a solitary at Châtres for fourteen years, attracted disciples whom he organized into a religious community, and then went to Rome. Pope Gregory II sent him to evangelize Germany (he may have been a bishop by then), and he settled at Fresing, Upper Bavaria. When he denounced his patron Duke Grimoald for the marriage of the Duke to his brother's widow, Biltrudis, Corbinian incurred her bitter enmity. When he learned she had plans to have him killed, he fled to Meran, where he remained until Grimoald was killed in battle. He spent the rest of his life in missionary work in Bavaria and founded a monastery at Obermais. His emblem of a bear is attributed to a legend that he made a bear who killed his pack horse take over the work of the horse. September 8.

CORMAC (d. 908). King of Munster, Ireland, he was probably the first bishop of Cashel and the compiler of the still-extant Psalter of Cashel. He was killed in battle. September 14.

CORNELIUS (1st century). A centurion of the Italica cohort stationed at Caesarea, Palestine, he had a vision telling him to send for Peter, who came to his home and baptized him and his household (Acts 10). According to tradition, he became the first bishop of Caesarea. February 2.

CORNELIUS (d. 253). A Roman priest, he was elected Pope to succeed Fabian in an election delayed fourteen months by Decius' persecution of the Christians. The main issue of his pontificate was the treatment to be accorded Christians who had apostatized during the persecution. He condemned those confessors who were lax in not demanding penance of these Christians and supported St. Cyprian, bishop of Carthage, against Novatus and his dupe, Felicissimus, whom he had set up as an antibishop to Cyprian, when Novatus came to Rome. On the other hand, he also denounced the Rigorists, headed by Novatian, a Roman priest, who declared that the Church could not pardon the *lapsi* (the lapsed Christians), and declared himself Pope—the first antipope. The two extremes eventually joined forces, and the Novatian movement had quite a vogue in the East. Meanwhile, Cornelius proclaimed that the Church had the authority and the power to forgive repentant *lapsi* and could readmit them to the sacraments and the Church after they had performed proper penances. A synod of Western bishops in Rome in October 251 upheld Cornelius, condemned the teachings of Novatian, and excommunicated him and his followers. When persecution of the Christians started up again in 253 under Emperor Gallus, Cornelius was exiled to Centum Cellae (Civita Vecchia), where he died a martyr, probably of hardships he was forced to endure. September 16.

CORNELIUS OF WYK (d. 1572). *See* Pieck, Nicholas.

COSMAS (d. 303). According to legend, Cosmas and Damian were twin brothers born in Arabia. They studied medicine in Syria and then lived at Aegeae, Cilicia, and became widely known for their great medical skills, which they offered without charge to all. As outstanding Christians, they were arrested during a persecution of Christians, tried before Lysias, governor of Cilicia, tortured, and then beheaded for their faith. Their three brothers, Anthimus, Euprepius, and Leontius, also died with them. Many miracles were reported after their deaths, and they are the patrons of barbers and of physicians after Luke. September 26.

COTTOLENGO, JOSEPH (1786–1842). Born at Bra, near Turin, Italy, he was ordained and engaged in pastoral work. When a woman he attended died from lack of medical facilities for the poor in Turin, he opened a small home for the sick poor. When it began to expand, he organized the volunteers who had been manning it into the Brothers of St. Vincent and the Daughters of St. Vincent (Vincentian Sisters). When cholera broke out in 1831, the hospital was closed, but he moved it just outside the city at Valdocco and continued ministering to the stricken. The hospital grew and he expanded his activities to helping the aged, the deaf, blind, crippled, insane, and wayward girls until his Piccola Casa became a great medical institution. To minister to these unfortunates, he founded the Daughters of Compassion, the Daughters of the Good Shepherd, the Hermits of the Holy Rosary, and the Priests of the Holy Trinity. Weakened by typhoid he had contracted, he died at Chieri, Italy, and was canonized in 1934. April 30.

COUDERC, TERESA (1805–85). Born on February 1 at Masle, Sablières, France, and christened Mary Victoria, she joined a community devoted to teaching founded by Fr. J. E. P. Terme in his parish at Aps. When he was sent as a missionary to the Vivrais in southeastern France in 1824, he summoned Teresa and two other sisters to run a hostel for women at the shrine of St. Francis Regis at La Louvesc in 1827 and appointed Teresa superior of the group, the Daughters of St. Regis, in 1829. They also began giving retreats for laywomen. When Fr. Terme died in 1834, the Jesuits took over the shrine and selected twelve Daughters of St. Regis headed by Mother Teresa to concentrate on giving retreats, and the Congregation of Our Lady of the Retreat in the Cenacle was founded. Mother Teresa resigned as superior in 1838 when financial difficulties beset the congregation, was sent to found a new house at Lyons, and spent the rest of her life as a simple sister of the community except for a short period when she was temporary superioress of the Paris convent. She died at Fourvière on September 26, and was canonized by Pope Paul VI in 1970.

CRESCENTIA (d. c. 300). *See* Vitus.

CRESCENTIUS (d. c. 90). *See* Romulus.

CRISPIN (c. 287). Unreliable legend has Crispin and Crispinian noble Roman brothers who with St. Quintinus went to Gaul to preach the gospel and settled at Soissons. They were most successful in convert work during the day and worked as shoemakers at night. By order of Emperor Maximian, who was visiting in Gaul, they were haled before Rictiovarus (whose position is unknown and even his existence is doubted by scholars), a hater of Christians, who subjected them to torture; when unsuccessful in trying to kill them, he committed suicide, whereupon Maximian had the two brothers beheaded. They are the patrons of shoemakers, cobblers, and leatherworkers. October 25.

CRISPIN OF VITERBO (1668–1750). Born at Viterbo, Italy, on November 13, Peter Fioretti had an early veneration for Mary. He studied at the Jesuit college, became an apprentice shoemaker, and in time a shoemaker. When twenty-five, he became a Capuchin brother at Viterbo and took the name Crispin. He was assigned menial tasks—gardener at Viterbo, cook at Tolfa—and reportedly effected many miraculous cures during epidemics at Tolfa and Bracciano. He was questor at Orvieto, where he became beloved of the populace, venerated for his miracles, prophecies, and wisdom. He died in Rome on May 19, and was canonized in 1982 by Pope John Paul II. May 21.

CRISPINIAN (c. 287). *See* Crispin.

CUMIAN (c. 590–c. 665). Son of King Fiachna of West Munster, Ireland, he became a monk in charge of the school at Clonfert and was later abbot of Kilcummin Monastery, which he had founded. He was noted for his learning and ably defended the Roman liturgical practices against the abbot of Iona, who was a stalwart defender of the Celtic practices. Cumian's defense is still extant, the *Paschal Epistle*, and he also wrote a hymn, some of which is still extant. He is often surnamed Fota or Fada, "the tall." November 12.

CURÉ OF ARS. *See* Vianney, John Baptist.

CUTHBERT (d. 687). Thought by some to be Irish and by others a Scot, Bede, the noted historian, says he was a Briton. Orphaned when a young child, he was a shepherd for a time, possibly fought against the Mercians, and became a monk at Melrose Abbey. In 661, he accompanied St. Eata to Ripon Abbey, which the abbot of Melrose had built, but returned to Melrose the following year when King Alcfrid turned the abbey over to St. Wilfrid, and then became prior of Melrose. Cuthbert engaged in missionary work and when St. Colman refused to accept the decision of the Council of Whitby in favor of the Roman liturgical practices and immigrated with most of the monks of Lindisfarne to Ireland, St. Eata was appointed bishop in his place and named Cuthbert prior of Lindisfarne. He resumed his missionary activities and attracted huge crowds until he received his abbot's permission to live as a hermit, at first on a nearby island and then in 676 at one of the Farnes Islands near Bamborough. Against his will, he was elected bishop of Hexham in 685, arranged with St. Eata to swap sees, and became bishop of Lindisfarne but without the monastery. He spent the last two years of his life administering his see, caring for the sick of the plague that decimated his diocese, working numerous miracles of healing, and gifted with the ability to prophesy. He died at Lindisfarne. March 20.

CYPRIAN (c. 200–58). Probably born at Carthage, Thascius Caecilius Cyprianus was a pagan rhetorician, lawyer, and teacher. He was converted to Christianity by Caecilius, an old priest, about 246, became a profound scholar of the Bible and the great religious authors, especially Tertullian, was ordained, and in 248, was elected bishop of Carthage. Cyprian was forced to flee Decius' persecution of Christians in 249 but continued to rule his see by letter from his hiding place. Greatly criticized for fleeing, he returned in 251 to find that many of the faithful had apostatized during the persecution and that a priest named Novatus who had opposed his election was in schism and was receiving back into the Church with no penance those who had lapsed from the faith (the *lapsi*). Cyprian denounced Novatus for his undue leniency and convened a council at Carthage in 251, which set forth the terms under which the *lapsi* could be received back into the Church, excommunicated the schismatic leaders, and asserted the supremacy of the Pope; it was at this council that Cyprian read his famous *De unitate ecclesiae*. Novatus then went to Rome and joined the antipope, Novatian, against Pope Cornelius, whom Cyprian actively supported, rallying the African bishops behind Cornelius. In 252–54 Carthage was stricken with a terrible plague. Although Cyprian was a leader in helping alleviate its effects, the Christians were blamed for the plague, and hatred for Cyprian and the Christians intensified. It was at this time that he wrote *De mortalite* to comfort his flock. Soon after, he and other African bishops came into conflict with Pope St. Stephen when they refused to recognize the validity of baptism by heretics and schismatics, which Stephen had proclaimed valid. Three African councils (255–56) demanded rebaptism for those baptized by schismatics, and Cyprian engaged in an acrimonius correspondence with Stephen, which was cut short when an imperial decree forbidding any assemblage of Christians and requiring all bishops, priests, and deacons to participate in the official state religion ushered in Valerian's persecution of the Christians. Cyprian was arrested, and when he refused to participate was exiled by Paternus, the proconsul, to Curubis, a small town fifty miles from Carthage. The following year an imperial decree ordered that all bishops, priests, and deacons were to be put to death. Cyprian was arraigned before a new proconsul, Galerius Maximus, and when Cyprian persisted in his refusal to sacrifice to pagan gods, he was beheaded on September 14. Cyprian wrote numerous theological treatises on the Church, ministry, the Bible, virginity, and the *lapsi*, and is considered a pioneer of Latin Christian literature. September 16.

CYPRIAN (3rd century). According to the fictional morality story that had great popularity though with no basis in fact, Cyprian was a native of Antioch who became a practitioner of sorcery and black magic. He traveled widely in Greece, Egypt, Macedonia, and the Indies to broaden his knowledge of the black arts. When Aglaïdes, a young pagan, fell in love with the beautiful Justina, a Christian of Antioch, he asked Cyprian to help him win her. Cyprian tried all his black magic and diabolical expertise to win her for himself but was repelled by her faith and the aid of Mary. He called on the Devil, who assailed Justina with every weapon in his arsenal, to no avail. When Cyprian realized the overwhelming power of the forces arrayed against him and the Devil, Cyprian threatened to leave the Devil's service; whereupon the Devil turned on Cyprian, only to be repulsed by the sign of the cross made by a repentant Cyprian, who realized the sinfulness of his past life. He then turned to a priest named Eusebius for instruction and was converted to Christianity. He destroyed his magical books, gave his wealth to the poor, and was baptized, as was Aglaïdes. Justina then gave away her possessions and dedicated herself to God. In time Cyprian was ordained and later was elected bishop of Antioch. He was arrested during Diocletian's persecution of the Christians and tortured at Tyre by the governor of Phoenicia, as was Justina. They were then sent to Diocletian, who had them beheaded at Nicomedia. September 26.

CYRIACA (d. 249). Also known as Dominica, she was a wealthy Roman who gave shelter to persecuted Christians in her home, which was also used as headquarters by St. Laurence and others for their charitable works. She was scourged to death for her Christianity. August 31.

CYRIACUS (d. c. 133). Bishop of Ancona, of which he is the patron, he is variously and unreliably conjectured to have been the legendary Jew named Judas Quiriacus who revealed where the Cross was hidden to Empress Helena, was baptized, became bishop of Jerusalem, and was martyred during the persecution of Julian the Apostate; or bishop of Ancona who died or was killed on a pilgrimage to Jerusalem; or as Judas, bishop of Jerusalem, who was killed during a riot there in 133. May 4.

CYRIL (c. 825–69) and **METHODIUS** (c. 826–84). Cyril and Methodius were brothers born at Thessalonika, Greece, of a senatorial family. Cyril was christened Constantine and sent at an early age to study at the imperial university at Constantinople under Photius, was ordained, and in time took over Photius' chair at the university, earning the sobriquet "the philosopher." Methodius became governor of one of the Slav colonies in Opsikion Province and then became a monk. Both were living in a monastery on the Bosporus in 861 when Emperor Michael III sent them to convert the Khazars in the Dnieper-Volga regions of Russia; they learned the Khazar language and made many converts. On their return, Methodius became abbot of a monastery in Greece. In 863, at the request of Prince Rostislav of Moravia, Photius, now patriarch of Constantinople, sent the two brothers to convert the Moravians, since German missionaries

had been unsuccessful in their attempts to evangelize them.
Their knowledge of the Slavonic tongue made them extremely
successful. They invented an alphabet called glagolothic,
which marked the beginning of Slavonic literature (the Cyril-
lic alphabet traditionally ascribed to Cyril was probably the
work of his followers), and Cyril, with the help of Methodius, translated the liturgical books into Slavonic. Meanwhile,
they had incurred the enmity of the German clergy because
of their use of Slavonic in Church services and because they
were from Constantinople, which was suspect to many in the
West because of the heresy rife there. Further, their missionary efforts were hampered by the refusal of the German
bishop of Passau to ordain their candidates for the priesthood.
They were summoned to Rome by Pope Nicholas I, who died
while they were on the way, and they were received by Pope
Adrian II, to whom they presented the relics of Pope St.
Clement they had brought with them from the Crimea, where
he had died. Adrian received them warmly, was convinced of
their orthodoxy, approved their use of Slavonic in the liturgy,
and announced that they were to be ordained bishops. While
they were in Rome, Cyril became a monk, taking the name
by which he has since been known, but died in Rome shortly
after, on February 14, and was buried in San Clemente
church there. It is uncertain whether he was consecrated before his death, but Methodius was and returned to Moravia a
bishop. There, at the request of the princess of Moravia and
Pannonia, Pope Adrian formed the archdiocese of Moravia
and Pannonia, independent of the German hierarchy, a move
fiercely opposed by the German hierarchy, and made Methodius archbishop at Velehrad, Czechoslovakia. In 870, King
Louis the German and the German bishops deposed Methodius at a synod at Ratisbon and imprisoned him. He was
released two years later by order of Pope John VIII, and he
returned to his see, though John deemed it politic to forbid
his use of Slavonic in the liturgy. He was again summoned to
Rome in 878 when his orthodoxy was impugned and for
again using Slavonic in the liturgy. John was convinced of his
orthodoxy, and impressed by Methodius' arguments, again
permitted the use of Slavonic in the liturgy. Methodius also
voyaged to Constantinople to finish the translation of Scriptures that he had begun with Cyril. Methodius' struggle with
the Germans was to continue all through the rest of his life,
until his death on April 6, probably at Stare Mesto

(Velehrad). He and Cyril are called "Apostles of the Slavs," and to this day the liturgical language of the Russians, Serbs, Ukrainians, and Bulgars is that designed by them. Their feast day was extended to the universal Church by Pope Leo XIII in 1880. February 14.

CYRIL OF ALEXANDRIA (c. 376–444). Born at Alexandria, Egypt, and nephew of the patriarch of that city, Theophilus, Cyril received a classical and theological education at Alexandria and was ordained by his uncle. He accompanied Theophilus to Constantinople in 403 and was present at the Synod of the Oak that deposed John Chrysostom, whom he believed guilty of the charges against him. He succeeded his Uncle Theophilus as patriarch of Alexandria on Theophilus' death in 412, but only after a riot between Cyril's supporters and the followers of his rival Timotheus. Cyril at once began a series of attacks against the Novatians, whose churches he closed; the Jews, whom he drove from the city; and Governor Orestes, with whom he disagreed about some of his actions. In 430 Cyril became embroiled with Nestorius, patriarch of Constantinople, who was preaching that Mary was not the Mother of God since Christ was divine and not human, and consequently she should not have the word *theotokos* (God-bearer) applied to her. He persuaded Pope Celestine I to convoke a synod at Rome, which condemned Nestorius, and then did the same at his own synod in Alexandria. Celestine directed Cyril to depose Nestorius, and in 431 Cyril presided over the third General Council at Ephesus, attended by some hundred bishops, which condemned all the tenets of Nestorius and his followers before the arrival of Archbishop John of Antioch and forty-two followers who believed Nestorius was innocent; when they found what had been done, they held a council of their own and deposed Cyril. Emperor Theodosius II arrested both Cyril and Nestorius but released Cyril on the arrival of papal legates who confirmed the council's actions against Nestorius and declared Cyril innocent of all charges. Two years later Archbishop John, representing the moderate Antiochene bishops, and Cyril reached an agreement and joined in the condemnation, and Nestorius was forced into exile. During the rest of his life Cyril wrote treatises that clarified the doctrines of the Trinity and the Incarnation and that helped prevent Nestorianism and Pelagianism from taking long-term deep root in the

Christian community. He was the most brilliant theologian of the Alexandrian tradition. His writings are characterized by accurate thinking, precise exposition, and great reasoning skill. Among his writings are commentaries on John, Luke, and the Pentateuch, treatises on dogmatic theology, and Apologia against Julian the Apostate, and letters and sermons. He was declared a Doctor of the Church by Pope Leo XIII in 1882. June 27.

CYRIL OF JERUSALEM (c. 315–86). Probably born of Christian parents, he was raised and well educated in Jerusalem and was ordained by St. Maximus. Cyril taught catechumens for several years and about 349 succeeded Maximus as bishop of Jerusalem. Cyril was expelled from the see in 357 by Acacius, the Arian bishop of Caesarea, who claimed ecclesiastical jurisdiction over Jerusalem and had an Arian synod condemn him for selling Church possessions to aid victims of a famine, but in reality because of his opposition to Arianism. He went to Tarsus but was recalled by the Council of Seleucia in 359. He was again expelled at Acacius' instigation by Emperor Constantius but recalled in 361 by Emperor Julian the Apostate when Constantius II died. Again Cyril was exiled, in 367, when Emperor Valens banished all churchmen recalled during Julian's reign; but Cyril returned once again, in 378. The following year the Council of Antioch sent St. Gregory of Nyssa to Palestine to investigate charges against Cyril arising from his questioning the word *homoousios*, the basic term in the Nicene Creed. Gregory reported that the see of Jerusalem was morally corrupt, torn by factionalism and Arianism, but that its faith and that of Cyril were orthodox. Cyril and Gregory attended the General Council of Constantinople in 381, and Cyril completely accepted the amended Nicene Creed and the term *homoousios*. Cyril was a scriptural scholar, a successful preacher, and his "Catecheses" delivered during Lent in about 347 gives a clear picture of the instruction given those preparing for baptism and of the Palestinian liturgy of the fourth century. Though friendly with many semi-Arian leaders and though Church historians Socrates and Sozomen claim that the criticism that caused Gregory to go to Palestine to investigate had some substance to it, Cyril was a firm opponent of Arianism, and his orthodoxy is unquestioned. He was declared a Doctor of the Church in 1882 by Pope Leo XIII. March 18.

D

DAFROSA (4th century). *See* Bibiana.

DAMASUS I (c. 304–84). Of Spanish descent, he was probably born in Rome, and became deacon in the church of his father, who was a priest. Damasus was elected Pope in 366 in a bitterly contested election and was faced with an antipope, Ursinus, who was elected by an opposing minority faction. The opposition was put down with great cruelty, and Ursinus was exiled by Emperor Valentinian. Damasus' opponents remained actively opposed to him and in 378 charged him with incontinence—a charge of which he was cleared by a Roman synod. He enforced Valentinian's edict of 370 forbidding gifts by widows and orphans to bishops, was a vigorous opponent of Arianism, and sent legates to the General Council of Constantinople in 381, which accepted papal teaching, again condemned Arianism, and denounced the teaching of Macedonius that the Holy Spirit is not divine. During Damasus' pontificate, in 380, Emperor Theodosius the Great in the East and Emperor Gratian in the West decreed Christianity to be the religion of the Empire. A biblical scholar, Damasus published the canon of Holy Scripture, specifying the authentic books of the Bible as decreed by a council in Rome in 374, and was the patron of St. Jerome, who served as his secretary for a time; it was at Damasus' request that Jerome began his biblical commentaries and translation of the Bible, the Vulgate. Damasus enhanced the prestige of the papacy; proclaimed Rome supreme among the churches; and restored the catacombs, shrines, and tombs of the martyrs, and encouraged pilgrimages to them. He died in Rome on December 11.

DAMIAN (c. 303). *See* Cosmas.

DAMIEN THE LEPER. *See* Veuster, Ven. Joseph de.

DANIEL (d. 309). *See* Elias.

DANIEL, ANTHONY (1601–48). Born on March 27 at Dieppe, France, he studied law but abandoned it to join the Jesuits at Rouen in 1621. He taught there for four years, studied theology at Clermont, was ordained in 1630, and was then assigned to the college at Eu. With three other priests he was sent as a missionary to Cape Breton Island, Arcadia, New France (Canada), in 1632, and a year later was sent to Quebec. He was most successful with his missionary work with the Huron Indians, founded a school for Indian boys at Quebec in 1636, and was martyred by a party of Iroquois, the traditional foe of the Hurons, on July 4 at the Indian village of Teanaustaye near Hillsdale, Ontario. He was canonized by Pope Pius XI in 1930 as one of the Martyrs of North America. October 19.

DANIEL THE STYLITE (c. 409–93). Born at Maratha, near Samosata on the Upper Euphrates, he entered a nearby monastery when twelve and became a monk there. He accompanied his abbot on a trip to Antioch, and on the way they stopped to see St. Simeon the Elder on his pillar. Daniel refused the request of the monks at the monastery to become abbot when the abbot died, made a pilgrimage to the Holy Land, and then after nine years as a hermit at Philempora, near Constantinople, he decided to emulate Simeon and live on a pillar. Daniel spent the next thirty-three years on a series of pillars built near Constantinople and was ordained on one of them when he refused to come down for his ordination. He prophesied a disastrous fire in Constantinople in 465 and became famed for his holiness and miracles of healing, attracting huge crowds with the sermons he delivered from the top of his pillar. He was consulted by Emperors Leo and Zeno, foretold the latter's banishment, and came down from his pillar only once, to denounce Basiliscus for usurping Zeno and supporting the Eutychians; Basiliscus' corruption and monophysite tendencies eventually led to the restoration of Zeno to the throne in 476. Daniel died on his pillar and was buried at its foot. December 11.

DAVID (5th–6th centuries). All the information we have about David, also known as Dewi, is based on the unreliable eleventh-century biography written by Rhygyfarch, the son of Bishop Sulien of St. David's. According to it David was the son of King Sant of South Wales and St. Non, became a priest, studied under St. Paulinus on an unidentified island for several years, and then engaged in missionary activities, founding some dozen monasteries, the last of which, at Mynyw (Menevia) in southwestern Wales, was noted for the extreme asceticism of its rule, which was based on that of the Egyptian monks. David attended a synod at Brefi, Cardiganshire, in about 550 where his eloquence is said to have caused him to be elected primate of the Cambrian Church with the understanding that the episcopal see would be moved from Caerleon to Mynyw, now St. David's. He was supposedly consecrated archbishop by the patriarch of Jerusalem while on pilgrimage to the Holy Land, and a council he convened, called the Synod of Victory because it marked the final demise of Pelagianism, ratified the edicts of Brefi, and drew up regulations for the British Church; both are events that seem to be without any factual foundation. He died at his monastery at Mynyw, and his cult was reputedly approved by Pope Callistus II about 1120. Even his birth and death dates are uncertain, ranging from c. 454 to 520 for the former and from 560 to 601 for the latter. He is the patron saint of Wales. March 1.

DAVID. *See* Gleb under Boris entry.

DAVID (d. 1321). *See* Theodore (d. 1299).

DAVID I OF SCOTLAND (1084–1153). The son of King Malcolm III and St. Margaret, he was sent to the Norman court in England in 1093, and married Matilda, widow of the earl of Northampton in 1113 (thereby becoming an English baron), and became the earl of Cumbria when his brother Alexander I became King. He succeeded his brother as King of Scotland in 1124 and engaged in a long struggle for the English crown on behalf of his niece Matilda against Stephen, who defeated him at Standard in 1138; he made peace with England the following year. He founded numerous sees and monasteries, established Norman law in Scotland, set up the office of chancellor, began the feudal court, and was noted for his justice, charities and piety. He died at Carlisle, Scotland, on May 24, and though listed in both Catholic and Protestant calendars, he has never been formally canonized.

DECLAN (c. 6th century). Born at Desi (Decies), Waterford, Ireland, he was baptized by a St. Colman, whose disciple he was, may have made two pilgrimages to Rome, and later became bishop of Ardmore. July 24.

DEICOLUS (c. 530–c. 625). Elder brother of St. Gall and born in Leinster, Ireland, Deicolus was one of the twelve disciples of Columban who accompanied him to France in 576. Deicolus worked with Columban in Austrasia and Burgundy, and when Columban was expelled by Thierry in 610, Deicolus was unable to accompany him into exile because of his age, and he settled at Lure, where he founded a monastery. He lived there as a hermit until his death. January 18.

DEINIOL. *See* Daniel (d. 584).

DEIRDRE. *See* Ita.

DEL BUFALO, CASPAR (1786–1837). Born in Rome, he was educated at the Collegio Romano and was ordained in 1808. He was exiled to Corsica for five years during the occupation of Rome by Napoleon's army for refusing to swear allegiance to Napoleon. On Caspar's return he engaged in pastoral work. While conducting a mission at Giano, he conceived the idea of founding a congregation for mission work and in 1815 received formal approval for the Missioners of the Most Precious Blood from Pope Pius VII. Caspar founded houses at Giano, Albano, and, despite great difficulties, in the kingdom of Naples; in time the congregation spread all over Italy. He was also active in charitable works and had as his goal for his missioners the evangelization of the world. He died on December 28 at Albano, a victim of cholera, and was canonized by Pope Pius XII in 1954. January 2.

DEMETRIA (4th century). *See* Bibiana.

DEMETRIUS (126–231). Made bishop of Alexandria in 188, he served for forty-three years and made the catechetical school at Alexandria famous. He appointed his young follower Origen (then eighteen) director of the school about 203, defended him in his early years, but later condemned him for preaching as a layman in Caesarea. Fifteen years later Demetrius expelled him from his diocese for being ordained without his permission. October 9.

DENIS (d. c. 258). Born in Italy, he was sent with six other bishops to Gaul in 250 as missionaries and became the first bishop of Paris. He was so effective in converting the inhabitants around Paris that he was arrested with his priest, St. Rusticus, and deacon, St. Eleutherius, and imprisoned. The three of them were beheaded on October 9 near Paris for their faith during Decius' persecution of the Christians. Their bodies were rescued from the Seine River, and a chapel built over their tomb later became the Benedictine abbey of Saint-Denis. He is the apostle and patron saint of France and is also known as Dionysius of Paris.

DERFEL GADARN (c. 5th century). According to legend, he was a great Welsh soldier who fought at Camlan where King Arthur was killed, may have been a monk at Bardsey, and was later a solitary at Llanderfel, Merionethshire, Wales. A wooden statue of him in the church there was greatly venerated until it was used for firewood in the burning of Bl. John Forest at Smithfield in 1538. April 5.

DESMAISIÈRES, MARY MICHAELEA (1809–65). Born at Madrid of a noble family, the Viscountess of Sorbalàn refused offers of marriage, accompanied her brother to Paris and Brussels when he was ambassador to France and Belgium, and was devoted to religious instruction and aiding the sick and the needy. On her return to Spain in 1848, she organized the Handmaids of the Blessed Sacrament and of Charity to help fallen women, was elected mother general in 1859, and died in Valencia of cholera while ministering to the plague-stricken. She was canonized in 1934. August 25.

DEUSDEDIT (d. 618). Son of a subdeacon, Stephen, he was born in Rome and was consecrated Pope on October 19, 615. Also known as Adeodatus I, he encouraged the secular clergy and devoted much of his time to aiding the needy, especially during the disastrous earthquake that devastated Rome in August 618. According to tradition, he was the first Pope to use lead seals (bullae) on papal documents, which in time came to be called bulls. He may have been a Benedictine. He died in Rome. November 8.

DEUSDEDIT OF CANTERBURY (d. 664). A South Saxon named Frithona, he became the first Anglo-Saxon to be primate when he succeeded Honorius as archbishop of Canterbury in 653. Nothing further of him is known beyond that he died, probably on October 28, during a plague. July 14.

DEVOTA (d. 303). A young Corsican girl, she was martyred for her faith by being racked to death during Diocletian's persecution of Christians. Her remains are interred at the Riviera di Ponenta in Monaco of which she is the patroness; she is also the patron saint of Corsica. January 17.

DEWI. *See* David (5th–6th centuries).

DICHU (5th century). Son of an Ulster chieftain, he succeeded to the kingdom of Lecale in County Down and bitterly opposed St. Patrick when he landed in Ireland in 432. He became Patrick's first Irish convert, gave Patrick a church in Saul, capital of Lecale, the first of Patrick's foundations in Ireland, and the two became close friends. April 29.

DIEGO DE AVEZEDO, BL. (d. 1207). A member of the clergy attached to the cathedral at Osma, Spain, he became provost and in 1201 was named bishop of Osma. In 1206, he was sent by King Alfonso IX of Castile to the Marches to escort back to Spain the bride-to-be of Prince Ferdinand. On arrival, Diego found the girl dead. He then went to Rome, taking with him a member of his party, St. Dominic, a visit that ultimately led to the founding of the Dominicans. In the same year Diego joined the Cistercians at Citeaux and became a leader in the crusade against the Albigensians in Languedoc. He returned to Osma late in 1207 and died there on December 30. February 6.

DIONYSIUS (d. 268). Possibly a Greek, he was a priest in Rome when he was elected Pope on July 22, 259, in an election delayed for a year by the violence of Valerian's persecution of the Christians. About 260 Dionysius issued an important doctrinal letter correcting the phraseology in the writings of Dionysius, bishop of Alexandria, regarding the Trinity, insisting on the true doctrine of three Persons in one divine nature, and condemning Sabellianism. He sent large sums of money to the churches of Cappadocia that had been devastated by marauding Goths and to ransom their Christian captives and was most successful in rebuilding the Church when Emperor Gallienus issued his edict of toleration shortly after Dionysius' election. He died in Rome, the first Pope not listed as a martyr. December 26.

DIONYSIUS OF ALEXANDRIA (d. 265). A native of Alexandria, Egypt, he was converted to Christianity by a vision, and became a student at the catechetical school in Alexandria under Origen. Dionysius was appointed head of the catechetical school by Bishop Heraclas in 232 and after fifteen years in that position was elected bishop of Alexandria in 247. He was arrested during Decius' persecution of the Christians in 249 but was rescued by a group of Egyptians and sought refuge in the Libyan desert, whence he ruled his see until the persecution died down. He supported Pope St. Cornelius against an antipope, Novatian, and denounced and fought Novatianism. Dionysius was an outstanding theologian and biblical scholar, was reproved by Pope St. Stephen I for his mistaken view in supporting Cyprian that baptism by heretics was invalid and by Pope St. Dionysius for his view on the Trinity, which Dionysius explained in an apologia to the Pope. Dionysius was banished to Kephro in Libya by Emilian, prefect of Egypt, when Valerian's persecution began in 257. Dionysius returned in 260 to a plague-stricken city in the throes of civil war, with mobs roaming the streets, and devoted himself to aiding the persecuted Christians and the victims of the plague. He died in Alexandria. An indefatigable defender of the faith, he is called "the Teacher of the Catholic Church" by St. Athanasius and is surnamed "the Great" by St. Basil. November 17.

DIONYSIUS THE AREOPAGITE (1st century). It is related (Acts 17:23–34) that Dionysius with a woman named Damaris was converted by St. Paul at the time he delivered his famous sermon on the Unknown God on the Hill of Mars (Areopagus) in Athens. St. Dionysius of Corinth says that he became first bishop of Athens, and Basil's Menology says he was burned to death during Domitian's persecution of the Christians about 95. The Roman Martyrology mistakenly identifies him with Dionysius of Paris, and it is now accepted that he was not the author of four treatises and ten letters on mysticism and theology that were so influential in the Middle Ages and were long attributed to him. October 9.

DIONYSIUS OF PARIS. *See* Denis.

DI ROSA, MARY (1813–55). Born at Brescia, Italy, on November 6 and christened Paula Frances Mary, and of a well-to-do family, her mother died when she was eleven and she was educated by the Visitandine nuns. When seventeen she left school to take over the running of her father's household. Early inclined to a religious life, she dissuaded her father from making a marriage for her and became involved in caring for the spiritual welfare of the girls in her father's textile mill at Acquafredda and his estate at Capriano. She worked in the hospital in Brescia, ministering to the victims of a cholera epidemic in 1836, became directress of a home for abandoned girls the following year, founded a home of her own for girls, and then started a school for deaf and mute girls. In 1840, she was appointed superioress of a religious society of women to care for the sick by her spiritual adviser, Msgr. Faustino Pinzoni, and took the name Maria Crocifissa. The society was called the Handmaids of Charity of Brescia. Despite initial difficulties, the institute received the approval of the bishop of Brescia in 1843, and in the wars that shook Europe in 1848 ministered to the wounded on the battlefields of northern Italy and in the hospitals of Brescia. In 1850, Mary received papal approval of her congregation and died five years later at Brescia on December 15. She was canonized in 1954.

DISMAS (1st century). All that is known of him is that he is the Good Thief crucified with Christ on Calvary; the other thief is known as Gestas (Luke 23:39–43). A completely unsubstantiated myth from the Arabic Gospel of the Infancy that enjoyed great popularity in the West during the Middle Ages had them two thieves who held up the Holy Family on the way to Egypt. Dismas bought off Gestas with forty drachmas to leave them unmolested, whereupon the Infant predicted they would be crucified with him in Jerusalem and that Dismas would accompany him to Paradise. March 25.

DOMINIC (1170–1221). Son of Felix Guzman and Bl. Joan of Aza, he was born at Calaruega, Spain, studied at the University at Palencia, 1184–94, was probably ordained there while pursuing his studies, and was appointed canon at Osma in 1199. There he became prior superior of the chapter, which was noted for its strict adherence to the rule of St. Benedict. In 1203, he accompanied Bishop Diego de Avezedo of Osma to Languedoc, where Dominic preached against the Albigensians and helped reform the Cistercians. Dominic founded an institute for women at Prouille in Albigensian territory in 1206 and attached several preaching friars to it. When papal legate Peter of Castelnan was murdered by the Albigensians in 1208, Pope Innocent III launched a crusade against them headed by Count Simon IV of Montfort, which was to continue for the next seven years. Dominic followed the army and preached to the heretics but with no great success. In 1214, Simon gave him a castle at Casseneuil, and Dominic, with six followers, founded an order devoted to the conversion of the Albigensians; the order was canonically approved by the bishop of Toulouse the following year. He failed to gain approval for his order of preachers at the fourth General Council of the Lateran in 1215 but received Pope Honorius III's approval in the following year, and the Order of Preachers (the Dominicans) was founded. Dominic spent the last years of his life organizing the order, traveling all over Italy, Spain, and France preaching and attracting new members and establishing new houses. The new order was phenomenally successful in conversion work as it applied Dominic's concept of harmonizing the intellectual life with popular needs. He convoked the first general council of the order at Bologna in 1220 and died there the following year on August 6, after being forced by illness to return from a preaching tour in Hungary. He was canonized in 1234, and is the patron saint of astronomers. August 8.

DOMINIC OF THE MOTHER OF GOD, BL. *See* Barberi, Bl. Dominic.

DOMINICA. *See* Cyriaca (d. 249).

DOMITILLA (1st century). Flavia Domitilla was the wife of Flavius Clemens, a Roman consul, and daughter of Emperor Domitian's sister. She was converted to Christianity and was banished to the island of Pandatania in the Tyrrhenian Sea for her faith after her husband was martyred in 96. A niece by marriage, also called Domitilla, was banished to the island of Ponza for her faith and may have been burned to death when she refused to sacrifice to the gods. May 12.

DOMNINA (no date). *See* Photina.

DOMNINA (d. c. 303). *See* Asterius.

DONALD (8th century). A resident of Ogilvy in Forfarshire, Scotland, he formed a religious group with his nine daughters on the death of his wife. They later entered a monastery at Abernethy. July 15.

DONATIAN (d. 289 or 304). Of a notable Roman-Gallo family living at Nantes, Brittany, he was charged with being a Christian and refusing to worship to the gods and was imprisoned during the persecution of the Christians by Emperor Maximian. Donatian was soon joined by his brother Rogatian, who professed Christianity but had not yet been formally professed because the local bishop was in hiding. Donatian and Rogatian were both tortured and then beheaded. May 24.

DONATUS (d. c. 303). *See* Honoratus.

DONATUS (d. c. 876). Legend has him an Irishman who, on his way back from a pilgrimage to Rome, stopped off in 829 at Fiesole, Italy, where the people were assembled to elect a new bishop. As he entered the cathedral, church bells began to ring and candles blazed alight, whereupon he was elected bishop. He later became a confidant of Lothair I and his son Louis II. October 22.

DOROTHY (d. 303). According to her apocryphal tradition, she was a resident of Caesarea, Cappadocia, who when she refused to sacrifice to the gods during Emperor Diocletian's persecution of the Christians was tortured by the governor and ordered executed. On the way to the place of execution, she met a young lawyer, Theophilus, who mockingly asked her to send him fruits from "the garden" she had joyously announced she would soon be in. When she knelt for her execution, she prayed, and an angel appeared with a basket of three roses and three apples, which she sent to Theophilus, telling him she would meet him in the garden. Theophilus was converted to Christianity and later was martyred. February 6.

DOROTHY OF MONTAU (1347–94). Born at Montau, Prussia, on February 6, she married a wealthy swordsmith, Albrecht of Danzig, when she was seventeen, and the couple had nine children. Her gentleness and humility completely changed the outlook of the surly Albrecht, and he accompanied her on various pilgrimages. He was not able to accompany her to Rome in 1390 because of illness; on her return she found he had died in her absence. She moved to Marienwerder in 1391 and two years later established her hermitage there, where she died on June 25. She was noted for her visions and her devotion to the Blessed Sacrament, and though never canonized, is considered a patroness of Prussia. October 30.

DROCTOVEUS (d. c. 580). Also known as Drotté, he was born at Auxerre, studied under St. Germanus at Saint-Symphorien Abbey at Autun, and was appointed abbot of the monastery in Paris built by King Childebert and attached to St. Germanus' church there when Germanus became bishop of Paris. It was renamed Saint-Germain after Germanus' death. March 10.

DROGO (c. 1105–89). Also known as Druon, he was born of noble Flemish parents, was orphaned at birth, and when eighteen became a penitential pilgrim, visiting several shrines. He then was a shepherd for six years at Sebourg, near Valen-

ciennes, revered by his neighbors for his holiness. He then resumed his pilgrimages and finally became a hermit at Sebourg
for forty years until his death there. He is the patron of shepherds. April 16.

DROTTÉ. *See* Droctoveus.

DRUON. *See* Drogo.

DUBRICIUS (c. 545). According to legend, he probably
was born at Madley, Wales, became a monk, and founded
monasteries at Henllan and Moccas. He attracted numerous
disciples to the two monasteries, and from them were founded
many other monasteries and churches. He and St. Deinol
were the two prelates who convinced David to attend the
synod of Brefi. Dubricius spent the last years of his life at
Ynys Enlli (Bardsey) and died there. Among other unreliable legends attached to his name are that he was the first
bishop of Llandaff, archbishop of Caerlon-on-Usk, the bishop
who crowned King Arthur at Colchester (he is the high
saint of *Idylls of a King*), and that David resigned in his
favor as metropolitan of Wales. Dubricius died and was
buried on Bardsey Island off the coast of Wales. He is also
known as Dyfrig. November 14.

DUCHESNE, BL. ROSE PHILIPPINE (1769–1852). Born
on August 29 at Grenoble, France, daughter of a wealthy
merchant, she was educated by the Visitation nuns of Sainte
Marie d'en Haut, near Grenoble, and when seventeen, despite
the objections of her parents, who wanted her married, she
joined the Visitation nuns. When they were expelled from
France during the Reign of Terror in 1791, she returned
home, ministered to the sick, taught, and visited priest prisoners of the Revolution. She attempted to rebuild the convent
at which she had been educated after the concordat of 1801
between Pope Pius VII and Napoleon had restored peaceful
relations between the state and the Church, but was unsuccessful. In 1804, she persuaded Mother Madelaine Sophie
Barat to accept it for her recently founded Society of the Sacred Heart, and with four others Bl. Rose became a postulant
of the Society and was professed the following year. In 1818,
she was sent as superioress with four nuns to the United
States and founded the first American Sacred Heart house at

St. Charles, near St. Louis, Missouri—a log cabin. They started the first free school west of the Mississippi there but moved to Florissant near St. Louis the following year; their first American postulant was accepted in 1820. Despite numerous difficulties, the community eventually flourished, and by 1828 it had six houses along the Mississippi River. She was allowed to resign as head of the American branch in 1840 and at the age of seventy-one began a school for Indians at Sugar Creek, Kansas, at the request of Jesuit Father De Smet. Ill health caused her to leave her Indian mission after a year, and she retired to St. Charles, where she died on October 18. She was beatified in 1940. November 17.

DUCKETT, BL. JAMES (d. 1602). Born at Gilfortriggs, Westmorland, England, he was raised a Protestant, became a printer's apprentice in London, and when he refused to attend Protestant religious services because of doubts about Protestantism, he was imprisoned and served two terms in prison. When released, he took instructions from a Catholic priest and became a Catholic. He devoted himself to spreading his faith by the printing and distribution of Catholic books, and after his marriage to a Catholic widow, he spent nine of the next twelve years in various prisons for his activities. He was accused of printing Father Southwell's *Supplications* (which he did not) by one Peter Bullock, who had bound books for him and was under sentence of death for another crime. When Duckett acknowledged he had Catholic books in his possession, he was found guilty of felony and sentenced to death. He was hanged with his betrayer, whom he forgave and exhorted to be constant in his faith on the gallows, at Tyburn. James was beatified in 1929. April 19.

DUNSTAN (c. 910–88). Born of a noble family at Baltonsborough, near Glastonbury, England, he was educated there by Irish monks and while still a youth was sent to the court of King Athelstan. He became a Benedictine monk about 934 and was ordained by his uncle, St. Alphege, bishop of Winchester, about 939. After a time as a hermit at Glastonbury, Dunstan was recalled to the royal court by King Edmund, who appointed him abbot of Glastonbury Abbey in 943. He developed the abbey into a great center of learning while revitalizing other monasteries in the area. He became adviser to King Edred on his accession to the throne when Edmund was murdered, and began a far-reaching reform of all the monasteries in Edred's realm. Dunstan also became deeply involved in secular politics and incurred the enmity of the West Saxon nobles for denouncing their immorality and for urging peace with the Danes. When Edwy succeeded his uncle Edred as King in 955, he became Dunstan's bitter enemy for the abbot's strong censure of his scandalous lifestyle. Edwy confiscated his property and banished him from his kingdom. Dunstan went to Ghent in Flanders but soon returned when a rebellion replaced Edwy with his brother Edgar, who appointed Dunstan bishop of Worcester and London in 957. When Edwy died in 959, the civil strife ended and the country was reunited under Edgar, who appointed Dunstan archbishop of Canterbury. The King and archbishop then planned a thorough reform of Church and state. Dunstan was appointed legate by Pope John XII, and with St. Ethelwold and St. Oswald, restored ecclesiastical discipline, rebuilt many of the monasteries destroyed by the Danish invaders, replaced inept secular priests with monks, and enforced the widespread reforms they put into effect. Dunstan served as Edgar's chief adviser for sixteen years and did not hesitate to reprimand him when he thought it deserved. When Edgar died, Dunstan helped elect Edward the Martyr King and then his half brother Ethelred when Edward died soon after his election. Under Ethelred, Dunstan's influence began to wane and he retired from politics to Canterbury to teach at the cathedral school and died there. Dunstan has been called the reviver of monasticism in England. He was a noted musician, played the harp, composed several hymns, notably *Kyrie Rex splendens*, was a skilled metalworker, and illuminated manuscripts. He is the patron of armorers, goldsmiths, locksmiths, and jewelers. May 19.

DUYNE (or DUYNEN), GODFREY VAN (d. 1572). *See* Vechel, Leonard.

DYFRIG. *See* Dubricius.

✗**DYMPHNA (d. c. 650).** Her popular legend has her the daughter of a pagan Celtic chieftain, whether Irish, Briton, or Amorican is uncertain, though probably Irish, and a Christian. She fled from home on the death of her mother to escape the incestuous interest of her father and went to Antwerp accompanied by her confessor, St. Gerebernus, and two companions. They then built an oratory at Gheel, near Amsterdam, where they lived as hermits. Tracked down by Dymphna's father, the two companions and the priest were murdered by his men, and Dymphna was beheaded by her father when she refused to return with him. When the bodies of Dymphna and Gerebernus were discovered at Gheel in the thirteenth century, many cures were reported at her tomb of epileptics, the insane, and those possessed. She is the patroness of epileptics and those suffering from mental illnesses. May 15.

E

EATA (d. 686). One of the twelve English boys brought to Northumbria by St. Aidan, Eata became abbot of Melrose. He accepted the Roman liturgical observances after the Synod of Whitby and replaced St. Colman (reportedly at Colman's request) as abbot of Lindisfarne when Colman refused to abandon the Celtic observations and migrated to the Isle of Inishbofin off the coast of Connacht. Eata was appointed bishop of Lindisfarne in 678 and later exchanged sees with St. Cuthbert and became bishop of Hexham, where he remained until his death. October 26.

EBERHARD, BL. (d. 958). Of Swabia's ducal family, he became provost of the Strasbourg cathedral but resigned in 934 to go to St. Benno's hermitage on Mount Etzel in Switzerland. There he built a Benedictine monastery he named Our Lady of the Hermits, which became famous as Einsiedeln, serving as its first abbot. August 14.

EDITH OF POLESWORTH (d. c. 925). The sister of King Athelstan of England, she married Viking King Sihtric at York in 925, and when he died the next year she became a Benedictine nun at Polesworth, Warwickshire, where she was noted for her holiness and may have become abbess. She may also have been the sister of King Edgar and aunt of St. Edith of Wilton; or possibly these were two different women named Edith of Polesworth. July 15.

EDMUND OF ABINGDON (c. 1180–1240). Born at Abingdon, Berkshire, England, on November 30, Edmund Rich studied at Oxford and Paris. He taught art and mathematics at Oxford, received his doctorate in theology, and was ordained. He taught theology for eight years and about 1222 became canon and treasurer of Salisbury Cathedral. He was an eloquent and popular preacher, preached a crusade against the Saracens at the request of Pope Gregory IX in 1227, was elected archbishop of Canterbury in 1233, and was consecrated in 1234 against his wishes. He was an adviser to King Henry III, undertook several diplomatic missions for the King, and in 1237 presided at Henry's ratification of the Great Charter. Edmund protested Henry's action in securing the appointment of a papal legate, Cardinal Otto, to England as an infringement of his episcopal rights. A rebellion by the monks of Christ Church at Canterbury, supported by Henry, to eliminate his rights there caused him to go to Rome in 1237, and on his return he excommunicated seventeen of the monks—an action that was opposed by his suffragans, Henry, and Cardinal Otto who lifted the excommunications. Edmund then became involved in a dispute with Otto over the King's practice of leaving benefices unoccupied so the crown could collect their revenues. When Rome withdrew the archbishop's authority to fill benefices left vacant for six months, he left England in 1240 and retired to the Cistercian abbey at Pontigny. He died at Soissons, France, on November 16 and was canonized in 1247 by Pope Innocent IV. The only surviving medieval hall at Oxford, St. Edmund's, is named in his honor, and according to tradition it was built on the site of his tomb.

EDWARD THE CONFESSOR (1003–66). Son of King Ethelred III and his Norman wife, Emma, daughter of Duke Richard I of Normandy, he was born at Islip, England, and sent to Normandy with his mother in 1013 when the Danes under Sweyn and his son Canute invaded England. Canute remained in England and the year after Ethelred's death in 1016, married Emma, who had returned to England, and became King of England. Edward remained in Normandy, was brought up a Norman, and in 1042, on the death of his half brother Hardicanute, son of Canute and Emma, and largely through the support of the powerful Earl Godwin, he was acclaimed King of England. In 1044, he married Godwin's daughter Edith. His reign was a peaceful one characterized by his good rule and remission of odious taxes but also by the struggle, partly caused by his natural inclination to favor the Normans, between Godwin and his Saxon supporters and the

Norman barons, including Robert of Jumièges, whom Edward had brought with him when he returned to England and whom he named archbishop of Canterbury in 1051. In the same year, Edward banished Godwin, who took refuge in Flanders but returned the following year with a fleet ready to lead a rebellion. Armed revolt was avoided when the two men met and settled their differences; among them was the archbishopric of Canterbury, which was resolved when Edward replaced Robert with Stigand, and Robert returned to Normandy. Edward's difficulties continued after Godwin's death in 1053 with Godwin's two sons: Harold who had his eye on the throne since Edward was childless, and Tostig, earl of Northumbria. Tostig was driven from Northumbria by a revolt in 1065 and banished to Europe by Edward, who named Harold his successor. After this Edward became more interested in religious affairs and built St. Peter's Abbey at Westminster, the site of the present Abbey, where he is buried. His piety gained him the surname "the Confessor." He died in London on January 5, and he was canonized in 1161 by Pope Alexander III. October 13.

EDWIN (c. 585–633). Son of King Aella of Deira (South Northumbria), he was only three when his father died. Edwin was deprived of the throne by King Ethelfrith of Bernicia (North Northumbria), who seized Aella's kingdom. Edwin spent the next thirty years in Mercia and finally was restored to the throne by King Baedwald of East Anglia, who defeated and killed Ethelfrith at the Battle of Idle River in 617. Edwin ruled ably and in 625, after the death of his first wife, married Ethelburga, sister of King Eadbald of Kent, and a Christian, who brought with her to Northumbria her confessor, Paulinus. Edwin established law and order in the kingdom and soon became the most powerful King in England. Through the efforts of Ethelburga and Paulinus, he was converted to Christianity in 627, and appointed Paulinus, who had baptized him, bishop of York. Many in Edwin's court were also converted, and thus began Christianity in Northumbria. His intention to build a stone church at York (an unprecedented event in those days) never materialized when his kingdom was invaded by pagan King Penda of Mercia and Cadwallon of North Wales. Edwin was defeated and killed at the Battle of Heathfield on October 12.

EEM, THEODORE VAN DER (d. 1572). *See* Pieck, Nicholas.

EGWIN (d. 717). Descended from the Mercian Kings, he became a religious in his youth and about 692 was named bishop of Worcester, England. He made a penitential pilgrimage to Rome to defend himself against charges of overseverity with his clergy, and on his return, aided by King Ethelred of Mercia, founded Evesham Monastery (purportedly as the result of a vision of Mary), which developed into one of the great Benedictine monasteries of medieval England. About 709, he made another pilgrimage to Rome, accompanied by King Cenred of Mercia and King Offa of the East Saxons. December 30.

ELEAZAR (d. 160 B.C.). *See* Maccabees, the Holy.

ELESBAAN (6th century). At the request of Emperor Justin I and the patriarch of Alexandria, Aksumite King Elesbaan led an expedition against Dunaan, a convert to Judaism, who had led a revolt of Jews and Arabs against the rule of Aksumite Ethiopians at Yemen and had slaughtered every Christian man, woman, and child in the town of Najran in southern Arabia who would not apostatize. Elesbaan defeated and killed Dunaan and then permitted atrocities against Dunaan's followers as dreadful as those committed by Dunaan. Elesbaan is said to have turned over his throne to his son, and he became an exemplary anchorite for the rest of his life. Though he is listed in the Roman Martyrology, he may have been a monophysite. October 24.

ELEUTHERIUS (d. c. 189). Son of one Habundius, he was a Greek of Nicopolis, Epirus, who became a deacon in Rome and was elected Pope about 174 to succeed St. Soter. He is known only for his decree that any food fit for humans was suitable for Christians—probably issued against the rigorism of the Gnostics and the Montanists. He probably died on May 24 in Rome. May 26.

ELEUTHERIUS (d. c. 258). *See* Dionysius.

ELIAS (d. 309). He and four companions, Daniel, Isaias, Jeremy, and Samuel, were Egyptians who visited Christians condemned to work in the mines of Cilicia during Maximus' persecution, to comfort them. Apprehended at the gates of Cilicia, Palestine, they were brought before the governor, Firmilian, and accused of being Christians. They were all tortured and then beheaded. When Porphyry, a servant of St. Pamphilus, demanded that the bodies be buried, he was tortured and then burned to death when it was found he was a Christian. Seleucus witnessed his death and applauded his constancy in the face of his terrible death; whereupon he was arrested by the soldiers involved in the execution, brought before the governor, and was beheaded at Firmilian's order. February 16.

ELIGIUS (c. 590–c. 660). The son of Roman-Gallo parents and also known as Eloi, he was born at Chaptel, Gaul. His father, Eucherius, was a metalsmith and apprenticed Eligius to Abbo, a goldsmith, who was master of the mint at Limoges. After his apprenticeship, Eligius worked under Bobbo, the royal treasurer, and became master of the mint for King Clotaire I in Paris. Eligius became a leading craftsman noted for his exquisite work and a close friend of Clotaire. Eligius' increased influence and affluence allowed him to be generous to the poor, to ransom numerous slaves, and to build several churches, and in 632 he founded and built a monastery at Solignac and a convent in Paris built on property granted him by Clotaire's son Dagobert I, who had appointed him his chief counselor in 629. Eligius went on a diplomatic mission to the Bretons for Dagobert in 636 and convinced Breton King Judicael to accept the authority of the Frankish King. Eligius was ordained in 640 and made bishop of Noyon and Tournai. He evangelized Flanders and converted many in the area around Antwerp, Ghent, and Courtrai despite great opposition. He founded a convent at Noyon, acted as counselor to Queen-regent St. Bathildis, and died at Noyon on December 1. He is the patron of metalworkers and metalsmiths and was one of the best-known and -loved persons of his time.

ELIZABETH (1st century). *See* Zachary.

ELIZABETH OF HUNGARY (1207–31). Daughter of Andrew II of Hungary and Gertrude of Andechs-Meran, she was born at Pressburg (Bratislava) or Saros-Patak, Hungary, and when four was brought to the court of Landgrave Herman I of Thuringia at Wartburg Castle, near Eisenach, as the betrothed of his son Ludwig. They were married in 1221 when Ludwig had become landgrave, had four children, and were an ideal married couple. She became known for her great charity, built a hospital at the foot of their castle, and another one. They were married six years when Ludwig went on crusade with Emperor Frederick II and died of the plague at Otranto. She was heartbroken, and to add to her troubles she was accused of mismanaging his estate because of her great charity; she was forced to leave Wartburg, probably forced out by her brother-in-law. She made provision for her children and in 1228 became a Franciscan tertiary. She lived for a time at Marburg and devoted herself to caring for the sick, the aged, and the poor at a hospice there. During this time her spiritual adviser was Conrad of Marburg, whose harsh methods of guiding her spiritual life have been sharply criticized. She led a life of exceptional poverty and humility and was allowed back to the castle four years before her death by the usurper, who also recognized her son's succession to the title of landgrave. She died at Marburg on November 17, not yet twenty-four, and soon miracles were reported at her tomb. She was canonized by Pope Gregory IX in 1235 and is the patroness of bakers.

ELIZABETH OF PORTUGAL (1271–1336). Daughter of King Peter III of Aragon, she was named after her grand-aunt, Elizabeth of Hungary. Elizabeth of Portugal was married when twelve to King Denis of Portugal, became known for her piety, charity, and concern for the poor, and founded convents, hospitals, foundling homes, and shelters for wayward girls. She was sometimes called "the Peacemaker" for her role in settling disputes between her husband and their son, Alfonso, who twice led rebellions against his father; between Ferdinand IV of Castile and his cousin Alfonso IV of Aragon; and between Ferdinand and her brother James II of Aragon. She was exiled for a time from the court when Denis thought she was favoring Alfonso. After Denis' death in 1325 she was persuaded to give up her idea of becoming a nun and became instead a Franciscan tertiary. She died on July 4 at Estremoz, Portugal, and was canonized in 1626. She is known as Isabella in Portugal.

ELIZABETH OF SCHÖNAU (c. 1129–64). Of humble birth, she entered the Benedictine double monastery of Schönau near Bonn, Germany, when she was twelve, was professed in 1147, and at once began to practice the greatest austerities. About 1152 she had her first vision, and throughout the rest of her life experienced many supernatural manifestations—visions, ecstasies, prophecies, and often diabolical visitations that left her bruised and beaten. She described her visions, especially of the Passion, Resurrection, and Ascension in three books recorded at first by her brother Egbert, who became a monk at Schönau and later was its abbot. Some of the visions described in her books are inaccurate and have been questioned by scholars, and in one of them she supported antipope Victor IV, a friend of her brother, but her sincerity was never questioned, and she was held in the highest esteem. She became abbess in 1157 and died at Schönau seven years later, on June 18. She has never been formally beatified or canonized, although she is referred to as St. Elizabeth in the Roman Martyrology.

ELMO. *See* Erasmus.

ELOI. *See* Eligius.

ELPHEGE. *See* Alphege.

EMERIC (1007–31). The only son of King St. Stephen of Hungary, who planned to have him succeed him as King, Emeric was killed while hunting. Many miracles were reported at his tomb at Szekesfehervar, and he was canonized, with his father, in 1083. November 4.

EMILIAN CUCULLATUS (d. 574). A shepherd at La Rioja, Navarre, Spain, he became a hermit when twenty and then after a brief stay at home spent the next forty years as a hermit in the mountains around Burgos when at the insistence of the bishop of Tarazona, he was ordained. He became a parish priest at Berceo but because of his excessive charity was forced to leave and with several disciples resumed his eremitical life. Tradition says the mountain hermitage he occupied near Burgos became the site of the Benedictine monastery of La Cogolla. He is known in Spain as San Millan de la Cogolla—the cowled St. Emilian. November 12.

EMILIANA (d. c. 550). Aunt of St. Gregory the Great, she and her sister Tharsilla lived a life of prayer and great austerity in Rome at the home of their brother, Gregory's father. Emiliana died on January 5, a few days after Tharsilla (also spelled Tarsilla). December 24.

EMILIANI, JEROME (1481–1537). Born at Venice, Italy, he became a soldier and was commander of the League of Cambrai forces at Castelnuevo near Treviso. When Castelnuevo fell to the Venetians, he was captured and imprisoned. He escaped, reformed his carefree lifestyle, became mayor of Treviso, and then returned to Venice, where he was ordained in 1518. While aiding plague and famine victims, he was especially touched by the plight of orphans and decided to devote himself to aiding orphans and founded orphanages at Brescia, Bergamo, and Como, a hospital at Verona, and a home for repentant prostitutes. About 1532, he and two other priests founded a congregation that became known as the Clerks Regular of Somascha, named after the town in which they established their first house, devoted to caring for orphans and educating children and priests. He died on February 8 at Somascha of an infectious disease he caught while ministering to its victims. His congregation was papally approved in 1540, and he was canonized in 1767. He was named patron saint of orphans and abandoned children in 1928.

EMILY DE RODAT. *See* Rodat, Emily de.

EMMA (d. c. 1045). A relative of Emperor St. Henry II and also known as Hemma, she was raised at Henry's court by St. Cunegund, and according to legend was married to Landgrave William of Friesach. Their two children were murdered during an uprising at mines owned by William. Grief-stricken, he made a pilgrimage to Rome and died on the way back; Emma decided to devote her life to God. She gave liberally to the poor, founded several religious houses and a double monastery at Gurk, Austria, and may have become a nun there. Despite the above legend, scholars believe she was of the Friesach family rather than William and that her son was killed in a battle twenty years after the death of her husband, Count William of Sanngan, about 1015, and it was at this time that she began her foundations. Her cult was confirmed in 1938. June 29.

EMMELIA (4th century). *See* Basil (d. c. 370).

EMYGDIUS (d. 304). According to legend, he was a pagan Teuton living in Trier who was converted to Christianity. He went to Rome and was forced to flee the wrath of the pagans when he destroyed an idol in a pagan temple. He was ordained and consecrated a bishop by Pope Marcellus I, who sent him to evangelize the region around Ascoli Piceno. His great success in making converts caused him to be arrested and beheaded during Diocletian's persecution of the Christians along with Eupolus, Germanus, and Valentius, three of his followers. He could not have been ordained by Marcellus, who was Pope 308–9, but could have been by Marcellinus, who reigned 296–304. Emygdius is the patron against earthquakes. August 9.

ENDA (d. c. 530). Legend has him an Irishman noted for his military feats who was convinced by his sister St. Fanchea to renounce his warring activities and marry. When he found his fiancée dead, he decided to become a monk and went on pilgrimage to Rome, where he was ordained. He returned to Ireland, built churches at Drogheda, and then secured from his brother-in-law King Oengus of Munster the island of Aran, where he built the monastery of Killeaney, from which ten other foundations on the island developed. With St. Finnian of Clonard, Enda is considered the founder of monasticism in Ireland. March 21.

ENECO. *See* Iñigo.

ENGELBERT (1187–1225). Son of the count of Berg, he was born at Berg and was made provost of several churches, including the Cologne cathedral while still a schoolboy studying at the cathedral school at Cologne. He was excommunicated for taking up arms against Emperor Otto IV, joined the crusade against the Albigensians, had the excommunication lifted, and was appointed archbishop of Cologne in 1217 when only thirty. He ruled the see well, restored clerical discipline, brought Franciscans and Dominicans into the diocese, held regular synods, encouraged monastic life, and was generous to the poor. He was also deeply involved in politics, supporting Emperor Frederick II (who appointed him regent during the minority of Henry's son in 1220 when the Emperor went to Sicily) and crowning Henry King of the Romans in 1222. He became embroiled in a dispute in 1225 with his cousin Count Frederick of Isenberg, whom he denounced for stealing the property of nuns in Essen for whom Frederick was acting as administrator. Frederick retaliated by waylaying Engelbert at Gevelsberg, Germany, and murdering him there on November 7. Although he has never been formally canonized, he is referred to in the Roman Martyrology as St. Engelbert, and his feast is observed in Cologne.

EOGHAN. *See* Eugene (d. c. 618).

EPAPHRODITUS (1st century). Mentioned with great affection and esteem by St. Paul (Phil. 1:25), he is traditionally considered the first bishop of Philippi, Macedonia. Both Andriaci in Lycia and Terracina in Italy also list an Epaphroditus as their first bishop. March 22.

EPHRAEM (c. 306–c. 373). Born at Nisibis, Mesopotamia, he was long thought to be the son of a pagan priest, but it is now believed his parents were Christians. He was baptized at eighteen, served under St. James of Nisibis, became head of his school, and probably accompanied him to the Council of Nicaea in 325. Syrian sources attribute the deliverance of Nisibis from the Persians in 350 to his prayers, but when Nisibis was ceded to the Persians by Emperor Jovian in 363, he took residence in a cave near Edessa in Roman territory, often preaching to the Christians, though he was probably only a deacon. It was here that he did most of his writing. Tradition says he visited St. Basil at Caesarea in 370 and on his return helped alleviate the rigors of the famine of winter 372–73 by distributing food and money to the stricken and helping the poor. He died at Edessa on June 9. Ephraem wrote voluminously in Syriac on exegetical, dogmatic, and ascetical themes, drawing heavily on scriptural sources. He wrote against the heretics—especially the Arians and the Gnostics—and on the Last Judgment, and was devoted to the Blessed Virgin (he is often invoked as a witness to the Immaculate Conception because of his absolute certainty of Mary's sinlessness). He was responsible in large measure for introducing hymns in public worship and used them effectively in religious instruction. His works were early translated into Greek, Armenian, and Latin. Particularly outstanding are his Nisibeian hymns and the canticles for the seasons. He was called "the Harp of the Holy Spirit," and in 1920 Pope Benedict XV declared him a Doctor of the Church, the only Syrian to be so honored. June 9.

EPIPHANIUS OF SALAMIS (c. 315–403). Born at Besanduk, Palestine, he became an expert in the languages needed to understand Scripture. After a time as a monk in Palestine, he went to Egypt and stayed at several desert communities. He returned to Palestine about 333, was ordained, and became superior of a monastery at Eleutheropolis, which he had built. He achieved a widespread reputation for his scholarship, austerities, mortifications, spiritual wisdom, and advice. Called "the Oracle of Palestine," he became bishop of Constantia (Salamis), Cyprus, and metropolitan of Cyprus in 367, although still continuing as superior of his monastery. His reputation was such that he was one of the few orthodox bishops not harassed by Arian Emperor Valens, though Epiphanius preached vigorously against Arianism. He supported Bishop Paulinus in 376 at Antioch against the claims of Metetius and the Eastern bishops, attended a council in Rome summoned by Pope Damasus in 382, and was embroiled in several unpleasant episodes with fellow prelates late in his life —denouncing his host, Bishop John of Jerusalem, in John's cathedral in 394 for John's softness to Origenism (he believed Origen responsible for many of the heresies of the times), ordaining a priest in another bishop's diocese, and in 402, at the behest of Theophilus of Alexandria, denouncing at Constantinople the four "Tall Brothers" and then admitting he knew nothing of their teachings. Epiphanius realized he was being used as a tool by Theophilus against John Chrysostom, who had given refuge to the monks who had been persecuted by Theophilus and were appealing to the Emperor, and started back to Salamis, only to die on the way home. He wrote numerous theological treatises, among them *Ancoratus*, on the Trinity and the Resurrection; *Panarion*, on some eighty heresies and their refutations; and *De mensuribus et ponderibus*, on ancient Jewish customs and measures. He was an authority on devotion to Mary and taught the primacy of Peter among the apostles. May 12.

ERASMUS (d. c. 303). Also known as Elmo, he was the bishop of Formiae, Campagna, Italy, and suffered martyrdom during Diocletian's persecution of the Christians. His unreliable legend has him confused with a Syrian bishop who was martyred at Antioch, and according to it he became a hermit on Mount Lebanon to escape Diocletian's persecution. He was captured and brought before the Emperor, tortured, and emerged from being hurled into fiery pitch unhurt. He was then imprisoned, and released by an angel who brought him to Illyricum, where his success with converts brought him further tortures, whereupon the angel again saved him and brought him to Formiae, where he died of his wounds. He is one of the Fourteen Holy Helpers and is patron of sailors (a blue light seen before a ship's masthead before and after a storm were called St. Elmo's lights by Neapolitan sailors). June 2.

ERASTUS (1st century). One of St. Paul's companions, he was sent with Timothy from Ephesus to Macedonia by the apostle (Acts 19:22). Paul also mentions Erastus as the city treasurer of Corinth (Rom. 16:23), who is probably the same Erastus he mentions in II Timothy 4:20, though not the same as the Erastus of Acts. Tradition says he became bishop of Philippi in Macedonia (of Philippi Paneas according to the Greeks) and suffered martyrdom. July 26.

ERIC IX OF SWEDEN (d. 1160). King of Sweden from 1150, he did much to aid Christianity in his realm and was responsible for codifying the laws of his kingdom, which became known as King Eric's Law (also the Code of Uppland). He led a victorious expedition against the marauding Finns and persuaded English Bishop Henry of Uppsala to remain in Finland to evangelize the Finns. Eric was killed and beheaded near Uppsala by rebelling Swedish nobles in the army of Magnus, son of the King of Denmark, who had invaded his territory, on May 18. Though never formally canonized, Eric was long considered the patron of Sweden.

ETHELBERT (d. 616). He became King of Kent about 560, married Bertha, daughter of Frankish King Charibert and a Christian, and though defeated by the West Saxons in 568, strengthened his rule and kingdom. He permitted St. Augustine of Canterbury to preach in his realm and in 597 was baptized by Augustine, the first Christian English King, and brought thousands of his subjects to Christianity with him. He granted religious freedom to his subjects, believing conversion by conviction was the only true conversion, encouraged the Christian missionaries, helped convert King Sabert of the East Saxons and King Redwald of the East Angles, codified the laws of the kingdom, and ruled wisely for fifty-six years. His name is spelled Aedilberct in Bede's history of the English Church. February 25.

ETHELBURGA (d. c. 647). Daughter of King Ethelbert of Kent, who had been converted to Christianity by St. Augustine of Canterbury, and Bertha, and also called Tata, she was married to pagan King Edwin of Northumbria. She and her chaplain, Paulinus, helped persuade Edwin to become a Christian in 627. He encouraged the advance of Christianity in his kingdom, but on his death in 633, paganism returned, and Ethelburga and Paulinus were forced to return to Kent. She founded an abbey at Lyminge and was its abbess until her death. April 5.

ETHELBURGA (d. c. 664). Daughter of Anna, King of the East Angles, she accompanied her half sister, Sethrida, to Gaul and became a nun at Faremoutier under St. Burgundofara. Sethrida succeeded Burgundofara as abbess, and on the former's death about 660, Ethelburga succeeded her. Ethelburga died at Faremoutier and is known in France as Aubierge. July 7.

ETHELBURGA (d. c. 678). Sister of SS. Erconwald, Etheldreda, Sexburga, and Withburga, all of whom are saints, and daughter of Anna, King of the East Angles, she was born at Stallington, Lindsey, England, became a nun, and was appointed first abbess of a double monastery founded by Erconwald at Barking, where she died. October 12.

ETHELDREDA (d. 679). Also known as Audrey, she was the daughter of Anna, King of the East Angles, and Bertha, and the sister of Erconwald, Ethelburga, Sexburga, and Withburga, all saints. Etheldreda was born in Exning, Suffolk, England, was married at an early age to Tonbert, prince of the Gryvii, but convinced him to allow her to retain her virginity during their married life. He died three years after their wedding, and Etheldreda lived in seclusion on the island of Ely for the next five years. She then married Egfrid, son of King Oswy of Northumbria, who was only a boy at the time. When, after twelve years of marriage, he demanded his conjugal rights, she refused, saying she had dedicated herself to God. The case was referred to St. Wilfrid, who upheld her claim. With Egfrid's consent she then became a nun at Coldingham Convent. The following year she returned to Ely, built a double monastery there about 672, was abbess of the convent for the rest of her life, and died there. June 23.

ETHELRED. *See* Aelred.

ETHELWOLD (c. 908–84). Born at Winchester, England, he was ordained by St. Alphege the Bald and in 944 became a Benedictine monk at Glastonbury Abbey under St. Dunstan and was made dean there. Ethelwold was appointed abbot of Abingdon in Berkshire about 954 and with St. Dunstan and St. Oswald was mainly responsible for the restoration of monasticism in England after its virtual destruction by the Danes during their raids. He was consecrated bishop of Winchester in 963, restored discipline among the canons of his cathedral by expelling them and replacing them with monks, and did the same thing the following year with the seculars of Newminster Monastery. He restored ruined monasteries and convents in his diocese and became known as "the Father of Monks." His reforms met with much opposition, but by the time of his death on August 1 he had rebuilt and reformed his see. He wrote several treatises and translated the rule of St. Benedict.

EUDES, JOHN (1601–80). Born at Ri, Normandy, France, on November 14, the son of a farmer, he went to the Jesuit college at Caen when fourteen and despite his parents' wish that he marry, joined the Congregation of the Oratory of France in 1623. He studied at Paris and at Aubervilliers, was ordained in 1625, and worked as a volunteer, caring for the victims of the plagues that struck Normandy in 1625 and 1631, and spent the next decade giving missions, building a reputation as an outstanding preacher and confessor and for his opposition to Jansenism. He became interested in helping fallen women, and in 1641, with Madeleine Lamy, founded a refuge for them in Caen under the direction of the Visitandines. He resigned from the Oratorians in 1643 and founded the Congregation of Jesus and Mary (the Eudists) at Caen, composed of secular priests not bound by vows but dedicated to upgrading the clergy by establishing effective seminaries and to preaching missions. His foundation was opposed by the Oratorians and the Jansenists, and he was unable to obtain papal approval for it, but in 1650, the bishop of Coutances invited him to establish a seminary in that diocese. The same year the sisters at his refuge in Caen left the Visitandines and were recognized by the bishop of Bayeux as a new congregation under the name of Sisters of Our Lady of Charity of the Refuge. John founded seminaries at Lisieux in 1653 and Rouen in 1659 and was unsuccessful in another attempt to secure papal approval of his congregation, but in 1666 the Refuge sisters received Pope Alexander III's approval as an institute to reclaim and care for penitent wayward women. John continued giving missions and established new seminaries at Evreux in 1666 and Rennes in 1670. He shared with St. Mary Margaret Alacoque the honor of initiating devotion to the Sacred Heart of Jesus (he composed the Mass for the Sacred Heart in 1668) and the Holy Heart of Mary, popularizing the devotions with his *The Devotion to the Adorable Heart of Jesus* (1670) and *The Admirable Heart of the Most Holy Mother of God,* which he finished a month before his death at Caen on August 19. He was canonized in 1925.

EUGENE (d. c. 618). Also known as Eoghan (Owen), unreliable sources have him born in Leinster, Ireland, and a relative of St. Kevin of Glendalough. Kidnaped into slavery while still a child and taken to Britain and then Brittany with two other boys, Tigernach and Coirpre, they were all released in time by their master and returned to Ireland. He spent fifteen years as a monk with St. Kevin at Kilnamanacg, helped Tigernach found Clones Monastery about 576 (Coirpre had meanwhile become bishop of Coleraine), and then settled with his disciples at Ardstraw, eventually being made its first bishop about 581. August 23.

EUGENE I (d. 657). A Roman priest who had held various positions in the Church and was known for his charity and sanctity, he was consecrated Pope on August 10, 654, while his predecessor, Pope St. Martin I, was still alive (he died on September 6), an exile and prisoner in the Crimea by order of Monothelite Emperor Constans II. Martin is reported to have approved the election, but many believed Eugene was a puppet of Constans. Eugene soon asserted his independence by refusing the Emperor's demands that he acknowledge Peter as Patriarch of Constantinople and allow toleration of the Monothelites. Constans was furious, and only the capture of Rhodes by the Moslems in 654 and their defeat of Constans at the naval battle of Phoenix in 655 saved Eugene from sharing the fate of his predecessor. Eugene died in Rome on June 2.

EUGENE III, BL. (d. 1153). Born at Montenagno, near Pisa, Italy, Pietro Paganelli became a canon at the Pisa cathedral and after meeting St. Bernard joined the Cistercians at Clairvaux in 1135, taking the name Bernard. He became abbot of St. Anastasius in Rome and was unexpectedly elected Pope on February 15, 1145, taking the name Eugene. Forced to flee the city when he refused to recognize the sovereignty of the Roman Senate and Arnold of Brescia, heading the opposition to his election, seized temporal power, he was secretly consecrated at Farfa Abbey on February 18. He moved to Viterbo and then returned to Rome under a truce, which the rebels immediately broke, pillaging churches and turning St. Peter's into an armory. At the invitation of King Louis VII, he went to France in 1147 and proclaimed the Second Crusade, which ended in failure, despite the efforts of St. Bernard, who preached it, when the armies of King Louis VII and Emperor Conrad II of Germany were defeated. Eugene held synods at Paris and Trier in 1147 and the following year at Rheims, where he condemned Gilbert de la Porrée, and at Cremona, where he excommunicated Arnold and threatened to use force against the Roman rebels. Terms were arranged and Eugene returned to Rome in 1149 but was again forced to leave the following year. He took up residence at Tivoli, concluded the Treaty of Constance in 1153 with Emperor Frederick I, guaranteeing the rights of the Church, and died at Tivoli on July 8. Eugene labored throughout a tumultuous pontificate to reunite the Eastern churches to Rome, to reform clerical conduct and discipline, removed unworthy clergymen (among them the archbishops of Mainz and York), fought the recurrence of Manichaeism, was known for his courage and simplicity, and lived according to the spiritual counsels of St. Bernard, who wrote *De consideratione* for his guidance. His cult was approved in 1872.

EUGENIA (d. c. 257). There definitely was a Roman martyr named Eugenia but the rest of her story is a romantic fictitious legend. According to it she was the daughter of Duke Philip of Alexandria, governor of Egypt during the reign of Emperor Valerian. She fled her father's house dressed in men's clothing and was baptized by Helenus, bishop of Heliopolis, who sent her to an abbey of which she later became abbot. Accused of adultery by a woman she had cured of a sickness and whose advances she had resisted, she was haled before a judge to answer the charges; the judge was her father. Exonerated when she revealed she was a woman and his daughter, she converted him to Christianity (he later became a bishop and was beheaded for his faith). Eugenia converted many others, including her mother, Claudia, and suffered martyrdom by sword for her faith in Rome, where she had gone with her mother. December 25.

EUGENIUS OF CARTHAGE (d. 505). A native of Carthage, he was noted for his learning, holiness, charity, and prudence. He was elected bishop of Carthage in 481 in an election permitted by King Huneric of the Vandals after the see had been vacant for fifty years. Huneric, who ruled the city and was an Arian, forbade him to occupy his episcopal chair, launched a persecution of Catholics, and forbade any Vandal to enter a Catholic church. He ordered a conference of bishops to be held, but when Eugenius learned it would be dominated by Arian bishops, he refused to attend. When the bishops assembled in 484 ostensibly to discuss relations between Catholics and Arians, Huneric seized the opportunity to plunder Catholic churches and banish many of the Catholic bishops, Eugenius among them. He was deported to the deserts of Tripoli and put in the custody of an Arian bishop, Anthony, who treated him with great cruelty. Huneric died in 484 and his nephew and successor, Gontamund, allowed Eugenius to return in 488 and later allowed the orthodox (Catholic) churches to be reopened. The next King, Thrasimund, renewed the persecution, sentenced Eugenius to death, but instead banished him to Languedoc, where he died at a monastery near Albi. July 13.

EULALIA OF BARCELONA (d. 304). Born at Barcelona, Spain, she was tortured and then put to death there for her faith during the persecution of Christians by Emperor Diocletian. She is known as Aulaire in French Catalonia and is probably the same as Eulalia of Mérida. February 12.

EULALIA OF MÉRIDA (d. c. 304). Though a Eulalia did live and suffer martyrdom in Mérida, Spain, all else about her is legendary. According to the legend, she was a twelve-year-old Spanish girl who despite her mother's efforts to prevent her from doing so, denounced Judge Dacian for attempting to get Christians to apostatize and was then tortured and put to death when she refused to sacrifice to the gods. She is mentioned by St. Augustine and had a hymn written in her honor by Prudentius. December 10.

EULOGIUS OF CORDOVA (d. 859). Of a prominent Christian family in Moorish-occupied Cordova, Spain, he was educated by Abbot Sperando and was ordained. He became noted for his learning and knowledge of Scripture and for the rules he drew up for many of the monasteries of Navarre and Pamplona. He was imprisoned in 850 when the Moors unleashed a persecution of the Christians in Cordova, and while in prison he wrote his *Exhortation to Martyrdom* for two Christian girls, Flora and Mary, who had been threatened with slavery. They were both beheaded, but a few days later Eulogius and the other prisoners were released. During the continued persecution that followed, he was tireless in his encouragement of his fellow Christians and was elected archbishop of Toledo but never occupied the see. Before he was consecrated, he helped a Christian convert from Mohammedanism, Leocritia, to escape (the penalty for a Moor who became a Christian was death), but she was discovered, and all who aided her were arrested. Eulogius tried to convert the kadi before whom he was tried but was ordered executed. He was beheaded, as was Leocritia four days later. He wrote *Memorial of the Saints*, describing the sufferings of martyred saints to encourage the persecuted Christians, and an *Apologia*, defending martyrs who sought death by proclaiming their faith. March 11.

EUPHROSYNE (5th century). A religious fiction makes her the daughter of wealthy Paphnutius, born after many years of his childless marriage. She was betrothed to a wealthy young man but began to give her possessions to the poor, and while her father was on retreat, she consulted with an old monk whose prayers had reputedly brought about her birth, and he gave her the veil. Fearful of her father's reaction, she donned men's clothing, became a monk at the monastery her father frequented, taking the name Smaragdus, and became famous for her holiness and spiritual wisdom. She was consulted by her father, who did not recognize her, and she did not reveal her identity to him until she was dying. After her death, her father became a monk and lived in her cell for ten years. January 1.

EUSEBIUS (d. 309). A Greek priest and the son of a physician, he was elected Pope to succeed Pope St. Marcellus on April 18, 309 or 310. Eusebius inherited the *lapsi* controversy from his predecessor, whose policy of readmitting the *lapsi* after suitable penance he followed. His election was opposed by a group of *lapsi*, who elected Heraclius antipope and demanded immediate return to the sacraments without penance. They caused such disturbances that Emperor Maxentius banished both Heraclius and the Pope to Sicily, where Eusebius died after a reign of only four months. August 17.

EUSEBIUS (c. 283–371). Born on Sardinia, son of a martyr, he was brought to Rome when an infant by his mother and raised there. He was ordained a lector and then went to Vercelli, where in 340 he was elected bishop of the city. He reformed his clergy, was the first Western bishop to unite the clerical and monastic life, and he lived in community with some of his clergy. He was sent by Pope Liberius in 354 with Bishop Lucifer of Cagliari to ask Emperor Constantius to call a council to settle the differences between Catholics and Arians, vehemently refused to sign the condemnation of St. Athanasius at the Council of Milan called by Constantius the following year, and demanded that all the bishops present sign the Nicene Creed before considering Athanasius' case. Eusebius was threatened with death by the Emperor and was banished to Scythopolis, Palestine, in the custody of Arian Bishop Patrophilus, by the furious Constantius when, with Dionysius of Milan and Lucifer of Cagliari, Eusebius adamantly refused the Emperor's demand that he sign Athanasius' condemnation. There Eusebius was persecuted and subjected to numerous humiliations by the Arians. He was moved first to Cappadocia and then to Upper Thebaid, Egypt, where he continued his uncompromising opposition to Arianism. He returned from exile to attend a council at Alexandria in 362 after Constantius died and Julian the Apostate permitted the exiled bishops to return to their sees. Eusebius was delegated by the council to go to Antioch to heal the breach between the Eustathians, the followers of St. Eustathius, who had been exiled from that see by the Arians in 331, and the Meletians, the followers of Bishop Meletius, who had been elected bishop of Antioch in 361 mainly by Arians, by recognizing Meletius as bishop, only to find that Lucifer of Cagliari, who had also been a delegate to the council, had complicated the situation further by consecrating Paulinus, leader of the Eustathians, bishop of Carthage. Lucifer's refusal to obey the council's decree began the Luciferian schism. Unable to accomplish anything at Antioch in the face of this development, Eusebius traveled throughout Illyricum visiting various churches to bolster their orthodoxy and returned to Vercelli in 363. He spent the rest of his life fighting Arianism in the Western Church, with St. Hilary of Poitiers, and was one of the chief opponents of Arian Bishop Auxentius of Milan. Eusebius died at Vercelli on August 1. He was one of the authors of the Athanasian Creed, and a manuscript copy of the Latin gospels he is reputed to have copied, the Codex Vercellensis, is the oldest such manuscript in existence. August 2.

EUSEBIUS (d. c. 379). A stanch defender of orthodoxy and bishop of Samosata, he was active at the synod of Antioch in 361, helping to elect Meletius bishop of Antioch. Most of those voting were Arians and expected Meletius to favor Arianism. When it became obvious that Meletius was orthodox, Emperor Constantius, an Arian, demanded that Eusebius surrender to him the election acts of the synod that were in his custody. When Eusebius refused, the Emperor threatened to cut off his right hand; when Eusebius still refused, Constantius, impressed by his courage, released him. Eusebius spent the next two years laboring to reconcile the orthodox (Catholics) and Arians but was unsuccessful. He helped elect St. Basil bishop of Caesarea in Cappadocia in 372, and the two became close friends. Eusebius traveled through Syria and Palestine encouraging the Catholics to resist Valens and his persecution, and in 374 was exiled to Thrace by Valens. Eusebius returned to Samosata when Valens died in 378 and died the following year at Dolikha, where he had gone to install a Catholic bishop, when struck on the head by a tile thrown from a rooftop by a woman who was an Arian. June 21.

EUSTACE (d. c. 118). According to his untrustworthy legend, he was a Roman general named Placida under Emperor Trajan who was converted to Christianity while hunting at Guadagnolo, Italy, when he saw a stag with the figure of Christ on the cross between its antlers. He changed his name to Eustace and sometime later he lost his fortune and was separated from his wife, Theopistis, and sons, Agapitus and Theopistus. Recalled to the army, he won a great victory, but when he refused to sacrifice to the gods during the victory celebration, he and his family, with whom he had been reunited, were roasted to death. It is not certain if he ever lived, and the whole story is probably a fictitious pious tale. He is one of the Fourteen Holy Helpers, and also known as Eustathius. September 20.

EUSTATHIUS. *See* Eustace.

EUSTOCHIUM (d. c. 419). Daughter of St. Paula, Eustochium Julia joined her mother in choosing St. Jerome as a spiritual director when he came to Rome in 382, and soon took the veil of perpetual virginity—an event that caused Jerome to write his famous *Concerning the Keeping of Virginity* for her in 384. She accompanied her mother to the Holy Land with Jerome and then to Bethlehem, where she and her mother helped Jerome in his translation of the Bible when his sight failed. She assisted her mother in directing the three communities of women founded by Jerome and succeeded her as directress when Paula died in 404. She revitalized the monasteries but never recovered from the destruction of her monastery by a band of marauders. St. Jerome often wrote of her and provides all that we know of her. She died at Bethlehem. September 28.

EUTHYMIUS (d. 1028). Son of St. John the Iberian and a native of Iberia (Georgia, U.S.S.R.), he accompanied John to Mount Athos when his father brought him back from Constantinople, where he and other Iberian youths had been held as hostages by the Emperor. Euthymius helped his father build Iviron Monastery on Mount Athos for Iberian monks, and in about 1002 he succeeded his father as abbot. Euthymius translated the Bible from Greek into Iberian as well as the works of the Church Fathers, among them Basil, Gregory of Nyssa, St. Ephrem, Pope St. Gregory the Great, and John Cassian. Euthymius resigned as abbot after fourteen years to devote himself to his translations. Summoned to Constantinople by Emperor Constantine VIII to explain the disturbances that were taking place at Iviron between the Greek and the Iberian monks, he died on May 13 while on the way of injuries he sustained in a fall from his mule. He is often called "the Enlightener" or "the Illuminator."

EUTHYMIUS THE GREAT (c. 378–473). Born of wealthy parents at Militene, Armenia, he studied under the bishop there and was ordained. He was appointed supervisor of the monasteries in the diocese but when twenty-nine he became a monk at the Pharan *laura* near Jerusalem. About 411, he left to live with a companion as a hermit in a cave near Jericho, attracted numerous disciples, left his companion, Theoctistus, as superior, and moved to a more remote spot. He still attracted many and converted so many, including a great many Arabs, that Patriarch Juvenal of Jerusalem consecrated him bishop to minister to them. Juvenal built him a *laura* on the road from Jerusalem to Jericho, which Euthymius ruled by vicars. He attracted enormous crowds, among them Eudoxia, the widow of Emperor Theodosius II, who followed his advice to give up her allegiance to the Eutychians and return to orthodoxy in 459. He died on January 20 after sixty-six years in the desert.

EUTHYMIUS THE YOUNGER (c. 824–898). Born at Opso, near Ancrya, Galatia, he was baptized Nicetas and married early, having one daughter, Anastasia. In 842 he left his family and entered a *laura* on Mount Olympus in Bithynia, where he took the name Euthymius and then entered the monastery of the Pissidion. When Abbot Nicholas was removed as abbot for supporting Patriarch Ignatius of Constantinople, who was deposed in 858, Euthymius became a hermit on Mount Athos with an *in situ* hermit, Joseph. In 863,

Euthymius visited the tomb of a fellow ascetic from Olympus, Theodore, at Salonika and lived for a time on a tower, preaching to crowds. He was ordained deacon there, returned to Mount Athos, but left to escape the crowds seeking him. After a time on a small island with two companions, he returned to Mount Athos and lived there with Joseph until Joseph's death. In response to a dream he had of Joseph, he took two disciples, Ignatius and Ephrem, to Mount Peristera in eastern Salonika, rebuilt ruined St. Andrew Monastery there, attracted numerous disciples, and served as their abbot for fourteen years. He built another double monastery, which he turned over to the metropolitan of Salonika, and then returned to Athos, where he remained until a few months before his death, when he went to Holy Island with George, a fellow monk, and died there on October 15. He is called "the Younger" to distinguish him from St. Euthymius the Great.

EUTICIUS (d. c. 305). *See* Januarius.

EUTYCHIAN (d. 283). Nothing is known of him except that he was born at Luni, Italy, succeeded Felix I as Pope on January 4, 275, died on December 7, and was buried in the catacomb of Callistus.

EUTYCHIUS (1st century). A native of Phrygia, he became a disciple of St. Paul and was raised from the dead by Paul when he fell out a window while listening to Paul preach (Acts 20:7–12). Eutychius is also believed to have been with St. John on Patmos while the evangelist wrote Revelation, preached the gospel in several countries, and was subjected to imprisonment and torture for his faith. August 24.

EVANS, PHILIP (1645–79). Born in Monmouthshire, Wales, and educated at Saint-Omer, he joined the Jesuits when twenty and was ordained at Liège in 1675. He was then sent to minister to the Catholics of southern Wales and was arrested in 1678 at Sker in Glamorgan, and when he refused to take the Oath of Supremacy was imprisoned in Cardiff Castle, where soon after he had Bl. John Lloyd as a fellow prisoner. They had both been arrested in the hysteria of the Titus Oates plot, but when no evidence of their complicity could be produced, they were charged and convicted of being priests illegally in England. They were both executed at

Cardiff on July 22. Evans was canonized as one of the Forty Martyrs of England and Wales by Pope Paul VI in 1970.

EVARISTUS (d. c. 105). The son of Juda, a Bethlehem Hellenic Jew, he was elected Pope succeeding St. Clement sometime between 97 and 100. He died sometime between 105 and 107 and was probably buried near St. Peter. October 26.

EVENTIUS (d. c. 113). *See* Alexander.

EVODIUS (d. c. 64). One of the seventy disciples, tradition has him ordained and consecrated bishop of Antioch by one of the apostles, probably Peter. It is believed Evodius was the first person to use the word Christian. May 6.

EWALD (d. c. 695). There were two Ewalds, brothers from Northumbria and educated in Ireland, who went as missionaries to Westphalia, Germany, about 694. Surnamed "the Dark" and "the Fair" to distinguish them, they were both murdered at Aplerbeke, Dortmund, by barbarians who feared that their friendship with a local chieftain would lead to the adoption of Christianity and the suppression of pagan rites. The chieftain put the murderers to death and destroyed their village. October 3.

EXUPERIUS (d. c. 287). *See* Maurice.

EYMARD, PETER JULIAN (1811–68). Born on February 4 at La Mure d'Isère near Grenoble, France, son of a cutler (at which trade he worked for a time), he entered the Grenoble seminary in 1831 and was ordained there in 1835. He engaged in pastoral work for the next five years and then joined the Marists. He served as spiritual director of the junior seminary at Belley and in 1845 was named provincial at Lyons. Always devoted to the Blessed Sacrament, he began to plan a religious congregation dedicated to Jesus in the Blessed Sacrament, and in 1856 his proposal for an institute of Priests of the Blessed Sacrament devoted to perpetual adoration of the Blessed Sacrament exposed was approved by Archbishop de Sibour of Paris. At first progress was slow, but in time the institute attracted new members, and in 1858 Peter began the Servants of the Blessed Sacrament (established as a religious

community in 1864), whose nuns devoted themselves to perpetual adoration of the Blessed Sacrament. His congregation
of priests was approved by Pope Pius IX during his lifetime
but did not receive final confirmation until 1895. He also
founded the Priests' Eucharistic League (it was not canonically erected until 1887), organized the Confraternity of the
Blessed Sacrament, and wrote several books on the Eucharist.
He died at La Mure on August 1, and was canonized by Pope
John XXIII in 1962.

EYSTEIN ERLANDSSON (d. 1188). Chaplain to King
Inge of Norway, he was appointed second archbishop of
Nidaros (Trondheim) in 1157 and then went on a pilgrimage to Rome from which he did not return until 1161, having
been made papal *legate a latere*. He labored to free the
Church in Norway from interference in its affairs by the nobles and to bring to the Norwegian Church the practices and
customs of the churches of Europe at that time, though celibacy for the clergy was largely unobserved in his country. He
crowned the child Magnus King of Norway at Bergen in
1164, and was closely associated with the boy's father, Jarl
Erling Skakke, who approved Eystein's code of laws. He was
forced to flee to England in 1181 when Sverre claimed the
throne on the grounds that he was the illegitimate son of King
Sigurd and the rightful heir; from there Eystein excommunicated Sverre. Eystein returned to Norway in 1183 and was
aboard a ship in Bergen Harbor when Sverre's fleet defeated
Magnus, causing the King to flee to Denmark. The following
year Magnus was killed in battle, Sverre became King, and
Eystein made peace with him. Eystein (Scandinavian for
Austin or Augustine) died on January 26. Though proclaimed a saint by a thirteenth-century Norwegian synod, he
has never formally been named a saint.

F

FABER, BL. PETER. *See* Favre, Bl. Peter.

FABIAN (d. 250). A Roman layman, he was elected Pope on January 10, 236, reportedly because a dove settled on his head during the election. Little is known of his pontificate. He condemned Bishop Privatus of Lambaesa, Africa, for heresy, had considerable restoration work done on the catacombs, and suffered martyrdom in the early stages of Decian's persecution of the Christians. January 20.

FABIOLA (d. 399). A wealthy Roman patrician of the famous Fabia family, she was for a time a member of St. Jerome's circle but fell away, divorced her husband for his dissolute life, and remarried. On the death of her second husband, she returned to the Church, devoted herself to charitable works and aiding churches, and built the first Christian public hospital in the West, where she personally tended the sick. She visited Jerome at Bethlehem in 395, supported him in his controversy with Patriarch John of Jerusalem, decided not to join Paula's community, and on her return to Rome, continued her charitable work, opening a hospice for poor pilgrims at Porto with St. Pammachius. Jerome wrote two treatises for her and is the source of most of our information about her. December 27.

FACHANAN (6th century). Born at Tulachteann, Ireland, he studied under St. Ita, founded Molana Monastery on an island in the Blackwater, and later the monastic school of Ross (Rosscarbery), Cork, which became one of the most famous monastic centers in Ireland. August 14.

FADA. *See* Cumian.

FAITH (2nd century). *See* Charity.

FAITH (3rd century). Her unreliable legend is that she was haled before Dacian, procurator at Agen, France, for her Christianity during Diocletian's persecution of the Christians. She was then tortured to death for her Christianity on a red-hot brazier. Also executed with her was St. Alberta (March 11); when some of the spectators objected, Dacian had them beheaded. October 6.

FALCONIERI, ALEXIS (c. 1200–1310). Son of Bernard Falconieri, a wealthy Florentine merchant and a Guelph, he with six other young Florentines joined the Confraternity of the Blessed Virgin in Florence about 1225. On the feast of the Assumption in 1233, they experienced a vision of the Blessed Virgin in which Mary inspired them to a life of prayer and solitude as hermits. They founded a house at La Camarzia on the outskirts of Florence and then moved to nearby Monte Senario, and in 1240, as the result of another vision of Mary, founded the Servants of Mary (the Servites), with Buonfiglio Monaldo superior general. They were all ordained except Alexis, who felt he was not worthy enough to be a priest and devoted himself to the material needs of the community and helped build the Servite church at Cafaggio. He was the only one of the seven still alive when the order was approved by Pope Benedict XI in 1304 and died at Monte Senario on February 17, reputedly at the age of 110. He and his six companions were canonized in 1888 by Pope Leo XIII as the Seven Holy Founders. February 17.

FALCONIERI, JULIANA (1270–1341). Of a wealthy Florentine family, she was raised by her mother and Uncle Alexis, one of the founders of the Servites, on the death of her father when she was quite young. She rejected her family's plans for her to marry and when she was fifteen was vested with the Servite habit by St. Philip Benizi. She became a Servite tertiary when sixteen, continuing to live at home. When her mother died in 1304, she headed a group of women dedicated to prayer and charitable works, was named superior, drew up a rule (which was approved for Servite nuns 120 years later by Pope Martin V), and is considered the foundress of the Servite nuns. She died in Florence and was canonized in 1731. June 19.

FARE. *See* Burgundofara.

FAUSTUS (d. c. 304). With Januarius and Martial, he was arrested for his Christianity during Diocletian's persecution of Christians at Cordova, Spain. All three were subjected to terrible tortures and then burned to death. They were called "the Three Crowns of Cordova" by Prudentius, the Christian Latin poet. October 13.

FAVRE, BL. PETER (1506–46). Born of a family of farmers at Vilardet, Savot, on April 13 and named Lefèvre, he was sent to St. Barbe College in Paris in 1525 and there roomed with Francis Xavier and met Ignatius Loyola; the three became close friends. Peter was ordained in 1534 and celebrated the Mass at Montmartre on August 15 when the Society of Jesus (the Jesuits) came into being. He went to Rome with Ignatius and Diego Laynez in 1537, was a professor at the university there, and was sent by Pope Paul III to diets at Worms in 1540 and at Ratisbon in 1541 convoked by Emperor Charles V in an unsuccessful attempt to reconcile religious differences in Germany. Peter was dismayed at the state of religion and of the clergy there and decided that the remedy was to reform the Church rather than by discussions with the Protestants. He then preached ceaselessly, giving retreats based on Ignatius Loyola's *Spiritual Exercises* to laypeople with tremendous success in Germany, France, Portugal, and Spain. Among the successful results of his preaching was attracting Peter Canisius and Francis Borgia to join the Jesuits. Peter Favre was selected by Pope Paul to be his theologian at the Council of Trent, but he died in Rome on August 1 while preparing for the council, and his cult was confirmed in 1872. His surname is sometimes spelled Faber. August 11.

FELICIAN (c. 159–254). A disciple of Pope St. Eleutherius, he worked as a missionary in Umbria, Italy, and was consecrated bishop of Foligno by Pope St. Victor I, who seems to have bestowed on him the pallium, the first recorded bishop to have received it. He was bishop for some fifty years when he was arrested during Decius' persecution of the Christians for refusing to sacrifice to the pagan gods. He was tortured, scourged, and died just outside Foligno while being conveyed to Rome for his execution. At the same time, Messalina (January 19), who had received the veil from him and ministered to him in prison, was clubbed to death when she too refused to sacrifice to the gods. January 24.

FELICIAN (d. c. 290). *See* Victor of Marseilles.

FELICIAN (d. c. 297). He and his eighty-year-old brother Primus were Roman patricians who had become Christians and devoted themselves to aiding the poor and visiting prisoners. About 297, during the persecution of Christians by Emperors Diocletian and Maximian, they were arrested, and when they refused to sacrifice to the pagan gods were imprisoned and scourged, again haled before a magistrate named Promotus at Nomentum, near Rome, tortured, and when they persisted in their Christianity, both were executed. June 9.

FELICISSIMUS (d. 258). *See* Sixtus II.

FELICITY (d. c. 165). A woman named Felicity was a martyr in Rome and was buried in the cemetery of Maximus on the Salarian Way, but all else about her is derived from various dubious legends. According to them, she was a woman with seven children and devoted herself to charitable works. She was so effective in conversion work that the pagan priests lodged a complaint against her with Emperor Antonius Pius, who caused her to be arraigned before Publius, the prefect of Rome. He used various threats and pleas in an unsuccessful attempt to get her to worship the pagan gods, and was equally unsuccessful with her seven sons. He remanded the case to the Emperor, who ordered them all executed. Felicity was beheaded with Alexander, Vitalis, and Martial; Januarius was scourged to death; Felix and Philip were beaten to death with clubs; and Silvanus was drowned in the Tiber. Seven martyrs with these names, commemorated on July 10, were buried in Roman cemeteries, one of them, Silvanus, near Felicity's tomb. The proximity gave rise to the legend that they were brothers (the so-called Seven

Brothers) and her sons, but there is no evidence that they were her sons nor even that they were brothers. July 10.

FELICITY (d. 203). *See* Perpetua.

FELIX (d. c. 165). *See* Felicity.

FELIX I (d. 274). Nothing is known of him except that he was a Roman, the son of one Constantius, was elected Pope to succeed Dionysius on January 5, 269, and ordered the celebration of Mass over the tombs of martyrs in the catacombs. He died on December 30 and was not martyred as the Roman Martyrology states. May 30.

FELIX (d. c. 303). *See* Honoratus.

FELIX (d. 304). *See* Optatus.

FELIX (d. c. 304). A priest in Rome, he was tortured and put to death during Diocletian's persecution of the Christians. On the way to the execution site, he encountered a Christian who was so impressed by Felix's faith that he publicly proclaimed his own Christianity and was ordered put to death with Felix. Both were beheaded. Since the name of the Christian he met is unknown, he was called Adauctus, "the added one," because his martyrdom was added to that of Felix. August 30.

FELIX II (III) (d. 492). Of an old Roman senatorial family, he was married, and when his wife died, he became a priest. He was elected Pope to succeed Simplicius in 483 and at once became embroiled in a dispute with Emperor Zeno when Felix denounced the Emperor's interference in ecclesiastical affairs with the publication of the imperial *Henoticon* in 482, which attempted to settle the difference between the monophysites and orthodox but instead exacerbated the dispute and implicitly condoned monophysitism. He sent legates to summon Acacius, orthodox patriarch of Constantinople, to Rome, only to find that his legates had held communion with the heretics and Acacius; and the Emperor had not removed Peter Mongus, a monophysite, as Patriarch of Alexandria, as he had demanded. A synod at Rome in 484 excommunicated the legates and Acacius who, supported by the Emperor, disregarded the excommunication, thus beginning the Acacian schism. Felix aided the African churches during the persecution of the Catholics there by Arian Vandal King Huneric and helped restore them when the persecution ended. Felix died on March 1. He is sometimes referred to as Pope Felix III to distinguish him from antipope Felix II, but he is II in the order of legitimate Popes.

FELIX III (IV) (d. 530). A native of Samnium and a priest, he was the choice of Emperor Theodoric for the papacy and was elected Pope and consecrated on July 12, 526, succeeding Pope John I. He ruled well, denounced semi-Pelagianism at the Council of Orange in 529, converted two pagan temples in the Forum at Rome to the basilica of SS. Cosmas and Damian, and secured a decree reserving the trial of clerics solely to the Pope. He is often called Felix IV because of the disruption in papal numbers for Popes named Felix by antipope Felix II but is III in the order of legitimate Popes. September 22.

FELIX OF NOLA (d. c. 260). The son of Hermias, a Syrian who had been a Roman soldier, he was born on his father's estate at Nola near Naples, Italy. On the death of his father, Felix distributed his inheritance to the poor, was ordained by Bishop St. Maximus of Nola, and became his assistant. When Maximus fled to the desert at the beginning of Decius' persecution of the Christians in 250, Felix was seized in his stead and imprisoned. He was reputedly released from prison by an angel, who directed him to the ailing Maximus, whom he brought back to Nola. Even after Decius' death in 251, Felix was a hunted man but kept well hidden until the persecution ended. When Maximus died, the people unanimously selected Felix as their bishop, but he declined the honor in favor of Quintus, a senior priest. Felix spent the rest of his life on a small piece of land sharing what he had with the poor, and died there on January 14. His tomb soon became famous for the miracles reported there, and when St. Paulinus became bishop of Nola almost a century later (410), he wrote about his predecessor, the source of our information about him, adding legendary material that had grown up about Felix in the intervening century.

FELIX OF VALOIS (1126–1212). A hermit at Cerfroid, France, he and his disciple, St. John of Matha, secured in 1198 the approval of the Holy See for the Order of the Most Holy Trinity (the Trinitarians) to ransom captives from the Moors. John worked in Spain and Barbary while Felix, now in his seventies, founded St. Mathurm Convent in Paris and administered the French province from Cerfroid, where he died on November 4. By 1240, the Order had some six hundred monasteries. The cult of the two men was approved by Pope Alexander VII in 1666, though members of the Order believe the two cofounders were canonized in 1262 by Pope Urban IV. November 20.

FERDINAND III OF CASTILE (c. 1199–1252). Son of King Alfonso IX of León and Berengaria, daughter of King Alfonso III of Castile, he was born near Salamanca and became King of Castile at eighteen when his mother relinquished her claim to the throne on the death of her brother Henry in 1217. Ferdinand married Beatrice, daughter of King Philip of Swabia, in 1219 and despite opposition from his two half sisters, also became King of León when his father died in 1230. He spent twenty years of his reign fighting the Moors, driving them from Ubeda, Cordova, Cadiz, and finally in 1249 from Seville. He ruled wisely, was an excellent administrator, and established internal peace in the two kingdoms. He had Archbishop Ximenes as his chancellor, founded the University of Salamanca in 1243, rebuilt the cathedral of Burgos, and converted the mosque in Seville to a church. He married Joan of Ponthieu on the death of Beatrice, and died in Seville on May 30. He was buried in the habit of a friar minor in the Seville cathedral, and was canonized in 1671.

FERDINAND OF PORTUGAL, BL. (1402–43). Son of King John I of Portugal and Philippa, daughter of John of Gaunt, he was born on September 29 at Santarem, Portugal. He led a life of piety unusual for a prince in those days, was appointed grand master of the Knights of Aviz (originally the New Militia to Fight the Moors), but refused a cardinalate from Pope Eugene IV. With his brother, Henry the Navigator, Ferdinand led an army against the Moors at Tangiers, Africa, an ill-conceived expedition approved by his brother, King Edward, and it ended in disaster with the Portuguese defeated. Henry escaped, but Ferdinand was captured and maltreated by his captor when Edward refused to ransom him with the stronghold of Ceuta. After six years of captivity, he died in prison at Fez on June 5, and his body was hung from the prison walls. He is often surnamed "the Constant," as he is the hero of one of the most popular tragedies, *El Principe Constante,* of the famous Spanish dramatist Pedro Calderón. Ferdinand's cult was approved in 1470.

FERGUS (8th century). An Irish bishop, possibly of Downpatrick, and surnamed "the Pict," he went to Scotland as a missionary, settled at Strathearn, Perthshire, and founded several churches there. He may be the same as Fergustus, bishop of the Scots, who attended a synod in Rome in 721. November 27.

FERRINI, BL. CONTARDO (1859–1902). Born on April 4 at Milan, Italy, son of a mathematics and physics teacher, he studied law at Borromeo College at Pavia, received his doctorate in 1880, and studied for two years at the University of Berlin. He returned to Italy in 1883 to edit an edition of Justinian's *Institutes.* Bl. Contardo was acquainted with some dozen languages, became reader in Roman criminal law in Pavia and then professor of Roman law, and in 1887 was made professor of Roman law at Messina. In 1894 he returned to the University of Pavia, where he was soon recognized as one of the outstanding authorities on Roman law. He was active in social work, was associated with the Ambrosian library, was a member of the St. Vincent de Paul Society and a Franciscan tertiary, helped found the St. Severinus Boethius Society for university students, and in 1895 was elected to the Milan Municipal Council. He died of typhoid at Suna (Novara), Italy, on October 17. He wrote some two hundred monographs and throughout his lifetime was regarded by his students and colleagues as one who lived a life of holiness in the midst of academia and while engaging in intellectual pursuits. He was beatified in 1947 and is the patron of universities. October 20.

FIACHRA. *See* Fiacre.

FIACRE (d. c. 670). Also known as Fiachra, he was a hermit at Kilfiachra, Ireland, left to go to France, and then lived as a solitary at Breuil, Brie, on land given him by St. Faro, bishop of Meaux. Fiacre built a hospice for travelers, attracted many disciples, was known for his charity and aid to the poor, and was consulted by many for his spiritual wisdom. His miracles of healing became legendary. He is the patron saint of gardeners and the cabdrivers of Paris, whose vehicles are called *fiacres*, since the first coach for hire in Paris was located near the Hotel Saint-Fiacre. September 1.

FILIPPINI, LUCY (1672–1732). Born at Tarquinia, Tuscany, Italy, on January 13, she was orphaned when quite young. She was brought to Montefiascone by Marcantonio Cardinal Barbarigo to participate in Maestre Pie Institute for training teachers and was put in charge of a school for young girls founded by the cardinal. She devoted the rest of her life to Maestre Pie, dedicating herself to improving the status of women, founding schools and educational centers for girls and women all over Italy, including the first Maestre Pie school established in Rome at the invitation of Pope Clement XI in 1707. Stricken with cancer the last years of her life, she died on March 25 at Montefiascone, and was canonized in 1930.

FINAN (d. 661). An Irishman, he became a monk at Iona and then succeeded St. Aidan as second bishop of Lindisfarne. Finan opposed the introduction of Roman liturgical practices to replace the Celtic usage, was a friend of King Oswy of Northumbria, and baptized Penda of the Middle Angles and later King Sigebert of the East Saxons, who had been converted by Oswy. February 17.

FINBAR (d. c. 633). Reportedly he was the illegitimate son of a master smith and a woman of royal background. Born in Connaught, Ireland, and baptized Lochan, he was educated at Kilmacahil, Kilkenny, where the monks named him Fionnbharr (white head); he is also known as Bairre and Barr. He went on pilgrimage to Rome with some of the monks, visiting St. David in Wales on the way back. Supposedly, on another visit to Rome the Pope wanted to consecrate him a bishop but was deterred by a vision, and Finbar was consecrated from heaven and then returned to Ireland. At any rate, he may have preached in Scotland, definitely did in southern Ireland, lived as a hermit on a small island at Lough Eiroe, and then, on the River Lee, founded a monastery that developed into the city of Cork, of which he was the first bishop. His monastery became famous in southern Ireland and attracted numerous disciples. Many extravagant miracles are attributed to him, and supposedly the sun did not set for two weeks after he died at Cloyne. September 25.

FINNIAN (d. c. 579). Born near Strangford Lough, Ulster, Ireland, reportedly of a royal family, he studied at Dromore under St. Colman, at Mahee Island under St. Mochae, and at Whitern in Strathclyde, where he became a monk. Forced to leave Whitern because of a prank he played on a Pictish princess who was enamored of him, he went to Rome and was ordained there. He returned to Ulster, founded several monasteries (one of which, Moville, was outstanding), and had St. Columba as a disciple. He and Columba became engaged in a dispute when Columba made a copy of the first copy of Jerome's psalter in Ireland, which Finnian had brought from Rome. He demanded Columba's copy, and Columba refused to give it to him. The dispute was finally settled by King Diarmaid, who ruled in Finnian's favor, and Columba was obliged to turn over his copy to Finnian. Finnian is reputed to have performed numerous extravagant miracles—moving a river, for example—and preached and founded a monastery at Holywood, Dumfries, Scotland. September 10.

FINNIAN OF CLONARD (c. 470–c. 549). Unreliable legend has him born at Myshall, Carlow, Ireland, and spending several years in Wales at monasteries under St. Cadoc and St. Gildas. He became a monk in Wales, returned to Ireland, and founded several monasteries, most notable of which was Clonard in Meath, which became a great center of learning, especially of Bible studies (Finnian was a great biblical scholar). He died at Clonard of yellow plague, which swept Ireland. Though called a bishop in Ireland, it is doubtful if he was ever consecrated. He is often called "the Teacher of Irish Saints" and at one time had as pupils at Clonard the so-called Twelve Apostles of Ireland, one of whom was St. Columba. December 12.

FINNIAN LOBHAR (d. c. 560). Born at Bregia, Leinster, Ireland, he may have been a disciple of St. Columba (or perhaps was trained at one of Columba's foundations), was ordained by Bishop Fathlad, and may have been consecrated

by him. He built a church that is believed to have been at
Innisfallen, and so is considered by some scholars to have
been the founder of that monastery. Later he lived at Clonmore and then went to Swords near Dublin, where he was
made abbot by Columba when he left. Another account has
him abbot of Clonmore Monastery for the last thirty years of
his life. Lobhar means "the Leper," a name he acquired when
he reputedly assumed the disease of a leper to cure a young
boy of an illness. As is evident, much of the information
about him is uncertain and conflicting, and it is not even certain what century he lived in. March 16.

FINTAN (d. c. 635). Also known as Munnu, he was a
monk under St. Seenell at Cluain Inis, Ireland, for eighteen
years and then left to become a monk at Iona. On his arrival,
he found that Columba had died (though one tradition has
him living at Iona for a time until Columba died in 597),
whereupon he returned to Ireland, founded a monastery at
Taghmon (Tech Munnu), Wexford, and became its abbot.
He was a firm supporter of the Celtic liturgical practices at
the synod of Magh Lene in 630, developed Taghmon into an
outstanding monastery, and reportedly contracted leprosy in
the late years of his life. October 21.

FISHER, JOHN (1469–1535). Born at Beverley, Yorkshire, England, son of a textiles dealer, he entered Cambridge
at fourteen, became a fellow of Michaelhouse, and was ordained when twenty-two. He served in various offices at the
university, becoming vice chancellor in 1501, but resigned in
1502 to be chaplain to Lady Margaret Beaufort, mother of
King Henry VIII. She made numerous gifts to Cambridge,
among them founding Christ's College and St. John's and
providing chairs of divinity at Oxford and Cambridge, which
Fisher administered and for which she is regarded as the outstanding benefactress in Cambridge history. Fisher helped
raise the standard of scholarship at Cambridge and in 1504
was named chancellor, a post he occupied until his death. He
was named bishop of Rochester the same year and became in-
ternationally known for his writings—against Luther, on
prayer and the sacraments, on the identity of Mary Magdalen
—and for his sermons. He was named one of Catherine of
Aragon's counselors in 1529 and became her leading champion against King Henry VIII's attempt to divorce her, incur-

ring Henry's enmity. Soon after the case was recalled to
Rome, Fisher became a leading opponent of Henry's attempt
to become supreme head of the Church in England and
brilliantly defended the supremacy of the Pope. Fisher was
twice imprisoned, and attempts were made on his life, but he
persisted. In 1534 he refused to accept the Bill of Succession
because the oath accompanying it was an oath of royal ecclesiastical supremacy; he was immediately arrested, imprisoned
in the Tower of London, and stripped of all his offices. While
he was in prison, Pope Paul III named him a cardinal, further
infuriating Henry. After ten months in prison and after a
farce of a trial Fisher was convicted of treason on trumped-
up charges and beheaded at Tyburn on June 22. Fisher was
not only one of the great scholars of his times, a close friend
of Thomas More and Erasmus, and possessor of one of the
finest libraries in Europe, but he was also an outstanding
bishop, devoted to the people of his diocese. He was canonized, with Thomas More, in 1935 by Pope Pius XI. June 22.

FLAVIA DOMITILLA. *See* Domitilla.

FLAVIAN (4th century). *See* Bibiana.

FLAVIAN (d. 449). A priest and treasurer of the church at
Constantinople, he succeeded St. Proclus as patriarch in 447.
Flavian incurred the enmity of Chrysaphius, chancellor of
Emperor Theodosius III, when Flavian refused to send an ex-
pensive gift to the Emperor on his coronation, declined to
make the Emperor's sister, Pulcherius, a deaconess, and condemned Eutyches, abbot of a nearby monastery, for his errors, which denied that Christ had two natures after the
Incarnation—the beginning of monophysitism. The condemnation was repeated by Eusebius of Dorylaeum at a
synod called by Flavian in 448, and Eutychius was deposed
and excommunicated. The decision was sustained by Pope
Leo I in a letter to Flavian, Leo's famous "Tome." Chrysaphius persuaded Theodosius to convene a council at Ephesus
in 449. Dioscorus of Alexandria presided, and in meetings
characterized by violence and intimidation by the Eutychian
faction and the Emperor's soldiers, who refused to allow the
papal legates to read a letter from Pope Leo, both Flavian
and Eusebius were ordered deposed, and Dioscorus was declared patriarch. The order was enforced by the Emperor's

soldiers, who forced the bishops present to sign the deposition order. Flavian was beaten so severely during the meeting that he died of the injuries three days later when sent into exile near Sardis, Libya. The acts of this "robber synod," as Leo called it, was undone when Theodosius died in 450 and the Council of Chalcedon in 451 reinstated Eusebius and deposed and exiled Dioscorus; on his accession to the throne in 451, Emperor Marcian had Chrysaphius executed. February 18.

FLORA (d. 851). Daughter of a Mohammedan, she was born in Cordova, Spain, and secretly raised a Christian by her Christian mother. Flora was betrayed by her brother, scourged, and put into his custody that he might persuade her to apostatize. She escaped, but later while praying in St. Acislus Church she met Mary, sister of a deacon who had just been martyred, and they both decided to give themselves up as Christians. They were sent to a brothel, and when their ordeal there failed to shake their constancy, they were beheaded. November 24.

FLORIAN (d. 304). An officer of the Roman army in Noricum (Austria), he surrendered himself to Aquilinus, the governor, at Lorsch when Aquilinus' troops were hunting Christians during Diocletian's persecution, declaring he was a Christian. He was scourged and then thrown into the River Enns with a rock around his neck. He is a patron of Poland and Upper Austria. May 4.

FLUË, BL. NICHOLAS VON. See Nicholas von Fluë, Bl.

FOILLAN (d. c. 655). Born in Ireland, he and his brothers, St. Fursey and St. Ultan, went to England about 630, built a monastery at Burgh Castle near Yarmouth, and worked as missionaries among the East Angles. When their monastery was destroyed by the Mercians under Penda, Foillan and Ultan decided to follow Fursey, who had gone to Gaul sometime earlier. They were welcomed to Neustria by King Clovis II, and Foillan founded a monastery, of which he became abbot, at Fosses on land given him by Bl. Itta near Nivelles Abbey, which she had founded. He had great success converting the Brabanters but with three disciples was murdered by a band of outlaws in the forest of Seneffe outside Nivelles, where he had just said Mass. October 31.

FOREST, BL. JOHN (d. 1538). He joined the Observant Franciscans when seventeen at Greenwich, England, studied theology at Oxford, and acquired a reputation for wisdom and learning. He returned to Greenwich, where he was Queen Catherine's confessor and knew King Henry VIII. He thought he had convinced Henry in 1529 not to suppress his Order for their opposition to his divorce of Catherine, but when the Pope denied the petition for divorce, Henry suppressed the Order in 1534 and John was imprisoned for a time in London. Reportedly he gained his freedom by submitting, but in 1538 he was at a Conventual house in Newgate under what amounted to house arrest. Accused of denouncing the Act of Supremacy, he was arrested, agreed to several propositions, but when asked to sign them refused, denying the King's ecclesiastical supremacy. He was then ordered burned at the stake, dragged on a hurdle to Smithfield, and burned to death. Also burned with him was a wooden statue of St. Derfel, of which centuries earlier it had been predicted would one day be used to set a forest afire. He was beatified in 1886. May 22.

FORTESCUE, BL. ADRIAN (1476–1539). Born at Punsbourne, England, of an old Devonshire family and a cousin of Anne Boleyn, he was twice married, first to Anne Stonor in 1499 and twelve years after her death to Anne Rede; he had two daughters by his first wife and three sons by Anne Rede. He became a Dominican tertiary at Oxford, was a knight of the Bath and in attendance at the royal court, served as a justice of the peace for Oxford County, fought in France in 1513 and 1523, was in Queen Catherine's retinue on her trip to Calais, and attended Anne Boleyn at her coronation. Deeply religious, he became caught up in the controversy over Henry VIII's divorce from Queen Catherine and his subsequent marriages. Fortescue was arrested late in August 1534 on grounds not now known but was released the following spring. He was again arrested and sent to the Tower of London in February 1539 for refusing to take the Oath of Supremacy. He was condemned by attainder in April for treason by Parliament; what the treason was was never stated, but it was probably for refusing to recognize royal supremacy in ecclesiastical matters over the Pope. He was permitted no trial and was beheaded with Ven. Thomas Dingley at Tower Hill, London, on July 8 or 9. Fortescue was beatified in 1895, July 11.

FORTUNATUS (1st century). *See* Hermagoras.

FORTUNATUS (d. c. 303). *See* Honoratus.

FOTA. *See* Cumian.

FOURIER, PETER (1565–1640). Born at Mirecourt, Lorraine, on November 30, he was sent to the Jesuit university at Pont à Mousson when fifteen and joined the Canons Regular of St. Augustine at Chaumousey when twenty. He was ordained in 1589, resumed his studies, received his doctorate, and was named vicar and procurator of the abbey parish of Chaumousey. In 1597, he was sent as parish priest to Mattaincourt, a rundown and neglected parish where he spent the next thirty years reforming the lives of the parishioners and combating Calvinism. He lived a simple, austere life, organized several confraternities, and supported education for poor children. He opened a free school with four women volunteers, with Alix Le Clerq as superior, and organized them into an institute in 1598. The institute received papal approval as the Canonesses Regular of St. Augustine of the Congregation of Our Lady in 1616 and soon spread all over France and later to other countries. In 1622, Bishop John de Maillane of Tours appointed him to reform and unite the houses of his order into one congregation, and the following year he headed the abbey of Lunéville. In 1629, the Observant canons regular of Lorraine were united into the Congregation of Our Savior, and Peter was elected superior in 1632. He was refused permission by the Holy See in 1627 to allow his congregation to teach boys in elementary schools, but it did become involved in some educational work. He fled to Gray in Franche-Comté in 1636 when he refused to take an oath of allegiance to King Louis XIII and spent the last years of his life as a chaplain in a convent there. He died on December 9 and was canonized in 1897.

FOURNET, ANDREW HUBERT (1752–1834). Born on December 6 at Maillé, near Poitiers, France, he resisted his mother's desire in his youth for him to be a priest and studied philosophy and law at Poitiers. A visit to a holy uncle who was a priest in a desolate parish turned him to the religious life. He studied theology, was ordained, and became his uncle's assistant. He became a parish priest at Maillé and completely changed his comfortable style of living for one of great austerity and simplicity. When the French revolutionary government outlawed priests who would not swear allegiance to it, he went into hiding and in 1792 went to Spain. He returned in 1797 but was at once forced to live the life of a fugitive. He resumed his pastorate when a concordat between Napoleon and the Holy See was signed in 1807, and with St. Elizabeth Bichier founded the Daughters of the Cross, a congregation dedicated to the education of children, for whom he composed a rule. He retired to La Puye in 1820 and devoted the rest of his life to the Daughters of the Cross and as a confessor and spiritual adviser. He died at La Puye on May 13, and was canonized in 1933. May 16.

FRANCES OF ROME (1384–1440). Daughter of Paul Busso and Jacobella dei Roffredeschi, a wealthy noble couple, she was born in the Trastevere, Rome, was married when thirteen to Lorenzo Ponziani, and for forty years was a model wife in an ideal marriage. With her sister-in-law, Vannozza, she ministered to the poor of Rome and led a life of great holiness. After she recovered from a serious illness during which she reported a vision of St. Alexis, they devoted themselves to the sick of Santo Spiritu Hospital until her son John Baptist was born in 1404. Despite her objections she was obliged to assume the responsibilities as head of the household when her mother-in-law died; Frances had two more children: a boy, Evangelist, and a girl, Agnes. During a plague and famine that struck Rome, Frances worked to alleviate its effects and even sold her jewels to aid the plague victims. The family fortunes suffered during the occupation of Rome by the antipapal forces of Ladislaus of Naples in 1408 (Lorenzo was wounded in the fighting), and in 1410, when Ladislaus again seized the city, Lorenzo was forced to flee, though the women remained. The Ponziani castle was looted, and the family holdings in the Campagna were burned and looted. In 1413 another plague took the life of Evangelist, and Frances turned her home into a hospital; two years later Agnes died. By 1414, when peace was restored and the Ponziani were recalled from banishment and their property restored,

Lorenzo's health was broken. Frances nursed her husband, continued her charitable activities, and organized the Oblates of Mary (later called the Oblates of Tor de' Specchi, after the building they moved into), a society of women living in the world, not bound by vows, but dedicated to helping the poor and affiliated with the Benedictines of Monte Oliveto. When Lorenzo died in 1436, she entered the foundation, was made superior, and spent the rest of her life practicing great austerities until her death in Rome on March 9. She experienced numerous visions and ecstasies, performed many miracles of healing, had the gift of prophecy (she is said to have prophesied the end of the Great Schism), and reportedly was guided the last twenty-three years of her life by an archangel visible only to herself. She was canonized in 1608 and is the patroness of motorists.

FRANCIS (d. 1597). *See* Miki, Paul.

FRANCIS OF ASSISI (c. 1181–1226). Son of Peter Bernadone, a wealthy silk merchant, he was born at Assisi, Italy, and christened John by his mother during his father's absence; on his return he insisted the child be renamed Francis. Francis spent his youth in extravagant living and pleasure-seeking, went gaily to war, and was taken prisoner in 1202. On his release he resumed his carefree ways, was seriously ill for a time, and returned to the wars in 1205. A vision of Christ he experienced at Spoleto, followed by another on his return to Assisi, caused him to change his whole lifestyle. He went on pilgrimage to Rome in 1206 and on his return devoted himself to a life of poverty and care of the sick and the poor. He was angrily denounced by his father as a madman and disinherited in one of the most dramatic scenes in religious history. After repairing several churches in Assisi, he retired to a little chapel, the Portiuncula, and devoted himself completely to his life's work of poverty and preaching. He soon attracted numerous disciples, among them several leading citizens, Bernard da Quintavalla, merchant, and Peter of Cattaneo, a canon of the cathedral, whom he robed on April 16, 1209, thus founding the Franciscans. In 1210, he received verbal approval of a rule he had drawn up from Pope Innocent III. Two years later Francis was joined by St. Clare, who joined him over the violent objections of her family. Obsessed with the desire to preach to the Mohammedans, he set out for

Syria in the fall of 1212, but was shipwrecked on the way; a second attempt, 1213–14, also failed when he fell ill in Spain while on the way to Morocco, and he was forced to return to Italy. He obtained the famous Portiuncula indulgence from Pope Innocent III in 1216 and the following year (when he probably met St. Dominic in Rome) Francis convened the first general chapter of his Order at the Portiuncula to organize the huge number of followers he had attracted to his way of life. In 1219, he sent his first missionaries to Tunis and Morocco from another general chapter, attended by some five thousand friars. He himself went to Egypt to evangelize the Mohammedans in Palestine and Egypt with twelve friars, but though he met with Sultan Malek al-Kamil at Damietta, Egypt, which was being besieged by Crusaders, his mission was a failure. Obliged to hasten back to Italy to combat a movement in his Order to mitigate his original rule of simplicity, humility, and poverty led by Matthew of Narni and Gregory of Naples, he secured the appointment of Cardinal Ugolino as protector of the Order and presented a revised rule to a general chapter of the Order at the Portiuncula in 1221, which maintained his ideals. A movement in the Order toward mitigating his rule, led by Brother Elias, began to spread and was met by Francis with still another revision, but this time he secured for it the approval of Pope Honorius III in 1223. By this time Francis had retired from the practical activities of the Order, and its direction was mainly in the hands of Brother Elias. At Christmas of 1223, Francis built a crèche at Grecchia, establishing the custom observed all over the Christian world to the present day. In 1224, while praying in his cell on Mount Alverna, he received on September 14 the stigmata, the climax of a series of supernatural events he had experienced throughout his lifetime. He died at Assisi on October 3, and was canonized in 1228. Though never ordained, Francis' impact on religious life since his times has been enormous. Probably no saint has affected so many in so many different ways as the gentle saint of Assisi who, born to wealth, devoted his life to poverty, concern for the poor and the sick, and so delighted in God's works as revealed in nature. October 4.

FRANCIS OF MIAKO. *See* Francis of Nagasaki.

FRANCIS OF NAGASAKI (d. 1597). A Japanese from

Miako, he became a physician and later was converted to Catholicism by the Franciscan missionaries in Japan. He became a Franciscan tertiary, served as a catechist, and was one of the twenty-six Catholics crucified for their faith near Nagasaki on February 5 during the persecution of Christians by the *taikō*, Toyotomi Hideyoshi. They were all canonized as the Martyrs of Japan in 1862. He is also known as Francis of Miako. February 6.

FRANCIS OF PAOLA (c. 1416–1507). Born at Paola, Italy, he was educated at the Franciscan friary at San Marco there and when fifteen became a hermit near Paola. In 1436, he and two companions began a community that is considered the foundation of the Minim Friars. He built a monastery where he had led his eremitical life some fifteen years later and set a rule for his followers emphasizing penance, charity, and humility, and added to the three monastic vows one of fasting and abstinence from meat; he also wrote a rule for tertiaries and nuns. He was credited with many miracles and had the gifts of prophecy and insight into men's hearts. The order was approved by Pope Sixtus IX in 1474 with the name Hermits of St. Francis of Assisi (changed to Minim Friars in 1492). Francis established foundations in southern Italy and Sicily, and his fame was such that at the request of dying King Louis XI of France, Pope Sixtus II ordered him to France, as the King felt he could be cured by Francis. He was not but was so comforted that Louis' son Charles VIII became Francis' friend and endowed several monasteries for the Minims. Francis spent the rest of his life at the monastery of Plessis, France, which Charles built for him. Francis died there on April 2, and was canonized in 1519.

FRANCIS OF ST. MICHAEL (d. 1597). Born at Parilla, near Valladolid, Spain, he joined the Franciscans as a lay brother and was sent from the Philippines to Japan to engage in missionary activities. He was arrested with his companion, St. Peter Baptist, in 1596, and with Peter and twenty-four others, was crucified near Nagasaki on February 5 during a persecution of Christians by the *taikō*, Toyotomi Hideyoshi. The twenty-six were canonized as the Martyrs of Japan in 1862. February 6.

FRANCIS DE SALES (1567–1622). Born in the family

castle at Thorens, Savoy, on August 21, he studied at Annecy and the Jesuit college of Clermont in Paris, 1580–88, and then studied law and theology at the University of Padua, receiving his doctorate in law when only twenty-four. Despite the opposition of his family and the offer of a senatorship, he abandoned his prospects for a brilliant secular career for the religious life and was ordained in 1593, when he was appointed provost of Geneva. He spent the next five years as a missionary in the Chablais, the residents of which were fiercely resisting the efforts of the duke of Savoy to impose Catholicism on them by military force. Despite repeated attacks on him by assassins and mobs of Calvinists, he was most successful in attracting thousands back to Catholicism and making new converts. He was named coadjutor to the bishop of Geneva in 1599 and succeeded to the see in 1602. He soon became one of the outstanding leaders of the Counter-Reformation, noted for his intellect and wisdom. An outstanding confessor (he was confessor of Bl. Marie Acarie in Paris for a time) and preacher, his theological knowledge and understanding impressed all. He founded schools, taught catechetics, and governed his diocese ably and well. In 1604, he met Frances de Chantal, became her spiritual adviser, and with her, in 1610, founded the Order of the Visitation (the Visitandines). He died in Lyons, France, on December 28. Two of his writings, *Introduction to the Devout Life* (1609) and *Treatise on the Love of God* (1616), stressing that sanctity is possible in everyday life, have become spiritual classics and are still widely read today. His beatification the year he died was the first formal beatification held in St. Peter's; he was canonized in 1665. He was declared a Doctor of the Church in 1877 and designated patron saint of the Catholic press in 1923. January 24.

FRANCIS XAVIER (1506–52). Born at the family castle of Xavier near Pamplona in the Basque area of Spanish Navarre on April 7, he studied at the University of Paris, received his licentiate in 1528, and while there met Ignatius Loyola. Despite initial opposition to Loyola's ideas, he was won over and was one of the first seven Jesuits who took their vows at Montmartre in 1534. He was ordained at Venice in 1537 with Ignatius and four other Jesuits, went to Rome in 1538, and in 1540 (the year the Pope formally approved the Society of Jesus), he and Fr. Simon Rodriguez were sent, as the first Jesuit missionaries, to the East Indies. They stopped off at Lisbon, where King John III made Rodriguez remain, and Francis lost eight months there before finally leaving for the Orient on April 7, 1541, with a brief from the Pope appointing him apostolic nuncio to the Indies. He arrived at Goa thirteen months later and spent the next five months preaching, ministering to the sick and imprisoned, teaching children, and laboring to correct the immorality of the Portuguese there, especially denouncing the practice of concubinage so prevalent in the city among the Westerners. He then spent three years at Cape Comorin at the southern tip of India opposite Ceylon (Sri Lanka), ministering to the Paravas, baptizing them by the thousands. He visited Malacca, 1545; the Moluccas, near New Guinea, and Morotai, near the Philippines, 1546–47; and Japan, 1549–51. He became the first provincial of India and the East in 1551 when Ignatius established the area as a separate province. Francis set out for China which he had always dreamed of evangelizing, in 1552 but died alone except for one companion, a Chinese youth named Antony, on the island of Shangchwan (Sancian) on December 3 in sight of the goal he was never to reach. Francis, with the possible exception of St. Paul, was the greatest of all Christian missionaries. He traveled thousands of miles to the most inaccessible places under the most harrowing conditions. His converts are estimated to have been in the hundreds of thousands; and his missionary impact in the East endured for centuries. Working with inadequate funds, little co-operation, and often actively opposed, he lived as the natives and won them to Christianity by the fervor of his preaching, the example of his life, and his concern for them. His miracles are legion, and his conversions are all the more remarkable in view of the fact that, contrary to a belief long held, he did not have the gift of tongues but worked through interpreters. He was called "the Apostle of the Indies" and "the Apostle of Japan," was canonized in 1622 by Pope Gregory XV, and was proclaimed patron of all foreign missions by Pope Pius X. December 3.

FREDERICK (d. 838). Grandson of King Radbon of the Frisians, he became a priest at Utrecht and soon was known for his holiness and learning. He was in charge of conversion work at Utrecht when he was elected bishop about 825. He labored to put the see in order, sent missionaries to the pagan areas in the northern part of his diocese, and incurred the enmity of Empress Judith when he reproached her for her immorality. He was stabbed to death at Maastricht, Flanders, by assassins; one story had them hired by the Empress; more probably they were from Walcheren, whose inhabitants deeply resented his missionary activities in their area.

FRONTO (1st century). An early missionary to Périgord, France, his untrustworthy legend has him born in Lycaonia, of the tribe of Juda. He became a follower of Christ, was baptized by Peter, and was one of the seventy-two disciples. He was with Peter in Antioch and Rome, whence he and a priest named George were sent to preach to the Gauls. Fronto made his center at Périgord, of which he is considered the first bishop, and was most successful in his missionary activities, as was George, who is considered the first bishop of Le Puy. Another legend has Fronto born at Leucuais in the Dordogne near Périgord. All kinds of extravagant miracles were attributed to him in these legends. October 25.

FRUMENTIUS (d. c. 380). He and another young man named Aedesius, who may have been his brother were natives of Tyre, and while on a voyage with their teacher, Meropius, about 330, everyone on the ship except them were killed by natives when the ship stopped off at Ethiopia. Taken to the King at Aksum, they were made members of his court, Aedesius as his cup bearer and Frumentius as his secretary. Freed on the death of the King, they remained on at the request of the widowed Queen to help rule the country, introduced Christianity, and brought in traders from the West. When the King's sons, Abreha and Asbeha, came of age, they resigned their posts. Aedesius returned to Tyre and was ordained. Frumentius went to Alexandria to ask St. Athanasius to send a missionary to the country he had just left. Athanasius consecrated Frumentius bishop of the Ethiopians and sent him back. He returned to Aksum and made numerous converts, including the two royal brothers, despite the attempts of Arian Emperor Constantius to discredit him because of his connection with Athanasius. Frumentius was called Abuna (our father) in Ethiopia, and to this day, the title of the dissident Ethiopian Church's primate is Abuna. October 27.

FULBERT (c. 952–1029). Born and raised in Italy, he

studied at Rheims under Gerbert, went to Rome when his
teacher was elected Pope Sylvester II, and returned to France
when Sylvester died in 1003. Fulbert became chancellor of
Chartres and head of the cathedral school there, which under
his direction became one of the most famous educational
centers in Europe. He later was elected bishop of Chartres,
rebuilt the cathedral when it burned down, had great
influence among the secular leaders of his day, fought simony, and opposed lay ecclesiastical endowments. Sermons,
hymns, letters, and several of his treatises are still extant.
April 10.

FULGENTIUS (468–533). Of a noble senatorial family of
Carthage, Fabius Claudius Gordianus Fulgentius helped man-
age the family estate when his mother was widowed, became
well known for his ability, and was appointed procurator and
tax receiver of Byzacena. When twenty-two, he entered a
monastery there governed by an orthodox bishop, Faustus,
who had been driven from his see by Arian King Huneric.
Fulgentius' mother caused such an uproar with her violent objections to Faustus' accepting her son into the monastery that
Faustus was obliged to leave, and Fulgentius also left, to enter
a nearby monastery where the abbot, Felix, insisted he rule
equally with him. The two ruled for six years until in 499
they were forced to flee invading Numidians and went to
Sicca Veneria. There they were arrested on the demand of an
Arian priest, scourged, and tortured, but refused to apostatize
from their orthodoxy and were then released. Fulgentius set
out to visit the monks in the Egyptian desert but instead went
to Rome in 500 to visit the tombs of the apostles. He returned to Byzacena soon after, built a monastery of which he
was abbot and lived as a hermit in a cell nearby. He was appointed bishop of Ruspe (Kudiat Rosfa, Tunisia) in 508
and began a monastery there to continue his austere lifestyle,
but before he could finish it was banished with scores of orthodox bishops to Sardinia by King Thrasimund. Encouraged
by supplies and money from Pope St. Symmachus, they
persisted in their faith. Fulgentius founded a monastery at
Cagliari, became spokesman for the exiled bishops, and wrote
several treatises, including his *An Answer to Ten Objections*,
a reply to objections raised to his orthodox position by King
Thrasimund when he summoned him before him, and *Three
Books to King Thrasimund*, a refutation of Arianism. The

King was so impressed that he allowed Fulgentius to return to Carthage, but complaints from the Arian bishops caused him in 520 to be again banished to Sardinia, where he built a new monastery near Cagliari. He was allowed to return from exile with the other bishops in 523 when Thrasimund died, and he set about reforming the abuses that had crept into his see during his absence. About 532, he retired to a monastery on an island named Circinia, but later in the year returned to Ruspe, where he died on January 1.

FULRAD (d. 784). Born in Alsace, he became a Benedictine, founded monasteries at Lièvre, Saint-Hippolyte, and Salone, and in 750 was elected abbot of St. Denis near Paris. He served in high office under Pepin, Carloman, and Charlemagne, and in the year he was elected abbot, he, with St. Burchard, went to Rome and secured the approval of Pope St. Zachary of Pepin as King of the Franks. Fulrad acted for Pepin in 756 in turning over the exarchate of Ravenna to the Holy See, the early seeds of the Papal States, and helped in setting up the Frankish Kings as supporters of the Holy See rather than the Byzantine Emperor, a move that was to have an incalculable impact on the future of Europe. Under his able guidance St. Denis flourished as one of the outstanding monasteries in Europe. July 16.

FURSEY (d. c. 648). Probably born on the island of Inisquin in Lough Corri, Ireland, of noble parents, he left home to build a monastery at Rathmat (probably Killursa), attracted throngs of disciples, and then after a time at home began preaching. After twelve years, about 630, he accompanied his brothers, St. Foillan and St. Ultan, to England, where he settled at East Anglia with them and built a monastery, probably at Burgh Castle near Yarmouth, on land donated by King Sigebert. Sometime about 542, he went to Gaul, settled in Neustria, built a monastery at Lagny, and died soon after. January 16.

G

GABRA MIKA'EL (1791–1855). Born in Ethiopia, he became a monk of the Church of Ethiopia and was known for his zeal and scholarship. He was fifty when named one of the party sent to Alexandria in 1841 to ask the Coptic patriarch to appoint one of his monks Abuna (primate) of the Ethiopian Church. Among the party was a Vincentian priest, Justin de Jacobis, whom he accompanied to Rome after their visit to Alexandria. As a result of Gabra's contact with Fr. Justin and his experience in Rome, he was converted to Catholicism in 1844 and helped Fr. Justin train Ethiopians for the priesthood, write a catechism, and found a college at Alitiena, with Gabra in charge. They were both banished to the island of Massawa as a result of the insistence of Abuna Salama, who had been named head of the Ethiopian Church during the visit to Alexandria in 1841. There Fr. Justin was consecrated bishop in 1846, returned to Ethiopia secretly, and ordained Gabra, then sixty, in 1851. They worked together and were quite successful in making converts until Kedaref Kassa, supported by Abuna Salama, led a successful revolt and became King Theodore II in 1855. To redeem a promise to Salama the new King unleashed a persecution of Catholics. Gabra Mika'el, with four colleagues, was imprisoned, tortured for months, and condemned to death on May 31, 1855; the sentence was commuted to life imprisonment through the intercession of the British consul, Walter Plowden. However, for the next three months the King had Gabra dragged in chains wherever he went until finally, on August 28, he died of his ill treatment. He was beatified in 1926. September 1.

GABRIEL. The archangel who was God's messenger to Daniel to explain his vision (Dan. 8:16–26) and prophecy (Dan. 9:21–27), he also foretold the birth of John the

Baptist to John's father, Zechariah (Luke 1:11–21) and proclaimed the birth of Christ to Mary (Luke 1:26–38). September 29.

GABRIEL (1578–97). *See* Miki, Paul.

GABRIEL OF FONSECA, BL. (d. 632). *See* Ixida, Bl. Antony.

GABRIEL OF OUR LADY OF SORROWS. *See* Possenti, Gabriel.

GAETANO. *See* Cajetan.

GAIANA. *See* Rhipsime.

GAIUS (1st century). Baptized with St. Crispus at Corinth by St. Paul (1 Cor. 1:14), the only two baptized there by Paul, he was Paul's host (Rom. 16:23) and was the "dear friend Gaius, whom I love in truth" to whom the third Johannine epistle is addressed. According to tradition, Crispin, who was president of the Corinth synagogue (Acts 18:8), became bishop of the island of Aegina; Gaius became bishop of Thessalonika and suffered martyrdom there. October 4.

GALGANI, GEMMA (1878–1903). Born at Camigliano, Tuscany, Italy, she experienced many supernatural manifestations—visions of Christ, diabolical assaults, and the stigmata—in her short lifetime. Ill with tuberculosis of the spine, she bore her illness and the scorn of her relatives and the townspeople who jeered at her visions with great fortitude and to a heroic degree. Many of her conversations while in ecstasy were recorded. After her death on April 11, a popular cult developed, which led to her canonization in 1940.

GALL (d. c. 635). Born in Ireland, he studied at Bangor under SS. Comgall and Columban, became versed in Scripture, and was ordained. Gall was one of the twelve who accompanied Columban to Gaul and was with him at Annegray and Luxeuil. He followed Columban into exile in 610 and then to Austrasia, where they preached with little success in the region around Lake Zurich, and for two years in the area near Bregenz. When Columban went to Italy in 612, Gall remained behind because of ill health and on his recovery became a hermit on the Steinach River, attracting numerous disciples. In time, St. Gall Monastery occupied this site and during the Middle Ages was a leading center of literature, the arts, and music. Reputedly he was twice offered bishoprics by King Sigebert, whose betrothed he had freed of a demon. He is also reported to have been offered the abbacy of Luxeuil on the death of St. Eustace but declined, to remain a hermit. He died sometime between 627 and 645 at Arbon, Switzerland, and is considered the apostle of that country. October 16.

GALLA (d. c. 550). The daughter of Quintus Aurelius Symmachus, who was consul in Rome in 485, she was widowed a year after her marriage and joined a community of consecrated women on Vatican Hill, where she lived until her death of cancer, devoted to the care of the sick and the needy. St. Gregory wrote of her in his *Dialogues,* and *Concerning the State of Widowhood* by Bishop St. Fulgentius of Ruspe is believed to have been written for her. October 5.

GAMALIEL (1st century). One of the great teachers of the law, honored in rabbinical circles with the title Rabban, he was Paul's teacher in Jerusalem (Acts 22:3), and it was Gamaliel's counsel to the Sanhedrin that caused that body to release Peter and the apostles, who had been arrested for preaching, with only a flogging (Acts 5:34–41). According to an ancient tradition, Gamaliel later became a Christian, and the finding of his body in Jerusalem is celebrated on August 3 in the Roman Martyrology.

GARNET, THOMAS (d. 1608). Of a distinguished English Catholic family and nephew of Jesuit Fr. Henry Garnet, he was born at Southwark, England, educated at St. Omer's in France, and then went to the English Jesuit college at Valladolid, Spain, where he arrived in 1596, and was ordained. He was sent on the English mission, with Bl. Mark Barkworth, in 1599, was admitted to the Jesuits by his uncle, who was superior of the Jesuits in England, and after ministering to the Catholics of Warwick for seven years was arrested in 1606,

the year his uncle was arrested and executed in connection
with the Gunpowder Plot. Thomas was tortured for information about the plot but after several months' imprisonment at
Newgate was released and deported to Flanders with forty-six
other priests. He made his Jesuit novitiate at Louvain and returned to England in the fall of 1607. He was arrested six
weeks later, charged with treason for his priesthood and for
being a Jesuit, and condemned to death. When he refused to
take the Oath of Supremacy, he was hanged, drawn, and
quartered at Tyburn on June 23. He was canonized in 1970
by Pope Paul VI as one of the English and Welsh Martyrs.

GARNIER, CHARLES (c. 1605–49). Son of the treasurer
of Normandy, he was born at Paris, educated at Louis-le-
Grand College there, and joined the Jesuits in Paris in 1624.
He continued his studies at Clermont, taught at the Jesuit college at Eu for three years, and was ordained in 1635. The following year he was sent to Quebec, Canada, with Fr. Pierre
Chastellain and two other priests as missionaries to the Huron
Indians. Charles was murdered by a war party of Iroquois,
the Hurons' traditional enemies, on December 7 at the Indian
village of Etarita, where he was stationed. He was canonized
in 1930 by Pope Pius XI as one of the North American Martyrs. October 19.

GELASIUS I (d. 496). Born in Rome, the son of an African named Valerius, he was a member of the Roman clergy
when he was elected Pope on March 1, 492, succeeding Pope
Felix II. Known for his holiness, justice, charity, and learning, Gelasius soon ran into difficulties with Euphemius, patriarch of Constantinople, over the matter of the Acacian heresy
when Euphemius refused to remove Acacius' name from the
diptychs in the churches of his see. Gelasius also defended the
rights of the patriarchates of Alexandria and Antioch against
the encroachments of Constantinople and eloquently defended the rights of the Church against Emperor Anastasius in
a famous letter to the Emperor. Gelasius caused the revived
pagan festival of Lupercalia in Rome to be abandoned and is
said to have ordered the reception of the Eucharist in both
forms, thus opposing the Manichaeans, who preached that
wine was impure and sinful. *Decretum de libris . . .* , listing

the canonical books of the Bible, and the Gelesian *Sacramentary*, long attributed to him, are no longer considered of his authorship. He died at Rome on November 21.

GENESIUS (3rd century). During a stage performance before Emperor Diocletian in Rome, the actor Genesius portrayed a catechumen about to be baptized in a play satirizing the Christian sacrament. In the midst of the ceremony he was suddenly converted to Christianity. When presented to the Emperor, he declared his Christianity. Enraged, Diocletian had him turned over to Plautian, prefect of the praetorium, who tortured him in an effort to force him to sacrifice to the pagan gods. When Genesius persisted in his faith, he was beheaded. Though the legend is an ancient one, it is no more than that. Genesius is the patron of actors. August 25.

GENEVIEVE (c. 422–500). Born at Nanterre, near Paris, and also known as Genovefa, she dedicated herself to God when only seven after meeting St. Germanus of Auxerre. When her parents died, she moved to Paris and became a nun at fifteen. Her visions and prophecies evoked hostility from the inhabitants of Paris, and an attempt was made on her life, but the support of Germanus and the accuracy of her predictions changed this attitude. She helped mitigate the rigor of the occupation of Paris by Childeric and his Franks and brought in boatloads of food for the people. She pleaded successfully with Childeric and later with Clovis to secure the release of captive prisoners. In 451, she predicted that Attila II and his Huns would bypass Paris, and after she led a crusade of prayer with the citizens, the city was left unmolested. She helped get a church built in honor of St. Dionysius and also convinced Clovis to build SS. Peter and Paul Church, where she was later buried. Many miracles were reported at her tomb in the church, which was later renamed in her honor. She is credited with saving Paris from many catastrophes, and an epidemic that swept the city in 1129 was reputedly ended through her intercession. She died in Paris. January 3.

GENNINGS, EDMUND (1567–91). Born at Lichfield, England, he was brought up a Protestant, but, impressed by the example of a Catholic named Mr. Sherwood, for whom he was a page, he became a Catholic about 1583. He followed

Sherwood to Rheims to study for the priesthood and was ordained in 1590 after recovering from a breakdown in his health. He was sent on the English mission but was arrested within a year while saying Mass at the home of St. Swithun Wells. Gennings was convicted of being a Catholic priest and hanged, drawn, and quartered with Wells at Gray's Inn Fields, London, on December 10. Arrested with him were St. Polydore Plasden, a priest; John Mason, a native of Kendal, Westmorland; and Sidney Hodgson, a layman. They too were hanged, drawn, and quartered on December 10, at Tyburn. Gennings and Plasden were canonized by Pope Paul VI in 1970 as two of the Forty Martyrs of England and Wales; Mason and Hodgson were beatified in 1929.

GEORGE (d. c. 303). Although he is the patron of England, Portugal, Germany, Aragon, Genoa, and Venice and is venerated in the East as one of the Fourteen Holy Helpers, all that is known of him with any certainty is that he suffered martyrdom at Lydda, Palestine, sometime before the reign of Emperor Constantine and that he may have been a soldier in the imperial army. All else is myth and legend that began to appear in the sixth century. The story of his slaying of the dragon does not appear until the twelfth century and became popular after its appearance in the *Golden Legend* in the thirteenth century. According to it he was a Christian knight who came to Sylene in Libya, where a dragon was terrorizing the city. The people were supplying the dragon with a victim at his demand; the latest victim was a princess. George sallied forth, attacked, and subdued the dragon; the princess led it back into the city, and George slew it after the inhabitants agreed to be baptized. A later accretion had him marry the princess. He was known in England as early as the eighth century and had tremendous appeal in the Middle Ages as the patron of knighthood and soldiers, particularly among the Crusaders. "St. George's arms," a red cross on a white background, became the basis of the uniforms of British soldiers and sailors; the red cross appears in the Union Jack; and the Order of the Garter, founded about 1347, is under his patronage. April 23.

GERALD (d. 732). Born in Northumbria, England, he became a monk at Lindisfarne, and when the Celtic liturgical practices were forbidden in Northumbria left England and

entered a monastery on the island of Inishbofin off the coast
of Mayo, Ireland. When the English and Irish monks there
quarreled, he built a monastery for the English monks on the
mainland for them. He succeeded St. Colman as abbot of the
English monastery (Colman had been abbot of both) and
may have founded two other monasteries and a convent.
March 13.

GERARD (935–94). Born at Cologne, Germany, he was
educated at the cathedral school there and after his mother
was killed by lightning devoted himself to the religious life.
He became a canon at the cathedral and in 963 was appointed bishop of Toul, which he ruled for thirty-one years.
He was a noted preacher, made Toul a center of learning by
bringing Irish and Greek monks into the diocese, rebuilt
churches and monasteries, and founded the Hôtel-Dieu Hospital in Toul. He also obtained from Emperor II a confirmation of the privilege granted his predecessor by which Toul
under the bishop had its independence recognized. Gerard
died at Toul on April 23, and was canonized in 1050 by Pope
St. Leo IX.

GERARD OF CLAIRVAUX (d. 1138). Brother of St. Bernard, he was a soldier when Bernard entered Cîteaux but
joined him after having been imprisoned after he was
wounded at the siege of Grancy. He followed Bernard to
Clairvaux, became cellarer there and Bernard's close
confidant and assistant, noted for his fervor and holiness.
June 13.

GERARD MAJELLA (1726–55). Born at Muro in southern Italy, son of a tailor, he was apprenticed to a tailor on the
death of his father, was turned down by the local Capuchins
when he tried to join (because of his youth), and became a
servant in the household of the bishop of Lacedonga. On the
death of the bishop in 1745, he returned home and opened a
tailor shop. He joined the Congregation of the Most Holy
Redeemer (the Redemptorists) as a lay brother in 1748 and
was professed by its founder, St. Alphonsus Liguori, in 1752.
He served as tailor and infirmarian and became known for his
extraordinary supernatural gifts—bilocation, prophecy, ecstasies, visions, and infused knowledge. He served as spiritual
adviser to several communities of nuns, was most successful

in converting sinners, and was widely known for his holiness
and charity. In 1754, he was accused of lechery by one Neria
Caggiano—a charge she later admitted was a lie. He was sent
to Naples soon after but when the house there was inundated
by visitors wanting to see him, he was sent to Caposele a few
months later, served as the porter there, and ministered to the
poor of the town. He spent the last months of his life raising
funds for new buildings at Caposele, where he died of con-
sumption on October 15. He was canonized in 1904 and is
the patron of childbirth. October 16.

GERARD SAGREDO (d. 1046). Born in Venice, he joined
the Benedictines at San Giorgio Maggiore Monastery there
and while on pilgrimage to Jerusalem was made the tutor to
the son of King St. Stephen while he was passing through
Hungary. Gerard was appointed first bishop of Csanad by
Stephen in 1035 and labored with some success to evangelize
his see. Stephen's death in 1038 unleashed a pagan reaction,
and a series of conflicts among claimants to the throne broke
out. Gerard was murdered by one of the competing factions
at Buda on September 24. He is considered the protomartyr
of Venice and is called "the Apostle of Hungary," where he
is known as Collert.

GEREON (d. c. 287). See Maurice.

GERLAC (d. c. 1170). A military man in his youth, he
went to Rome on the death of his wife and spent seven years
nursing the sick and doing penance for the sins of his youth.
He then returned to his native Holland, gave his possessions
to the poor, and became a hermit on his estate near Valken-
burg. The last years of his life were embittered by a dispute
with neighboring monks who wanted him to enter their monastery. He has never been canonized but is honored locally.
January 5.

GERMAIN. See Germanus of Auxerre.

GERMANUS (14th century). All that is known of him is
that he and St. Sergius were Greek monks who founded the
Russian monastery of Valaam (Valamo) on an island in
Lake Ladoga, southeastern Finland, and that they evangelized the Karelians in the area. An untrustworthy legend says

that Germanus was a Karelian pagan named Munga who was converted to Christianity by Sergius. Even the date of the foundation of Valaam is uncertain, with some authorities believing it was founded in the tenth century, while others believe that 1329 is more likely. June 28.

GERMANUS OF AUXERRE (c. 378–448). Born at Auxerre, Gaul, of Christian parents and also known as Germain, he studied at Gallic schools and then law at Rome and became a lawyer. After his marriage to Eustochia, he was named governor of the Amorican border provinces of Gaul and in 418 was named bishop of Auxerre. He changed his lifestyle, embraced a life of poverty and austerity, built a monastery, and endowed various poor churches in the diocese. In 429, he and St. Lupus, bishop of Troyes, were sent to Britain to combat the Pelagian heresy so rife there and were most successful in restoring orthodoxy. It was on this trip that occurred the famous incident in which Germanus is reputed to have saved a force of Britons from destruction by a superior force of marauding Picts and Saxons. He led the Britons to a narrow ravine between two high mountains, and when the enemy approached had the Britons shout "Alleluia!" three times. The echoes magnified the shouts causing the invaders to believe they were confronted by a far superior force, and they fled. Also at this time Germanus baptized many of the Britons in the army. On his return to Gaul, he convinced Auxiliaris, prefect of Gaul, to reduce taxes (reputedly by healing Auxiliaris' sick wife), and in about 440 again returned to Britain to combat Pelagianism. Again he was successful, eliminating the heresy, and founded numerous schools to teach true doctrine. When he returned to Gaul, he found that Aetius, a Roman general, had dispatched a barbarian army under Goar to put down a revolt in Amorica. Fearful of the savagery of the barbarian forces, Germanus persuaded Goar to desist and then went to Ravenna in an unsuccessful attempt to persuade Emperor Valentinian III to call off the attack. Germanus' effort came to naught when news of another Amorican uprising reached the Emperor. Germanus died on July 31 while he was still in Ravenna.

GERTRUDE (c. 1256–c. 1302). Of unknown parentage and often surnamed "the Great," she was placed in the care of the Benedictine nuns at Helfta in Saxony when five and became a pupil of and close friend of St. Mechtilde. When older Gertrude became a nun and when twenty-six had the first of many visions of Christ she was to experience during her lifetime. She became versed in the Bible and the writings of Augustine, Gregory, and Bernard and began to record her supernatural and mystical experiences, a record that eventually appeared in her *Book of Extraordinary Grace* (*Revelation of St. Gertrude*), together with Mechtilde's mystical experiences *Liber Specialis Gratiae*, which Gertrude recorded. She also wrote with St. Mechtilde a series of prayers that became very popular, and through her writing helped spread devotion to the Sacred Heart. She died on November 17 at Helfta and though never formally canonized, Pope Clement XII directed that her feast be observed throughout the Church in 1677. She is a patroness of the West Indies. November 16.

GERTRUDE OF NIVELLES (626–59). The younger daughter of Bl. Pepin of Landen and Bl. Itta, she was born at Landen and early devoted herself to a religious life. On the death of Pepin in 639, Itta built a double monastery at Nivelles, and mother and daughter entered it, with Gertrude as abbess. She resigned in 656 and spent the rest of her life studying Scripture and doing penances, gifted with visions. She died on March 17 and is considered the patroness of travelers (for her hospitality to travelers) and of gardeners.

GERVASE (1st century). Untrustworthy tradition has Gervase and his twin brother, Protase, the sons of Vitalis and Valeria, who suffered martyrdom for their faith. Both children were also martyred for their faith; Gervase was beaten to death with a lead-tipped whip, and Protase was beheaded. They are considered the first martyrs of Milan ever since St. Ambrose, guided by a vision, supposedly unearthed their remains there. June 19.

GERVINUS (d. 1075). Born at Rheims, France, he studied at the episcopal school there, was ordained, and became a canon at Rheims. He then became a monk at Saint-Vanne Abbey at Verdun, was known for his learning, and in 1045 was appointed abbot of Saint-Riquier by King Henry I. Gervinus traveled widely on preaching tours, acquired an extensive collection of Greek and Latin manuscripts for his library (he was a scholar of Latin classics), and was a much-sought-after confessor. He visited England several times on abbey business, became a close friend of Edward the Confessor, and accompanied Pope St. Leo IX back to Rome after the Pontiff had consecrated St. Remigius Church in Rheims. Afflicted with leprosy the last four years of his life, Gervinus died on March 3.

GHÈBRE, MICHAEL. *See* Gabra Mika'el.

GIANELLI, ANTONY (1789–1846). Born at Cerreto, near Genoa, Italy, he studied there and was ordained in 1812 by special dispensation, since he was not of canonical age for ordination. He engaged in pastoral and educational work, gave numerous missions, and became known for his preaching and as a confessor. He founded a congregation of men, Missioners of St. Alphonsus Liguori, and one of women, Sisters of Mary dell' Orto, devoted to teaching poor children and caring for the sick, which spread to the United States and Asia. In 1838, he was appointed bishop of Bobbio, where he ruled wisely until his death. He was canonized in 1951. June 7.

GILBERT OF SEMPRINGHAM (c. 1083–1189). Born at Sempringham, England, son of Jocelin, a wealthy Norman knight, he was sent to France to study and returned to England to receive the benefices of Sempringham and Tirington from his father. He became a clerk in the household of Bishop Robert Bloet of Lincoln and was ordained by Robert's successor, Alexander. He returned to Sempringham as lord on the death of his father in 1131. In the same year he began acting as adviser for a group of seven young women living in enclosure with lay sisters and brothers and decided the community should be incorporated into an established religious order. After several new foundations were established, Gilbert went to Cîteaux in 1148 to ask the Cistercians to take over the community. When the Cistercians declined to take on the governing of a group of women, Gilbert, with the approval of Pope Eugene III, continued the community with the addition of canons regular for its spiritual directors and Gilbert as master general. The community became known as the Gilbertine Order, the only English religious order originating in the medieval period; it eventually had twenty-six monasteries, which continued in existence until King Henry VIII suppressed monasteries in England. Gilbert imposed a strict rule on his order and became noted for his own austerities and concern for the poor. He was imprisoned in 1165 on a false charge of aiding Thomas of Canterbury during the latter's exile but was exonerated of the charge. He was faced with a revolt of some of his lay brothers when he was ninety but was sustained by Pope Alexander III. Gilbert resigned his office late in life because of blindness and died at Sempringham. He was canonized in 1202. February 16.

GILES (c. 712). A well-known legend of the Middle Ages has Giles, also known as Aegidius, an Athenian who, to escape the adulation showered on him for a miracle he performed, left Athens and went to Marseilles. He spent two years with St. Caesarius at Arles and then became a hermit at the mouth of the Rhone River. Supposedly he was fed by the milk of a deer that took refuge with him while being hunted by Gothic King Flavius. When one of the hunters shot into a thicket at the deer, he found Giles pierced with the arrow and holding the deer. Later King Flavius built a monastery with Giles as abbot. He attracted many disciples and his reputation reached Charlemagne, who sent for him for spiritual advice. In confessing to him, the King failed to mention a sin he had committed, which was revealed to Giles by an angel while he was saying Mass; he revealed this to the amazed King, who admitted the sin and repented. These are just two of the many fabled stories told of him, though it is probably true that he was a hermit of the sixth (or perhaps eighth) century who founded a monastery. He is also one of the Fourteen Holy Helpers, and his shrine was a great medieval pilgrimage center. He is the patron of cripples and beggars. September 1.

GILES OF ASSISI, BL. (d. 1262). A native of Assisi, Italy, he was one of the earliest followers of St. Francis, from whom he received the habit in 1208. He accompanied Francis on many of his missions around Assisi, made a pilgrimage to Compostela, visited Rome and the Holy Land, and then made an unsuccessful visit to Tunis to convert the Saracens. The Christians in Tunis, fearful of the repercussions of his religious fervor, forced him back on a boat as soon as he landed. He spent the rest of his life living in Italy, living from about 1243 at the Monte Rapido hermitage on the outskirts of Perugia, where he died. He experienced ecstasies, had a vision of Christ at Cetona, and is considered the most perfect example of the primitive Franciscan. He is spoken of at length in *The Little Flowers of St. Francis,* and Francis called him his "Knight of the Round Table." Known for his austerity and silence, his *The Golden Sayings of Brother Giles* is noted for its humor, deep understanding of human nature, and optimism. April 23.

GILES OF PORTUGAL (1185–1265). Born at Vaozela, Portugal, son of Rodrigues de Vagliaditos, governor of Coïmbra under King Sancho the Great, he studied at Coïmbra and started out for Paris to study medicine. On the advice of a stranger he met on the way, he went to Toledo instead and became a student of the black arts, reportedly signing a pact in blood with the Devil. After seven years, he went to Paris and became a successful physician. Troubled by nightmarish visions in which he was exhorted to amend his life, he repented, destroyed his magic books and potions, and started back to Portugal on foot. At Valencia, Spain, he joined the Dominicans, was troubled with diabolical attacks, but was finally set at peace by a vision of our Lady. He served at Santarem, Portugal, and Paris, and was elected prior general of the Dominicans in Portugal. He later resigned because of age, and spent his last years at Santarem, where he was gifted with ecstasies and the ability to prophesy. Many of the sensational episodes reported in his life are unverified. His cult was approved in 1748. May 14.

GIULIANI, VERONICA (1660–1727). Born at Mercatello, Urbino, Italy, and christened Ursula, she was early attracted to things religious, refused her father's wish that she marry, and in 1677 joined the Capuchins at Città di Castello, taking the name Veronica. She began to experience Christ's Passion and received the stigmata in 1697; a personal investigation by the bishop of Città di Castello resulted in a declaration that these manifestations were authentic. She combined her contemplative life with one of great activity, was novice mistress for thirty-four years, and in 1716 was elected abbess, a position she held until her death. She received many supernatural gifts, including levitation, and is considered one of the most extraordinary mystics of the eighteenth century. Afflicted with apoplexy in her later life, she died on July 9, leaving an account of her spiritual life and experiences, which she wrote at the order of her confessor. She was canonized in 1839. July 10.

GIUSTINIANI, LAURENCE (d. 1381–1455). Born at Venice of a noble family, his mother was widowed when he was a child and she devoted herself to raising her children. He refused his mother's wish for him to marry, and instead at nineteen, joined his Uncle Marino Querino, a canon regular of St. George's Chapter, in a community on the island of Alga near Venice. Laurence practiced the most severe austerities, went about the city begging, and was ordained in 1406. He was made provost of St. George's, preached widely, taught religion, and was appointed bishop of Castello (which then included Venice in its diocesan boundaries) in 1433. He became noted for his piety, charitable works, reforms, and peacemaking abilities. In 1451, Pope Nicholas suppressed the see of Castello and transferred the metropolitanship of Grado to Venice with Giustiniani as archbishop (and referred to by the honorary title of patriarch). He was venerated for his spiritual knowledge, his gifts of prophecy and miracles, and he wrote several mystical treatises, among them *The Degree of Perfection*. He died at Venice on January 8, and was canonized in 1670. September 4.

GLADYS. See Gundleus.

GLEB (d. 1015). See Boris.

GODEFRIED OF MERVEL (d. 1572). See Pieck, Nicholas.

GODEHARD (962–1038). Also known as Gothard, he was born at Reichersdorf, Bavaria, was educated by the canons of Nieder-Altaich abbey there, and was taken to Rome by Archbishop Salzburg, who made him provost of canons when he was nineteen. He was ordained, became a monk at Nieder-Altaich in 990 when the Benedictine rule was restored there, and in time became abbot. His success as abbot caused Emperor Henry II to name him to reform several monasteries, and he was so successful that Henry named him bishop of Hildesheim in 1022. He built churches, schools, and a hospice, imposed strict discipline on the canons, encouraged education in his diocese, and ministered to the sick and the poor. St. Gothard Pass in the Alps takes its name from a chapel built on its summit named after him. He was canonized in 1131. May 4.

GODFREY (1065–1115). Born at Soissons, France, he was placed in the care of the abbot of Mont-Saint-Quentin Abbey when he was five, was raised there, and became a monk. He was ordained, was named abbot of rundown Nogent Abbey in Champagne, restored discipline, and rebuilt it into a flourishing community. He refused the abbacy of Saint-Remi but in 1104 was appointed bishop of Amiens. There his strict discipline, insistence on clerical celibacy, and struggle against simony aroused much bitter opposition and even caused an attempt on his life. He died on the way to Soissons to visit his metropolitan see. November 8.

GODRIC (d. 1170). Born at Walpole, Norfolk, England, he was a peddler in his youth and then was a sailor for sixteen years. He became quite wealthy from his trading activities on his various voyages (one account says he was a pirate), but after a visit to Lindisfarne Monastery, he went on pilgrimage to Jerusalem, stopping off at Compostela on the way back. He became a steward to a landowner in Norfolk on his return, resigned after a time, and went on pilgrimage to St. Giles' shrine in Provence and to Rome. He was a hermit for two years with a recluse named Aelric, whom he met at Wolsingham, made another pilgrimage to Jerusalem, and on his return resumed his eremitical life near Durham. He spent the last sixty years of his life there, venerated for his austerity, gifts of prophecy, knowledge of distant events, and visions. He died at his hermitage at Finchdale on May 21.

GONZAGA, ALOYSIUS (1568–91). The oldest son of Marquis Ferrante of Castiglione, who was in the service of Philip II of Spain, he was born on March 9 at the family castle in Lombardy. He was destined for the military by his father, but early in his childhood decided on a religious life. He was sent to Florence to be educated in 1577, joined the court of the Duke of Mantua, who had appointed his father governor of Montserrat two years later, suffered a kidney attack that was to leave him with digestive trouble the rest of his life, and began to practice great austerities and to devote himself to religious practices and teaching catechism to the poor of Castiglione. While at the court of Prince Diego of the Asturias in Spain, he desired to enter the Jesuits, was refused permission by his father, and on their return to Italy in 1584 renewed his plea. He finally broke down his father, joined the Jesuits in Rome in 1585, and was sent to Milan to study. Because of his poor health he was recalled to Rome, made his vows in 1587, and when a plague struck the city in 1587, served in a hospital opened by the Jesuits. He caught the plague while ministering to its victims and died on June 21 after he received the last rites from St. Robert Bellarmine. Aloysius Gonzaga was canonized in 1726, was declared protector of young students by Pope Benedict XIII and patron of Catholic youth by Pope Pius XI. June 21.

GONZALEZ, BL. ROQUE (1576–1628). Born of noble Spanish parents at Asunción, Paraguay, he was educated and ordained there when he was twenty-three. He began his priestly career working among the Indians, joined the Jesuits in 1609, and was active in the formation of the Paraguayan reductions devoted to improving the conditions of the Indians. With other Jesuits, he opposed Spanish imperialism, the imported Spanish Inquisition, and enslaving the Indians—for all of which he was bitterly opposed by the Spanish authorities. He worked among and for the Indians for two decades, heading the first Paraguayan reduction for three years and establishing another six in the Paraná and Uruguay rivers areas. In 1628, with two other Jesuits, Alonso Rodriguez and Juan de Castillo, he founded a new reduction near the Ijuhi River and then with Fr. Rodriguez established another reduction at Caaró in southern Brazil. He was opposed by the local medicine man, who instigated a raid by the Indians on the reduction during which both he and Fr. Rodriguez were tomahawked to death on November 15. Two days later, Ijuhi was attacked, and Fr. Castillo was stoned to death. The three Jesuits were beatified in 1934 as the Martyrs of Paraguay—the first martyrs in the Americas to be so honored. November 17.

GORETTI, MARIA (1890–1902). Born at Corinaldo, near Ancona, Italy, on October 16, she was the daughter of a farmworker who moved the family to Ferriere di Conca, near Anzio. She was stabbed to death on July 6 by Alexander

Serenelli, son of her father's partner, who lived in the same house with the Gorettis, while resisting his attempt to seduce her. She was canonized for her purity in 1950 by Pope Pius XII in the presence of her murderer, who completely reformed his life after he had a vision of Maria. July 6.

GORGONIA (d. c. 372). Daughter of St. Gregory Naziazen the Elder and St. Nonna and sister of St. Gregory Naziazen and St. Caesarius, she married and lived a life of great holiness, which her brother Gregory described in a panegyric at her funeral. December 9.

GOTHARD. *See* Godehard.

GOTTSCHALK (d. 1066). A prince of the Wends and a Christian, he gave up his religion when his father was killed by a Christian Saxon. He served in the army of Canute of Denmark, accompanied Sweyn to England, married his daughter, and returned to his Christian religion. When he reconquered his realm, he was active in the conversion of his subjects to Christianity, brought in Saxon monks, and founded monasteries, but was killed at Lenzen on the Elbe by adherents of his brother-in-law, who was the leader of an anti-Christian uprising against him. Many scholars question his designation as either saint or martyr. June 7.

GOUPIL, RENÉ (1606–42). Born at Anjou, France, he joined the Jesuits, was forced to leave because of ill health, and became a successful surgeon. He went to Quebec to work among the Jesuits' missions there in 1638, was attached to the hospital in Quebec, and became a *donné* (a lay assistant) for the mission to the Huron Indians in 1640. While on a journey with Isaac Jogues in 1642, he was captured by a group of Iroquois Indians, implacable foes of the Hurons. He was subjected to torture and mutilations for two months and then tomahawked to death on September 29 before Jogues at Osserneon, near Albany, New York—the first of the North American Martyrs. He was canonized in 1930 by Pope Pius XI. October 19.

GREGORY I THE GREAT (c. 540–604). Son of a wealthy patrician, Gordianus, he was born and educated at Rome. He was prefect of Rome when the Lombard invasion of Italy was threatening Rome in 571. Long attracted to the religious life, about 574 he converted his home in Rome into St. Andrew's Monastery under Valentius, became a monk there, and founded six monasteries on his estates in Sicily. After several years of seclusion at St. Andrew's, he was ordained by Pope Pelagius II and was made one of the seven papal deacons in 578. He served as papal nuncio to the Byzantine court, 579–85, was recalled in 586, resumed his monastic life, and became abbot of St. Andrew's. He set out to evangelize England but was brought back to Rome by Pope Pelagius when plague struck Rome, 589–90. Pelagius was stricken and died, and Gregory was elected Pope and consecrated on September 3, 590. He restored ecclesiastical discipline, removed unworthy clerics from office, abolished clerical fees for burials and ordinations, and was prodigious in his charities. He administered papal properties wisely and justly, ransomed captives from the Lombards, protected Jews from unjust coercion, and fed the victims of a famine. In 593, he persuaded the invading Lombards under Agilulf to spare Rome, and he negotiated a peace with the Lombard King—an unprecedented move that effectively set aside the authority of the Byzantine Emperor's representative, the exarch. This was the beginning of a series of actions by which Gregory resisted the arrogance, incompetence, and treachery of Byzantine authorities by which he appointed governors of the Italian cities, providing them with war materials and denouncing the heavy taxes levied on the Italians by Byzantine officials. He thus started on its course the acquisition and exercise of temporal power by the papacy. He was responsible for the conversion of England to Christianity by his interest in that country and his dispatch of St. Augustine of Canterbury and forty monks from St. Andrew's there (though the story in Bede's history of the English Church that he was motivated to do so by the sight of a group of blond, handsome Saxon slaves up for sale in the marketplace may be apocryphal). He was untiring in his efforts to ensure that the papacy was the supreme authority in the Church, and denouncing John, Patriarch of Constantinople, for his use of the title Ecumenical Patriarch (he himself preferred as his own title "Servant of the Servants of God," a title used by Popes to this day, fourteen centuries later). He was an eloquent preacher and was mainly responsible for the restoration of a Rome devastated by the invasions, pillages, and earthquakes of the century be-

fore his pontificate. He wrote treatises, notably his *Dialogues,*
a collection of visions, prophecies, miracles, and lives of Italian saints, and *Liber regulae pastoralis* (on the duties of
bishops), and hundreds of sermons and letters. Whether he
was the compiler of the Antiphony on which the Roman
schola cantorum was based and several hymns attributed to
him is uncertain, but he did greatly influence the Roman liturgy. The custom of saying thirty successive Masses for a
dead person goes back to him and bears his name, and to
Gregory is due the Gregorian Chant. He actively encouraged
Benedictine monasticism, and his grants of privileges to
monks often restricting episcopal jurisdictions was the beginning of later exemptions that were to bring religious orders
directly under papal control. He is the last of the traditional
Latin Doctors of the Church, is justly called "the Great," and
is considered the founder of the medieval papacy. He died in
Rome on March 12 and was canonized by acclamation immediately after his death. September 3.

GREGORY II (d. 731). Born at Rome, he became involved
in ecclesiastical affairs in his youth, served as treasurer of the
Church and librarian under four Popes, and became widely
known for his learning and wisdom. He distinguished himself
by his replies to Emperor Justinian when he accompanied
Pope Constantine to Constantinople to oppose the Council of
Trullo canon that had declared the patriarchate of Constantinople independent of Rome and helped to secure Justinian's
acknowledgment of papal supremacy. He was elected Pope
on May 19, 715, to succeed Constantine, put into effect a program to restore clerical discipline, fought heresies, began to
rebuild the walls around Rome as a defense against the Saracens, and helped restore and rebuild churches, hospitals, and
monasteries, including Monte Cassino, which had been destroyed by the Lombards a century and a half earlier. He sent
missionaries to Germany, among them St. Corbinian and St.
Boniface in 719, whom he consecrated bishop. The outstanding concern of his pontificate was his difficulties with
Emperor Leo III the Isaurian. Gregory opposed his illegal
taxation on the Italians, though Gregory counseled against the
planned revolt of Italy against Byzantium and the election of
an Emperor in opposition to Leo. He also demanded that Leo
stop interfering with ecclesiastical matters, vigorously opposed iconoclasm supported by the Emperor, and severely re-

buked him at a synod in Rome in 727; Gregory also supported Germanus, patriarch of Constantinople, against Leo.
Gregory's relations with the Lombards who were intent on
conquering Italy were friendly mainly due to his influence
with their leader, Liutprand. February 11.

GREGORY III (d. 741). The son of a Syrian named John,
he became a priest in Rome, and his reputation for learning
and holiness was so great that he was acclaimed Pope while
accompanying the funeral cortege of his predecessor, Gregory
II, on February 11, 731. He continued Gregory II's opposition to iconoclasm and convoked two synods in Rome in 731,
which condemned the heresy. In response, Emperor Leo the
Iconoclast seized papal patrimonies in Calabria and Sicily and
transferred ecclesiastical jurisdiction of those two provinces
and Illyrium to the patriarch of Constantinople. Gregory supported the missionary activities of St. Boniface in Germany
and sent St. Willibald to assist him. Gregory completed rebuilding the walls around Rome begun by Gregory II and
sought the assistance of Charles Martel against the attacks of
Liutprand and his Lombards on the exarchate of Ravenna,
the dukes of Spoleto and Benevento, and the duchy of Rome
rather than from the Eastern Emperor, an appeal that was to
have far-reaching historical implications. In the midst of this
turmoil, Gregory died on November 28.

GREGORY VII (c. 1021–85). Born at Soana, Tuscany,
Italy, and baptized Hildebrand, he was sent at an early age to
St. Mary on the Aventine Monastery in Rome, where his
uncle was superior. Hildebrand studied under John Gratian at
the Lateran school and when Gratian was elected Pope as
Pope Gregory VI, he appointed Hildebrand his secretary. According to tradition, Hildebrand became a monk at Cluny
under St. Odilo when Gregory died in 1047. When Bishop
Bruno of Toul was elected Pope as Pope Leo IX in 1049, he
appointed Hildebrand his counselor and put him in charge of
the treasury. He restored solvency to the Church's finances,
was active in Leo's reforms, and was a most influential counselor for the next four Popes. He was made a cardinal-
deacon, was legate to France during the controversy over the
Eucharist between Lanfrance and Berengarius of Tours, and
presided in 1054 at the Council at Sens, which condemned
Berengarius. He was influential in securing the election of

Bishop Gebhard of Eichstätt as Pope Victor II in 1055, was papal legate to Empress-regent Agnes of Germany's court in 1057 to get her to accept the election of Pope Stephen, and helped secure the election of Bishop Gerhard of Florence as Pope Nicholas II in 1059. During the pontificate of Nicholas, Hildebrand was instrumental in the publication of the papal decree mandating that the election of Popes was to be vested in the college of cardinals and was responsible for negotiating a treaty of alliance with the Normans in the Treaty of Melfi in 1059. By now he was the best-known and most powerful prelate in the Church. He was appointed chancellor of the Apostolic See by Pope Alexander II, and when Alexander died in 1073, he was elected Pope by acclamation and consecrated on June 30, taking the name Gregory VII. He immediately set to work to reform a very corrupt and decadent Church. He deposed Archbishop Godfrey of Milan for simony, enacted decrees against simony and married clergy at his first synod in Rome, in 1074, and ordered an end to lay investiture at his second synod, in 1075—decrees that aroused great opposition. He appointed monks as papal legates to enforce the decrees. He was generally successful with his reforms in England except in the matter of lay investiture, which right William the Conqueror refused to surrender; gradually Gregory succeeded in France by replacing practically the whole episcopate; but in Germany he was resisted by Emperor IV and by the clergy in Germany and northern Italy. Even the papal nobles in Rome objected and kidnaped him while he was celebrating Christmas Mass. Henry convened a diet at Worms in 1076 and sent legates to Rome, informing the Pope that the diet had decided he was deposed, whereupon Gregory excommunicated Henry—the first deposition of a King by a Pope—and declared that his subjects were free of allegiance to him. The German nobles then stated that they considered Henry to be dethroned if he did not receive the Pope's absolution. In January 1077, in a bitter winter, Henry's famous submission to the Pope took place at Canossa as barefoot and in penitential garb he stood in the snow and begged the Pope's forgiveness. Though suspicious of Henry's motives and the validity of his repentance, Gregory lifted the ban of excommunication. Later in the year a group of German nobles elected Rudolf of Swabia, Henry's brother-in-law, King of Germany, and civil war broke out. At first neutral, Henry supported Rudolf when Henry violated all his agreements with him, and Gregory again excommunicated Henry, in 1080. When Henry triumphed over Rudolf, who was killed in battle in October 1080, he arranged the election of Archbishop Guibert of Ravenna as antipope Clement III, declared Gregory deposed, invaded Italy, and laid siege to Rome. He took the city in 1084, but Gregory had taken refuge in Sant' Angelo Castle. When he refused Henry's demand that he crown him Emperor, Henry had Guibert consecrated Pope, and then Guibert crowned Henry Emperor. Gregory remained in Sant' Angelo until rescued by the Normans under Robert Guiscard, duke of Normandy, with whom Gregory had signed an alliance. When the Normans sacked the city, the Romans turned on Gregory and he was forced to flee to Monte Cassino and then to Salerno, where he died on May 25, lifting all of his excommunications except those on Henry and Guibert. In large measure, Gregory was successful in rejuvenating the Church, and the reforms of his pontificate marked a turning point in the history of the Church. It is now generally agreed among historians that his struggles with the monarchs of Europe were not a bid for great personal power, as some historians in the past contended, but a titanic defense of the freedom of the Church against secular domination. Though he did not clearly and unequivocally win the struggle, he did delineate the issues, particularly that of lay investiture, which thirty-seven years after his death was won by the Concordat of Worms in 1122, when Emperor Henry V guaranteed the free election of bishops and abbots and renounced the right to invest them with the ring and staff—the symbols of their spiritual authority. Gregory was unsuccessful in his efforts to reunite the Eastern churches to Rome, and his struggle with Henry prevented him from launching a crusade against the Turks and to drive the Saracens from Spain. He was canonized in 1606 by Pope Paul V, and despite French and Austrian objections, Pope Benedict XIII made his feast day of May 25 universal in the Church.

GREGORY X, BL. (1210–76). Of a distinguished family, Theobald Visconti was born at Piacenza, Italy, studied canon law at Paris and Liège, and became archdeacon of Liège. He accompanied Cardinal Ottoboni on a mission to England and was at Acre on pilgrimage to the Holy Land when he was informed that though he was not yet ordained, he had been selected as Pope by a committee of six cardinals who had been chosen to select a Pope when a candidate had not been elected by the cardinals at Viterbo to fill the pontifical throne, which had been vacant for three years. He returned to Rome, was ordained a priest on March 19, and then was consecrated Pope on March 27, 1272, taking the name Gregory X. He labored to end the warfare between the Guelphs and the Ghibellines, placed Florence under interdict for refusing efforts at reconciliation with its neighbors, and approved Rudolph of Hapsburg as German Emperor. Gregory convoked the fourteenth General Council at Lyons in 1274, which effected a short-lived reunion of the Eastern churches with Rome but was unsuccessful in launching a crusade. He died at Rezzo, Italy, on his way back from the Council on January 10. His cult was approved in 1713.

GREGORY THE ENLIGHTENER (d. c. 330). Also surnamed "the Illuminator," he is of unknown origins, but unreliable tradition has him the son of Anak, a Parthian who murdered King Khosrov I of Armenia when he was a baby. The infant Gregory was smuggled to Caesarea to escape the dying Khosrov's order to murder the entire family, was baptized, married, and had two sons. When King Khosrov's son, Tiridates, regained his father's throne, Gregory was permitted to return, but he incurred the King's displeasure by his support of the Armenian Christians and his conversion activities. In time Tiridates was converted to Christianity by Gregory and proclaimed Christianity the official religion of Armenia. Gregory was consecrated bishop of Ashtishat, set about organizing the Church in Armenia and building a native clergy, and worked untiringly to evangelize the Armenians. Curiously enough, he set into motion the process that was to make his see a hereditary episcopate when he consecrated his son Aristakes to succeed him. He then retired to a hermitage on Mount Manyea in Taron and remained there until his death. Many extravagant legends and miracles were attributed to him, many of which are celebrated as feasts by the Armenians. He is considered the apostle of Armenia. September 30.

GREGORY MAKAR (d. c. 1010). Born in Armenia, he became a monk at a monastery near Nicropolis, Little Armenia. He was ordained by the bishop of Nicropolis, was a successful preacher, and was chosen bishop of Nicropolis on the death of his predecessor. Desirous of living as a solitary, he went to Italy and then France, where he lived as a recluse at Pithiviers. His reputation for spiritual wisdom and as a miracle healer spread and attracted crowds of people. He spent the last seven years of his life at Pithiviers and died there. March 16.

GREGORY NAZIANZEN (c. 329–89). Son of St. Gregory Nazianzen the Elder, bishop of Nazianzus for forty-five years, and St. Nonna, he was born at Nazianzus, Cappadocia, studied at Caesarea, Cappadocia (where he met St. Basil), the rhetorical school at Caesarea, Palestine, and then for ten years at Athens (where both Basil and the future Emperor Julian the Apostate were also studying). When about thirty, Gregory returned to Nazianzus but soon joined Basil at Pontus on the Iris River to live the life of a solitary. After two years there, Gregory returned home to assist his father, now over eighty, in running his see, was ordained most unwillingly about 362 by his father, and in about 372 was named bishop of Sasima. The see was in Arian territory, was rent by civil strife, and had been created by his friend Basil, now metropolitan of Caesarea in Cappadocia, who had created it in an attempt to offset the jurisdictional claims of Bishop Anthimus of Tyana to the area. Gregory was consecrated but never went to Sasima, to the dismay of Basil, remaining instead as coadjutor to his father. When his father died in 374, he continued administering the see until a new bishop was chosen. He suffered a breakdown in 375 and spent the next five years at Seleucia, Isauria. On the death of Emperor Valens and the mitigation of his persecution of the orthodox, a group of bishops invited Gregory to Constantinople to help revitalize the Church in the East by restoring orthodoxy to the Arian-dominated city. There his eloquent preaching at the Church of Anastasia (a house he had converted to a church) brought floods of converts, and torrents of abuse and persecution from the Arians and the Apollinarists. He came into controversy with one Maximus, who tried to depose him while he was ill, but Gregory finally prevailed, and in 380 the newly baptized Emperor Theodosius decreed that his subjects must be orthodox, ordered the Arian leaders to submit or leave (they left), and named Gregory archbishop of Constantinople. A few months after his installation hostilities began anew, and the validity of his election was questioned at the Council of Constantinople in 381, at which he presided. He resigned the see in the hope of restoring peace now that he had restored orthodoxy to Constantinople. He retired to private life, lived a life of great austerity, and died at Nazianzus on January 25. A Doctor of the Church, Gregory is often surnamed "the Theologian" for his eloquent defense of orthodoxy and the decrees of the Council of Nicaea in his sermons and treatises, notably his celebrated sermons on the Trinity, *Five Theological Orations,* delivered at St. Anastasia in Constantinople. He also wrote a long poem, *De vita sua,* letters, and with St. Basil, compiled a selection of writings by Origen. January 2.

GREGORY NAZIANZEN THE ELDER (c. 276–374). A native of Nazianzus, Cappadocia, he was an official there when converted to Christianity by his wife, Nonna. They had three children, all saints: Gregory Nazianzen, Caesarius, and Gorgonia. Gregory the Elder became bishop of Nazianzus about 328, fell into heresy, but was brought back to orthodoxy in 361 by his son Gregory, who became his coadjutor in 372. Gregory the Elder continued as bishop until his death, having ruled for some forty-five years. January 1.

GREGORY OF NYSSA (c. 330–c. 395). Son of St. Basil and St. Emmilia, he was born at Caesarea, Cappadocia, and raised by his brother St. Basil and his sister Macrina. Gregory was well educated, became a rhetorician, and married Theosebeia. He became a professor of rhetoric and, depressed by his students, he was turned to the religious life by St. Gregory Nazianzen and was ordained a priest. He may have lived in seclusion at Iris in Pontus the first years of his priesthood and at the suggestion of his brother Basil, who was bishop of Caesarea, was named bishop of Nyssa, Lower Armenia, in 372. He found his see infested with Arianism, was falsely accused of stealing Church property by the governor of Pontus, Demosthenes, and was imprisoned. He escaped but was deposed by a synod of Galatian and Pontic bishops in 376 and remained in exile until 378, when Emperor Gratian restored him to his see. In 379 he attended the Council of Antioch, which denounced the Meletian heresy, and was sent by that council to Palestine and Arabia to combat heresy there. He was active in 381 in the General Council of Constantinople, which attacked Arianism and eloquently reaffirmed the de-

crees of the Council of Nicaea. By this time he was widely
venerated as the great pillar of orthodoxy and the great opponent of Arianism. Greatly influenced by the writings of Origen and Plato, he wrote numerous theological treatises, which
were considered the true exposition of the Catholic faith.
Among them were his *Catechetical Discourse,* treatises
against Eunomius and Appolinaris, a book on virginity, and
commentaries on Scripture. The second General Council of
Nicaea, 680–81, called him "Father of the Fathers."
March 9.

GREGORY THAUMATURGUS (c. 213–68). Of a distinguished pagan family, he was born at Neocaesarea, Pontus,
and studied law there. About 233, he and his brother, Athen-
odorus, accompanied his sister, who was joining her husband
in Caesarea, Palestine, while they continued on to Beirut to
continue their law studies. They met Origen and instead of
going to Beirut, entered his school at Caesarea, studied theology, were converted to Christianity by Origen, and became
his disciples. Gregory returned to Neocaesarea about 238, in-
tending to practice law, but was elected bishop by the seventeen Christians of the city. It soon became apparent that he
was gifted with remarkable powers. He preached eloquently,
made so many converts he was able to build a church, and
soon was so renowned for his miracles that he was surnamed
Thaumaturgus (the wonder worker). He was a much-
sought-after arbiter for his wisdom and legal knowledge and
ability, advised his flock to go into hiding when Decius' persecution of the Christians broke out in 250, and fled to the desert with his deacon. On his return, he ministered to his flock
when plague struck his see and when the Goths devastated
Pontus, 252–54, which he described in his "Canonical Letter." He participated in the Synod of Antioch, 264–65,
against Samosata, and fought Sabellianism and Tritheism. It
is reported that at his death at Neocaesarea, only seventeen
unbelievers were left in the city. He is invoked against floods
and earthquakes (at one time he reportedly stopped the
flooding Lycus, and at another, he moved a mountain). According to Gregory of Nyssa, Gregory Thaumaturgus experienced a vision of our Lady, the first such recorded vision. He
wrote a panegyric to Origen, a treatise on the Creed, and a
dissertation addressed to Theopompus; St. Gregory of Nyssa
wrote a panegyric to Gregory Thaumaturgus. November 17.

GREGORY OF TOURS (538–94). Of a well-known Auvergne family, Gregorius Florentius was born at Clermont-Ferrand, Gaul, and later took the name Gregory. He was raised by his uncle, St. Gallus of Clermont, on the death of his father, studied Scripture under St. Avitus, a priest of Clermont, and in 573 was made bishop of Tours. He soon came into conflict with King Chilperic when Tours came under the King's control in 576, and Gregory supported Meroveus, the King's son, against the King. The differences culminated in a charge of treason against Gregory by Leudastis, whom Gregory had removed as count of Tours. The charges were proved false by a council appointed to investigate them, and Leudastis was punished for perjury. Things improved with subsequent monarchs after Chilperic's death in 584. Gregory rebuilt the cathedral and several churches, converted heretics, and was known for his ability, justice, charity, and religious fervor. He wrote books on the martyrs, saints, and Fathers, but is particularly remembered for his *History of the Franks*, one of the outstanding original sources of early French history. November 17.

GREGORY THE WONDER WORKER. *See* Gregory Thaumaturgus.

GRIGNION, LOUIS MARY (1673–1716). Born on January 31 of poor parents at Montford, France, he was educated at the Jesuit college in Rennes and was ordained there in 1700. He became a chaplain in a hospital at Poitiers, but his reorganization of the hospital staff there caused such resentment that he resigned. Before leaving, he organized a group of women into what became the congregation of the Daughters of Divine Wisdom. His missionary preaching to the poor caused his critics to complain to the bishop of Poitiers, who forbade him to preach in his diocese. He went to Rome, was named missionary apostolic by Pope Clement XI, and began preaching missions in Brittany, which he was to continue until his death. Though his sermons aroused much opposition for their emotionalism, he was tremendously successful, particularly in fostering devotion to Mary and the rosary; he wrote his *True Devotion to the Blessed Virgin* to foster this devotion, and it achieved great popularity. In 1715, he organized several priests into a group that developed into the Missionaries of the Company of Mary. He died at Saint-Laurent-sur-Sèvre, France, and was canonized in 1947. April 28.

GUDWAL (6th century). Probably a Welshman or a Briton, he was one of the early missionaries to Brittany, founded Plecit Monastery near Locoal and several other monasteries in Brittany, and died at one of them. He might have been a regionary bishop and is now considered to be the same as Gurval, who succeeded St. Malo at Aleth in Brittany. June 6.

GUIBERT (892–962). Of a noble Latharingian family, he was a well-known military leader, but he abandoned his military career for the religious life. He became a hermit on his estate at Gembloux, Brabant, and with the help of his Grandmother Gisla, in 936 founded a Benedictine monastery on the estate with Herluin as abbot and donated the estate to the monastery. Guibert then became a monk at Gorze but was summoned before Emperor Otto I to defend his right to donate the estate (it was an imperial fief) to the monastery—which he did successfully. He was again obliged to defend the monastery when the count of Namur seized its revenues, claiming it belonged to his wife, and again successfully defended the monastery against the count, his brother-in-law. Guibert was active in missionary work among the Hungarian and Slav soldiers who remained in Brabant after an invasion in 954. He died on May 23, and was canonized in 1211.

GUNDLEUS (6th century). According to legend, Gundleus (Latin for Gwynllyw) was a Welsh chieftain who desired to marry Gwladys, daughter of Brychan of Brecknow. When Brychan refused his daughter's hand, Gundleus kidnaped Gwladys (Gladys) and married her (one aspect of the legend has King Arthur helping to defeat the pursuing Brychan and being dissuaded from capturing Gwladys for himself by two of his knights). At any rate, Gundleus and Gwladys led a riotous life, engaging in violence and banditry until their first son, St. Cadoc, convinced them to adopt and follow a religious life together at Newport, Monmouthshire; later he had them separate and live as hermits, with Gwladys eventually living at Oencarnau, Bassaleg. The Anglicized version of Gundleus is Woolo. March 29.

GURVAL. *See* Gudwal.

GUTIERREZ, BL. BARTHOLOMEW (c. 1580–1632). Born in Mexico of Spanish parents, he joined the Augustinians in 1596, was ordained at Puebla, and was sent to the Philippines in 1606. He was then sent to Japan, was prior at Ukusi in 1612, and worked among the Japanese until 1629, when he was arrested. After three years in prison at Omura, he was burned to death at Nagasaki. He was beatified in 1867. September 28.

GUYARD, BL. MARIE. *See* Martin, Bl. Marie of the Incarnation.

GWENFREWI. *See* Winifred.

GWLADYS. *See* Gundleus.

GWYN, RICHARD (1537–84). Born at Llanidloes, Montgomeryshire, Wales, he was raised a Protestant, studied briefly at Oxford and then at St. John's College, Cambridge. He returned to Wales in 1562, opened a school at Overton, Flintshire, married, and had six children. He left Overton after becoming a Catholic, when his absence from Anglican services was noticed, but was arrested in 1579 at Wrexham, Wales. He escaped but was again arrested in 1580 and imprisoned at Ruthin. He was brought up before eight assizes, tortured, and fined in between, and four years later, in 1584, he was convicted of treason on charges by perjuring witnesses and sentenced to death. He was hanged, drawn, and quartered at Wrexham on October 15—the first Welsh martyr of Queen Elizabeth I's reign. He was canonized by Pope Paul VI in 1970 as one of the Forty Martyrs of England and Wales and is the protomartyr of Wales. October 17.

GWYNLLYW. *See* Gundleus.

H

HADRIAN. *See* Adrian.

HARDING, STEPHEN. *See* Stephen Harding.

HARVEY. *See* Hervé.

HEDWIG (c. 1174–1243). Also known as Jadwiga, she was the daughter of Count Berthold IV of Andechs, Bavaria, where she was born. She was educated at Kitzingen Monastery in Franconia and when she was twelve, she was married to Duke Henry of Silesia. In 1202, on the death of his father, Henry succeeded to the dukedom and at Hedwig's request built a Cistercian monastery for nuns at Trebnitz, the first monastery for women in Silesia; the couple founded numerous other monasteries and hospitals. They had seven children, and two of them, Henry and Conrad, despite Hedwig's efforts, warred over the division of territories made by Duke Henry in 1112; and in 1227 Henry and Duke Ladislaus of Sandomir warred against Swatopluk of Pomerania. They were successful but when Ladislaus was killed, Henry went to war against Conrad of Masovia over Ladislaus' lands; Hedwig acted as peacemaker between the two and restored peace. On the death of Henry in 1238, Hedwig moved into the monastery at Trebnitz. Her son Henry was killed in 1240 in a battle against the Mongol Tartars near Wahlstadt, and she died at Trebnitz, Poland, on October 15. Many miracles were attributed to her and she was canonized in 1267. She is the patroness of Silesia. October 16.

HEDWIG, BL. (1374–99). The youngest daughter of King Louis I of Hungary, nephew and successor in 1370 to King Casimir III of Poland as Louis the Great of Poland. She suc-

ceeded to the throne on Louis' death in 1382 and at thirteen
was married to pagan Duke Jagiello of Lithuania—a marriage
that began a four-hundred-year alliance between Poland and
Lithuania when Jagiello by the marriage also became King
Ladislaus II of Poland. As part of the marriage pact, Jagiello
became a Christian, destroyed pagan temples, and forced baptism on his people. Hedwig became known for her charity,
concern for the poor, and her asceticism. She died in childbirth. Venerated in Poland and honored on February 28 with
a popular cult, Hedwig's cause for beatification was introduced but has never been approved.

HEGESIPPUS (d. c. 180). A Jewish convert to Christianity
at Jerusalem, he spent twenty years in Rome, returned to
Jerusalem in 177 after visiting most of the important Christian churches, and probably died at Jerusalem. He is considered the father of Church history for his five books on the
history of the Church from the death of Christ up to the
pontificate of St. Eleutherius (c. 174–c. 189); Eusebius
drew on it heavily for his *Ecclesiastical History*. Unfortunately, only a few chapters of Hegesippus' work are extant.
April 7.

HELEN OF POLAND, BL. *See* Jolenta, Bl.

HELENA (c. 250–c. 330). Probably the daughter of an
innkeeper, and born sometime between 248 and 255 at Dre-
panum, Bithynia (a legend that she was the daughter of an
English prince has long since been disproved), she met
Roman General Constantius Chlorus about 270, and despite
her lowly station, they were married. Sometime between 274
and 288, their son Constantine was born. When Constantius
was named Caesar in 293 under Emperor Maximian, he
divorced Helena for political reasons and married Maximian's
stepdaughter, Theodora. When Maximian died at York, England, in 306, Constantine, who was with him, was declared
Emperor by the troops there but did not win a clear title to
the throne until his dramatic victory at the Milvian bridge in
312. He conferred the title Augusta on his mother, ordered
all honor be paid to her as the mother of the sovereign, and
had coins struck with her likeness on them. In 313, he and his
fellow Emperor, Licinius, issued the Edict of Milan, permit-

ting Christianity in the Empire and releasing all religious prisoners. About this time, Helena was converted to Christianity (she was then sixty-three, according to historian Eusebius). She zealously supported the Christian cause, built numerous churches, aided the poor, and ministered to the distressed. After several wars between them, Constantine defeated Licinius a final time, in 324; Licinius was executed, Constantine became sole Emperor of both East and West, and moved the capital to Constantinople. Helena went to Palestine, and while there, according to Rufinus, Sulpicius Severus, and a sermon of St. Ambrose, all dating from the late fourth century, she discovered the True Cross. She built basilicas on the Mount of Olives and at Bethlehem, traveled all over Palestine, and was known for her kindness to soldiers, the poor, and prisoners. She died somewhere in the East, probably at Nicomedia, and was buried at Constantinople. August 18.

HELGA. *See* Olga.

HEMMA. *See* Emma.

HENRY II (972–1024). Son of Duke Henry II of Bavaria, and Gisela of Burgundy, he was born probably at Hildesheim, Bavaria, on May 6, succeeded his father as duke of Bavaria in 995, married Kunigunda about 998, and in 1002 was chosen Emperor on the death of his cousin Emperor Otto III. In the early years of Henry's reign he was involved in constant warfare as he strove to consolidate Germany into political unity. He defeated Arduin of Ivrea, leader of the opposition in Italy, in Lombardy when Arduin had himself crowned King of Italy in 1004. He drove Boleslaus I of Poland from Bohemia in 1004, though peace did not come until 1018, and in 1014 was crowned Holy Roman Emperor by Pope Benedict VIII. Henry founded and richly endowed the see of Bamberg in 1006 (in large measure to effect the Germanization of the Wends), restored the sees of Hildesheim, Magdeburg, Strasbourg, and Meersburg, made numerous foundations, and was benefactor of many churches. He often interfered in ecclesiastical matters, though he was usually supported by Rome. For example, the bishops of Würzburg and Eichstätt opposed his creation of the see of Bamberg, but Pope John XIX approved it. Henry quarreled with Aribo, his appoint-

ment as archbishop of Mainz, who had denounced appeals to
Rome without episcopal approval and adamantly opposed the
Cluniac reforms, both of which Henry supported. Henry went
to Italy in an unsuccessful expedition against the Greeks in
Apulia in 1021, was taken ill at Monte Cassino, reportedly
was miraculously cured by St. Benedict, but was lame thereaf-
ter. He was a monarch of great ability and outstanding piety
and asceticism. An interesting story, perhaps apocryphal, had
him desirous of becoming a monk at Saint-Vanne at Verdun.
He pledged obedience to the abbot, whereupon the abbot
commanded him under obedience to continue as Emperor.
He died in his palace of Grona, near Göttingen, Germany, on
July 13, and was canonized in 1146 by Pope Eugene III.
July 15.

HENRY OF UPPSALA (d. c̄. 1156). An Englishman living
in Rome, he accompanied the papal legate, Nicholas Cardinal
Breakspear (later Pope Adrian IV), to Scandinavia in 1151
and was consecrated bishop of Uppsala, Sweden, the next
year by the cardinal. Henry was with King Eric of Sweden in
the latter's invasion of Finland to punish Finnish pirates and
remained behind when Eric returned to Sweden. Henry was
murdered by a convert named Lalli, on whom he had imposed a penance for a murder he had committed. Henry is
considered the patron saint of Finland, though he does not
appear to have ever been formally canonized. January 19.

HERACLAS (c. 180–247). An Egyptian, he and his
brother, St. Plutarch, were Origen's first pupils at his catechetical school at Alexandria and were converted to Christianity
by him. Heraclas became Origen's assistant, was ordained,
and succeeded Origen as head of the school when Bishop
Demetrius of Alexandria condemned Origen in 231. Heraclas
succeeded Demetrius as bishop of Alexandria the same year,
and when Origen returned to Alexandria, Heraclas excommunicated him and drove him from the city. July 14.

HERIBERT (d. 1021). Born at Worms, Germany, he studied at Gorze Abbey in Lorraine and on his return to Worms
was given a canonry and ordained. He became chancellor for
Emperor Otto III and in 998 was named archbishop of Cologne. He accompanied Otto on a trip to Italy and brought

the Emperor's body back to Aachen when he died at Paterno
in Italy in 1002. Heribert incurred the dislike of Duke Henry
of Bavaria, who became Emperor Henry II through a misun-
derstanding, but the two men were later reconciled, and Heribert served as Henry's chancellor. Heribert built a monastery
at Deutz on the Rhine (where he was buried on his death),
was an active peacemaker, was devoted to the poor, maintained strict clerical discipline, and is reputed to have performed miracles, one of which caused a heavy rainfall ending
a severe drought and that causes him to be invoked for rainfall. He died at Cologne on March 16, and was canonized by
Pope Gregory VII sometime between 1073 and 1075.

HERMAGORUS (1st century). According to tradition, he
was chosen by St. Mark to tend his converts in Aquileia,
Italy, of which he was consecrated first bishop by St. Peter.
With his deacon Fortunatus, Hermagorus preached in the
area until arrested by Sebastius, a representative of Emperor
Nero, and then was tortured and beheaded with Fortunatus.
Fortunatus' connection with Hermagorus, despite the tradi-
tion, has never been proven, but he did suffer martyrdom in
Aquileia. July 12.

HERMAN CONTRACTUS. *See* Herman the Cripple.

HERMAN THE CRIPPLE, BL. (1013–54). Born a cripple
on February 18 at Altshausen, Swabia, and so terribly deformed he was almost helpless, he was placed in Reichenau
Abbey in Lake Constance, Switzerland, in 1020 when seven
and spent all his life there. He was professed at twenty, became known to scholars all over Europe for his keen mind,
wrote the hymns *Alma Redemptoris mater* and, in all probability, *Salve Regina* to our Lady, poetry, a universal chronicle, and a mathematical treatise. He died at Reichenau on
September 21 and is sometimes called Herman Contractus.
September 25.

HERVÉ (6th century). According to legend, he was the son
of a British bard named Hyvarnion and was born blind in
Brittany. He was raised by one Arthian and later his uncle at
Plouvien, where he worked as a farmhand and as a teacher in

his uncle's monastic school at Plouvien. On the death of his
mother, who had lived as a hermitess since he was seven, he
became head of his uncle's monastery and then moved to
Lanhouarneau, where he founded a new monastery and remained until his death, venerated for his holiness and miracles. He is invoked against eye trouble. One of the most extravagant and most popular miracles ascribed to him is the
story of the wolf that ate the donkey with which Hervé was
plowing; at Hervé's prayers, the wolf put himself into the
donkey's harness and finished the plowing. The Anglicized
version of Hervé is Harvey. June 17.

HIERONYMUS OF WEERT (d. 1572). *See* Pieck, Nicholas.

HILARY (d. 468). Born on Sardinia, he was one of the
papal legates to the Robber Council of Ephesus in 449 who
barely escaped with their lives. He was an archdeacon when
he was elected Pope and consecrated on November 19, 461.
During his pontificate, he labored to improve ecclesiastical
discipline and strengthen the church organization in Gaul and
Spain. He adjudicated several disputes between contending
bishops and held councils in Rome in 462 and 465 to settle
the matters; the latter is the first council in Rome of which
the original records are still extant. He rebuilt many Roman
churches and built the chapel of St. John the Apostle in the
baptistery of St. John Lateran in thanksgiving for his escape
at Ephesus. He publicly rebuked Emperor Anthemius in St.
Peter's for allowing one of his favorites, Philotheus, to promulgate the Macedonian heresy in Rome, and sent an encyclical letter to the East confirming the decisions of the General Councils of Nicaea, Ephesus, and Chalcedon, and the
contents of Pope Leo I's letter to Flavian. Hilary died in
Rome on February 28.

✳ **HILARY OF GALATEA** (c. 476–558). A native of Tuscany, he was first attracted to the religious life when only
twelve. Soon after, he left home, built a hermitage, and was
founding abbot of Galatea Monastery. He persuaded the invading Theodoric the Goth not to destroy his monastery and
even convinced him to grant him land. May 15.

HILARY OF POITIERS (d. c. 368). Born at Poitiers, Gaul, of a noble family, he was converted from paganism to Christianity by his study of the Bible and was baptized when well on in years. He had been married before his conversion, and his wife was still alive when, despite his objections, he was elected bishop of Poitiers about 350. Almost at once he became involved in the Arian controversy. He refused to attend a synod at Milan called by Emperor Constantius in 355, at which the bishops present were required to sign a condemnation of St. Athanasius, and was condemned for his orthodoxy by the synod of Béziers in 356, presided over by Arian Bishop Saturninus of Arles and composed mainly of Arian bishops. Later in the year he was exiled by the Emperor to Phrygia. He was so successful in refuting Arianism at a council of Eastern bishops at Seleucia in 359 and in encouraging the clergy to resist the heresy that the Arians requested the Emperor to send him back to Gaul. The Emperor ended his banishment and ordered him back to Gaul in 360. A synod he was instrumental in convoking deposed and excommunicated Saturninus; in 361, the death of Constantius ended the Arian persecution of the Catholics. In 364, Hilary held a public dispute at Milan with Auxentius, the Arian usurper of that see, and was ordered from Milan by Auxentius' protector, Emperor Valentinian. Hilary died at Poitiers, probably on November 1. Hilary was one of the leading and most respected theologians of his times. He wrote numerous treatises, notable among which were his *De Trinitate* (written while he was in exile against the Arians), *De synodis*, and *Opus historicum*. He was declared a Doctor of the Church by Pope Pius IX in 1851. January 13.

HILDA (614–80). Daughter of the nephew of King Edwin of Northumbria, England, Hereric, she was baptized at the same time as Edwin by St. Paulinus in 627, when she was thirteen. She lived the life of a noblewoman of her times until she was thirty-three, when she proposed to go to Chelles Monastery in France, where her sister Hereswitha was a nun. Hilda returned to Northumbria at the request of St. Aidan, spent some time in a nunnery on the banks of the Wear River, and then became abbess of a double monastery at Hartlepool. She was transferred sometime later to the Streaneschalch (Whitby) double monastery as abbess. She became renowned for her spiritual wisdom, and her monas-

tery for the caliber of its learning and of its nuns. She favored
the Celtic liturgical customs at the Synod of Whitby, which
she had convened in 664, but accepted the Roman usage
when the synod and King Oswy's decree ordered them observed in the churches of Northumbria. She died on November 17.

HILDEBRAND. *See* Gregory VII.

HILDEGARD, BL. (c. 754–83). Probably of a noble family, she was seventeen when Charlemagne put Queen Her-
mengard aside and married her. She bore him nine children
and died at Thionville (Diedenhofen), France. Said to have
been the daughter of the duke of Swabia, she was known for
her aid to nuns and monks and was greatly venerated at the
time of her death. Her tomb is at Kempten Abbey, of which
she is considered the foundress. April 30.

HILDEGARD (1098–1179). Born at Böckelheim, Germany, possibly of noble parents (her father may have been
a soldier in the service of Count Meginhard of Spanheim),
she was sickly as a child and when eight was placed in the
care of Count Meginhard's sister Jutta, a recluse near Speyer.
By the time Hildegard was old enough to become a nun, a
community had grown up around Jutta. When she died in
1136, Hildegard became prioress of the community. About
1147, with eighteen nuns, she moved her community to Rupertsberg on the Rhine near Bingen and founded a convent;
she founded another convent at Eibingen about 1165. From
her childhood, Hildegard was favored with supernatural experiences—visions, prophecies, and revelations. When about
forty, she began to relate these experiences to her spiritual adviser, a monk named Godfrey, who had them copied down by
a monk named Volmar. They were approved as coming from
God by Archbishop Henry of Mainz and were also approved
by Bishop Albero of Chiny when he was appointed to investigate them by Pope Eugene II. Huge crowds from all over
Germany and France flocked to see and consult with her. She
was hailed as both a saint and as a fraud and sorceress. In the
last year of her life she was involved in a dispute with ecclesiastical authorities when she permitted the burial of a young
man who had been excommunicated in the cemetery adjoining her convent. Her defense that he had received the last

rites was not accepted and the convent was put under interdict. The interdict was finally removed, and she died at Rupertsberg on September 17. She is called "the Sibyl of the Rhine" for her powers as seeress and prophetess. She wrote hundreds of letters to Popes, Emperors, bishops, abbots, clergy, and laity, many of which are still extant. Her best-known work is *Scrivias*, written between 1141 and 1151, which tells of twenty-six of her visions, written symbolically of the relationship between God and man as seen in the Creation, redemption, and the Church. She has long been venerated as a saint but has never been formally canonized. September 17.

HIPPARCHUS (d. 297 or c. 308). He and Philotheus were magistrates at Samosata on the Euphrates who had been converted to Christianity. On his return from a campaign against the Persians, Emperor Maximinus noticed that his magistrates were missing from the public celebration, which included sacrifices to the pagan gods, as he had ordered. When he found they had not made sacrifices for three years he had them and Abibus, James, Lollian, Paregrus, and Romanus, whom they had converted, brought before him. When they all refused to sacrifice to the gods, he had them all tortured and then imprisoned for two months. When they still persisted in their refusal, he had them all crucified at Samosata. They are known as the Martyrs of Samosata. December 9.

HIPPOLYTUS (d. c. 235). A priest at Rome known for his learning, he may have been a disciple of St. Irenaeus and became a major theological writer of the early Church. He denounced Pope St. Zephrinus for his leniency to the Christological heresies abroad in Rome, especially Modalism and Sabellianism. When Pope St. Callistus I was elected Pope in 217, Hippolytus allowed himself to be elected antipope by his small band of followers and opposed Callistus' successors, Popes Urban and Pontian as well. Hippolytus was banished to Sardinia during Emperor Maximinus' persecution of the Christians in 235 with Pope Pontian, who reconciled him and brought him back into the Church. He died on Sardinia, a martyr from the sufferings he endured. His most important work was *A Refutation of All Heresies;* he also wrote commentaries on Daniel and the Song of Songs and *The Apostolic Tradition*. He is often confused with the Hippolytus

(mentioned in the Roman Martyrology on August 13) of St.
Lawrence's unreliable *acta,* which names him the officer in
charge of Lawrence's imprisonment who was baptized by
Lawrence, was brought before the Emperor when he attended
the saint's funeral, and was then scourged and torn apart by
horses at the order of the Emperor. At the same time Hippolytus' nurse, Concordia, and nineteen other Christians of
his household were beaten to death with leaden whips.
August 3.

HODGSON, BL. SIDNEY (d. 1591). *See* Gennings, Edmund.

HOFBAUER, CLEMENT MARY (1751–1820). Born at
Tasswitz, Moravia, on December 26 and baptized John, he
was the ninth child of a butcher who changed his Moravian
name of Dvorak to the German Hofbauer. He was an apprentice baker in his youth, worked in the bakery of the
Premonstratensian monastery at Bruck, and then became a
hermit. When Emperor Joseph II abolished hermitages, he became a baker in Vienna but again became a hermit with a
friend, Peter Kunzmann, with the permission of Bishop
Chiaramonti of Tivoli (later Pope Pius VII). Clement studied at the University of Vienna and in Rome with a friend,
Thaddeus Hubl, and both of them joined the Redemptorists
(when Clement took the name Mary) in Rome and were ordained in 1785. They were sent to Vienna, but when unable
to establish a Redemptorist foundation since Emperor Joseph
II had banned many religious foundations in Austria-Hun-
gary, they were sent to Courland. On the way, Clement's old
friend Kunzmann joined them as a lay brother. At the request
of the papal nuncio, they went to Warsaw, and using St.
Benno Church as their center, engaged in missionary work. In
the twenty years they were there they were highly successful
with the Poles, Germans in Warsaw, Protestants, and Jews.
Clement worked among the poor, built orphanages and
schools, and sent Redemptorist missionaries to Germany and
Switzerland. When Napoleon suppressed the religious orders
in his territories, Clement and his fellow Redemptorists were
arrested and imprisoned in 1808, and then each was expelled
to his native country. Clement decided to settle in Vienna and
worked in the Italian quarter there. When appointed chaplain
of the Ursuline nuns and rector of the church attached to

their convent, he began to attract attention by his sermons, the holiness of his life, and his wisdom and understanding as a confessor. He founded a Catholic college in Vienna and became enormously influential in revitalizing the religious life of the German nations, even defeating, with Prince Rupert of Bavaria, an effort at the Congress of Vienna to establish a national German church. Clement also fought vigorously the whole concept of Josephinism (secular domination of the Church and hierarchy by the secular ruler), a stand for which he was bitterly opposed; his expulsion was demanded by the Austrian chancellor but forbidden by Emperor Francis I. Clement died in Vienna on March 15 and was canonized in 1909.

HOMER. *See* Angilbert.

HOMOBONUS (d. 1197). Son of a Cremona, Lombardy, Italy, merchant, he was taught the business by his father, married, and led a life of the utmost rectitude and integrity, known for his charity and concern for the poor. He died on November 13 while attending Mass at St. Giles Church in Cremona, was canonized in 1199, and is the patron of tailors and clothworkers. November 13.

HONORATUS (d. c. 303). He, Arontius, Fortunatus, Savinian, Felix, Januarius, Septimus, Repositus, Sator, Vitalis, Donatus, and another Felix were all natives of Hadrumetum, Africa, and are known as the Twelve Brothers, although they were probably not related. They were arrested at Hadrumetum during the reign of Emperor Maximian, tortured at Carthage, and then sent to Italy. The first four were beheaded at Potenza on August 27; Felix, Januarius, and Septimus suffered a similar fate at Venosa on August 28; Repositus, Sator, and Vitalis at Velleiano on August 29; and Donatus and the second Felix were beheaded on September 1 at Sentiana. September 1.

HONORATUS (d. c. 600). Born at Port-le-Grand, near Amiens, Gaul, he became bishop of Amiens and governed the see until his death there. He had a widespread cult in France following reports of numerous miracles when his body was elevated in 1060. He is the patron of bakers and confectioners; the famous Rue Saint-Honoré in Paris is named after him. May 16.

HONORIUS (d. 653). Born at Rome, he became a Benedictine monk and was sent to England by Pope Gregory the Great at the request of St. Augustine of Canterbury. Honorius was named archbishop of Canterbury in 627 and governed that see for a quarter century. He was granted authority to consecrate bishops by Pope Honorius I, gave refuge to St. Paulinus when he fled Cadwallon of Wales, who had defeated and killed King Edwin, and named him bishop of Rochester. When Paulinus died in 644, Honorius appointed as his successor St. Ithmar, the first English-born bishop. Honorius died on September 30.

HOORNAER, JOHN VAN (d. 1572). A Dominican priest from the Dominican province of Cologne, he was parish priest at a town near Gorkum, Holland, when he heard that the Franciscan community there had been captured by a Calvinist mob. He hastened to the city to administer the sacraments to the Franciscans and was himself seized. After imprisonment at Gorkum they were all sent to Briel and summarily executed when they would not apostatize. They were canonized as the Martyrs of Gorkum in 1867. July 9.

HOPE (2nd century). *See* Charity.

HORMISDAS (d. c. 420). A Persian noble and son of a provincial governor, he was stripped of his rank and possessions and made a camel tender when he refused to denounce his Christianity at the demand of Bahram, King of Persia. When the King offered to restore his position if he would apostatize, Hormisdas again refused, was relegated again to his demeaning position, and eventually suffered martyrdom for his faith. August 8.

HORMISDAS (d. 523). Born at Frosinone, Compagna di Roma, Italy, he was married and then was widowered (his son became Pope Silverius). Hormisdas was a deacon in Rome when he was elected Pope, succeeding St. Symmachus, on July 21, 514. The outstanding event of his pontificate was the ending of the Acacian schism, which had divided East and West since 484. The Church in Constantinople was reunited to Rome in 519 as a result of the *Formula* of Hormisdas, which formally condemned Acacius and unequivocally stated the primacy and infallibility of the Roman see. It was signed by Patriarch John of Constantinople and in time by some 250 Eastern bishops. It is a landmark statement of the authority and primacy of the Pope and has been quoted down through the ages to substantiate that claim. Early in his pontificate, Hormisdas also received back into the Church the last group of Laurentian schismatics. He died at Rome on August 6.

HOUGHTON, JOHN (1487–1535). Born in Essex, England, he served as a parish priest for four years after his graduation from Cambridge and then joined the Carthusians. He was named prior of Beauvale Charterhouse in Northampton but a few months later became prior of the charterhouse in London. In 1534, he and his procurator, Bl. Humphrey Middlemore, were arrested for refusing to accept the Act of Succession, which proclaimed the legitimacy of Anne Boleyn's children by Henry VIII, but were soon released when they accepted the Act with the proviso "as far as the law of God allows." He was again arrested when he refused, the following year, to accept the Act of Supremacy of King Henry, the first man to so refuse, together with St. Robert Lawrence and St. Augustine Webster, while they were seeking an exemption from the Oath from Thomas Cromwell. They were dragged through the streets of London, treated with the utmost savagery, and then hanged, drawn, and quartered at Tyburn on May 4. After his death, John Houghton's body was chopped to pieces and hung in different parts of London. He was canonized by Pope Paul VI in 1970 as one of the Forty Martyrs of England and Wales.

HOWARD, PHILIP (1557–95). Eldest son of Thomas Howard, fourth duke of Norfolk, who had been beheaded under Queen Elizabeth I in 1572, he had Philip II of Spain as his godfather and was earl of Arundel and Surrey on his mother's side. Baptized a Catholic but raised a Protestant, he was married at twelve to Ann Dacres, studied at Cambridge for two years, and was a wastrel at Elizabeth's court. Deeply impressed by St. Edmund Campion when he debated at London, Philip reformed his life, was reconciled to his neglected wife, and returned to the Catholic Church in 1584. Impris-

oned for a time in his own home for his religion, he wrote to
the Queen and then tried to flee to Flanders with his family
and brother William. He was captured at sea, returned to
London, and accused of treason for working with Mary
Queen of Scots. The charge was not provable, but he was
fined ten thousand pounds. At the time of the Spanish Ar-
mada, he was again accused of treason (though he was in
the Tower at the time) and ordered executed—a sentence
that was never carried out. He was kept imprisoned in the
Tower and died there six years later, on October 19, perhaps
poisoned. He was canonized by Pope Paul VI in 1970 as one
of the Forty Martyrs of England and Wales.

HUBERT (d. 727). A married courtier serving Pepin of
Heristal, he turned to the religious life after his wife died, reputedly after seeing a crucifix between the horns of a stag
while he was hunting (for which he is the patron of
hunters). He became a priest under St. Lambert, bishop of
Maastricht, and when Lambert was murdered at Liège about
705, Hubert was elected to succeed him. He moved his see to
Liège, where he had built a church to house Lambert's
remains. He ended idol worship in his diocese, made numerous conversions, and became known for his miracles. He
died on May 30 at Tervueren near Brussels while on a trip to
consecrate a new church. November 3.

HUGH (1024–1109). Eldest son of the count of Semur, he
entered the monastery at Cluny, France, when fifteen, was ordained five years later, was named prior shortly after, and in
1049 succeeded St. Odilo as abbot. Hugh attended the Council of Rheims and eloquently supported the reforms of Pope
St. Leo X, denouncing simony and the relaxation of clerical
discipline. Hugh went back to Rome with Leo, attended a
synod condemning Berengarius of Tours in 1050, and in
1057, as papal legate, effected peace between Emperor Henry
IV and King Andrew of Hungary. Hugh assisted Pope Nicholas II in drawing up the decree on papal elections at a council
in Rome in 1059 and continued his close relations with the
Holy See when Hildebrand, who had been a monk at Cluny,
was elected Pope as Gregory VII. Hugh worked closely with
Gregory to reform the Church and revive spiritual life in it.
He tried to mediate the bitter feud between Gregory and Emperor Henry IV and in 1068 settled the usage for the whole

Cluniac order. He had Pope Urban II consecrate the high
altar of the basilica at Cluny, then the largest church in
Christendom, and in 1065 was a leader at the Council of
Clermont in organizing the First Crusade. Hugh was abbot of
Cluny for sixty years and under his abbacy the prestige of
Cluny reached its highest point as new houses were opened all
over Europe. He served nine Popes, was adviser of Emperors,
Kings, bishops, and religious superiors. Universally admired
for his intellectual and spiritual attainments and as a simple
man of great prudence and justice, he exercised a dominant
influence on the political and ecclesiastical affairs of his times.
He died at Cluny, and was canonized by Pope Callistus III
in 1120.

HUGH OF GRENOBLE (1052–1132). Born at Cha-
teauneuf, France, he became a canon of the cathedral in
nearby Valence though a layman. He became an aide of
Bishop Hugh of Die, was active in the bishop's campaign
against simony, and while attending a synod at Avignon in
1080 to discuss the problems besetting the vacant see of
Grenoble, was elected bishop of that see. He was ordained by
the papal legate and consecrated by the Pope in Rome. Hugh
at once set in motion plans to reform the see, denounced
simony and usury, restored clerical discipline and clerical celibacy, and rebuilt the empty diocesan treasury. Discouraged
by his lack of progress, he became a Benedictine at Chaise-
Dieu Abbey but was ordered back to his see by Pope Gregory
VII. Hugh repeatedly tried to resign the see but each time the
Pope in office turned down his request because of his outstanding ability. He welcomed St. Bruno and his companions,
gave them the land on which the Grande Chartreuse was
built, and encouraged the Order. He died on April 1 and was
canonized two years later by Pope Innocent II.

HUGH OF LINCOLN (1140–1200). Son of William, lord
of Avalon, he was born at Avalon Castle in Burgundy and
was raised and educated at a convent at Villard-Benoît after
his mother died when he was eight. He was professed at
fifteen, ordained deacon at nineteen, and was made prior of a
monastery at Saint-Maxim. While visiting the Grande Chartreuse with his prior in 1160, he decided to become a Carthusian there and was ordained. After ten years, he was named
procurator and in 1175 became abbot of the first Carthusian

monastery in England, built by King Henry II as part of his penance for the murder of Thomas Becket. On Hugh's arrival at the site of the monastery at Witham in Somersetshire, he found not a building started but soon built the monastery. His reputation for holiness and sanctity spread all over England and attracted many to the monastery. He chided Henry for keeping sees vacant to enrich the royal coffers (since income from vacant sees went to the royal treasury), and was then named bishop of the eighteen-year-old vacant see of Lincoln in 1186—a post he accepted only when ordered to do so by the prior of the Grande Chartreuse. Hugh quickly restored clerical discipline, labored to restore religion to the diocese, and became known for his wisdom and justice. He was one of the leaders in denouncing the persecution of the Jews that swept England, 1190–91, repeatedly facing down armed mobs and making them release their victims. He had differences with Henry over the appointment of seculars to ecclesiastical positions and with King Richard I (flatly refusing to contribute to Richard's war chest to finance foreign wars in 1197, the first time a direct levy by an English King had been refused), but remained on good terms with both monarchs. He went on a diplomatic mission to France for King John in 1199, visiting the Grande Chartreuse, Cluny, and Citeaux, and returned from the trip in poor health. A few months later, while attending a national council in London, he was stricken and died two months later at the Old Temple in London on November 16. He was canonized twenty years later, in 1220, the first Carthusian to be so honored. November 17.

HUGH THE LITTLE (d. 1255). One of the most tragic stories of the Middle Ages had nine-year-old Hugh lured into the home of a Jew named Koppin, scourged, crowned with thorns, and crucified. His body was then thrown into a well. Koppin and ninety-two other Jews were arrested; Koppin confessed to the crime, denounced his fellow Jews, and said it was a Jewish custom to crucify a Christian child each year. He and eighteen others were executed at Lincoln; the others were imprisoned but eventually released when a group of Franciscans interceded for them and they paid heavy fines. Miracles were reported when Hugh's body was recovered from the well. That a Christian child may have been killed by a Jew or Jews may have taken place; but it was never proven nor is there any evidence of any ritual killing of the type described above. Hugh's story is told in Chaucer's *Prioresse's Tale*. August 27.

HUMBELINE, BL. (1092–1135). Sister of St. Bernard, she was born at Dijon, France, married the noble Guy de Marcy, and lived the life of the nobility of the day. Reproved by Bernard for her ostentatious dress and lifestyle while she was visiting him one day, she took his reproof to heart and several years later, with her husband's permission, she became a nun at Benedictine Jully-les-Nonnais nunnery. She succeeded her sister-in-law, Elizabeth, as abbess, lived a life of great austerity, and died at Jully in Bernard's arms. Her cult was approved in 1703. August 21.

HUMILITY (1226–1310). Born at Faenza, Italy, of a wealthy family, she was named Rosana and was married, when fifteen, to a nobleman named Ugoletto. They had two children who died in infancy and after a near-fatal illness of Ugoletto when she was twenty-four, they both entered St. Perpetua double monastery near Faenza, he as a lay brother and she as a nun with the name Humility. She lived as a recluse in a cell adjoining St. Apollinaris Church for twelve years, living a life of great austerity under the direction of the Vallombrosan abbey of St. Crispin. At the suggestion of the abbot general of the Vallumbrosans, she became founding abbess of Santa Maria Novella Convent at Malta, near Faenza (the first Vallombrosan convent for nuns), and later of a second house at Florence, Italy, where she died on May 22.

HUNNA (d. c. 679). The daughter of an Alsatian duke, and also known as Huva, she was married to Huno of Hunnaweyer and devoted herself to the poor of Strasbourg, earning the title of "holy washerwoman" when she even washed for the poor. A local cult developed after her death, and she was canonized in 1520 by Pope Leo X. April 15.

HUVA. *See* Hunna.

HYACINTH (1185–1257). Born at Oppeln, Poland, he joined the Dominicans, possibly in Rome in 1217 or 1218, and was sent to Silesia with a group of Dominicans to evangelize the area. He preached over a wide area including Scandinavia, Prussia, and Lithuania, is venerated as an apostle of Poland, and is credited with numerous miracles. He died on August 15 and was canonized in 1594. August 17.

HYGINUS (d. c. 142). Little is known of him or his pontificate beyond that he was a Greek and was Pope, probably 138–42, succeeding Pope Telesphorus. It is known that two Gnostics, Valentinus and Cerdo, were in Rome while he was Pope, but what action if any he took about them is unknown. January 11.

IA (d. c. 360). Unreliable sources have her a Greek, perhaps a slave, who was so successful in converting Persian ladies to Christianity that she was arrested during the persecution of the Christians by King Sapor II of Persia. Tortured for months in an attempt to force her to apostatize, to no avail, she was eventually lashed to death and then beheaded. August 4.

IBAR (5th century). Perhaps a missionary to Ireland before Patrick but more probably one of his disciples, Ibar preached in Leinster and Meath and founded a monastic school on the island of Beg-Eire (Beggery). April 23.

IBARAKI, LOUIS (d. 1597). See Karasumaru, Leo.

IBARAKI, PAUL (d. 1597). See Karasumaru, Leo.

IGNATIUS OF ANTIOCH (d. c. 107). Probably a convert to Christianity and perhaps a disciple of St. John, legend has him appointed and consecrated bishop of Antioch by St. Peter after Peter left the deathbed of Evodius, previous bishop of the see. Ignatius governed for forty years but was arrested during the persecution of Emperor Trajan (untrustworthy legend has him questioned by the Emperor himself) and sent to Rome. The ship he was sent on traveled along the coast of Asia Minor, then Greece, and finally reached Rome. Ignatius was greeted by crowds of Christians wherever the ship touched port, but he received ill treatment from his captors. He arrived in Rome on December 20, the last day of the public games, was escorted to the amphitheater, and there was killed by lions in the arena. A detailed description of the trip to Rome is provided by Agathopus and a deacon named

Philo, who were with him, and who also wrote at his dictation seven letters of instruction on the Church, marriage, the Trinity, the Incarnation, Redemption, and the Eucharist, which are among the most important of the earliest Christian writings. He is often surnamed Theophorus (God bearer). October 17.

IGNATIUS OF CONSTANTINOPLE (c. 799–877). Son of Byzantine Emperor Michael I and the daughter of Emperor Nicephorus I and named Nicetas, he and his brother were mutilated and exiled to a monastery when their father was deposed by Leo the Armenian in 813. Ignatius later became a monk, was ordained, and in time was elected abbot of his monastery. He was named patriarch of Constantinople in 846, vigorously assailed evil in high places, and in 857, when he refused communion to Bardas because of alleged incestuous sexual relationships, he was deposed and exiled by Bardas' nephew, Emperor Michael III. Banished to the island of Terebinthos, Ignatius seems to have resigned his see, and Bardas secured the election of his secretary Photius, a layman, as patriarch. A long factional struggle ensued, and in 867 Michael was murdered and his successor, Basil the Macedonian, deposed Photius and recalled Ignatius, as much to secure the support of Ignatius' supporters as to secure justice. Ignatius then asked Pope Adrian II to convoke a council, and at the eighth General Council, 869–70, Photius and his supporters were condemned, and Photius was excommunicated. Ignatius later came into conflict with Rome when he claimed jurisdiction over the Bulgars and convinced their prince to expel Latin priests and replace them with the Greek priests he sent. Pope John VIII's legates, threatening Ignatius with excommunication, arrived in Constantinople to find he had died on October 23. Though he is recognized as personally holy, he was evidently deeply engaged in the politics of his times.

IGNATIUS LOYOLA (1491–1556). Of a noble family and the son of Don Beltran Yáñez de Loyola and Maria Sáenz de Licona y Balda, he was born in the family castle in the Basque province of Gúipuzcoa, Spain, the youngest of thirteen children, and was christened Iñigo. He entered the military service of the Duke of Nagara, was wounded in the right leg during the siege of Pamplona in 1521, and while recuperating was so impressed by a life of Christ and biographies of the saints he read that he decided to devote himself to Christ. After he recovered he went on pilgrimage to Monserrat, where he hung up his sword at Our Lord's altar and then spent 1522–23 on retreat at Manresa, where he experienced visions and probably wrote the bulk of his *Spiritual Exercises* (which was not published until 1548). He spent the years 1524–35 studying at Barcelona, Alcalá, Salamanca (where he was accused and then exonerated of preaching heresy), and Paris. He received his master of arts degree in 1534, when he was forty-three, and in the same year founded the Society of Jesus (the Jesuits) with fellow students Francis Xavier, Peter Favre, Diego Laynez, Alfonso Salmeron, Simon Rodriguez, and Nicholas Bobadilla in Paris, though the formal title Society of Jesus was not adopted until 1537, when Ignatius and seven of his band were ordained in Venice after he had spent a year on pilgrimage in Spain. Unable to go on pilgrimage to Jerusalem, as they had vowed, they went to Rome and offered their services to the Pope. It was on the way to Rome that Ignatius had the famous vision of La Storta, in which Christ promised all would go well in Rome. The Society was approved by Pope Paul III in 1540, and the group took their final vows in 1541, with Ignatius named superior general. Jesuits were sent at once to missionary areas, soon Jesuit houses, schools, colleges, and seminaries were founded all over Europe, and the Jesuits became renowned for their prowess in the intellectual sphere and in the field of education. By the time Ignatius died in Rome on July 31, his three goals for the Church—reform of the Church (especially through education and more frequent use of the sacraments), widespread activity in the missionary field, and the fight against heresy—were well established as the bases of Jesuit activities. He was canonized in 1622 and was proclaimed patron of retreats and spiritual exercises by Pope Pius XI. July 31.

ILDEPHONSUS (607–67). Of distinguished parents and perhaps a pupil of St. Isidore of Seville, he was born at Toledo, became a monk at Agli (Agalia) near Toledo despite his parents' objections, was ordained, and in time was elected abbot. He attended councils in Toledo in 653 and 655, was named archbishop of Toledo about 657, and governed until his death on January 23. He had an intense devotion to Mary, wrote several theological treatises, notably *De virginitate perpetua sanctae Mariae* (according to a legend Mary appeared to him and presented him with a chasuble), and is honored as a Doctor of the Church in the Spanish Church.

ILLTUD. *See* Illtyd.

ILLTYD (450–535). Also known as Illtud, his life is derived mainly from legend and unreliable sources, though he is one of the most celebrated of the Welsh saints. According to them, he was the son of a Briton living in Letavia, Brittany (some scholars believe Letavia is an area in central Brednock, England, rather than in Brittany), who came to visit his cousin King Arthur of England about 470. Illtyd married Trynihid and then served in the army of a Glamorgan chieftain. When one of his friends was killed in a hunting accident, he and Trynihid lived as recluses in a hut by the Nadafan River. He left her to become a monk under St. Dubricius, but after a time resumed his eremitical life. He attracted many disciples and organized them into Llanilltud Fawr Monastery (Llanwit Major in Glamorgan), which soon developed into a great monastic foundation and a center of missionary activity in Wales. Another legend has him a disciple of St. Germanus of Auxerre, who ordained him, famed for his learning and wisdom, which caused him to be named head of the monastic school at Llanwit. Many extravagant miracles were attributed to him (he was fed by heaven when forced to flee the ire of a local chieftain and take refuge in a cave, his miraculous restoration of a collapsed seawall), and he is reputed to have sent grain to relieve a famine in Brittany. His death is variously reported at Dol, Brittany, where he had retired in his old age, Llanwit, and Defynock. One Welsh tradition has him one of the three knights put in charge of the Holy Grail by Arthur, and another even has him Galahad. November 6.

IMBERT, BL. LAURENCE (d. 1839). A native of Aix-en-Provence, France, he joined the Paris Foreign Missionary Society and was sent to China in 1825. He worked there as a missionary for twelve years and was named titular bishop of Capsa. In 1837, he was sent to Korea and entered the country secretly, as Christianity was forbidden there. He was successful in his missionary activities, but in 1839 a wave of violent persecutions of the Christians swept the country. In the hope of ending the persecutions of native Christians, he, Fr. Philibert Maubant, and Fr. James Honoré Chastan, who had preceded him into Korea, surrendered to the authorities. They were bastinadoed and then beheaded at Seoul on September 21. During the same persecution, John Ri was bastinadoed and suffered martyrdom, and Agatha Kim was hanged from a cross by her arms and hair, driven over rough country in a cart, and then stripped and beheaded. In 1925, Bl. Laurence and his companions and many others, eighty-one in all, who had been executed for their faith, were beatified as the Martyrs of Korea. September 22.

INGENES (d. 250). *See* Ammon.

IÑIGO (d. 1057). Also known as Eneco, he is believed to have been a native of Calatayud, Bilbao, Spain. He became a hermit, then a monk at San Juan de Peña in Aragon, and after serving as prior, resumed his eremitical life in the Aragon Mountains. He was persuaded by King Sancho the Great about 1029 to be abbot of a group of monks the King had chosen to reform the monastery at Oña founded by the King's father-in-law in 1010. Iñigo was most successful in his reforms, became known for his peacemaking ability, and was reputed to have performed miracles. He died at Oña on June 1, and was probably canonized by Pope Alexander III.

INNOCENT I (d. 417). Born at Albano, Italy, he became Pope, succeeding Pope St. Anastasius I, on December 22, 401. During Innocent's pontificate, he emphasized papal supremacy, commending the bishops of Africa for referring the decrees of their councils at Carthage and Milevis in 416, condemning Pelagianism, to the Pope for confirmation. It was his confirmation of these decrees that caused Augustine to make a remark that was to echo through the centuries: "*Roma locuta, causa finita est*" (Rome has spoken, the matter is ended). Earlier Innocent had stressed to Bishop St. Victrius and the Spanish bishops that matters of great importance were to be referred to Rome for settlement. Innocent strongly favored clerical celibacy and fought the unjust removal of St.

John Chrysostom. He vainly sought help from Emperor Honorius at Ravenna when the Goths under Alaric captured and sacked Rome. Innocent died in Rome on March 12. July 28.

INNOCENT V (c. 1225–76). Born at Tarentaise-en-Forez, France, and known as Peter of Tarentaise, he became a Dominican under Bl. Jordan of Saxony when sixteen, received his master's degree in theology from the University of Paris in 1259, and then occupied a chair at the university. He soon became famous as a preacher and theologian, and in 1259, with a committee including his friend Thomas Aquinas, composed a plan of study that is still the basis of Dominican teaching. When thirty-seven, Innocent was appointed prior provincial of France, visited on foot all Dominican houses under him, and was then sent to Paris to replace Thomas Aquinas at the University of Paris. Pope Gregory V named Innocent archbishop of Lyons in 1272 and cardinal-bishop of Ostia the next year while still administering the see of Lyons. He was a prominent and active delegate to the General Council of Lyons in 1274 and was largely responsible for the short-lived healing of the Greek schism. After preaching the panegyric of St. Bonaventure, who died at the council, he returned to Italy with Pope Bl. Gregory X and was with Gregory when he died at Arezzo in 1276. He was unanimously elected his successor on January 21, 1276, the first Dominican Pope, and took the name Innocent V. During his short five-month pontificate, he struggled to reconcile Guelphs and Ghibellines, restored peace between Pisa and Lucca, and acted as mediator between Rudolph of Hapsburg and Charles of Anjou. Innocent attempted to consolidate the reunion with the Byzantines achieved at the General Council of Lyons but died suddenly on June 22. His cult was confirmed in 1898. He wrote several theological and philosophical treatises, chief of which was his *Commentary on the Sentences of Peter Lombard.*

INNOCENT XI, BL. (1611–89). Born at Como, Italy, on May 16, Benedetto Odescalchi studied under the Jesuits there, law at Rome and Naples, held numerous posts under Pope Urban VIII, among them administrator of Macerata and governor of Picena and was created a cardinal by Pope Innocent X in 1645. He served as legate to Ferrara, was appointed bishop of Novara in 1650, resigned in favor of his brother in

1656 and then returned to Rome. Known for his holiness and desire for reform, he was unanimously elected pope on September 21, 1676 and was consecrated on October 4. Throughout his entire pontificate he struggled against the absolutism of King Louis XIV of France, who had bitterly opposed his election, in Church matters. When an assembly of French bishops called by Louis in 1682 passed *Declaration du clergy français* declaring the pope subject to a general council and the king subject to the pope only in spiritual matters, Innocent annulled the *Declaration* and refused to confirm any episcopal nomination made by those who had participated in the council. He disapproved Louis' Revocation of the Edict of Nantes in 1685 and sought milder treatment for the French Protestants. In 1687 Innocent's abolishment of diplomatic immunity to persons sought by papal courts sheltered in foreign consulates in Rome led to the occupation of the papal palace in Rome by French forces. The following year Innocent appointed Joseph Clement archbishop of Cologne against Louis' wishes; whereupon the French king imprisoned the papal nuncio, occupied papal Avignon and threatened to cut off the French Church's ties with Rome. Innocent supported James II in England but disapproved the Declaration of Indulgence in 1687 and feared the English king too was attracted by the concepts of Gallicanism. Innocent encouraged Christian resistance to the Turks in Austria and Hungary, put ecclesiastical reforms into effect and encouraged daily communion, and condemned quietism in 1687 with *Coelestis pastor*. He died in Rome on August 12, and was beatified in 1956 by Pope Pius XII.

IRENAEUS (c. 125–c. 203). Born in Asia Minor, probably at Smyrna, he was well educated and probably knew and was influenced by men who knew the apostles, especially St. Polycarp, who had been a pupil of St. John. According to Gregory of Tours, Polycarp sent him as a missionary to Gaul, where he was a priest under St. Pothinus at Lyons. Irenaeus was sent to Rome in 177 with a letter from his fellow Christians to Pope St. Eleutherius pleading for leniency to the Montanists in Phrygia. In Irenaeus' absence a violent persecution of Christians broke out at Lyons, claiming Pothinus as one of its martyrs, and Irenaeus returned to Lyons in 178 as bishop. He was active in evangelizing the area around Lyons and was the fierce opponent of Gnosticism in Gaul, which he refuted in a five-book treatise, *Adversus omnes haereses*. He was successful in 190 in reconciling the Quartodecimans, who had been excommunicated by Pope Victor III for refusing to celebrate Easter on the date of Western usage adopted by Rome. Irenaeus was the first great Catholic theologian. His treatise against the Gnostics is witness to the apostolic tradition and in it, at this early date, is a testimony to the primacy of the Pope. June 28.

IRENE (d. 304). *See* Agape.

ISAAC OF CORDOVA (c. 825–52). Born at Cordova, Spain, he was a Christian and so proficient in Arabic, he became a notary under the Moors. He resigned to become a monk at Tabanos near Cordova, emerged from the monastery to debate the chief magistrate, and in the course of the debate denounced Mohammed. He was arrested for his denunciation, tortured, and then executed. June 3.

ISAAC THE GREAT (d. 439). Son of Catholicos (Patriarch) St. Nerses I of Armenia, he studied at Constantinople, married, and on the early death of his wife became a monk. He was appointed Catholicos of Armenia in 390 and secured from Constantinople recognition of the metropolitan rights of the Armenian Church, thus terminating its long dependence on the Church of Caesarea in Cappodocia. He at once began to reform the Armenian Church. He ended the practice of married bishops, enforced Byzantine canon law, encouraged monasticism, built churches and schools, and fought Persian paganism. He supported St. Mesrop in his creation of an Armenian alphabet, helped to promote the translation of the Bible and the works of the Greek and Syrian doctors into Armenian, and was responsible for establishing a national liturgy and the beginnings of Armenian literature. He was driven into retirement in 428 when the Persians conquered part of his territory but returned at an advanced age to rule again from his see at Ashtishat, where he died. He was the founder of the Armenian Church and is sometimes called Sahak in Armenia. September 9.

ISABEL OF FRANCE, BL. (d. 1270). Sister of St. Louis and daughter of King Louis VIII of France and Blanche of Castile, she refused offers of marriage from several noble suitors to continue her life of virginity consecrated to God. She ministered to the sick and the poor, and after the death of her mother founded the Franciscan Monastery of the Humility of the Blessed Virgin Mary at Longchamps in Paris. She lived there in austerity but never became a nun and refused to become abbess. She died there on February 23, and her cult was approved in 1521. February 26.

ISABELLA OF PORTUGAL. *See* Elizabeth of Portugal.

ISAIAS (d. 309). *See* Elias.

ISIDORE THE FARMER (1070–1130). Born at Madrid, Spain, of poor parents, he became a hired hand on the estate of wealthy John de Vergas just outside of Madrid. He lived a life of great devotion, is reputed to have performed numerous miracles, and despite his own poverty, shared what little he had with the poor. He died on May 15 at Madrid. His wife, Maria Torribia, who shared his devotion and poverty, is also honored as a saint under the name of Santa Maria de la Cabeza. Many miracles were reported at Isidore's shrine, and over the centuries his aid has been sought and granted to several Spanish monarchs. He was canonized in 1622 and is the patron of farmers and of the city of Madrid.

ISIDORE OF PELUSIUM (d. c. 450). Born at Alexandria, he left the city in his youth and became a monk at the monastery of Lychnos near Pelusium. He was ordained and in time became abbot. He was revered for his devotion to his religious duties and was famous for his voluminous correspondence; some two thousand letters of pious exhortation and theological instruction are still extant, though he is reported to have written ten thousand letters in his lifetime. He was a vigorous opponent of Nestorianism and Eutychianism and wrote *Adversus gentiles* and *De fato,* neither of which has survived. February 4.

ISIDORE OF SEVILLE (c. 560–636). Of a noble Hispanic-Roman family of Cartagena, Spain, and brother of SS. Leander, Fulgentius, and Florentina, he was born at Seville, was educated under the supervision of his elder brother, Leander, and succeeded him as bishop of Seville in about 600. Isidore became noted as one of the most learned men of his times, continued Leander's work of converting the Arian Visigoths, and presided over several important councils, including that of Seville in 619 and Toledo in 633. Greatly interested in education, he founded schools in each diocese similar to our present-day seminaries and broadened the curriculum to include liberal arts, medicine, and law as well as the conventional subjects. He compiled the *Etymologies*, an encyclopedia of the knowledge of his times, wrote treatises on theology, astronomy, and geography, histories (his history of the Goths is the principal source of information about them), biographies, and completed the Mozarabic liturgy begun by Leander. Isidore was known for his austerities and charities and is considered the last of the ancient Christian philosophers. He died on April 4, was canonized in 1598, and was declared a Doctor of the Church by Pope Benedict XIV in 1722.

ITA (d. c. 570). Reputedly of royal lineage, she was born at Decies, Waterford, Ireland, refused to be married, and secured her father's permission to live a virginal life. She moved to Killeedy, Limerick, and founded a community of women dedicated to God. She also founded a school for boys, and one of her pupils was St. Brendan. Many extravagant miracles were attributed to her (in one of them she is reputed to have reunited the head and body of a man who had been beheaded; in another she lived entirely on food from heaven), and she is widely venerated in Ireland. She is also known as Deirdre and Mida. January 15.

IVO OF CHARTRES (c. 1040–1116). Born at Beauvais, France, he was a canon at Nesles and then became a canon regular of St. Augustine at Saint-Quentin. After teaching Scripture, theology, and canon law there, he became prior about 1078 and was elected bishop of Chartres in 1191. He was councilor of King Philip I, but when he denounced the King's plan to divorce his wife, Bertha, to marry Bertrada, third wife of Count Fulk of Anjou, Ivo was imprisoned in 1192 and had his revenues confiscated by the crown. He was freed through the intercession of the Pope and later reconciled Philip to the Holy See after Bertha died. Ivo acted as mediator in several investiture disputes and openly protested the simony of several members of the papal court. He wrote widely on canon law, and his *Decretum* had a great influence

IVO HÉLORY OF KERMARTIN **260**

on its development; he was also a voluminous letter writer, and many of his letters reflecting the religious issues of his time are still extant. He died on December 23. May 23.

IVO HÉLORY OF KERMARTIN (1253–1303). Son of the lord of the manor of Kermartin, Brittany, where he was born, he studied theology, canon law, and philosophy at Paris and civil law at Orléans. On his return to Brittany, he became a judge of the Rennes diocesan court and then of his own diocese, Tréguier, where he became known as "the poor man's advocate" for his defense of the poor and his refusal to accept fees from his poor clients. In 1284, he was ordained, resigned his legal position in 1287 to be parish priest at Trédrez, and later filled the same role at Lovannec. He built a hospital, tended the ill, ministered to the poor, and acquired a reputation for his preaching ability. He was much sought after as a mediator and was noted for the austerity and piety of his life. He died on May 19, was canonized in 1347, and is the patron of lawyers.

IXIDA, BL. ANTONY (1569–1632). A Japanese, he joined the Jesuits, was ordained, and became famed for his learning and eloquent preaching. He was successful in conversion work in Arima Province until he was captured while on a sick call in Nagasaki and imprisoned for two years at Omura. He was then returned to Nagasaki with three Augustinians, Bl. Bartholomew Gutierrez, a Mexican, Francis Ortega, and Vincent Carvalho, and two Franciscans, Bl. Jerome, a Japanese priest, and Bl. Gabriel of Fonseca, a lay brother. They were scalded for thirty-three days with boiling water to force them to apostatize, and when they persisted in their faith they were burned to death on September 3 at Nagasaki. They were beatified in 1867 as among the Martyrs of Japan.

J

JACOBIS, JUSTIN DE (1800–60). Born at San Fele, Italy, on October 9, he was taken to Naples when a child by his parents, joined the Vincentians when eighteen, and was ordained. After helping found a Vincentian house at Monopoli, he served as superior at Lecce and in 1839 was sent as the first prefect and vicar apostolic to the new Catholic mission at Adua, Ethiopia. His efforts to evangelize met with great opposition, but in 1841 he was included in a delegation of Ethiopian prelates to Cairo to request the Coptic patriarch of Alexandria to appoint one of his monks Abuna (Patriarch) of the Ethiopian Church. In Cairo, the patriarch denounced the presence of Fr. de Jacobis on the delegation and intrigued to appoint one Salama as Abuna. Some of the delegation then accompanied Fr. de Jacobis to meet the Pope in Rome. On his return, Fr. de Jacobis founded a college and seminary at Guala, and in 1846 a vicariate apostolic of the Galla was established, with William Massaia its first bishop. These developments caused Salama to launch an anti-Catholic campaign. The college was closed, Catholicism was proscribed, and Bishop Massaia was forced to return to Aden. In 1848, he secretly consecrated Fr. de Jacobis, now a fugitive, bishop at Massawa, with authority to administer the sacraments in the Ethiopian rite. By 1853, the new bishop had ordained some twenty Ethiopians, was ministering to five thousand Catholics, and was able to reopen the college. In 1860, Kedaref Kassa became King as Theodore II and in return for the backing he had received from Abuna Salama launched a persecution of the Catholics. Bishop de Jacobis was arrested and after several months' imprisonment was released and managed to find his way to Halai in southern Eritrea. He spent the rest of his life in missionary work along the Red Sea coast and died in the valley of Alghedien on July 31 of fever he contracted while on a missionary trip. He was canonized by Pope Paul VI in 1975.

JACOBUS DE VORAGINE. *See* James of Voragine, Bl.

JACOPO DE VORAGINE. *See* James of Voragine, Bl.

JACOPONE OF TODI, BL. (c. 1230–1306). Of the Benedetti family of Todi, Italy, he studied law at Bologna, where he probably received his doctorate, and returned to Todi to practice. He married Vanna di Guidone in 1267, and they lived a worldly life until the following year, when Vanna was tragically killed when a balcony on which she was standing collapsed. Blaming himself for her death, Jacopone completely changed his lifestyle, performed the most humiliating penances, and acquired a widespread notoriety for his eccentricities. In 1278, he became a Franciscan lay brother at San Fortunato friary in Todi and began to write religious hymns and poetry, some in Latin but chiefly in the Umbrian dialect, which became immensely popular. He was soon attracted to the Spiritual branch of the Franciscans (though San Fortunato was a Conventual house), and in 1294 he and some of his brethren were granted permission by Pope Celestine V to live in a separate community and follow the Franciscan rule in its original strictness. This permission was revoked by Pope Boniface VIII after his election to succeed Pope Celestine, who had resigned in 1294. With Cardinals Jacopo and Pietro Colonna, Jacopone issued a manifesto in 1297 declaring that Boniface, an opponent of the Spirituals, had been elected invalidly; when papal forces captured the Colonnas' stronghold, Palestrina, Jacopone was captured, excommunicated, and imprisoned for five years. While in prison, he wrote many of his best-known poems. He was freed in 1303 when Boniface died, lived as a hermit near Orvieto, and then moved to a Poor Clare convent at Collazzone, where he died on Christmas Day. He was one of the most important poets of the Middle Ages and is reputed to have written *Stabat Mater dolorosa* and *Stabat Mater speciosa*, though this is questioned by many authorities. Though referred to as Blessed, his cult has never been approved.

JADWIGA. *See* Hedwig.

JAMES (d. 297). *See* Hipparchus.

JAMES THE GREATER (d. 42). Son of Zebedee, he and his younger brother, John, were natives of Galilee and fishermen when called by Jesus to follow him as they were mending their nets with their father in a fishing boat on Lake Genesareth (Matt. 4:21–22; Mark 1:19–20; Luke 5:10). They were with Jesus when he cured Peter's mother-in-law at the house of Peter and Andrew (Mark 1:29–31), asked Christ if they could sit on either side of him in his glory and assured him they could drink his cup (Matt. 20:20–28; Mark 10:35–45), and were nicknamed Boanerges (Sons of Thunder) by Jesus (Mark 3:17), probably on the occasion when they asked Jesus if they should ask heaven to strike the inhospitable Samaritans with fire (Luke 9:54–56). James was with Peter and John at the raising of Jairus' daughter from the dead (Mark 5:37; Luke 8:51), and the three of them were the only apostles at the Transfiguration (Matt. 17:1–8; Mark 9:2–8) and the agony at Gethsemane (Matt. 26:37–46; Mark 14:33–42). James was the first of the apostles to be martyred when he was beheaded in Jerusalem by Herod Agrippa I (Acts 12:1–2). An old tradition, now largely discredited by scholars, says he preached in Spain before his martyrdom, and a Spanish tradition had his body translated to Santiago de Compostela in Spain, which was one of the great pilgrimage centers of the Middle Ages. He is the patron saint of Spain. July 25.

JAMES THE LESS (d. 62). James, the son of Alpheus, is named in the lists of the apostles in Matthew, Mark, and Luke and in Acts 1:13 is one of the eleven apostles in the upper room in Jerusalem after Christ's Ascension. James is mentioned as one of the brothers of the Lord (Matt. 13:55; Mark 6:3) with Joseph, Simon, and Jude, and is called the "brother of the Lord" (Galatians 1:19). It was to James that Peter wanted the news of his miraculous escape transmitted (Acts 12:17), and James seems to have been regarded as the head of the primitive Church in Jerusalem. It was he who suggested that only four Jewish practices be imposed on Gentiles wishing to be followers of Christ (Acts 15:13–21), beginning this statement with the words "I rule, then, that . . ." Paul reported to him and sought his approval several times. This James seems to be the James of the Epistle of James who opens the epistle by calling himself "servant of God and of the Lord Jesus Christ," which may indicate it was an official Church title; James uses the tone of authority of one well known in the Church and accustomed to wielding authority. Traditionally, biblical exegetes have considered James, the son of Alpheus, as the same James called "the brother of the Lord," the James who speaks with the voice of authority in the early Church; many modern scholars, however, hold that there may have been two Jameses, one the son of Alpheus and one of the Twelve, and the other "the brother of the Lord," the author of the Epistle of James, and an authoritative figure in the early Church. Among the reasons they cite for this belief is the fact that in his epistle, James speaks of the apostles in the past tense and does not identify himself as an apostle; the apparent distinction between this James and the apostle James in 1 Corinthians 15:7; and the elegant Greek literary style used by the author of the epistle, a style hardly likely to be used by a Galilean peasant. The name James the Less is usually applied to James, son of Alpheus, because of the reference in Mark 15:40, where he is called "James the Less" in the King James and Douay versions of the Bible; he is called James the Younger in the Jerusalem, Revised Standard version, New English Bible, Living Bible, and the New International version. According to Hegesippus, a second-century ecclesiastical historian, James was thrown from the pinnacle of the Temple in Jerusalem by the Pharisees and then stoned to death. May 3.

JAMES OF NISIBIS (d. 338). A Syrian, he became a monk and in about 308 was named first bishop of Nisibis, Mesopotamia. He built a basilica there and founded the theological school of Nisibis, which became famous. A fierce opponent of Arianism at the Council of Nicaea in 325 (according to the legend repeated in the Roman Martyrology, the prayers of James and Alexander of Constantinople were responsible for the death of Arius and his "bowels gushing out"), he was renowned for his great holiness, learning, and miracles. He died at Nisibis. July 15.

JAMES OF VORAGINE, BL. (c. 1230–98). Born at Viraggio (Varazze) near Genoa, Italy, he became a Dominican when fourteen, taught theology and Scripture, was named prior at Genoa, and in 1267 was elected provincial of Lombard Province, a post he was to hold for nineteen years. He was famous for his eloquent and powerful preaching and was named archbishop of Genoa in 1286 but refused the appointment. In 1288, Pope Nicholas IV appointed him to raise the interdict placed on Genoa for aiding a revolt against the King of Naples. In 1292 James was again elected archbishop of Genoa and again refused; this time he was obliged to accept. The six years of his reign were spent in an unsuccessful attempt to reconcile the warring Guelphs and Ghibellines, in aiding the needy, building and repairing churches, monasteries, and hospitals, and maintaining clerical discipline. He is reputed to have translated the Bible into Italian (though no copy has ever been found), but he is probably best known today as the author of one of the most famous and most popular collections of legends and lives of the saints ever written, *The Golden Legend*, which has appeared in hundreds of editions over the centuries since it was first published in Latin in 1470. He died on July 13, and his cult was confirmed by Pope Pius VII in 1816.

JAMES THE YOUNGER. *See* James the Less.

JANE FRANCES DE CHANTAL. *See* Chantal, Bl. Jane Frances de.

JANSSEN, BL. ARNOLD (1837–1909). Born at Goch, Germany, on November 5, he studied at Gaesdonck, Münster, and Bonn, and was ordained in 1861. He served as a parish priest, was chaplain of an Ursuline convent at Kempen in 1873, and two years later established the mission house of St. Michael at Steyl, Holland, which developed into the Society of the Divine Word, devoted to foreign missions, which received its formal approval in 1901. He founded the Servant Sisters of the Holy Ghost with the same purpose in 1889. He died at Steyl on January 15, and was beatified in 1975 by Pope Paul VI.

JANSSEN-POPPEL, NICHOLAS (d. 1572). *See* Vechel, Leonard.

JANUARIUS (d. c. 165). *See* Felicity.

JANUARIUS (d. 258). *See* Sixtus II.

JANUARIUS (d. c. 303). *See* Honoratus.

JANUARIUS (d. c. 304). *See* Faustus.

JANUARIUS (d. c. 305). According to legend, he was born at Naples, or perhaps Benevento, Italy, and was bishop of Benevento when Emperor Diocletian launched his persecution of the Christians. On hearing that his friend, Sossus, a deacon of Miseno, had been imprisoned for his faith at Pozzuoli with Proculus, a deacon of Pozzuoli, and two laymen, Euticius and Acutius, Januarius went to visit them in prison. He was arrested with his deacon, Festus, and a lector, Desiderius, on order of the governor of Campania. They were all thrown to the wild beasts, and when the animals would not harm them, they were beheaded near Pozzuoli. Januarius' relics ended up in Naples, and for the past four centuries a vial containing a solid red substance reputed to be his blood liquefies and often bubbles and boils when exposed in the cathedral there. No satisfactory scientific explanation has been adduced for this phenomenon, and devout Neapolitans accept it as a miracle. September 19.

JASON (1st century). In Acts 17:5–9, it is recounted that St. Paul stayed at Jason's house while in Salonika during his second missionary journey. Jason was a prominent convert to Christianity and is probably the same Jason referred to in Romans 16:21 with Sosipater. Greek legend has Jason the bishop of Tarsus, Cilicia, who, with Sosipater, evangelized Corfu, where Jason died. Syrian legend has him evangelizing the area around Apamea and martyred there by being thrown to wild beasts. July 12.

JAVOUHEY, BL. ANNE (1798–1851). Daughter of a well-to-do farmer, she was born at Jallanges, France, on November 10 and early decided to devote her life to the poor and the education of children. After failing to adjust to life in several convents (it was in a convent at Besançon in 1800 that she had a vision of black children, which was to so influence her later life), she and eight companions were clothed by the bishop of Autun in 1807 and with their purchase of a friary at Cluny in 1812, the Congregation of St. Joseph of Cluny dedicated to the education of children was founded. The congregation became famous for its successful teaching methods, and Anne established houses in Africa and South America as well as in Europe. She was in French Guiana, 1828–32, and in 1834 was sent there by the French Government to educate six hundred Guianan slaves who were to be set free. She left French Guiana in 1843 and spent her remaining years establishing new houses in Tahiti, Madagascar, and elsewhere. She died at Paris on July 15 and was beatified in 1950.

JEREMY (d. 309). *See* Elias.

JEROME (c. 342–420). Born at Strido, near Aquileia, Dalmatia, Eusebius Hieronymus Sophronius studied at Rome under Donatus, the famous pagan grammarian, acquired great skill and knowledge of the Latin, Greek, and great classical authors, and was baptized by Pope Liberius at Rome in 360. After further study at Treves and travel in Gaul, Jerome became an ascetic at Aquileia in 370, joining a group of scholars under Bishop Valerian, among whom was Rufinus. When a quarrel broke up the group, Jerome traveled in the East and in 374 settled at Antioch, where he heard Apollinarius of Laodicea lecture. A vision of Christ caused Jerome to go to Chalcis in the Syrian desert, after a serious illness, and he lived as a hermit for four years, praying and fasting, learning Hebrew, and writing a life of St. Paul of Thebes. On Jerome's return to Antioch, he was ordained by St. Paulinus and entered into the Meletian schism controversy, supporting Paulinus and denouncing the schism in a treatise, *Altercatio luciferiani et orthodoxi*. Jerome went to Constantinople to study Scripture under St. Gregory Nazianzen, and in 382 Jerome went to Rome with Paulinus and St. Epiphanius to attend a council and remained there as secretary to Pope Damasus. While there, at the suggestion of Damasus, he revised the Latin version of the four gospels, St. Paul's epistles, and the Psalms, and wrote *Adversum Helvidium*, denouncing a book by Helvidius declaring that Mary had had several children besides Jesus. Jerome encouraged a group of noble

ladies to study Scripture and made numerous enemies by his
sermons to them on the virtues of celibacy and by his fiery attacks on pagan life and some influential Romans. On the
death of Damasus, his protector and patron, in 384, his enemies and the vicious rumors that were circulated about him
(including a scandalous rumor concerning his relations with
St. Paula) decided him to return to the East, which he did
in 385. He visited Antioch, where Paula, Eustochium, and
others of the Roman group joined him, Egypt and Palestine
and in 386, they all settled at Bethlehem, where Paula built
three convents for women and a monastery for men, which
Jerome headed. Most of his time was devoted to his translation of the Bible into Latin from the original tongues, which
had been suggested to him by Pope Damasus, but Jerome
found time to become involved in numerous controversies. In
393, he wrote *Adversus Jovianianum* to refute Jovinian's belief that Mary had other children besides Jesus and attacking
the desirability of virginity; and Jerome's *Contra Vigilantium*
denounced Vigilantius' condemnation of celibacy and the
veneration of relics. But Jerome's bitterest controversy was
with Rufinus, his old friend from Aquileia, who supported
Origen and translated many of his works into Latin, when
Jerome attacked Origenism in *Apologetici adversus Rufinum*
in 395. Soon after he even attacked St. Augustine, who had
questioned Jerome's exegesis of the second chapter of St.
Paul's epistle to the Romans. Jerome's greatest achievement
was his translation of the Old Testament from Hebrew and
his revision of the Latin version of the New Testament in
390–405, a feat of scholarship unequaled in the early Church.
This version, called the Vulgate, was declared the official
Latin text of the Bible for Catholics by the Council of Trent,
and it was from it that almost all English Catholic translations were made until the middle of the twentieth century,
when scholars began to use original sources. It remained the
official Latin text of the Bible for the Catholic Church until
Pope John Paul II replaced it with the New Vulgate in 1979.
From 405 until his death he produced a series of biblical
commentaries notable for the range of linguistic and topo-
graphical material he brought to bear on his interpretations.
In 415, his denunciation of Pelagianism in *Dialogi contra
Pelagianos* caused a new furor, and in 416, groups of armed
Pelagian monks burned the monasteries at Bethlehem, though

he escaped unharmed, and left them poverty-stricken. He died at Bethlehem after a lingering illness on September 30. In addition to the works mentioned above, Jerome corresponded widely (some 120 of his letters, of great historical interest and importance, are still extant); he also compiled a bibliography of ecclesiastical writers, *De viris illustribus* and he translated and continued Eusebius' *Chronicle*. Jerome is venerated as a Doctor of the Church.

JEROME, BL. (d. 1632). *See* Ixida, Bl. Antony.

JOACHIM (1st century). Joachim is the name traditionally given to the father of Mary. According to the apocryphal and uncanonical *Protoevangelium of St. James,* he was born at Nazareth, married St. Anne at a youthful age, and when publicly reproached for their childlessness, fasted for forty days in the desert. An angel appeared to him and promised the couple a child. He died soon after witnessing the presentation of Jesus at the Temple. July 26.

JOAN OF ARC (1412-31). The daughter of Jacques d'Arc, a peasant farmer, she was the youngest of five children and was born on January 6 at Domrémy, France. A pious child, she was only thirteen when she experienced the first of her supernatural visions, which she described as a voice accompanied by a blaze of light. As time went on she identified the voices she heard as those of St. Michael, St. Catherine, St. Margaret, and others who she claimed revealed to her that her mission in life was to save France by aiding the Dauphin. Laughed at by Robert de Baudricourt, the French commander at Vaucouleurs, at first, his skepticism was overcome when her prophecies came true and the French were defeated in the Battle of Herrings outside Orléans in February 1429. He sent her to the Dauphin. Son of the insane King Charles VI, he had been kept from the French throne by the British in the Hundred Years' War and preferred the life of pleasure he had been pursuing since his father's death in 1422 to taking on the responsibilities of kingship if he mounted the throne. When she recognized him despite a disguise he had assumed and gave him a secret signal that he recognized, he was convinced of her mission. After an examination by theologians at Poitiers cleared her of all suspicion of heresy, she was allowed to lead an expedition to relieve besieged Orléans, and in a suit of white armor, she led her forces to victory. She followed this with a great victory over the British on June 18 and the capture of Troyes shortly after. Finally, on July 17, 1429, Charles was crowned as King Charles VII at Rheims, with Joan at his side. She failed in an attempt to capture Paris in August, and in the spring of 1430, she set out on a new campaign. She was captured on May 24 near Compiègne and sold to the British by John of Luxemburg on November 21. Charged with heresy and witchcraft before the court of Bishop Pierre Cauchon, her visions were declared to be of diabolical origin. She was tricked into signing a form of recantation on May 23, 1431, but when she again dressed in male attire, which she had agreed to abandon, she was condemned as a lapsed heretic and burned to death at the stake at Rouen on May 30, 1431, the victim of her enemies' determination to destroy her. A court appointed by Pope Callistus III found her innocent in 1456 and she was canonized in 1920. She is the second patron of France and is known as the Maid of Orléans.

JOAN OF AZA, BL. (d. c. 1190). Born in the castle of Aza, near Aranda, Old Castile, she was married to Felix de Guzman, warden of Calaruega in Burgos. They had four children, one of whom was St. Dominic. She was known for her physical and spiritual beauty, and on her death a cult developed, which was confirmed in 1828. Legend says she prayed for a son when her two eldest boys were grown and dreamed she bore a dog in her womb, while she was bearing Dominic, which would set the world afire with the torch in its mouth; the dog became the symbol of the Dominicans and gave rise to the expression *Domini canes* (watchdogs of the Lord) to describe the Dominicans. August 8.

JOAN OF FRANCE. *See* Joan of Valois.

JOAN OF LESTONNAC. *See* Lestonnac, Joan de.

JOAN OF PORTUGAL, BL. (1452–90). Daughter of King Alphonsus V of Portugal and Elizabeth of Coimbra, she was born at Lisbon and became heir to the throne because of the illness of her brother and the death of her mother. She lived austerely from her early youth in the midst of the court and was refused permission by her father to enter the religious life. She was regent when her father and brother went to war against the Moors, and when they defeated the Moors in 1471, her father, in the first flush of victory, granted her request and she entered the Benedictine convent of Odivellas in 1472; later she transferred to the Dominican convent at Aveiro. Because of her family's objections she was unable to take vows until 1485, when the succession to the throne was settled, repeatedly refusing offers of marriage from royal suitors in the meanwhile. At Aveiro, she lived as a simple nun and devoted her income to charity and to redeeming captives. She died there, and her cult was authorized in 1693. May 12.

JOAN OF VALOIS (1464–1505). Sometimes called Joan of France, she was the deformed daughter of King Louis XI and Charlotte of Savoy. She was married to the King's cousin, Duke Louis of Orléans, in 1476 and saved the duke's life when her brother King Charles VIII determined to execute him for rebellion. When the duke ascended the throne as King Louis XII, he had Pope Alexander VI declare his marriage to Joan void on the grounds that he had been forced to marry her by King Louis XI. Joan offered no objections and retired to the duchy of Berry given her by Louis and lived a secluded life of prayer at Bourges, where in 1501 she founded the Annonciades of Bourges, a contemplative order of nuns; she was professed in 1504. Joan suffered much throughout her life for her deformed body, which she accepted with great patience and equanimity. She was canonized in 1950. February 4.

JOANNA (1st century). Wife of Chuza, steward of King Herod Antipas, tetrarch of Galilee, she was one of the women who helped provide for Jesus and the apostles (Luke 8:3) and was one of the three women who discovered the empty tomb of Jesus on the first Easter morning (Luke 24:10). May 24.

JOGUES, ISAAC (1607–46). Born at Orléans, France, of well-to-do parents, he studied at the Jesuit school there and joined the Jesuits in 1624. After his ordination in 1636, he requested and was sent to Quebec. He worked with great success among the Hurons until 1642, when a war party of Iroquois, the traditional enemies of the Hurons, captured a group of Jesuits, among them Isaac and René Goupil, who was murdered. After a year of terrible torture and mutilation, Isaac escaped with the aid of the Dutch at Albany to New York and returned to France. At his request, he was sent back to Quebec in 1644. Two years later, he and Jean de Lalande set out for Iroquois country after a peace treaty with the Iroquois had been signed. They were captured by a Mohawk war party and he was tomahawked and beheaded at Ossernenon, near Albany, New York, on October 18; Jean de Lalande suffered martyrdom the next day. They were canonized with a group of other Jesuits in 1930 by Pope Pius XI as the Martyrs of North America. October 19.

JOHN I (d. 526). Born in Tuscany, he became an archdeacon in Rome, and on August 13, 523, was elected Pope, succeeding St. Hormisdas. Despite his protests, he was sent by King Theodoric of the Ostrogoths, a champion of Arianism, to Constantinople to secure a moderation of Emperor Justin's decree of 523 against the Arians, compelling them to surrender to Catholics the churches they held. Theodoric also resented the increasing cordiality between the Latin and Greek churches, fearing it might lead to the restoration of imperial Byzantine authority in Italy, which he ruled. John was warmly received by Justin and huge crowds but returned to find that Theodoric had murdered the great philosopher Boethius and his father-in-law, Symmachus. Theodoric had John arrested as soon as he landed in Italy and had him imprisoned at Ravenna, where he died of ill treatment on May 18 or 19. May 18.

JOHN THE ALMSGIVER (c. 550–c. 619). Of a noble family, he was born at Amathus, Cyprus, the son of Epiphanius, governor of the island. He married when quite young but when his wife and child died he entered the religious life, gave his income to the poor, and became widely known for his holiness and charity. He was named patriarch of Alexandria in 608, immediately distributed the wealth of his see to aid the poor, helped refugees from Syria and Jerusalem fleeing the marauding Persians in 614, visited the sick in hospitals, and built churches. He fought simony, ended corruption in his diocese, was generous to those in difficulty, and worked to alleviate the onerous new taxes levied by Nicetas, the governor. His concern for and financial aid to the poor were so well known he was surnamed "the

Almsgiver." Throughout his patriarchate, he labored to end monophysitism and restore orthodoxy by peaceful means. He was forced to leave Alexandria when the Persians drew near to the city and was on the way to Constantinople with Nicetas to visit Emperor Heraclius when a vision of his own impending death caused him to return to his native Amathus, where he died on November 11. January 23.

JOHN OF ÁVILA (1499–1569). Born of wealthy parents at Almodóvar del Campo, New Castile, Spain, on January 6, he was sent to the University of Salamanca when fourteen to study law. He was attracted to the religious life instead and left to live a life of austerity. Three years later he went to Alcalà to study philosophy under Dominic Soto and met Peter Guerrero and was ordained. Left wealthy when his parents died, he disposed of his wealth to aid the poor. He soon achieved fame as a powerful preacher and served as a missionary in Andalusia, drawing huge crowds to his missions. He made enemies by his fearless denunciation of evil even in high places, which led to his imprisonment by the Inquisition at Seville for his harshness and preaching that the rich could not reach heaven. When the charges were dismissed and he was released, his popularity reached new heights. He continued preaching all over Spain and was spiritual adviser to St. Teresa of Ávila, St. John of the Cross, St. Francis Borgia, and St. Peter of Alcantara, among others. John of Ávila died at Montilla on May 10, and was canonized by Pope Paul VI in 1970.

JOHN THE BAPTIST (1st century). Son of Zachary, a priest of the Temple in Jerusalem, and Elizabeth, a kinswoman of Mary who visited her, he was probably born at Ain-Karim southwest of Jerusalem after the angel Gabriel had told Zachary that his wife would bear a child even though she was an old woman. He lived as a hermit in the desert of Judea until about A.D. 27, when he was thirty, he began to preach on the banks of the Jordan against the evils of the times and called men to penance and baptism "for the kingdom of heaven is close at hand." He attracted large crowds, and when Christ came to him John recognized him as the Messiah and baptized him, saying, "It is I who need baptism from you" (Matt. 3:14). When Christ left to preach in Galilee, John continued preaching in the Jordan Valley. Fearful of his great power with the people, Herod Antipas, tetrarch of Perea and Galilee, had him arrested and imprisoned at Machaerus Fortress on the Dead Sea when John denounced his adulterous and incestuous marriage with Herodias, wife of his half brother Philip. John was beheaded at the request of Salome, daughter of Herodias, who asked for his head at the instigation of her mother. John inspired many of his followers to follow Christ when he designated him "the lamb of God," among them Andrew and John, who came to know Christ through John's preaching. John is presented in the New Testament as the last of the Old Testament prophets and the precursor of the Messiah. June 24 (August 29 for his beheading).

JOHN BAPTIST DE LA SALLE. *See* La Salle, John Baptist de.

JOHN BOSCO. *See* Bosco, John.

JOHN OF BRIDLINGTON. *See* Thwing, John.

JOHN CANTIUS (1390–1473). Born on June 23 at Kanti, Poland, and also known as John of Kanti, he studied at the University of Cracow, was ordained, and then was appointed lecturer in Scripture at the university. He became famed for his preaching but was forced from his position by jealous associates and became parish priest at Olkusz. Fearful of the responsibility of the care of souls, he returned to Cracow as professor of Scripture, a position he held until his death at Cracow on December 24. He was noted for his scholarship, learning, austerities, and concern for the poor, was declared the patron of Poland and Lithuania by Pope Clement XII in 1737, and was canonized in 1767 by Pope Clement XIII. December 23.

JOHN OF CAPISTRANO (1386–1456). Born at Capistrano, Abruzzi, Italy, he studied law at Perugia, was appointed governor of that city in 1412, and married. Imprisonment during a war between Perugia and Malatesta caused him to change his life. He obtained a dispensation to enter a religious order, despite his marriage, and publicly repented of his sins. In 1416, he joined the Friars Minor, studied under Bernardino of Siena, and was ordained in 1420. He began preaching and met with immediate success, drawing thousands to his sermons and converting many more to a more religious way of life. He also labored with his friend Bernardino of Siena to heal the wounds among the Franciscans, drawing up the plans approved by the general chapter of the Franciscans held at Assisi in 1430 for a short-lived reunion of the various groups in the Order. The following year he was active at the Observant chapter at Bologna, and according to Gonzaga was appointed commissary general. In 1430, John had helped elect Bernardino vicar general of the Observants and soon after met St. Colette in France and joined her efforts to reform the Poor Clares. He was inquisitor in the proceedings against the Fraticelli and the charges made against the Gesuats and was frequently sent on papal diplomatic missions: In 1439 he was legate to Milan and Burgundy to oppose the claims of antipope Felix V; in 1446 he was sent on a mission to the King of France; and in 1451 he was selected by Pope Nicholas V, in response to an appeal from Emperor Frederick, to go as commissary and inquisitor general with twelve Franciscans to combat the Hussites. He preached in Bavaria, Saxony, and Poland, bringing about great revivals of the faith, though some of the methods he employed against the heretics have been severely criticized. His campaign ended when the Turks captured Constantinople in 1453, and he devoted his energies to preaching a crusade against them. Unsuccessful in Bavaria and Austria, he joined Janos Hunyady in exhorting the Hungarians to resist the invading Turks and personally led the left wing of the Christian army at the Battle of Belgrade in 1456. The failure of the Turks to capture the city in the ensuing siege saved Europe from being overrun by the Turks. He died at Villach, Austria, on October 23 of the plague that followed, as had Hunyady a few weeks earlier. He was canonized in 1690.

JOHN CASSIAN (c. 360–c. 433). Probably born in Provence, though Gennadius, writing in the fifth century, says, probably erroneously, that he was born in Scythia, of wealthy parents, and about 380, went to Palestine with a friend, Germanus. They became monks at Bethlehem and then went to Egypt, where they lived as hermits under Archebius for a time and then went to Skete. In about 400 he became a follower of St. John Chrysostom at Constantinople and was ordained a deacon by him. When Chrysostom was deposed, he was one of the delegation that went to Rome in 405 to defend him before Pope Innocent I and may have been ordained a priest while there. Several years later he went to Marseilles and lived there until his death. He founded two monasteries about 415, importing to Gaul the plan and spirit of Egyptian asceticism and spirituality in them. He wrote two books of instructions for his monks, *Institutes of the Monastic Life*, setting forth rules for the monastic life and listing eight chief hindrances to a monk's perfection, and *Conferences on the Egyptian Monks*, conversations with the leaders of Eastern monasticism. His *Institutes* greatly impressed St. Benedict and through him were to affect Western monasticism for centuries to come. John's *Conferences* was censured by Pope Pelagius for containing erroneous doctrine in some of its passages. His *De Incarnatione Domini*, against Nestorius, was written at the request of a Roman archdeacon who later became Pope Leo the Great, but it was evidently written in haste and does not compare with the other two works. In it he denounces Pelagianism but is considered the founder of semi-Pelagianism for his views on free will in several sections of the *Conferences*, for which he was condemned by St. Augustine. He died at Marseilles on July 23. He is considered a saint in the Eastern Church but has never been canonized in the West.

JOHN CHRYSOSTOM (c. 347–407). Born at Antioch, Syria, the son of an imperial military officer, he studied rhetoric under the famous pagan rhetorician Libanius at Antioch and theology under Diodorus of Tarsus, leader of the Antiochene school. John was baptized by Bishop Meletius in about 369 and in about 374 became a hermit under St. Basil and Theodore of Mopsuestia. John returned home when his austere life in a cave undermined his health, became a deacon in 381, and was ordained in 386 by Bishop Flavian of Antioch, whom he served the next twelve years. He became famed for his preaching, which earned him the sobriquet Chrysostom (golden-mouthed) and had a tremendous effect on the spiritual life of the city. Beginning in 390, he preached a series of homilies on books of the New Testament (including eighty-eight on John, ninety on Matthew, and thirty-two on Romans), which established him as one of the great expositors of the Christian faith. In 398, against his wishes, he was named Patriarch of Constantinople and at once began to reform the Church there. He made extraordinary donations to the poor, abolished ecclesiastical pomp and luxury, sent missionaries to the East, and made friends but also many enemies by his honesty, his asceticism, and his firm opposition to idolatry, immoral entertainment, and aristocratic extravagances. Among the enemies he made were Empress Eudoxia, who resented his criticism of her vanity, lack of charity, and dress; Gainas, commander-in-chief of the army and leader of the Arians, when John curbed his exactions; the churchmen he antagonized by curtailing their power and restricting their extravagant lifestyle; and Archbishop Theophilus of Alexandria, who had aspired to be Patriarch of Constantinople when John was appointed. In 403, led by Theophilus, thirty-six hostile bishops at the Synod of the Oak condemned him on twenty-nine charges (among them an unjustified charge of Origenism and for an imagined attack on the Empress in a sermon in which he had denounced the luxury of women) and ordered him deposed and exiled. Civil war threatened and when an earthquake shook the city, Eudoxia revoked the banishment order. Soon after, though, when John denounced the excesses of the public games held to celebrate the erection of a silver statue of Eudoxia, she renewed her enmity. On June 24, 404, Emperor Arcadius ordered John into exile at Cucusus, Armenia, despite the support of the people of Constantinople, Pope Innocent I, and the whole Western Church. From Cucusus, John wrote at least 238 letters that are still extant. Arcadius remained adamant about his banishment, and five bishops sent by the Pope and Emperor Honorius were imprisoned in Thrace by Theophilus' followers, who knew they had been sent to demand the restoration of John to his patriarchal see. Meanwhile, John was ordered exiled to a more distant location, Pityus, at the far end of the Black Sea, and died on the way at Comana, Pontus, on September 14 from exhaustion brought on by long forced marches on foot in the stifling heat and inclement weather. In addition to his sermons and letters, several of John's treatises are still extant, among them *The Priesthood*, which he wrote soon after his ordination in 386. He was declared a Doctor of the Universal Church at the Council of Chalcedon in 451 and was named patron of preachers by Pope Pius X. September 13.

JOHN CLIMACUS (c. 569–c. 649). Probably born in Syria, though perhaps in Palestine, he joined the monks on Mount Sinai when sixteen and was professed four years later.

He lived as a hermit nearby, and later when he was thirty-five continued his eremitical life at Thole. He was learned in Scripture and the Church Fathers and became a sought-after spiritual adviser, noted for his ability to console distraught souls. When seventy years old, and over his objections, he was elected abbot of the monks on Mount Sinai and ruled until shortly before he died in the hermitage he had lived in for forty years. He is particularly known as the author of *Scala Paradisi* (*Ladder of Paradise*, sometimes called *Ladder of Perfection*), describing the thirty steps of the ladder required to attain religious perfection, which was enormously popular during the Middle Ages. He died on Mount Sinai on March 30. He is also known as John Scholasticus.

JOHN OF THE CROSS (1542–91). Born at Fontiveros, Old Castile, Spain, on June 24, Juan de Yepes y Alvarez was the youngest son of a silk weaver. John was educated at the catechism school at Medina del Campo, where his mother settled when his father died soon after his birth. When seventeen, he began working for the director of a hospital at Medina while at the same time studying at the Jesuit college there, 1559–63. He joined the Carmelites at Medina in 1563, taking the name Juan de Santo Matía, continued his studies at Salamanca, and was ordained in 1567. He met St. Teresa on a visit home to Medina and told her he was contemplating becoming a Carthusian to embrace a life of deeper solitude and prayer than that offered by the Carmelites, but she persuaded him to remain in the Carmelites and join her efforts to effect a reform in the Order. On November 28, 1568, John and four others, including the former prior of the Carmelite monastery in Medina, Antonio de Heredia, founded the first men's house of the reform at Duruelo, the beginning of the Discalced Carmelites, and John took the name John of the Cross. In 1570, he became rector of the newly established Discalced house of studies at Alcalá and in 1572 became spiritual director of Teresa's Convent of the Incarnation at Avila, where he spent the next five years. Meanwhile, dissension between the Calced and the Discalced Carmelites reached a climax, and in 1577 John was arrested by the Calced Carmelites and ordered to abandon the reform; when he refused to do so, he was imprisoned at Toledo. After being subjected to great hardships in prison and intense pressure during the next nine months, he escaped. In 1579, the Discalced Carmelites

were recognized and a separate province was established. He
founded and became head of the Discalced college at Baeza,
1579–81; was elected prior of Granada in 1582; was appointed provincial of Andalusia in 1585; was elected prior at
Segovia in 1587; and established several houses of his Order
during these years. In 1590 controversy among the Discalceds
broke out into the open, and the following year the Madrid
general chapter deprived John of all his offices for his support
of the moderates in the bitter dispute that had been raging in
the Order for nine years and sent him as a simple monk to La
Peñuela Monastery in Andalusia, though his enemies really
wanted him expelled from the Order. Soon after he arrived at
La Peñuela, he contracted a fever, went to the priory at
Ubeda for medical attention, and died there on December 14.
John of the Cross is now recognized as one of the great mystics of all time, and his writings are among the world's
greatest spiritual classics. Among them are *Dark Night of the
Soul*, which he wrote while in prison in Toledo, where he also
wrote parts of his *Spiritual Canticle* and *Living Flame of
Love*, which he probably finished at Granada. He was canon-
ized in 1726, and was proclaimed a Doctor of the Church by
Pope Pius XI in 1926.

JOHN DAMASCENE (c. 675–c. 749). Born of a wealthy
Christian family at Damascus, he spent all his life under
Mohammedan rule. He was educated by a brilliant monk
named Cosmas, who had been captured in a Mohammedan
raid on Sicily and was bought by John's father, Mansur. John
succeeded his father as chief revenue officer and counselor of
Caliph Abdul Malek. In 726, when Emperor Leo the Isaurian
issued his first edict prohibiting the veneration of images,
John defended the practice and soon became a leading champion of the Catholic position, arousing the bitter enmity of
the Byzantine Emperors, who could not molest him physically, since he was under the caliph's rule and protection. He
resigned his position about 726, and with his adopted brother,
another Cosmas, became a monk at St. Sabas' *laura* outside
Jerusalem. He was denounced at a pseudosynod in Constantinople by iconoclast Emperor Constantine Copronymus,
successor of Emperor Leo the Isaurian, but was ordained in
Constantinople by Patriarch John V, who also appointed
Cosmas bishop of Majuma. John soon after returned to the
monastery and led the defenders of orthodoxy and ex-

pounders of the Catholic position in the iconoclasm controversy. Among his outstanding writings are the *Fount of Wisdom*, on philosophy, heresies, and the orthodox faith; *De Fide Orthodoxa*, a comprehensive presentation of the teachings of the Greek Fathers on the main Christian doctrines; and *Sacra Parallela*, a compilation of scriptural and patristic texts on Christian moral and ascetical works. His writings, especially his *De Fide Orthodoxa*, one of the most notable theological works of antiquity, has had great influence on theologians of both East and West. He also wrote poetry, and some of his poems are used in the Greek liturgy. The elegance of his Greek caused him to be called Chrysorrhoas (gold-pouring). He died at Sabas, probably on December 5, the last of the Greek Fathers, and was made a Doctor of the Church by Pope Leo XIII in 1890. December 4.

JOHN THE DIVINE. *See* John the Evangelist.

JOHN THE DWARF (5th century). A native of Basta in Lower Egypt, he retired to the desert of Skete when a young man and became a disciple of St. Poemen. John lived a life of obedience, humility, and austerity the rest of his days. When he first arrived at Skete he is reputed to have watered a stick stuck in the ground unquestioningly when his spiritual director ordered him to do so; in the third year of his ministrations, it bore fruit. He left Skete to escape marauding Berbers and settled on Mount Quolzum, where he died. October 17.

JOHN EUDES. *See* Eudes, John.

JOHN THE EVANGELIST (c. 6–c. 104). Born in Galilee, the son of Zebedee and Salome and younger brother of James the Greater, he was a fisherman on Lake Genesareth until with James he was called by Christ to follow him (Matt. 4:21–22; Mark 1:19–20). He was the youngest of the apostles. James the Greater and John were called "Sons of Thunder" by the Lord because of their volatile temperaments (Mark 3:17), and John became the beloved disciple (John 13:23; 19:26; 20:2ff.; 21:7; 21:24). That he was one of those closest to Christ was attested to by the fact that only he, Peter, and James were present at such events as the Transfiguration (Matt. 17:1; Mark 9:2; Luke 9:28), the healing of Peter's mother-in-law (Mark 1:29–31), the raising of Jairus' daughter from the dead (Mark 5:22–43; Luke 8:40–56), and the agony in the garden of Gethsemane (Matt. 26:37ff.; Mark 14:33ff.). He and Peter were sent to prepare the Passover (Luke 22:8ff.) and were the first apostles at the tomb of the risen Christ. He was the only apostle at the Crucifixion, where Jesus placed Mary in his care (John 19:25–27). He was imprisoned with Peter and appeared before the Sanhedrin (Acts 4:1–21), accompanied Peter to Samaria (Acts 8:14) to transmit the Holy Spirit to the new converts, and was at the Council of Jerusalem in 49. Soon after, he went to Asia Minor and in all probability was present at the passing away of Mary. He was named, with Peter and James, by Paul as "these leaders, these pillars" of the Church in Jerusalem (Gal. 2:9). According to tradition, he went to Rome during the reign of Emperor Domitian, miraculously escaped martyrdom (he emerged unscathed from a cauldron of boiling oil, according to Tertullian), and was exiled to the island of Patmos, where he wrote Revelation. He returned to Ephesus on the death of Domitian in 96, wrote the fourth gospel and three epistles, and died there, the only one of the apostles who did not suffer martyrdom. Although traditionally he has been considered the author of the fourth gospel, Revelation, and the three epistles, some modern scholars questioned his authorship; however, the preponderance of opinion among most contemporary biblical scholars now accepts the early tradition that he is the author of these New Testament books. John is often surnamed "the Divine" because of his theological brilliance and is represented in art as an eagle for the soaring majesty of his gospel. December 27.

JOHN THE GEORGIAN. *See* John the Iberian.

JOHN OF GOD (1495–1550). Born at Montemoro Novo, Portugal, on March 8, he served as a soldier in the wars between France and Spain and against the Turks in Hungary, as overseer of slaves in Morocco, and as a shepherd near Seville. At forty he decided to make amends for his dissolute life by going to Africa to rescue Christian slaves. Instead he accompanied a Portuguese family from Gibraltar to Ceuta, Barbary, and when he returned to Gibraltar, he became a peddler of holy pictures and religious books. He opened a shop in Granada in 1538, went berserk when a sermon by St. John of

Avila filled him with remorse and guilt for his wastrel life,
and was confined to a lunatic asylum. Helped by John, he
found a new purpose in life and on his release in 1539
devoted himself to helping the sick and the poor and opened
a house to serve the sick poor (the beginnings of the Order
of Brothers Hospitalers, also known as the Brothers of St.
John of God). His holiness and dedication brought donations
from the wealthy to carry on his work. He died in Granada,
Spain, on March 8, and was canonized in 1690. He is the patron of the sick, nurses, and hospitals.

JOHN GUALBERT (d. 1073). Of the noble Visdomini
family, he was born at Florence, Italy, and had his life
changed when, bent on revenge for the murder of his brother
Hugh, he met the murderer, drew his sword to kill him, and
then forgave him. He became a Benedictine monk at San
Miniato del Monte Monastery, left to seek greater solitude
when it seemed he might be made abbot, and while at the
hermitage of Camaldoli decided to found a monastery of his
own, which he did at Vallombrosa (Vallis Umbrosa), near
Fiesole. Following the primitive rule of St. Benedict, the
Vallumbrosans, as his followers came to be called, stressed
charity and poverty and admitted lay brothers, an innovation
for religious congregations of that time. John became known
for his aid to the poor, his fierce opposition to simony, his
miracles, gift of prophecy, and spiritual wisdom, which attracted great crowds seeking his advice. The Vallumbrosans
soon spread all through Italy, particularly in Tuscany and
Lombardy. He died at Passignano, near Florence, and was
canonized in 1193.

JOHN THE IBERIAN (d. c. 1002). Of a noble Iberian
(Georgian, U.S.S.R.) family and also known as John the
Georgian, he was an outstanding military commander until
middle age, when he resigned his position and with his wife's
consent left her and their family to become a monk on Mount
Olympus in Bithynia. He went to Constantinople for his son
Euthymius, who with other young Iberian men was being
held hostage by the Emperor, and brought him back to
Olympus with him. Their reputation for holiness attracted so
many disciples that they retired to St. Athanasius *laura* on
Mount Athos in Macedonia in quest of greater solitude. With
John's brother-in-law, retired General John Thornikios, who

had become a monk, the father and son, about 980, founded a monastery for Iberians on Mount Athos, the beginning of the famous Iviron Monastery, with John as abbot. On the death of Thornikios, who had handled all the details of running the monastery, John and several of his disciples set out for Spain but were intercepted and brought to Constantinople, where Emperor Constantine VIII persuaded him to return to Athos. He was confined to bed the last years of his life and died at Iviron, after designating Euthymius as the new abbot. July 12.

JOHN OF KANTI. *See* John Cantius.

JOHN OF MATHA (1160–1213). Born at Faucon, Provence, on June 23, he was educated at Aix, but on his return to Faucon lived as a hermit for a time. He then went to Paris where he received his doctorate in theology, was ordained there in 1197, and then joined St. Felix of Valois in his hermitage at Cerfroid. He confided to Felix his idea of founding a religious order to ransom Christian prisoners from the Moslems, and late in 1197, the two went to Rome and received the approval of Pope Innocent III for the Order of the Most Holy Trinity (the Trinitarians), with John as superior, in 1198; they also secured the approval of King Philip Augustus of France. The Order flourished, spread to France, Spain, Italy, and England, sent many of its members to North Africa, and redeemed many captives. John died at Rome on December 17, and his cult was approved in 1655 and again in 1694. February 8.

JOHN NEPOMUCEN (c. 1340–93). Born at Nepomuk, Bohemia, he used the name of his native town for his surname instead of his family name of Wölflein or Welflin. He studied at the University of Prague and was ordained. In time, he became vicar general of Archbishop John of Genzenstein at Prague and according to tradition incurred the enmity of dissolute King Wenceslaus IV when he refused to reveal what the Queen had told him in confession. He became involved in a dispute between Wenceslaus and the archbishop when the King, in 1393, sought to convert a Benedictine abbey into a cathedral for a new diocese he proposed to create for a favorite when the aged abbot died. The archbishop and John thwarted him by approving the election of a new abbot immediately on the death of the old abbot. At a meeting with John and other clerics, Wenceslaus flew into a rage, tortured them so that John was seriously injured, and then on March 20 had him murdered and thrown into the Moldau River at Prague. He was canonized in 1729 and is the patron of confessors and principal patron of Bohemia. May 16.

JOHN OF PENNA, BL. (c. 1193–1271). Born at Penna, Ancona, Italy, he joined the Franciscans at Recanati about 1213 and was sent to France, where he worked for a quarter century in Provence, founding several Franciscan houses there. About 1242 he returned to Italy, where he spent the last thirty years of his life, mainly in retirement, although he did serve as guardian several times. He experienced visions and had the gift of prophecy, but was also afflicted with extended periods of spiritual aridity. He died on April 3, and his cult was approved in 1806. His life is described in Chapters 4 and 5 of *The Little Flowers of St. Francis*.

JOHN SCHOLASTICUS. *See* John Climacus.

JOLENTA, BL. (d. 1299). Daughter of King Bela IV of Hungary, she was raised by her elder sister Bl. Cunegund, wife of Boleslaus V of Poland. Jolenta married Duke Boleslaus of Kalisz, and when he died in 1279, she, Cunegund (now widowed), and one of her daughters retired to the Poor Clare convent that Cunegund had founded at Sandeck. Later Jolenta became superior of the convent at Gnesen, which she had founded, and died there. Her cult was approved in 1827 and she is known as Helen of Poland in Poland. June 12.

JONES, JOHN (d. 1598). Born of a Catholic family at Clynog Fawr, Carnarvonshire, Wales, he was ordained at Rheims and in 1587 was working among the Catholic prisoners in Marshalsea Prison in London. He was discovered, imprisoned at Wisbech Castle, but managed to escape to the Continent. He joined the Franciscans of the Observance, probably at Pontoise, France, and was professed at Ara Coeli Convent in Rome. He received permission to return to England in 1592, using the alias John Buckley, worked in London and other parts of England, and was arrested again in

1596. He was imprisoned for two years (he brought Bl. John Rigby back to the faith while in prison), and when convicted of being a Catholic priest guilty of treason for having been ordained abroad and returned to England, he was hanged, drawn, and quartered at Southwark in London on July 12. He was canonized by Pope Paul VI in 1970 as one of the Forty Martyrs of England and Wales.

JOSAPHAT (c. 1580–1623). Born at Vladimir, Volhynia, Poland, John Kunsevich in his youth became an apprentice to a merchant at Vilna. Interested in pursuing a religious life, he refused a partnership in the business and marriage to his master's daughter and in 1604 became a monk in the Ukrainian Order of St. Basil at Holy Trinity Monastery at Vilna with a friend, Joseph Rutsky, taking the name Josaphat. He was ordained a priest of the Byzantine rite in 1609 and soon achieved a reputation as a compelling preacher and a leading advocate for the union of the Ukrainian Church with Rome. His friend Rutsky became abbot of Holy Trinity, and Josaphat was sent to found new houses in Poland, but returned in 1614 as abbot of the monastery when Rutsky was named metropolitan of Kiev. In 1617, Josaphat was named bishop of Vitebsk, Russia, with the right of succession to Polotsk, and a few months later succeeded to that see when Archbishop Brolnitsky died. He found the diocese in a deplorable condition—widespread opposition to Rome, married clergy, lax discipline, churches in a rundown state—and called synods to put into effect his reforms, which by 1620 were effective. At that time, one Metetius Smotritsky was appointed archbishop of Polotsk by a group of dissident bishops and began to sow the seeds of dissension, claiming that Josaphat was really a Latin priest and declaring that Roman Catholicism was not for the Ruthenian people. Riots broke out as people chose sides, and Josaphat was falsely accused of fomenting trouble and using force against the dissidents by the chancellor of Lithuania, Leo Sapiaha, a Catholic, thus stirring up further dissent. Not being given the support he should have received from the Latin bishops of Poland because of his insistence on maintaining Byzantine rites and customs, he went to Vitebsk, the hotbed of the opposition, in 1623 to meet it head on despite threats of violence against him. On November 12, a priest named Elias who had harassed Josaphat several times, was locked up by one of Josaphat's deacons when Elias again abused the archbishop. A mob assembled demanding Elias' release, and though Josaphat released Elias, Josaphat was beaten and shot to death on November 12 by the mob and his body thrown into the Divina River at Vitebsk, Russia. He was canonized in 1867, the first Eastern saint to be formally canonized.

✱ **JOSEPH** (1st century). Our only reliable information about Joseph is to be found in the Infancy narratives of Matthew 1–2 and Luke 1–2. According to them Joseph is of royal descent from David. Joseph's family came from Bethlehem in Judea but he had moved to Nazareth in Galilee, where he was a builder. He was betrothed to Mary, became alarmed when he found Mary was pregnant though she had not lived with him, and was dissuaded from divorcing her by the angel of the Lord who told him her pregnancy was "by the Holy Spirit." He was with Mary at the birth of Jesus and the visit by the Magi at Bethlehem. He took Mary and the child to Egypt to escape Herod's massacre of the infants, and after the death of Herod, brought them back to Nazareth. He and Mary had Jesus circumcised and presented to the Lord in the Temple in Jerusalem. When Jesus was twelve Joseph and Mary took him to Jerusalem, lost him, and found him discoursing with the doctors in the Temple. Thereafter the name of Joseph is absent from the New Testament except in Luke 4:22, where he is mentioned by name as the father of Jesus. Joseph was probably dead by the time of the Passion and death of Christ; the apocryphal *Protoevangelium of James* says he was an old man when he married Mary. Special veneration to Joseph began in the East, where the apocryphal *History of Joseph* enjoyed great popularity in the fourth to the seventh centuries. In the West the ninth-century Irish *Félire* of Oengus mentions a commemoration, but it was not until the fifteenth century that veneration of Joseph in the West became widespread, when his feast was introduced into the Roman calendar in 1479; his devotion was particularly popularized by St. Teresa and St. Francis de Sales. Joseph was declared Patron of the Universal Church by Pope Pius IX in 1870; a model for fathers of families by Pope Leo XIII, who confirmed that his pre-eminent sanctity places him next to the Blessed Virgin among the saints, in his encyclical *Quanquam pluries* in 1889; a protector of workingmen by Pope Benedict XV; the patron of social justice by Pope Pius

XI; and in 1955, Pope Pius XII established the feast of St. Joseph the Worker on May 1. March 19.

JOSEPH OF ARIMATHEA (1st century). Mentioned in all four gospels, he was a secret follower of Jesus for fear of the Jewish authorities. He was present at the Crucifixion, and after the death of Jesus persuaded Pontius Pilate to let him have Jesus' body. He wrapped it in fine linen and herbs and laid it in a tomb carved from rock in the side of a hill. Beyond that all that is known of him is from medieval legend, according to which he accompanied Philip to Gaul to preach the gospel and was sent to England at the head of twelve missionaries. Supposedly inspired by the archangel Gabriel, they built a church made of wattles in honor of our Lady on an island given them by the King of England, which in time became Glastonbury Abbey; supposedly Joseph died there. Pious legend also had him catch the blood of Christ while he was dying on the cross; Joseph is also supposed to have inherited the chalice used at the Last Supper. March 17.

JOSEPH BARSABBAS (1st century). A follower of Christ and surnamed "the Just," he was probably one of the seventy-two disciples. In Acts 1:23–26 he was nominated with Matthias (who was chosen) to take Judas' place among the twelve apostles. July 20.

JOSEPH CALASANCTIUS. *See* Calasanz, Joseph.

JOSEPH OF CUPERTINO (1603–63). Born of poor parents at Cupertino, Italy, on June 17, Joseph Desa was an apprentice shoemaker in his youth, was refused admittance by the Conventual Franciscans when he was seventeen, and then became a Capuchin lay brother. He was dismissed after eight months for clumsiness and low intelligence but was later accepted as a servant and Franciscan tertiary by the Conventual Franciscans at Grottela, where he was to remain for the next seventeen years. He was admitted as a novice in 1625 and though he was a poor scholar, was ordained in 1628. He became famous for his ecstasies, miracles, and supernatural gifts, particularly the gift of levitation, which he is reputed to have experienced some seventy times, all reported by numerous reputable eyewitnesses. He was accused of seeking publicity, and though even Pope Urban VIII was impressed by his holiness and sincerity, he was sent to Assisi in 1639. For a time he experienced the desolation of spiritual aridity and suffered great temptations but gradually he regained great spiritual joy and happiness. Despite the attempts to keep him secluded in Assisi, his fame spread all over Europe, and in 1653 the Inquisition of Perugia sent him to an isolated Capuchin friary in the hills of Pietrarossa, where he was cut off completely from communication with the outside world. But word he was there soon attracted pilgrims and he was again moved—this time to another Capuchin house, at Fossombrone. Finally, in 1657, he was allowed to return to his own order at Osimo and again kept in the strictest seclusion; he experienced daily supernatural manifestations until his death there on September 18. He was canonized in 1767 and is the patron of air travelers and pilots.

JUDAS QUIRIACUS. *See* Cyriacus.

JUDE (1st century). In the list of the Twelve in Luke 6:16 and Acts 1:13, he is called Jude; in the lists in Matthew and Mark appears the name Thaddeus, and scholars believe they are the same. In the Epistle of Jude, the author calls himself the brother of James, and in Matthew 13:55 and Mark 6:3, Jude is mentioned as among the brethren of the Lord. Some modern scholars believe that Jude of the Twelve and Jude the author of the Epistle of Jude are different individuals (in verse 17, the author refers to the apostles in the past tense, which seems unlikely if he was one of them). According to legend, he preached in Mesopotamia, and the apocryphal *Passion of Simon and Jude* describes the preaching and martyrdom of those two apostles in Persia. October 28.

JUGAN, BL. JEANNE (1792–1879). Born at Petites-Croix, Brittany, France, on October 25, she worked as a domestic and then in hospital work. In 1842, with two women who aided her, Virginia Tredaniel and Marie Jumet, she founded the Little Sisters of the Poor with Jeanne as superior. Re-elected in early December in 1843, she was suddenly deposed two weeks later by Fr. Le Pailleur, the community's moderator. In 1845 she received an award from the French Academy for her work in aiding the poor. In 1852, she was sent to the mother house and spent the rest of her life in ob-

scurity. She died at Pern, France, on August 29, and was
beatified by Pope John Paul II in 1982.

JULIA OF CORSICA (5th century). According to legend,
she was of a noble Carthaginian family who was sold as a
slave to a Syrian merchant named Eusebius when Genseric
captured Carthage in 439. While on the way to Gaul, the ship
on which she was a passenger with her master stopped off at
Cape Corso, northern Corsica. When the governor of the island, Felix, learned she was a Christian when she did not
debark with her master to participate in a pagan ceremony,
he ordered her to sacrifice to the gods. When she refused to
do so, he offered her her freedom if she would apostatize.
When she still refused, he had her tortured and then crucified.
Some scholars believe she may have lived a century or two
later and was murdered by Saracen raiders. She is the patroness of Corsica. May 22.

JULIAN THE HOSPITALER (no date). According to a
pious fiction that was very popular in the Middle Ages, Julian
was of noble birth and while hunting one day was reproached
by a hart for hunting him and told he would one day kill his
mother and father. He was richly rewarded for his services by
a King and married a wealthy widow. While he was away his
mother and father arrived at his castle seeking him; when his
wife realized who they were she put them up for the night in
the master's bedroom. When Julian returned unexpectedly
later that night and saw a man and a woman in his bed, he
suspected the worst and killed them both. When his wife returned from church and he found he had killed his parents,
he was overcome with remorse and fled the castle, resolved to
do a fitting penance. He was joined by his wife and they built
an inn for travelers near a wide river, and a hospital for the
poor. He was forgiven for his crime when he gave succor to a
leper in his own bed; the leper turned out to be a messenger
from God who had been sent to test him. He is the patron of
hotelkeepers, travelers, and boatmen. February 12.

JULIANA OF FALCONIERI. *See* Falconieri, Juliana.

JULIANA OF MOUNT CORNILLON, BL. (1192–1258).
Born at Retinnes near Liège, Flanders, she was orphaned
when five and placed in the care of the nuns of Mount Cor-

nillon. She experienced visions when she was young in which the Lord pointed out that there was no feast in honor of the Blessed Sacrament. She became a nun at Mount Cornillon and in 1225 was elected prioress. She began to agitate for the establishment of the feast day of her vision, received support and opposition, and was driven from the monastery by the lay directors, who accused her of mismanaging the funds of a hospital under her control. An inquiry by the bishop of Liège exonerated her and resulted in her recall in 1246, when he introduced the feast of Corpus Christi to Liège. When he died, she was again driven from the monastery, in 1248, and found refuge at the Cistercian monastery of Salzinnes at Namur but was again homeless when the monastery was burned down during the siege of Namur by the troops of Henry II of Luxembourg. She then retired to Fosses and spent the rest of her days until her death on April 5 there. Her struggle for the establishment of the feast of Corpus Christi was carried on by her friend Bl. Eva of Liège and was sanctioned by Pope Urban IV in 1264 (the office for the feast was written by Thomas Aquinas). Juliana's cult was confirmed in 1869.

JULIANA OF NORWICH, BL. (c. 1342–1423). Of her early life before she became an anchorite outside the walls of St. Julian's Church in Norwich, England, nothing is known. In 1373, she experienced a series of sixteen revelations, while in a state of ecstasy, of Christ's passion and the Trinity, and spent the next twenty years meditating on them and the suffering she had endured just prior to the revelations. The result was her *Revelations of Divine Love*, on the love of God, the Incarnation, redemption, sin, penance, and divine consolation, one of the most important of English writings. At the time of her death she had a far-spread reputation for sanctity, which attracted visitors from all over Europe to her cell. Though she is often called Blessed, there has never been any formal confirmation of this title. May 13.

JULIUS I (d. 352). Son of a Roman named Rusticus, he was elected Pope to succeed Pope St. Mark on February 6, 337. Julius was soon involved in the Arian controversy when Eusebius of Nicomedia opposed the return of Athanasius to the see of Alexandria in 338. Eusebius and his followers elected George, whereupon the Arians elected Pistus. Julius convened a synod in Rome in 340 or 341 that neither group attended, and in a letter to the Eusebian bishops, Julius declared that Athanasius was the rightful bishop of Alexandria and reinstated him. The matter was not finally settled until the Council of Sardica (Sofia), summoned by Emperors Constans and Constantius in 342 or 343, declared Julius' action correct and that any deposed bishop had the right of appeal to the Pope in Rome. Julius built several basilicas and churches in Rome and died there on April 12.

JUSTIN MARTYR (c. 100–c. 165). Born at Flavia Neapolis, of pagan Greco-Roman parents, he studied philosophy, rhetoric, history, and poetry, and was inspired by a meeting with an old man at Ephesus, where he taught for a time, to study Christian Scripture. When about thirty, Justin became a Christian and devoted himself to expounding his new faith to his fellow men. He traveled about debating with pagan philosophers and eventually he came to Rome, where he opened a school of philosophy. He incurred the enmity of a Cynic named Crescens for besting him in debate and was denounced, probably at the instigation of Crescens, to the authorities as a Christian. He was brought to trial with six companions, Charita, Chariton, Euelpistus, Hierax, Liberianus, and Paeon, before the Roman prefect, Rusticus. When they refused to sacrifice to the gods, they were scourged and beheaded. Justin is the first Christian apologist, and a layman, to have written on Christianity at any length, and in his writings he sought to reconcile the claims of faith and reason. Two of his most important works are still extant: His *Apologies,* addressed to Emperor Antoninus and the first document addressed to the enemies of Christianity, defends the Christians, replies to charges of immorality leveled against them, explains how they are loyal subjects based on their beliefs in the teaching of Christ, and goes on to explain immortality, free will, and fasting; and *Dialogue with Trypho,* in which he debates the merits of Christianity over Judaism in a dialogue with Trypho, a Jew. June 1.

JUSTUS OF CANTERBURY (d. c. 627). Among the missionaries sent to Britain by Pope St. Gregory the Great to aid St. Augustine in 601 was a Benedictine named Justus. He was consecrated first bishop of Rochester by Augustine in 604, but when the death of King Ethelbert in 616 caused a revival of paganism in his Kingdom of Kent under his son and successor Eadbald, Justus returned to Gaul with Mellitus of London. Justus came back to Britain the following year and succeeded St. Laurence as fourth archbishop of Canterbury in 624. It was Justus who consecrated St. Paulinus when Paulinus accompanied Ethelburga of Kent to her marriage with King Edward of Northumbria, November 10.

JUVENTINUS (d. 363). He and Maximinus were officers in the guard of Julian the Apostate. During a campaign against the Persians, they were overheard decrying the Emperor's edicts against the veneration of relics. Haled before Julian, they were stripped of their estates, scourged, and beheaded at Antioch on January 25 when they refused to recant and sacrifice to the pagan gods. St. John Chrysostom wrote their eulogy.

K

KAGGWA, CHARLES. *See* Lwanga, Charles.

KARASUMARU, LEO (d. 1597). A native of Korea, he became a pagan priest and then was converted to Christianity and baptized by the Jesuits in Japan in 1589. He became the first Korean Franciscan tertiary and was the chief catechist for the Friars. During the persecution of the Christians in Japan by the *taikō*, Toyotomi Hideyoshi, he and twenty-five other Catholics were crucified near Nagasaki on February 5. With him was crucified his brother Paul Ibaraki and their twelve-year-old nephew Louis Ibaraki. They were all canonized as the Martyrs of Japan in 1862. February 6.

KATERI TEKAKWITHA, BL. *See* Tekakwitha, Bl. Kateri.

KATHERINE. *See* Catherine.

KEMBLE, JOHN (1599–1679). Born of Catholic parents at St. Weonard's, Herefordshire, England, he went to Douai to study for the priesthood and was ordained there in 1625. He was sent on the English mission and worked in Herefordshire and Monmouthshire for fifty-three years. He became a victim of the Titus Oates plot hysteria and was arrested in 1678 at Pembridge Castle, his brother's home, which he had used as his headquarters, and charged with complicity in the Titus Oates plot to assassinate King Charles II. When no evidence was found of his involvement in that notorious fraudulent "plot" when he was examined by the Privy Council in London, he was found guilty of being a Catholic priest. He was hanged, drawn, and quartered at Hereford on August 22 when he was eighty years old. He was canonized by Pope Paul VI in 1970 as one of the martyrs of England and Wales.

KENELM (d. c. 812). According to a popular legend of the Middle Ages, he was seven when his father, King Kenulf of Mercia, died, and he succeeded to the throne. His sister Quendreda bribed his teacher, Ascebert, to murder him so she could claim the throne. Ascebert did, but when the body was discovered and enshrined at Winchcombe in Gloucestershire, all kinds of marvels occurred at his grave. All three are actual figures, but Kenelm did not die at seven and may even have died before his father. July 17.

KENNETH. *See* Canice.

KENTIGERN (c. 518–603). Also known as Mungo ("dear one" or "darling"), his mother was a British princess named Thenaw (or Thaney or Theneva). When it was discovered that she was pregnant of an unknown man, she was hurled from a cliff and, when discovered alive at the foot of the cliff, was set adrift in a boat on the Firth of Forth. She reached Culross, was given shelter by St. Serf, and gave birth to a child to whom Serf gave the name Mungo (darling). Raised by the saint, he became a hermit at Glasghu (Glasgow) and was so renowned for his holiness that he was consecrated bishop of Strathclyde about 540. Driven to flight because of the feuds among the neighboring chieftains, he went to Wales, met St. David at Menevia, and founded a monastery at Llanelwy. About 553, Kentigern returned to Scotland, settled at Hoddam, and then returned to Glasghu, where he spent his last days. He is considered the first bishop of Scotland and with Thenaw (July 18) is joint patron of Glasgow. January 14.

KESSOG (d. c. 560). Son of the King of Cashel where he was born, he left Ireland to go to Scotland as a missionary and was consecrated a missionary bishop. Using Monks' Island in Loch Lomond as his headquarters, he evangelized the surrounding area until he was martyred, though where is uncertain—some claim at Bandry, and others abroad. Many extravagant miracles were ascribed to him. March 10.

KEUMURGIAN, BL. GOMIDAS (c. 1656–1707). Born at Constantinople, the son of a dissident Armenian priest, he

married when twenty, was ordained, and was assigned to St.
George Armenian Church. He became known for his eloquence and religious fervor, and in 1696, when he was forty,
with his wife, was reconciled to Rome. He stayed on at St.
George's, and his success in reuniting five of the twelve
priests there to Rome caused much opposition from the dissidents, who complained to the Turkish authorities. He then
went to Jerusalem, where his activities at St. James Armenian
Monastery incurred the opposition of a John of Smyrna.
When Gomidas returned to Constantinople in 1702, John was
vicar of Patriarch Avedik. Avedik was exiled for a time to
Cyprus, and while there was kidnaped by the French ambassador. This angered the dissidents and they persuaded the
Turkish authorities to move against the Catholics. Gomidas
was arrested in 1707 and condemned to the galleys, but was
ransomed by friends. He continued to preach reunion with
Rome and was again arrested later in the same year at the instigation of dissident Armenian priests. By now John of
Smyrna had become patriarch of the Armenians. Gomidas
was accused of being a Frank (which meant being either a
foreigner or a Latin Catholic), though he had been born in
Constantinople, and of fomenting trouble among the Armenians in the city. Though the judge, Mustafa Kamal, the
chief kadi, knew Gomidas was an Armenian priest, Kamal
was unable to do anything in the case when a stream of perjured witnesses testified that Gomidas was a troublemaker, a
Frank, and an agent of hostile Western powers, and Gomidas
was found guilty. He was offered his freedom if he would
apostatize to Islam, and was beheaded at Parmark-Kapu, on
the outskirts of Constantinople, when he refused. He is sometimes mistakenly called Cosimo di Carbognano, but this was
his son's name. Gomidas was beatified in 1929. November 5.

KEVIN (d. c. 618). Known in Ireland as Coemgen as well
as Kevin, according to tradition he was born at the Fort of
the White Fountain in Leinster, Ireland, of royal descent. He
was baptized by St. Cronan and educated by St. Petroc, was
ordained, and became a hermit at the Valley of the Two
Lanes in Glendalough. After seven years there he was persuaded to give up his solitary life, went to Disert-Coemgen,
where he founded a monastery for the disciples he attracted,
and later moved to Glendalough. He made a pilgrimage to
Rome, bringing back many relics for his permanent founda-

tion at Glendalough, was a friend of St. Kieran of Clonmacnois, and was entrusted with the raising of the son of King Colman of Ui Faelain by the King. Many extravagant miracles were attributed to Kevin, and he was reputed to be 120 at his death. June 3.

KIERAN OF CLONMACNOIS (d. c. 556). Born in Connacht, Ireland, the son of Beoit, a carpenter, he studied at St. Finnian's School at Clonard and taught the daughter of the King of Cuala, as he was considered the most learned monk at Clonard. Kieran spent seven years at Inishmore on Aran with St. Enda and then went to a monastery in the center of Ireland called Isel. Forced to leave by the monks because of what they considered his excessive charity, he spent some time on Inis Aingin (Hare island) and with eight companions migrated to a spot on the bank of the Shannon River in Offaly, where he built a monastery that became the famous Clonmacnois, renowned for centuries as the great center of Irish learning, and was its abbot. Many extravagant miracles and tales are told of Kieran, who is one of the Twelve Apostles of Ireland. He is often called St. Kieran the Younger to distinguish him from St. Kieran of Saighir. September 9.

KIERAN OF SAIGHIR (d. c. 530). Often called St. Kieran the Elder, to distinguish him from St. Kieran of Clonmacnois, and Ciaran, the story of his life is based on conflicting and untrustworthy legends according to which he was born in Ossory (or Cork), went to Rome when he was thirty to learn more about his religion, and was consecrated bishop (some say in Rome; others that he was one of the twelve consecrated by St. Patrick when he arrived in Ireland). He lived for a time as a hermit, attracted numerous disciples, and built a monastery that developed into the town of Saighir; he is considered the first bishop of Ossory. His legend is replete with extravagant miracles and tall tales. March 5.

KILIAN (d. c. 689). An Irish monk, he was consecrated bishop, went to Rome with eleven companions in 686, and received permission from Pope Conon to evangelize Franconia (Baden and Bavaria). He was successful, with two followers —Colman, a priest, and Totnan, a deacon—in his missionary endeavors until he converted Gosbert, duke of Würzburg, who had married Geilana, his brother's widow. According to legend, while Gosbert was away on a military expedition, Geilana is reputed to have had the three missionaries beheaded when she found that Gosbert was going to leave her after Kilian had told him the marriage was forbidden by the Church. July 8.

KIM, BL. AGATHA (d. 1839). *See* Imbert, Bl. Laurence.

KINUYA, LEO (1569–97). *See* Miki, Paul.

KIRBY, LUKE (d. 1582). Born at Bedale, Yorkshire, England, he graduated from Cambridge, became a Catholic, and in 1576 went to Douai to study for the priesthood. After further study at Rome, he was ordained in 1577, was sent on the English mission in 1580, and was soon arrested and charged with conspiring against the Queen, though in reality because he was a Catholic priest. He was imprisoned in the Tower in London, subjected to the terrible torture known as "the scavenger's daughter," and then hanged, drawn, and quartered at Tyburn on May 30. He was canonized by Pope Paul VI in 1970 as one of the Forty Martyrs of England and Wales.

KNUD. *See* Canute Lavard.

KNUTE. *See* Canute.

KOLBE, MAXIMILIAN (1894–1941). Born at Zdunska-Wola, near Lodz, Poland, on January 7 and baptized Raymond, he joined the Conventual Franciscans, taking the name Maximilian. He pronounced his temporary vows in 1911 and in 1917 founded the Militia of Mary Immaculate in Rome to advance devotion to Mary. He was ordained in Rome in 1918, returned to Poland, and founded *Militia of the Immaculate Mary,* a monthly bulletin. In 1927, he founded Niepokalanów ("cities of the Immaculate Conception") about twenty-five miles from Warsaw to house some eight hundred religious and established similar foundations in Japan and India. He became superior of the Polish Niepokalanów in 1936, and in 1941 was arrested by the Gestapo when the Germans invaded Poland, and imprisoned in the notorious prison camp in Auschwitz in Poland. He took the place of a married man with a family who was one of ten men arbitrarily selected by the commandant to be executed in retaliation for a prisoner who had escaped. Fr. Kolbe was killed on August 14 by an injection of carbolic acid, and was canonized by Pope John Paul II in 1982.

KOSTKA, STANISLAUS (1550–68). Son of a Polish senator and born in Rostkovo Castle in Poland about October 28, he was educated by a private tutor and then sent to the Jesuit college in Vienna when he was fourteen. He was soon known for his studious ways, deep religious fervor, and mortifications. After he recovered from a serious illness during which he experienced several visions, he decided to join the Jesuits. Opposed by his father and refused admission by the Vienna provincial, who feared the father's reaction if he admitted the youth, Stanislaus walked 350 miles to Dillengen where Peter Canisius, provincial of Upper Germany, took him in and then sent him to Rome, where Francis Borgia, father general of the Society of Jesus, accepted him into the Jesuits in 1567, when he was seventeen. He practiced the most severe mortifications, experienced ecstasies at Mass, and lived a life of great sanctity. He died in Rome on August 15, only nine months after joining the Jesuits, and was canonized in 1726. He is one of the lesser patrons of Poland. November 13.

L

LABOURÉ, CATHERINE (1806–76). Daughter of a farmer, she was born at Fain-les-Moutiers, France, on May 2 and named Zoé. She never went to school, as her mother died when she was eight, and she took care of the family. She joined the Sisters of Charity of St. Vincent de Paul at Chatillon in 1830, taking the name Catherine, and was sent to the Rue du Bac Convent in Paris. Almost at once she began to experience a series of visions of our Lady in the chapel of the convent, and in several of them was asked by the Lady in the vision to strike a medal showing the Lady and honoring the Immaculate Conception. Her confessor, Fr. Aladel, secured permission from Archbishop Quelen of Paris to have the medals struck, and in 1832 the first fifteen hundred of what were to be millions of medals were minted—the famous Miraculous Medal. The visions were approved as authentic in 1836 by a special commission appointed by the archbishop, and the popularity of the medal spread all over the world. Catherine spent the years from 1831 until her death performing menial tasks at the Hospice d'Enghien, revealing none of her visions to any but her confessor until a few months before her death on December 31 at Enghien. A widespread popular cult developed on her death, and she was canonized in 1947. November 28.

LABRE, BENEDICT JOSEPH (1748–83). Born at Amettes, France, on March 25, the eldest of eighteen children, he studied under his uncle, the parish priest at Erin, was unsuccessful in attempts to join the Trappists, Carthusians, and Cistercians, and in 1770 made pilgrimages to many of the major shrines in Europe. In 1774, he stayed in Rome, lived in the Colosseum, and became known as "the beggar of Rome" for his poverty and sanctity. He was noted for his attendance at and devotion to Forty Hours' devotion, died in Rome on April 16, and was canonized in 1883.

LADISLAUS OF HUNGARY (1040–95). Son of King Bela of Hungary, he was born at Neustra on July 29 and was elected King of Hungary by the nobles in 1077. He was at once faced with the claims of a relative and son of a former King, Solomon, to the throne, and defeated him on the battlefield in 1089. He supported Pope Gregory VII in his investiture struggle against Emperor Henry IV, and Rupert of Swabia, Henry's rival; Ladislaus married Adelaide, daughter of Duke Welf of Bavaria, one of Rupert's supporters. Ladislaus successfully repelled Cuman attempts to invade Hungary, encouraged Christian missionaries, and built many churches, but allowed religious freedom to the Jews and Mohammedans in his realms. In 1091, he marched to the aid of his sister Helen, Queen of Croatia, against the murderers of her husband, and when she died childless, annexed Croatia and Dalmatia despite objections from the Pope, the Emperor in Constantinople, and Venice. At the Synod of Szabolcs in 1092, he promulgated a series of laws on religious and civil matters. He was chosen to lead the armies of the First Crusade but before he could do so died at Nitra, Bohemia, on July 29. He is one of the great national heroes of Hungary and made Hungary a great state, extending its borders and defending it successfully against invasion. He was venerated from the time of his death for his zeal, piety, and moral life, and was canonized in 1192 by Pope Celestine III. Ladislaus is known in Hungary as Laszlo. June 27.

LALANDE, JOHN DE (d. 1646). Born at Dieppe, France, he went to Quebec, Canada, where he became a *donné* (lay assistant) to the Jesuit missionaries there. In 1646, he accompanied Isaac Jogues on a trip to the territory of the Iroquois Indians after a peace treaty with them had just been signed. They were captured by a war party of Mohawks, and John was tomahawked and beheaded at Ossernenon near Albany, New York, on October 19, the day after Fr. Jogues had suffered a similar fate there. They were canonized by Pope Pius XI in 1930 as two of the Martyrs of North America.

LALEMENT, GABRIEL (1610–49). Born at Paris, France, he joined the Jesuits in 1630, taught at Moulins for three years, and after further study at Bourges, was ordained in 1638. After teaching at La Flèche and Moulins, he was sent to New France (Canada) at his request in 1646 as a missionary. He worked among the Hurons, became assistant to St. John de Brébeuf at St. Ignace in 1649, and was with him in the village when the Iroquois, traditional enemies of the Hurons, attacked and destroyed it on March 16, killing all the inhabitants except the two priests. After torturing them, the Iroquois tomahawked them to death the next day. They were canonized by Pope Pius XI in 1930 as two of the Martyrs of North America. October 19.

LAMBERT OF MAESTRICHT (c. 635–c. 705). Born of a noble family at Maestricht, Flanders, he was educated by St. Theodard and was chosen to succeed him as bishop of Tongres-Maestricht in 668 when Theodard was murdered. Lambert was expelled from his see by Ebroin, mayor of the palace, for his support of Childeric II when the King was murdered in 674, and Lambert retired to Stavelot Monastery. When Ebroin was murdered in 681, his successor, Pepin of Herstal, reinstated Lambert, who devoted himself to building a convent at Munsterbilzen, converting pagans in the area, and tending his flock. He denounced Pepin for his adulterous affair with Alpais, sister of his wife, Plectrudis, and was murdered in Liège, allegedly by Alpais' brother, Dodo, and a group of his followers. Another version is that Lambert was killed with two relatives, Peter and Andolet, who had killed relatives of Dodo. September 17.

LANFRANC, BL. (c. 1005–89). Born at Pavia, Italy, he studied law there, was a lawyer for a time, and in about 1035 went to France. He continued his studies at Avranches, Normandy, taught there, and in 1042 became a monk at Bec. He was made prior in 1045 and head of the monastery school, which under him became famous for its scholarship. He became embroiled in the quarrel over the Eucharist with Berengar and was brought by Pope Leo IX to the Councils of Rome and Vercelli in 1050, where Berengar was condemned. Lanfranc's opposition to the proposed marriage of Duke Wil-

liam of Normandy to Matilda of Flanders in 1053 caused
William to draw up a decree of exile, but the two were reconciled, and Lanfranc became a close adviser of the Duke and
secured a papal dispensation for the marriage in 1059. Lanfranc was appointed abbot of St. Stephen's in Caen about
1063, accompanied William on his conquest of England, and
was named archbishop of Canterbury in 1070. He brought
Norman practices to the English Church, built churches,
founded new sees, and in 1072 compelled the archbishop of
York to accept the primacy of Canterbury when a council of
bishops and abbots of Winchester so decreed. Lanfranc was
regent for William in 1074 and put down a revolt against the
Conqueror, fought any secular intrusion on ecclesiastical
rights, and in 1076, at a synod at Winchester, ordered clerical
celibacy for future ordinands. Though he persuaded William
to name his son William Rufus his heir to the throne and
crowned him on his father's death in 1087, he never had the
influence over William Rufus that he had had over William.
Lanfranc's *De Sacramento Corporis et Sanguinis Christi* became the classic statement of transubstantiation in the Middle
Ages. He died at Canterbury on May 24, and though he has
always been honored with the title Blessed, there does not
seem to have ever been any public cult.

LA SALLE, JOHN BAPTIST DE (1651–1719). Born at
Rheims, France, on April 30, the eldest of ten children of a
wealthy and noble family, he was tonsured at eleven, became
a canon at Rheims in 1667, studied at St. Sulpice Seminary in
Paris, 1670–72, and was ordained in 1678. He was sent to
Rheims, met Adrian Nyel, a layman who was opening a
school for poor boys in 1679, and became involved in educational work. He resigned his canonry in 1683, distributed his
fortune to the poor in 1684, and devoted himself to improving the caliber of teachers. He began to attract men desirous
of receiving his training and formed twelve of his teachers
into the Institute of the Brothers of the Christian Schools
(which did not receive papal approval until 1725). He
began to establish teachers' colleges (Rheims in 1687, Paris
in 1699, Saint-Denis in 1709) and established a junior novitiate in 1685 for younger men. He steadily increased the
number of schools for boys under his control. He decided to
exclude priests from his institute and in about 1695 drew up

in Paris a draft of his rule in which it was stated that no
Christian Brother could become a priest and no priest could
become a Christian Brother, and wrote his *Conduite des
écoles Chrétiennes,* revolutionizing teaching methods by replacing individual instruction with classroom teaching; it also
required teaching in the vernacular rather than in Latin. In
1698 he opened a college for the Irish followers of King
James II of England who had followed him into exile in
France. In later years he encountered opposition from secular
teachers for his ideas and reported severity to novices, for
which he was officially deposed in 1702. However, he remained in control of the Institute when the brothers all
threatened to leave. Later, spurred by the Jansenists, an attack on teaching anything but manual education to poor students caused his schools in Paris to be closed, but the storm
soon subsided, and they reopened. His schools spread to Italy
and in time all over the world. He established a reformatory
for boys at Dijon in 1705, and in 1717 a school for adult
prisoners. He resigned in 1717 and died at St. Yon, Rouen,
where he had retired to spend the last years of his life, on
April 7. He was canonized by Pope Leo XIII in 1900 and
was named patron of teachers by Pope Pius XII in 1950.

LASZLO. *See* Ladislaus of Hungary.

LAURENCE. *See* Lawrence.

LAVAL, MARTYRS OF (d. 1794). During the French
Revolution a group of priests, nuns, and a laywoman were executed at Laval, the capital of Mayenne, in Western France,
for refusing to subscribe to the Civil Constitution of the
Clergy which was condemned by Pope Pius VI in 1791. They
were all beatified in 1955. They are: Françoise Mézière, a
laywoman, who was guillotined at Laval on February 5,
1794, after having been found guilty of nursing wounded
Vendean soldiers; two sisters of the Sisters of Charity de la
Chapelle-au-Ribout, Françoise Trehet, executed March 13,
and Jeanne Véron, executed March 20; Marie Lhullier
(Sister Monica), an illiterate lay sister of the Hospital
Sisters of the Mercy of Jesus; and fifteen priests: René Am-
broise, Jacques André, Jacques Burin, François Duchesne,
André Duliou, Jean Gallot, Louis Gastineau, François Mi-

goret, Julien Morin de la Girardière, Julien Moulé, Joseph Pellé, Augustine Philipott, Pierre Thomas, Jean Baptiste Turpin du Cormier, all secular priests, and Jean Baptiste Triquerle, a Conventual Franciscan.

LAWRENCE (d. 258). One of the seven deacons of Rome, he was born, according to tradition, at Huesca, Spain, and suffered martyrdom in Rome during Emperor Valerian's persecution of the Christians. According to several early Christian writers, among them St. Ambrose and Prudentius, he was a deacon of Pope Sixtus II and was overwhelmed with grief when Sixtus was condemned to death in 258. Overjoyed when Sixtus predicted he would follow him in three days, he sold many of the Church's possessions and donated the money to the poor. When the prefect of Rome heard of his action, he had Lawrence brought before him and demanded all the Church's treasures for the Emperor. Lawrence said he would need three days to collect them and then presented the blind, the crippled, the poor, the orphans, and other unfortunates to the prefect and told him they were the Church's treasures. Furious, the prefect prepared a red-hot griddle and bound Lawrence to it; Lawrence bore the agony with unbelievable equanimity and in the midst of his torment instructed the executioner to turn him over, as he was broiled enough on the one side. According to Prudentius, his death and example led to the conversion of Rome and signaled the end of paganism in the city. There is no doubt that his death inspired a great devotion in Rome, which quickly spread throughout the entire Church. August 10.

LAWRENCE OF BRINDISI (1559–1619). Caesare de Rossi was born at Brindisi, Kingdom of Naples, on July 22, was educated by the Conventual Franciscans there and by his uncle at St. Mark's in Venice, and when sixteen joined the Capuchins at Verona, taking the name Lawrence. He pursued his higher studies in theology, philosophy, the Bible, Greek, Hebrew, and several other languages at the University of Padua, was ordained, and began to preach with great effect in northern Italy. He became definitor general of his order in Rome in 1596, a position he was to hold five times, was assigned to conversion work with Jews, and was sent to Germany, with Bl. Benedict of Urbino, to combat Lutheranism. They founded friaries at Prague, Vienna, and Gorizia, which were to develop into the provinces of Bohemia, Austria, and Styria. At the request of Emperor Rudolf II, Lawrence helped raise an army among the German rulers to fight against the Turks, who were threatening to conquer all of Hungary, became its chaplain, and was among the leaders in the Battle of Szekesfehevar in 1601; many attributed the ensuing victory to him. In 1602, he was elected vicar general of the Capuchins but refused re-election in 1605. He was sent to Spain by the Emperor to persuade Philip III to join the Catholic League, and while there founded a Capuchin house in Madrid. He was then sent as papal nuncio to the court of Maximilian of Bavaria, served as peacemaker in several royal disputes, and in 1618 retired from worldly affairs to the friary at Caserta. He was recalled at the request of the rulers of Naples to go to Spain to intercede with King Philip for them against the duke of Osuna, Spanish envoy to Naples, and convinced the King to recall the duke to avert an uprising. The trip in the sweltering heat of summer exhausted him, and he died a few days after his meeting with the King at Lisbon on July 22. Lawrence wrote a commentary on Genesis and several treatises against Luther, but Lawrence's main writings are in the nine volumes of his sermons. He was canonized in 1881 and proclaimed a Doctor of the Church by Pope John XXIII in 1959. July 21.

LAWRENCE OF CANTERBURY (d. 619). One of the thirteen monks from St. Andrew's Monastery in Rome who accompanied St. Augustine of Canterbury to England in 597, he succeeded Augustine as archbishop of Canterbury in 604. Lawrence was unsuccessful in convincing the Britons to accept the Roman liturgical practices and was faced with great difficulties when Edbald succeeded his father, Ethelbert, as King of Kent in 616, married his father's wife, and allowed the country to lapse into pagan practices. Lawrence considered returning to Gaul but in a dream was rebuked by St. Peter for considering abandoning his flock and was lashed physically by the apostle for the thought. Lawrence decided to remain, and the day after his vision converted Edbald to Christianity when he displayed the stripes on his back to the King and told him their origin. Lawrence died on February 2. February 3.

LAWRENCE JUSTINIAN. *See* Giustiniani, Laurence.

LAWRENCE O'TOOLE (1128–80). Son of Murtagh, chief of the Murrays, he was born near Castledermot, Kildare, Ireland, was taken as hostage by the raiding King Dermot McMurrogh of Leinster, but was turned over to the bishop of Glendalough after two years. Lawrence became a monk at Glendalough, was named abbot in 1153, ruled well though there were some objections to his strict rule, and in 1611 was named archbishop of Dublin. He instituted reforms among the clergy, upgraded the caliber of new clerics, and imposed strict discipline on his canons. When a revolt drove Dermot McMurrogh from Ireland, the King sought the help of King Henry II of England, who dispatched an army of his nobles headed by Richard de Clare, earl of Pembroke. He landed in Ireland in 1170 and marched on Dublin. While Lawrence was negotiating with him, Dermot's men and allies raped and looted the city. When Dermot suddenly died, Pembroke declared himself King of Leinster as the husband of Dermot's daughter Eva (Lawrence's niece), but was recalled to England by Henry. Before Pembroke could return, the Irish united behind Rory O'Conor, and the earl barricaded himself in Dublin as the Irish forces attacked. While Lawrence was trying to effect a settlement, Pembroke suddenly attacked and won an unexpected victory. Henry himself then went to Ireland in 1171, received the submission of most of the Irish chieftains, and the great tragedy of Ireland, the beginning of the "troubles" with England that were to endure for eight centuries, had started. In 1172, a synod Lawrence convened at Cashel confirmed a bull of Pope Adrian IV imposing the English form of the liturgy on Ireland, and Lawrence accepted the decrees when Pope Alexander III confirmed them. In 1175, he went to England to negotiate a treaty between Henry and Rory O'Conor, and during his visit had an attack made on his life while he was visiting the shrine of Thomas Becket. He attended the General Lateran Council in Rome in 1179 and was appointed papal legate to Ireland. On his way home he stopped off in England to conduct further negotiations on behalf of Rory O'Conor and was forbidden to return to Ireland by Henry. He journeyed to Normandy where Henry was, received his permission to return, but died on the way back at Eu, near Rouen, on November 14. He was canonized in 1225.

LAWRENCE, ROBERT (d. 1535). Prior of the char-

terhouse at Beauvale, Nottinghamshire, England, he was on a
visit to the London charterhouse when he and St. Augustine
Webster accompanied its prior, St. John Houghton, to see
Thomas Cromwell, who had them seized and imprisoned in
the Tower. When they refused to accept the King's Act of Supremacy they were treated savagely and hanged at Tyburn on
May 4. They were canonized by Pope Paul VI in 1970 as
three of the Forty Martyrs of England and Wales.

LAZARUS (1st century). All that is really known of Lazarus
is from John 11:1–44, which tells us he was a friend of
Jesus, brother of Martha and Mary, and that he was raised
from the dead by Jesus after being in the tomb for four days;
and from John 12:1–11, where he is mentioned as among
those present at a dinner in Bethany. According to tradition,
Lazarus, Mary Magdalen, Martha, Maximus, and others were
put into an oarless, rudderless boat and set adrift. It brought
them to southwestern Gaul, where Lazarus made numerous
converts, became the first bishop of Marseilles, and was martyred during the persecution of Christians by Emperor Domitian. In another tradition, Lazarus was put into a leaking boat
with his sisters and others by the Jews at Jaffa and was conducted supernaturally in safety to Cyprus, where he became
bishop of Kition (Larnaka), ruled for thirty years, and died
there. Still another tradition has him following St. Peter to
Syria. December 17.

LAZARUS (1st century). He is the poor man at the gate of
the rich man in Christ's parable related in Luke 16:19–31.
His name was perpetuated in the Middle Ages by such words
as *lazaretto* (hospital), *lazarone* (a beggar in the streets),
and the Order of St. Lazarus, which though a military order
had as one of its objectives the care of lepers. June 21.

LAZIOSI, PEREGRINE (1260–1345). Born at Forlì, Italy,
of well-to-do parents, he was active in his youth in the antipapal party in Romagna but after an encounter with St.
Philip Benizi changed his lifestyle. He joined the Servites at
Siena, was ordained, and then went to Forlì and founded a
new Servite house. He became famed for his preaching, austerities, holiness, and as a confessor, a fame that became
widespread when an advanced cancer of his foot was seemingly miraculously cured overnight after he had experienced a

vision. He was canonized in 1726 and is the patron against cancer. May 1.

LEANDER (c. 534–c. 600). Of a noble Hispanic-Roman family of Cartagena, Spain, and brother of SS. Fulgentius, Isidore, and Florentina, he was born at Cartagena and in 554 went to Seville when his family moved there. He became a monk there, fought Arianism in Spain, met St. Gregory the Great at Constantinople in 583 while on a diplomatic mission from King Leovigild to the Emperor, and on his return in about 584 was appointed bishop of Seville. He was banished by King Leovigild, who had executed his son Hermenegild for refusing communion from an Arian bishop. While in exile Leander wrote treatises against Arianism, was recalled by Leovigild who, on his deathbed, charged him with raising his son Reccared, who was his successor, in the Catholic faith. In the next few years Leander converted many of the Arian bishops and brought most of the Visigoths and Spanish Suevi to the Catholic faith. He presided at the third council of Toledo in 589 at which Visigothic Spain abjured Arianism and added the Nicene Creed to the Mass. In 590, he held a synod at Seville that solidified the work of conversion. He was responsible for the reform of the Spanish liturgy and wrote a rule for nuns that is still extant. It was at his suggestion that St. Gregory wrote his treatise on Job, *Moralia.* Leander died at Seville on March 13 and is considered a Doctor of the Church in the Spanish Church. February 27.

LEGER. *See* Leodegarius.

LELLIS, CAMILLUS DE (1550–1614). Born at Bocchianico, Italy, he fought for the Venetians against the Turks, was addicted to gambling, and by 1574 was penniless in Naples. He became a Capuchin novice, was unable to be professed because of a diseased leg he contracted while fighting the Turks, devoted himself to caring for the sick, and became director of St. Giacomo Hospital in Rome. He received permission from his confessor (St. Philip Neri) to be ordained and decided, with two companions, to found his own congregation, the Ministers of the Sick (the Camellians), dedicated to the care of the sick. They ministered to the sick of Holy Ghost Hospital in Rome, enlarged their facilities in 1585, founded a new house in Naples in 1588, and attended the plague-stricken aboard ships in Rome's harbor and in Rome. In 1591, the congregation was made into an order to serve the sick by Pope Gregory XIV, and in 1591 and 1605, Camillus sent members of his order to minister to wounded troops in Hungary and Croatia, the first field medical unit. Gravely ill for many years, he resigned as superior of the Order in 1607 and died in Rome on July 14, the year after he attended a general chapter there. He was canonized in 1746, was declared patron of the sick, with St. John of God, by Pope Leo XIII, and patron of nurses and nursing groups by Pope Pius XI. July 14.

LEO I THE GREAT (d. 461). Probably born in Rome of Tuscan parents, he served as deacon under Popes Celestine I and Sixtus III, acted as peacemaker between Aetius and Albinus, the imperial generals whose quarrels were leaving Gaul open to attacks by the barbarians, and was elected Pope to succeed Sixtus III while he was in Gaul. He was consecrated on September 29, 440, and at once began his pastoral duties with a series of ninety-six still extant sermons on faith and charity and strenuous opposition to Manichaeanism, Pelagianism, Priscillianism, and Nestorianism. In 448, he was faced with the Eutychian problem. Eutyches, an archimandrite in a monastery at Constantinople, had been deposed as abbot by Patriarch Flavian of Constantinople for denying the two natures of Christ. Supported by Emperor Theodosius II, Eutyches appealed to Leo for reinstatement. The Emperor summoned a packed council at Ephesus in 449 (the notorious Robber Synod), which acquitted Eutyches and at which Flavian was physically assaulted (he later died from the attack), and refused to allow papal legates to read a letter from Leo; it also declared Flavian deposed. In 451, Leo called the General Council of Chalcedon at which his letter of 449 clarifying the doctrine of the Incarnation and vindicating Flavian was read; it excommunicated and deposed Dioscorus, Eutyches' friend, who had been intruded as patriarch of Constantinople in place of Flavian by Theodosius. It was Leo's famous *Tome* and was received with great acclamation. In 452, Attila and his Huns invaded Italy and were about to attack defenseless Rome when he was dissuaded by Leo in a face-to-face meeting with Leo at Peschiera. Three years later Leo was not so successful with the Vandal Genseric, who plundered Rome, though he agreed not to burn the city. Leo ministered to the stricken populace and worked to rebuild the city and the churches. He sent missionaries to Africa to minister to the captives Genseric took back with him. Leo died in Rome on November 10. Leo advanced the influence of the papacy to unprecedented heights with his authoritative approach to events, buttressed by his firm belief that the Holy See was the supreme authority in human affairs because of divine and scriptural mandate. In a time of great disorder, he forged an energetic central authority that stood for stability, authority, action, and wisdom; his pontificate was to affect the concept of the papacy for centuries to come. He was declared a Doctor of the Church in 1754. November 10.

LEO II (d. 683). Born in Sicily, he was elected Pope to succeed Pope St. Agatho on January 10, 681, though he was not consecrated until August 17, 682. He was an eloquent preacher, was interested in music, and was known for his concern for the poor. He confirmed the acts of the sixth General Council of Constantinople, 680–81, which condemned monothelitism and censured Pope Honorius I for not formally condemning that heresy. Leo died on June 28. July 3.

LEO III (d. 816). A Roman, son of Atypius and Elizabeth, he was chief of the pontifical treasury or wardrobe (*vestiarius*) and a cardinal-priest of Santa Susanna when he was elected Pope on the day his predecessor, Pope Hadrian (Adrian) I, was buried, December 26, 795. In 799 he was the victim of a plot by relatives of Hadrian to oust him from the papacy and was attacked by armed men who attempted to gouge out his eyes and cut out his tongue. He managed to escape to St. Erasmus Monastery, where he quickly recovered, a recovery many considered miraculous. He fled to Charlemagne's protection at Paderborn and was escorted back to Rome a few months later by a contingent of Charlemagne's men. In 800 Charlemagne came to Rome and at a synod completely exonerated Leo of charges brought against him by his enemies, though Leo insisted on taking an oath that he was innocent before the assembled bishops. On Christmas Day, Leo crowned Charlemagne in St. Peter's, an action that founded the Holy Roman Empire and was to have a profound effect on European history for centuries to come. In 804, Leo visited the Emperor and came to an agreement with him about the division of the Empire among Charlemagne's

sons, which Leo formally agreed to two years later. With
Charlemagne's help adoptionism was fought in Spain, but
when Charlemagne wanted the expression *Filioque* (and the
Son) added to the Nicene Creed, Leo refused, in part because
he would not permit secular interference in ecclesiastical
affairs, and in part because he did not wish to offend the
Byzantine Church. Generally, the two acted in concert most
of the time. They recovered his throne for Eardulf of Northumbria, settled the dispute between Canterbury and York,
and in the quarrel between Archbishop Wulfred and King
Cenulf of Mercia, Leo intervened, suspended the archbishop,
and put the kingdom under interdict. He also created a fleet
at the suggestion of Charlemagne to combat the Saracens,
recovered some of the Church's patrimony in Gaeta with the
Emperor's help, and was the beneficiary of much treasure
from him. When Charlemagne died in 814 and Leo's protection was gone, his enemies again rose against him, but he
crushed one conspiracy by executing the ringleader, and another revolt by the nobles of Campagna, who planned to
march on Rome, was suppressed by the duke of Spoleto. Leo
was a patron of the arts, using much of Charlemagne's gifts
to help the poor and to rebuild and decorate churches in
Rome and Ravenna, where the relationship between the two
men is portrayed in magnificent mosaics. Leo died in Rome in
June, and was canonized in 1673. June 12.

LEO IV (d. 855). Born in Rome, probably of Lombard an-
cestry, he studied at St. Martin's Monastery in Rome, was
made subdeacon of the Lateran Basilica by Pope Gregory IV,
and soon after was named cardinal by Pope Sergius II. Leo
was unanimously elected Pope to succeed Sergius and was
consecrated on April 10, 847. He immediately began to repair
the fortifications of Rome in anticipation of another Saracen
attack on the city, built a wall around St. Peter's and Vatican
Hill, giving the area its name of the Leonine City, and also
restored many churches in Rome. He tightened clerical discipline with a synod at Rome in 853 and was confronted with
numerous problems during his pontificate. A papal legate he
sent to Archbishop John of Ravenna and his brother, the
duke of Emilia, was murdered by the duke, and Leo went to
Ravenna, tried him, and found him guilty. Duke Nomenoë
deposed a number of bishops and erected a metropolitan see
at Dol without papal permission, actions the Pope was unable

to do anything about. Patriarch Ignatius of Constantinople had deposed Gregory Asbestas, the bishop of Syracuse, and Archbishop Hincmar of Rheims, and was forbidding clerics from appealing to Rome, actions that Leo refused to confirm. In 850, Leo crowned Louis, son of Lothair, Emperor, and in 853 King Ethelwulf of the West Saxons sent his son, Alfred, whom Leo adopted as his spiritual son, to be crowned. Just before his death on July 17, Leo was accused by a military officer (a *magister militum*) named Daniel of plotting with the Greek Emperor to overthrow Emperor Louis, a charge he easily disproved, though his death sentence on Daniel was remitted through the intercession of the Emperor.

LEO IX (1002–54). Born at Egisheim, Alsace, and named Bruno, on June 21, he was sent to study under his cousin Adalbert at Toul and received a canonry there in 1017. Although a deacon, he commanded troops under Emperor Conrad II when he invaded Italy in 1026 and made quite a reputation as a military man. He was elected bishop of Toul while in Italy and ruled for twenty years, instituting many reforms among the clergy and introducing the Cluny reform in the monasteries of his see. In 1048, with the support of his relative Emperor Henry III, he was elected Pope to succeed Pope Damasus II and was consecrated on February 12, 1049. He at once called a synod at Rome, which denounced simony and clerical incontinence, and he began a series of reforms, traveling all over Western Europe in his efforts to have them enforced, earning the title Peregrinus Apostolicus (the Apostolic Pilgrim). He condemned Berengarius of Tours for his denial of transubstantiation, acted as peacemaker in an attempt to reconcile the differences between the Emperor and King Andrew of Hungary in 1052, and succeeded in adding Benevento and territories in southern Italy to Peter's patrimony. Leo led an army against the Norman invaders in 1053 but was defeated and captured at Civitella and imprisoned at Benevento. He was severely criticized by St. Peter Damian for this action—a Pope acting as a military commander and leading an army. Leo also became involved in 1053 in a dispute with Patriarch Michael Cerularius of Constantinople (a dispute that was the beginning of the complete separation of Rome and the Eastern churches) for increasing the ritual differences with the Latin Church. Leo's proposal that the Pope be elected only by cardinals was put into effect five years after his death and endures to the present day. He died in Rome on April 19. Many miracles were attributed to him, and he was canonized in 1087.

LEO OF SAINT-BERTIN, BL. (d. 1163). Born at Furnes, Flanders, he was almoner at the court of the Count of Flanders when twenty but left to become a monk at the monastery at Auchin. He was appointed abbot of Lobbes Abbey, restored the abbey and discipline there, and in 1138 was named abbot of the famous Saint-Bertin Monastery. In 1146, he accompanied Thierry of Alsace, Count of Flanders, to Jerusalem during the Second Crusade, bringing back reputed drops of the blood of Christ supposedly collected by Joseph of Arimathea while he was washing the Savior's body. In 1152, his monastery was destroyed by fire but with the help of William of Ypres, he rebuilt it. He was blind the last two years of his life. February 26.

LEOCRITIA (d. 859). Also known as Lucretia, she was the daughter of wealthy Moorish parents in Cordova, Spain, which at that time was under Moorish rule. She was secretly converted to Christianity and was driven from her home when her parents learned of her conversion. With the help of St. Eulogius, she went into hiding and was sheltered by several Christian families. In time she was captured, with Eulogius, condemned for her Christianity, scourged, and beheaded, as was Eulogius. March 15.

LEODEGARIUS (c. 616–79). Also known as Leger, he was raised at the court of King Clotaire II and by his uncle, Bishop Didon of Poitiers. Leodegarius was made archdeacon by Didon, was ordained, and in about 651 became abbot of Maxentius Abbey, where he introduced the rule of St. Benedict. He served Queen regent St. Bathildis and helped her govern when Clovis II died in 656, and was named bishop of Autun in 663. He reconciled the differing factions that had torn the see apart, introduced reforms, fortified the town, and was known for his concern for the poor. On the death of Clotaire III, he supported young Childeric II for King against his brother Thierry, who had been backed by Ebroin, mayor of the palace. Ebroin was exiled to Luxeuil and became a bitter enemy of Leodegarius, who became Childeric's adviser. When Leodegarius denounced the marriage of Childeric to his uncle's daughter, he also incurred the enmity of Childeric, and in 675 Leodegarius was arrested at Autun and banished to Luxeuil. When Childeric was murdered in 675, his successor, Theodoric III, restored Leodegarius to his see. Ebroin was also restored as mayor of the palace after he had the incumbent Leudesius murdered and persuaded the duke of Champagne and the bishops of Chalons and Valence to attack Autun. To save the town, Leodegarius surrendered. Ebroin had him blinded, his lips cut off, and his tongue pulled out. Not satisfied, several years later, he convinced the King that Childeric had been murdered by Leodegarius and his brother Gerinus. Gerinus was stoned to death, and Leodegarius was tortured and imprisoned at Fécamp monastery in Normandy. After two years Leodegarius was summoned to a court at Marly by Ebroin, deposed, and executed at Sarcing, Artois, protesting his innocence to the end. Though the Roman Martyrology calls him Blessed and a martyr, there is doubt among many scholars that he is entitled to those honors. October 2.

LEONARD (d. c. 559). According to unreliable sources, he was a Frank courtier who was converted by St. Remigius, refused the offer of a see from his godfather, King Clovis I, and became a monk at Micy. He lived as a hermit at Limoges and was rewarded by the King with all the land he could ride around on a donkey in a day for his prayers, which were believed to have brought the Queen through a difficult delivery safely. He founded Noblac monastery on the land so granted him, and it grew into the town of Saint-Leonard. He remained there evangelizing the surrounding area until his death. He is invoked by women in labor and by prisoners of war because of the legend that Clovis promised to release every captive Leonard visited. November 6.

LEONARD OF PORT MAURICE. *See* Casanova, Leonard.

LEONARDI, JOHN (c. 1550–1609). Born at Diecimo, Italy, he became a pharmacist's assistant at Lucca, studied for the priesthood, and was ordained in 1572. He gathered a group of laymen about him to work in hospitals and prisons, became interested in the reforms proposed by the Council of Trent, and proposed a new congregation of secular priests. Great opposition to his proposal developed, but in 1583, his association (formally designated Clerks Regular of the

Mother of God in 1621) was recognized by the bishop of Lucca with the approval of Pope Gregory XIII. John was aided by St. Philip Neri and St. Joseph Calasanctius, and in 1595 the congregation was confirmed by Pope Clement VIII, who appointed John to reform the monks of Vallombrosa and Monte Vergine. He died in Rome on October 9 of plague contracted while he was ministering to the stricken. He was venerated for his miracles and religious fervor and is considered one of the founders of the College for the Propagation of the Faith. He was canonized in 1938 by Pope Pius XI. October 9.

LEONIDES OF ALEXANDRIA (d. 202). Father of Origen and a noted scholar, he was imprisoned at Alexandria, Egypt, during the persecution of Christians in the reign of Emperor Septimus Severus by Laetus, governor of Egypt, had his property confiscated, and was beheaded for being a Christian. April 22.

LEOPOLD (1073–1136). Born at Melk, Austria, he was educated by Bishop Altman of Passau and succeeded his father as margrave of Austria when he was twenty-three. He married the daughter of Emperor Henry IV, by whom he had eighteen children; in 1106, founded the monasteries of Heiligenkreuz in the Wienerwald, Klosterneuburg, near Vienna, and Mariazell in Styria, and was known for his piety and charity. He refused the imperial crown when his brother-in-law Henry V died in 1125. Leopold died after reigning as margrave for forty years at Klosterneuburg. He was surnamed "the Good" by his people and was canonized in 1486. November 15.

LESTONNAC, JOAN DE (1556–1640). Born at Bordeaux, France, she refused to follow the urging of her mother (Montaigne's sister) to become a Calvinist. When she was seventeen, she married Gaston de Montferrant, and the couple had a happily married life and four children. Gaston died in 1597 and when her children were old enough to take care of themselves, she, at the age of forty-seven and despite the objections of her son, joined the Cistercians at Toulouse. The harsh regimen caused her health to give way, and she was obliged to leave. Imbued with the idea of founding her own community, she gathered a group of women about her on her estate, La Mothe, ministered to the victims of a plague that struck Bordeaux, and with the help of two Jesuits, Frs. de Bordes and Raymond, formulated plans for a community of nuns devoted to teaching young girls. She and her followers received the habit from Cardinal de Sourdis, archbishop of Bordeaux, in 1608, and the religious of Notre Dame of Bordeaux were founded. She was elected superior in 1610, and the order spread and flourished but was shaken when one of the nuns, Blanche Hervé, circulated false rumors about Joan, caused her to be deposed as superior, and had herself elected superior. Eventually the two women were reconciled in Joan's old age, and a new superior was elected. Joan spent the last years of her life in retirement. Miracles were reported at her tomb at Bordeaux, and she was canonized in 1949. February 2.

LEWIS, DAVID (1616–79). Born at Abergavenny, Monmouthshire, Wales, the son of a Protestant schoolteacher and a Catholic mother, he was the only one of their nine children raised a Protestant. He studied law at the Middle Temple in London, went to Europe as tutor for a nobleman's son, and while in Paris was converted to Catholicism. In 1638 he entered the English college in Rome, was ordained in 1642, and in 1644 joined the Jesuits. He was sent on the English mission but a short time later was brought back to Rome as spiritual director of the English college. In 1648, he was sent to Wales and made his headquarters at Cwm in Monnow Valley at a farmhouse that was the College of St. Francis Xavier, the center for Jesuit missionary activities in western England. He worked from there for thirty-one years until 1679, when the Titus Oates plot unleashed a wave of persecution of Catholics. He escaped from Cwm but was betrayed by a servant and captured at Llanfihangel Llantarnam. He was imprisoned at Monmouth jail and after two months was tried at Usk. When no evidence could be produced linking him with the Titus Oates plot, he was convicted of being a Catholic priest and hanged, drawn, and quartered at Usk on August 27. He was canonized by Pope Paul VI as one of the Forty Martyrs of England and Wales in 1970. August 27.

LIDWINA. *See* Lydwina, Bl.

LIGUORI, ALPHONSUS MARY DE (1696–1787). Born

on September 21 at Marianelli near Naples, Italy, son of a captain of the royal galleys, he received his doctorate in both canon and civil law at the University of Naples when only sixteen and practiced law very successfully for the next eight years. He abandoned the practice of law when through an oversight he lost an important case, decided to become a priest, joined the Oratorians, and was ordained in 1726. He served as a missionary around Naples for two years, taught for a year, and in 1730, at the invitation of Bishop Thomas Falcoia, whom he had met while teaching, he went to Castellamare. During a nuns' retreat he was conducting at Scala, he met Sister Mary Celeste and became convinced that her vision of a new religious order, which coincided with a vision Bishop Falcoia had experienced earlier in Rome, was genuine, and reorganized her convent according to the rule she had been given in the vision in 1731, thus founding the Redemptorines. He moved to Scala and in 1732 organized the Congregation of the Most Holy Redeemer (the Redemptorists), devoted to mission work, and using a hospice of the nuns at Scala for headquarters, with Bishop Falcoia as nominal superior. Dissension broke out almost immediately; Sister Mary Celeste left and founded a convent at Foggia, and in 1733 all the members of Alphonsus' group except one lay brother left to found their own congregation. New postulants were recruited, and in 1734 a second foundation was made at Villa degli Schiavi, and Alphonsus went there to live. In 1738 Scala had to be abandoned after Villa degli Schiavi had been closed the previous year. Despite all the difficulties, the congregation grew, and in 1743, on the death of Bishop Falcoia, a general council elected Alphonsus superior; Pope Benedict XIV approved the rule of the men in 1749 and of the women the following year. During this time Alphonsus was personally active in preaching missions in rural areas and small villages but was increasingly devoting himself to writing. He refused an appointment to the see of Palermo but in 1762 was obliged to accept appointment as bishop of Sant' Agata dei Goti. He inaugurated a program designed to reform the clergy, monasteries, and the entire diocese, and worked to alleviate the condition of the poor and the ignorant. Ill and inflicted with rheumatism that left him paralyzed until his death, he resigned his see in 1775 and retired to Nocera. Meanwhile, during this entire period, he had been engaged in running disputes with the anticlerical Marquis Bernard Tanucci, who governed Naples, 1734–76, as Prime Minister of Charles III of Spain, who had conquered Naples in 1734. Tanucci refused to grant royal approval for the Redemptorists and constantly threatened to suppress Alphonsus' congregation as disguised Jesuits (the Jesuits had been expelled from Spanish domains in 1767). In 1780, with a new governor in power, Alphonsus was tricked into signing and submitting for royal approval a new rule that completely altered his own rule, which had been papally approved in 1750; when this fraudulent rule was approved by the King at Naples, a storm burst around Alphonsus. Pope Pius VI refused to accept the new rule, recognized the Redemptorists in the Papal States as the true Redemptorists, and a new superior was appointed to replace Alphonsus. For the last few years of his life, in addition to his ill health, he experienced deep spiritual depression and he went through a "dark night of the soul." But this period was replaced by a time of peace and light when he experienced visions, ecstasies, made prophecies that were later fulfilled, and reportedly performed miracles. He died on August 1 at Nocera. Alphonsus wrote profusely on moral, theological, and ascetical subjects (notably his *Moral Theology*), was constantly engaged in combating anticlericalism and Jansenism, and was involved in several controversies over probabilism. His devotional writings were most successful, especially his *Glories of Mary*. He was canonized in 1839 and was declared a Doctor of the Church in 1871 by Pope Pius IX.

LILY OF QUITO, THE. *See* Paredesy y Flores, Mariana de.

LINE, ANNE (d. 1601). Born at Dunmow, Essex, England, the daughter of William Heigham, who disowned her when she became a Catholic, she married Roger Line, a Catholic. He was arrested for his religion but was permitted to go to Flanders, where he died in 1594. Anne spent the rest of her life aiding fugitive priests at her home and later in a house in London that had been set up to provide shelter for Catholic priests by Jesuit Fr. John Gerard. She was arrested there and hanged for harboring Catholic priests, with Fr. Roger Filcock, a Jesuit priest who was her confessor, at Tyburn on February 27. She was canonized by Pope Paul VI in 1970 as one of the Forty Martyrs of England and Wales.

LINUS (d. c. 76). A native of Tuscany, he succeeded St. Peter as Pope about 67. St. Irenaeus says he is the Linus mentioned by St. Paul in 2 Timothy 4:21 and that he was consecrated bishop by St. Paul. September 23.

LIPHARD. *See* Liudhard.

LIUDHARD (d. c. 602). Chaplain of Bertha, daughter of King Charibert of Paris, he accompanied her to England, when she married King Ethelbert of Kent. According to tradition, he helped prepare Ethelbert for baptism by St. Augustine and died at Canterbury. An unverifiable legend had Liphard archbishop of Canterbury and murdered at Cambrai while on the way back from a pilgrimage to Rome; however, there is no record of an archbishop of Canterbury named Liphard, as Liudhard is sometimes called. May 7.

LLOYD, JOHN (d. 1679). A native of Breconshire, Wales, he was educated at Ghent and Valladolid, where he was ordained in 1653. The following year he returned to Wales and ministered to the Catholics of his native land for the next twenty-four years. He was arrested at Penllyn, Glamorgan, in 1678 and was imprisoned in Cardiff Castle at the same time as St. Philip Evans and charged with complicity in the Titus Oates plot to assassinate King Charles II. Though no proof was produced to implicate them, they were both convicted of being Catholic priests unlawfully in the kingdom and were executed at Cardiff on July 22. They were canonized as among the Forty Martyrs of England and Wales by Pope Paul VI in 1970.

LOLLIAN (d. 297). *See* Hipparchus.

LOMAN (d. c. 450). Unreliable legend has him the son of St. Patrick's sister Tigris. He accompanied Patrick to Ireland and was left to navigate their boat up the Boyne while Patrick went to Tara. On the way, he met Fortchern, son of the chieftain of Trim, his mother, a Christian, and his father, Fedelmid, a pagan. In time, he converted Fedelmid and his whole household to Christianity. Fedelmid gave Patrick land at Trim for a church, and Loman became bishop of Trim. Some scholars believe that in reality Loman was a bishop of Trim in the seventh century and in no way related to Patrick. February 17.

LONGINUS (1st century). According to tradition, Longinus was the name of the centurion at the Crucifixion who acknowledged Christ as "the son of God" (Matt. 27:54; Mark 15:39; Luke 23:47). This centurion is also identified, with no evidence, with the soldier who "pierced his side with a lance" (John 19:34). Untrustworthy legend says he was converted, left the army, took instructions from the apostles, and then became a monk at Caesarea in Cappadocia. The legend further says he was arrested for his faith and tortured, destroyed idols in the presence of the governor who was trying him, and was beheaded; whereupon the governor was converted. March 15.

LONGINUS (d. c. 290). *See* Victor of Marseilles.

LOPEZ Y VICUÑA, VINCENTIA MARÍA (1847–96). Daughter of a lawyer, she was born at Cascante, Spain, on March 22 and was sent to school at Madrid. While living there with her Aunt Eulalia de Vicuña, Vincentia was so impressed with her aunt's work with serving girls that she took a vow of chastity and dedicated herself to helping working girls. With her aunt she gathered a group of followers who lived a communal life, 1871–76, drew up a constitution, and in 1878 pronounced her vows with three others, and the congregation of the Daughters of Mary Immaculate for Domestic Service was founded. The institute soon spread through Spain, then to other parts of Europe and to Latin America, and received the approval of the Holy See in 1888. Vincentia died in Madrid on December 26 and was canonized by Pope Paul VI in 1975.

LOUIS IX (1214–70). Born at Poissy, France, on April 25, son of King Louis VIII and Blanche of Castile, he was raised in a religious atmosphere by his mother. His father died in 1226 when he was twelve, and Blanche became regent. She defended his throne against Thibaut of Champagne and other ambitious nobles by alliances, and when necessary, by war. He married Margaret, daughter of Count Raymund Berenger of Provence, in 1234, and the couple had eleven children. On reaching his majority in the same year, he assumed the reins of ruler, though Blanche was his adviser until her death. He put down revolts in southern France, 1242–43, defeated King Henry III of England at Taillebourg in 1242, securing suzerainty over Guienne by his victory, and in the same year forced Poitou to submit to him; in 1243 he compelled Raymond VII of Toulouse to submit to him. He went on crusade in 1248 and captured Damietta in 1249 but suffered a disastrous defeat at the hands of the Saracens at El Mansura in 1250 and was taken prisoner. After he ransomed himself and his men, he went to the Holy Land and remained there until 1254, when Blanche died and he returned to France. He imposed peace on Flanders in 1256, and ceded Limoges, Cahors, and Perigueux to King Henry III of England in return for Henry's renunciation of any claims he had to Normandy, Anjou, Maine, Touraine, and Poitou with the Treaty of Paris ratified in 1259. He ended Aragon's claims to Provence and Languedoc by yielding French claims to Roussillon and Barcelona in the Treaty of Corbeil in 1258. He set forth on a new crusade in 1270 but contracted typhoid soon after landing in Tunisia and died there near Tunis on August 25. Noted for his justice, ability, charity, and personal piety, Louis founded numerous religious and educational institutions (he rebuilt the Sainte-Chapelle in Paris, 1245–48, to house the Crown of Thorns given him by Emperor Baldwin II in 1239, and supported the founding of the Sorbonne in 1257) and forbade war among the feudal lords. He protected vassals from oppression by their lords and made the lords live up to their obligations. A man of his word, he was often sought out as an arbitrator and settled disputes about succession in Flanders, Navarre, and Hainaut and between King Henry III and his barons in 1263. Under his reign, France enjoyed unprecedented prosperity and peace as he followed a policy of peaceful coexistence with his European neighbors, improved the tax system, simplified administration, extended the appellate jurisdiction of the crown to all cases, and encouraged the use of Roman law. Gothic architecture flowered during his regime and he built the first French navy. He was one of the greatest of all French Kings and embodied the highest ideals of medieval kingship in the forty-four years of his rule. He was canonized in 1297 by Pope Boniface VII. August 25.

LOUIS OF ANJOU (1274–97). Son of King Charles II of

Naples and Sicily and Mary, daughter of King Stephen V of Hungary, he was born at Brignolles, Provence. When his father was captured by the King of Aragon in 1284, he was sent to Barcelona with two of his brothers in 1288 as hostages of his father's release. He was freed after seven years there by a treaty in 1295 between his father and King James II of Aragon. Louis refused to marry James's sister, surrendered his rights to the throne, and after much opposition, was ordained when he was twenty-three, was named bishop of Toulouse, and joined the Friars Minor at Rome. He lived a life of great austerity despite his royal background, resigned his bishopric after a few months because he felt he was unequal to its demands, and died at Brignolles on August 19. He was canonized in 1317.

LOUIS OF MONTFORT. *See* Grignion, Louis Mary.

LOUISE DE MARILLAC. *See* Marillac, Louise.

LOYOLA, IGNATIUS. *See* Ignatius Loyola.

LUCIAN OF ANTIOCH (d. 312). Born at Samosata, Syria, he studied Scripture under Macarius at Edessa and after he was ordained served as a priest in Antioch. He prepared an accurate version of the Old and New Testaments that was used by St. Jerome in preparing the Vulgate. Separated from the Church for a time (probably because he followed the teachings of Paul of Samosata), he was later reconciled. He was arrested at Nicomedia in 303 when Emperor Diocletian's persecution of the Christians began. After a long imprisonment, when he refused to sacrifice to pagan gods, he was convicted of being a Christian, racked, and sworded to death on January 7 at Nicomedia, Bithynia.

LUCIUS I (d. 254). A Roman, he was elected Pope to succeed Pope St. Cornelius on June 25, 253, and ruled only eighteen months. He was exiled briefly during the persecution of Emperor Gallus but was allowed to return to Rome. A letter of St. Cyprian praises him for condemning the Novatians for their refusal of the sacraments to penitent *lapsi*. He did not suffer martyrdom, as erroneously stated in the *Liber Pontificalis,* but died probably on March 4 in Rome and was buried in St. Callistus' catacomb.

LUCRETIA. *See* Leocritia.

LUCY (d. 304). According to unreliable tradition, she was born of noble parents at Syracuse, Sicily. When she refused marriage to a suitor during Emperor Diocletian's persecution of the Christians, he denounced her as a Christian. The governor sentenced her to a brothel, but when the guards tried to take her there they were unable to move her. She was then ordered burned to death, but the flames made no impression on her. Finally, she was stabbed through the throat. She is invoked by those with eye trouble, perhaps because of her name, which means light; one tradition has her eyes torn out by her judge, while another has her tearing them out to present to a suitor she disliked who admired them; in both cases they were miraculously restored. December 13.

LUKE (1st century). The author of the third gospel and the Acts of the Apostles is of unknown origin, though Eusebius and Jerome say he was probably a Greek and may have come from Antioch. He was a physician (Col. 4:14), accompanied Paul on his second missionary journey about 51, and then stayed at Philippi as a leader of the Christian community there until 57, when he rejoined Paul on his third missionary journey. He was with Paul in Rome during Paul's imprisonment, 61–63, and also during his second imprisonment. After Paul's death in 66, he seems to have gone to Greece. An improbable legend has him the painter of several portraits of Mary, though he may very well have visited her in Jerusalem. Where and when he wrote his gospel are uncertain, though it was probably between 70 and 90 (Eusebius says before Paul's death, Jerome says after, and an early tradition says in Greece). It was unquestionably written by a Gentile Christian for Gentile Christians. His Acts, probably written in Rome (Eusebius and Jerome agree in saying during Paul's imprisonment, though Irenaeus says after Paul's death), is the story of the growth of the Church under the inspiration of the Holy Spirit from about 35 to 63. Legend has him one of the seventy disciples, and some scholars identify him with Lucius of Cyrene, a teacher and prophet at Antioch (Acts 13:1) and with Lucius, Paul's companion at Corinth (Rom. 16:21). He is believed to have died at Boetia when eighty-four. He is the patron of painters and physicians and is represented in art as an ox. October 18.

LULL (d. 786). Probably a native of Britain, he was educated at Malmesbury Monastery, where he became a deacon,
and when twenty went to Germany, where he labored as a
missionary, noted for his learning, under St. Boniface, who
ordained him. He was sent to Rome on a mission to Pope St.
Zachary by Boniface, was consecrated his coadjutor when he
returned, and succeeded to the see of Fulda on Boniface's
death. He became involved in a jurisdictional dispute with St.
Sturmi, abbot of Fulda, deposed him, but saw him restored
and the abbey declared independent by King Pepin. Luke
refounded the monastery of Hersfeld, where he retired late in
life, and died there. October 16.

LUTGARDIS (1182–1246). Born at Tongres, Brabant, she
was sent to St. Catherine Benedictine Convent near Saint-
Trond when she was twelve presumably because her dowry
had been lost in a business venture. She had no particular vocation to the religious life until one day a vision of Christ
caused a change in her outlook on life and she became a
Benedictine nun when twenty. During the next twelve years
she experienced numerous ecstasies, during which she had visions of our Lord, our Lady, and several of the saints, was
levitated, and dripped blood when sharing in the Passion of
Christ. Though the nuns of her convent wanted to make her
abbess, she left in quest of a stricter rule and became a Cistercian at their convent at Aywières. She lived there the thirty
remaining years of her life, famed for her spiritual wisdom,
miracles, and prophecies. Blind the last eleven years of her
life, she died on June 16 and is considered one of the leading
mystics of the thirteenth century.

LWANGA, CHARLES (d. 1886). A master of pages at the
court of King Mwanga of Uganda, he had succeeded Joseph
Mkasa, a Catholic, whose censure of the King for his murder
of a Protestant minister and his homosexuality and corruption
of the young pages had intensified Mwanga's hatred of Catholics. Mwanga ordered Lwanga and fourteen of the pages who
were Christians sent to Namugango. Three of them were
murdered on the way; Lwanga and the others, with two soldiers, were burned to death. Among them were a thirteen-
year-old, Kizito, and Mbanga, a boy who was killed by his
uncle, who was the chief executioner, before being thrown on
the pyre. Some one hundred people died in the persecution;

among those martyred were a young catechist, Denis Sebuggawo, speared to death by Mwanga himself; Andrew Kaggwa, a native chief, beheaded; Pontain Ngondwe, a soldier; and Mathias Kalemba, a Membo judge, tortured to death. Also among those martyred in the same persecution were Matthias Murumba, an assistant judge to the provincial chief who was attracted to Christianity by Protestant missionaries and then was baptized a Catholic by Fr. Livinhac; also Andrew Kagwas, chief of Kigowa, who had been active in conversion work. In all, twenty-two martyrs were canonized in 1964 by Pope Paul VI as the Martyrs of Uganda. June 3.

LYDIA PURPURARIA (1st century). Born at Thyatira (Ak-Hissar), a town in Asia Minor famous for its dye works (hence her name, which means purple seller), she "was in the purple-dye trade" when she became Paul's first convert at Philippi. She was baptized with her household, and Paul stayed at her home there (Acts 16:12–15).

LYDWINA, BL. (1380–1433). Born at Schiedam, Holland, one of nine children of a workingman, she was injured in 1396 while ice skating and became a lifelong invalid, suffering intensely, with each year bringing increasing pain. She bore the pain as reparation for the sins of others. Beginning in 1407, she began to experience supernatural gifts—ecstasies and visions in which she participated in the Passion of Christ, saw purgatory and heaven, and visited with saints. The last nineteen years of her life she took no sustenance but Communion, slept little if at all the last seven years of her life, and became almost completely blind. Her extraordinary suffering attracted widespread attention, and when a new parish priest accused her of hypocrisy, the people of the town threatened to drive him away. An ecclesiastical commission appointed to investigate declared her experiences to be valid. Thomas à Kempis wrote a biography of her, and her cult was approved in 1890. April 14.

M

MACANISIUS (d. 514). According to unreliable legends, Aengus MacNisse was baptized by St. Patrick, who years later consecrated him bishop. After a pilgrimage to the Holy Land and Rome, he founded a church and monastery at Kells, which developed into Connor, of which he is considered the first bishop. His story is filled with extravagant miracles, such as changing the course of a river for the convenience of his monks and rescuing a child about to be executed for his father's crime by causing him to be carried by the wind from the executioners to his arms. September 3.

MACARIUS (d. c. 335). Named bishop of Jerusalem in 314, he fought the Arian heresy and was one of the signers of the decrees of the Council of Nicaea. According to legend he was with Helena when she found three crosses and was the one who suggested that a seriously ill woman be touched with each of the crosses; when one of them instantly cured her it was proclaimed the True Cross. He was commissioned by Constantine to build a church over Christ's sepulcher and supervised the building of the basilica that was consecrated on September 13, 335. He died soon after. March 10.

MACARIUS OF ALEXANDRIA. *See* Macarius the Younger.

MACARIUS THE ELDER (c. 300–90). Born in Upper Egypt, he was a cattleherder in his youth but early became a hermit, practicing the greatest austerities. He was accused of assaulting a woman but proved his innocence and became somewhat of a hero for his patience and humility during this trying ordeal. To escape the adulation, he retired to the desert of Skete when he was thirty, was ordained, and was much sought after for his spiritual wisdom. He was exiled for a time on a small island in the Nile with Macarius the Younger and other monks when Arian Lucius of Alexandria tried to drive out the desert monks, but was later allowed to return. He died after living in Skete for sixty years and is believed to be the first hermit to live there. January 15.

MACARIUS THE WONDER WORKER (d. c. 830). Born at Constantinople and baptized Christopher, he became a monk at Pelekete, taking the name Macarius. In time he was elected abbot and became known for the miracles he was reputed to have performed. He was ordained by Patriarch Tarasius of Constantinople, was imprisoned and tortured for his opposition to the iconoclasm proclaimed by Emperor Leo the Armenian, and was released by Leo's successor, Emperor Michael the Stammerer. When he refused Michael's demands that he support the iconoclastic heresy, he was exiled to the island of Aphusia off the coast of Bithynia and died there on August 18. April 1.

MACARIUS THE YOUNGER (d. c. 394). A successful businessman in Alexandria, Egypt, he gave up his business about 335 to become a monk in the Thebaid, Upper Egypt, and spent the remaining sixty years of his life as a hermit. In 373, he moved to Lower Egypt, where he built cells in the deserts of Skete and Nitria, but spent most of his time in the area called the Cells. He was ordained, lived a life of great austerity, and was known for his miracles. He was banished for a time with Macarius the Elder and other monks to an island in the Nile for his unswerving fidelity to orthodoxy by Lucius, the intruded Arian Patriarch of Jerusalem, but was later allowed to return. Macarius wrote a constitution for the monastery in Nitria named after him, and some of its rules were adopted by St. Jerome for his monastery. He is often surnamed "of Alexandria." January 2.

MACCABEES, THE HOLY (d. 160 B.C.). This is the name given to a group of Jews who were executed for resisting the attempts of King Antiochus IV Epiphanes to impose Greek paganism on the Jews and thus subvert their religion in his efforts to Hellenize them. Most prominent among the Maccabees are Eleazar, a prominent scribe who though ninety

years old refused to succumb to the bribes and cajolery of the
King's men, refused to violate the Jewish Torah by eating the
flesh of swine, and was executed for his resistance; also tortured and executed were seven brothers who, encouraged by
their mother, remained adamant in refusing to give up their
Jewish faith. All seven and their mother were executed (2
Mac. 6–7), and their remains are believed to be enshrined in
the Church of St. Peter in Chains in Rome. These are the
only persons in the Old Testament liturgically venerated in
the Western Church and are honored on August 1.

MACIAS, JOHN. See Massias, John.

MACRINA THE ELDER (c. 270–340). Grandmother of
St. Basil the Great and St. Gregory of Nyssa, both of whom
she influenced with her religious fervor, she and her husband
lived at Neocaesarea, Pontus, and suffered great hardships
when they were forced to flee into hiding during Emperor
Diocletian's persecution of the Christians. January 14.

MACRINA THE YOUNGER (c. 330–79). Granddaughter
of Macrina the Elder and sister of St. Basil, St. Gregory of
Nyssa, and St. Peter of Sebastea, she was well educated, especially in Scripture, was engaged to be married when twelve,
but when her fiancé died, she decided to dedicate her life to
God. On the death of her father, she and her mother retired
to the family estate in Pontus and lived a life of prayer and
contemplation in a community they formed there. Macrina
became head of the group when her mother died and lived in
Pontus until her death there. July 19.

MAEDOC. See Aidan.

MAGI. See Balthasar.

MAGNUS (d. 258). See Sixtus II.

MAHARSAPOR (d. 421). A Christian Persian of noble
family, he was seized with Narses and Sabutaka when King
Yezdigerd, angered at the destruction of a Mazdean temple,
unleashed a persecution of Christians. They were tortured,
and then Narses and Sabutaka were executed. Maharsapor

was imprisoned for three years and was then thrown into a cistern to die of starvation and was found dead three days later. October 10.

MAINCIN. *See* Munchin.

MAJOLUS (c. 906–94). Also known as Mayeul, he was born at Avignon, France, was forced to flee from his large estates near Rietz to relatives at Mâcon, Burgundy, to escape marauding Saracens. He received a canonry from his uncle, Bishop Berno, who sent him to Lyons to study under Abbot Antony of L'Isle Barbe, was named archdeacon on his return to Mâcon, and soon after was named bishop of Besançon. He became a monk at Cluny to escape this unwanted post and in 965 was elected abbot. The monasteries of Germany were entrusted to him by Emperor Otto the Great, and Majolus reformed many of them. He was noted for his scholarship and held in the greatest esteem by the rulers of his time, at one time settling a disagreement between Empress St. Adelaide and her son Emperor Otto II. Majolus appointed St. Odilo his coadjutor in 991 and devoted himself to prayer and penance. He died at Souvigny Abbey on May 11 on the way to reform St. Denis Abbey near Paris at the request of Hugh Capet.

MALACHY (1095–1148). Malachy O'More (Mael Maedoc Ua Morgair) was the son of a schoolteacher and was born and raised in Armagh, Ireland. When his parents died, he became a disciple of Eimar, a hermit, and was ordained by St. Celsus when he was twenty-five. He continued his studies under Bishop St. Malchus of Lismore, was assigned the abbacy of rundown Bangor Abbey, and in 1125 was named bishop of Connor, using Bangor as his headquarters. He soon restored religious fervor to the people of his see. When marauding Norsemen overran Bangor in 1127, he and his monks fled to Lismore and then established a monastery at Iveragh, Kerry. St. Celsus named Malachy his successor as metropolitan of Armagh on his deathbed in 1129, but instead Celsus' family installed his cousin Murtagh, as the archbishopric had been hereditary for generations. Malachy refused to try to occupy the see but after three years was ordered to do so by the papal legate and others. He governed the see but would not enter the city until 1134, when Murtagh died, naming Celsus' brother Niall his successor. Armed conflict broke out between the followers of the two, but Malachy finally obtained possession of his cathedral. When Niall fled with two relics that were supposed to be in the possession of the true archbishop, a book (probably the Book of Armagh), and a crozier, both reputed to have been St. Patrick's, the division and conflict continued as many of the people turned to Niall as possessor of these all-important symbols. Malachy eventually recovered them, restored peace and discipline to the see, and became uncontested archbishop. He then resigned the archbishopric of Armagh and returned to Connor in 1137. He then divided Connor into two dioceses, Connor and Down, became bishop of the latter, and established a monastery on the ruins of Bangor. He went to Rome two years later, met St. Bernard on the way, and wanted to become a monk at Clairvaux but was refused permission to resign his see and do so by Pope Innocent II. Instead his actions in Ireland were approved and he was appointed papal legate to Ireland. He returned to his native land in 1142, founded Mellifont Abbey with four of his companions who had become Cistercian monks at Clairvaux on their return trip from Rome, and in 1148 was appointed by a synod on Inishpatrick to go to Rome to secure *pallia* for the two metropolitans from Pope Eugene III. Delayed in England by King Stephen for political reasons, Malachy set off for Rome, and when he found that the Pope had left France and returned to Rome, decided to stop off on the way to see Bernard at Clairvaux. Malachy was stricken there and died in Bernard's arms on November 2. Bernard proclaimed him a saint at his requiem Mass, an action formally confirmed by Pope Innocent III in 1190, the first papal canonization of an Irish saint. Malachy was one of the great saints of Irish history, being responsible for the unification of the Irish clergy, the restoration of discipline, the revival of religious fervor, and the restoration of morality by his determination, humility, and lack of any desire for self-aggrandizement. He is reputed to have performed many miracles, among them curing Henry, son of King David of Scotland, of a grave disease, but is probably best known for the so-called Prophecies of Malachy, a list of Popes from Celestine II (d. 1144) "to the end of the world." The Popes are not named but are described in general, symbolic terms, quite accurate to 1590 but extremely vague after that. One theory is that they were forgeries from the conclave of 1590 to support the aspirations of one of the papal candidates. Another theory is that Malachy wrote them while he was in Rome, showed them to Pope Innocent II, and then they were buried in the papal archives until found by a Dom Arnold de Wyon, a Benedictine in 1597, 449 years after Malachy's death. Who wrote them is unknown but almost certainly it was not Malachy; they are considered spurious by scholars. November 3.

MALCHUS (4th century). According to the story he told St. Jerome, he was born in Nisibia, fled to avoid the marriage his parents had planned for him, and became a monk with a group of recluses at Khalkis near Antioch. When his father died, he set out for home, despite the refusal of his abbot to grant him permission to do so. The caravan he was with was attacked by marauding Bedouins, and he and a young woman were carried off as slaves. When his master decided he should marry the girl, they lived as brother and sister after Malchus had told her he would rather die than marry. They decided to flee, he to return to the monastery and she to her husband, and were pursued by their master and an aide. Malchus and the girl hid near a cave, and the master, thinking they had taken refuge in the cave, went into it with his aide, and both were killed by a lioness. Malchus returned to Khalkis, and when she was unable to find her husband, she joined him as a hermitess. She died there and Malchus ended up in Maronia, where Jerome found him, old and venerated for his holiness. October 21.

MAMERTIUS (d. c. 475). Elder brother of the poet Claudian, he was known for his learning, he was named bishop of Vienne, Gaul, in 461, and in 463 was condemned by Rome for consecrating, without the authority to do so, a new bishop of Die, which had been transferred from his jurisdiction to Arles; but no papal action seems to have been taken in the matter. He is particularly remembered as the originator of the penitential practice of rogation days, which was marked by processions and psalm singing the three days before the feast of the Ascension. May 11.

MANNES, BL. (d. c. 1230). Son of Felix de Guzmán and Bl. Joan of Aza and brother of St. Dominic, he was born at Calaruega, Burgos, Spain, and was one of the original sixteen members of the Dominicans, making his profession at Prouille in 1217. He and six others were sent to Paris to make the first French Dominican foundation in the same year. He then became chaplain to the Dominican nuns at Prouille, in 1218 was sent to Madrid as chaplain to a convent of Dominican nuns there, and spent the rest of his life in Madrid. He died at St. Peter Monastery at Gumiel d'Izan near Caleruega, and Pope Gregory XVI, in 1834, approved his cult. There is a possibility he may not have died until 1235. July 30.

MARCELLA (d. 410). A Roman matron, she was widowed after nine months of marriage, refused to marry Cerealis, the consul, and formed a group of noble ladies to live a life of austerity and asceticism. She was tortured by the Goths looting Rome in 410 to force her to reveal the whereabouts of her wealth, which she had long since given to the poor, was released, but died shortly after, in August. She had a correspondence with St. Jerome in which he answered queries she put to him about spiritual matters. January 31.

MARCELLINUS (d. 304). Born at Rome, the son of Projectus, he was elected Pope to succeed Pope St. Caius on June 30, 296, and witnessed the beginnings of Emperor Diocletian's persecution of the Christians. According to an ancient legend that may have been Donatist-inspired, he seems to have apostatized and surrendered the sacred books and offered incense to pagan gods but later repented and died a martyr's death by being beheaded. He died in Rome on October 25, but whether he died a martyr or from natural causes is still very uncertain. April 26.

MARCELLINUS (d. 413). Tribunal secretary to Emperor Honorius, he was sent to Carthage by the Emperor to chair a meeting between Catholic and Donatist bishops. At the end of the conference, Marcellinus ordered the Donatists to return to the Catholic faith and with his brother Apringius enforced his decree with great severity. Angered, the Donatists accused them of being implicated in a rebellion led by Heraclion to Marinus, the general in charge of putting down the insurrection. Marinus had Marcellinus and Apringius peremptorily executed at Carthage, an action for which he was later reprimanded by the Emperor. St. Augustine dedicated his *City of God* to "My dear friend Marcellinus." April 6.

MARCELLUS I (d. 309). After the death of Pope Marcellinus in 304, the intensity of Emperor Diocletian's persecution of the Christians prevented the election of a new Pope for years, and it was not until Diocletian abdicated in 305 and Maxentius became Emperor in 306 that a new election could be contemplated. Marcellus, a priest in Rome, was elected Pope in May or June 308. He reorganized the Church in Rome and was soon embroiled in the controversy concerning the *lapsi* when he insisted that they do penance before being readmitted to the sacraments. His decree caused widespread civil disorders, which caused Maxentius to exile Marcellus, who died shortly after leaving Rome on January 16 (although this may be the date of his burial) after a pontificate of about eighteen months.

MARCELLUS THE CENTURION (d. 298). A centurion in the Roman army at Tingis (Tangiers), he denounced the festivals held to celebrate the Emperor's birthday for their paganism and declared his Christianity. He was imprisoned and brought before Aurelius Agricolan, deputy for the praetorian prefects, after the festival was over. After an exchange between the two that is still preserved, Marcellus was condemned to death and was executed by sword. October 30.

MARCHIONI, JOHN CHARLES (1616–70). Born at Sezze, Italy, on October 19, of humble parents, he became a shepherd and wanted to become a priest. When unable to do so because of his poor scholarship (he barely learned to read and write), he became a lay brother at Naziano, served in various menial positions—cook, porter, gardener—at different monasteries near Rome and became known for his holiness, simplicity, and charity. He wrote several mystical works, lived a life of great mortifications, and worked heroically to help the stricken in the plague of 1656. He died in Rome on January 6. His family name may have been Melchior, and he is also known as Charles of Sezze. He was canonized by Pope John XXIII in 1959. January 5.

MARCOUL. *See* Marculf.

MARCULF (d. c. 558). Also known as Marcoul, he was born at Bayeux, Gaul, of noble parents, was ordained when he was thirty, and did missionary work at Coutances. Desirous of living as a hermit, he was granted land by King Childebert at Nanteuil, attracted numerous disciples, and built a monastery, of which he was abbot. It became a great pilgrimage center after his death on May 1. He is considered the patron of skin diseases.

MARGARET (no date). Nothing certain is known of her, but according to her untrustworthy legend, she was the daughter of a pagan priest at Antioch in Pisidia. Also known as Marina, she was converted to Christianity, whereupon she was driven from home by her father. She became a shepherdess and when she spurned the advances of Olybrius, the prefect, who was infatuated with her beauty, he charged her with being a Christian. He had her tortured and then imprisoned, and while she was in prison she had an encounter with the devil in the form of a dragon. According to the legend, he swallowed her, but the cross she carried in her hand so irritated his throat he was forced to disgorge her (she is patroness of childbirth). The next day attempts were made to execute her by fire and then by drowning, but she was miraculously saved and converted thousands of spectators witnessing her ordeal—all of whom were promptly executed. Finally she was beheaded. That she existed and was martyred are probably true; all else is probably fictitious embroidery added to her story, which was immensely popular in the Middle Ages, spreading from the East all over Western Europe. She is one of the Fourteen Holy Helpers, and hers was one of the voices heard by Joan of Arc. July 20.

MARGARET OF CORTONA (1247–97). Daughter of a farmer, she was born at Laviano, Tuscany, Italy, and was raised by an unsympathetic stepmother after the death of her mother, when she was seven. She ran away to become the mistress of a young nobleman from Montepulciano, bore him a son, and lived ostentatiously in great luxury. Nine years after she went to live with him, he was murdered and she resolved to change her lifestyle. She made a public confession of her sins in the church at Cortona where she had gone to seek the aid of the Friars Minor, but her father refused to take her back into his home. She and her son were taken in by two ladies, Marinana and Raneria, living in Cortona. Margaret became a Franciscan tertiary and Frs. John da Castiglione and Giunta Bevegnati became her spiritual advisers and helped her through three years of spiritual despair and aridity, frequently admonishing her to moderate the severity of the penances and mortifications she imposed on herself. After a brief period as a recluse, she devoted herself to caring for the poor and the sick. She began to experience ecstasies and visions of Christ, acted as a peacemaker, often admonishing worldly prelates, and in 1286 received approval from Bishop William of Arezzo for her plan to form a community of women to care for the sick poor called the Poverelle. She founded a hospital at Cortona and the Confraternity of Our Lady of Mercy to support it. About 1289 false and vicious rumors about her relations to the friars began to circulate, and Fr. Giunta was transferred to Siena, but it was later proved that the rumors were the work of vicious gossips, and the holiness of her life became apparent to all. She converted great numbers of sinners and was sought after for spiritual advice and her miraculous healing powers by people from all over Italy, France, and Spain. She died at Cortona, acclaimed a saint at once, though she was not formally canonized until 1728. May 16.

MARGARET MARY. *See* Alacoque, Margaret Mary.

MARGARET THE PENITENT. *See* Pelagia the Penitent.

MARGARET OF SCOTLAND (1045–93). Daughter of Prince Edward d'Outremer (the Exile) and a German princess, Agatha, who was probably the niece of King St. Stephen of Hungary's wife, Margaret was probably born in Hungary and raised at Stephen's court, where her father was an exile. When she was twelve she was brought to the court of King Edward the Confessor in England, but was forced to flee England with her mother, brother, and sister after the Battle of Hastings in 1066. They were given refuge at the court of King Malcolm III of Scotland, and in 1070 she and Malcolm were married at Dunfermline Castle. She became known for her great personal piety expressed in prayer, austerities, and fasting, her great concern for the poor and the needy, and for her royal benefactions. She supported synods that reformed abuses so prevalent at the time, such as simony and usury, regulated degrees of relationship in marriage, and set regulations for the Lenten fast and Easter Communion. She encouraged arts and education, acted as adviser in state matters, and with Malcolm, founded Holy Trinity Church at Dunfermline. She died at Edinburgh Castle on November 16 soon after learning that her husband and son had been killed by rebels attacking Alnwick Castle and while rebel forces were attacking Edinburgh. She was canonized in 1250 and declared patroness of Scotland in 1673. November 16.

MARI (d. c. 180). *See* Addai.

MARIA CROCIFISSA. *See* Di Rosa, Mary.

MARIA GORETTI. *See* Goretti, Maria.

MARIANA OF QUITO. *See* Paredes y Flores, Marian de.

MARIE OF THE INCARNATION, BL. *See* Martin, Bl. Marie of the Incarnation.

MARIE OF THE URSULINES. *See* Martin, Bl. Marie of the Incarnation.

MARILLAC, LOUISE DE (1591–1660). Born probably at Ferrières-en-Brie near Meux, France, on August 12, she was educated by the Dominican nuns at Poissy. She desired to become a nun but on the advice of her confessor, she married Antony Le Gras, an official in the Queen's service, in 1613. After his death in 1625, she met St. Vincent de Paul, who became her spiritual adviser, and she devoted the rest of her life to working with him. She helped direct his Ladies of Charity in their work of caring for the sick, the poor, and the neglected, and in 1633 she set up a training center, of which she was directress, in her own home for candidates seeking to help in the work. This was the beginning of the Sisters (or Daughters, as Vincent preferred) of Charity of St. Vincent de Paul (though it was not formally approved until 1655). She took her vows in 1634 and attracted great numbers of candidates, wrote a rule for the community, and in 1642, Vincent allowed four of the members to take vows. Formal approval placed the community under Vincent and his Congregation of the Mission, with Louise superior. She traveled all over France establishing her Sisters in hospitals, orphanages, and other institutions, and by the time of her death in Paris on March 15, the congregation had more than forty houses in France. Since then they have spread all over the world. She was canonized by Pope Pius XI in 1934 and was declared patroness of social workers by Pope John XXIII in 1960.

MARINA (no date). The daughter of Eugenius, a Bithynian who became a monk, she was brought into the monastery as a boy by her father. She dressed as a boy and lived the life of a monk until her father died when she was seventeen. She was accused of making the daughter of the local innkeeper pregnant but concealed her identity and was dismissed from the monastery. She became a beggar at the gates of the monastery and still maintained her silence about her sex when the innkeeper's daughter made her take custody of the child and was readmitted to the monastery with her "son" five years later. She was assigned the lowliest tasks and made to perform the most severe penances. Her sex was finally revealed at her death, when of course all concerned in the affair were filled with remorse. The whole story is typical of the pious fictions telling of women saints masquerading as men. February 12.

MARINA. *See* Margaret (no date).

MARK (d. c. 74). The son of Mary at whose house in Jerusalem the apostles stayed and a cousin of Barnabas, he was probably a Levite and perhaps a minor minister in the synagogue. He may have been the young man who attempted to follow Jesus after his arrest, was caught, but wiggled out of his cloak and fled naked (Mark 14:51–52), but this is uncertain. He accompanied Paul and Barnabas to Antioch in 44 (Acts 12:25), then to Cyprus, and with Barnabas was on Paul's first missionary journey (Acts 13:5), but left Paul at Pamphylia and returned to Jerusalem (Acts 13:13). Whatever the reason, he had evidently offended Paul, who did not take him on his second missionary journey, which was the occasion of the disagreement and separation of Paul and Barnabas (Acts 15:36–40). Mark accompanied Barnabas to Cyprus (Acts 15:39) and then, evidently back in Paul's good graces, was with him in Rome during his first imprisonment (Col. 4:10), where he was evidently a disciple of Peter, who affectionately called him "my son, Mark" (1 Pet. 5:13). An early uncertain tradition has him first bishop of Alexandria, and he is probably the same as the John Mark (Acts 12:25) mentioned several times in the New Testament. In the East this John Mark is believed to have been a separate person who became bishop of Biblos; his feast is celebrated on September 27. Mark was the author of the second gospel, written probably between 60 and 70 and based on the teaching of Peter. Papias, the bishop of Hierapolis in Asia Minor, called him the interpreter of Peter, in 130, and an ancient tradition had it written in Rome for Gentile Christians. Many modern scholars believe that Mark provided Matthew and Luke with a common source for their gospels. Mark is the patron of Venice, which claims his body is in St. Mark's Cathedral there, where it is reported to have been brought from Alexandria. In art he is represented as a lion. April 25.

MARK (d. 336). Son of Priscus, he became a priest in Rome and was elected Pope to succeed Pope St. Sylvester on January 18, 336. Mark built two basilicas in Rome on land granted by Emperor Constantine and is believed to have decreed that the bishop of Ostia was to consecrate the bishop of Rome. Mark died in Rome on October 7 after a pontificate of only eight months.

MARTHA (1st century). Sister of Mary and Lazarus, with whom she lived in Bethany, she was evidently the eldest and in charge of the household. They were all friends of Jesus, who often stayed at their home, and she was most solicitous of his welfare. In the famous incident in Luke 10:38–42, she asked Christ to tell her sister Mary, who was listening to the Lord, to help her in the household preparations; whereupon he chided her for bustling about so, concluding, "it is Mary who has chosen the better part." She has thus become the prototype of the activist Christian and Mary the symbol of the contemplative life. It was Martha who went out to meet Jesus after the death of Lazarus, while Mary remained at home (John 11:20). According to a medieval legend, she, Mary, and Lazarus went to France after the death of Jesus and evangelized Provence. She is the patron of cooks. July 29.

MARTIAL (d. c. 165). *See* Felicity.

MARTIAL (d. c. 250). According to tradition, he was one of the seven missionary bishops sent from Rome before 250 to preach the gospel in Gaul. He evangelized the Limousin area and founded Limoges, of which he was the first bishop. Later legends extravagantly (and erroneously) had him one of the followers of Christ, one of the seventy-two disciples, and the boy with the barley loaves when the Savior performed the miracle of the loaves and the fishes. June 30.

MARTIAL (d. c. 304). *See* Faustus.

MARTIN I (d. c. 656). Born at Todi, Umbria, Italy, he came to Rome and was known for his great learning and piety. He was Pope Theodore I's nuncio to Constantinople and succeeded him as Pope on July 21, 649. He called a council at the Lateran the same year, which condemned monothelitism and censured the imperial decrees of Heraclius, *Ekthesis,* and of Constans II, *Typos.* When Martin's condemnations were published in the East, Constans, who was a monothelite, was furious and sent Theodore Calliopas to Rome to bring Martin to Constantinople. Though Martin was ill and had taken refuge in the Lateran, Calliopas' soldiers broke in and forcibly took the Pope captive to Constantinople, where he arrived in the fall of 653. He was imprisoned for three months under terrible conditions and then tried and convicted, without being heard, by the Senate of treason and sent back to prison for another three months. His life was spared at the plea of the dying Patriarch Paul of Constantinople and he was exiled to Kherson in the Crimea, where he died on September 16 of neglect and ill treatment, the last of the Popes to die a martyr. November 12.

MARTIN, BL. MARIE OF THE INCARNATION (1599–1672). The daughter of a baker, Marie Guyard was born in Tours, France, on October 28 and married a silk manufacturer named Claude Martin when she was seventeen; the couple had one son. Claude died two years later and Marie became a bookkeeper for her brother-in-law. In 1629, she joined the Ursulines at Tours, taking the name Marie of the Incarnation. In 1639, she was sent to Canada where she laid the cornerstone of the first Ursuline convent in Quebec in

1641; she rebuilt it when it was destroyed by fire in 1650. She compiled dictionaries in Algonquin and Iroquois and taught the Indians the rest of her life until her death in Quebec on April 30. She experienced mystical visions and suffered periods of spiritual aridity about which she wrote and her *Letters* give a valuable account of life in Quebec in 1639–71. Also known as Marie of the Ursulines, she was beatified in 1980 by Pope John Paul II.

MARTIN DE PORRES. *See* Porres, Martin de.

MARTIN, THÉRÈSE. *See* Thérèse of Lisieux.

MARTIN OF TOURS (c. 316–97). Born at Sabaria, Pannonia (Hungary), perhaps in 315, the son of a pagan army officer, he was taken to Pavia when his parents moved there, and when fifteen, against his will, was inducted into the army. About 337 occurred the famous incident at Amiens where he was stationed in which he cut his cloak in half and gave half of it to a poorly clad beggar in the freezing cold; that night he had a vision of Christ clad in his half cloak. He became a convert to Christianity, refused to fight, and was discharged soon after. He returned to Pannonia, converted his mother and others, and then went to Illyricum, where he was so active in opposing Arianism that he was scourged and forced to leave the country. He returned to Italy but was driven away by Bishop Auxentius of Milan, an Arian. After a time as a recluse on the island of Gallinaria in the Tyrrhenian Sea, he returned to Gaul in 360. When St. Hilary, bishop of Poitiers, was allowed to return to Poitiers from the exile imposed on him by Emperor Constantius, Martin joined him at Poitiers and became a hermit on land granted him by Hilary at Ligugé. When other hermits joined Martin, a monastic community was organized—the first monastic community in Gaul. After ten years at Ligugé, despite his objections, Martin was named bishop of Tours in 371. He lived privately at Marmoutier as a monk, establishing the great monastic center of Marmoutier, while publicly devoting himself to his episcopal duties with great zeal. He worked ceaselessly to spread the faith and convert pagans, ruthlessly destroyed pagan temples, and was often saved from harm by seemingly miraculous means. He is reputed to have experienced visions and revelations and was gifted with the ability to prophesy. An opponent of Priscillianism, Martin interceded with Emperor Maximus at Trier in 384 to spare Priscillian's life when Bishop Ithacius of Ossanova demanded he be put to death for his heresy and was accused of the heresy himself. Priscillian was eventually beheaded by Prefect Evodius, to whom Maximus remanded the case—the first judicial death sentence for heresy and an infringement of the secular authority into ecclesiastical affairs that Martin vigorously opposed. Both Maximus and Ithacius were censured by Pope St. Siricius for their roles in the affair. Martin again returned to Trier to plead with the Emperor against the bloodbath about to be unleashed against the Priscillianists in Spain. Maximus agreed to do so only provided Martin became reconciled to Ithacius, which he did, though later bitterly reproaching himself for doing so. Martin made a visit to Rome and then went to Candes in Touraine, where he had established a religious center, and died there on November 8. Martin was one of the great saints of Gaul and the outstanding pioneer of Western monasticism before St. Benedict. Martin's shrine at Tours became one of the most popular pilgrim centers in Europe, and he is one of the patron saints of France. November 11.

MARTINIAN (1st century). Although early venerated in Rome, the story of Martinian and Processes seems to be based on an unreliable sixth-century legend according to which they were the wardens of Peter and Paul when the two apostles were in Mammertine Prison in Rome. They were converted by the two (Peter is reputed to have baptized them from a spring that miraculously sprung into being in the prison), were tortured by their superior, Paulinus, when they would not sacrifice to Jupiter, and were then sworded to death. July 2.

MARUTHAS (d. c. 415). Bishop of Maiferkat, Mesopotamia, near the Persian border, he petitioned Emperor Arcadius at Constantinople in 399 to ask newly crowned King Yezdigerd of Persia to mitigate the deplorable conditions under which Christians in Persia were forced to live. While on a diplomatic mission to Yezdigerd for Emperor Theodosius, Maruthas gained the King's favor and despite the opposition of the Mazdeans, received permission from him to restore a Church organization in Persia and to build churches there wherever he pleased. Maruthas is considered the father of the Syrian Church, was known for his knowledge of medicine, compiled a record of Christians martyred in Persia during the persecution of Christians during the reign of King Sapor, and brought so many martyrs' relics to Maiferkat that it was renamed Martyropolis. He composed several hymns used in the Syriac liturgy and was the author of several theological treatises. December 4.

MARY (1st century). "Mary has by grace been exalted above all the angels and men to a place second only to her Son, as the most holy mother of God who was involved in the mysteries of Christ: She is rightly honored by a special cult in the Church. From the earliest times the Blessed Virgin is honored under the title Mother of God, [under] whose protection the faithful take refuge together in prayer in all their perils and needs." (Dogmatic Constitution on the Church, No. 66). Pre-eminent among the saints, all the factual information we have about Mary is to be found in the New Testament, and it is from this source that the role of Mary in the Church has been developed. Aside from the Infancy narratives (Matt. 1–2; Luke 1–2), in which, of course, she plays a prominent role, there are only a few scattered references to her elsewhere in the New Testament. The Infancy narratives have been the subjects of prolonged and intensive study by biblical scholars, and they clearly and unequivocally declare her divine maternity, Jesus' messianic character, and Mary's virginity. Nothing is known of her childhood, though tradition has it that she was the daughter of Joachim and Anne, was born in Jerusalem, as a child was presented in the Temple, and took a vow of perpetual virginity. According to the evangelists, she was betrothed to Joseph when she was visited by the angel Gabriel, who announced to her that she was to be the mother of Jesus. She became pregnant of the Holy Spirit and then married Joseph after he was assured by an angel that "she has conceived what is in her by the Holy Spirit" (Matt. 1:20). Soon after she visited her Cousin Elizabeth, who was bearing John the Baptist; when Elizabeth acknowledged Mary as the Mother of God, Mary replied with the Magnificat (Luke 1:5–25; 39–56). Shortly after the birth of Jesus, she and Joseph were forced to flee with Jesus to Egypt to escape the wrath of Herod, who feared the child as a rival to his throne. On the death of Herod, they returned and settled at Nazareth. Nothing is known of her life during

the years she lived there except for Jesus' presentation in the
Temple (Luke 2:22) and an incident recounted in Luke
2:41 on a trip back from Jerusalem when Jesus was twelve
during which Mary and Joseph lost him; they finally found
him in the Temple discoursing learnedly with the doctors
there. Mary was instrumental in having Jesus perform his first
miracle, changing water into wine at Cana (John 2:1–5),
and then returned with him to Capernaum (John 2:12),
which may mean they no longer lived at Bethlehem. There
are references to her as the mother of Jesus in Matthew
13:55 and Mark 6:3, and she is again mentioned in Matthew
12:46–50, Mark 3:31–35, and Luke 8:19–21 when Jesus
describes his "mothers and brothers" as "anyone who does
the will of God." She was at the Crucifixion (but only in
John 19:25–27), where she was given into John's care, which
would seem to indicate that she had no relatives to care for
her. She was present with the disciples at Jerusalem in the
days before Pentecost (Acts 1:14), and it is believed that
she was present at the Resurrection and Ascension, though
this is not in Scripture; there is no further mention of her in
the New Testament. According to tradition, she went to
Ephesus, where she died; but another tradition has her living
in Jerusalem until her death, which is believed to have occurred in 48. The belief her body was assumed into heaven is
one of the oldest traditions in the Church and was declared
dogma by Pope Pius XII in 1950; the feast of the Assumption
is celebrated on August 15. Also declared dogma is that she is
the Mother of God, the Second Person of the Holy Trinity,
and hence free from original sin from the moment of her
conception, the dogma of the Immaculate Conception proclaimed by Pope Pius IX in 1854 (celebrated on December
8), the only human being to be so honored. Catholics believe
in the motherhood and perpetual virginity of Mary and that
"the Blessed Virgin stands out in eminent and singular fash-
ion as exemplar of virgin and mother" (ibid., No. 63). Her
birthday has been celebrated since before the seventh century
on September 8. Among her other feast days are: the Solem-
nity of Mary, Mother of God (January 1); the Purification
of the Blessed Virgin, now called the Presentation of the Lord
(February 2); the Annunciation of the Blessed Virgin Mary,
now called the Annunciation of the Lord (March 25); the
Visitation (May 31); the Assumption of Blessed Mary the
Virgin (August 15); the Queenship of Mary (August 22);

Our Lady of Sorrows (September 15); Our Lady of the Rosary (October 7); the Immaculate Conception of Blessed Mary the Virgin (December 8) and the Immaculate Heart of Mary (the Saturday following the second Sunday of Pentecost), under which title Pope Pius XII dedicated the whole human race in 1944. One of the pre-eminent features of modern Catholicism has been the reported appearances of Mary in the last century and a half, notably at Lourdes, Fatima, and La Salette.

MARY (1st century). Mother of John Mark, her home in Jerusalem was a gathering place of the apostles and was the first place Peter went when released from Herod's imprisonment. (Acts 12:12ff.). June 29.

MARY (d. 851). *See* Flora.

MARY OF CEREVELLON (d. 1290). Born at Barcelona, Spain, daughter of a nobleman, she decided to devote herself to aiding Christian slaves of the Moors after hearing a sermon by Bernard Corbaria, a Mercedarian. Under his direction, she and a group of women formed a community that became the third order regular of the Mercedarians (Order of Our Lady of Ranson), with Mary as first prioress. She was called Mary of Help for her prayers and work for the slaves. She died at Barcelona. She is considered the patroness of sailors in Spain, and her cult was confirmed in 1692. September 19.

MARY CLEOPHAS. *See* Mary Clopas.

MARY CLOPAS (1st century). Mother of James the Younger and Joseph (Matt. 27:56; Mark 15:40) and wife of Clopas and sister of Mary (John 19:25), she was present at the Crucifixion (Matt. 27:56; Mark 15:40; John 19:25) and accompanied Mary Magdalen to the tomb of Christ on the first Easter (Mark 16:1; Luke 24:10). Later legend had her going to Spain, where she died at Ciudad Rodrigo; another legend had her accompanying Lazarus, Mary Magdalen, and Martha to Provence. Mary Clopas' name is also spelled Cleophas. April 9.

MARY DI ROSA. *See* Di Rosa, Mary.

MARY OF EGYPT (5th century). In Cyril of Scythopolis' life of St. Cyriacus, he tells of a woman named Mary found by Cyriacus and his companions living as a hermitess in the Jordanian desert. She told him she had been a famous singer and actress who had sinned and was doing penance in the desert; when they returned, she was dead. Around this story was built an elaborate legend that had tremendous popularity during the Middle Ages according to which she was an Egyptian who went to Alexandria when she was twelve and lived as an actress and courtesan for seventeen years. She was brought to the realization of her evil life before an icon of the Blessed Virgin, and at Mary's direction went to the desert east of Palestine, where she lived as a hermitess for forty-seven years, not seeing a single human being and beset by all kinds of temptations, which were mitigated by her prayers to the Blessed Virgin. She was discovered about 430 by a holy man named Zosimus, who was impressed by her spiritual knowledge and wisdom. He saw her the following Lent, but when he returned, he found her dead and buried her. When he returned to his monastery near the Jordan, he told the brethren what had happened and the story spread. April 2.

MARY OF THE GAEL. *See* Brigid (c. 450–525).

MARY MAGDALEN (1st century). Probably from Magdala on the western shore of the Sea of Galilee near Tiberias, she became a follower of Christ and has been the classic example of the repentant sinner from earliest times. She is identified with the unknown sinner who anointed Christ's feet in Simon's house (Luke 7:36ff.) and with Mary, the sister of Martha, but there are no real justifications for these identifications in the Gospels, and modern scholars do not believe they are the same. She had seven devils cast out of her by the Lord (Mark 16:9; Luke 8:2), ministered to him in Galilee (Luke 8:2), was among the women at the Crucifixion (Matt. 27:56; Mark 15:40; John 19:25), and with Joanna and Mary, the mother of James and Salome, discovered the empty tomb and heard the angelic announcement of the resurrection of Christ (Matt. 28:1ff.; Mark 16:1–8; Luke 24:1–10). She was the first person to see Christ later the same day (Matt. 28:9; Mark 16:9; John 20:1–18). According to an ancient tradition, she accompanied John to Ephesus, where she died; a later unfounded pious legend in the West had her going to Provence, France, with Martha and Lazarus and dying there. July 22.

MARY SALOME (1st century). *See* Salome.

MASON, BL. JOHN (d. 1591). *See* Gennings, St. Edmund.

MASSIAS, JOHN (1585–1645). Born at Ribera del Fresno, Estramadura, Spain, on March 2, of an impoverished noble family, he was orphaned in his youth and worked as a shepherd. He went to Peru, worked on a cattle ranch for two years, and then went to Lima, where he became a Dominican lay brother and worked as a porter. He became known for his austerities, miracles, and visions, and attracted the poor and the sick of the city, ministering to them spiritually and physically. He died in Lima on September 16, and was canonized by Pope Paul VI in 1975. His name is sometimes spelled Macias.

MATILDA (c. 895–968). Daughter of Count Dietrich of Westphalia and Reinhild of Denmark and also known as Mechtildis and Maud, she was raised by her grandmother, the abbess of Eufurt convent. Matilda married Henry the Fowler, son of Duke Otto of Saxony, in 909. He succeeded his father as duke in 912 and in 919 succeeded King Conrad I to the German throne. She was noted for her piety and charitable works, was widowed in 936, and supported her son Henry's claim to his father's throne. When her son Otto (the Great) was elected, she persuaded him to name Henry duke of Bavaria after he had led an unsuccessful revolt. She was severely criticized by both Otto and Henry for what they considered her extravagant charities, resigned her inheritance to her sons, and retired to her country home but was recalled to the court through the intercession of Otto's wife, Edith. When Henry again revolted, Otto put down the insurrection in 941 with great cruelty. Matilda censured Henry when he began another revolt against Otto in 953 and for his ruthlessness in suppressing a revolt by his own subjects; at that time she prophesied his imminent death. When he did die in 955, she devoted herself to building three convents and a monastery, was left in charge of the kingdom when Otto went to Rome in 962 to be crowned Emperor (often regarded as the beginning of the Holy Roman Empire), and spent most of the declining years of her life at the convent at Nordhausen she had built. She died at the monastery at Quedlinburg on March 14 and was buried there with Henry.

MATRONA (date unknown). According to the Roman Martyrology, she was the Christian maid of a Jewish mistress in Thessalonica. When her mistress discovered she was Christian, she subjected her to many tribulations; Matrona was later beaten to death at the instigation of her mistress. Another Matrona, a native of Barcelona, Spain, was taken to Rome and was executed there for ministering to Christian prisoners. And a third St. Matrona is reputed to have been a Portuguese of royal birth, was supernaturally instructed to go to Italy for a cure of her dysentery, and died there. She is venerated in Capua and is the patroness of those suffering from dysentery. March 15.

MATTHEW (1st century). Called Levi (though this may have been merely a tribal designation—that is, Matthew the Levite), he was probably born in Galilee, and was a publican tax collector (Matt. 9:9–13; 10:3) at Capharnaum when Christ called him to follow him (Mark 2:14; Luke 5:27–32), and he became one of the twelve apostles. He was the author of the first Gospel, written sometime between 60 and 90, perhaps originally in Aramaic (Papias in 130 records that Matthew wrote the Logia, presumably our Gospel, "in the Hebrew tongue"), though the Gospel we now have was in Greek and at the very least is a thorough and substantial revision of the original Aramaic, of which no traces have ever been found. It was without question written by a Jewish Christian of Palestinian origins for Jewish Christians. Some scholars believe it was written sometime after 70 and perhaps at Antioch, Syria. According to tradition, Matthew preached in Judea and then went to the East, where he suffered martyrdom in Ethiopia, according to the Roman Martyrology; in Persia, according to another legend. He is the patron of bankers and bookkeepers. September 21.

MATTHIAS (1st century). Mentioned in the New Testament only in Acts 1:21–26, where he was selected by the apostles to replace Judas, unreliable legend had him preaching in Judea, Cappadocia, and on the shores of the Caspian

Sea, where he endured great persecutions; he suffered martyr-dom at Colchis. May 14.

MAUBANT, BL. PHILIBERT (d. 1839). *See* Imbert, Bl. Laurence.

MAUD. *See* Matilda.

MAURA (5th century). *See* Brigid.

MAURICE (d. c. 287). An officer of the Theban Legion of Emperor Maximian Herculius' army, which was composed of Christians from Upper Egypt, he and his fellow legionnaires refused to sacrifice to the gods as ordered by the Emperor to insure victory over rebelling Bagaudae. When they refused to obey repeated orders to do so and withdrew from the army encamped at Octodurum (Martigny) near Lake Geneva to Agaunum (St. Maurice-en-Valais), Maximian had the entire legion of over six thousand men put to death. To the end they were encouraged in their constancy by Maurice and two fellow officers, Exuperius and Candidus. Also executed was Victor (October 10), who refused to accept any of the belongings of the dead soldiers. In a follow-up action, other Christians put to death were Ursus and another Victor at Solothurin (September 30); Alexander at Bergamo; Oc-tavius, Innocent, Adventor, and Solutar at Turin; and Gereon (October 10) at Cologne. Their story was told by St. Eu-cherius, who became bishop of Lyons about 434, but scholars doubt that an entire legion was massacred; but there is no doubt that Maurice and some of his comrades did suffer mar-tyrdom at Agaunum. September 22.

MAXIMINUS (d. 363). *See* Juventinus.

MAXIMINUS OF AIX (5th century). According to legend, he was one of Christ's seventy-two disciples and accompanied Mary Magdalen, Martha, Lazarus, and Mary Clopas to Pro-vence to evangelize the area. He made his headquarters at Aix, where he is considered its first bishop, and was reputed to have given communion to Mary Magdalen when she was miraculously transported to him from her cave at Sainte-Baume. In one legend, he is identified as "the man who had been blind from birth" in John 9:1–38. However, factual information about him is lacking, including even the century in which he lived, though he may have been a fifth-century bishop of Aix. June 8.

MAXIMUS (date unknown). *See* Cecilia.

MAXIMUS THE CONFESSOR (c. 580–662). Maximus Homologetes was born of a noble family at Constantinople and became secretary to Emperor Heraclius but resigned to become a monk at nearby Chrysopolis (Skutari), where he became abbot. He was one of the leaders in the struggle against monothelitism and Emperor Constans II, who favored the heresy. Maximus defended Pope Honorius against charges of monothelitism, was a supporter of papal authority, and in 645 refuted Pyrrhus in a public debate so decisively that Pyrrhus went to Rome to abjure the heresy. When Constans issued his decree *Typhos,* favoring monothelitism, Maximus was at the Lateran Council of 649, convened by Pope St. Martin I, which condemned the decree, a step that caused the Pope's exile and martyrdom from ill treatment at the Chersonese in 653. Maximus was seized at Rome, brought to Constantinople, and charged with conspiracy against the Empire. He was exiled to Bizya, Thrace, next to a monastery at Rhegium, and then spent the next six years at Perberis, with two of his supporters, both named Anastasius, subjected to great hardships. They were then brought back to Constantinople, tortured and mutilated (their tongues and right hands were cut off), and sentenced to life imprisonment. Maximus, after a terrible journey, died soon after his arrival at Skhemaris on the Black Sea; one Athanasius died before Maximus, and the other four years later. Maximus was a foremost exponent of Byzantine mysticism and wrote prolifically, theological, mystical, and ascetical treatises, biblical commentaries, a dialogue on the spiritual life between two monks, and *Mystagogia,* a treatise on liturgical symbolism. August 13.

MAYEUL. *See* Majolus.

MAYNE, CUTHBERT (1544–77). Born at Youlston, Devonshire, England, he was raised a Protestant by his uncle, a schismatic priest, and was ordained a minister when he was about nineteen. He studied at Oxford, where he received his M.A. and met Edmund Campion, at whose urging he became

a Catholic in 1570. He was forced to flee England when letters from Campion were intercepted and went to Douai to
study for the priesthood, was ordained in 1575, and was sent
back to England the following year. He became estate steward of Francis Tregian at Golden, Cornwall, and was arrested
the following year. He was found guilty of treason for being a
Catholic priest and was hanged, drawn, and quartered at
Launceton on November 25 when he refused to accept the
supremacy of the Queen in ecclesiastical matters. He was the
first Englishman trained for the priesthood at Douai to be
martyred and is the protomartyr of English seminaries. He
was canonized in 1970 by Pope Paul VI as one of the Forty
Martyrs of England and Wales. November 30.

MAZENROD, BL. CHARLES JOSEPH EUGENE
(1782–1861). Born at Aix-la-Chapelle, France, on August
1, he was forced to flee to Italy during the French Revolution
but later returned and was ordained at Amiens in 1811. He
was assigned to pastoral work at Aix, became interested in
missionary work, and in 1816 founded an institute that became the Oblates of Mary Immaculate, approved by Pope
Leo XII, and served as superior until his death. He was appointed titular bishop of Icosium in 1832, and five years later
was named bishop of Marseilles, where he restored ecclesiastical discipline and became a leader in the defense of the
papacy against the civil authorities and the Gallicanists. He
died at Marseilles on May 21, and was beatified by Pope Paul
VI in 1975.

MAZZARELLO, MARY (1837–81). Born at Mornese near
Genoa, Italy, daughter of a peasant, she worked in the fields
as a child, and when seventeen joined the sodality of Daughters of Mary Immaculate founded at the inspiration of St.
John Bosco. Stricken by typhoid in 1860 and unable to work
in the fields, she started a dressmaking business with a friend,
Petronilla, and the two became interested in working with
girls, as Don Bosco was doing with boys. In 1872 Don Bosco
received permission from Pope Pius IX to found a congregation of nuns for that purpose and appointed Mary superioress of the Daughters of Our Lady Help of Christians,
popularly known as the Salesian Sisters, at Mornese. The congregation spread rapidly (by 1900 there were nearly eight
hundred of its foundations in existence) and expanded its ac-

tivities to charitable works as well as teaching. Mary died at
Nizza Monferrato, where the mother house had been trans-
ferred in 1879, on April 27, and was canonized in 1951 by
Pope Pius XII. May 14.

MECHTILDIS. *See* Matilda.

MEL (d. c. 488). According to untrustworthy legend, he
and his brother Melchu were sons of Conis and St. Patrick's
sister, Darerca. They accompanied Patrick to Ireland, joined
him in his missionary work, and became bishops. Patrick appointed Mel bishop of Armagh, and Melchu is reputed to
have been bishop of Ardagh. Some scandal was circulated
about Mel, who lived with his Aunt Lupait but both cleared
themselves by miraculous means to Patrick, who ordered
them to live apart. Two other brothers, Muinis and Rioch,
also became missionary bishops. February 6.

MELANIA THE YOUNGER (383–439). Daughter of
Publicola, a Roman senator who was the son of Melania the
Elder, and Albina, the Christian daughter of a pagan priest,
Melania the Younger was married against her will to Valerius
Pinianus by her father when she was fourteen. After two children died soon after birth, Pinianus agreed to respect her
desire to devote her life to God, and when her father died,
leaving his enormous wealth to her, she, Pinianus, and her
mother, Albina, left Rome and turned their country villa into
a religious center. Melania sold some of her property for
charitable purposes, encountered much family opposition, and
finally appealed to Emperor Honorius, who granted her his
protection. She became one of the great religious philan-
thropists of all time, endowing monasteries in Egypt, Syria,
and Palestine, helping churches and monasteries in Europe,
aiding the poor, sick, and captives, helping pilgrims, and free-
ing some eight thousand slaves in two years. In 406, she and
her followers were forced to flee the invading Goths, went to
Messina, and then decided to go to Carthage. They were
shipwrecked on the island of Lipari, which she ransomed
from pirates, and then settled at Tagaste in Numidia in about
410. She founded a monastery for men and another for
women, where she lived in great austerity. In 417, with Pinianus and Albina, she made a pilgrimage to the Holy Land
and visited the Egyptian desert monks. On their return they

settled at Jerusalem, where Melania met her Cousin Paula, niece of St. Eustochium, who introduced her to the group in Bethlehem presided over by St. Jerome, whose friend she became. Albina died fourteen years after their arrival in Jerusalem, and Pinianus the following year. Melania built a cell near their tombs, and when she attracted numerous disciples, built a convent for them, of which she was superior for the rest of her life. She died at Jerusalem on December 31. Although she has been venerated in the Eastern Church for centuries, she has had no cult in the West, although Pope Pius X approved the observance of her feast in 1908 for the Somaschi, an observance followed by the Latin Catholics of Constantinople and Jerusalem.

MELCHIADES. *See* Miltiades.

MELCHIOR (1st century). *See* Balthasar.

MELCHIOR, CHARLES. *See* Marchioni, John Charles.

MELCHU. *See* Mel.

MELETIUS OF ANTIOCH (d. 381). Born at Melitene, Lower Armenia, of a distinguished family, he was appointed bishop of Sebastea about 358 but fled to the desert and then to Beroea in Syria when the appointment caused great dissension. In 361 a group of Arians and Catholics elected him archbishop of Antioch as a compromise candidate between the two groups, and though confirmed by Emperor Constantius II, he was opposed by some Catholics because Arians had participated in his election. The Arians' hope that he would join them was dashed when he expounded the Catholic position before the pro-Arian Emperor, who was persuaded by Arian Bishop Eudoxus of Constantinople to exile Meletius to Lower Armenia only a month after he occupied his see and to appoint Arian Euzoius to his episcopal chair. On the death of the Emperor in 361, his successor, Emperor Julian, recalled Meletius, who found that in his absence, a faction of the Catholic bishops, led by Lucifer Cagliari, had elected Paulinus archbishop—the beginning of the Meletian schism, which was to rend the Church of Antioch for years to come. The Council of Alexandria in 362 was unsuccessful in healing the breach, and an unfortunate rift between St. Athanasius

and Meletius in 363 exacerbated the matter. During the next
decade and a half, Meletius was exiled, 356–66 and 371–78,
by Emperor Valens while the conflict between the Arian and
the Catholic factions raged. Gradually, Meletius' influence in
the East grew as more and more bishops supported him (by
379 the bishops backing him numbered 150, in contrast to his
26 supporters in 363), but the rift between the contending
Catholic factions continued despite the untiring efforts of St.
Basil, who was unswerving in his support of Meletius, to resolve the matter. In 374 the matter was further complicated
when Pope Damasus recognized Paulinus as archbishop, appointed him papal legate in the East, and St. Jerome allowed
himself to be ordained presbyter by Paulinus. In 378, the
death of avidly pro-Arian Valens led to the restoration of the
banished bishops by Emperor Gratian, and Meletius was reinstated. He was unable to reach an agreement with Paulinus
before his death in Constantinople in May while presiding at
the third General Council of Constantinople. February 12.

MERCURIUS (d. c. 250). That he was a real martyr is all
that is really known of him. All else is pious fiction, according to which he was the son of a Scythian officer in the
Roman army, became a soldier himself, and led the army to a
great victory with a sword an angel had given him in a battle
against the barbarians attacking Rome. When Emperor
Decius asked him why he did not participate in sacrifices to
the gods after the victory, Mercurius proclaimed his Christianity, whereupon Decius sent him to Caesarea in Cappadocia, where he was tortured and beheaded for his faith.
He was venerated as a warrior saint and is reputed to have
appeared at various times in history to lend his sword to
worthy causes, notably, with St. George and St. Demetrius, at
Antioch during the First Crusade. November 25.

MERICI, ANGELA (c. 1470–1540). Born at Desenzano,
Lombardy, on March 21, she was orphaned at ten and raised
by her uncle at Salo. She became a Franciscan tertiary when
she was thirteen and began a life of great austerity. She returned to Desenzano and on the death of her uncle became
interested in the education of poor children and began, with a
group of friends, to teach young girls. She was invited to
Brescia by a noble couple to open a school there, temporarily
lost her sight while on pilgrimage to the Holy Land, went to

Rome during the 1525 Holy Year, and refused an offer of
Pope Clement VII to head a congregation of nursing sisters.
In 1533, she began training a group of women in Brescia, and
on November 25, 1535, twenty-eight women dedicated themselves to the service of God under the protection of St.
Ursula, and the Ursulines, devoted to the religious education
of girls, especially poor children, were founded, with Angela
as superior. The congregation was formally recognized by
Pope Paul III four years after Angela's death at Brescia on
January 27. Angela experienced many visions during her lifetime, one of which foretold that she would found the Ursulines. She was canonized in 1807.

MESROP (d. 441). Born in Taron, Armenia, he became a
government official in Armenia and then was a hermit and a
disciple of St. Nerses the Great. Mesrop was ordained and
devoted himself to the study of Greek, Syriac and Persian
(Armenia had recently been partitioned between Persia and
the Empire). He joined St. Isaac the Great as a missionary to
the Armenians, helped compose an Armenian alphabet, and
translated the New Testament and Proverbs into Armenian.
He organized schools in Armenia and Georgia, created a
Georgian alphabet, founded his own school in Armenia, and
continued preaching until his death at Valarshapat on February 19, when he was well past eighty. He was surnamed "the
Teacher" for his educational activities and teaching ability.

MESSALINA (d. c. 254). *See* Felician.

METHODIUS. *See* Cyril.

METHODIUS I (d. 847). Born at Syracuse, Sicily, he was
educated at Syracuse, went to Constantinople in quest of a
position at the imperial court, but instead became a monk. He
built a monastery on the island of Chios, returned to Constantinople under Patriarch Nicephorus, and opposed iconoclasm
when Emperor Leo the Armenian launched his persecution of
opponents of that heresy in 815. Methodius went to Rome
when Nicephorus was exiled but returned in 821 when Emperor Michael the Stammerer was enthroned, bringing a letter
from Pope Paschal asking the new Emperor to permit Nicephorus to return to his see. Instead the Emperor had Methodius scourged and exiled to prison. On his release from prison

seven years later, he resumed his opposition to iconoclasm under Emperor Theophilus, but when the Emperor died in 842 his widow Theodora, the regent, repealed all decrees against images, and Methodius was named Patriarch of Constantinople to replace iconoclast supporter John the Grammarian. Methodius convoked a synod at Constantinople that endorsed the second Council of Nicaea's decrees regarding icons, became involved in a controversy with the monks under St. Theodore Studites, over some of Theodore's writings, and died of dropsy on June 14 at Constantinople. Though reputedly a prolific writer, few of his writings have survived, notable among those that have survived being a life of St. Theophanes.

MICHAEL. He is one of the three angels, with Gabriel and Raphael, liturgically venerated by the Church. He appears twice in the Old Testament (Dan. 10:13ff.; 12:1, as the helper of the Chosen People) and twice in the New Testament (Jude v. 9, where he disputes with the devil over Moses' body; and Rev. 12:7–9, where he and his angels fought the dragon and hurled him and his followers from heaven). He repeatedly appears in apocryphal literature and was early regarded in the Church as the captain of the heavenly host, the protector of the Christian against the devil, especially at the hour of death, when he conducts the soul to God, and as the helper of Christian armies against heathen armies. His cult apparently originated in Phrygia but soon spread to the West, where it received great impetus as a result of the legend that he appeared at Mount Garganus in northern Italy during the pontificate of Pope Gelasius (492–96) and indicated a spot at which a shrine in his honor was to be erected. Usually he is represented with a sword fighting with or standing over a conquered dragon. A feast day on September 29 (Michaelmas Day), celebrated since the sixth century to honor the dedication of a basilica in his honor on the Salerian Way in Rome, is no longer commemorated, and in 1970 his feast was joined with those of Gabriel and Raphael on that date.

MIDA. *See* Ita.

MIKI, PAUL (1562–97). Son of a Japanese military leader, he was born at Tounucumada, Japan, was educated at the

Jesuit college at Anziquiama, joined the Jesuits in 1580, and became known for his eloquent preaching. He was crucified on February 5 with twenty-five other Catholics during the persecution of Christians under the *taikō*, Toyotomi Hideyoshi, ruler of Japan in the name of the Emperor. Among the Japanese laymen who suffered the same fate were: Francis, a carpenter who was arrested while watching the executions and then crucified; Gabriel, the nineteen-year-old son of the Franciscans' porter; Leo Kinuya, a twenty-eight-year-old carpenter from Miyako; Diego Kisai (or Kizayemon), temporal coadjutor of the Jesuits; Joachim Sakakibara, cook for the Franciscans at Osaka; Peter Sukejirō, sent by a Jesuit priest to help the prisoners, who was then arrested; Cosmas Takeya from Owari, who had preached in Osaka; and Ventura from Miyako, who had been baptized by the Jesuits, gave up his Catholicism on the death of his father, became a bonze, and was brought back to the Church by the Franciscans. They were all canonized as the Martyrs of Japan in 1862. February 6.

MILBURGA (d. c. 700 or 722). Daughter of Merewald, an Anglian chieftain, and St. Ermenburga, a princess of Kent, and sister of SS. Mildred and Mildgytha, Milburga was founding abbess of Wenlock convent in Shropshire, built with funds from her father and King Wulfhere, her uncle. She was venerated for her humility, holiness, the miracles she is reputed to have performed, and for the gift of levitation she is said to have possessed. February 23.

MILDGYTHA (d. c. 676). Daughter of Anglian chieftain Merewald and St. Ermenburga, a Kentish princess, she was the sister of SS. Mildred and Milburga, became a nun at Minster on the Isle of Thanet, of which her mother was founding abbess, and later was abbess of a convent in Northumbria. January 17.

MILDRED (d. c. 700 or 725). Daughter of Merewald, an Anglian chieftain, and St. Ermenburga, a Kentish princess, she was the sister of SS. Milburga and Mildgytha and was educated at a convent at Chelles near Paris. She rejected an ardent suitor and on her return from France entered the monastery of Minster on the Isle of Thanet, which had been founded by her mother, whom she succeeded as abbess. She attended a council in Kent, was known for the fervor of her religion and her aid to the poor and the afflicted, and was widely venerated in England after her death. July 13.

MILLAN DE LA COGOLLA. *See* Emilian Culcullatus.

MILTIADES (d. 314). Also called Melchiades, he was probably an African and was elected Pope on July 2, 311, succeeding Pope St. Eusebius. Miltiades' reign saw the end of Christian persecutions with the victory of Constantine over Maxentius at the Milvian Bridge in 312, the granting of religious freedom throughout the Empire by Constantine in 313, and the beginnings of Donatism in Africa. He held a synod in 313 at the Lateran palace, given him by Constantine's wife, Fausta, which condemned Donatus. Miltiades died in Rome on January 10 or 11. December 10.

MKASA, JOSEPH (d. 1885). A Christian in charge of the pages at the court of King Mwanga of Uganda, he was beheaded on November 15 when he denounced the King's notorious immoralities and his murder of Joseph Harrington, a Protestant missionary, and his group. Joseph was canonized by Pope Paul VI as one of the Martyrs of Uganda in 1964. June 3.

MOCHTA (c. 445–c. 535). Born in Britain, he was brought to Ireland as a child by his Christian parents, became a disciple of St. Patrick, and supposedly, while on a visit to Rome, was made a bishop by Pope St. Leo I. He collected a group of twelve disciples and returned to Ireland, where he eventually built a monastery at Louth, of which he was probably made bishop by Patrick. He died, reportedly at ninety, the last of Patrick's personal followers. August 19.

MOCHUDA. *See* Carthach.

MODESTUS (d. c. 300). *See* Vitus.

MOGROBEJO, TORIBIO ALFONSO DE (1538–1605). Born at Mayorga, Spain, he studied law, became a lawyer and a professor of law at the University of Salamanca, and was named chief judge of the Inquisition court at Granada by King Philip II. He was named archbishop of Lima, Peru, in

1580 despite his objections and the fact that he was a layman, was ordained and consecrated, and arrived in Peru in 1581. He came into immediate conflict with the secular authorities over the treatment of the Indians whose rights he defended, restored ecclesiastical discipline in the see, fought for the poor, founded numerous churches, schools, and hospitals, and in 1591 he founded the first seminary in the New World. He learned to speak Indian dialects, was known for his charities, and despite great physical privations managed to visit every part of his dioceses, teaching and preaching with great effect. He died at Santa, Peru, on March 23 while on his way back to Peru from a visit, and was canonized in 1726. March 23.

MONALDO, BUONFIGLIO (d. 1261). He and six fellow Florentine merchants, Bartholomes Amidei (Amadeus), Benedict Dell' Antell (Manettus), John Buonagiunta (Buonagiunta), Alexis Falconieri (Alexis), Gerardino Sostegni (Sostenes), and Ricovero Ugoccione (Hugh), all members of noble Florentine families, joined the Confraternity of the Blessed Virgin (the Laudesi—Praisers) in Florence about 1225, with James of Poggibonsi their spiritual director; the Confraternity was dedicated to Mary, especially in her Seven Sorrows. On the feast of the Assumption in 1233, they experienced a vision in which the Blessed Virgin inspired them to live a life of prayer and solitude as hermits. They pursued an eremitical way of life at La Camarzia on the outskirts of Florence and then moved to nearby Monte Senario, where another vision of Mary in 1240 caused them to found a religious community—the Servants of Mary (the Servites)—and revealed to them the habit they were to wear. They were all ordained, except Alexis Falconieri, taking the names indicated above in parentheses after their real names, and Buonfiglio (Bonfilius) was elected their first superior general. He served until 1256 (he died on January 1) and was succeeded by John Buonagiunta, who died soon after his election. Their first foundation outside of Florence was a church at nearby Cafaggio, which was finished in 1252, and the Order soon spread to other Italian cities. In 1260, it was divided into two provinces: Tuscany, under Manettus, and Umbria, under Sostenes. At the invitation of King St. Louis, Manettus introduced the Order to France, and Sostenes brought it to Germany; in time it spread all over Europe, and when Manettus became fourth prior general, he sent missionaries to Asia. Though the Order was approved by the seven founders' superiors from the beginning and had the approval of Raniero Cardinal Capocci, papal legate to Tuscany, in 1249, it was not papally approved until 1304, by Pope Benedict XI, at which time only Alexis of the original seven founders was still alive. He reportedly was 110 when he died on February 17, 1310, at Monte Senario. The seven founders were co-jointly canonized by Pope Leo XIII in 1888 as the "Seven Holy Founders." February 17.

MONICA (c. 331–87). Probably born at Tagaste, North Africa, of Christian parents, she was married to Patricius, a pagan, known for his dissolute habits and violent temper. They had three children: Augustine, Navigius, and Perpetua. Through her patience and prayers, she was able to convert Patricius and his mother in 370. She was widowed in 371 and for years prayed for the conversion of Augustine, who from the time he went to study at Carthage when he was seventeen lived a wayward life, embraced Manichaeism, dabbled in other philosophies, and had a mistress. She followed him to Rome in 383 and then to Milan where, in 386, he embraced Christianity and was baptized on Easter in 387. She lived with Augustine, his son Adeodatus, and his associates at Cassiciacum while Augustine was preparing for baptism, and she died at Ostia, Italy, soon after as they were awaiting a ship to take them back to Africa. Monica is the patroness of married women and is regarded as a model for Christian mothers. August 27.

MORAND (d. c. 1115). Born of noble parents near Worms, Germany, he was educated at the Worms cathedral school, was ordained, and after a pilgrimage to Compostela, became a Benedictine monk under St. Hugh at Cluny. He spent several years at Cluniac monasteries in Auvergne, but about 1100 he was sent as a missionary to lower Alsace at the request of Count Frederick Pferz, who had just restored St. Christopher Church at Altkirch. Morand became the confidant of the count and was highly regarded for his holiness, concern for the people, and miracles. He is regarded as the patron of wine growers because of the tradition that he once fasted throughout Lent eating nothing except a bunch of grapes. June 3.

MORE, THOMAS (1478–1535). Born in London on February 6, the son of John More, a lawyer and a judge, he became a page in the household of Archbishop John Morton of Canterbury when he was about twelve. He went to Oxford, studied law at Lincoln's Inn, was admitted to the bar in 1501, and entered Parliament in 1504. He decided against becoming a Carthusian and married Jane Holt in 1505. Their home became a center of medieval and Renaissance culture in England, and he became one of the leading intellectual figures of his time, noted for his learning, intellect, and wit. He became England's leading humanist and one of the outstanding scholars of the age. He wrote poetry, history, treatises against Protestantism, devotional books and prayers, and translated Lucian from the Latin. His *Utopia* (1515–16), an account of an imaginary society ruled by reason, has become a classic, and his *Vindication of Henry Against Luther* (1523) was a spirited defense of King Henry VIII, whom he had tutored. He was undersheriff of London in 1510, and in 1511, a month after the death of his wife, Jane, he married Alice Middleton, a widow. When Henry became King he sent More on several diplomatic missions to France and Flanders, appointed him to the Royal Council in 1517, and knighted him in 1521. He was selected speaker of the House of Commons in 1523, was High Steward of Cambridge in 1525, and succeeded Cardinal Wolsey as Lord Chancellor in 1529 despite his grave misgivings about Henry's defiance of the Pope in divorcing Catherine of Aragon. More's silence about the matter disturbed Henry, who was angered when More refused to sign a petition to the Pope requesting permission for Henry to divorce Catherine. After opposing a series of measures against the Church, More resigned the chancellorship and retired, penniless, to his home in Chelsea in 1532 to write. When he refused to sign the oath in the Act of Succession recognizing the offspring of Henry and his second wife, Anne Boleyn, as heir to the throne, declaring that Henry's first marriage, to Catherine, was not a true marriage and repudiating the Pope, he was arrested in 1534 and imprisoned in the Tower of London. He remained there for fifteen months until July 1, 1535, and when asked by Cromwell to comment on the Act of Supremacy, he remained silent; whereupon he was accused of treason. Despite his refusal to break his silence, he was convicted of treason, and five days later, on July 6, was beheaded. As he mounted the scaffold, he proclaimed that he was "the King's good servant but God's first." He was canonized in 1935. He is a patron of lawyers. June 22.

MORONE, PETER DI. *See* Celestine V.

MORSE, HENRY (1595–1645). Born at Broome, Suffolk, England, he was raised a Protestant, studied at Cambridge and law at Barnard's Inn, and in 1614 he became a Catholic at Douai. When he returned to England to settle an inheritance, he was arrested and spent the next four years in New Prison in Southwark for his faith. He was released in 1618 when a general amnesty was proclaimed by King James, returned to Douai to study for the priesthood, and continued his studies in Rome, where he was ordained in 1623. He was sent on the English mission the following year and was almost immediately arrested and imprisoned at York. While in prison, he became a Jesuit, and after three years in prison was exiled to Flanders, where he served as chaplain to English soldiers in the army of King Philip IV of Spain. He returned to England in 1633, worked in London under the pseudonym of Cuthbert Claxton, made many converts by his heroic labors in the plague of 1636–37, and was arrested for his priesthood. Released on bail through the intercession of Queen Marietta, he again left England in 1641 when a royal decree ordered all Catholic priests from the country, but returned again in 1643. He was arrested in Cumberland eighteen months later, escaped, but was captured and brought to trial. He was convicted of being a Catholic priest at the Old Bailey and was hanged, drawn, and quartered at Tyburn on February 1. His hanging was attended by the French, Spanish, and Portuguese ambassadors in protest. He was canonized as one of the Forty Martyrs of England and Wales by Pope Paul VI in 1970.

MOSES THE BLACK (c. 330–c. 405). An Ethiopian born a slave, he was a servant in the household of an Egyptian official. Moses was dismissed from the official's service because of his viciousness, thievery, and evil propensities, and became the leader of a notorious band of outlaws who terrorized the area. How he was converted is not known, though it is believed by the hermits of the Skete Desert in Lower Egypt, where he was hiding out after some particularly vicious crime. He became a monk at Petra Monastery, was known for his extreme mortifications while living as a hermit, and was ordained by Archbishop Theophilus of Alexandria. Moses was murdered, with six other monks, by a band of marauding Berbers when he refused to defend himself by force. August 28.

MUINIS. *See* Mel.

MUNCHIN (7th century). Venerated as the patron of Limerick, Ireland, and called "the Wise," he may have come to Limerick from County Clare, and tradition has him a bishop, though scholars doubt this. He is also known as Maincin (Little Monk) in Ireland. January 2.

MUNGA. *See* Germanus (14th century).

MUNGO. *See* Kentigern.

MUNNU. *See* Fintan (d. c. 635).

MURUMBA, MATTHIAS. *See* Lwanga, Charles.

N

NARCISSUS (d. c. 215). A Greek, he was named bishop of Jerusalem in his old age, imposed strict discipline on his see, and was forced to flee his see when some of his opponents denounced him for his support of Roman customs at the Council of Jerusalem. He lived as a hermit for several years, then returned and was persuaded to resume his bishopric by the faithful of the city. He appointed St. Alexander his coadjutor, who stated that Narcissus was 116 years old in 212. October 29.

NARCISSUS (d. 320). *See* Argeus.

NARSES. Another form of Nerses.

NARSES (d. 421). *See* Maharsapor.

NATALIA (d. c. 304). *See* Adrian.

NATHANAEL. *See* Bartholomew.

NAZARIUS (c. 68). Unreliable legend has him born in Rome the son of a pagan Roman army officer and a Christian mother and taught by St. Peter. Nazarius was beheaded in Milan, with a young companion, Celsus, for preaching Christianity, during Emperor Nero's first persecution of the Christians. It is a fact that St. Ambrose discovered the bodies in Milan soon after 395 (reputedly Nazarius' blood was still liquid and red) and enshrined them there, but that is all that is really known of them factually. July 28.

NEALE, JOHN. *See* John Roche under Ward, Margaret.

NENNIUS (6th century). All that is known of him is that he was Irish, became a disciple of St. Finnian of Clonard, and is one of the Twelve Apostles of Ireland. January 17.

NERI, PHILIP (1515–95). Born at Florence, Italy, on July 22, he was the son of a notary and was educated by the Dominicans of San Marco in Florence. When he was eighteen, he was sent to San Germano to pursue a business career, but a mystical experience he had turned him to the religious life. He went to Rome in 1533, lived there almost as a recluse for two years while tutoring two sons of a wealthy Florentine, and then studied philosophy and theology at the Sapienza and Sant' Agostino for three years. He began to preach on the streets and in the markets to the Romans, whose religious practices had become lukewarm and were frequently neglected; the city was corrupt and the Church reflected the current malaise of the secular society. In 1548, with Fr. Persiano Rossa, his confessor, Philip founded the Confraternity of the Most Holy Trinity, composed of laypeople to minister to needy pilgrims (it developed into the famous Santa Trinità dei Pellegrini Hospital) and to spread the Forty Hours' devotion. He was ordained in 1551 and soon achieved fame as a confessor, attracting huge crowds of penitents to San Girolamo della Carità, where he lived in a community of priests. He had remarkable success in making converts and attracted many priests to aid him in ministering the informal conferences he devised for the throngs seeking spiritual advice and solace, and in time they became known as Oratorians because they summoned their groups to their oratory (room) for prayer. However, the actual founding of the Oratorians dates to 1564, when Philip became rector of San Giovanni Church, and five of his disciples were ordained and installed there and followed the spiritual directions he established. The new society received formal approval in 1575, by which time Philip was the most popular person in Rome, from Pope St. Gregory XIII, who gave it the rundown Church of Sta Maria in Vallicela and named Philip superior. He demolished the old church and erected a new one on its site, naming it Chiesa Nuova, which became headquarters for the Oratorians in 1577, though Philip did not come to Vallicela from San Girolamo until 1583. By this time he was

known as "the Apostle of Rome" and was venerated by
popes, cardinals, rulers, and ordinary people. He was consulted by rich and poor, powerful and helpless for his spiritual wisdom and his ability to look into men's minds. He experienced ecstasies and visions, was credited with performing
miracles, and had the gift of prophecy. He resigned as superior in 1593 because of ill health and in the same year
prevented a serious conflict between France and the Holy See
when he insisted on the absolution of Henry IV. He died in
Rome on May 26, venerated as a saint, and was canonized in
1622 by Pope Gregory XV. May 26.

NERSES I THE GREAT (d. c. 373). Born at Caesarea,
Cappadocia, in 333 or 337, of royal descent, he married a
princess, and when she died he became a chamberlain at the
court of King Arshak of Armenia. Nerses was ordained, and
in 353, against his will, was made Katholikos of the Armenians. He instituted reforms he had learned under St. Basil
at Caesarea with the first national synod at Ashtishat in 365,
founded hospitals, and encouraged monasticism. His vigorous
new ecclesiastical program alienated Arshak, and when
Nerses denounced the King for the murder of his wife,
Nerses was banished to Edessa by Arshak, who intruded another bishop in his place. When Arshak was killed in battle
with the Persians he was succeeded by Pap, and Nerses returned. However, his relationship with Pap was as strained as
it had been with the previous King, and he refused to allow
Pap into his church until he reformed his evil life. Seemingly
repentant, Pap invited Nerses to a banquet and poisoned him
at Khakh on the Euphrates. November 19.

NERSES KLAIËTSI (d. 1173). Born at Hromkla, Cilicia,
he was educated by his uncle, Katholikos Gregory II, and
Stephen Manuk, and was ordained by his brother, Katholikos
Gregory III. Like his uncle, he favored the reunion of Rome
and the Armenian Church, was himself reunited to Rome
when he met Roman bishops with the crusaders, and when he
succeeded his brother as Katholikos in 1166 remained in
union with Rome, though formal reunion did not take place
until 1198, when Leo II became King. He worked actively for
the reunion of Rome and the Orthodox Greeks and unsuccessfully for the union of the Greek and Armenian

churches. He wrote poetry, prayers, hymns, and a history of Armenia, and is considered one of the outstanding figures of twelfth-century Armenian culture; he was surnamed "the Great" because of the quality of his writing. He died on August 13. August 3.

NERSES LAMPRONATS (1153–98). Born at Lampron, Cilicia, the son of the prince of Lampron, he was educated at Skeyra Monastery and became an outstanding scholar, theologian, and exegete, skilled in Greek, Latin, Syriac, and Coptic. When his father died, he was ordained in 1169, lived as a hermit for a time, and in 1176 was consecrated archbishop of Tarsus. He strongly supported the reunion of the Armenian Church with Rome at a council at Hromkla in 1179, but nothing came of it when the supporter of the move, Emperor Manuel Comnenus, died the next year. Nerses actively engaged in the negotiations that led to the reunion with Rome in 1198 and died six months after the reunion was confirmed by the crowning of Leo II as King of Lower Armenia by the papal legate with a crown sent by Pope Celestine III. Nerses wrote on the liturgy, scriptural commentaries, hymns, and lives of the desert saints, and translated St. Benedict's Rule and St. Gregory's *Dialogues* into Armenian. He died at Tarsus on July 14.

NEUMANN, JOHN NEPOMUCENE (1811–60). Born at Prachatiz, Bohemia, on March 28, the third of six children of Agnes and Philip Neumann, he was early attracted to the religious life, entered the diocesan seminary of Budweis in 1831, and two years later the archiepiscopal seminary at Prague University. Unable to be ordained because of a surplus of priests in Bohemia, he went to the United States in 1836, was ordained in New York later the same year, and devoted the next four years to missionary work, especially among German-speaking Catholics, in upstate New York. In 1840, he joined the newly established branch of the Redemptorists at St. Philomena's in Pittsburgh and became the first Redemptorist to take his vows in the United States, in 1842. He continued his missionary activities in Maryland, Ohio, Pennsylvania, and Virginia, became rector of St. Philomena's in 1844, and was named vice regent and superior of the American Redemptorists in 1847. He was consecrated fourth bishop of Philadelphia in 1852 and reorganized the diocese, inaugurating a widespread program of new church and school building. He was an active proponent of Catholic education, and two catechisms he wrote were endorsed by the American bishops at their first Plenary Council in 1852 and were widely used in Catholic schools the next thirty-five years. At the time of his death in Philadelphia on January 5, he was renowned for his holiness, charity, pastoral work, and preaching. He was canonized in 1977 by Pope Paul VI, the first American male saint.

NICANOR (1st century). A resident of Jerusalem, he was one of the seven selected by the apostles to minister to the needs of the needy. Tradition says he later went to Cyprus, where he suffered martyrdom during the reign of Emperor Vespasian (69–79), though this is uncertain. January 10.

NICASIUS VAN HEEZE (d. 1572). *See* Pieck, Nicholas.

NICEPHORUS (758–828). The son of the secretary of Emperor Constantine Copronymus who had been tortured and exiled when he refused to accept the Emperor's decrees banishing holy images, Nicephorus grew up a stanch opponent of iconoclasm. He became imperial commissioner known for his eloquence, scholarship, and statesmanship, and built a monastery near the Black Sea. Though he was a layman, he was named against his wishes Patriarch of Constantinople in 806, succeeding St. Tarasius. Nicephorus incurred the enmity of St. Theodore Studites for forgiving a priest who had illicitly married Emperor Constantine VI and Theodota while Constantine's wife, Mary, was still alive. The two were later reconciled and Nicephorus devoted himself to reforming his see, restoring monastic discipline, and reinvigorating the religion of his flock. He resisted the efforts of Emperor Leo the Armenian who became Emperor in 813, to reimpose the heresy of iconoclasm, was deposed by a synod of iconoclastic bishops assembled by Leo, had several attempts made on his life, was exiled to the monastery he had built on the Black Sea, and spent the last fifteen years of his life there. He wrote several treatises against iconoclasm and two historical works, *Breviarum* and *Chronographia*. He died on June 2 at the monastery. March 13.

NICETAS (d. 824). A native of Caesarea, Bithynia, his father entered a monastery a few years after his mother died when he was a week old, and he was raised in the monastery. He became a monk at Medikion Monastery at the foot of Mount Olympus, Bithynia, was ordained in 790 by St. Tarasius, and in time became abbot. When he and a group of other abbots refused the demand of Emperor Leo the Armenian that they recognize the intruded Theodotus as Patriarch of Constantinople, whom Leo had appointed to replace the exiled Patriarch Nicephorus, Nicetas was exiled to Anatolia, where he was subjected to ill treatment. When he was brought back to Constantinople, he accepted Theodotus as patriarch and was returned to his monastery. He soon repented publicly, withdrew his allegiance to the patriarch, and denounced iconoclasm. He was exiled to the isle of Glyceria in 813, released when Michael the Stammerer became Emperor in 820, and lived as a hermit near Constantinople until his death there. April 3.

NICETAS OF CONSTANTINOPLE (d. c. 838). Of a Paphlagonian family related to Empress Irene, he was a courtier at her court and reportedly was one of her official representatives at the second General Council of Nicaea, in 787. He was appointed prefect of Sicily, a position he retained when Nicephorus' palace revolution put him on the throne in 802, but became a monk at Khrysonike Monastery in Constantinople when Nicephorus was killed in 811. Nicetas fled the monastery with an icon of Christ with some of the monks when Emperor Leo V began his attacks on icons, and was made a house prisoner at a country house when Leo's soldiers forcibly possessed the icon. Twelve years later Nicetas and three other monks were driven from the monastery when they refused to accept iconoclast Antony as Patriarch of Constantinople when Emperor Theophilus demanded they do so. They were driven from one place to another because of their refusal to accept iconoclasm until they finally found refuge on a farm at Katisia, Paphlagonia, where Nicetas lived the rest of his life. October 6.

NICETAS OF REMESIANA (c. 335–c. 414). A close friend of St. Paulinus of Nola, he was bishop of Remesiana in

Dacia (modern Romania and Yugoslavia) and was noted for his successful missionary activities, especially among the Bessi, which Paulinus commemorates in a poem. Nicetas wrote several dissertations on faith, the creed, the Trinity, and liturgical singing, and is believed by some scholars to be the author of *Te Deum*. June 22.

NICHOLAS (d. c. 350). Probably born at Patara, Lycia, Asia Minor, of wealthy parents, he was named bishop of Myra, a rundown diocese, and became known for his holiness, zeal, and miracles. He was imprisoned for his faith during the persecution of Christians under Emperor Diocletian, was present at the Council of Nicaea, where he denounced Arianism and died at Myra. To these meager facts of his life were added colorful details from legends and untrustworthy biographies, according to which he was born at Patara and when his wealthy parents died, he devoted himself to the conversion of sinners and his wealth to the poor and to charitable works. One such is the story of three poverty-stricken girls whose father was about to turn them into prostitutes since he could not afford a dowry for them; Nicholas on three occasions threw bags of gold into their house, and all three were married. He destroyed pagan temples, forced a governor, Eustathius, to admit he had been bribed to condemn three innocent men to death (Nicholas saved them), and appeared in a dream to Emperor Constantine to tell the Emperor that three imperial officers condemned to death at Constantinople were innocent (Constantine freed them the next morning). His popularity, already great, increased enormously in the West when his relics were brought to Bari in 1087, and his shrine was one of the great pilgrimage centers of medieval Europe. He is the patron of storm-beset sailors (for miraculously saving doomed mariners off the coast of Lycia), of prisoners, of children (in some accounts the story of the three bags of gold and the three girls became the heads of three murdered children restored to life by the saint), which led to the practice of children giving presents at Christmas in his name and the metamorphosis of his name, St. Nicholas, into Sint Klaes into Santa Claus by the Dutch. It should be noted though that the figure of Santa Claus is really non-Christian and is based on the Germanic god Thor, who was associated with winter and the Yule log and rode on a chariot drawn by goats named Cracker and Gnasher. Nicholas is also the patron of Greece, Apulia, Sicily, Lorraine, and Russia. December 6.

NICHOLAS I (d. 867). Surnamed "the Great," he was born at Rome between 819 and 822 of a distinguished family, became a member of the Roman clergy, served in the Curia under Pope Sergius II, became a deacon under Pope Leo IV, and was a trusted adviser of Pope Benedict III. Nicholas was elected pope on April 22, 858, succeeding Benedict, and immediately exhibited the courage and energy for which he was famed. He insisted on the sanctity and indissolubility of marriage, despite the threat of an invasion of Rome, when he denounced the irregularity of the marriage of the Emperor's nephew, King Lothaire II of Lorraine, and insisted on the freedom to marry when he forced King Charles the Bald of Burgundy to accept the marriage of his daughter Judith to Baldwin of Flanders without the King's consent and compelled the Frankish bishops to withdraw the excommunication they had imposed on her for marrying without her father's consent. In 861 Nicholas compelled Archbishop Hincmar of Rheims to accept papal appellate jurisdiction in important cases when he obliged Hincmar to restore Bishop Rothad of Soissons, whom he had deposed. Twice he excommunicated recalcitrant and powerful Archbishop John of Ravenna, who counted on imperial support, for infringing on the rights of the Holy See and for abuses of his office, and made him submit to papal authority. Nicholas was involved in controversy with Constantinople throughout his pontificate over the illegal deposition of Ignatius and the appointment of Photius as Patriarch of Constantinople by Emperor Michael III, and Nicholas excommunicated Michael in 863; the matter was not finally resolved until newly crowned Emperor Basil I expelled Photius, who had declared the Pope deposed, on the day Nicholas died. He encouraged missionary activities, sending St. Anskar as papal missionary to Scandinavia and bringing about the conversion of Bulgaria with missionaries he sent there. Nicholas is also known for his correspondence with King Boris, which led to Nicholas' famous *Responsa Nicolai ad consulta Bulgarum,* a classic summary of Christian faith and discipline. A champion of papal primacy and the ascendancy of the Church over Emperors, Kings, and other secular rulers in matters concerning the Church, he was responsible for restoring the papacy to the highest prestige. He was one of the most forceful of early medieval Popes, was famous for his concern for the poor, his justice, and for the reforms he instituted among the clergy and laity, was a patron of learning and the arts, and was a man of the highest personal integrity. He died at Rome on November 13.

NICHOLAS VON FLÜE (1417–87). Born on the Flüeli (hence his name), a fertile plain near Sachseln, Obwalden (Unterwalden) Canton, Switzerland, on March 21, he married Dorothea Wissling, and during their happily married life they had ten children. He fought in the forces of his canton in the war with Zurich in 1439, was a captain in the occupation of the Turgau in 1453, served as magistrate and councillor for Obwalden, and consistently refused the position of governor. In 1467, when he was fifty, with the consent and approval of his wife and children, he embraced the eremitical life in a cell at Ranft, near Sachseln, and spent the last nineteen years of his life there, subsisting solely on Holy Communion. He became famed for his holiness and wisdom and was consulted by a constant stream of leaders and common folk from all walks of life. He was responsible for the inclusion of Fribourg and Soleure in the Swiss Confederation in 1481 after independence had been won from Charles the Bold of Burgundy and Switzerland's leaders could not come to an agreement and civil war threatened. He was the outstanding religious figure in Swiss history, known affectionately as "Bruder Klaus." He died on March 21 in his cell at Ranft, and was canonized in 1947. March 22.

NICHOLAS STUDITES (793–863). Born at Sydonia (Canea), Crete, he was educated at Studius Monastery at Constantinople from the age of ten, and when he was eighteen he became a monk there. He aided those exiled by the iconoclast persecution until it ended in 842 on the death of Emperor Theophilus, and Nicholas was later elected abbot. When Emperor Michael III exiled St. Ignatius and made Photius Patriarch of Constantinople in 858, Nicholas refused to recognize Photius as Patriarch and went into voluntary exile; Michael then appointed a new abbot. After several years of exile, Nicholas was brought back to his monastery and imprisoned. He died at Studius on February 4.

NICHOLAS OF TOLENTINE (1245–1305). Born at Sant' Angelo, Ancona, Italy, he joined the Augustinians there and was professed in 1263, studied at San Ginesio, and was ordained at Cingoli about 1270. He served as master of novices at Sant' Elpidio for a time, and in 1274 was sent to Tolentino, where he became famous for the eloquence of his preaching and as a confessor, converting hardened sinners and ministering to the poor, the sick, criminals, and the needy. He died at Tolentino, where he had labored for thirty years, on September 10, venerated for the many miracles he is reported to have performed. He was canonized in 1446.

NICODEMUS (1st century). A leading Jew of Jerusalem and probably a member of the Sanhedrin, he visited Jesus secretly at night, acknowledged him as "a teacher who comes from God," and in response to his questions, the Lord discoursed on baptism (John 3:1ff.). Nicodemus spoke on Jesus' behalf before the chief priests and the Pharisees, pointing out to them that the Law demanded the accused be given a hearing before judgment was passed (John 7:50–52). He brought large quantities of costly myrrh and aloes to Jesus' tomb, and with Joseph of Arimathea wrapped Christ's body "with spices in linen cloths" (John 19:39–42). It is believed that he became a disciple, though this is nowhere stated in the New Testament. August 1.

NICOSTRATUS (d. c. 306). *See* Castorius.

NILUS THE ELDER (d. c. 430). An imperial official, perhaps a prefect, at Constantinople, he became a disciple of St. John Chrysostom. Though married with two children, Nilus became a monk on Mount Sinai, taking his son Theodulus, after Nilus and his wife mutually agreed to leave the secular world. During a raid on the monastery by Arabs, Theodulus was kidnaped and Nilus went looking for him, finally tracing him to Eleusa, where he had been given shelter by the local bishop, who ordained both of them. Nilus is reputed to have written theological and ascetical treatises and numerous letters (among them two to Emperor Arcadius rebuking the Emperor for his exile of St. John Chrysostom from Constantinople), but many authorities believe that Nilus the author was a monk called "the Wise" at Ancryna, Galatia

(Ankara), and different from the Nilus described above. November 12.

NINIAN (d. c. 432). According to the untrustworthy twelfth-century life of Ninian by St. Aelred, he was the son of a converted chieftain of the Cumbrian Britons, studied at Rome, was ordained, was consecrated a bishop, and returned to evangelize his native Britain. He had a stone church built by masons from St. Martin's Monastery in Tours, which became known as the White House (Whitern), and a monastery, which became known as the Great Monastery and was the center of his missionary activities. From it Ninian and his monks evangelized neighboring Britons and the Picts of Valentia. Ninian was known for his miracles, among them curing a chieftain of blindness, which cure led to many conversions. September 16.

NINO (4th century). A captive slave in Iberia (Georgia), variously reported as a native of Cappadocia, Asia Minor, Rome, Jerusalem, and Gaul, she impressed those around her with her prayers, virtue, and the miracles she wrought, which she proclaimed were performed through her by Christ. When she cured the Queen of an illness and aided the King on a hunting expedition, they took instructions from her and were converted to Christianity, and with them their people. The King requested Emperor Constantine to send bishops and priests to his realm, which the Emperor did, and Georgia became Christian. When this was accomplished, Nino is reputed to have become a hermitess on the slopes of a mountain at Bodbe in Kakheti, where she died and was buried; it eventually became an episcopal see, and Nino is entombed in the Cathedral of Mtzkheta. The story is first told by Rufinus who said that he had received it from Iberian Prince Bakur in Palestine late in the fourth century, and though embellished by later legend, is believed to be true and was translated into many Eastern languages. The girl's name is not given in the legend narrated by Rufinus, but she is called Nino by Georgians and Christiana in the Roman Martyrology and is the apostle of Georgia in the U.S.S.R. Legend also has her the only one of St. Rhipsime's community at Valarshapat to escape slaughter by King Tiridate's soldiers. December 15.

NON (6th century). Also known as Nonnita, according to

unreliable sources she was of noble birth and resided at a convent at Ty Gwyn near present-day St. Davids in Wales and was seduced by a local chieftain named Sant. The child born was St. David, and some sources say she was married to Sant either before or after the birth of the child. She was said to have gone later to Cornwall and then to Brittany. March 3.

NONIUS. *See* Pereira, Bl. Nonius Alvares de.

NONNA (d. 374). A Christian, she married Gregory, a magistrate at Nazianzus, Cappadocia, who was a member of the Hypsistarians, a Jewish-pagan group, and converted him to Christianity. He became a priest and then bishop and is St. Gregory Nanianzen the Elder. Their three children all became saints; St. Gregory Nazianzen, St. Caesarius of Nazianzen, and St. Gorgonia. August 5.

NONNITA. *See* Non.

NORBERT (c. 1080–1134). Born at Xanten, duchy of Cleves, Prussia, son of Count Heribert of Gennep and Hedwig of Guise, he received minor orders and several benefices but lived a life of pleasure at the court of Emperor Henry V, where he was almoner. Norbert avoided the priesthood and declined the bishopric of Cambrai in 1113, but when struck by lightning and hearing the words that Saul heard on the road to Damascus, Norbert reformed his life, was ordained in 1115, and took the monastic habit. His attempts to reform his brother canons at Xanten coupled with his extreme asceticism caused them to denounce him and his unauthorized preaching at the Council of Fritzlar in 1118. In response, he resigned his canonry, sold his possessions, and gave the proceeds to the poor, and on a visit of penance to Pope Gelasius II was given permission to preach where he wished. He became an itinerant preacher in northern France, was soon renowned for his preaching prowess, and was credited with performing miracles. Bl. Hugh of Fosses became his follower, close confidant, and eventually his successor. After unsuccessfully attempting to reform the canons regular of St. Martin's at Laon, Norbert received a grant of land from Bishop Bartholomes of Laon at Prémontré. In 1120, with thirteen followers, Norbert began the foundation, and in 1121, their number increased to forty, they made their profession, and the Canons Regular of

Prémontré were founded. Eight abbeys and two convents were soon founded, and in 1125 Norbert's constitutions received papal approval from Pope Honorius II. When Count Theobald of Champagnes desired to enter the Order, Norbert counseled him to remain in the world, marry, and follow religious practices prescribed by Norbert—the first instance of a tertiary of a religious order. Norbert was appointed archbishop of Magdeburg by Emperor Lothair II in 1126 and was the victim of several assassination plots as he put into effect stringent reforms in the see, especially in upholding ecclesiastical rights against local secular officials. He traveled throughout France, Belgium, and Germany preaching, and he successfully opposed the heresy of Tranchelm of Antwerp in 1124. He won the confidence and support of Lothair, supported Pope Innocent II against the claims of antipope Anacletus II, and persuaded Lothair to lead an army, which he accompanied, to Rome to place Innocent on the papal throne in 1133. The Emperor named him chancellor of Italy in 1133, and he died shortly after, on June 6, at Magdeburg, Saxony. He was canonized in 1582 by Pope Gregory XIII.

NOTHELM (d. c. 740). A priest in London, he was named archbishop of Canterbury in 734. In his preface to his *Ecclesiastical History*, the historian Bede acknowledges that the chief authority for his work was Abbot Albinus, who passed along to him the recollections of Nothelm, including the research Nothelm had done in Roman archives on the history of Kent and adjacent areas. October 17.

NUÑES. *See* Pereira, Bl. Nonius Alvares de.

O

OCTAVIUS (d. c. 287). *See* Maurice.

ODHRAN. *See* Otteran.

ODHREN. *See* Adrian (d. c. 875).

ODILIA (d. c. 720). Also known as Ottilia and Adilia, according to legend she was born at Obernheim in the Vosges Mountains, the blind daughter of Adalric, an Alsatian lord. Dissuaded from putting her to death by his wife, Bereswindis, only on condition that the child be sent away to someone who was not to be told of her background, Bereswindis gave Odilia to a peasant woman. Bereswindis told the woman the story and sent her to Baume-les-Dames near Besançon. When she was twelve, Odilia was put in a convent at Baume, where she was baptized by Bishop St. Erhard of Regensburg and recovered her sight when the bishop touched her eyes with chrism during the baptism ceremony. The bishop told Adalric of the miracle but, angered at the prospect of her return, which had been arranged by his son Hugh, Adalric struck Hugh and killed him. He then changed his attitude toward his daughter and lavished affection on her, but she fled when he wanted her to marry a German duke. Miraculously saved from his murderous anger when he caught her, he was so struck by what had happened that he agreed to allow her to turn his castle at Hohenburg (Odilienbeg, Alsace) into a convent, and she became its abbess. She founded another monastery, Niedermünster, and lived there until her death, venerated for her visions and the miracles attributed to her. She died at Niedermünster on December 13, and her shrine became a great pilgrimage center. She is the patroness of the blind and of Alsace.

ODILO (962–1049). A monk at Cluny, he was named abbot in 994, practiced great austerities, and sold Church treasures to feed the poor during a famine in 1006. During his abbacy, he increased substantially the number of abbeys dependent on Cluny, and with Abbot Richard of Saint-Vanne was responsible for the acceptance in France of "the truce of God" and the rule guaranteeing sanctuary to those seeking refuge in a church. He was devoted to the Incarnation and the Blessed Virgin, inaugurated All Souls' Day with an annual commemoration of the departed faithful, and experienced ecstasies. Ill the last five years of his life, he died while on a visitation of his monasteries at a priory at Souvigny on January 1. He had been abbot for more than fifty years.

ODO (801–80). Born near Beauvais, France, he chose the military as a profession in his youth but abandoned this calling to become a Benedictine monk at Corbie. He taught Charles Martel's sons while he was a monk there and in 851 was elected abbot. He was named bishop of his native city in 861 and in the two decades of his bishopric helped reform the Church in northern France and mediated the differences between Pope Nicholas I and Archbishop Hincmar of Rheims over Hincmar's deposition of Rothadius of Soissons in 862 and Rothadius' restoration by the Pope in 865. His cult was approved by Pope Pius IX. January 28.

ODO OF CANTERBURY (d. 959). Born of Danish parents in East Anglia, he became a monk at Fleury-sur-Loire and was later named bishop of Ramsbury. He was with King Athelstan when the King defeated the Danes, Scots, and Northumbrians at the Battle of Brunanburh in 937, and in 942 became archbishop of Canterbury. He played an active role in secular as well as ecclesiastical affairs, established East Anglia as a separate diocese, and supported St. Dunstan's monastic reforms at Glastonbury. He was called Odo the Good and was reputed to have performed several miracles. July 4.

ODO OF CLUNY (c. 879–942). Born near Le Mans, France, he was raised in the households of Count Fulk II of Anjou and Duke William of Aquitaine, received the tonsure when he was nineteen, received a canonry at St. Martin's in

Tours, and then spent several years studying at Paris, particularly music, under Remigius of Auxerre. Odo became a monk under Berno at Baume-les-Messieurs near Besançon in 909, was named director of the Baume Monastery school by Berno, who became abbot of the newly founded Cluny, and in 924 was named abbot of Baume. He succeeded Berno as second abbot of Cluny in 927, continued Berno's work of reforming abbeys from Cluny, and in 931 was authorized by Pope John XI to reform the monasteries of northern France and Italy. Odo was called to Rome by Pope Leo VII in 936 to arrange peace between Alberic of Rome and Hugh of Provence, who was besieging the city, and succeeded temporarily by negotiating a marriage between Alberic and Hugh's daughter; Odo returned to Rome twice in the next six years to reconcile Alberic and Hugh. Odo spread Cluny's influence to monasteries all over Europe, encountering and overcoming much opposition, and successfully persuaded secular rulers to relinquish control of monasteries they had been illegally controlling. He died at Tours on the way back to Rome on November 18. He wrote hymns, treatises on morality, an epic poem on the Redemption, and a life of St. Gerald of Aurillac.

OGILVIE, JOHN (c. 1579–1615). Born in Banffshire, Scotland, son of the baron of Drum-na-Keith and Lady Douglas of Lochleven, he was raised a Calvinist and was sent to study at Louvain when he was thirteen. In 1596 he became a Catholic there, continued his studies at Ratisbon and Olmütz, and in 1600 joined the Jesuits at Brünn. He was ordained at Paris in 1610, worked in Austria and France, and in 1613 received permission to go to Scotland to minister to the persecuted Catholics there. Using the alias John Watson, purportedly a horse trader and/or a soldier back from the wars in Europe, he worked in Edinburgh and Glasgow and in time was most successful in winning back a number of converts to the Church. He was betrayed by one Adam Boyd, who trapped him by pretending to be interested in being converted. He was imprisoned, tortured for months, found guilty of high treason for refusing to acknowledge the spiritual supremacy of the King and for refusing to apostatize, and was hanged at Glasgow on March 10. He was canonized in 1976 by Pope Paul VI, the first Scottish saint since St. Mary of Scotland in 1250.

OLAF (995–1030). The son of Harold Grenske, a lord in Norway, Olaf Haraldsson, often called "the Fat," spent his youth as a pirate, was baptized in Rouen, and in 1013 went to England to aid King Ethelred against the Danes. He returned to Norway in 1015, captured most of Norway back from the Danes and Swedes, defeated Earl Sweyn at the battle of Nesje in 1016, and became King. He set about unifying and Christianizing his realm, but the harshness of his rule precipitated a revolt of the nobles in 1029, and aided by Canute of Denmark, they defeated him and forced him to flee to Russia. He returned in 1031 and attempted to recover his kingdom but was slain at the Battle of Stiklestad in Norway on July 29. Though not too popular during his lifetime, miracles were reported at his shrine, and a chapel was built, which became the Cathedral of Trondheim; it became a great pilgrimage center for all Scandinavia. He is one of the great heroes of Norway for his efforts to unify and Christianize Norway, of which he is patron. He was canonized in 1164.

OLAF SKOTTKONUNG (d. 1024). A son of Eric the Conqueror, he was King of Sweden in 993–1024 and was converted by St. Sigfrid and established Christianity in Sweden. In a coalition with King Sweyn of Denmark and Eric, jarl of Lade, he defeated King Olaf I Tryggvesson of Norway at the battle of Svolder in 1000 and annexed part of his territory. He was murdered by rebellious followers at Stockholm when he refused to sacrifice to pagan gods. July 30.

OLGA (c. 879–969). Also called Helga, she was born at Pskov, Russia, and in 903 married Igor, Varangarian prince of Kiev, Russia. After the assassination of Igor in 945, she punished the murderers of her husband by having them scalded to death and then had hundreds of their followers murdered. She ruled the country ably and well as regent for her son Svyastoslav until he came of age in 964. She became a Christian, was baptized at Constantinople about 957, and changed her lifestyle. She devoted herself to converting her people to Christianity, requesting missionaries from Emperor Otto I in 959, but was not too successful, unable to convert even Svyastoslav; but her grandson Vladimir evangelized Russia. She died at Kiev on July 11.

OMER (c. 595–c. 670). Also known as Audomarus, he was born near Coutances, France, and on the death of his mother he and his father became Benedictine monks at Luxeuil under St. Eustace. In 637, after twenty years at Luxeuil, Omer was named bishop of Thérouanne, a see that had become relaxed in religion and morals, and at once put into effect reforms. He ministered to the poor, the sick, and the needy, and with SS. Mommolinus, Bertrand, and Bertinus, monks from Luxeuil, he founded Sithiu Monastery and developed it into one of the great spiritual centers in France. He was noted for the passion and eloquence of his preaching, was credited with performing miracles, and late in life became blind. September 9.

ONESIMUS (1st century). According to St. Paul's epistle to Philomena (10–18), Onesimus was a slave of Philemon in Colossae, Phrygia, who ran away. He met St. Paul while the apostle was in prison in Rome, was baptized, and became Paul's spiritual son. Paul sent him back to Philemon asking him to accept Onesimus "not as a slave . . . but . . . [as] a dear brother. . . ." Evidently Philemon did, as Paul mentions Onesimus again in Colossians (4:7–9), with Tychichus as the bearer of the epistle to the Colossians. According to St. Jerome, Onesimus became a preacher of the Word and later was a bishop, though probably not the bishop of Ephesus who succeeded St. Timothy and was stoned to death in Rome, as stated in the Roman Martyrology. February 16.

ONUPHRIUS (d. c. 400). While on a visit to the hermits of Thebaïd in Egypt to find out if the eremitical life was for him, Abbot Paphnutius met Onuphrius, who told him he had been a monk in a monastery but had left to follow the eremitical life, which he had done for seventy years. During the night the abbot stayed with the hermit; the next morning, after food had miraculously appeared the previous evening, Onuphrius told Paphnutius that the Lord had told him he, Onuphrius, was to die and that Paphnutius had been sent by the Lord to bury him. Onuphrius did die, Paphnutius buried him in a hole in the mountainside, and the site immediately disappeared, as if to tell the abbot that he was not to remain there. The story was put into writing by one of his monks and was already popular in the sixth century. June 12.

OPTATUS (d. c. 387). A convert from paganism to Christianity, he became bishop of Milevis, Numidia, North Africa, was highly praised by St. Augustine, and was ranked with Ambrose and Augustine by St. Fulgentius. Optatus was a leading opponent of Donatism and wrote a famous treatise, *Against Parmenian the Donatist*, in about 370, refuting the teachings of Donatist Bishop Parmenian of Carthage; the treatise is still extant. It is a historically important document, since in it he speaks of the supremacy of the Pope, the validity of the sacraments, and refers to the veneration of relics. June 4.

OSMUND (d. 1099). Said to have been the son of Count Henry of Séez and Isabella, half sister of William the Conqueror, he accompanied the Normans to England, served as chancellor, and in 1078 was named bishop of Salisbury by William. Osmund finished the cathedral there, established a cathedral chapter of canons regular and a clergy school, helped prepare the Domesday survey, and was at Old Sarum when the Domesday Book was presented to William. Osmund supported King William II in an investiture dispute against Anselm at the Council of Rockingham, though Osmund later admitted his error and asked Anselm's pardon. Osmund drew up new liturgical books regulating the Mass, the Divine Office, and the administration of the sacraments that in the next century and a half were widely adopted in England, Ireland, and Wales. He assembled an extensive collection of manuscripts for the cathedral library, was an expert copyist and a skilled binder of books, and wrote a life of St. Aldhelm. Osmund died on December 4 and was canonized in 1457, the last English saint to be canonized until John More and John Fisher were canonized in 1935.

OSWALD OF NORTHUMBRIA (c. 605–42). Forced to flee from Northumbria to Scotland when his father, Aethelfrith, was defeated and killed by Raedwald in 617, Oswald was converted to Christianity at Iona while he was in Scotland. When his uncle, King St. Edwin of Northumbria, was killed in battle against pagan King Penda of Mercia and Welsh King Cadwallon in 633, Oswald assembled an army and in 634 defeated a superior force under Cadwallon, who was killed in a battle near Hexham, and Oswald became King of Northumbria. He attributed his victory to a vision he had had of St. Columba promising him victory and to a huge cross he had erected the night before the battle. He brought St. Aidan to his kingdom to preach Christianity, gave him the island of Lindisfarne for his see, and acted as his interpreter. He built churches and monasteries, brought in monks from Scotland to bring his people back to Christianity, and was known for his personal piety and charity. He married Cyneburga, daughter of Cynegils, first Christian king of Wessex, and died a few years later, on August 5, while fighting against the superior forces of Penda at Maserfield. He was only thirty-seven at his death. August 9.

OSWIN (d. 651). When his father, King Osric of Deira, was killed by Welsh King Cadwallon in 633, he was taken to Wessex, was baptized, and was educated there. When St. Oswald was killed in battle against King Penda of Mercia in 642, Oswin became King of Deira, which Oswald had united to Bernicia, and Oswald's brother, Oswy, became King of Bernicia. Soon after, Oswy declared war on Oswin who, rather than precipitate a bloody battle, went into hiding at the estate of Earl Hunwald at Gilling near Richmond, York. Hunwald betrayed him and he was murdered there by Ethelwin on orders from Oswy. August 20.

OTTERAN (d. 563). Also known as Odhran, he was said to be a Briton who became abbot of Meath and was one of the twelve who accompanied Columba to Iona. He died soon after their arrival, the first of the monks from Ireland to die at Iona. He may have founded the monastery at Leitrioch Odrain (Latteragh, Tipperary). October 27.

OTTILIA. *See* Odilia.

OTTO (d. 1139). Of a noble Swabian family, he was ordained while quite young, entered the service of Emperor Henry IV in 1090, and became his chancellor about 1101. He opposed Henry in the Emperor's struggle with the Holy See and when appointed bishop of Bamberg in 1103 by Henry refused to accept consecration until Pope Paschal II approved and consecrated him at Rome in 1106. He labored to heal the breach between the Pope and the Emperor under Emperor

Henry V, and in 1124, at the invitation of Boleslaus III of Poland, headed a group of missionaries to eastern Pomerania, where they made thousands of converts. He returned in 1128 to reconvert the cities of Stettin and Julin and died at Bamberg on June 30, 1139. He was canonized in 1189. July 2.

OUEN (c. 610–84). Also known as Owen and Audoenus, he was the son of St. Authaire and was born at Sancy near Soissons, France. He was educated at St. Médard Abbey, served at the courts of King Clotaire II and his son Dagobert I, who made him his chancellor and in 636 built a monastery at Rebais. He was persuaded not to become a monk there by Dagobert, and despite the fact that Ouen was a layman, he was active in promoting religion and combating simony. He was continued as chancellor by King Clovis II, was ordained and in 641, was consecrated archbishop of Rouen. He encouraged learning and the founding of new monasteries, was known for his personal austerities and his charities, and supported missionary activities to pagan areas of his see. He supported Ebroin, mayor of the palace, against the nobles, and at the invitation of Thierry III negotiated a peace between Neustria and Austrasia in Cologne. He died at Clich near Paris on August 24 while returning from Cologne.

OWEN. *See* Eugene (d. c. 618).

OWEN. *See* Ouen.

OWEN, NICHOLAS (d. 1606). Born at Oxford, England, he became a carpenter or builder and served Jesuit priests in England for two decades by constructing hiding places for them in mansions throughout the country. He became a Jesuit lay brother in 1580, was arrested in 1594 with Fr. John Gerard, and despite prolonged torture would not give the names of any of his Catholic colleagues; he was released on the payment of a ransom by a wealthy Catholic. Nicholas is believed responsible for Fr. Gerard's dramatic escape from the Tower of London in 1597. Nicholas was again arrested in 1606 with Fr. Henry Garnet, whom he had served eighteen years, Fr. Oldcorne, and Fr. Oldcorne's servant, Brother Ralph Ashley, and imprisoned in the Tower of London. Nicholas was subjected to such vicious torture that he died of it on March 2.

He was known as Little John and Little Michael and used the aliases of Andrewes and Draper. He was canonized by Pope Paul VI in 1970 as one of the Forty Martyrs of England and Wales. March 22.

P

PACHOMIUS (c. 292–348). Born of heathen parents in the Upper Thebaid, Egypt, he was drafted into the army against his will and was so impressed by the kindness of the Christians of Latopolis to the recruits that he became a Christian after he left the army. He became the disciple of a hermit named Palaemon, and in response to a vision bidding him to build a monastery at Tabennisi on the Nile, he built a cell there in about 320. He soon attracted numerous disciples, organized them into a community, and founded six other monasteries in the Thebaid and a convent for his sister across the Nile from Tabennisi. He opposed Arianism, was denounced to a council of bishops at Latopolis, but was completely exonerated, and by the time of his death on May 15, there were some three thousand monks and nuns in the nine monasteries and two convents he governed, though he was never ordained. He was really the founder of cenobitic monasticism, and St. Benedict made generous use of his rule in formulating the Rule of St. Benedict. May 9.

PAINE, JOHN. *See* Payne, John.

PALLADIUS (d. 432). A deacon at Rome, he was responsible for sending St. Germanus of Auxerre to Britain in 429 to combat Pelagianism and in 431 was consecrated by Pope Celestine I and sent as a missionary to Ireland—the first bishop of the Irish. He worked in Leinster, encountered much opposition, but made some converts and built three churches. Acknowledging his lack of success in Ireland, he went to Scotland to preach to the Picts, and died soon after he arrived at Fordun, near Aberdeen. July 7.

PALLOTTI, VINCENT (1795-1850). Born at Rome on April 21, the son of a grocer, he was ordained when he was twenty-three, received his doctorate in theology, and taught theology at the Spaienza in Rome. He served in several parishes in his native city, suffering rebuffs from fellow curates for a decade, and then was involved in organizing a group of clergy and laity for conversion work and social justice on a worldwide scale. In 1835, he founded the Society of the Catholic Apostolate (called for a time the Pious Society of Missions), composed of priests, nuns, and laity, organized trade schools with evening classes for poor boys, worked among the poor, was a sought-after confessor and exorcist, and brought many back to the Church. He died in Rome on January 22, and was canonized in 1963 by Pope John XXIII. January 23.

PAMBO (d. c. 390). A disciple of St. Antony in his youth, he was one of the founders of the Nitrian Desert monasteries in Egypt and was noted for his austerities, mortifications, and wisdom. He was consulted by many, among them St. Athanius, St. Rufinus, and St. Melania the Elder, who was with him when he died. July 18.

PAMMACHIUS (d. 410). Of the Furii family, he was a Roman senator and a friend of St. Jerome. Pammachius married St. Paula's daughter Paulina in 385. His denunciation to Pope St. Siricius of Jovinian, who was later condemned at a synod at Rome, and by St. Ambrose at Milan, caused Jerome to write a treatise against Jovinian's teachings that Pammachius criticized, which led to two more letters from Jerome defending his treatise. Paulina died in 397, and Pammachius devoted the rest of his life to study and charitable works. With Fabiola he built a hospice at Porto for poor and sick pilgrims coming to Rome (the first such in the West) and had a church in his house (a site now occupied by the Passionists' SS. Peter and Paul Church). He often tried, unsuccessfully, to tone down the polemics of some of Jerome's controversial treatises and particularly the bitterness of Jerome's controversy with Rufinus. Pammachius urged Jerome to translate Origen's *De principiis*, and Pammachius' letter to tenants on his estate in Numidia in 401 to abandon

Donatism evoked a letter of thanks from St. Augustine. Pammachius died in Rome. August 30.

PAMPHILUS (d. 309). Born of a wealthy family at Berytus (Beirut), Phoenicia, he studied there and at the catechetical school at Alexandria under Pierius, a follower of Origen. Pamphilus was ordained at Caesarea, Palestine, accumulated a large library, was noted for his learning, and was considered the leading biblical scholar of his time. He founded a Bible school at Caesarea (one of his students was the historian Eusebius), produced an accurate version of the Bible, lived an austere, hard-working life, and gave away his wealth to the poor. He was arrested in 308 for his Christianity by Urban, governor of Palestine, tortured, and imprisoned when he refused to sacrifice to pagan gods. After almost two years in prison, Firmilian, Urban's successor, found him, Paul of Jamnia, and Valens, an old deacon from Jerusalem, guilty of being Christians and sentenced them to death by beheading. At the same time he had one of his servants, Theodulus, crucified when he found he was a Christian; Porphyrius, a student of Pamphilus, was tortured and burned to death when Firmilian heard he had requested Pamphilus' body and was a Christian; and Seleucus, a Cappadocian, was decapitated when Firmilian heard him applauding Porphyrius' firmness under torture. Eusebius wrote a now lost biography of Pamphilus and praises him highly in his *Ecclesiastical History;* he collaborated with Pamphilus on *Apology for Origen* while Pamphilus was in prison and may have been a fellow prisoner. June 1.

PANCRAS (d. c. 304). According to unreliable sources, he was a native of Syria or Phrygia who when orphaned was brought by his uncle to Rome, where both were converted to Christianity. When only fourteen, Pancras was beheaded in Rome for his faith during the persecution of Christians under Emperor Diocletian and was buried in the cemetery of Calepodius, which was later named after him. May 12.

PANTALEON (c. 305). That he lived, was also known as Panteleimon, and was martyred are facts, but all else is dubious legend, according to which he was the son of a pagan father, Eustorgius of Nicomedia, and raised a Christian by his mother, Eubula. He became Emperor Maximian's physician and enjoyed the dissolute life of the court to such a degree that he lost his faith. He was brought back to Christian ways by Hermolaos, donated his medical skills to the poor free of charge, sold his possessions, and gave the proceeds to the poor. When the persecution of Christians under Emperor Diocletian broke out in Nicomedia in 303, he was denounced as a Christian by fellow physicians and was arrested with Hermolaos and two other Christians. They were condemned to death, and Pantaleon was finally executed by beheading after being miraculously saved from execution by six other methods, including drowning, by fire, and by wild beasts. He is one of the Fourteen Holy Helpers and is called the Great Martyr and Wonder Worker in the East. His blood is reputed to liquefy on his feast day, as does that of St. Januarius in Naples. July 27.

PANTELEIMON. *See* Pantaleon.

PAPHNUTIUS (d. c. 350). Sometimes called "the Great," he was an Egyptian who served as a monk under St. Antony in the desert for several years and was then named bishop of Upper Thebaid. He was tortured and lost his right eye during Emperor Maximinus' persecution of Christians and was condemned to labor in the mines, as were so many other Christians at the time. On his release, he was an uncompromising opponent of Arianism, successfully convinced the Council of Nicaea in 325 to allow married men to be ordained and to be consecrated bishops, though opposing marriage after ordination, and at the Council of Tyre in 335 brought Bishop Maximus of Jerusalem back to orthodoxy from Arianism. September 11.

PAREDES Y FLORES, MARIANA DE (1618–45). Born at Quito, Ecuador (then part of Peru), of noble Spanish parents, she was orphaned as a child and raised by her elder sister and her husband. Mariana early was attracted to things religious and became a solitary in her sister's home under the direction of Mariana's Jesuit confessor. Mariana practiced the greatest austerities, ate hardly anything, slept for only three hours a night for years, had the gift of prophecy, and reputedly performed miracles. When an earthquake followed by an

epidemic shook Quito in 1645, she offered herself publicly as
a victim for the sins of the people. When the epidemic began
to abate, she was stricken and died on May 26. She is known
as Mariana of Quito and is often called "the Lily of Quito."
She was canonized in 1950.

PAREGORIUS (d. c. 260). *See* Leo.

PAREGRUS (d. 297). *See* Hipparchus.

PARMENAS (d. c. 98). He was one of the seven chosen by
the apostles in Jerusalem to minister to the needs of the
Hellenic Jewish converts to Christianity there (Acts 6:5).
According to tradition, he preached for years in Asia Minor
before being martyred at Philippi, Macedonia, during the persecution of the Christians under Emperor Trajan. January 23.

PASCHAL I (d. 824). Son of Bonosus, a Roman, he studied at the Lateran, was named head of St. Stephen's Monastery, which housed pilgrims to Rome, and was elected Pope
to succeed Pope Stephen IV (V) on the day Stephen died,
January 25, 817. Emperor Louis the Pious agreed to respect
papal jurisdiction, but when Louis' son Lothair I came to
Rome in 823 to be consecrated King, he broke the pact by
presiding at a trial involving a group of nobles opposing the
Pope. When two papal officials who had testified for the nobles were found blinded and murdered, Paschal was accused
of the crime. He denied any complicity but refused to surrender the murderers, who were members of his household, declaring that the two dead officials were traitors and the secular authorities had no jurisdiction in the case. The result was
the Constitution of Lothair, severely restricting papal judicial
and police powers in Italy. Paschal was unsuccessful in attempts to end the iconoclast heresy of Emperor Leo V, encouraged SS. Nicephorus and Theodore Studites in Constantinople to resist iconoclasm, and gave refuge to the many
Greek monks who fled to Rome to escape persecution from
the iconoclasts. Paschal built and redecorated many churches
in Rome and transferred many relics from the catacombs to
churches in the city. Although listed in the Roman Martyrology, he has never been formally canonized. February 11.

PASCHASIUS RADBERTUS (d. c. 860). Abandoned as an infant at the doorway of Notre Dame convent in Soissons, France, he was adopted by the nuns there, was educated by the monks of St. Peter's, Soissons, and became a monk at Corbie. In 822, he was one of the monks sent to found New Corbie in Westphalia, helped make the Corbie schools famous while he served as master of novices there, and was abbot of Corbie for seven years, though he never became a priest. After a time at Saint-Riquier Abbey, he returned to Corbie, where he died. He wrote numerous treatises, chief of which was *De Corpore et Sanguine Christe*, biblical commentaries, and biographies of two Corbie abbots, St. Adalhard and his brother Wala, whose friend and confidant Paschasius had been. April 26.

PATRICIA (d. c. 665). According to legend, she was of a noble and perhaps royal family in Constantinople who fled to Italy to escape marriage and became a virgin consecrated to God in Rome. She returned to Constantinople, distributed her wealth to the poor, and then went back to Italy, where she died soon after, at Naples. She is a patron of Naples, and like St. Januarius there, a vial believed to be filled with her blood reportedly liquefies thirteen hundred years after her death. August 25.

PATRICK (c. 389–c. 461). So much of the life of the apostle of Ireland is enshrouded in myth and legend that much of his biography must be conjecture. The son of a Romano-British official, Calpurnius, he was born somewhere in Roman Britain, perhaps in a village called Bannavem, but possibly in Gaul; or perhaps at Kilpatrick near Dunbarton, Scotland. He was captured by raiders when he was about sixteen and carried off in slavery to pagan Ireland. After sheepherding for six years, probably in Antrim or Mayo, he escaped, probably to Gaul. When about twenty-two, he returned to Britain and then seems to have studied at the monastery of Lérins, 412–15. He spent the next fifteen years at Auxerre and was probably ordained about 417. About 432 he was probably consecrated a bishop by St. Germanus and sent to Ireland to succeed St. Paulinus, who had died the previous year. Patrick traveled the length and breadth of the island meeting fierce opposition from hostile chieftains and Druids, whom he repeatedly overcame by miraculous means; eventually he converted most of the island to Christianity. He visited Rome in 442 and 444, founded the cathedral church of Armagh, and it soon became the center of the Church's activities in Ireland. During his three decades in Ireland, he raised the standards of scholarship, encouraged the study of Latin, brought Ireland into closer relations with the rest of the Western Church, and of course converted the Irish to the faith they have so fiercely defended through the centuries. He wrote *Confessio*, an apology against his detractors and the chief source of biographical information about him, and a *Letter to the Soldiers of Coroticus*, denouncing the slaughter of a group of Irish Christians by Coroticus' raiding Welshmen, who were also Christian. His cult began on his death, perhaps at Saul on Strangford Lough in Downpatrick, and has flourished ever since. March 17.

PAUL (d. c. 67). Born of Jewish parents of the tribe of Benjamin sometime between 5 and 15 in Tarsus, which also made him a citizen of Rome, Saul studied under the famous Jewish rabbi, Gamaliel, in Jerusalem. A tentmaker by trade, Saul became a rigid Pharisee and a rabid persecutor of the Christians. He was present at the stoning of Stephen but only as a spectator. On the way to Damascus to arrest some Christians and bring them back to Jerusalem, he experienced his famous vision (sometime between 34 and 36), which led not only to his dramatic conversion but (in view of the tremendous impact he was to have on early Christianity) was to shape the whole Christian experience. He spent the next three years in Arabia (probably the Nabatean kingdom) and then returned to Damascus to preach. He immediately encountered resistance from the Jews, a resistance that was to continue throughout his life and travels. Forced to flee secretly from Aretas, the Nabatean King, he went, sometime between 36 and 39, to Jerusalem, where he met the apostles, and through the sponsorship of Barnabas was accepted by the Christian community. He returned to Tarsus for several years, then about 43 was brought to Antioch by Barnabas and was made a teacher in the church there. After accompanying Barnabas to Jerusalem in 44 with a donation from the church at Antioch to the church at Jerusalem, Saul was sent out, with Barnabas, to preach the gospel on the first of his three missionary journeys. During 45–49, it took them to Cyprus, Perga, Antioch in Pisidia, and the cities of Lycaonia; it was on this journey that Saul was changed to Paul. On his return he went to Jerusalem in 49 and was successful in convincing Peter, James, and the other apostles that Gentile Christians need not be circumcised and have Jewish law forced on them—a decision that ensured the universality of Christianity—and secured the approval of the Jerusalem Church for his mission to the Gentiles. Shortly after his return to Antioch, Paul and Barnabas set out on their second missionary journey (49–52). After revisiting the churches founded on the first journey, Paul crossed to Macedonia (as a result of a dream) and preached the gospel in Europe for the first time. He founded churches at Philippi (where he and Silas were imprisoned and miraculously escaped), Thessalonica, and Beroea; preached, with little effect, on the Unknown God in Athens; and then spent 50–52 at Corinth, where he founded a flourishing church. He then returned to Antioch but soon set out on a third journey (53–58). He spent two years at Ephesus teaching and working miracles there and in the surrounding areas but was driven out by rioting silversmiths, whose trade in statues and shrines of Diana was being adversely affected by Christianity; from there he went to Macedonia and then in 58 back to Jerusalem with contributions for the mother church. At Jerusalem, he was attacked by a mob for his missions to the Gentiles and put under protective arrest by the Roman soldiers. A plot against his life caused the Roman captain to send him to Governor Felix at Caesarea, where his trial was delayed two years (58–60) until Festus succeeded Felix, when Paul as a Roman citizen demanded and was granted a trial in Rome. On the way to Rome in 60–61, he was shipwrecked off the coast of Malta but eventually reached Rome, where he remained under house arrest in his own lodgings for two years, 61–62—the last time he is mentioned in the Acts of the Apostles, the major source of biographical material about him. According to Clement of Rome, writing only thirty years after Paul's death, Paul went to Spain after his imprisonment, and on his return, according to the pastoral epistles, revisited Ephesus, Macedonia, and Greece, 63–67. According to tradition he was again arrested, probably at Troas, and returned to Rome, where he was executed on the same day as St. Peter (in 67, according to Eusebius) during the persecution of Christians under Emperor Nero (by beheading, according to Tertullian). One of the most creative of Christian writers, Paul wrote epistles to

the Romans (from Corinth, 57–58); 1 Corinthians (from
Ephesus in 54); 2 Corinthians (probably from Philippi in
57); Galatians (from Ephesus about 54); Colossians, Philemon, Ephesians, and Philippians (probably from Rome in
61–63); 1 and 2 Thessalonians (from Corinth in 51–52);
and two pastoral epistles to Timothy and one to Titus. The
epistle to the Hebrews is now believed to have been written
by another author of Alexandrian background; it was not accepted canonically in the West before 350 and was probably
written sometime between 60 and 90. June 29; Paul's conversion is celebrated on January 25.

PAUL I (d. 767). The brother of Pope Stephen III, he was
educated at the Lateran school, ordained at Rome, and served
on diplomatic missions for Stephen, including one to Lombard King Desiderius, who promised to return several papal
cities to the Pope. Paul was elected to succeed his brother as
Pope on April 26, 757. Paul maintained friendly relations
with King Pepin throughout his pontificate, resisted Byzantine
attempts to encroach on papal temporal power, and finally
succeeded in 765 in coming to an agreement with Desiderius
about the boundaries of their respective territories. Paul rebuilt churches and monasteries in Rome, opposed the iconoclasm of Emperor Constantine Copronymus, and died at St.
Paul's Outside the Walls in Rome on June 28.

PAUL OF THE CROSS (1694–1775). Born at Ovada,
Italy, on January 3, Paul Francis Danei, the eldest son of impoverished noble parents, adopted a lifestyle of rigorous austerity and great mortifications at his home at Castellazzo,
Lombardy, when he was fifteen. In 1714, he joined the Vene-
tian army to fight against the Turks, and when discharged a
year later resumed his life of prayer and penance. He refused
marriage, spent several years in retreat at Castellazzo, and in
1720 had a vision of our Lady in a black habit with the name
Jesus and a cross in white on the chest in which she told him
to found a religious order devoted to preaching the Passion of
Christ. He received permission to proceed from the bishop of
Alessandria, who decided the visions were authentic, and Paul
drew up a rule during a forty-day retreat that became the
basic rule for the congregation he was to found. With his
brother, John the Baptist, who became his inseparable companion and closest confidant, he went to Rome for papal ap-

proval, was refused at first, but on their return to Rome in 1725 were granted permission to accept novices from Pope Benedict XIII, who ordained them in 1727. They set up a house on Monte Argentaro, lost many of their first novices because of the severity of the rule, opened their first monastery in 1737, and in 1741 received approval of a modified rule from Pope Benedict XIV, and the Barefooted Clerks of the Holy Cross and Passion (the Passionists) began to spread throughout Italy, in great demand for their missions, which became famous. Paul was elected first superior general, against his will, at the first general chapter at Monte Argentaro and held that position the rest of his life. He preached all over the Papal States to tremendous crowds, raised them to a fever pitch as he scourged himself in public, and brought back to the faith the most hardened sinners and criminals. He was blessed with supernatural gifts—prophecy, miracles of healing, appearances to people in visions in distant places—and was one of the most celebrated preachers of his time. People fought to touch him and to get a piece of his tunic as a relic. One of his particular concerns was for the conversion of sinners, for which he prayed for fifty years. The Passionists received final approbation from Pope Clement XIV in 1769, and two years later, Paul's efforts to create an institute of nuns came into being with the opening of the first house of the Passionist nuns, at Corneto. Ill the last three years of his life, he died in Rome on October 18, and was canonized in 1867. October 19.

PAUL THE HERMIT (c. 229–342). Born in Lower Thebaid, Egypt, he was orphaned when he was fifteen, went into hiding to escape the persecution of Christians under Emperor Decius, and then fled to the desert when he was twenty-two when he learned that his brother-in-law planned to report him as a Christian to take over his estate. He decided to stay a hermit when he found that the eremitical life suited him. Reportedly, St. Jerome visited Paul in his old age, found him an exemplar of what a holy man should be, and buried him when he died; Jerome also wrote a life of Paul, who reputedly lived to be 113 years old, more than 90 of which were spent as a hermit. He is sometimes called Paul the First Hermit to distinguish him from other hermits named Paul. January 15.

PAUL THE SIMPLE (d. c. 339). A working man all his

life, he left his unfaithful wife when he was sixty and sought out St. Antony in the Egyptian Thebaid to become one of his disciples. Antony at first refused to accept him because of his advanced age but was so impressed by Paul's persistence that he took him in. Antony subjected Paul to an arduous training in an attempt to discourage him, but was convinced by Paul's humility, eagerness, and obedience, and assigned a cell to him. There Paul performed miracles of healing, revealed his power to read men's minds, and so impressed Antony that he referred to him as the ideal of what a monk should be. Paul was surnamed "the Simple" because of his childlike innocence. March 7.

PAULA (347–404). Born in Rome of a noble family on May 5, she married Toxotius, and the couple had five children—Toxotius, Blesilla, Paulina, Eustochium, and Rufina. They were regarded as an ideal married couple, and on his death in 379, she renounced the world, lived in the greatest austerity, and devoted herself to helping the poor. She met St. Jerome in 382 through St. Epiphanius and Paulinus of Antioch and was closely associated with Jerome in his work while he was in Rome. The death of her daughter Blesilla in 384 left her heartbroken, and in 385 she left Rome with Eustochium, traveled through the Holy Land with Jerome, and a year later settled in Bethlehem under his spiritual direction. She and Eustochium built a hospice, a monastery, and a convent, which Paula governed. She became Jerome's closest confidante and assistant, taking care of him and helping him in his biblical work, built numerous churches, which were to cause her financial difficulties in her old age, and died at Bethlehem on January 26. She is the patroness of widows.

PAULINUS (c. 584–644). Sent as a missionary from Rome to England by Pope St. Gregory I, he worked in Kent and was consecrated bishop in 625. He accompanied Ethelburga, daughter of King Ethelbert of Kent, to Northumbria, when she married pagan King Edwin of Northumbria. Two years later he baptized Edwin on Easter at his see city of York, bringing Christianity to Northumbria; Paulinus and his assistants baptized thousands, who followed their King into Christianity. When Edwin was slain by the pagan Mercians at the Battle of Hatfield Chase in 633 and Northumbria reverted to paganism, Paulinus returned to Kent with Ethelburga, her two children, and Edwin's grandson Osfrid. Paulinus was named administrator of the vacant see of Rochester, administered it for ten years, and died there on October 10.

PAULINUS OF NOLA (c. 354–431). Born near Bordeaux, France, the son of the Roman prefect of Gaul, Pontius Meropius Anicius Paulinus studied rhetoric and poetry under the poet Ausonius and became a successful and prominent lawyer. He held several public offices, among them probably the prefecture of New Epirus, traveled extensively throughout Gaul, Italy, and Spain, and married a Spanish lady, Therasia. He resigned his public offices and retired to Aquitaine, where he met Bishop Delphinus of Bordeaux, who baptized him and his brother. In about 390 Paulinus moved to Therasia's estate in Spain and when their only child died a week after he was born they gave much of their property to the Church and to the poor and began living lives of great austerity. In about 393, the bishop of Barcelona, by popular demand of the populace, ordained him a priest. He then moved to an estate near the tomb of St. Felix at Nola near Naples, Italy, in about 395, and over the vehement objections of his relatives, sold his estate and belongings in Aquitaine and gave most of it to the poor. He became known for his charities, built a church at Fondi, an aqueduct at Nola, a basilica near the tomb of St. Felix, a hospice for travelers at Nola, and housed many of the poor and needy in his own home, where he lived a semimonastic life with several of his friends. In about 409, he was elected bishop of Nola, a position he held until his death there. Paulinus had a wide circle of friends, and a wide correspondence with, among others, St. Augustine and St. Jerome (Augustine's *On the Care of the Dead* was written in reply to an inquiry from Paulinus), and was a friend of SS. Ambrose and Martin of Tours. Of Paulinus' many writings some fifty-one letters, thirty-two poems, and a few prose pieces are still extant. His poetry, most of it written for the annual celebration in honor of St. Felix, has caused him to be ranked with Prudentius as the foremost Christian Latin poets of the patristic period. June 22.

PAYNE, JOHN (d. 1582). Born at Peterborough, England, he may have been a convert to Catholicism. He went to Douai in 1574, was ordained in 1576, and was sent at once on the English mission with St. Cuthbert Mayne. Payne was

most successful in his work, bringing back many to the
Church, until he was arrested a year after his arrival. He was
released and left England but returned in 1579. He was again
arrested in Warwickshire, where he was acting as steward for
Lady Petre at Ingatestone Hall, which Lady Petre used as a
hiding place for priests. He was accused of plotting to murder
the Queen by one John Eliot, a seasoned criminal and murderer who denounced dozens of priests for money. Payne was
imprisoned and tortured in the Tower for nine months before
being condemned to death. He was hanged, drawn, and quartered at Chelmsford on April 2, and was canonized in 1970
by Pope Paul VI as one of the Forty Martyrs of England and
Wales. His name is also spelled Paine.

PAZZI, MARY MAGDALEN DEI (1566–1607). Born at
Florence, Italy, of a distinguished Florentine family, and baptized Catherine, she was educated at St. John Convent at
Florence, resisted attempts to have her marry, and joined the
Carmelites at St. Mary of the Angels Convent in her native
city in 1582, taking the name Mary Magdalen when professed
the following year. She became seriously ill, during which she
experienced numerous ecstasies, recovered, practiced great
mortifications, and then spent five years in the depths of spiritual depression and aridity, from which she did not emerge
until 1590. She had the gifts of prophecy and the ability to
read people's minds and to perform miracles of healing. Her
utterances while in ecstasy and descriptions of her revelations
were copied down by some of the sisters in the convent and
were later published. Bedridden the last three years of her
life, she died at the convent on May 25. She was canonized in
1669.

PELAGIA THE PENITENT (no date). Often called Margaret, she was an actress at Antioch known for her great
beauty and dissolute life. During a synod at Antioch, she
passed Bishop St. Nonnus of Edessa, who was struck with her
beauty; the next day she went to hear him preach and was so
moved by his sermon that she asked him to baptize her,
which he did. She gave her wealth to Nonnus to aid the poor
and left Antioch dressed in men's clothing. She became a hermitess in a cave on Mount of Olivet in Jerusalem, where she
lived in great austerity, performing penances and known as
"the beardless monk" until her sex was discovered at her

death. Though a young girl of fifteen did exist and suffer martyrdom at Antioch in the fourth century, the story here told is a pious fiction, which gave rise to a whole set of similar stories under different names. October 8.

PELLETIER, MARY EUPHRASIA (1796–1868). Born on July 31 on the island of Noirmoutier off the Brittany coast and baptized Rose Virginia, she studied at Tours and in 1814 joined the Institute of Our Lady of Charity, founded by St. John Eudes in 1641 to help wayward women. She was professed in 1816, taking the names Mary Euphrasia, was elected superior in 1825, made a new foundation at Angers, and then decided that a new congregation under a central authority was needed rather than individual foundations under separate bishops. She founded the Institute of Our Lady of Charity of the Good Shepherd, dedicated to working with wayward girls, at Angers, and received papal approval in 1835. The Institute spread rapidly and by the time of Mother Euphrasia's death had almost three thousand nuns in foundations all over the world. She died at Angers, France, on April 24, and was canonized in 1940. April 24.

PEPIN OF LANDEN, BL. (d. c. 639). Duke of Brabant, husband of Bl. Itta, and often called Pippin, he served as mayor of the palace under Kings Clotaire II, Dagobert I, and Sigebert III. Pepin and Bishop Arnulf of Metz aided King Clotaire II of Neustria in overthrowing Queen Brunhilda of Austrasia in 613, and Clotaire appointed them mayors of the palace to rule Austrasia for Clotaire's son Dagobert I from 623. When Pepin rebuked Dagobert (who had succeeded his father about 629) for his licentious life, Dagobert discharged him and he retired to Aquitaine. Dagobert appointed him tutor of his three-year-old son Sigebert before his death in 638, and Pepin returned and ruled the kingdom until his own death the next year. He worked to spread the faith, defended Christian towns from Slavic invaders, and chose responsible men to fill vacant sees. The marriage of his daughter, St. Begga, and Arnulf's son, Segisilius, produced Pepin of Herstal, the first of the Carolingian dynasty in France. Pepin has never been canonized but is listed as a saint in some of the old martyrologies. February 21.

PERCY, BL. THOMAS (1528–72). Son of Sir Thomas

Percy, who was hanged at Tyburn in 1537 as one of the
leaders of the Pilgrimage of Grace, he became earl of Northumberland in 1557. He served Queen Mary during her reign
and in 1558 married Anne Somerset, daughter of the earl of
Worcester; they had four children. Though viewed with suspicion by Queen Elizabeth I's followers because of his Catholicism, Elizabeth bestowed the Order of the Garter on him in
1563. He supported Mary, Queen of Scots, when she took
refuge at Carlisle in 1568. He and Charles Neville, earl of
Westmorland, refused to appear before Elizabeth when ordered to do so in 1569 and became the leaders of what came
to be known as the Rising of the North. They were defeated
by Elizabeth's troops under the earl of Sussex, who destroyed
towns and hanged hundreds to avenge the uprising. Percy fled
to Scotland but was captured by the earl of Moray, the
Scottish regent. Percy was held prisoner at Lochleven Castle
for two and a half years until the earl of Mar became regent
and sold him to Elizabeth for £2,000. He was brought to
York, offered his freedom if he would apostatize, and when
he refused, was beheaded there on August 22. He was
beatified in 1896. August 26.

PEREGRINE LAZIOSI (1260–1345). *See* Laziosi, Peregrine.

PEREIRA, BL. NONIUS ALVARES DE (1360–1431).
Also known as Nuñes and Nonius, he was born at Bomjardin
near Lisbon, Portugal, married when he was seventeen, and
was named commander of Portugal's armies in 1383, when
he was only twenty-three, by the grand master of the knights
of Aviz, who became King John I. They revolted against
Spanish domination and established Portugal as an independent state when they defeated the Castilian army at the battle
of Aljubarrota in 1385, and John became King. After the
death of his wife in 1422, Nuñes became a Carmelite lay
brother in a friary he had founded in Lisbon and died there
on November 1. Called the Great Constable, he is one of the
great national heroes of Portugal, celebrated in the sixteenth-
century epic *Chronica Condestavel;* his cult was approved for
Portugal and the Carmelites in 1918. November 6.

PERPETUA (d. 203). A matron of noble birth in Carthage
with one child, an infant, Vivia (or Vibia), she was arrested

during the persecution of Christians under Emperor Severus with fellow catechumens Revocatus and the pregnant Felicity, both slaves, Saturninus and Secundulus, and imprisoned in a private home. There they were all baptized, probably by Saturus, their instructor, who had joined them. Later they were moved to a prison, where Secundulus died and Felicity gave birth to a daughter. They were then examined by Hilarion, procurator of the province, and sentenced to death at the public games in the amphitheater. They were exposed to wild beasts, and when Perpetua and Felicity were unharmed, they were sworded to death. The descriptions of their passion written by Perpetua and Saturus and their death written by an unknown eyewitness (once thought by some to be Tertullian) are considered among the most remarkable of such acts and achieved such popularity that Augustine protested against their being read in African churches along with Scripture. March 7.

PETER (d. c. 64). A native of Bethsaida, a village near Lake Tiberias, he was the son of John, was called Simon, and lived and worked as a fisherman on Lake Genesareth. His brother Andrew introduced him to Jesus, who gave him the name Cephas, the Aramaic equivalent of the Greek Peter (the Rock). He was present at Christ's first miracle at Cana and at his home at Capernaum when Jesus cured his mother-in-law, and his boat was always available to the Savior. When Peter acknowledged Jesus as "the Christ . . . the son of the living God" (Matt. 16:16), the Lord replied, "You are Peter and on this rock I will build my Church" (Matt. 16:18) and "I will give you the keys of the kingdom of heaven: Whatever you bind on earth will be considered bound in heaven; whatever you loose on earth shall be considered loosed in heaven," statements underlying Catholic teaching that Peter was the first Pope and the whole Catholic concept of the primacy of the papacy. Peter is mentioned more frequently in the gospels than any of the other apostles, was with Christ during many of his miracles, but denied him in the courtyard of Pontius Pilate's palace, where Christ was being held prisoner. He was the head of the Christians after the Ascension, designated Judas' successor, was the first of the apostles to preach to the Gentiles, was the first apostle to perform miracles, and converted many with his preaching. He was imprisoned by Herod Agrippa in about 43, but guided by

an angel, escaped and firmly proclaimed that Christ wanted
the Good News preached to all at the assembly at Jerusalem.
After this episode, he is not mentioned in the New Testament
again, but a very early tradition says he went to Rome, where
he was Rome's first bishop and was crucified there at the foot
of Vatican Hill in about 64 during the reign of Emperor
Nero. Excavations under St. Peter's Basilica have unearthed
what is believed to be his tomb, and bones found in the tomb
are still under intensive study. June 29.

PETER (d. 311). Born at Alexandria, Egypt, and known
for his learning and knowledge of Scripture, he was named
head of the catechetical school in Alexandria and in 300 was
named Patriarch of that city. He fought Arianism and Origenism and spent the last nine years of his episcopate encouraging his flock to stand fast against the persecution of
Christians launched by Emperor Diocletian. Peter eventually
was forced into hiding, whereupon Bishop Meletius of Lycop-
olis began to usurp Peter's authority as metropolitan and accused Peter of treating the *lapsi* with too great leniency.
When Peter excommunicated Meletius, a schism developed.
Peter continued administering his see from hiding and returned to Alexandria when the persecutions were temporarily
suspended. When Emperor Maximin renewed the persecution,
Peter was arrested and then executed—the last Christian martyr put to death in Alexandria by the authorities. Peter's instructions on how *lapsi* were to be received back into the
Church were later adopted throughout the East. November
26.

PETER OF ALCÁNTARA (1499–1562). Son of the governor of Alcántara, Estremadura, Spain, where he was born,
Peter Garavito studied locally and law at Salamanca University, and when he was sixteen, joined the Observant Franciscans at Manjaretes. He practiced great austerities and penances, was sent to Badajoz to found a friary when he was
twenty-two, and was ordained in 1524. He preached in Estremadura, served as superior at Robredillo, Plasencia, Lapa,
and Estremadura, and had his request for solitude granted
with an appointment to the friary at Lapa, though he was also
named its superior. He served as a court chaplain for a time
to King John III of Portugal and in 1538 was elected minister
provincial of the Observants' province of St. Gabriel at Es-

tremadura. He formulated a strict rule but when unable to
convince the entire province to accept it at a provincial chapter at Placensia in 1540, he resigned as minister provincial.
He lived as a hermit with Friar Martin of St. Mary on
Arabida Mountain near Lisbon and was named superior of
Palhaes community for novices when numerous friars were
attracted to their way of life. Unable to secure approval for a
stricter congregation of friars from his minister provincial, his
idea was accepted by the bishop of Coria and he secured permission from Pope Julius III to build a friary under the Conventuals, but with his rule, in 1555—the beginnings of the
Franciscans of the Observance of St. Peter of Alcántara (the
Alcantarines), devoted to a life of penance and austerity.
When other houses accepted his rule, St. Joseph Province was
erected in 1561 and moved from Conventual to Observant jurisdiction despite much opposition from his former colleagues, the Conventuals. In 1560, he met St. Teresa of Avila,
who included much of what he told her about himself and his
life in her autobiography, became her confessor and adviser,
and encouraged her in her work of reforming the Carmelites.
He wrote *Treatise on Prayer and Meditation*, which was later
used by St. Francis de Sales, and was gifted with many supernatural experiences. He died in the convent at Estremadura
on October 18, was canonized in 1669, and was declared patron of Brazil in 1862. October 22.

PETER OF ASSCHE (d. 1572). *See* Pieck, Nicholas.

PETER OF ATROA (773–837). Born near Ephesus, Asia
Minor, and christened Theophylact, he became a monk when
he was eighteen and joined St. Paul the Hesychast, who
named him Peter, at Crypta, Phrygia. He was ordained several years later, set out with Paul on a pilgrimage to Jerusalem, but instead they went to Mount Olympus, where Paul
founded St. Zachary Monastery near Atroa. When Paul died
in 805, Peter succeeded him as abbot, but after ten years
closed the monastery because of the iconoclastic persecution
under Emperor Leo the Armenian. Peter went to Ephesus
and Crete, and when he returned found he was a wanted
man. He escaped the imperial troops seeking him by miraculous means, and wandered from place to place, settling for
several years at Kalonaros near the Hellespont. He was accused of practicing magic and using the devil because of the

miracles he performed, but he was completely cleared by St. Theodore Studites. Peter again resumed his eremitical life near Atroa, restored St. Zachary Monastery, and reorganized several other monasteries, but when another outburst of iconoclastic persecution erupted, dispersed the monks and sent them into hiding. When the persecution became more violent, Peter retired to St. Porphyry Monastery on the Hellespont but eventually returned to his hermitage at St. Zachary and died there on January 1.

PETER BAPTIST (1545–97). Born near Avila, Spain, he joined the Franciscans in 1567, worked as a missionary in Mexico, was sent to the Philippines in 1583, and then in 1593 was sent to Japan, where he served as commissary for the Franciscans. He was crucified with twenty-five other Christians on February 5 near Nagasaki during the persecution of Christians by the *taikō*, Toyotomi Hideyoshi. They were all canonized in 1862 as the Martyrs of Japan. February 6.

PETER OF CANTERBURY (d. 606). A Benedictine monk at St. Andrew's Monastery in Rome, he was one of the first group of missionaries under St. Augustine of Canterbury sent to England by Pope St. Gregory the Great in 596. Peter became first abbot of SS. Peter and Paul at Canterbury in 602. He was drowned at Ambleteuse near Boulogne while on a mission to Gaul. His cult was confirmed in 1915. January 6.

PETER CHRYSOLOGUS (406–c. 450). Born at Imola, Emilia, Italy, he studied under the direction of Bishop Cornelius of Imola, who ordained him deacon. An unlikely legend has him named bishop of Ravenna in 433 by Pope St. Sixtus III, who reputedly selected him in place of another elected by the people because of a vision Sixtus had telling him to do so. At any rate, he at once set about the reform of his lax see and to eradicate paganism, was known for his charities, and preached with such effect that he was surnamed Chrysologus ("the golden-worded"). His first sermon impressed Empress Galla Placidia so much that thereafter she generously supported his ambitious building projects. He advised Eutyches to stop attempting to justify himself after his condemnation by the synod of Constantinople in 448 and officiated at the funeral of St. Germanus of Auxerre after his death at Ravenna in 448. Peter died at Imola on July 31, and his homilies, many still extant, caused Pope Benedict XIII to declare him a Doctor of the Church in 1729. July 30.

PETER CLAVER. *See* Claver, Peter.

PETER OF CLUNY, BL. *See* Peter the Venerable, Bl.

PETER DAMIAN (1001–72). Born of poor parents at Ravenna, Italy, he was orphaned when very young and raised by a brother for whom he tended swine in his youth. Another brother, a priest at Ravenna named Damian whose name he adopted as his surname, sent him to Faenza and then to Parma to be educated. Peter became a professor, began to practice great austerities, and in 1035 joined the Benedictines at Fonte Avellana, living as a hermit and devoting himself to intensive study of Scripture. About 1043 he was elected abbot by the monks, founded five other hermitages, and became famous for his uncompromising attitude toward worldliness and denunciations of simony. In 1057, he was named cardinal-bishop of Ostia by Pope Stephen IX but soon attempted to resign his see; refused by Pope Nicholas II, he finally persuaded Pope Alexander II to allow him to do so. He returned to the life of a monk but remained active in the work of ecclesiastical reform. He opposed the antipopes, especially Honorius II, and engaged in several papal diplomatic missions to France and Germany, notably to King Henry IV of Germany, whom he persuaded to abandon his plan to divorce his wife, Bertha. Peter died at Faenza while on the way back from Ravenna, which he had just reconciled with the Holy See. He wrote prolifically on purgatory, the Eucharist, in favor of the validity of sacraments administered by simoniacal priests, and clerical celibacy, and denounced immorality and simony. He was never formally canonized, but local cults developed on his death, and in 1828 Pope Leo XII extended his feast to the Universal Church and declared him a Doctor of the Church. February 21.

PETER GONZALEZ, BL. (1190–1246). Of a noble Castilian family, he was born at Astorga, Spain, and was educated by his uncle, the bishop of Astorga, who appointed him a canon of the cathedral. He resigned his canonry to join the Benedictines, became famed for his preaching, was appointed King Ferdinand III's chaplain, and labored to reform the court despite great opposition. He preached a crusade against the Moors and then persuaded the victors to be magnanimous to the defeated enemy after Cordova and Seville were captured. He then left the court to preach in Cilicia and along the coast and attracted huge crowds. He was particularly concerned with the welfare of sailors and is considered the patron of Spanish and Portuguese sailors with St. Erasmus; both are called Elmo or Telmo by them. Peter died at Tuy, Spain, and his cult was confirmed in 1741. April 14.

PETER NOLASCO (c. 1189–1258). Born at Mas-des-Saintes Puelles, France, of a noble family, he inherited a fortune when his father died when Peter was fifteen. He went to Barcelona and used his wealth to ransom Christian prisoners from the Moors, who ruled most of Spain at that time. In response to a vision (which according to legend was also experienced by St. Raymond of Peñafort and King James of Aragon), Peter decided to found a religious congregation dedicated to ransoming Christian slaves from the Moors. The Order of Our Lady of Ransom (the Mercedarians) developed from the decision, with the aid of St. Raymond, Peter's spiritual director, who is considered the cofounder of the Order; it was approved by Bishop Berengarius of Barcelona in 1223 (1218, 1222, 1228, and 1234 are also given as possible dates), with Peter as master general, and supported by King James of Aragon; papal approval came from Pope Gregory IX in 1235. In addition to the three traditional religious vows, the Mercedarians took a fourth—to give themselves if necessary in exchange for a slave. Peter traveled to Moorish-dominated Spain several times and to Algeria, where he was imprisoned for a time. He resigned his position as master general several years before his death on December 25 at Barcelona, and was canonized in 1628. January 28.

PETER OF SEBASTEA (c. 340–91). Son of St. Basil the Elder and St. Emmelia, brother of SS. Basil, Gergory of Nyssa, and Macrina, and the youngest of ten children, Peter was raised and educated by Macrina after their father died when he was an infant. He entered a monastery in Armenia on the Iris River founded by his mother and father and headed by Basil, and in time became abbot, in 362. Peter helped alleviate the distress of the famine that afflicted Pontus and Cappadocia, was ordained in 370, and was named bishop of Sebastea in 380. He labored to eliminate Arianism in his see and attended the General Council of Constantinople in 381. January 9.

PETER OF TARENTAISE. *See* Innocent V.

PETER THE VENERABLE, BL. (1092–1156). Peter de Montboissier was born of a noble Auvergne family, was educated at Sauxillanges, a Cluniac monastery, and when he was twenty was prior of Vézelay. He was elected abbot of Cluny in 1122 when he was thirty and in 1125 was faced with an armed force led by Pontius, the abbot he had succeeded, who took over Cluny while he was away. Both Peter and Pontius were summoned to Rome, where Pope Honorius II sentenced Pontius to prison. Peter then became involved in a controversy with St. Bernard, who accused Cluny of too relaxed a rule—a charge that led Peter to put into effect reforms in the Cluniac houses. He visited England in 1130 and Spain in 1139. He offered Peter Abelard shelter at Cluny in 1140, convinced the Pope to lighten Abelard's sentence, and reconciled Abelard and Bernard. He wrote against Petrobrusian heretics in southern France, defended the Jews, attended the synod of Rheims that denounced the teachings of Bishop Gilbert de la Porrée, and had a voluminous correspondence with his contemporaries. He ruled Cluny for thirty-four years, during which Cluny was the greatest and most influential abbey in Christendom. He died at Cluny on December 25, and though his cult has never been formally approved, he is venerated in the diocese of Arras on December 29.

PETROC (6th century). Born in Wales, possibly the son of a Welsh King, he became a monk and with some of his friends went to Ireland to study. They immigrated to Cornwall in England and settled at Lanwethinoc (Padstow). After thirty years there, he made a pilgrimage to Rome and Jerusalem, at which time he is also reputed to have reached the Indian Ocean, where he lived for a time as a hermit on an island. He then returned to Cornwall, built a chapel at Little Petherick near Padstow, established a community of his followers, and then became a hermit at Bodmir Moor, where he again attracted followers and was known for his miracles. He

died between Nanceventon and Lanwethinoc while visiting
some of his disciples there. June 4.

PETRONILLA (d. c. 251). A martyr in third-century
Rome, she is erroneously called the daughter of St. Peter in
legends and gnostic apocrypha and was executed when she refused to sacrifice her virginity by marrying a nobleman
named Flaccus. May 31.

PHILEMON (1st century). A Christian of Colossae, Phrygia,
he was converted by St. Paul, probably at Ephesus, and
was the recipient of the Epistle to Philemon, a private personal letter in which Paul tells him that he is sending back to
him his runaway slave Onesimus so that he could have him
back "not as a slave anymore, but . . . [as] a dear brother."
According to tradition, Philemon freed Onesimus and was
later stoned to death with his wife, Apphia, at Colossae for
their Christianity. November 22.

PHILIP (1st century). Born in Bethsaida, Galilee, he may
have been a disciple of John the Baptist and is mentioned as
one of the apostles in the lists of Matthew (10:3), Mark
(3:18), Luke (6:14), and in Acts (1:13). Aside from
the lists, he is mentioned only in John in the New Testament.
He was called by Jesus himself (John 1:43–48) and brought
Nathanael to Christ. Philip was present at the miracle of the
loaves and fishes (John 6:1–15), when he engaged in a brief
dialogue with the Lord (John 6:5–7), and was the apostle
approached by the Hellenistic Jews from Bethsaida to introduce them to Jesus (John 12:21ff.). Just before the Passion,
Jesus answered Philip's query to show them the Father
(John 14:8ff.), but no further mention of Philip is made in
the New Testament beyond his listing among the apostles
awaiting the Holy Spirit in the upper room (Acts 1:13). According to tradition he preached in Greece and was crucified
upside down at Hierapolis under Emperor Domitian. May 3.

PHILIP (d. c. 165). *See* Felicity.

PHILIP BENIZI (1233–85). Born of a noble family at
Florence, Italy, on August 15, he studied medicine at Paris
and Padua, where he received his doctorate in medicine and
philosophy when he was nineteen and began practicing medi-

cine at Florence. After a year in his practice, he joined the
Servites at Monte Senario near Florence in 1254, was sent to
the Servite house in Siena in 1258, and was ordained there.
He became known for his preaching, served as master of novices at Siena in 1262, was superior of several friaries, and in
1267, despite his protests, he was elected prior general. He
codified the rules of the Order, began to have miracles attributed to him, and in 1268, when Cardinal Ottobuoni proposed his name as a papal candidate on the death of Pope
Clement IV, Philip fled and hid in a cave until a new Pope
was elected. He attended the General Council of Lyons in
1274, helped to reconcile the Guelphs and the Ghibellines in
1279, attracted many converts to the Church, and reconciled
many others. He helped St. Juliana establish a Servite third
Order in 1284 and sent the first Servite missionaries to the
Far East. In declining health, he resigned the generalship at a
general chapter in 1285, naming his close confidant and long-
time friend, Lottaringo Stufa, his successor, and retired to an
impoverished Servite house at Todi, where he died on August
22. He was canonized in 1671. August 23.

PHILIP THE DEACON (1st century). All that is known of
him is what we are told in Acts. He was one of the seven chosen to assist the apostles (6:5) by ministering to the needy
members of the Church so the apostles could be free to
preach the gospel. He was the first to preach in Samaria
(8:5–13), where he converted Simon Magus and then a
eunuch who was chief treasurer of the Queen of Ethiopia on
the road from Jerusalem to Gaza (8:26–40). Philip
preached in the coastal cities on the way to his home at
Caesarea, and twenty-four years later, St. Paul stayed at his
home in Caesarea, where he still lived with his four un-
married daughters (21:8–9). A Greek tradition has him become bishop of Tralles, Lydia. He was so successful in his
preaching that he was sometimes surnamed "the Evangelist,"
which has sometimes caused him to be confused with Philip
the apostle. June 6.

PHILIP OF JESUS. *See* Casas, Philip de las.

PHILIP NERI. *See* Neri, Philip.

PHILOMENA. A cult began with the discovery of the bones

of a young girl, a small vial containing what was believed to be blood, and a tablet nearby with an inscription that when translated read, "Peace be with you, Philomena" in St. Priscilla catacomb in Rome. When the remains were moved in 1805 to the church of Mugnano del Cardinale near Nola, miracles were reported at her tomb, and devotion to Philomena became widespread. Her cult was authorized by Pope Gregory XVI in 1837, with a feast day of August 11. However, her name was removed from the calendar of the saints in 1961, since nothing was known of her beyond the facts listed here to justify sainthood.

PHILOTHEUS (d. 297). *See* Hipparchus.

PHOCAS THE GARDENER (date unknown). A gardener at Sinope, Paphlagonia, he lived as an anchorite pursuing an austere life of prayer and contemplation, offering shelter to travelers, and suffered martyrdom for his faith. According to legend, he was denounced as a Christian and sentenced to death. When a squad of soldiers arrived at his house, he gave them shelter; when they told him they were seeking one Phocas, he told them he would tell them where to find Phocas in the morning. After preparing his soul for death, he dug his grave and then told them who he was. Overcome by his courage and kindness, they hesitated, but at his urging they beheaded him. September 22.

PHOEBE (1st century). A deaconess of the church at Cenchreae, the port of Corinth, she was recommended to the Christian congregation at Rome by St. Paul, who praised her for her assistance to him and to many others (Rom. 16:1–2). She may have brought Paul's epistle to the Romans to Rome with her. September 3.

PHOTINA (no date). Untrustworthy legend has her the Samaritan woman of Sychar with whom Jesus talked at the well (John 4). She preached the gospel, was imprisoned for three years, and died for her faith at Carthage. She also reputedly converted Emperor Nero's daughter Domnina and one hundred of her servants to Christianity before suffering martyrdom in Rome. March 20.

PIECK, NICHOLAS (d. 1572). Guardian of the Observant

Franciscan house at Gorkum, Holland, he was engaged in missionary activities among the Calvinists when he and four other priests were seized when Calvinist forces opposed to the Spanish rule seized the town in June. They were tortured, subjected to all kinds of indignities, and offered their freedom if they would abjure Catholic teaching on the Eucharist and the primacy of the Pope. When they refused, despite a letter from the prince of Orange ordering their release, he and eighteen other priests and religious were hanged at deserted Ruggen Monastery on the outskirts of Briel on July 9, and their bodies were callously thrown into a ditch. They were all canonized in 1867 as the Martyrs of Gorkum. Among those of the Franciscan community who were thus martyred were Jerome Weerden, vicar; Antony of Hoornaer; Antony of Weert; Theodore van der Eem of Amersfoort; Godefried of Mervel; Nicasius Jannsen, a native of Heeze, Brabant, also known as Nicasius van Heeze; Antony van Willehad of Denmark; Andrew Wouters; and two lay brothers, Cornelius of Wyk near Utrecht, and Peter of Assche near Brussels.

PIGNATELLI, JOSEPH (1737–1811). Born of a noble family at Saragossa, Spain, he joined the Jesuits at Tarragona when he was sixteen, was ordained in 1763, and was assigned to Saragossa. When Charles III banished the Jesuits from Spain in 1767, Fr. Pignatelli and his fellow Jesuits went to Corsica, where they were forced to leave when the French, who had also banished the Jesuits, occupied the island. They then settled at Ferrara, Italy. When Pope Clement XIV suppressed the Jesuits in 1773, Joseph and the members of the Society of Jesus were secularized. He lived for the next twenty years at Bologna, aiding his less fortunate fellow Jesuit exiles. Meanwhile, Empress Catherine had refused to allow the bull of suppression to be published in Russia, and the Society continued in existence there. In 1792, the duke of Parma invited three Italian Jesuits in Russia to establish themselves in his realm, and after receiving permission from Pope Pius VI, Fr. Pignatelli became superior, thus bringing the Jesuits back to Italy. He began a quasinovitiate at Colorno in 1799 and saw Pope Pius VII give formal approval to the Jesuit province in Russia in 1801. Fr. Pignatelli worked to revive the Jesuits, and in 1804 the Society was re-established in the Kingdom of Naples, with Fr. Pignatelli as provincial. The province was dispersed when the French invaded Naples

later the same year, whereupon he went to Rome and was
named provincial for Italy. He restored the Society in Sardinia and helped conserve it when the French occupied
Rome. Though the Society of Jesus was not fully restored
until 1814, three years after his death in Rome on November
11, Pope Pius XII called him the "restorer of the Jesuits"
when he canonized him in 1954. November 28.

PIPPIN. *See* Pepin of Landen, Bl.

PIUS I (d. c. 154). A native of Aquileia and son of
Rufinus, he may have been the brother of Hermes, author of
The Shepherd, and was perhaps a slave later freed. He succeeded Pope Hyginus as pope in about 140 and during his
pontificate opposed the Valentinians and Gnostics under Marcion, whom he excommunicated. July 11.

PIUS V (1504–72). Born at Bosco near Alessandria, Italy,
on January 17, of an impoverished noble family, Antonio
Michael Ghislieri joined the Dominicans at Voghera when he
was fourteen and was ordained in 1528. He taught theology
and philosophy for sixteen years, served as master of novices
and as prior of several Dominican houses, and was appointed
bishop of Nepi and Butri by Pope Paul IV in 1556. Bishop
Ghislieri was also named inquisitor of Milan and Lombardy
and in 1557 was created a cardinal and inquisitor general of
the entire Church. He was translated to Mondovi in 1559, restored wartorn Piedmont, opposed Pope Pius IV's attempt to
make thirteen-year-old Ferdinand de' Medici a cardinal, and
defeated the attempt of Emperor Maximilian II of Germany
to abolish clerical celibacy. Cardinal Ghislieri was elected
Pope to succeed Pope Pius IV on January 7, 1566, and at
once set about putting into effect the decrees of the Council
of Trent. He restored simplicity to the papal court, completed
the new catechism (1566), reformed the breviary (1568)
and the missal (1570), and ordered a complete new edition
of the works of Thomas Aquinas, whom he proclaimed a
Doctor of the Church in 1567. Pius gave large sums to the
poor, lived a life of great austerity and piety, and personally
visited the sick in hospitals. Throughout his entire pontificate,
he fought Protestantism, and in 1570 he excommunicated
Queen Elizabeth I of England and supported Mary Stuart. He
re-energized the Inquisition and has been severely criticized

for his harshness to heretics. He persistently sought to unite Christian monarchs against the Turks and ardently supported Don Juan of Austria and Marcantonio Colonna, rejoicing in their success in 1571 when they halted the Moslem tide at the Battle of Lepanto. He was attempting to form an alliance of the Italian cities, France, Poland, and other Christian nations of Europe to march against the Turks when he died in Rome on May 1. He was canonized in 1712. April 30.

PIUS X (1835–1914). The second of ten children of a cobbler and postman, Giuseppe Melchior Sarto was born on June 2 at Riese near Trevino, Italy, was educated there, and entered the seminary at Padua in 1850. He was ordained there in 1858, engaged in pastoral work at Tombolo and Salzano during the next seventeen years, and was diocesan chancellor at Treviso, 1875–84. He was appointed bishop of Mantua in 1884 and in the next nine years successfully revived that rundown diocese. He was named cardinal and patriarch of Venice but did not occupy his see for eighteen months until 1894 because of the claim of the Italian Government that it had the right to nominate the patriarch of Venice. He was elected Pope to succeed Pope Leo XIII, when Austria vetoed the nomination of front-running Cardinal Rampolla, on August 4, 1903. He began a codification of canon law, set up a commission to revise the Vulgate, reorganized the papal court and ordered a revision of the psalter and the breviary. He urged frequent reception of Holy Communion, especially by children, told Italian Catholics to become more actively involved in politics, and in 1905 broke off diplomatic relations with France when the antireligious government of that country unilaterally denounced the Concordat of 1801, demanded control of ecclesiastical affairs, and confiscated Church property when Pius refused its demands. Throughout his pontificate, he was concerned with the heresy of modernism, which he denounced in his encyclicals *Lamentabilis sane exitu* (1907) and *Pascendi dominici gregis* (1907), and he demanded an oath against modernism by every priest. In 1910, he condemned the "Sillon," a French social movement that was attempting to spread an adapted concept of the French Revolution, and Action Française, which was advocating an intransigent nationalism. He died in Rome on August 20, and was canonized by Pope Pius XII in 1954, the first Pope to be so honored since the canonization of Pope Pius V in 1712. August 21.

PLASDEN, POLYDORE (d. 1591). Born at London, England, he studied for the priesthood at Rheims and Rome and was ordained in Rome in 1586. He was sent on the English mission, was captured with St. Edmund Gennings and convicted of being a Catholic priest, and was hanged, drawn, and quartered at Tyburn on December 10. He was canonized in 1970 by Pope Paul VI as one of the Forty Martyrs of England and Wales.

PLEASINGTON, WILLIAM. *See* Plessington, John.

PLECHELM (d. c. 730). *See* Wiro.

PLEGMUND (d. 914). Born in Mercia, England, he became a hermit on an island near Chester and was noted for his holiness. He became a member of the court of Alfred the Great and at Alfred's request was named archbishop of Canterbury in 890 and consecrated in Rome by Pope Formosus. Plegmund went to Rome in 908 probably to secure approval of his archbishopric by Pope Sergius III, since Formosus' consecrations were condemned in 897 and 905. Plegmund probably died at Canterbury on August 2.

PLESSINGTON, JOHN (d. 1679). Born at Dimples Hall, Lancashire, England, son of a Royalist Catholic, he was educated at St. Omer's in France, and the English college at Valladolid, Spain, and was ordained at Segovia in 1662. He returned to England the next year and worked in the Cheshire area, using the aliases Scarisbrick and William Pleasington, and in 1670 became tutor to the children of a Mr. Massey at Puddington Hall near Chester. Fr. Plessington was arrested and charged with participating in the "popish plot," fabricated by Titus Oates, to murder King Charles II. Despite the clear evidence of Oates' perjury, Fr. Plessington was found guilty and hanged at Barrowshill at Boughton outside Chester on July 19. He was canonized by Pope Paul VI in 1970 as one of the Forty Martyrs of England and Wales.

PLUNKET, OLIVER (1629–81). He was born on November 1 at Loughcrew, Meath, Ireland, of a noble family that supported King Charles I and the cause of Irish freedom. He studied at St. Mary's Benedictine Abbey in Dublin, went to the Irish college in Rome when he was sixteen, and was ordained in 1654. He spent the next fifteen years in Rome serving as professor of theology at the College of the Propagation of the Faith, was consultor of the Sacred Congregation of the Index, and was procurator for the Irish bishops. In 1669, he was named archbishop of Armagh and Primate of All Ireland and was consecrated at Ghent. He returned to Ireland in 1670 and spent the next four years reorganizing his diocese, reforming the abuses that had arisen during the absences of persecuted bishops, enforcing clerical discipline, and improving relations between secular and order clergy. In 1673 the renewed persecution of Catholics forced many bishops to flee, and he was forced into hiding. In 1678, in the aftermath of the Titus Oates plot, all Catholic priests and bishops were ordered expelled from Ireland, and on December 6, 1679, he was imprisoned in Dublin Castle on charges of conspiring to bring about a rebellion against the British crown. The charges were obviously false but he was removed to Newgate Prison in London, where he was kept in solitary confinement for nine months. In a travesty of a trial, he was convicted of high treason, complicity in the Titus Oates plot, and hanged, drawn, and quartered on July 1 at Tyburn, the last Catholic to suffer martyrdom there. He was canonized by Pope Paul VI in 1975, the first Irish saint to be canonized since St. Lawrence O'Toole in 1226. July 1.

POLE, BL. MARGARET (1471–1541). Margaret Plantagenet, daughter of the duke of Clarence and niece of Kings Edward IV and Richard III of England, was born at Farley Castle near Bath, England, on August 14, and in about 1491 married Sir Richard Pole. When Henry VIII became King, she was widowed with five children and had her estates, which had been forfeited by attainder, returned by Henry, who made her countess of Salisbury. She was governess of the King's daughter Anne, but incurred his enmity by her disapproval of his marriage to Anne Boleyn, despite his remark that she was the holiest woman in England, and was forced to leave the court. When her son Reginald Cardinal Pole wrote against the Act of Supremacy, Henry swore to destroy the family. In 1538, two other sons were arrested and executed on a charge of treason, even though Cromwell wrote that

their only crime was being brothers of the cardinal. Margaret
was arrested ten days later and in May 1539 Parliament
passed a bill of attainder against her for complicity in a revolt
in the North, and she was imprisoned in the Tower. When another uprising occurred in Yorkshire in April 1541, she was
summarily beheaded on May 28 at the Tower. She was never
tried and no guilt was ever proven against her except her possession of a white silk tunic embroidered with the Five
Wounds, which was supposed to connect her with the uprising in the North. She was beatified in 1886.

POLYCARP (c. 69–c. 155). A disciple of St. John the
apostle, he became bishop of Smyrna and was reputedly consecrated by John. Polycarp was a stanch defender of orthodoxy and an energetic opponent of heresy, especially Valen-
tinianism and Marcionism. A letter to him from St. John has
survived, as has his *Epistle to the Philippians*, in which he
quotes from 1 John 4:3 and warns the Philippians against the
false teachings of Marcion, whom he once called "the
firstborn of Satan," and which was widely read in Asian
churches. Toward the end of his life he visited Pope Anicetus
in Rome, and when they could not agree on a date for Easter
decided each should observe his own date. Soon after Polycarp's return to Smyrna, when he was eighty (according to
Eusebius), he was arrested when the persecution of Christians
under Emperor Marcus Aurelius broke out. When Polycarp
refused to sacrifice to the gods and acknowledge the Emperor's divinity, he was ordered burned to death at the stake.
When the flames failed to consume him, he was speared to
death on February 23. Polycarp was probably the leading
Christian in Roman Asia in the second century and an important link between the apostolic age and the great Christian
writers of the late second century. The *Martyrium Polycarpi*,
written in the name of the church of Smyrna and evidently
from eyewitness accounts of his arrest, trial, and martyrdom,
is the oldest authentic example of the *acta* of a martyr. February 23.

POLYXENA (1st century). *See* Xantippa.

PONTIAN (d. c. 236). A Roman and son of Calpurnius, he
was elected Pope to succeed Pope St. Urban I on July 21,
230. He held a synod at Rome in 232 that confirmed the con-

demnation of Origenism at Alexandria, 231–32. At the beginning of the persecution of Christians under Emperor Maximinus, Pontian was exiled to Sardinia, probably to the mines there, where he met exiled antipope Hippolytus and reconciled him to the Church. Pontian resigned his office on September 28, 235, to allow the election of a nephew and probably died of ill treatment, though a tradition says he was beaten to death. August 13.

PORPHYRY (d. 309). *See* Elias.

PORRAS, RAPHAELA (1850–1925). Born at Pedro Abad near Cordova, Spain, on March 1, she was the daughter of the mayor, who died when she was four. She and her sister Dolores joined the Sisters of Marie Reparatrice in 1873; when the bishop of the diocese, Ceferino Gonzalez, asked the community to leave his diocese, Raphaela and fifteen other novices remained behind to form a new community. When ready to take their vows in 1877, Bishop Gonzalez presented them with an entirely new rule; whereupon they left Cordova and settled at Madrid. After much initial confusion, Raphaela and Dolores took their vows later in 1877, and the Handmaids of the Sacred Heart, devoted to teaching children and helping at retreats, was founded. Approval from the Holy See was granted in the same year, with Raphaela as mother general. The new congregation was disturbed by differences between Raphaela and Dolores but despite this friction spread throughout Spain and abroad. Mother Raphaela resigned in 1893, lived the remaining thirty-two years of her life in obscurity in the Roman house of the congregation, and died there on Jan. 6. She was canonized in 1977 by Pope Paul VI.

PORRES, MARTIN DE (1579–1639). Born at Lima, Peru, on November 9, he was the illegitimate son of John de Porres, a Spanish knight, and Anna, a freed Panamanian. He was apprenticed to a barber-surgeon when he was twelve and in 1594 became a Dominican lay brother at Rosary Convent in Lima. He served in various offices in the convent—barber, infirmarian, wardrobe keeper—and was active in caring for the sick throughout the city. He founded an orphanage and foundling hospital, was put in charge of the convent's food distribution to the poor, and ministered to African slaves brought to Peru. A close friend of St. Rose of Lima, his prodigious efforts to help the poor and his holiness and penances caused him to be venerated by all. He is reputed to have been gifted with supernatural gifts, among them bilocation and aerial flights. He died at Rosary Convent on November 3, and was canonized in 1962 by Pope John XXIII. He is the patron of interracial justice.

POSSENTI, GABRIEL (1838–62). The eleventh of thirteen children of Sante Possenti, a lawyer in Assisi, Italy, he was christened Francis and was educated at the Jesuit college at Spoleto. He joined the Jesuits when he was seventeen after he had vowed to do so if cured of an almost fatal illness, but delayed entering the novitiate and finally in 1856 became a Passionist at Morroville with the name Br. Gabriel of Our Lady of Sorrows. He led an exemplary life as a religious, filled with penances and self-effacement, was ordained but stricken with tuberculosis, and died at Isola di Gran Sasso in the Abruzzi on February 27 when he was only twenty-four. He was canonized in 1920.

POSTEL, MARY MAGDALEN (1756–1846). Born at Barfleur, France, on November 28 and baptized Julia Frances Catherine, she was educated at the Benedictine convent at Valognes, and when eighteen she opened a school for girls at Barfleur. When the French Revolution broke out, the revolutionaries closed the school and she became a leader in Barfleur against the constitutional priests and sheltered fugitive priests in her home, where Mass was celebrated. When the concordat of 1801 between Napoleon and the Holy See brought peace to the French Church, she worked in the field of religious education, and in 1807, at Cherbourg, she and three other teachers took religious vows before Abbé Cabart, who had encouraged her in her work—the beginning of the Sisters of the Christian Schools of Mercy. She was named superior and took the name Mary Magdalen. During the next few years the community encountered great difficulties and was forced to move several times before settling at Tamersville in 1815. It was not until she obtained the abbey of St. Sauveur le Vicomte that the congregation finally began to expand and flourish. She died on July 16 at St. Sauveur, venerated for her holiness and miracles, and was canonized in 1925. July 17.

PRIMUS (d. c. 297). *See* Felician.

PRISCA (1st century). *See* Aquila; Priscilla.

PRISCA (d. c. 270). Also known as Priscilla, she had a very early cult in Rome, seems to have suffered martyrdom, and was buried in the catacomb of Priscilla there. Beyond that nothing is known of her. January 18.

PRISCILLA (d. c. 98). Wife of Mancius Aeilius Glabrio, who was executed by Domitian probably because he was a Christian, she is probably the mother of St. Pudens, the senator, and her home on Via Salaria was used by St. Peter as his headquarters in Rome. The catacomb of Priscilla under her home was named after her. She is also known as Prisca. January 16.

PRISCILLA (1st century). *See* Aquila.

PRISCILLA (d. c. 270). *See* Prisca.

PROBUS (d. 304). *See* Tarachus.

PROCESSUS (1st century). *See* Martinian.

PROCLUS (d. 446). Born at Constantinople, he was a disciple of St. John Chrysostom, became a lector, and then was secretary to John's opponent, Patriarch Atticus of Constantinople, who ordained him. He was named bishop of Cyzicus but the people there would not accept him. In 428 Nestorius was named Patriarch of Constantinople by Emperor Theodosius II, and Proclus, by now famed for his preaching, opposed his teachings. In 434, Maximian, who had succeeded Nestorius when he was deposed in 431, died, and Proclus was named Patriarch of Constantinople. He continued his opposition to Nestorianism, ministered to the people of the city when it was struck with a devastating earthquake, and was known for his dedication and tactful handling of those with whom he disagreed. He wrote several treatises, notably *Tome to the Armenians*, which opposed the Nestorian-flavored teaching of Theodore of Mopsuestia without mentioning him by name. Several of his letters and sermons have survived. He died on July 24. October 24.

PROCOPIUS (c. 980–1053). Born in Bohemia, he studied at Prague and was ordained there. He became a canon, was a hermit for a time and then was founding abbot of the Basilian abbey of Sazaba in Prague. He was canonized by Pope Innocent III in 1204 and is one of the patrons of Czechoslovakia. July 14.

PROCULUS (d. c. 305). *See* Januarius.

PROSPER OF AQUITAINE (c. 390–c. 465). Probably a layman who may have been married, he left Aquitaine for Provence and settled at Marseilles. He wrote to St. Augustine in 428, and in response, Augustine wrote his treatises on perseverance and predestination. Prosper opposed the semi-Pelagianism of St. John Cassian, accompanied his friend Hilary, who had asked him to write to Augustine, on a trip to visit Pope St. Celestine I in Rome, and is said to have become a secretary to Pope St. Leo the Great in Rome, where Prosper died. He wrote poetry and treatises, notably his *Chronicle*, a universal history from creation to the Vandal capture of Rome in 455. June 25.

PROTASE (1st century). *See* Gervase.

PRUDENTIUS (d. 861). Born in Spain and baptized Galindo, he fled to Gaul to escape the Saracens' persecutions and studied at the Palatine school, where he changed his name to Prudentius. He was elected bishop of Troyes in 840 or 845 and was known for his learning and as a theologian. He was appointed by Bishop Hincmar of Rheims to judge the case of a monk named Gottschalk, whom Hincmar had tortured, imprisoned, and excommunicated for teaching that God would save only the elect and condemn most of humanity. Prudentius defended the theory of double predestination and that Christ died only for those who are saved—a theory that set off a widespread dispute. He wrote a still extant treatise against John Scotus Erigena in 851, *De praedistinatione contra Johannem Scotem*, a defense of his own theory, *Epistola tractoria ad Wenilonem*, in 856 and a history of the western Franks, *Annales Bertiani*. He died at Troyes on April 6.

PTOLEMY (d. 250). *See* Ammon.

PUBLIUS (d. c. 112). Prefect of the island of Malta, he was host to Paul when the apostle was on his way to Rome as a prisoner; Paul cured his father of fever and dysentery (Acts 28:7–10). According to tradition, Publius later became the first bishop of Malta, though another tradition has him bishop of Athens and suffering martyrdom there during the reign of Emperor Trajan. January 21.

PUDENS. *See* Pudentiana.

PUDENTIANA (d. c. 160). A lady of Rome, the daughter of Pudens, whom some scholars believe is the same Pudens mentioned in 2 Timothy 4:21, she gave her wealth to the poor and helped bury martyred Christians. May 19.

PULCHERIA (399–453). Daughter of Emperor Arcadius and Empress Eudoxia, she was born on January 19 and lost her father in 408 when she was nine. Her younger brother Theodosius was proclaimed Emperor, and in 414 she was named *augusta* and regent of Theodosius by the Senate. She took a vow of virginity, devoted herself to the raising and education of her brother, changed the atmosphere of the court to an almost monastic environment, and in effect ran the Empire. In 421, Theodosius married Athenais, who was then baptized Eudocia, and two years later named her *augusta*. The clash between the two *augustae* was inevitable. Eudocia supported Nestorius, but Pulcheria was stanchly orthodox and eventually convinced Theodosius to condemn Nestorius. Court intrigue, encouraged and abetted by Eudocia, caused Pulcheria to be banished from the court, but in 441, Eudocia was exiled to Jerusalem because of infidelity to the Emperor, and Pulcheria was recalled. When Theodosius supported Eutyches and his monophysitism and approved the decrees of the Robber Synod of Ephesus in 449, Pulcheria supported the plea of Pope St. Leo the Great for orthodoxy. In 450, Theodosius was killed in a fall from his horse while hunting, and Pulcheria was proclaimed Empress. She then married the aged General Marcian, with the condition he respect her virginity, and the two ruled the Empire. They sponsored the Council of Chalcedon in 451 (she attended the third session), which condemned monophysitism, and in a letter to her in 451, Pope Leo credited her with overcoming the Nestorian and Eutychian heresies and for the recall of the Catholic bishops who had been exiled by Theodosius. She built many churches, hospitals, and hospices and encouraged the building of a university in Constantinople, where she died in July. September 10.

PUSICIUS (d. 341). *See* Simeon Barsabae.

Q

QUADRATUS (d. c. 129). Possibly a disciple of the apostles, he is believed to have been bishop of Athens and perhaps the author of a defense of Christianity addressed to Emperor Hadrian. May 26.

QUENTIN (d. 287). Also known as Quintinus, according to legend he was a Roman, went to Gaul as a missionary with St. Lucian of Beauvais, and settled at Amiens in Picardy. He was so successful in preaching that he was imprisoned by Prefect Rictiovarus, tortured, and then brought to Augusta Veromanduorum (Saint-Quentin), where he was again tortured and then was beheaded. October 31.

QUENTIN. *See* Quintius.

QUINTA (d. 249). *See* Apollonia.

QUINTINUS. *See* Quentin.

QUINTIUS (d. c. 570). Born at Tours, Gaul, and also known as Quentin, he became an official at the Frankish court. When he rejected the attempts of the Queen, probably Fredegunde, to seduce him, she had him murdered at L'Indrois near Montresor. October 4.

QUINZANI, BL. STEPHANA (1457–1530). Born near Brescia, Italy, she became a Dominican tertiary at Soncino when she was fifteen, devoted herself to ministering to the poor and the sick, and founded a convent at Soncino. She experienced ecstasies, including participating in the various stages of the Passion, which was attested to by twenty-one witnesses in 1497 in an account that is still extant, and was credited with performing numerous miracles of healing. She died on January 2, and her cult was confirmed in 1740.

QUIRIACUS. *See* Cyriacus (d. c. 133).

QUIRICUS. *See* Julitta.

QUIRINUS (d. 308). Bishop of Siscia (Sisak, Croatia) during the persecution of Christians under Emperor Diocletian, he fled the city to escape arrest but was captured. Haled before Maximus, the magistrate, he refused to sacrifice to the gods and was brought to Amantius, the governor of Pannonia Prima. When he persisted in his refusal, he was drowned in the Raab River at Sabaria (Szombathely, Hungary). June 4.

QUITERIA (5th century). According to legend, she was the daughter of a Galician prince who fled to escape his demand that she marry and give up her Christianity. His followers found her at Aire, Gascony, and on his orders, beheaded her there. May 22.

R

RABANUS MAURUS, BL. (c. 776 [784?]–856). Probably born at Mainz, Germany (though possibly in Ireland or Scotland), he was educated at the monastery school of Fulda under Abbot Bangulf and at Tours under Alcuin, whose favorite he became. He returned to Fulda as a monk, became known for his learning and knowledge of the early Church Fathers and the Bible, and in about 799 became master of Fulda's monastery school. He was ordained in 815, became abbot in 822, completed the monastery buildings, and founded several churches and monasteries. He resigned his abbacy to go into retirement, but in 847, at seventy-one, he was named archbishop of Mainz. He imposed strict discipline on his clergy (which led to an abortive conspiracy on his life), held two synods that condemned the heretical teaching of Gottschalk, a monk in his see, and helped alleviate a famine by feeding the poor at his house. He wrote a martyrology; poetry, including the hymn *Veni Creator Spiritus;* and some sixty-four of his homilies are still extant. He died at Winkel, near Mainz. February 4.

RADULF. *See* Ralph (d. 866).

RAFAELA MARIA OF THE SACRED HEART. *See* Porras, Raphaela.

RALPH (d. 866). Also known as Raoul and Radulf, he was the son of Count Raoul of Cahors. He was educated under Abbot Bertrand of Solignac, served as abbot of several abbeys, though he does not seem to have been a monk, and in 840 was named bishop of Bourges. He attended numerous synods, among them the Synod of Meaux in 845, founded several monasteries and convents, was known for his learning, and compiled a summary of pastoral instructions for his clergy. He died on June 21.

RAMÓN LULL. *See* Raymond Lull.

RAOUL. *See* Ralph (d. 866).

RAPHAEL. One of the seven archangels "who stand before the Lord" (Tb. 12:12, 15), he was sent by God to minister to Tobias and Sara and accompanied young Tobias into Media disguised as a man named Azarias. His name in Hebrew means "God heals," and he is identified as the angel who "healed" the earth when it was defiled by the sins of the fallen angels in the apochryphal Enoch (10:7) and who moved the waters of the healing sheep pool (John 5:1–4). He is one of only three archangels identified by name, with Michael and Gabriel, in the Bible and has been venerated for ages in both the Jewish and the Christian traditions. He is the patron of the blind. September 29.

RAYMOND (d. 1242). *See* William Arnaud.

RAYMOND OF CAPUA, BL. (1330–99). Raymond delle Vigne was born at Capua, Italy, became a Dominican while studying at Bologna, was named prior of the Minerva in Rome, and then served as lector in Florence and Siena, where he met Catherine of Siena. He became her spiritual director in 1376 and was her close confidant. He helped care for the victims of a plague that had stricken Siena, was stricken himself, and was cured through Catherine's prayers. With Catherine he worked to launch a crusade, attempted to effect a peace between Florence and the Tuscan League and the Pope, who was then living at Avignon, and tried to persuade Pope Gregory XI to return to Rome. When Gregory died in 1378, they supported Pope Urban VI against antipope Clement VII, whose election began the Great Schism. Bl. Raymond was sent to France by Urban to win the support of King Charles V, an effort that was unsuccessful, and had his life threatened while on the trip by soldiers of Clement. After Catherine's death in 1380, he continued her efforts to end the schism, and in the same year he was elected master general of the Dominicans, remaining faithful to Urban. Bl. Raymond labored to reform the order and established several houses following a strict rule. He wrote biographies of Catherine and St. Agnes of Montepulciano and died at Nuremberg, Germany, on October 5. He was beatified in 1899.

RAYMOND LULL, BL. (c. 1232–1316). Son of one of the military leaders who reconquered Majorca from the Moslems, he was born at Palma, Majorca, entered the service of King James I of Aragon, was appointed grand senechal by James, and in 1257 married Blanca Picany. Despite his marriage and two children, he led a dissolute life, but changed his lifestyle in 1263 when he had a vision of Christ while writing to a woman with whom he was having an affair, followed by five more visions. After pilgrimages to Compostela and Rocamadour, he became a Franciscan tertiary, provided for his family, gave the rest of his wealth to the poor, and determined to devote the rest of his life to converting the Mohammedans. He spent the next nine years learning all he could of Moslem philosophy, religion, and culture, and learning Arabic. He founded the short-lived Trinity College on Majorca in 1276 to put into effect his idea of a missionary college, visited Rome in 1277 to enlist the Pope's support, went to Paris in 1286, and in 1290 joined the Friars Minor at Genoa. After a serious illness, he went to Tunis in 1292, began preaching, but was almost immediately forcibly deported by the Moors. Further appeals to Popes Boniface VIII and Clement V for aid in his mission to the Mohammedans were fruitless, as was a visit to Cyprus. After lecturing at Paris on Arabic metaphysics for a time, he was successful in getting to Bougie in Barbary in 1306 but was again imprisoned and deported. He continued his appeals for aid to the Pope and to the Council of Vienne in 1311 but with no success, resumed lecturing at Paris, and again returned to Bougie in 1315. This time he was stoned and left for dead but was rescued by Genoese sailors and died on board ship near Majorca on September 29. He wrote voluminously—more than three hundred treatises (many in Arabic) on philosophy, music, navigation, law, astronomy, mathematics, and theology, chief among his writings being *Arbre de philosophia de armor*. He also wrote mystical poetry of the highest order and is considered the forerunner of Teresa of Avila and John of the Cross; his

Blanquera is the first novel written in Catalan. His cult was confirmed in 1858 by Pope Pius IX. June 30.

RAYMOND NONNATUS (c. 1204–40). Born at Portella, Catalonia, Spain, he was delivered by caesarian operation when his mother died in childbirth, hence his name *non natus* (not born). He joined the Mercedarians under St. Peter Nolasco at Barcelona, succeeded Peter as chief ransomer, and went to Algeria to ransom slaves. He remained as hostage for several slaves when his ransom money ran out and was sentenced to be impaled when the governor learned that he had converted several Mohammedans. He escaped the death sentence because of the ransom he would bring, but was forced to run the gantlet. He was then tortured for continuing his evangelizing activities but was ransomed eight months later by Peter Nolasco. On his return to Barcelona in 1239, he was appointed cardinal by Pope Gregory IX but died at Cardona (Cerdagne) a short distance from Barcelona the next year while on the way to Rome. He was canonized in 1657 and is the patron saint of midwives. August 31.

RAYMOND OF PEÑAFORT (1175–1275). Born at Peñafort, Catalonia, Spain, he was teaching philosophy by the time he was twenty at Barcelona. He resigned his chair there in 1210 to study law at Bologna, where he received his doctorate in 1216. He was made archdeacon by Bishop Berengarius of Barcelona in 1219 and joined the Dominicans there in 1222. He became famed for his preaching and went all over Spain preaching to Moors and Christians returned from Moorish slavery. He preached the Spanish crusade that freed Spain from the Moors and is considered by many to be cofounder with St. Peter Nolasco of the Mercedarians, though the claim is disputed. In 1230, he was confessor to Pope Gregory IX in Rome and spent three years collecting and codifying papal decrees from 1150, which became the cornerstone of canon law until the revision of 1917. He was named archbishop of Tarragona, despite his protests, in 1235, and persuaded Pope Gregory to recall the appointment when he became seriously ill. He returned to Spain in 1236 to convalesce, resumed his work as a preacher and confessor, was tremendously successful in making conversions, and in 1238 was elected master general of the Dominicans. He drew up a revision of the Dominican constitution, which was to remain in effect until 1924, but resigned his generalship, citing his age, sixty-five, as a factor. But he was to live another thirty-five years, active in the conversion work that was to bring thousands to the Church. He established friaries at Tunis and Murcia, helped to establish the Inquisition at Catalonia, introduced the study of Arabic and Hebrew into several Dominican houses, and was responsible for Thomas Aquinas writing *Summa contra Gentiles*. Raymond died at Barcelona on January 6 and was canonized by Pope Clement VIII in 1601. His *Summa de poenitentia* (also called *Summa casuum*), which he compiled between 1223 and 1238, had a profound influence on the development of the penitential system of the later Middle Ages. January 7.

REALINO, BERNARDINO (1530–1616). Born at Carpi, Italy, he became a lawyer, and when he was 34, he joined the Jesuits. He engaged in pastoral work at Naples for 10 years and then went to the college at Lecce, of which in time he became rector. His reputation for holiness increased as he grew older. Just before his death, blood emerging from an unhealed leg wound he had sustained 6 years earlier was collected in vials, and reputable witnesses over the next 250 years testified that they had seen the blood in these vials, which remained in a liquid state, bubble and boil. He was canonized in 1947 by Pope Pius XII. July 3.

REGINA (2nd century). Also known as Reine, legend says she was the daughter of pagan Clement of Alise in Burgundy. She was raised by a Christian woman, when her mother died at her birth, as a Christian. When her father discovered she was a Christian he put her out of his house and she went to live with the woman who had raised her, working as a shepherdess. When Regina refused to marry Olybrius, the prefect, she was imprisoned, tortured, and beheaded at Autun, Gaul. September 7.

REINE. *See* Regina.

REINOLD (d. c. 960). The youngest of the four sons in William Caxton's romantic poem *Aymon*, he became a monk at St. Pantaleon Monastery in Cologne, was put in charge of building, and was murdered by a group of stonemasons he had been overseeing who were annoyed because he worked harder and longer than they did. He is patron of stonemasons. January 7.

REMI. The French form of Remigius.

REMIGIUS (c. 437–530). Also known as Remi, he was born at Laon, the son of Count Emilius of Laon and St. Celina. He became known for his preaching, and in 459, when he was only twenty-two, he was appointed bishop of Rheims. He was ordained and consecrated and reigned for more than seventy years, devoting himself to the evangelization of the Franks. In 496, Clovis, pagan King of northern Gaul, supposedly in response to a suggestion by his wife, Clotildis, a Christian, invoked the Christian God when the invading Alemanni were on the verge of defeating his forces, whereupon the tide of battle turned and Clovis was victorious. St. Remigius, aided by St. Vedast, instructed him and his chieftains in Christianity, and soon after baptized Clovis, his two sisters, and three thousand of his followers. Remigius was a zealous proponent of orthodoxy, opposed Arianism, and converted an Arian bishop at a synod of Arian bishops in 517. He was censured by a group of bishops for ordaining one Claudius, whom they felt was unworthy of the priesthood, but St. Remigius was generally held in great veneration for his holiness, learning, and miracles. He was the most influential prelate of Gaul and is considered the apostle of the Franks. He died at Rheims on January 13. October 1.

REPOSITUS (d. c. 303). *See* Honoratus.

REVOCATUS (d. 203). *See* Perpetua.

REYNOLDS, RICHARD (c. 1490–1535). Born in Devon, England, he studied at Cambridge, was elected a fellow of Corpus Christi College in 1510, and was appointed university preacher in 1513. He joined the Briggitine monks at Syon Abbey, Isleworth, the same year and became known for his sanctity and as one of the most learned monks of his time. He was imprisoned when he refused to subscribe to King Henry VIII's Act of Supremacy and was hanged on May 4 at

Tyburn, one of the first group of martyrs there, after having been forced to witness the butchering of four other martyrs. He was canonized by Pope Paul VI in 1970 as one of the Forty Martyrs of England and Wales. May 11.

RHIPSIME (d. c. 312). According to untrustworthy legend, she was a member of a community of dedicated virgins, headed by Gaiana, in Rome during the reign of Emperor Diocletian. Rhipsime was a great beauty, and when Emperor Diocletian saw her portrait, he desired her, but Rhipsime would have no part of him. To escape his wrath when Rhipsime refused him, Gaiana took her community from Rome to Alexandria, and eventually they settled at Valarshapat, Armenia. There Rhipsime's beauty caused such a stir that news of her whereabouts reached Diocletian in Rome, and he wrote about her to King Tiridates. He had her seized and brought to his palace, where she resisted him and then escaped. Enraged, he sent his troops to the community and they roasted Rhipsime to death and executed Gaiana and thirty-five of her companions; only one, Nino (called Christiana in the Roman Martyrology), escaped, and in time she became the apostle of Georgia. The cult is an ancient one in Armenia, and they probably were martyred under Tiridates, but all the other details seem to be a fictional embellishment of that fact. September 30.

RI, BL. JOHN (d. 1839). *See* Imbert, Bl. Laurence.

RICHARD DE WYCHE (c. 1197–1253). Also known as Richard of Chichester, he was born at Wyche (Droitwich), Worcestershire, England. He was orphaned when he was quite young, retrieved the fortunes of the mismanaged estate he inherited when he took it over, and then turned it over to his brother Robert. Richard refused marriage and went to Oxford, where he studied under Grosseteste and met and began a lifelong friendship with Edmund Rich. Richard pursued his studies at Paris, received his M.A. from Oxford, and then continued his studies at Bologna, where he received his doctorate in canon law. After seven years at Bologna, he returned to Oxford, was appointed chancellor of the university in 1235, and then became chancellor to Edmund Rich, now archbishop of Canterbury, whom he accompanied to the Cistercian monastery at Pontigny when the archbishop retired there. After Rich died at Pontigny, Richard taught at the Dominican house of studies at Orléans and was ordained there in 1243. After a time as a parish priest at Deal, he became chancellor of Boniface of Savoy, the new archbishop of Canterbury, and when King Henry III named Ralph Neville bishop of Chichester in 1244, Boniface declared his selection invalid and named Richard to the see. Eventually, the matter was brought to Rome, and in 1245 Pope Innocent IV declared in Richard's favor and consecrated him. When he returned to England, he was still opposed by Henry and was refused admittance to the bishop's palace; eventually Henry gave in when threatened with excommunication by the Pope. The remaining eight years of Richard's life were spent in ministering to his flock. He denounced nepotism, insisted on strict clerical discipline, and was ever generous to the poor and the needy. He died at a house for poor priests in Dover, England, while preaching a crusade, and was canonized in 1262. April 3.

RICTRUDIS (c. 612–88). Of a distinguished Gascon family, she married St. Adalbald, a Frankish nobleman serving King Clovis II, despite some opposition from her family, and the couple had four children—Adalsind, Clotsind, Eusebia, and Mauront—all of whom became saints. After sixteen years of a happy married life at Ostrevant, Flanders, Adalbald was murdered by relatives of Rictrudis while visiting in Gascony. After several years, King Clovis ordered her to marry, but with the aid of her old friend and director, St. Amandus, Clovis relented and permitted her to become a nun at Marchiennes, Flanders, a double monastery she had founded. Adalsind and Clotsind joined her, and sometime later Mauront left the court and became a monk there. Rictrudis became abbess of Marchiennes and ruled for forty years. May 12.

RIGBY, JOHN (c. 1570–1600). Born near Wigan, Lancashire, England, the son of an impoverished gentleman, he was a Catholic but was obliged to earn his living as a servant in a Protestant household. He attended Protestant services to conform with the law but repented of his actions and returned to his Catholic faith. While appearing to answer a summons for the daughter of his employer, he admitted he was a Catholic and was imprisoned at Newgate Prison. When he refused his freedom if he would attend Protestant services, he was sentenced to death and hanged, drawn, and quartered at Southwark on June 21. He was canonized by Pope Paul VI in 1970 as one of the Forty Martyrs of England and Wales.

RINIERI. *See* Rizzerio, Bl.

RIOCH. *See* Mel.

RITA OF CASCIA (1381–1457). Born at Roccaporena near Spoleto, Italy, of elderly parents, she was married against her will when twelve, had two sons, and after eighteen years of an unhappy marriage, her husband, who had treated her cruelly, was killed in a brawl. When her two sons died, she tried to enter the Augustinians at Cascia three times but was refused each time, as its rule permitted only virgins, but was finally allowed to become a nun there in 1413. She became known for her austerities, penances, and concern for others, and brought many back to their religion with her prayers. She experienced visions and in 1441 suffered a seemingly thorn-induced wound on her forehead after hearing a sermon on the crown of thorns. Several miracles were attributed to her after her death on May 22 at Cascia. She was canonized in 1900 and is venerated as the saint of desperate causes.

RIZZERIO (d. 1236). Of a wealthy family, he was born at Muccia in the Marches, became a student at the University of Bologna, and while there he and his friend Bl. Peregrine preach so impressed by a sermon they heard Francis of Assisi preach at Bologna in 1222 that they joined the Franciscans. Rizzerio was ordained, became a close associate of Francis, and served as provincial of the Marches. He practiced great austerities and mortifications and was the recipient of a miracle from Francis that dissolved his despair of God's mercy. He died on March 26, and his cult was confirmed in 1836. He is called Rinieri in *The Little Flowers of St. Francis*. February 7.

ROBERT (d. 1159). Born at Gargrave, Yorkshire, England, he was ordained, served as rector at Gargrave, and then became a Benedictine at Whitby. He and a group of monks from St. Mary's Abbey in York settled in Skeldale to follow a strict Benedictine rule and founded Fountains Abbey in 1132.

They affiliated with the Cistercians, and the abbey became famous for the holiness and austerity of its members. In 1138, Robert and twelve monks left Fountains to people Newminster Abbey, built by Ralph de Merly, lord of Morpeth, and Robert was named abbot. He founded houses at Pipewall, Sawley, and Roche, wrote a commentary on the Psalms, and ruled until his death on June 7. He was buried at Newminster, and his tomb became a pilgrimage center.

ROBERT OF ARBRISSEL, BL. (c. 1047–1117). Born at Arbrissel (Arbressec), Brittany, he studied at Paris, was ordained, and then became archpriest in Rennes in 1089 at the invitation of Bishop Sylvester de Gerche, who invited him to assist him in reforming that see. Robert was forced to flee the enemies he had made with his reforms when the bishop died, and he became a hermit in the Craon Forest in 1095. The following year he was founding abbot of La Roé monastery, which he established for the many disciples he had attracted with his holiness. He was appointed "preacher" by Pope Urban II the same year, attracted huge crowds, and in 1099 founded the double monastery of Fontvrault for the many postulants La Roé could not accommodate. He was at the Council of Poitiers in 1100, where he favored the excommunication of King Philip I of France, and attended the Council of Nantes in 1110. He called a chapter to set up a permanent organization of his monks in 1116, and died the next year at Orsan on February 25. Although called Blessed, he has never been formally beatified.

ROBERT OF MOLESMES (c. 1024–1110). Born of noble parents near Troyes, Champagne, France, he became a Benedictine at Moutier-la-Celle when he was fifteen, and when he finished his novitiate he was named prior. He was then named abbot of St. Michael of Tonnere, was unsuccessful in his attempts to reform that abbey, and after his recall to Moutier-la-Celle, Pope Alexander II named him superior of a group of hermits he had been instructing. He moved the community from Collan to Molesmes in 1075. The austerity and holiness of the members of the community led to a great influx of ill-qualified candidates, and when he was unsuccessful in raising the standards to their previous level, he, St. Stephen Harding, and St. Alberic with several others left and founded a new community, dedicated to strict observance of the rule of St.

Benedict, at Cîteaux in 1098. It was designated an abbey with Walter as abbot by Bishop Walters of Chalon, and thus the Cistercians began. Robert was ordered back to Molesmes by Pope Urban II in 1099, was successful with his reform, and lived there until his death on March 21. He was canonized in 1222. April 29.

ROBERTS, JOHN (1577–1610). Born near Trawsfynydd, Merionethshire, Wales, he was brought up a Protestant, studied at St. John's College, Oxford, and law at Furnivall's Inn. Though a Protestant, he had leanings toward the Catholic Church and left Oxford rather than take the Oath of Supremacy. He went to Paris in 1598, became a Catholic there, went to the English college at Valladolid, and joined the Benedictines. He was ordained in 1602, and within three weeks after the English monks at St. Martin's Monastery were granted permission to go on the English mission, he and Fr. Augustine Bradshaw returned to England, the first monks to return as missionaries since the suppression of the monasteries. They were soon arrested in London and expelled from the country; Fr. Roberts soon came back, ministered to the victims of the plague that killed 30,000 Londoners in the winter of 1603, and was again arrested, early in 1604. He was released when he was not recognized as a priest, but was arrested and imprisoned during the Gunpowder Plot, and was again released after eight months in prison through the intercession of the French ambassador. Fr. Roberts remained on the Continent for a year helping found a monastery for the English monks of Valladolid at Douai, and then returned to England. Arrested in 1607, he escaped, was rearrested in 1609, was banished through the intercession of the French ambassador, went to Spain and then went to Douai. He returned to England, was arrested once again with Bl. Thomas Somers, and this time he was convicted of being a Catholic priest. When he refused to take the Oath of Supremacy, he was hanged, drawn, and quartered at Tyburn with Fr. Somers on December 10. Fr. Roberts was canonized by Pope Paul VI in 1970 as one of the Forty Martyrs of England and Wales.

ROCCO. *See* Roch.

ROCH (1295–1378). Untrustworthy sources say he was probably born at Montpellier, France, son of the governor there. When he was orphaned when he was twenty, he went on pilgrimage to Rome and devoted himself to caring for the victims of a plague that was ravaging Italy. He became a victim himself at Piacenza but recovered and was reputed to have performed many miracles of healing. On his return to Montpellier, he was imprisoned for five years as a spy in pilgrim's disguise when his uncle, who was governor, ordered him imprisoned. (His uncle failed to recognize him, and Roch failed to identify himself.) Roch died in prison and was only then identified as the former governor's son by a birthmark in the form of a cross on his chest. Another biographer says that he was arrested as a spy at Angers, Lombardy, and died in prison there. When miracles were reported at his intercession after his death, a popular cult developed, and he is invoked against pestilence and plague. He is known as Rocco in Italy and Roque in Spain. August 16.

ROCHE, BL. JOHN (d. 1588). *See* Ward, Margaret.

RODAT, EMILY DE (1787–1852). Born at Rodez, France, Marie Guillemette Emilie de Rodat was raised by her grandmother near Villefranche-de-Rouerge, attended school there at Maison Saint-Cyr, and when eighteen began to teach children there. With the approval of her spiritual adviser, Abbé Marty, she joined successively the Ladies of Nevers, the Picpus Sisters, and the Sisters of Mercy, but felt she did not fit in with any of these congregations. In 1815, she decided that teaching poor children was her vocation, and with three companions began teaching in her own room at Maison Saint-Cyr, and the Congregation of the Holy Family of Villefranche was founded. She started her own free school in 1816, and when the Saint-Cyr community broke up, she bought their property for her new congregation which, despite her constant ill health, she expanded to thirty-eight foundations in the next thirty-six years. In time, she extended the scope of the congregation to nursing sick poor, visiting prisoners, and caring for the aged, orphans, and wayward women; she also founded several cloistered convents. She died on September 19, and was canonized by Pope Pius XII in 1950.

RODRIGUEZ, BL. ALONSO (d. 1628). *See* Gonzalez, Bl. Roque.

ROE, ALBAN BARTHOLOMEW (c. 1583–1642). Born probably at Bury St. Edmunds, England, he was a student at Cambridge when he met an imprisoned Catholic and was so impressed by his faith that he was converted to Catholicism. He studied at Douai but was dismissed for infraction of discipline and then became a Benedictine monk at Dieulouard, France, in 1612, taking the name Alban, was ordained, and was sent on the English mission. He was arrested in 1615, imprisoned, and then banished; he was back in England in four months and again was arrested, in 1618, and imprisoned in New Prison until 1623, when he was released through the intercession of the Spanish ambassador. Fr. Roe was banished but after a short stay at Douai, he returned to England and worked until his arrest in 1625. He spent the next seventeen years in prison until he was finally tried, and when convicted of being a Catholic priest was hanged, drawn, and quartered on January 21, two days after his sentencing, at Tyburn with Bl. Thomas Reynolds. Fr. Roe was canonized in 1970 by Pope Paul VI as one of the Forty Martyrs of England and Wales.

ROGATIAN (d. 289 or 304). *See* Donatian.

ROLLE, BL. RICHARD (c. 1300–49). Born at Thornton, Yorkshire, England, he studied at Oxford, left when he was nineteen, was probably at the Sorbonne in Paris, 1320–26, probably received a doctorate in theology there, and may have been ordained. He returned to England in about 1326 and lived as a hermit on the estate of John Dalton, perhaps at Topcliffe, then at several other places before settling at Hampole in a cell near the priory of a community of Cistercian nuns who were under his spiritual guidance; he died there on September 29. He was one of the first religious writers to write in the vernacular as well as in Latin and is one of the best known of the mystical writers of his time. Among his numerous works are *De emendatione vitae,* which he wrote for another recluse he directed, Margaret Kirby of Ainderby; a translation of the Psalms; the ninety-six-hundred-line poem *Pricke of Conscience* (though some modern scholars dispute his authorship), denouncing contemporary abuses; and the mystical *De incendium amoris.* He had a popular cult, which was never formally approved, although the Cistercian nuns of

Hampton wrote a service for a proposed feast day on January 20.

ROMANUS (d. 258). According to unreliable sources, he was a soldier in Rome, was instructed and baptized in prison by St. Lawrence, and when Romanus announced he had been converted, was beheaded the day before Lawrence suffered his martyrdom. August 9.

ROMANUS (d. 297). *See* Hipparchus.

ROMANUS (d. c. 550). A monk at a monastery near Monte Subiaco, it was he who encouraged St. Benedict, brought him to the cave where Benedict lived as a hermit for three years, and supplied him with food during that time. According to legend, Romanus left Italy during the invasion of the Vandals, went to France, and founded Fontrouge abbey near Auxerre, where he died. May 22.

ROMANUS. *See* Boris (d. 1015).

ROMUALD (c. 950–1027). Of the noble Onesti family of Ravenna, Italy, he retired when he was twenty to San Apollinare Monastery at Classe to expiate his father's killing of a relative in a duel and became a monk there. After three years at the monastery, he left in quest of a more austere life and became a disciple of a hermit named Marinus near Venice. About 978, the two of them with Abbot Guarinus of Cuxa in Catalonia persuaded Peter Orseolo, doge of Venice, to resign (he had become doge by acquiescing in the murder of his predecessor). Peter accompanied Marinus and Romuald back to Cuxa and became a Benedictine there, while Romuald and Marinus built a hermitage near the monastery and lived as hermits. Romuald returned to Italy ten years later to help his father, Sergius, who had become a monk after his duel, resolve his doubts about his vocation. Emperor Otto III appointed Romuald abbot of San Apollinare in Classe, but he left after two years to live as a hermit near Pereum. He then set out to evangelize the Magyars in Hungary but was forced to turn back because of illness and probably by his age. He spent the rest of his life founding monasteries and hermitages in northern and central Italy, notably at Vallombrosa in 1012, and in 1023 at Camaldoli near Arezzo. The five hermitages he built at Camaldoli developed into the mother house of the Camaldolese Order, which combined the cenobitic and eremitical life under a modified Benedictine rule that he drew up. He died at Valdi Castro near Fabiano on June 19.

ROMULUS (d. c. 90). According to tradition, he was a Roman converted by St. Peter who became the first bishop of Fiesole, Italy, and suffered martyrdom there with Carissimus, Dulcissimus, and Crescentius during the reign of Emperor Domitian. A worthless eleventh-century fiction has him the illegitimate son of Lucerna and her father's slave Cyrus. Romulus was abandoned, suckled by a wolf, and captured by St. Peter when Emperor Nero was unable to do so. Romulus later performed all kinds of extravagant miracles after being instructed by Peter's companion Justin. After evangelizing much of central Italy, Romulus was put to death by the governor, Repertian. July 6.

ROQUE. See Roch.

ROSE OF LIMA (d. 1586). Isabel de Santa Maria de Flores was born at Lima, Peru, of Spanish parents and took the name Rose at confirmation. Noted for her beauty, she resisted her parents' efforts to have her marry and practiced great austerities, taking St. Catherine of Siena as her model from her childhood days. She became a Dominican tertiary, lived as a recluse in a shack in the garden she had worked to help her parents, who had fallen on difficult times, and experienced mystical gifts and visions of such an extraordinary nature that a commission of priests and doctors was appointed to examine her. They decided they were of supernatural origin. Stories of her holiness spread, and her garden became the spiritual center of the city; when earthquakes struck nearby, her prayers were credited with sparing Lima. In ill health, she accepted the offer of Don Gonzalo de Massa and his wife to take care of her, and she spent the last three years of her life in their home in Lima and died there on August 24. She was canonized in 1671 by Pope Clement X, the first saint of the New World. She is patroness of South America. August 23.

ROYO, BL. JOACHIM (1690–1747). See Sanz, Bl. Peter.

RUADAN (d. c. 584). Born in Leinster, Ireland, he became a disciple of St. Finian of Clonard, was founding abbot of Lothra Monastery in Tipperary, where he directed 150 monks, and is considered one of the 12 apostles of Ireland. April 15.

RUDESIND (907–77). Of a noble Spanish Galician family and also known as Rosendo, he was named bishop of Dumium (Mondoñedo) against his wishes when he was only eighteen. He was put in charge of the see of Compostela when his wastrel cousin Bishop Sisnand was imprisoned by King Sancho for neglect of his ecclesiastical duties. During an absence of King Sancho, Rudesind headed an army that drove invading Norsemen from Galicia and then drove invading Moors from Portugal. When Sancho died in 967, Sisnand escaped from prison and threatened Rudesind with death if he did not relinquish the see of Compostela. Rudesind retired to St. John of Caveiro Monastery, which he had founded, built another monastery, Celanova, at Villar, and then founded several others. He became abbot of Celanova when Abbot Franquila died, was sought after for advice by ecclesiastics from all parts of Portugal, and was credited with many miracles of healing. He was canonized in 1195. March 1.

RUFUS (d. c. 107). He and Zosimus were citizens of Antioch (or perhaps Philippi) who were brought to Rome with St. Ignatius of Antioch during the reign of Emperor Trajan. They were condemned to death for their Christianity and thrown to wild beasts in the arena two days before the martyrdom of Ignatius. December 18.

RUPERT (c. 795–c. 815). *See* Bertha (d. c. 840).

RUSTICUS (d. c. 258). *See* Dionysius.

RUYSBROECK, BL. JOHN (1293–1381). Born at Ruysbroeck near Brussels, Flanders, he was raised from the age of eleven and educated by his uncle John Hinckaert, a canon at St. Gudule's in Brussels, and was ordained in 1317. For the next twenty-six years, he, his uncle, and another canon named Francis van Coudenberg lived a life of extreme austerity, retirement, and contemplation. During this time, John actively fought the heresies and false mysticism of the Brethren of the

Free Spirit, writing several pamphlets attacking their teaching. In 1343, John, his uncle, and Francis retired to a hermitage at Groenendael near Brussels to live as hermits. They attracted so many disciples that in 1349 they formed a community of Canons Regular of St. Augustine, with John as prior. His fame as a contemplative, director of souls, and man of God spread, bringing visitors from all over Europe. Groenendael became a school of sanctity, and John's *Devotio moderna* was to influence deeply the Brethren of the Common Life and the Canons Regular of Windesheim, notable among them Thomas à Kempis and Dionysius the Carthusian. John was the foremost Flemish mystic, and his treatises on mysticism and sanctity, all written in Flemish, had an enormous impact on his time. Among his works are *Spiritual Espousals, Spiritual Tabernacles,* and *The Kingdom of God's Lovers.* He died at Groenendael on December 2, and his cult was approved in 1908.

S

SABAS (439–532). Born at Mutalaska, Cappadocia, near Caesarea, he was the son of an army officer there who when assigned to Alexandria left him in the care of an uncle. Mistreated by his uncle's wife, Sabas ran away to another uncle, though he was only eight. When the two uncles became involved in a lawsuit over his estate, he again ran away, this time to a monastery near Mutalaska. In time the uncles were reconciled and wanted him to marry, but he remained in the monastery. In 456, he went to Jerusalem and there entered a monastery under St. Theoctistus. When he was thirty, he became a hermit under the guidance of St. Euthymius, and after Euthymius' death spent four years alone in the desert near Jericho. Despite his desire for solitude, he attracted disciples, organized them into a *laura* in 483, and when his 150 monks asked for a priest and despite his opposition to monks being ordained, he was obliged to accept ordination by Patriarch Sallust of Jerusalem in 491. He attracted disciples from Egypt and Armenia, allowed them a liturgy in their own tongue, and built several hospitals and another monastery near Jericho. He was appointed archimandrite of all hermits in Palestine who lived in separate cells, but his custom of going off by himself during Lent caused dissension in the monastery, and 60 of his monks left to revive a ruined monastery at Thecuna. He bore them no ill will and aided them with food and supplies. In 511, he was one of a delegation of abbots sent to Emperor Anastasius I, a supporter of Eutychianism, which Sabas opposed, to plead with the Emperor to mitigate his persecution of orthodox bishops and religious; they were unsuccessful. Sabas supported Elias of Jerusalem when the Emperor exiled him, was a strong supporter of theological orthodoxy, and persuaded many to return to orthodoxy. He was a vigorous opponent of Origenism and monophysitism. In

531, when he was ninety-one, he again went to Constantinople, this time to plead with Emperor Justinian to suppress a Samaritan revolt and protect the people of Jerusalem from further harassment by the Samaritans. He fell ill soon after his return to his *laura* from this trip and died on December 5 at Laura Mar Saba, after naming his successor. Sabas is one of the most notable figures of early monasticism and is considered one of the founders of Eastern monasticism. The *laura* he founded in the desolate, wild country between Jerusalem and the Dead Sea, named Mar Saba after him, was often called the Great Laura for its pre-eminence and produced many great saints; it is still inhabited by monks of the Eastern Orthodox Church and is one of the three or four oldest inhabited monasteries in the world.

SABAS. *See* Sava.

SABAS THE GOTH (d. 372). A Goth who had been converted to Christianity in his youth, he became lector to Sansala, a priest in Targoviste in Romania. Sabas denounced the practice of certain Christians of pretending to eat meat offered to pagan gods though in reality it had not been eaten and was forced out of the town but was later allowed to return. In another persecution of the Christians, he loudly proclaimed his Christianity but was allowed to go unharmed. During a third persecution a group of pagan Gothic soldiers under Atharidus arrested Sansala and Sabas. Despite the tortures to which he was subjected, he emerged from each of them unscathed. Finally Atharidus ordered him to be drowned, and though the leaders of the execution party offered to let him go free, he refused and was drowned in the Mussovo River near Targoviste. Another fifty Christians suffered martyrdom in the same persecution. April 12.

SABUTAKA (d. 421). *See* Maharsapor.

SAHAK. *See* Isaac the Great.

SAKAKIBARA, JOACHIM (1557–97). *See* Miki, Paul.

SALOME (1st century). Wife of Zebedee and mother of the apostles James and John (Matt. 20:20; 27:56), she asked

Christ to allow her sons to sit next to him in his kingdom
(Matt. 20:20ff.). She was present at the crucifixion (Matt.
27:56; Mark 15:40) of Christ and was one of the women
who discovered the empty tomb (Mark 16:1ff.). She is
sometimes called Mary Salome. October 22.

SAMSON (c. 485–565). Born at Glamorgan, Wales, he was
dedicated to God as a child and enrolled under St. Illtud at
his monastery at Llanwit, Glamorgan. Samson was ordained,
had an attempt made on his life by two of Illtud's nephews
jealous of his ordination, and then lived for a time as a hermit under Piro on the island of Caldey (Ynys Byr) off the
coast of Pembrokeshire. His father, Amon, and his Uncle
Umbrafel joined him there after Amon recovered from a serious illness when he received the last rites from his son. When
Piro died, Samson succeeded him as abbot but resigned after
a trip to Ireland and resumed his eremitical life with Amon
and two others. Samson was soon after appointed abbot of St.
Dubricius Monastery and consecrated bishop. He then traveled through Cornwall where he worked as a missionary,
founded monasteries and churches at Southill and Golant,
probably visited the Scilly Islands, and then went to Brittany
to continue his missionary activities. He founded monasteries
at Dol, of which he was abbot, and at Pental in Normandy,
successfully supported Judual as ruler of Brittany against
Conmor in 555, and is reported to have been named bishop
of Dol by King Childebert. Samson died at Dol. July 28.

SAMUEL (d. 309). See Elias.

SANZ, BL. PETER (1680–1747). Born at Asco, Catalonia,
Spain, he joined the Dominicans in 1697, in 1714 was sent as
a missionary to the Philippines, and from there was sent to
Fukien Province in China. In 1730, he was made bishop of
Mauricastro and vicar apostolic of Fukien. A renewed persecution of Christians flared up in 1746 and he was accused of
breaking the laws by converting thousands to Christianity by
a man to whom he had refused to lend money. Imprisoned
with him were fellow Spanish Dominicans Frs. Joachim Royo
and John Alcober, and they were soon joined by Frs. Francis
Serrano and Francis Diaz. After a year in prison at Foochow,
Bl. Peter was beheaded; when word arrived that Fr. Serrano

(October 20) had been appointed titular bishop of Tipsa and coadjutor to Bl. Peter, he and the other three were summarily executed at Fukien. They were all beatified by Pope Leo XIII in 1893. May 26.

SATOR (d. c. 303). *See* Honoratus.

SATURNINUS (d. 203). *See* Perpetua.

SATURUS (d. 203). *See* Perpetua.

SATYRUS (d. c. 379). Brother of St. Ambrose and St. Marcellina, he was probably born at Trier, Gaul, moved to Rome with his family when his father, praetorium of the Gauls, died about 354, and became a lawyer. He was appointed prefect of one of the provinces, resigned to take care of the secular affairs of the see of Milan when Ambrose was appointed its bishop in 374, and after being shipwrecked on a voyage to Africa, was baptized. He died unexpectedly in Milan and was eulogized by Ambrose in his famous funeral sermon "On the Death of a Brother." September 17.

SAULI, ALEXANDER (1534–92). Born at Milan, Italy, of a well-known Genoese family, he became a Barnabite when he was seventeen, studied at the Barnabite college at Pavia, and was ordained in 1556. He taught at the university at Pavia and soon achieved a reputation as a fiery preacher. He became spiritual adviser to St. Charles Borromeo and Cardinal Sfondrati (later Pope Gregory XIV), was named provost general of his Order in 1567, resisted the efforts of Borromeo to incorporate a group of Humiliati friars with the Barnabites, and in 1570 was appointed bishop of Aleria, Corsica. During the next twenty years he put into effect numerous reforms with such success that he was called "the Apostle of Corsica." He refused translation to the see of Tortona and then Genoa, but in 1591 Gregory translated him to Pavia. He died on October 11 while on a visitation to Colozza the following year. He was reputed to have performed miracles during his lifetime and after his death, and was canonized in 1904 by Pope St. Pius X.

SAVA (1174–1237). Son of Stephen I, founder of the

Nemanydes dynasty, and also known as Sabas, he became a monk on Mount Athos in Greece when he was seventeen. With his father, who abdicated in 1196, he founded Khilandrai Monastery on Mount Athos for Serbian monks and became abbot. He returned home in 1207 when his brothers, Stephen II and Vulkan, began to quarrel, and civil war broke out. Sava brought many of his monks with him, and from the headquarters he established at Studenitsa Monastery, he founded several monasteries and began the reformation and education of the country, where religion and education had fallen to a low estate. He was named metropolitan of a new Serbian hierarchy by Emperor Theodore II Laskaris at Nicaea; was consecrated, though for political reasons unwillingly, by Patriarch Manuel I in 1219; returned home bringing more monks from Mount Athos; and in 1222 crowned his brother Stephen II, King of Serbia. Through his efforts, he finished the uniting of his people that had been begun by his father, translated religious works into Serbian, and gave his people a native clergy and hierarchy. He made a pilgrimage to the Holy Land, was later sent on a second visit there on an ecclesiastical mission, and died on the way back at Tirnovo, Bulgaria, on January 14. He is the patron of Serbia.

SAVINIAN (d. c. 303). *See* Honoratus.

SAVIO, DOMINIC (1842–57). Born of peasant family at Riva, Italy, he became a student under St. John Bosco at St. Francis de Sales oratory in Turin when he was twelve. There he formed the Company of the Immaculate Conception to help Don Bosco in his work. Though only a young boy, he was blessed with spiritual gifts far beyond his age—knowledge of people in need, knowledge of the spiritual needs of those around him, and the ability to prophesy. A vision of his is reported to have strongly influenced Pope Pius IX to restore a hierarchy to England in 1850. Dominic died at Mondonio, Italy, and was canonized by Pope Pius XII in 1954. He is the patron of choirboys. March 9.

SCHERVIER, MARY FRANCES (1819–76). Born at Aachen, Germany, on January 3, she began helping the sick and the poor early in her life and in 1840 joined a charitable group devoted to aiding the poor. In 1845, she and four other women founded the Sisters of the Poor of St. Francis, with Frances as superior. They set up an infirmary at Aachen during a smallpox plague, cared for cholera victims, and by 1850 had established a hospital for incurables, several relief kitchens, and home nursing centers. The foundation received papal approbation after the bishop of Cologne had approved, spread to other parts of Germany with the opening of new homes and hospitals, and in 1855 sent a group of six sisters to establish a hospital in the United States at Cincinnati, Ohio. Frances died at Aachen on December 14, and was beatified in 1974 by Pope Paul VI. December 15.

SCHOLASTICA (d. 543). The sister of St. Benedict (and perhaps his twin), she founded and was abbess, probably under Benedict's direction, of a convent at Plombariola near Monte Cassino. She died there days after a visit to her brother, which St. Gregory describes in detail. She is considered the first Benedictine nun. February 10.

SEACHNALL. *See* Secundinus.

SEBASTIAN (d. c. 288). According to his untrustworthy legend, he was born at Narbonne, Gaul, became a soldier in the Roman army at Rome in about 283, and encouraged Marcellian and Marcus, under sentence of death, to remain firm in their faith. Sebastian made numerous converts, among them the master of the rolls, Nicostratus, who was in charge of prisoners, and his wife, Zoé, a deaf mute whom he cured, the jailer Claudius, Chromatius, prefect of Rome, whom he cured of gout, and his son Tiburtius. Chromatius set the prisoners free, freed his slaves, and resigned as prefect. Sebastian was named captain in the praetorian guards by Emperor Diocletian, as did Emperor Maximian when Diocletian went to the East, neither knowing that Sebastian was a Christian. When it was discovered during Maximian's persecution of the Christians that Sebastian was a Christian, he was ordered executed. He was shot with arrows and left for dead, but when the widow of St. Castulus went to recover his body, she found he was still alive and nursed him back to health. Soon after, Sebastian intercepted the Emperor, denounced him for his cruelty to Christians, and was beaten to death on the Emperor's orders. That Sebastian was a martyr and was venerated at Milan as early as the time of St. Ambrose and was buried on the Appian Way is fact; all else is pious fiction dating back no earlier than the fifth century. He is patron of archers, athletes, and soldiers, and is appealed to as protection against plague. January 20.

SECHNALL. *See* Secundinus.

SECUNDINUS (c. 375–447). Also known as Sechnall and Seachnall, he was sent from Gaul in 439 to assist St. Patrick in Ireland, together with Auxilius and Iserninus, became the first bishop of Dunslaughlin in Meath, and then auxiliary bishop of Armagh. He wrote several hymns, notably *Audites, omnes amantes Deum* in honor of Patrick and the earliest Latin hymn written in Ireland, and, *Sancti, venite, Christi corpus sumite*. November 27.

SECUNDIUS (1st century). *See* Torquatus.

SECUNDULUS (d. 203). *See* Perpetua.

SELEUCUS (d. 309). *See* Elias.

SEPTIMUS (d. c. 303). *See* Honoratus.

SERAPION (d. 249). *See* Apollonia.

SERENUS THE GARDENER (d. c. 302). Also known as Cerneuf, according to his probably fictitious legend he was born in Greece, immigrated to Sirmium (Metrovica, Yugoslavia), and was known for his garden. He went into hiding for a time to escape a persecution of Christians that had just begun, and on his return rebuked a lady for walking in his garden at an unseemly time. She reported to her husband that he had insulted her, and the husband, a member of the imperial guards, reported the matter to Emperor Maximian. Upon orders from the Emperor, the governor investigated the matter, found Serenus innocent of insulting the woman, but while examining him found he was a Christian. When Serenus refused to sacrifice to pagan gods, he was beheaded. February 23.

SERF (6th century). Also known as Servanus, untrust-

worthy legend has him an Irishman who was consecrated
bishop by St. Palladius, founded a monastery at Culross,
Scotland, and died and was buried there. One particularly extravagant story has him the son of the King of Canaan who
renounced the throne, became Patriarch of Jerusalem, then
Pope, and resigned the papacy to preach to the Scots. He is
the patron of the Orkney Islands, though it is doubtful if he
ever preached there. July 1.

SERGIUS (d. 303). His legend has Sergius an officer in the
Roman army and Bacchus an officer under him, and both
were friends of Emperor Maximian. When they did not enter
a temple of Jupiter with the Emperor, he ordered them to do
so. When they further refused his order that they sacrifice to
pagan gods, they were humiliated by being led through the
streets of Arabissus in women's garb and then sent to Rosafa,
Mesopotamia, where they were scourged so terribly that Bacchus died of the scourging; Sergius was then tortured further
and beheaded. October 7.

SERGIUS I (d. 701). Son of an Antioch, Syria, merchant,
he was born and brought up at Palermo, Italy, and educated
at Rome, where he became a priest. He was elected Pope on
December 15, 687, succeeding Pope Conon, despite the
claims of Pascal and Theodosius, when he was supported by
the exarch John. However, Sergius was forced to pay John
the amount of the bribe that Pascal had promised John to
support his (Pascal's) nomination. He became embroiled in
a controversy with Emperor Justinian II in 693 when he refused to sign the decrees of the previous year's Council of
Trullanum, called by Justinian, because the council, except
for one bishop, was attended only by Eastern bishops but
passed canons applicable to the whole Church. If Sergius accepted these decrees, it would have meant that Constantinople
was on an ecclesiastical level with Rome. The Emperor sent
Zachary, his bodyguard commander, to Rome to bring Sergius to Constantinople, but the people of Rome and Ravenna
resisted Zachary, who was forced to seek the protection of the
Pope; eventually, Zachary was forced to leave the city. The
matter ended when Justinian was deposed in 695. Sergius
baptized Caedwalla, King of the West Saxons, in 689, consecrated St. Willibrod in 695, and encouraged English missions
in Germany and Friesland. Interested in music (he had at-

tended the *schola cantorum* in Rome), Sergius encouraged liturgical music, decreeing that the *Agnus Dei* be sung at Mass. He died on September 7 in Rome. September 8.

SERGIUS (c. 1315–92). Of a noble Russian family, he was born near Rostov and christened Bartholomew. When he was fifteen he was forced to flee with his family from the attack on Rostov by the rulers of Moscow. They lost all and became peasant farmers at Radonezh near Moscow. In 1335, after his parents died, he and his brother Stephen lived as hermits at Makovka until Stephen left to enter a monastery. Sergius received the tonsure from an abbot in the area, taking the name Sergius, and continued his eremitical way of life in the bitter cold and isolation of the Russian winter. But word of his holiness spread, and he soon attracted disciples, whom he organized into the famous Holy Trinity Monastery, of which he was named abbot, and he was ordained at Pereyaslav Zalesky. He thus re-established community life in Russia, which had disappeared from the Russian scene because of the Tartar invasion. In 1354 Sergius' decision in favor of cenobitical life for the community caused disagreement when a faction led by Stephen, who had joined him, objected, whereupon Sergius left and became a hermit on the banks of the Herzhach River. When many of the monks followed him, the monastery went into decline until he returned four years later at the request of Metropolitan Alexis of Moscow. On the advice of Sergius, Prince Dmitry Donskoy of Moscow decided to do battle with the Tartars and defeated them in the momentous Battle of Kulikovo Polye in 1380, a victory that freed Russia from Tartar domination. Its attribution to Sergius' inspiration and prayers further enhanced his reputation. He then traveled widely, promoting peace among rival Russian princes and establishing some forty monasteries. He refused the metropolitan see in 1378, resigned his abbacy early in 1392, and died six months later, on September 25. Sergius is considered the greatest of Russian saints. Many miracles were attributed to him, and he experienced visions and ecstasies. He had great influence with all classes (he is reputed to have stopped four civil wars between Russian princes) and was sought by all for his spiritual wisdom and love of his people.

SERGIUS (14th century). According to legend, he was the head of a trading group at Novgorod, Russia (another legend says he was from Byzantium), and became a hermit at Vaage, engaging in stonemasonry to support himself. With St. Germanus, he founded and was abbot of a Russian monastery on Valaam (Valamo) Island in Lake Ladoga in southeastern Finland, whence they evangelized the pagan Karelians around the lake. When the monastery was founded is uncertain, but tradition says late in the tenth century; another more probable date is 1329. June 28.

SERVANUS. *See* Serf.

SETHRIDA (d. c. 660). *See* Ethelburga (d. 664).

SETON, ELIZABETH ANN (1774–1821). Born at New York City on August 28, she was the daughter of Richard Bayley, professor of anatomy at King's College (now Columbia) in New York and the stepsister of Archbishop James Roosevelt Bayley of Baltimore. She was educated by her father, married William Magee Seton in 1794, and became involved in social work, helping to found the Society for the Relief of Poor Widows with Small Children in 1797. She was widowed with five children in 1803 when her husband died at Pisa, Italy, where they had gone for his health. She returned to the United States and in 1805 became a Catholic—a step that led to her ostracization by her family and friends. She was invited to open a school in Baltimore by Dr. Dubourg, rector of St. Mary's Seminary there, and in 1809 with four companions founded a religious community, the Sisters of St. Joseph, and a school for poor children near Emmitsburg, Maryland, the beginning of the far-reaching Catholic parochial school system in the United States. The new community's rule was approved by Archbishop Carroll of Baltimore in 1812, she was elected superior, and with eighteen sisters she took vows on July 19, 1813, the founding of the Sisters of Charity, the first American religious society. The order spread throughout the United States and numbered some twenty communities by the time of her death at Emmitsburg on January 4. She was canonized by Pope Paul VI in 1975, the first American-born saint.

SEVERINUS BOETHIUS (c. 480–524). Born in Rome of the famous Anicia family, the son of Flavius Manlius Boethius, who was a consul in 487, Ancius Manlius Severinus

Boethius was orphaned as a child and was raised by Q. Aurelius Symmachus, whose daughter Rusticiana he married. He was known even in his youth for his learning, began to translate Plato and Aristotle into Latin, and made available translations of Pythagoras, Ptolemy, Nichomachus, Euclid, and Archimedes in Latin. He was knowledgeable in astronomy, music, logic, and theology, and wrote several theological treatises that are still extant, notably *De sancta Trinitate*. He was named consul by Ostrogoth Emperor Theodoric in 510 and then was named master of the offices. However, when he defended ex-Consul Albinus against charges of conspiring with Eastern Emperor Justin to overthrow the Ostrogoth rulers, he too was arrested. He was charged with treason and sacrilege for allegedly using astronomy for impious purposes and was imprisoned at Ticinum (Pavia). During the nine months he was in prison, he wrote *The Consolation of Philosophy*. He was then tortured and executed. Boethius is considered the first of the scholastics and had great influence in the Middle Ages. His *Consolation of Philosophy* was tremendously popular, and for long his translations of the Greek philosophers were the only translations available. He was canonized by Pope Leo XIII in 1883. October 23.

SEXBURGA (d. c. 699). Daughter of King Anna of the East Angles and sister of SS. Etheldreda, Ethelburga, Erconwald, and Withburga, she married King Erconbert of Kent in 640 and on his death in 664 finished Minster Monastery, which she had founded on Sheppey Island, and joined the nuns there. She appointed her daughter St. Ermenilda abbess and then went to Ely Abbey, where she succeeded her sister Etheldreda as abbess and where Sexburga died on July 6.

SHENOUTE. *See* Shenute.

SHENUTE (d. c. 450). Born at Shenalolet, Akhym, Egypt, he became a monk in 370 at the double monastery at Dair-al-Abiad near Atripe in the Thebaid and in 385 succeeded his Uncle Bgôl, who had founded the abbey as abbot. Shenute's rigorous austerities, severe rule, rigid discipline, and severe punishment for slight infractions attracted many to the monastery (at one time it is estimated that some two thousand monks and eighteen hundred nuns lived there). He accompanied St. Cyril of Alexandria to the Council of Ephesus in 431, where Shenute was active in his opposition to Nestorius. He was a leader in the development of monastic communal life and in time was regarded as archimandrite of all the surrounding monasteries. He wrote extensively in Coptic, mainly letters of spiritual direction and sermons, is believed to have died when he was 118, and may have died as late as 466. His name is also spelled Schenute, Shenoute, and Sinuthius. July 1.

SHERWIN, RALPH (d. 1581). Born at Rodsley, Derbyshire, England, he was granted a fellowship at Oxford, studied at Exeter College there, and became a classical scholar of distinction, receiving his M.A. in 1574. He became a Catholic in 1575, went to Douai to study for the priesthood, and was ordained there in 1577. He continued his studies at the English college at Rome and was sent on the English mission in 1580. He arrived in England on August 1 and was arrested in London in November; he was imprisoned in the Tower, tortured, and offered the bribe of a bishopric if he would apostatize. Brought to trial the next year with Edmund Campion and others, he was convicted of attempting to foment a rebellion and condemned to death. He was hanged, drawn, and quartered at Tyburn on December 1 with Edmund Campion and Alexander Briant, and was canonized in 1970 by Pope Paul VI as one of the Forty Martyrs of England and Wales.

SIDONIUS APOLLINARIS (c. 430–c. 480). Caius Sollius Apollinaris Sidonius was born at Lyons, Gaul, on November 5 of a noble family, received a classical education at Arles, and was a student of Claudianus Mamertus of Vienne. He married Papianilla, daughter of Avitus (who became Emperor in 455), in about 450 and lived at the imperial court at Rome for several years. He served under several Emperors, for whom he wrote panegyrics after Avitus was deposed in 456, retired for a time after Emperor Majorian's death in 461, but returned and was prefect of Rome in 468. He then retired to the life of a country gentleman in Auvergne, carrying on a large correspondence, much of it still extant, which gave valuable insights into the life of the times. Against his will, in 469, he was named bishop of Avernum (Clermont), partly because it was felt he was the only one able to defend crumbling Roman prestige against the Goths, abandoned his worldly lifestyle for a more humble mode, and was soon recognized as a leading ecclesiastical authority. He was a benefactor of monks, spent much of his wealth in charities, and provided food for thousands during a great famine. He led the populace against King Euric of the Goths, and when Clermont fell to the Goths in 474, he was exiled but returned in 476 and devoted the last few years before his death at Clermont to a collection of his letters. He was an outstanding orator, was famed as a poet (twenty-four of his poems have survived), and was one of the last representatives of the classical school. August 21.

✶**SIGFRID** (d. c. 1045). Untrustworthy sources say he was born in Northumbria, became a priest at York or perhaps Glastonbury, was consecrated missionary bishop, and with two other bishops, Grimkel and John, was sent to Norway at the request of King Olaf Tryggvason (who had just been converted to Christianity) for missionaries. Sigfrid went to Sweden in 1008, converted the King, also named Olaf, and was so successful he is called the Apostle of Sweden. He also labored in Denmark. He is reported to have been canonized by Pope Adrian IV, but there is no proof of such a canonization. February 15.

SILAS (1st century). One of the leaders of the Church of Jerusalem, he was sent with Paul and Barnabas to Antioch to communicate the decisions of the Council of Jerusalem to the Gentile community in Syria. When Paul and Barnabas quarreled over Paul Mark, Silas was chosen by Paul to accompany him on his second missionary journey to Syria, Cilicia, and Macedonia (Acts 15:38–40). Silas was beaten and imprisoned with Paul at Philippi (Acts 16:19ff.), was involved with Paul in the riot of the Jews at Thessalonica that drove Paul and Silas from the city to Beroea (Acts 17:5–10), remained at Beroea with Timothy when Paul left, but rejoined him at Corinth (Acts 18:5). The Silvanus mentioned with Timothy by Paul and who helped him preach at Corinth (2 Cor. 1:19) is believed to be the same as Silas, since Silvanus is a Greek variant of the Semitic Silas. Silvanus is also mentioned as the man through whom Peter communicated (1 Peter 5:12) and is considered by some scholars to be the author of that epistle. Tradition says he was the first bishop of Corinth and that he died in Macedonia. July 13.

SILVA MENESES, BEATRICE DA (1424–90). Daughter of the count of Viana and sister of St. Amadeus of Portugal, she was born at Ceuta, Portugal, where she is known as Brites. She was raised in the household of Princess Isabel and accompanied the princess to Spain when she married John II of Castile. Disenchanted with court life after being unjustly imprisoned by Isabel, she shortly after left the court and became a Cistercian nun at St. Dominic of Silos Convent at Toledo. In 1484, she founded the Congregation of the Immaculate Conception of the Blessed Virgin Mary (the Conceptionists), headquartered at the Castle of Galliana, donated by Queen Isabella. Beatrice died at Toledo on September 1, and was canonized by Pope Paul VI in 1976.

SILVANUS. *See* Silas (1st century).

SILVANUS (d. c. 165). *See* Felicity.

SILVERIUS (d. c. 537). Son of Pope Hormisdas, he was born at Frosinone, Campania, Italy. He became a sub-deacon in Rome and on the death of Pope St. Agapitus I was named Pope in April 536 by Ostrogoth King Theodehad of Italy to forestall the election of a Byzantine nominee; on Silverius' consecration on June 1 or 8, he was accepted by the Roman clergy as Pope. He soon incurred the bitter enmity of Empress Theodora and the Byzantines when he refused to accept monophysites Anthimus and Severus as Patriarchs of Constantinople and Antioch, respectively, as she requested. In an attempt to save Rome from Ostrogoth General Vitiges, Silverius invited the imperial General Belisarius into the city after Vitiges had overrun and devastated the suburbs of Rome. A forged letter accusing Silverius of being responsible for Vitiges' destruction proved unsuccessful in implicating Silverius, whereupon he was kidnaped and brought to Patara, Lycia, at the instigation of Theodora; as soon as he was kidnaped, Belisarius proclaimed Vigilius, a deacon, Pope in his stead. When Emperor Justinian learned what had happened, he ordered Silverius freed, and the Pope returned to Italy, where he was promptly captured by Vigilius' adherents and taken to the island of Palmarola off Naples, where he died of starvation or was murdered at the behest of Antonina, Belisarius' wife, who had engineered the whole plan to make

Vigilius Pope. Silverius died on the island on December 2.
June 20.

SILVESTER. *See* Sylvester.

SIMEON (1st century). A resident of Jerusalem, he had his
wish to see the Messiah before he died when he was privi-
leged to hold the infant Jesus in his arms when Mary and
Joseph brought the child to the Temple and uttered the words
of praise to God that we know as the *Nunc dimittis* (Luke
2:25–35) and made his famous prophecy (Luke 2:34–35).
October 8.

SIMEON (d. c. 107). Mentioned in Matthew 13:55 and
Mark 6:3 as one of the brothers of the carpenter, he was, ac-
cording to the Roman Martyrology, son of Cleophas, St.
Joseph's brother, and hence first cousin of the Lord. He was
elected successor to James as bishop of Jerusalem when
James was martyred. According to tradition, Simeon was su-
pernaturally warned of the destruction of Jerusalem by the
Romans in 66 and led a group of Christians to the city of
Pella, where they remained until it was safe for them to return to Jerusalem. He escaped the death ordered by Emperors
Vespasian and Domitian when they decreed that all of Jewish
origin were to be executed, but was arrested by the Roman
Governor Atticus during the persecution of Christians under
Emperor Trajan, was tortured, and then crucified, reputedly
when he was well over one hundred years old. He may be the
same as the apostle Simeon the Zealot (Matt. 10:4; Mark
3:18; Luke 6:15; Acts 1:13). February 18.

SIMEON BARSABAE (d. 341). Bishop of Seleucia and
Ctesiphon, he was arrested during the persecution of King
Sapor II of Persia, and when he refused to worship the sun,
was tortured and imprisoned. After being forced to witness
the beheading of some one hundred of his followers, he was
himself beheaded. Among those who suffered martyrdom
were Usthazanes, the King's tutor, who had apostatized but
was brought back to the faith by Simeon; Abdechalas and
Ananias, two of Simeon's priests; and Pusicius, who had encouraged Ananias. April 21.

SIMEON THE LOGOTHETE. *See* Simeon Metaphrastes.

SIMEON METAPHRASTES (d. c. 1000). He was probably a Logothete (Secretary of State) to Emperor Constantine VII Porphyrogenitus, at whose order he compiled a *Menology* of legends and stories of the Byzantine saints under the name Simeon the Logothete. It is the most famous of the medieval Greek collections, comparable to *The Golden Legend* of Bl. James Voragine in the West. Simeon also wrote a chronicle, prayers, letters, and collections of maxims of Basil and Macarius of Egypt. Simeon's feast is celebrated in the Orthodox Church on November 28 but has never been formally recognized in Rome.

SIMEON STYLITES (c. 390–459). Son of a Cilician shepherd and born on the Syrian border of Cilicia, he was a shepherd in his childhood and when he was thirteen had a vision that he later interpreted as foretelling his later life on pillars. He spent two years in a nearby monastery and then became a monk at a stricter monastery at Heliodorus, where he practiced such severe mortifications that he was dismissed from the monastery. He then became a hermit at the foot of Mount Teleanissae near Antioch and after three years moved to the top of the mountain, where word of his holiness began to attract huge crowds. To escape them, in 423, he erected a ten-foot-high pillar and lived on top of it; he spent the rest of his life living on successively higher pillars (*stylites* is from the Greek word *stylos,* meaning pillar), which were no wider than six feet in diameter at the top; his last pillar was sixty feet high. He practiced the greatest austerities, slept little if at all, was clad only in the skins of wild beasts, and fasted completely during Lent for forty years. He soon became greatly venerated as a holy man and had extraordinary influence. He preached daily exhorting his endless stream of listeners to greater holiness, converted many, and was listened to and consulted by all, from Emperors and prelates to commoners. He died on September 2 (or perhaps July 24), the first of the pillar ascetics.

SIMEON STYLITES THE YOUNGER (c. 517–92). Born at Antioch, his father died when he was five, and when he was seven, he became a stylite under the tutelage of the well-known St. John Stylite, and lived on a pillar that was to be his home for the next sixty-eight years. By the time he was twenty, his reputation for holiness attracted such crowds that he retired to a more inaccessible spot in the mountains near Antioch, which was soon called the Hill of Wonders. When he was thirty, in response to a vision, he founded a monastery, and when he was thirty-three he was ordained on one of his pillars. Huge crowds were attracted to his pillars because of his preaching, and he was venerated for his holiness, spiritual wisdom and advice, prophecies, and the miracles reported of him. He was said to have gone for long periods of time with hardly any sleep or nourishment. September 3.

SIMON. The Greek form of the Hebrew Simeon.

SIMON (1st century). Surnamed the Zealot for his rigid adherence to the Jewish law in Luke 6:15 and Acts 1:13 and the Canaanite in Matthew 10:4 and Mark 3:18, he was one of the original followers of Christ. Western tradition is that he preached in Egypt and then went to Persia with St. Jude, where both suffered martyrdom; Eastern tradition says Simon died peacefully at Edessa. October 28.

SIMON PETER. *See* Peter (d. c. 64).

SIMON STOCK (c. 1165–1265). Born at Aylesford, Kent, England, he became a hermit and then went on pilgrimage to Jerusalem, where he joined the Carmelites. He returned to Kent when the Moslems drove the Carmelites out and in 1247 was elected superior general of the Carmelites. He greatly expanded the Order, established new foundations in England, Ireland, Scotland, France, and Italy, and revised the rule, which revision was approved by Pope Innocent IV in 1237. At about this time Simon experienced the controversial vision of Mary promising salvation to all Carmelites who wore the brown scapular she showed him—a vision that led to the widespread devotion to Mary over the next centuries of wearing this scapular in her honor. He died at Bordeaux on May 16. Though never formally canonized, he has long been venerated, and celebration of his feast was permitted to the Carmelites by the Holy See on May 16. The surname Stock may come from the legend that he lived inside a tree trunk in his youth.

SIMON OF TRENT (1472–75). According to reports of the time, Simon was a 2½-year-old Christian boy living in

Trent, Italy, who was kidnaped by a Jewish doctor who allegedly crucified him out of hatred of Christ. Under intensive and terrible torture, those arrested for the crime admitted to it and were executed after further torture. Though the murder was blamed on the Jews of Trent, there never has been any proof that such a crime was committed for ritualistic purposes. Miracles were later reported at the child's tomb. March 24.

SIMPLICIAN (d. 400). A close friend of St. Ambrose, he was a confidant of St. Augustine and played a leading role in his conversion. Simplician was highly praised by Ambrose for his learning and zeal, and when an old man he succeeded Ambrose as bishop of Milan in 397. He ruled for only three years, until his death in May. August 13 (August 16 in Roman Martyrology).

SIMPLICIUS (d. 483). Born at Tivoli, Italy, he was elected Pope to succeed Pope St. Hilarus on March 3, 468. He defended the action of the Council of Chalcedon against the monophysite heresy, labored to help the people of Italy against the marauding raids of barbarian invaders, and saw the Heruli mercenaries in Roman service revolt and proclaim Odoacer King in 476 during his pontificate. Odoacer's deposition of the last Roman Emperor, Romulus Augustus, and his occupation of Rome in 476 marked the end of the Roman Empire. March 10.

SINUTHIUS. *See* Shenute.

SIRICIUS (d. 399). Son of Tiburtius, he was born in Rome, became a deacon, and was known for his learning and piety. He was elected Pope in December 384, succeeding Pope Damasus. Siricius' pontificate was marked by his denunciation of the monk Jovinian for denying the perpetual virginity of Mary and for a decretal Siricius sent to Bishop Himerius of Tarragona in Spain requiring married priests to desist from cohabitation with their wives; this is the earliest insistence on clerical celibacy and also the earliest papal decree that has survived in its entirety. He supported St. Martin of Tours, excommunicated Felix of Trier for his role in bringing about the execution of Priscillian by the Emperor, and died in Rome on November 26.

SIXTUS I (d. c. 127). Born at Rome, he succeeded Pope St. Alexander I as Pope and reigned for about ten years. He is believed to have suffered martyrdom, but no details have survived. Two of his decrees directed that the people should join in saying the *Sanctus* at Mass and that only the clergy could touch the sacred vessels. April 3.

SIXTUS II (d. 258). Possibly a Greek and a philosopher, he was elected Pope on August 30, 257. His pontificate is known only for his correspondence with Dionysius of Alexandria and Firmilian of Antioch, in which Sixtus upheld the Roman position that heretical baptisms were invalid, though he did not break off relations with those African and Asian churches that held otherwise. During Emperor Valerian's persecution of the Christians, he was seized in the cemetery of Praetextatus outside Rome while saying Mass and executed on August 6. Also seized and executed were six deacons: Agapitus, Felicissimus, Januarius, Magnus, Stephen, and Vincent. August 7.

SIXTUS III (d. 440). A member of the Roman clergy, he was elected Pope to succeed Pope Celestine I on July 31, 432. He denounced Pelagianism and Nestorianism, but his kindness to the Pelagians and Nestorians caused some of his critics to accuse him of leanings toward these heresies. He restored St. Mary Major Basilica and dedicated St. Peter in Chains and several other churches. He died on August 19.

SMARAGDUS. *See* Euphrosyne.

SOLANO, FRANCIS (1549–1610). Born at Montilla, Spain, on March 10, of noble and pious parents, he joined the Observant Franciscans at Montilla in 1569 and was ordained in 1576. He served as master of novices at the convent of Arifazza and became known for his preaching and conversions. At his request he was sent as a missionary to Peru in 1589, and for the rest of his life he worked for the welfare of the Indians and the Spanish colonists in South America. He learned the dialects and customs of Indian tribes, served as custodian of Franciscan houses in Argentina, Paraguay, and finally in Lima, Peru, and had phenomenal success in his preaching and in making converts, earning the sobriquet "the Wonder Worker of the New World" for his extraordinary

achievements. He died at Lima, and was canonized by Pope
Benedict XIII in 1726. July 14.

SOLUTAR (d. c. 287). *See* Maurice.

SOPATER (1st century). Son of Pyrrhus, a Christian of
Beroea, he accompanied St. Paul on his journey from Greece
to Jerusalem (Acts 20:4) and is considered by many
scholars to be the same as the Sosipater whom Paul calls a
compatriot and includes in his greetings to the Romans from
Corinth (Rom. 16:21). According to tradition he later went
to Corfu. June 25.

SOPHIA (2nd century). *See* Charity.

SOPHRONIUS (d. c. 638). Born at Damascus, Syria, he
lived as a hermit, traveling throughout his native land, Asia
Minor, and Egypt with another hermit named John Moschus.
Sophronius became a monk in Egypt in about 580, lived for a
time with Moschus at St. Sabas *laura* and then at St. Theodosius Monastery near Jerusalem. After visiting various Egyptian monasteries, he spent ten years at Alexandria under Patriarch St. John the Almsgiver, made a pilgrimage to Rome,
where Moschus died in about 620, and then returned to
Jerusalem, where he was elected patriarch. He called a synod
that condemned monothelitism, became a leader of the orthodox, and sent Bishop Stephen of Dor to Rome to secure papal
condemnation of monothelitism (which was finally condemned by the Lateran Council in 649). He was forced to
flee Jerusalem when the Saracens captured the city in 638 and
probably died at Alexandria soon after. He wrote several
biographies, doctrinal theses, homilies, and poems. March 11.

SOSIPATER. *See* Sopater.

SOSSUS (d. c. 305). *See* Januarius.

SOSTEGNI, GERARDINO (1204–76). *See* Monaldo,
Buonfiglio.

SOTER (d. 175). Born at Fondi, Italy, nothing is known of
his life beyond that he succeeded Pope St. Anicetus as Pope
about 167, opposed the Montanist heresy, and according to a

letter of Bishop St. Dionysius of Corinth, was known for his charity. April 22.

SOUBIROUS, MARIE BERNARDE (1844–79). Born at Lourdes, France, on January 7, the oldest child of miller Francis Soubirous and his wife, Louise, she was called Bernadette as a child, lived in abject poverty with her parents, was uneducated, and suffered from asthma. On February 11, 1858, while collecting firewood on the banks of the Gave River near Lourdes, she saw a vision of the Virgin Mary in a cave above the riverbank. Her report provoked skepticism, but her daily visions of the Lady from February 18 through March 4 drew great crowds of people. Despite great hostility on the part of the civil authorities, she persisted in her claims, and on February 25 caused a spring to flow where none had been before. On March 25, the vision told her it was the Immaculate Conception and directed her to build a chapel on the site. In 1866, she became a Sister of Notre Dame at Nevers, and she remained there until she died at Nevers on April 16. Lourdes soon became one of the great pilgrimage centers of modern Christianity, attracting millions of visitors. Miracles were reported at the shrine and in the waters of the spring, and after painstaking investigation the apparitions were ecclesiastically approved. Bernadette was canonized in 1933 by Pope Pius XI.

SOUTHWELL, ROBERT (c. 1561–95). Born at Horsham Saint, Norfolk, England, the son of a favorite at the royal court (his father had conformed and married Queen Elizabeth's governess), he was sent abroad to study at Douai and then Paris. He joined the Jesuits at Rome in 1578, became prefect of studies at the English college at Rome, and was ordained in 1584. He was sent on the English mission, with Fr. Henry Garnet, in 1586, became chaplain to Countess Anne of Arundel in London in 1587, and ministered with great success to the Catholics, including Anne's husband imprisoned in the Tower, in and around London until 1592, when he was betrayed by Anne Bellamy, daughter of Richard Bellamy, whom he was visiting at Harrow. He was repeatedly tortured over the next three years before he was brought to trial, condemned to death for being a Catholic priest, and hanged, drawn, and quartered at Tyburn on February 21. He wrote a large number of moving poems, most of which were probably written in prison to encourage his fellow Catholics but which soon became very popular among both Catholics and Protestants. They were collected soon after his death as *St. Peter's Complaint and Other Poems* and *Maeoniae;* he also wrote prose treatises, among them *Mary Magdalen's Funeral Tears, Epistle of Comfort,* and *The Triumph over Death.* He was canonized in 1970 by Pope Paul VI as one of the Forty Martyrs of England and Wales.

SOUTHWORTH, JOHN (1592–1654). Born in Lancashire, England, he was sent to Douai to study for the priesthood in 1613, was ordained in 1618, lived as a Benedictine for a few months, and then decided to remain a secular priest. He was sent on the English mission in 1619, worked around London for three years, and then returned to Belgium. He went back to England, was arrested in 1627, and was condemned to death for being a Catholic priest, but was released three years later with fifteen other priests through the intercession of Queen Henrietta Maria, the Catholic wife of King Charles I and sister of King Louis XIII of France. John apparently remained in England and was again in prison in 1632. He worked with St. Henry Morse to help victims of the London plague of 1635–36 but was required to stay in prison when complaints were made of his freedom to go in and out of prison as he wished. He was released again through the intercession of Henrietta Maria and then disappeared from view until he was arrested in 1654. Though there was no evidence against him, he insisted on proclaiming that he was a Catholic priest and was hanged, drawn, and quartered for his priesthood at Tyburn on June 28. His body was bought by the Spanish ambassador and sent to Douai; hidden during the French Revolution, it was discovered in 1927 and is now in Westminster Cathedral in London. He was canonized by Pope Paul VI in 1970 as one of the Forty Martyrs of England and Wales.

STANISLAUS (1030–79). Born of noble parents on July 26 at Szczepanow near Cracow, Poland, he was educated at Gnesen and was ordained. He was given a canonry by Bishop Lampert Zula of Cracow, who made him his preacher, and soon he became noted for his preaching. He became a much sought after spiritual adviser, was successful in his reforming efforts, and in 1072 was named bishop of Cracow. He in-

curred the enmity of King Boleslaus the Bold when he denounced the King's cruelties and injustices and especially his
kidnaping of the beautiful wife of a nobleman. When Stanislaus excommunicated the King and stopped services at the
cathedral when Boleslaus entered, Boleslaus himself killed
Stanislaus while the bishop was saying Mass in a chapel outside the city on April 11. Stanislaus has long been the symbol
of Polish nationhood; he was canonized by Pope Innocent IV
in 1253 and is the principal patron of Cracow. April 11.

STANISLAUS KOSKKA. *See* Kostka, Stanislaus.

STEEB, BL. KARL (1773–1856). Born in Tubingen, Germany, he was converted to Catholicism and ordained a priest,
and founded the Sisters of Mercy of Verona. He died at
Verona, Italy, on December 15, and was beatified by Pope
Paul VI in 1975.

STEPHEN (d. c. 35). A learned Greek-speaking Jew probably born in a foreign land but living in Jerusalem, he may
have been educated at Alexandria, was converted to Christianity, and was one of the seven chosen by the Twelve to
take care of the secular needs of the Hellenic Jewish Christian community in Jerusalem. They were ordained deacons by
the Twelve and began to perform miracles. His success as a
preacher caused some of the elders of some of the Jewish
synagogues, unable to best him in debate, to charge him with
blasphemy to the Sanhedrin; he was arrested and brought before that body. He spoke eloquently in his own defense,
denounced his accusers, and then described a vision of Christ
standing at the right hand of God after denouncing them for
resisting the Holy Spirit, as had their fathers. At this those assembled seized him, dragged him to the outskirts of the city,
and stoned him to death—the first Christian martyr. His story
is told in Acts 6–7. The finding of his body is celebrated on
August 3. December 26.

STEPHEN I (d. 257). Born in Rome, he became a priest
there, succeeded Pope St. Lucius as Pope, and was consecrated on May 12, 254. He was subjected to much criticism,
when he decreed that baptism by heretics was valid, by St.
Cyprian and other African bishops, and refused to see a delegation from an African council in 255 that had declared such

baptisms invalid. It is now believed he did not die a martyr, as was once thought. August 2.

STEPHEN (d. 258). *See* Sixtus II.

STEPHEN I (975–1038). Vaik, son of the Magyar *voivode* (duke) of Geza in Hungary, he was born at Asztergom and baptized in 985 when he was ten, at the same time as his father, and christened Stephen. He married Gisela, sister of Duke Henry III of Bavaria (who was to become Emperor Henry II in 1002) and became ruler of the Magyars on his father's death in 977. Through a series of wars against rival leaders who opposed his Christianization policies, he consolidated the country and in 1001 was crowned the first King of Hungary with a crown sent to him by Pope Sylvester II, the famous crown of St. Stephen captured in World War II by the American army and returned to Hungary by the United States in 1978. Stephen organized a hierarchy under St. Astrik (also known as Anastasius), who became Hungary's first archbishop and began establishing sees, building churches, and ordering tithes to be paid for their support. Stephen finished building St. Martin's Monastery (Pannonhalma), begun by his father, inaugurated widespread reforms, including a new legal code and a reorganization of the government in the kingdom, ruled wisely, and was very generous to the poor. He united the Magyars, made the nobles vassals to him, and was the founder of an independent Hungary. His later years were embittered by squabbles about the succession (his only son, Bl. Emeric, had died in a hunting accident in 1031). Stephen died at Szekesfehervar, Hungary, on August 15, and was canonized by Pope Gregory VII in 1083, when his relics were enshrined at the Church of Our Lady in Buda. August 16.

STEPHEN HARDING (d. 1134). Born at Sherborne, Dorsetshire, England, he was educated at Sherborne Abbey, traveled to Scotland, Paris, and Rome, and on his way back joined a group of hermits near Molesmes under Abbot St. Robert and Prior St. Alberic. In 1094, the abbot, the prior, Stephen, and four other monks obtained permission from Archbishop Hugh of Lyons, the papal delegate to France, to leave Molesmes to seek a more spiritual way of life. Robert, with twenty monks, then founded Cîteaux with Robert as abbot, Alberic as prior, and Stephen as subprior in 1098. Robert returned to Molesmes the following year, and Alberic became abbot and Stephen prior. When Alberic died in 1109, Stephen was elected abbot and immediately put into effect a series of austere regulations that cut off much of the abbey's income and discouraged new candidates. When a mysterious malady killed many of the monks, it seemed that the young community was doomed. Then dramatically one day in 1112, a troop of thirty horsemen led by a dashing young noble appeared requesting admission. His name was Bernard, and from then on the Cistercians flourished. By 1119, ten monasteries had been founded from Cîteaux, among them Clairvaux, with Bernard as abbot, though he was only twenty-four at the time; in that year Stephen drew up the rule for the Order, the Charter of Charity, which organized the Cistercians into an Order. He resigned in 1133 because of old age and blindness and died at Cîteaux. He was canonized in 1623. April 17 (July 16 among the Cistercians).

STEPHEN OF NARBONNE (d. 1242). *See* William Arnaud.

STONE, JOHN (d. c. 1539). A native of Canterbury, England, he became an Augustinian friar of the Canterbury community, was a Doctor of Divinity, and was highly regarded for his learning. He served as professor and prior at Droitwich for a time but was back at Canterbury when Henry VIII began his divorce proceedings. John denounced the claims of Henry to ecclesiastical supremacy from the pulpit, was arrested in December 1538, imprisoned at Westgate Prison, and when he reiterated his condemnation of the Act of Supremacy, was hanged, drawn, and quartered at Canterbury sometime before December 1539. He was canonized by Pope Paul VI in 1970 as one of the Forty Martyrs of England and Wales. December 27.

STRAMBI, VINCENT (1745–1824). Son of a druggist, he was born on January 1 at Civitavecchia, Italy, resisted his parents' wish that he become a diocesan priest, and though he studied at the diocesan seminary and was ordained in 1767, he joined the Passionists in 1768 after attending a retreat given by St. Paul of the Cross. Vincent became a professor of theology, was made provincial in 1781, and in 1801 was ap-

pointed bishop of Macerata and Tolentino. He was expelled
from his see when he refused to take an oath of allegiance to
Napoleon in 1808 but returned in 1813 with the downfall of
Napoleon. When Napoleon escaped from Elba, Murat made
Macerata his headquarters, and when his troops were defeated
by the Austrians, Vincent dissuaded him from sacking and
destroying the town. He imposed reforms in his see that
caused threats to his life, labored for his people during a ty-
phus epidemic, and resigned his see on the death of Pope Pius
VII to become one of the advisers of his old friend Pope Leo
XII in Rome. Vincent died on January 1, and was canonized
by Pope Pius XII in 1950. September 25.

STURMI (d. 779). Born of Christian parents in Bavaria, he
was placed in the custody of St. Boniface, who had him
educated by St. Wigbert at Fritzlar Abbey. Sturmi was ordained, engaged in missionary work in Westphalia for three
years, and then became a hermit at Hersfeld. Forced to leave
by raiding Saxons, he founded Fulda Monastery in 744 and
was appointed its first abbot by Boniface. He studied Benedic-
tinism at Monte Cassino, was granted complete autonomy for
Fulda by Pope St. Zachary, and under Sturmi's direction it
became a great center of monastic learning and spirituality.
He later became involved in a drawn-out dispute with Bishop
St. Lull of Mainz, who claimed jurisdiction over the monastery, and in 763 Pepin banished Sturmi from Fulda. The
monks rebelled at his banishment and persuaded Pepin to recall him after two years of exile. He was unsuccessful in attempts to convert the Saxons due in no small measure to the
conquests and harsh treatment accorded them by Charlemagne and Pepin. When Charlemagne led an expedition
against the Moors of Spain, the Saxons rose up, drove out the
monks, and threatened Fulda. On his return in 779, Charlemagne put down the uprising, but Sturmi was stricken at
Fulda before he could reorganize his missions and died there
on December 17. Known as "the Apostle of the Saxons," he
was the first German to become a Benedictine and was canonized in 1139.

SUKEJIRŌ, PETER (d. 1597). See Miki, Paul.

SUSANNA (d. 295). The beautiful daughter of Gabinius, a
priest, and niece of Pope Caius, she refused Emperor Diocle-

tian's request that she marry his son-in-law Maximian and converted two of her uncles, Claudius and Maximus, who were court officers sent by Diocletian to persuade her to marry, to Christianity. Diocletian was so enraged by what she had done that he sent one of his favorites, Julian, to deal with the matter. Julian had Maximus, Claudius and his wife Praepedigna, and their two sons burned to death at Cumae, and then had Susanna and her father beheaded. There was a Susanna who lived in Rome, but the details of the story are fictitious. August 11.

SUSO, BL. HENRY (c. 1295–1365). Born at Bihlmeyer near Constance, Switzerland, he early began to use his mother's name, Suso, instead of his father's, von Berg. When he was thirteen, he entered the Dominicans at Constance, was professed, and went to Cologne for further study. He studied under Johann Eckhart, 1324–28, and defended him against charges of heresy in *Little Book of Truth*. His mystical life began when at eighteen he made himself "Servant of the Eternal Wisdom," to whom he devoted himself the rest of his life. For ten years he inflicted the most rigorous mortifications and penances on himself, endured arid periods of spirituality, and experienced visions of Christ, Our Lady, and the saints. When he was forty, he began preaching and was tremendously successful in making converts and causing sinners to repent, and was a much sought after spiritual director in Dominican convents. He suffered innumerable slanders, was accused of theft, sacrilege, heresy, adultery, and even poisoning, but was completely exonerated of all charges. The climax came when his sister ran away from her convent; but he convinced her to return, and she lived an exemplary life thereafter. He was elected prior, probably of Diessenhofen, in 1343 and was at the Dominican house in Ulm, Germany, when he died on January 25. He wrote mystical treatises, notably *Book of Eternal Wisdom* (one of the most influential treatises in mystical literature), and an autobiography purportedly pieced together by Elizabet Stagel from material he gave her. His beatification was confirmed by Pope Gregory XVI in 1831. March 2.

SUZUKI, PAUL (1563–97). A native of Owari, Japan, he was baptized by the Jesuits in 1584, became a Franciscan tertiary, and was an outstanding catechist until he was crucified for his faith with twenty-five other Catholics near Nagasaki on February 5. They were all canonized as the Martyrs of Japan in 1862. February 6.

SWITHBERT (647–713). Born in Northumbria, he became a monk at a monastery near the Scottish border, studied in Ireland under St. Egbert for a time, and was one of the missionaries who accompanied St. Willibrod to Germany in 690 to convert the Frisians. Swithbert worked in southern Holland and northern Brabant with great success, converting many with his eloquence and zeal. He was consecrated regionary bishop by St. Wilfrid in England in 693 and on his return extended his missionary activities to the Rhine and converted many of the Boructuari. He was obliged to withdraw to Frankish territory when the Saxons invaded the area, built a monastery on an island in the Rhine near Düsseldorf given him by Pepin of Herstal (the town of Kaiserwerth grew up around the monastery), and died there. He is the patron saint invoked against angina. March 1.

SWITHIN. *See* Swithun.

SWITHUN (d. 862). Also spelled Swithin, he was born in Wessex, England, was educated at the Old Monastery, Winchester, and was ordained. He became chaplain to King Egbert of the West Saxons, who appointed him tutor of his son Ethelwulf, and was one of the King's counselors. Swithun was named bishop of Winchester in 852 when Ethelwulf succeeded his father as King. Swithun built several churches and was known for his humility and his aid to the poor and needy. He died on July 2. A long-held superstition declares it will rain for forty days if it rains on his feast day of July 15, but the reason for and origin of this belief are unknown.

SYBIL OF THE RHINE. *See* Hildegard.

SYLVESTER I (d. 335). The son of Rufinus, a Roman, he was ordained and succeeded Pope Miltiades as Pope on January 31, 314. He had representatives at the Council of Arles and at the first General Council of Nicaea in 325, which condemned Donatism and Arianism, respectively. The tradition that he cured Emperor Constantine of leprosy when he baptized him and in return received great grants of territory (the Donation of Constantine) has no basis in fact. During his pontificate, many new churches were built, notably the basilicas of St. Peter and St. John Lateran. December 31.

SYLVESTER GOZZOLINI (1177–1267). Born of a noble family of Osimo, Italy, he studied law at Bologna and Padua but then switched to the study of theology and Scripture. He was ordained and became a canon at Osimo until he berated his bishop for the dissolute life he was leading; Sylvester resigned his canonry in 1227, when he was fifty, and became a hermit near Osimo and then at Grotta Fucile. Directed by a vision of St. Benedict, he organized the disciples he had attracted into a monastery at Monte Fano near Fabriano in 1231, thus founding the Silvestrine Benedictines, known as the Blue Benedictines from the color of their habit. The congregation was approved by Pope Innocent IV in 1247, and Sylvester ruled it for thirty-six years until his death at Fabiano, by which time eleven monasteries were under his rule. He was equivalently canonized in 1598 by Pope Clement VIII. November 26.

SYMMACHUS (d. 514). Born on the island of Sardinia, the son of Fortunatus, he was baptized in Rome, where he became archdeacon of the Church under Pope Anastasius II and succeeded him as Pope on November 22, 498. The same day the archpriest of St. Praxedes, Laurence, was elected Pope by a dissenting faction with Byzantine leanings, which was supported by Emperor Anastasius, but Gothic King Theodoric ruled against him and in favor of Symmachus. In 501 the pro-Byzantine group, led by Senator Festus, accused Symmachus of various crimes, but the Pope refused to appear before the King to answer the charges, asserting that the secular ruler had no jurisdiction over him. A synod called by Theodoric exonerated Symmachus, whereupon Theodoric installed Laurence in the Lateran as Pope. The schism continued for four years when Theodoric ended it by withdrawing his support of Laurence. Symmachus helped the African bishops exiled to Sardinia by the Arian Thrasimund, founded three hospices, aided the victims of the barbarians' raids in northern Italy, helped ransom captives, and was known for his help to the poor. He died on July 19.

SYMPHORIAN (d. c. 306). *See* Castorius.

T

TAKEYA, COSMAS (d. 1597). *See* Miki, Paul.

TARACHUS (c. 239–304). A Roman born at Claudiopolis, Isauria, he became a soldier in the Roman army but left the army when he became a Christian. When he was sixty-five, he was arrested with Andronicus and Probus at Pompeiopolis in Cilicia during the persecution of Christians under Emperors Diocletian and Maximian. They were tried before Numerian Maximus, the governor, subjected to three interrogations (at Tarsus, Mopsuestia, and Anazarbus), and cruelly tortured. They remained steadfast in their faith and were ordered thrown to wild beasts in the arena near Anazarbus; when the beasts did not harm them, gladiators killed them by sword. Probus was a plebeian born at Side in Pamphylia of a Thracian father, and Andronicus was a patrician of Ephesus. October 11.

TARSICIUS (3rd century). An acolyte or perhaps a deacon at Rome, he was accosted and beaten to death on the Appian Way by a mob while carrying the Eucharist to some Christians in prison. The incident is included in Cardinal Wiseman's novel *Fabiola*, and Pope Damasus wrote a poem about it. Tarsicius is the patron of first communicants. August 15.

TARSILLA. *See* Tharsilla under Emiliana.

TASSACH. *See* Asicus (d. 470).

TASSACH (d. c. 495). The first bishop of Raholp, Down, Ireland, and also known as Asicus, he was a skilled artisan and a disciple of St. Patrick, for whom he made croziers, patens, chalices, credences, and crosses for the many churches Patrick founded; Tassach gave the last rites to Patrick when Patrick was dying. April 14.

TATA. *See* Ethelburga (d. c. 647).

TEKAKWITHA, BL. KATERI (c. 1656–80). The daughter of a Christian Algonquin who was captured by Iroquois Indians and married to a pagan Mohawk chieftain, she was born at the Indian village of Osserneon (Auriesville), New York (where two Jesuit priests, St. Isaac Jogues and St. Jean de Lalande, had suffered martyrdom in 1646), and was orphaned as a child when her parents and brother died during an epidemic of smallpox, which left her with seriously impaired eyesight and a disfigured face. She was converted to Catholicism by Fr. Jacques de Lamberville, a Jesuit priest-missionary, in 1676 and was soon subjected to great abuse and ostracism by her relatives and the other Indians for her new religion. Fearful for her life, she fled her native village and trekked some 200 miles through the wilderness to the Christian Indian village of Sault Ste. Marie, near Montreal, Canada, in 1677. She made her First Communion on Christmas of that year, lived a life of great holiness and austerity, and in 1679 took a vow of chastity and dedicated herself to Christ. She died at Caughnawaga, Canada, on April 17, venerated for her holiness and concern for others. She was known as the Lily of the Mohawks, many miracles were attributed to her, and in 1943 she was declared Venerable by Pope Pius XII; she was beatified in 1980 by Pope John Paul II.

TELEMACHUS. *See* Almachius.

TELESPHORUS (d. c. 136). Born in Greece, he succeeded Pope St. Sixtus I as Pope, reigned for ten years, and according to tradition suffered martyrdom under Emperor Hadrian. January 5.

TERESA OF ÁVILA (1515–82). Born at Ávila, Castile, Spain, on March 28, the daughter of Alonso Sanchez de

Cepeda and his second wife, Beatrice Davila y Ahumada, she was educated by Augustinian nuns but was forced to leave their convent at Ávila in 1532 because of ill health. Long attracted to the religious life, she became a Carmelite at Ávila in 1536, was professed the next year, left in 1538 because of illness, but returned in 1540. She experienced visions and heard voices, 1555–56, which caused her great anguish until St. Peter of Alcántara became her spiritual adviser in 1557 and convinced her that they were authentic. Despite bitter opposition, she founded St. Joseph Convent at Ávila in 1562 for nuns who wished to live an enclosed spiritual life rather than the relaxed style so prevalent in convents of that time. In 1567, Fr. Rubeo, prior general of the Carmelites, gave her permission to establish other convents based on the strict rule followed at St. Joseph's; in time she was to found sixteen convents. While establishing her second convent, at Medino del Campo, she met a young friar named John Yepes (John of the Cross), founded her first monastery for men (the first reform Carmelite monastery) at Duruelo in 1568, and then turned the task of founding Carmelite reformed monasteries over to John. She traveled all over Spain, tireless in her struggle to reform the Carmelites, but violent opposition from the calced Carmelites developed, and at a general chapter of the Carmelites at Piacenza in 1575 Fr. Rubeo put strict restrictions on her reforming group. For the next five years a bitter struggle took place within the Carmelites until in 1580, Pope Gregory XIII, at the instigation of King Philip II, recognized the Discalced Reform as a separate province. During these turbulent years, while traveling all over Spain, Teresa wrote letters and books that are widely regarded as classics of spiritual literature, among them her *Autobiography* (1565), *The Way of Perfection* (1573), and *Interior Castle* (1577). One of the great mystics of all times, she was intelligent, hardheaded, charming, deeply spiritual, and successfully blended a highly active life with a life of deep contemplation. She died at Alba de Tormes, Spain, on October 4 (October 14 by the Gregorian calendar, which went into effect the next day and advanced the calendar ten days), and was canonized in 1622 by Pope Gregory XV. She was declared a Doctor of the Church in 1970 by Pope Paul VI—the first woman to be so honored. October 15.

TERESA OF PORTUGAL (d. 1250). Eldest daughter of King Sancho I of Portugal and sister of SS. Mafalda and Sanchia, she married her cousin, King Alfonso IX of León. The couple had several children, but when the marriage was declared invalid because of consanguinity, she returned to Portugal and founded a Benedictine monastery on her estate at Lorvão. She replaced the monks with nuns following the Cistercian rule, expanded the monastery to accommodate three hundred nuns, and lived there. In about 1231, at the request of Alfonso's second wife and widow, Berengaria, she settled a dispute among their children over the succession of the throne of León, and on her return to Lorvão probably became a nun. Her cult, with that of her sister Sanchia, was approved by Pope Clement XI in 1705. June 17.

THADDEUS. See Jude.

THAIS (no date). According to legend, she was raised a Christian but became a famous courtesan in Alexandria, Egypt. She decided to mend her sinful ways when she was visited by the aged St. Paphnutius, destroyed her ill-gotten wealth, and entered a convent selected by Paphnutius, who sealed her up in a cell. After three years of penances, Paphnutius, on the advice of St. Antony and his monks, released her to live with the other women in the convent; she died fifteen days after her release. October 8.

THALELAEUS (d. 284). The son of a Roman general, he was born in Lebanon, became a physician at Anazarbus, where he was called "the Merciful" for his services to the sick poor, and fled to escape the persecution of Christians under Emperor Numerian. Thalelaeus was captured, brought to Aegea, Cilicia (mistakenly called Edessa, Syria, in the Roman Martyrology), and then beheaded when an attempt to drown him failed. Also martyred with him were Alexander and Asterius, two bystanders who may have been the officers in charge of his execution, because of their compassion for him. May 20.

THANEY. See Kentigern.

THARASIUS. See Tarasius.

THARSILLA (d. c. 550). *See* Emiliana.

THENAW (6th century). *See* Kentigern.

THENEVA (6th century). *See* Kentigern.

THEOBALD (1017–66). Son of Count Arnoul of Champagne, he was born at Provins, Brie, France, was raised to be a soldier, but decided he wanted to lead an ascetic life. He left the military life, with his father's permission, and after a time at St. Remi Abbey in Rheims, he and another nobleman named Walter became hermits at Suxy, Ardennes, and in 1135 moved to Pettingen Forest in Luxemburg. They worked as masons and field hands during the day to earn their keep and spent the night in prayer. In quest of greater solitude, they went on pilgrimage to Compostela and Rome and then resumed their eremitical life at Salanigo near Vicenza, Italy; Walter died two years later. Theobald's sanctity attracted numerous disciples, and he was ordained and became a Camaldolese. His fame spread and reached his parents, who came to visit him, and his mother, Gisela, became a hermitess nearby. Theobald died at Salanigo on June 30, and was canonized by Pope Alexander II in 1073.

THEODORA (d. c. 304). There is a pious fiction according to which Theodora, a beautiful Christian girl of Alexandria, was sentenced to a brothel during the persecution of Christians under Emperor Diocletian when she refused to sacrifice to the gods. She fell dead when she was rescued by Didymus; when Didymus' act was discovered, he was beheaded. April 28.

THEODORE (c. 775–c. 841). He and his brother Theophanes (b. c. 778) were born at Kerak, Moab (Transjordan), were brought to Jerusalem in their youth by their parents, and became monks at St. Sabas Monastery there. Theodore was ordained, was sent by the Patriarch of Jerusalem to protest to Emperor Leo the Armenian against the Emperor's persecution of those opposed to his iconoclasm, and was scourged and exiled with Theophanes to an island in the Black Sea. They returned to Constantinople on the death of Leo in 820 but were again banished by Emperor Theophilus in 829. Brought back to Constantinople by the Emperor in 831, they were tortured and had twelve lines of verses cut into their skins for their opposition to iconoclasm. They were then banished to Apamea, Bithynia, where Theodore died. Soon after the death of Theophilus, Theophanes was brought back and later was named bishop of Nicaea, where he was venerated for the suffering he had endured and where he died on October 11, 845. Theophanes wrote poetry, for which he is surnamed "the Poet," and both brothers are called Graptoi (the written-on) because of their branding. December 27.

THEODORE OF CANTERBURY (602–90). Born at Tarsus, Cilicia, he studied at Athens and became a Basilian monk at Rome. When he was sixty-six, he was named archbishop of Canterbury by Pope St. Vitalian in 668 and took possession of his see the following year. He made a visitation of all the churches in England, filled vacancies, restored clerical discipline, opened schools, instituted reforms, and introduced liturgical chant to the English churches. He settled the controversy between St. Wilfrid and St. Chad over the see of York, recognizing Wilfrid as bishop, and was famed for his learning and knowledge of Scripture. He held the first nationwide English Church council at Hertford in 673 where he introduced a new set of ten canons, which among other things set the date of Easter according to the Roman custom and established the diocesan system in England. Another council, at Hatfield in 680, condemned monophysitism while endorsing the decrees of the first five general councils of the Church. In 678, a controversy erupted between Wilfrid of York and King Egfrid of Northumbria, whom Wilfrid had condemned for not allowing his wife to enter a convent, and over the division of the see of York into the dioceses of Hereford, Lindsey, and Worcester without Wilfrid's permission, and for which Egfrid appointed bishops. Wilfrid appealed to Rome, and Pope St. Agatho ruled that the see should remain divided but that Wilfrid should appoint the suffragans. When Egfrid refused to obey the Pope's order and exiled Wilfrid, Theodore evidently made no attempt to prevent Egfrid's action but was later reconciled to Wilfrid. In 679, Theodore acted as peacemaker between King Egfrid and King Ethelred, ending their war and establishing a peace between the two Kings for years. Theodore was the first metropolitan of all England. He changed the Church in England from a missionary body to an organized Church, with Canterbury as its metropolitan see. He died at Canterbury on September 19, universally mourned, after reigning for twenty-two years during which, according to the historian Bede, "the English Church made greater progress during his pontificate than they had ever done before." He is also known as Theodore of Tarsus.

THEODORE OF HERACLEA (no date). A resident of Heraclea in Pontus, he became a general in the army of Emperor Licinius and governor of Pontus and the surrounding area. When it was discovered that he was a Christian, he was tortured and then beheaded by order of Licinius. Theodore is often surnamed Stratelates (general) and is one of the four honored by the Greeks as "a great martyr." February 7.

THEODORE STRATELATES (d. 319). *See* Theodore Tiro.

THEODORE STUDITES (759–826). Born at Constantinople and nephew of Abbot St. Plato of Symboleon on Mount Olympus in Bithynia, he became a novice at a monastery established by his father on his estate at Saccudium near Constantinople, where he was sent to study by Plato, who had become abbot of Saccudium. Theodore was ordained in 787 at Constantinople, returned to Saccudium, and in 794 succeeded Plato as abbot. He and Plato denounced the action of Emperor Constantine VI in leaving his wife and marrying Theodota, and in 796, Theodore and his monks were exiled to Thessalonica. He returned a few months later when Constantine's mother, Irene, seized power, dethroned, and then blinded her son. Theodore reopened Saccudium but moved to Constantinople to escape Saracen raids, was named abbot of the famous Studios Monastery, founded in 463 but now neglected and rundown, built it from a dozen monks to a thousand, and made it the center of Eastern monastic life. He encouraged learning and the arts, founded a school of calligraphy, and wrote a rule for the monastery that was adopted in Russia, Bulgaria, Serbia, and even on Mount Athos. When he opposed the appointment of a layman, Nicephorus, to succeed Tarasius, who had died in 806 as patriarch of Constantinople by Emperor Nicephorus, Theodore was imprisoned by the emperor. When in 809 Nicephorus, the Patriarch, and a synod of bishops reinstated the priest, Joseph,

who had married Constantine and Theodota and declared the
marriage valid, Theodore's denunciations of the decision
caused him to be exiled to Princes' Island with Plato and
Archbishop Joseph of Thessalonica, Theodore's brother, and
the monks of Studios were dispersed. Theodore returned on
the Emperor's death in 811 and was reconciled to Patriarch
Nicephorus in a common fight against the iconoclasm of Emperor Leo V the Armenian. When Nicephorus was banished,
Theodore became the leader of the orthodox and was himself
banished in 813 to Mysia by Leo. When Theodore's correspondence (among it letters to Pope St. Pascal I emphasizing the primacy of the bishop of Rome) was discovered, he
was removed to Bonita in Anatolia. He endured great hardships the three years he was in prison there and then was
transferred to Smyrna and put in the custody of an iconoclast
bishop who wanted him beheaded and treated him with great
harshness. Released on the murder of Leo in 820, he was
again faced with a renewed iconoclasm under Emperor Michael the Stammerer, who refused to restore him as abbot or
to restore any of the orthodox bishops to their sees. Theodore
left Constantinople and visited monasteries in Bithynia,
founded a monastery on Akrita for many of his monks who
had followed him, and died there on November 11. Many of
his letters, treatises, sermons, and hymns are still extant.

THEODORE OF TARSUS. *See* Theodore of Canterbury.

THEODORE TIRO (d. c. 306). A recruit (*tiro*) in the
Roman army at Pontus on the Black Sea, he was brought before his tribune and the governor of the province when he refused to participate in the pagan rites of his comrades in
arms. Temporarily freed, he set fire to the pagan temple of
Cybele near Amasea in Pontus, was brought before his judges
again, and tortured. After a third examination he was condemned to be executed and was burned to death in a furnace.
His cult was enormously popular in the East, and he was one
of the best known of the "warrior saints," though the facts of
his life, beyond that he was martyred, are from unreliable
sources. He may have been the same as Theodore Stratelates
who is also known as Theodore of Heraclea, a general in the
army of Emperor Licinius. Theodore of Heraclea was reported to have been tortured and beheaded at Heraclea,
Thrace, in 319; his feast day is February 7. November 9.

THEODOSIUS PECHERSKY (d. 1074). The son of well-to-do parents, he abandoned their easy way of life, despite their opposition, labored in the fields with the serfs, apprenticed himself to a baker, and in about 1032 became a monk at the Caves of Kiev, founded by Antony Pechersky. Theodosius succeeded Barlaam as abbot and replaced the founding Antony's concept of monasticism based on the drastic austerities of the Egyptian hermits with the more moderate approach of the Palestinian monks, stressed the need for corporal work as well as prayer and mortifications, urged common sense rather than fanatical austerities and penances in their religious life, recommended that his monks participate in secular affairs, and emphasized a harmony between the active and the contemplative life. He expanded the number of buildings at the monastery, established a hospital and a hostel, and with his monks evangelized Kiev. He took part in secular affairs to help and defend the poor, and bitterly denounced Svyastoslav for driving his brother from the throne of Kiev, comparing him to Cain. During the four decades of his abbacy, Theodosius developed the Caves of Kiev into a great monastery, which marked the real beginning of Russian monasticism. His directions to the monks of the Caves of Kiev were to endure for generations. He died in one of the caves of the original monastery, and was canonized by the bishops of Kiev in 1108. With Antony Pechersky, he is the founder of Russian monasticism. July 10.

THEODULUS (d. c. 113). *See* Alexander.

THEOPHANES (d. 817). Born at Constantinople and left a large fortune in his youth when his father died, he was raised at the court of Emperor Constantine V, married, but by mutual agreement he and his wife separated, she to become a nun and he to become a monk. He built monasteries on Mount Sigriana and on the island of Kalonymos; after six years at the latter, he became abbot of Mount Sigriana. He attended the General Council of Nicaea in 787 and when he supported the decrees of the Council approving the veneration of sacred images, he came into conflict with Emperor Leo the Armenian, who supported iconoclasm. When Theophanes refused to accede to the Emperor's demands, he was scourged, imprisoned for two years, and then banished to

Samothrace, where he died on March 12, soon after his arrival, of the ill treatment he had received in prison. He is called "the Chronicler" for his *Chronographia*, a history covering the years 284–813.

THEOPHANES (d. 845). *See* Theodore (d. c. 841).

THEOPHILUS (d. 250). *See* Ammon.

THEOPHILUS (d. 303). *See* Dorothy.

THEOPHILUS THE PENITENT (no date). A tenth-century Latin play by Hrosvitha of Gandesheim depicts Theophilus as administrator of Adan, Cilicia, who declined a bishopric because of his humility. He was deposed of his office in the Church by the man who became bishop and was so furious that he made a pact with Satan, who had him restored to his position. He later repented, appealed to our Lady, found the pact he had signed with Satan on his chest when he awoke one morning, did penance for his deed, made a public confession of his sin, and had the bishop burn the pact before the congregation. Theophilus is a legendary figure often listed as a saint on February 4 and is the precursor of the Faust theme.

THÉRÈSE OF LISIEUX (1873–97). Marie Françoise Martin was born at Alençon, France, on January 2, the youngest of the nine children of Louis Martin, a watchmaker, and Zélie Guérin. Her mother died when she was five, and the family moved to Lisieux, where she was raised by her older sisters and an aunt. Two of her sisters became Carmelite nuns, and she resolved to emulate them. She was refused admission at first but a year later was admitted to the Carmel at Lisieux. She was professed in 1890, taking the name Thérèse of the Child Jesus. Afflicted with tuberculosis, she bore her illness with great patience and fortitude, devoting herself to prayer and meditation and serving for a time as mistress of novices. By order of the prioress, Mother Agnes (her sister Pauline), she began in 1894 to write the story of her childhood, and in 1897, after finishing it the previous year, she was ordered by the new prioress, Mother Marie de Gonzague, to tell of her life in the convent. Both were combined into *The Story of a Soul*, which became one of the most widely read modern spiritual autobiographies. She died of tuberculosis on September 30 at Lisieux, quickly attracted a tremendous following as "the Little Flower" and "the saint of the little way," and was canonized in 1925 by Pope Pius XI. She was declared copatron of the missions, with St. Francis Xavier, in 1927, is the patroness of aviators, and in 1944 was named copatroness of France with Joan of Arc. October 1.

THIBAUD. The French spelling of Theobald.

THOMAS (1st century). Born probably in Galilee and surnamed Didymus (the twin), he became one of the twelve apostles, though where and when are uncertain. He was one of those with Jesus at the raising of Lazarus from the dead, but is best known for the incident in John 20:24–29 when he refused to believe that Christ had appeared to the apostles, saying he would do so only if he could "see the holes that the nails made in his hands and can put my finger into the holes they made, and . . . put my hand into his side . . . ," giving rise to the expression "doubting Thomas." When Christ appeared to him, he exclaimed, "My Lord and my God," thus becoming the first to acknowledge explicitly the divinity of Christ. He was also one of the group fishing to whom Jesus appeared in John 21. According to Eusebius, Thomas later preached in Parthia, and an ancient tradition has him bringing the gospel to India, where he was martyred and buried at Mylapore near Madras. He is the patron saint of architects and was declared the apostle of India by Pope Paul VI in 1972. July 3.

THOMAS AQUINAS (c. 1225–74). Born at the family castle of Roccasecca near Aquino, Italy, the son of Count Landulf of Aquino, a relative of the Emperor and of the King of France, and Theodora, he was sent to nearby Benedictine Monte Cassino Monastery as an oblate when he was five years old to be educated. In about 1239 he went to the University of Naples to finish his education and joined the Dominicans there in 1244, a move so strongly opposed by his family that they kidnaped him and held him captive at Roccasecca Castle for fifteen months in an attempt to deter him from the Dominicans. He persisted, rejoined the Order in 1245, and studied at Paris, 1245–48. He accompanied Albertus Magnus to a new Dominican *studium generale* at Co-

logne in 1248, was ordained there sometime in 1250–51, and
in 1252 returned to Paris as *sententarius*, lecturing on the
Sentences of Peter Lombard. He was master of theology at
Paris in 1256 and taught at Naples, Anagni, Orvieto, Rome,
and Viterbo, 1259–68, finishing his *Summa contra Gentiles*
and beginning his *Summa theologiae* during those years. He
returned to Paris in 1269, became involved in the struggle between the Order priests and the seculars, and opposed the
philosophical teachings of Siger of Brabant, John Peckham,
and Bishop Stephen Tempier of Paris. When dissension
racked the university in 1272, he was sent as regent to head a
new Dominican house of studies at Naples. He was appointed
to attend the General Council of Lyons, called to discuss the
reunion of the Greek and Latin churches by Pope Gregory X
in 1274, but died on the way to Lyons at the Cistercian abbey
of Fossa Nuova near Terracina, Italy, on March 7. He was
canonized by Pope John XXII in 1323, was declared a Doctor of the Church by Pope St. Pius V in 1567, and was
named patron of all universities, colleges, and schools in 1880
by Pope Leo XIII, whose bull *Aeterni Patris* required all
theological students to study his thought; the substance of his
work became the official teaching of the Catholic Church.
Aquinas was probably the greatest theological master of
Christianity, and his thought dominated Catholic teaching for
seven centuries after his death. His writings were voluminous,
characterized by his sharp distinction between faith and reason, but emphasizing that the great fundamental Christian
doctrines, though impossible to establish by reason, are not
contrary to reason and reach us by revelation; nevertheless,
he believed that such truths as the existence of God, his eter-
nity, his creative power, and his providence can be discovered
by natural reason. His *magnum opus*, the unfinished *Summa
theologiae*, is probably the greatest exposition of theological
thought ever written and became the accepted basis for modern Catholic theology. Among his other writings are *Quaestiones disputatae, Quaestiones quodlibetales, Summa contra
Gentiles, De unitate intellectus contra Averroistas*, and his
commentaries on the *Sentences* of Peter Lombard, on
Boethius, on Dionysius, and on Aristotle. In addition to his
towering intellect, Aquinas was a man of great humility and
holiness. He experienced visions, ecstasies, and revelations
(he left *Summa theologiae* unfinished because of a revelation he experienced while saying Mass in 1273), composed

the office for the feast of Corpus Christi, and wrote hymns still used in Church services, notably *Pange lingua, Verbum supernum, Lauda Sion,* and *Adoro te devote.* He wrote commentaries on the Lord's Prayer, the Apostles' Creed, and parts of the Bible. In him the Middle Ages reached its full flowering and Christianity received its most towering and influential intellect. January 28.

THOMAS BECKET (1118–70). Son of Gilbert, sheriff of London, and Matilda, both of Norman descent, he was born on December 21 in London, studied at Merton Priory in Surrey and law in London, and continued his studies at the University of Paris. His father's death left him in straitened circumstances, and in about 1141 he joined the household of Archbishop Theobold of Canterbury, who sent him on several missions to Rome and in 1144 to Bologna and Auxerre to study canon law. He was ordained deacon in 1154 and then became archdeacon of Canterbury when nominated by Theobold. Thomas became a favorite of Henry of Anjou when he convinced Pope Eugene III not to recognize the succession of King Stephen of Blois' son, Eustace, thus ensuring Henry's right to the English throne as Henry II. Thomas was appointed chancellor of England by Henry in 1155, soon became the most powerful man in England next to Henry, and was famed for the luxury and magnificence of his style of life. He accompanied Henry on his military expedition to Toulouse in 1159 at the head of his own troops. On the death of Theobold in 1161, Henry nominated Thomas as archbishop of Canterbury, and despite Becket's vigorous objections, he was elected in 1162. He resigned his chancellorship, was ordained a priest the day before his consecration, and became archbishop. He changed his life completely, lived a life of great austerity, and soon clashed with the King over clerical and Church rights. In 1164, Thomas refused to accept the Constitutions of Clarendon, which among other things denied clerics the right to be tried in ecclesiastical courts and to appeal to Rome, and he was forced to flee to France. He appealed to Pope Alexander III, then at Sens, but the Pope, not wishing to offend Henry, would not support Thomas. When Henry and Thomas both remained adamant, Thomas, at Alexander's suggestion, entered the Cistercian abbey at Pontigny. When Henry threatened to expel all Cistercians from his realm in 1166, Thomas moved to St. Columba

Abbey near Sens, which was under the protection of King Louis VII of France. Through the efforts of Louis, Henry and Thomas patched up a peace in Normandy in 1170, and Thomas returned to England. But warfare between the two soon broke out again when Becket refused to lift the excommunication of the archbishop of York and those bishops who had participated at the coronation of Henry's son, a flagrant infringement of the rights of the archbishop of Canterbury, unless they swore obedience to the Pope. Henry reacted violently and in a fit of rage said aloud in public that he wished he was rid of this troublesome prelate, though it is most doubtful that he really meant it. Four of his knights took him at his word and on December 29 murdered the archbishop in his cathedral. The act shocked all of Europe. Thomas was at once proclaimed a martyr, and in 1173 Pope Alexander III declared him a saint. The following year Henry did public penance, and the shrine of St. Thomas became one of the most popular pilgrimage centers in Europe. December 29.

THOMAS CANTELUPE (c. 1218–82). Of a distinguished Norman family, and son of Baron William of Cantelupe, steward of King Henry III's household, he was born at Hambleden, England, and was educated by his uncle, Bishop Walter of Worcester, at Oxford, and at Paris. Thomas was with his father at the General Council of Lyons in 1245 and was probably ordained then. After studying law at Orléans and Paris, he became a lecturer in canon law at Oxford and in 1262 was named chancellor. He supported the barons against King Henry III, was one of three delegates to plead their cause to King St. Louis at Amiens in 1264, and when Henry was defeated at Lewes was named chancellor of England in 1265. He filled the office with great integrity and justice, but on the death of Simon de Montfort in 1265, he was dismissed and retired to Paris. He was again named chancellor of Oxford in 1274, and the following year became bishop of Hereford. He restored the fortunes of the see, recovered the rights that had been infringed on by the lords of the area, and ruled his see with great prudence and ability. Though the holder of many benefices (with the permission of Pope Innocent IV), he carefully supervised the administration of his benefices, a rare concern of those holding plural benefices in those times. The last years of his life were saddened by a jurisdictional dispute with Archbishop John Peckham of Canterbury. Thomas was the leader of the bishops opposing Peckham at the Council of Reading in 1279 and was excommunicated by the archbishop in 1282. He went to Orvieto to appeal his case personally to Pope Martin IV, but worn out by the trip, died at nearby Montefiascone on August 25 and was buried at Orvieto. When his body was returned to Hereford and enshrined in the cathedral, hundreds of miracles were reported, and it became a popular pilgrimage center. He was canonized by Pope John XXII in 1320. He is also known as Thomas of Hereford. October 3.

THOMAS OF HEREFORD. *See* Thomas Cantelupe.

THOMAS OF VILLANOVA (1488–1555). Son of Alonzo Tomás García and Lucía Martínez Castellanos, he was born at Fuentellana, Castile, Spain, near the birthplace of his parents, Villanueva de los Infantes (hence his surname), spent ten years at the University of Alcalá, where he received his masters in art and his licentiate in theology, and became a professor there when he was only twenty-six. He declined the chair of philosophy at Salamanca and joined the Augustinians there in 1516. He was ordained in 1518, served as prior of several houses, was named provincial of Andalusia and Castile in 1527, and was provincial of Castile in 1533, whence he sent the first Augustinian missionaries to America (to Mexico). He became chaplain to Emperor Charles V, refused the see of Granada, but in 1544 was appointed archbishop of Valencia by the Emperor. The see had been vacant for ninety years, but he soon reformed the diocese. He was noted for the austerity and poverty of his life, was known for his generosity to the poor and the needy, labored among the Moors, and gave funds for priests to be especially trained for this work, founding a college for the children of new converts and another for poor students. He did not attend the Council of Trent but was active in influencing the Spanish bishops to promote reform in the Church in Spain. He died at Valencia on September 8, and was canonized in 1658. September 22.

THORLAC THORHALLSSON (1133–93). Born in Iceland, he became a deacon when he was fifteen and was ordained when he was eighteen. He was sent abroad to study, reportedly visited London, and returned to Iceland in 1161.

He founded a monastery at Thykkviboer, became its abbot, and in 1178 was named bishop of Skalholt, one of the two dioceses of Iceland. He reformed the see, insisted on clerical discipline and celibacy, abolished lay patronage, and fought simony. He planned to resign and retire to Thykkviboer, but he died on December 23 before he could do so. He was canonized by the Iceland Althing five years later, but his cult has never been formally approved by the Holy See.

THWING, JOHN (1319–79). Born at Thwing near Bridlington, Yorkshire, England, he went to Oxford when he was seventeen and two years later became a Canon Regular of St. Augustine in his native town. He filled various offices in the monastery there and in time was elected prior, a position he held for seventeen years until his death there on October 10. He was canonized by Pope Boniface IX as John of Bridlington in 1401 and is patron of women in difficult labor. October 21.

TIBURTIUS (date unknown). *See* Cecilia.

TIGRIS (5th century). One of five sisters of St. Patrick, she married Gollit, and the two had five sons, all of whom became bishops. Where and when she died are uncertain.

TIMOTHY (d. c. 97). Born at Lystra, Lycaenia, he was the son of a Greek father and Eunice, a converted Jewess. He joined St. Paul when Paul preached at Lystra, replacing Barnabas, and became Paul's close friend and confidant. Paul allowed him to be circumcised to placate the Jews, since he was the son of a Jewess, and he then accompanied Paul on his second missionary journey. When Paul was forced to flee Berea because of the enmity of the Jews there, Timothy remained but after a time was sent to Thessalonica to report on the condition of the Christians there and to encourage them under persecution, a report that led to Paul's first letter to the Thessalonians when he rejoined Timothy at Corinth. Timothy and Erastus were sent to Macedonia in 58, went to Corinth to remind the Corinthians of Paul's teaching, and then accompanied Paul into Macedonia and Achaia. Timothy was probably with Paul when the apostle was imprisoned at Caesarea and then Rome, and was himself imprisoned but then freed. According to tradition, he went to Ephesus, became its first bishop, and was stoned to death there when he opposed the pagan festival of Katagogian in honor of Diana. Paul wrote two letters to Timothy, one written about 65 from Macedonia and the second from Rome while he was in prison awaiting execution. January 25.

TITUS (1st century). Converted by St. Paul, he became his secretary and accompanied him to the Council of Jerusalem, where Paul refused to allow him to be circumcised. Paul sent him to Corinth to correct errors and settle dissensions that had arisen there and again later to collect alms for the poor Christians of Jerusalem. He was ordained bishop of Crete by Paul, to carry on Paul's work, met Paul at Nicopolis in Epirus, and was the recipient of a letter from Paul written from Macedonia in about 65 giving him instructions on spiritual matters, advising him on the qualities needed by a good bishop, the need to maintain strict discipline among the Cretans, and telling him to establish presbyters in all the cities of Crete. He visited Dalmatia and then returned to Crete, where he probably died at an advanced age. He is represented in the Acts of Titus, supposedly written by Zenas the lawyer (who is mentioned in Titus 3:13), as having been born of royal descent on Crete and went to Judea when he was twenty in response to a heavenly command and to have lived on Crete until he died there when in his nineties, but these Acts are considered a work of fiction by scholars. Other equally untrustworthy sources have him born at Iconium and at Corinth. January 26.

✳ **TORQUATUS** (1st century). According to legend, he was one of the first seven missionaries sent out by Peter and Paul to evangelize Spain. The others were Caecilius at Granada, Ctesiphon at Verga, Euphrasius at Andujar, Hesychius at Gibraltas, Indaletius at Urci near Almeria, and Secundius at Avila. Torquatus worked with great success at Guadix, Granada. Apparently all seven were martyrs, Torquatus at Cadiz. May 15.

TOTNAN (d. c. 689). *See* Kilian.

TROPHIMUS (1st century). A Gentile from Ephesus, he accompanied St. Paul on his third missionary journey (Acts 20:4) and to Jerusalem, where his presence in the Temple provoked violent protests against Paul that almost resulted in Paul's death (Acts 21:26–36). The only other mention of Trophimus is in 2 Timothy 4:20, in which Paul says he "left Trophimus ill at Miletus." He is often confused with Trophimus, the first bishop of Arles. December 29.

TURIBIUS. *See* Mogrobejo, Toribio Alfonso de.

U

UGOCCIONE, RICOVERO (1206–82). *See* Monaldo, Buonfiglio.

ULRIC (890–973). Born at Augsburg, Germany, he was educated at St. Gall Abbey in Switzerland and by his uncle, St. Adalbeo, bishop of Augsburg. Ulric succeeded to the see as bishop in 923, and when Augsburg was plundered and ravaged by the Magyars, he led its inhabitants in the task of rebuilding the city and its cathedral. In his old age, he retired to St. Gall, named his nephew as his successor, and was accused of nepotism for his action. His canonization by Pope John XV in 993 is the first recorded canonization by a Pope. July 4.

ULTAN (d. 686). Brother of SS. Fursey and Foillan and like them an Irish monk, he went to East Anglia, founded Burgh Castle Monastery near Yarmouth but left and went to France to escape raiding Mercians. He built and became abbot of Fosses Monastery on land given him by St. Ita and St. Gertrude and then became abbot of a monastery at Péronne, where he died. May 2.

URBAN I (d. c. 230). Son of Pontianus, he was born at Rome and was elected Pope in about 222, succeeding Pope St. Callistus I, and ruled during a relatively peaceful period of the early Church. He died at Rome on May 23 and was buried there on May 25, which is celebrated as his feast day.

URBAN II, BL. (c. 1042–99). Of a noble family, Odo of Lagery was born at Châtillons-sur-Marne, Champagne, France, studied under St. Bruno at Rheims, became archdeacon there, and in about 1070 became a Benedictine monk at Cluny. He was named prior by St. Hugh, was sent to Rome to assist Pope Gregory VII's reform of the Church, became his chief adviser, and was named cardinal-bishop of Ostia in 1078. He was legate to Germany, 1082–85, was briefly imprisoned there by Emperor Henry IV, and on March 12, 1088, he was elected Pope to succeed Pope Bl. Victor III and took the name Urban II. He was faced by antipope Clement III, who held Rome and whom he had anathematized at the Synod of Quedlinburg in Saxony he had held in 1085 and who was supported by Emperor Henry IV. Urban held a synod at Melfi in 1089 that decreed against lay investiture, simony, and clerical marriages, but it was not until 1094 that he was able to sit on the papal throne in Rome. In 1095, he summoned a council at Clermont-Ferrand, France, at which the Gregorian decrees requiring clerical celibacy and denouncing lay investiture and simony were reiterated and "the Truce of God" was proclaimed a law of the Church. It also anathematized King Philip I of France for putting aside his wife, Bertha, and marrying Bertrada, wife of the count of Anjou, and as the result of a request from Eastern Emperor Alexis I, Urban preached the First Crusade. His appeal was greeted with tremendous enthusiasm; launched in 1097, the crusade led to the capture of Jerusalem in 1099. When Emperor Henry IV left Italy in 1097 and the party of antipope Clement III (Guibert) left Rome the following year, Urban was finally triumphant over his most persistent opponents. He called a council at Bari in 1098 that was unsuccessful in an attempt to effect a reconciliation between Rome and Constantinople. His entire pontificate was marked by conflicts with secular rulers, especially Emperor Henry IV; Urban excommunicated Henry, King Philip I of France, and would have excommunicated William Rufus of England except for the intercession of St. Anselm. Urban died at Rome on July 29, and was beatified by Pope Leo XIII in 1881.

URBAN V, BL. (1310–70). Of a noble family, William de Grimoard was born at Grisac, Languedoc, France, became a Benedictine monk at Chirac, studied at Montpellier, Toulouse, Paris, and Avignon, and was ordained and received his doctorate. He taught canon law at Montpellier and Avignon and served as vicar general at Clermont and Uzès. He was appointed abbot of St. Germanus at Auxerre by Pope Clement VI in 1352 and served on several diplomatic missions to Italy.

Pope Innocent VI appointed him abbot of St. Victor's in Marseilles in 1361 and legate to Queen Joanna of Naples. While there he was elected Pope to succeed Innocent VI on September 28, 1362, and took the name Urban V. He at once began to reform the Church, made peace with Barnabo Visconti in 1364, was unsuccessful in attempts to suppress the *condottieri* (marauding bands of soldiers) in France and Italy, and though Peter de Lusignan temporarily occupied Alexandria in 1365, his crusade against the Turks did not succeed. At the urging of Emperor Charles IV, he returned the papacy to Rome from Avignon (where it had been for half a century), despite the opposition of the French court and cardinals, when Cardinal Albornoz reconquered the Papal States in 1367. Urban worked to restore the rundown city, restore clerical discipline, and revive religion. In 1368, he crowned Emperor Charles IV's consort German Empress, and Charles agreed to respect Church rights in Germany. The following year Urban received Greek Emperor John V Palaeologus back into the Church, but the Emperor was unable to bring his people with him into the Church. When Perugia revolted and unrest beset Italy and war broke out between England and France in the same year, he decided to return to Avignon despite the prediction of St. Bridget that he would die an early death if he left Rome. He died at Avignon on December 19, three months after he left Rome. His cult was approved by Pope Pius IX in 1870.

URSULA (date unknown). According to a legend that appeared in the tenth century, Ursula was the daughter of a Christian King in Britain and was granted a three-year postponement of a marriage she did not wish to a pagan prince. With ten ladies in waiting, each attended by a thousand maidens, she embarked on a voyage across the North Sea, sailed up the Rhine to Basle, Switzerland, and then went to Rome. On their way back they were all massacred by pagan Huns at Cologne in about 451 when Ursula refused to marry their chieftain. According to another legend, Amorica was settled by British colonizers and soldiers after Emperor Magnus Clemens Maximus conquered Britain and Gaul in 383. The ruler of the settlers, Cynan Meiriadog, called on King Dionotus of Cornwall for wives for the settlers, whereupon Dionotus sent his daughter Ursula, who was to marry Cynan, with eleven thousand noble maidens and sixty thousand common women. Their fleet was shipwrecked and all the women were enslaved or murdered. The legends are pious fictions, but what is true is that one Clematius, a senator, rebuilt a basilica in Cologne that had originally been built, probably at the beginning of the fourth century, to honor a group of virgins who had been martyred at Cologne. They were evidently venerated enough to have had a church built in their honor, but who they were and how many of them there were are unknown. From these meager facts, the legend of Ursula grew and developed. October 21.

URSULINA (1375–1410). Born at Parma, Italy, she experienced visions and ecstasies, and when fifteen, in response to a supernatural voice's direction, went to Avignon in an unsuccessful attempt to convince antipope Clement VII to give up his claim to the papal throne. She next went to Rome to ask Pope Boniface IX to resign and then returned to Avignon in another unsuccessful attempt to persuade Clement to resign. After a pilgrimage to Rome and the Holy Land, she returned to Parma, where she was expelled from the city during a civil war there. After a time at Bologna, she went to Verona, where she died. April 7.

URSUS (d. c. 287). *See* Maurice.

USTHAZANES (d. 341). *See* Simeon Barsabae.

V

VACLAV. *See* Wenceslaus.

VALENTINE (d. c. 269). A priest in Rome and a physician, he was beheaded there under Claudius the Goth on February 14 and buried on the Flaminian Way, where a basilica was erected in 350. On the same day in the Roman Martyrology is celebrated another Valentine who was bishop of Interamna (Terni) about sixty miles from Rome and who was scourged, imprisoned, and then beheaded there by order of Placidus, prefect of Interamna. Many scholars believe that the two are the same, and it is suggested that the bishop of Interamna had been a Roman priest who became bishop and was sentenced there and brought to Rome for his execution. The custom of sending Valentines on February 14 stems from a medieval belief that birds began to pair on that day.

VALERIAN (date unknown). *See* Cecilia.

VAUDRU. Otherwise Waudru, q.v.

VECHEL, LEONARD (d. 1572). Born in Bois-le-Duc, Holland, he studied at Louvain, was ordained, became parish priest at Gorkum, and was active in his opposition to Calvinism. He and his assistant Nicholas Jannsen Poppel of Welde, Belgium, were among those seized by a Calvinist mob when the Calvinists captured Gorkum. Also arrested at the same time was Godefried Van Duynsen, who was a native of Gorkum and a priest there. They were sent to Briel, Holland, and then hanged with sixteen other Catholics. They were all canonized as the Martyrs of Gorkum in 1867. July 9.

VENANTIUS FORTUNATUS (c. 535–c. 605). Venantius

Honorius Clementianus Fortunatus was born near Treviso, Italy, was educated at Ravenna, and in 565 went to Germany. For some twenty years (567–87) he lived at Poitiers, where he was ordained and became adviser and secretary of King Clotaire I's wife, Radegund, and her adopted daughter at their convent there. In about 600 Venantius was appointed bishop of Poitiers, where he died. A fluent versifier, he wrote voluminously. Among his works were metrical lives of St. Martin de Tours, Hilary of Poitiers, Germanus of Paris, Radegund, and other religious figures; poems on a trip on the Moselle, on church construction, and on the marriage of King Sigebert and Brunehilde in 566; elegies on the deaths of Brunehilde's sister, Queen Galeswintha, and Radegund's cousin, Amalafried; and several outstanding hymns, notably *Pange Lingua gloriosi* and *Vexilla Regis*. His poems revealed much valuable information about his times, Merovingian figures and customs, family life, descriptions of buildings, works of art, and the status of women. December 14.

VÉNARD, BL. THEOPHANE (1829–61). Born on November 21 at Poitiers, France, he studied at the college of Doué and the seminaries at Montmorillon and Poitiers, where he was ordained a subdeacon in 1850. He entered the Society of Foreign Missions in Paris the following year, was ordained in 1852, and was sent to Hong Kong later the same year. He remained there until he was sent as a missionary to West Tonkin (Vietnam) in 1854. He was captured during an outbreak of persecution of Christians in 1860, chained in a tiny cage for months, and on February 2 was beheaded at Ke Cho. He was beatified in 1900.

VENTURA (d. 1597). *See* Miki, Paul.

VERONICA (1st century). According to legend, when Christ was carrying his cross to Calvary an unknown woman offered him a cloth to wipe his brow, and when he returned it to her it bore the imprint of his face. In time she came to be known as Veronica (Vera—true; icon—image). Her fate after this incident is told in several different legends. In one she came to Rome and cured Emperor Tiberius with her relic; on her death she bequeathed it to Pope St. Clement. In another she is the wife of Zacchaeus (the tax collector in the sycamore tree in Luke 19:1–10), accompanied him to France, where he was known as Amadour, and helped convert the inhabitants of southern France. And in the apocryphal *The Arts of Pilate*, she is identified with the woman Jesus cured of a hemorrhage she had suffered for twelve years (Matt. 9:20–22). In truth there is no factual information about her. July 12.

VEUSTER, VEN. JOSEPH DE (1840–89). Born at Tremeloo, Belgium, on January 3, he studied at the College of Braine-le-Comte, and in 1860 joined the Fathers of the Sacred Hearts of Jesus and Mary (the Picpus Fathers), taking the name Damien. At his request he was sent as a missionary to Hawaii in 1864, was ordained the same year in Honolulu, and spent the next nine years working to evangelize the peoples of Puno and Kohala. In 1873, again at his request, he was sent to the leper colony at Molokai and spent the rest of his life ministering to the lepers. He contracted the dread disease himself in 1885 but continued to live and work with and aid the lepers until his death on Molokai on April 15. Though he was often slandered during his lifetime, his holiness and dedication were quickly recognized after his death (Robert Louis Stevenson wrote an impassioned defense of his character in 1905), and he was declared Venerable by Pope Paul VI in 1977.

VIALAR, EMILY DE (1797–1856). Daughter of Baron James de Vialar and Antoinette de Portal, she was born at Gaillac, Languedoc, France, studied at Paris, and became estranged from her father when, on the death of her mother when she was fifteen, she refused to marry. He was further antagonized when she began to teach abandoned and poor children and to treat and help the sick and the destitute at his house. When her grandmother died and left her a fortune in 1832, she bought a house at Gaillac and with the help of her spiritual director, Abbé Mercier, began with several companions, a congregation that was formally approved by Archbishop de Gauly of Albi as the Congregation of the Sisters of St. Joseph of the Apparition in 1835, dedicated to the care of the sick and needy and the education of young children in France and abroad. She traveled constantly, and the congregation soon spread all over the Near East—Algiers, Tunis,

Malta, Jerusalem, and the Balkans. A jurisdictional dispute with Bishop Dupuch, bishop of Algiers, though decided in her favor, forced the closing of the house in Algiers. On her return to Gaillac in 1845 she found the organization in chaos and its existence threatened by lawsuits, quarrels among the nuns, and financial instability. She moved the mother house to Toulouse (and in 1854 to Marseilles), and by the time of Emily's death on August 14, there were some forty houses all over the world, from Europe to Burma to Australia. She was canonized in 1951. June 17.

VIANNEY, JOHN BAPTIST (1786–1859). Born at Dardilly, France, on May 8, he was a shepherd on his father's farm as a boy, was early attracted to the priesthood, and when twenty began his studies at Ecully, under Abbé Balley, encountering great difficulties with his studies, especially Latin. Though an ecclesiastical student, through an error he was drafted into the army in 1809 but deserted. He was able to return home when Napoleon granted amnesty to all deserters in 1810, and the following year was tonsured and went to the major seminary at Lyons in 1813. Beset by difficulties with his studies, he was finally ordained in 1815 through the intercession of Abbé Balley and the decision that his goodness was sufficient to offset his deficiencies in learning. He spent the next years as curate to Abbé Balley at Ecully until the abbé died in 1817; early in 1818 was appointed curé of Ars, where he spent the rest of his life. He labored to improve the indifferent religious attitude of his parishioners, and his war on immorality, indifference, and frivolities was unceasing, making him some enemies, but all charges against him were disproved. Eventually he was to reform the entire village. At his encouragement Catherine Lassagne and Benedicta Lardet in 1824 opened a free school for girls that three years later developed into La Providence, a shelter for orphans and deserted children. His reputation as a spiritual director and confessor (he often spent sixteen to eighteen hours a day in the confessional) spread, and a shrine he built to St. Philomena became a place of pilgrimage. Though he had the gift of insight into men's minds and souls, he was often referred to scornfully for his lack of learning and rejected for higher positions by his superiors. Even more trying were the continuing diabolical attacks he was subjected to over a thirty-year period. Attracted all his life to the Carthusians, he left Ars three times in search of solitude but returned each time to aid the sinners who sought him in ever-increasing numbers. He refused all honors offered him late in life and died at Ars on August 4, venerated as the beloved "curé of Ars." He was canonized in 1925 by Pope Pius XI, who made him patron of parish priests in 1929.

VICTOR I (d. c. 199). A native of Africa, he succeeded Pope St. Eleutherius as Pope in about 189. During his pontificate Victor was embroiled in a dispute with a group of Christians from the province of Asia in Rome who celebrated Easter on a date of their choosing, and he was also faced with the arrival of Theodotus from Constantinople and his teaching that Christ was only a man endowed with supernatural powers by the Holy Spirit. July 28.

VICTOR (d. c. 287). *See* Maurice.

VICTOR III (c. 1027–87). Only son of Duke Dauferius Benevento, Daufar was born at Benevento, Italy, resisted his father's efforts to have him marry, and when his father was killed in battle in 1047, he became a hermit. He was forced to return home by his family but escaped a year later, entered La Cava Monastery, and then, at the insistence of his family, transferred to St. Sophia Abbey at Benevento, where he was given the name Desiderius. He then spent several years wandering about—a time at an island monastery, a period studying medicine at Salerno, a time as a hermit in the Abruzzi—helped to negotiate a peace with the Normans for Pope Leo IX in 1053, and the following year joined the court of Victor II in Florence in 1054. Later the same year he joined the Benedictines at Monte Cassino, was elected abbot-designate in 1057, and was on his way to Constantinople as papal legate when Pope St. Stephen, who had retained the abbacy of Monte Cassino after he was elected Pope, died, and he was installed as abbot on Easter in 1058. He rebuilt Monte Cassino and developed it into one of the great centers of learning and culture in Europe, noted for the strict rule of its monks and the magnificence of its buildings and the art there. He became papal vicar for Campania, Apulia, Calabria, and Capua, served on diplomatic missions to the Normans for Pope St.

Gregory VII, attempted to effect a reconciliation between Emperor Henry IV and Gregory in 1083, and was known as a firm upholder of papal rights. Despite his attempt to flee the honor, he was elected Pope to succeed Gregory and was forcibly vested on May 24, 1086, with the name Victor III. Four days later he was forced to flee to Monte Cassino from the imperial prefect and was not consecrated until May 9, 1087, at which time Guibert of Ravenna (antipope Clement III), who had been occupying the city, was temporarily driven out by Norman troops. Victor returned to Monte Cassino but came back to Rome a few weeks later, only to be forced to leave again when the forces of Countess Matilda of Tuscany attacked those of Guibert but were unsuccessful in their attempt to drive the antipope from the city. Stricken while presiding at a synod at Benevento, where he renewed the excommunication of Guibert, he returned, dying, to Monte Cassino, where he died on September 16 after a reign of only four months. His cult was approved by Pope Leo XIII in 1887.

VICTOR OF MARSEILLES (d. c. 290). According to legend, he was a soldier in the Roman army at Marseilles when he was haled before the prefects, Asterius and Eutychius, who sent him to Emperor Maximian for his exhortations to Christians to be firm in their faith in the face of an impending visit by the Emperor. He was dragged through the streets, racked, imprisoned (he converted three guards, Alexander, Felician, and Longinus while in prison), was again tortured after the guards were beheaded when it was discovered he had converted them to Christianity, and when he refused to offer incense to Jupiter, he was crushed in a millstone and beheaded. His tomb became one of the most popular pilgrimage centers in Gaul. July 21.

VIGRI, CATHERINE DE' (1413–63). Daughter of a lawyer and diplomat for Marquis Nicholas d'Este of Ferrara, she became Margaret d'Este's maid of honor and companion at eleven, left the court on the death of her father, and became a Franciscan tertiary at Ferrara with a group of women living a semimonastic life; they later became Poor Clares. She soon began to experience visions of Christ and Satan, and wrote of her experiences, one of which occurred one Christmas. It was a vision of Mary with the infant Jesus in her arms, a vision reproduced often in art since. Through her efforts the monastery in Ferrara received papal approval to be enclosed, but she left to become prioress of the new Poor Clares' Corpus Christi Convent in Bologna. The convent became famous for the sanctity and supernatural gifts of Catherine. She died there on March 9, was canonized in 1712, and is the patron of artists. She is also known as Catherine of Bologna.

VINCENT (d. 258). *See* Sixtus II.

VINCENT FERRER (1350–1419). Born at Valencia, Spain, on January 23, the son of William Ferrer and Constantia Miguel, both of noble families, he was educated at Valencia and joined the Dominicans in 1367. He was sent to Barcelona for further studies, taught philosophy at Lerida when twenty-one, and then returned to Barcelona in 1373. Three years later he continued his education at Toulouse, and in 1379 he became a member of Pedro Cardinal de Luna's court, the beginning of a long friendship that was to end in grief for both of them (De Luna had voted for Pope Urban VI in 1378, but convinced the election had been invalid, joined a group of cardinals who elected Robert of Geneva Pope as Clement VII later in the same year, thus creating a schism and the line of Avignon Popes). De Luna was elected to succeed antipope Clement VII in 1394 and became known in history as antipope Benedict XIII. Vincent was convinced of the legitimacy of the Avignon Popes and was their ardent champion. He taught at the cathedral in Valencia, 1385–90, was confessor to Queen Yolanda of Aragon, 1391–95, and was cited for heresy to the Inquisition for teaching that Judas had done penance. The charge was dismissed by the newly elected antipope Benedict XIII, who brought him to his papal court and made him his confessor and apostolic penitentiary. Vincent refused a cardinalate from the antipope and after recovering from a serious illness in 1398, during which he had a vision of Christ accompanied by SS. Dominic and Francis directing him to preach penance, he devoted himself to preaching. Released by Benedict to do so, he began preaching in 1399, and in the next two decades he traveled all over western Europe preaching penance for sin and preparation for the Last Judgment, attracting enormous crowds wherever he went and followed by thousands of disciples; among his converts were Bernadine of Siena and Margaret of Savoy. So successful was he in preaching in different countries, though he only knew his own language, that many believed he had the gift of tongues. In 1408, while ministering to the plague-stricken of Genoa, he tried and failed to persuade Benedict to withdraw his claims to the papacy so Christendom might be united under one Pope. Vincent then went to Spain, where his preaching was as phenomenally successful as it had been in other parts of Europe, making converts by the tens of thousands, including thousands of Jews and Moors. He was one of the judges of the Compromise of Caspe to resolve the royal succession and was instrumental in electing Ferdinand King of Castile. Still a friend of Benedict, he again begged him to resign after the Council of Constance had deposed a third claimant to the throne, antipope John XXIII, and demanded that the other two resign. When Benedict refused, he advised Ferdinand in 1416 to withdraw his allegiance to Avignon; when Ferdinand did so, Benedict was deposed, and the great Western Schism ended. Vincent spent the last three years of his life preaching in France and died at Vannes, Brittany, on April 5. He was canonized in 1455.

VINCENT DE PAUL (c. 1580–1660). Son of Jean de Paul and Bertrande de Moras, French peasants, the third of six children, he was born at Pouy, France, on April 24. He was educated at the college at Dax and the University of Toulouse and was ordained in 1600. While returning from Marseilles, where he had gone to claim a legacy left him, in 1605, he was captured by pirates and sold as a slave in Algeria. He eventually escaped in 1607 to Avignon, went to Rome for further studies, was sent back to France on a secret mission to Henry IV in 1609, and became chaplain to Queen Margaret of Valois in Paris. In the following years his work with the poor and his preaching attracted widespread attention. His meeting with St. Francis de Sales in Paris in 1618 made him a disciple of Francis, who had him appointed ecclesiastical superior of the Visitation. He was tutor in the household of Count de Gondi, general of the galleys, 1613–25, and began to minister to the galley slaves. In 1619 he became chaplain of galley slaves waiting to be shipped abroad, and in 1625 he founded the Congregation of the Mission (known as the Vicentians and Lazarists), devoted to missionary work among the peasants, and it soon spread all over France. He also began establishing parish confraternities to aid the poor, and in 1633, with Louise de Marillac, founded the Sisters of Charity. He established hospitals and orphanages, ransomed Christian slaves in northern Africa, helped better priest formation by founding new seminaries, sent his priests abroad to preach missions, organized far-flung relief among the victims of the wars of the Fronde, and wrote widely on spiritual topics. The friend of royalty and the nobility, his whole life was devoted to the alleviation of human suffering and misery. During his lifetime he vigorously opposed Jansenism and was active in securing its condemnation. He died in Paris on September 27, was canonized by Pope Clement XII in 1737, and was declared patron of all charitable groups by Pope Leo XIII in 1885.

VITALIAN (d. 672). Born at Segni, Campania, he was elected Pope to succeed Pope Eugene I and was consecrated on July 30, 657. During his pontificate the conflict between English and Irish bishops over the date of Easter was resolved, and relations with the Church in England were strengthened when he sent SS. Adrian and Theodore of Tarsus there. However, the monothelite heresy in the East continued throughout his reign. He died on January 27.

VITALIS (d. c. 165). *See* Felicity.

VITALIS (d. c. 303). *See* Honoratus.

VITALIS (d. c. 304). *See* Agricola.

VITUS (d. c. 300). Unreliable legend has Vitus, the only son of a senator in Sicily, become a Christian when he was twelve. When his conversions and miracles became widely known to the administrator of Sicily, Valerian, he had Vitus brought before him to shake his faith. He was unsuccessful, but Vitus with his tutor, Modestus, and servant, Crescentia, fled to Lucania and then to Rome, where he freed Emperor Diocletian's son of an evil spirit. When Vitus would not sacrifice to the gods his cure was attributed to sorcery. He, Modestus, and Crescentia were subjected to various tortures from which they emerged unscathed, and were freed when during a storm temples were destroyed and an angel guided them back to Lucania, where they eventually died. So much for the legend. What is fact is that their cult goes back centuries and that they were Christians who were martyred in Lucania. A great devotion to Vitus developed in Germany when his relics were translated to Saxony in 836. He is one of the Fourteen Holy Helpers and is the patron of epileptics, those afflicted with St. Vitus dance (named after him), dancers, and actors, and is a protector against storms. June 15.

VIVIANA. *See* Bibian.

VLADIMIR I OF KIEV (c. 975–1015). Illegitimate son of Grand Duke Sviastoslav and his mistress, Malushka, he was given Novgorod to rule by Sviastoslav. Forced to flee to Scandinavia in 977 when his half brother Yaropolk defeated and killed another half brother, Oleg, and captured Novgorod, he returned with an army, recaptured Novgorod, and captured and killed Yaropolk at Rodno in 980. Notorious for his cruelty and barbarity, he was now ruler of Russia. He conquered Kherson in the Crimea in 988, and impressed by the progress of Christianity, married Anne, daughter of Emperor Basil II, and became a Christian in about 989. His conversion marked the beginning of Christianity in Russia. He reformed his life (putting aside his five former wives), built schools and churches, destroyed idols, brought Greek missionaries to his realms, exchanged ambassadors with Rome, and aided St. Boniface in his mission to the Pechangs. In his later years he was troubled by rebellions led by the sons of his earlier marriages, but two of his sons by Anne, Romanus (Boris) and David (Gleb), became saints. He died at Beresyx, Russia, while leading an expedition against his rebellious son Yaroslav in Novgorod. Vladimir reportedly gave all his possessions to his friends and to the poor on his deathbed. He is the patron of Russian Catholics. July 15.

W

WALDEBERT (d. c. 665). A Frankish nobleman also known as Gaubert, he renounced his military career to become a monk at Luxeuil, France, and donated his wealth to the monastery. He was allowed to live as a hermit, but on the death of Abbot St. Eustace he was elected third abbot of Luxeuil in 628. He ruled for almost forty years, replaced the rule of St. Columban with that of St. Benedict, secured freedom from episcopal control for the monastery from Pope John IV, and helped build Luxeuil into one of the outstanding monasteries in France. He helped St. Salaberga found her convent at Laon and established many monasteries and convents from Luxeuil. May 2.

WALL, JOHN (1620–79). Born in Lancashire, England, he was sent to study at Douai in his youth, went to the Roman college in 1641, and was ordained there in 1645. He served as a missionary for a time, joined the Franciscans at St. Bonaventure Friary at Douai in 1651, taking the name Joachim of St. Anne, and in 1656 was sent on the English mission. Using the aliases Francis Johnson, Dormer, and Webb, he worked among the Catholics in Worcestershire for twenty-two years until December 1678, when he was arrested near Bromsgrove and charged with being a Catholic priest. After five months' imprisonment, he was exonerated of any complicity in the Titus Oates plot, but when he refused to renounce his Catholic faith, he was hanged, drawn, and quartered for his priesthood at Redhill, Worcester, on August 22. He was canonized as one of the Forty Martyrs of England and Wales by Pope Paul VI in 1970. June 12.

WALPOLE, HENRY (1558–95). Born in Docking, Norfolk, England, he studied at Cambridge and law at Gray's

Inn, was reconciled to the Church when he witnessed the execution of Edmund Campion, gave up the study of law, and went to Rheims. He became a Jesuit in Rome in 1584 and was ordained there in 1588. He was sent on the missions to Lorraine, and in 1589, while acting as chaplain to the Spanish troops in the Netherlands, he was imprisoned by the Calvinists at Flushing for a year. When released he taught at Seville and Valladolid, engaged in missionary activities in Flanders, and in 1593 was sent on the English mission. Arrested almost on landing, he was imprisoned for a year in York and then the Tower, subjected to numerous tortures, and then convicted of treason for his priesthood at York. He was hanged, drawn, and quartered at York with Bl. Alexander Rawlins on April 7. He was canonized as one of the Forty Martyrs of England and Wales in 1970 by Pope Paul VI.

WANDREGISILUS. *See* Wandrille.

WANDRILLE (d. 668). Also known as Wandregisilus, he was born near Verdun, France, of a noble family related to Bl. Pepin of Landen. When Wandrille came of age he was sent to the court of King Dagobert of Austrasia and married in deference to his parents' wishes but against his. In about 628, by mutual agreement, they separated, she to become a nun and he to become a Benedictine monk at Montfaucon Abbey in Champagne under St. Baudry. A few months later he left to become a hermit at St. Ursanne in the Jura. He remained there for about five years, then went to Bobbio and later to Romain-Moûtier Abbey on the Isère, where he spent the next decade and where he was ordained. He left to be founding abbot of Fontenelle Abbey in Normandy, which he developed into a missionary and spiritual center, founded a school there, and became involved in helping and preaching to the inhabitants of the surrounding area. July 22.

WARD, MARGARET (d. 1588). Born in Congleton, Cheshire, England, she was a gentlewoman in service in London when arrested with her Irish servant, John Roche, alias Neale, for helping Fr. Richard Watson escape from Bridewell Prison. They were offered their freedom if they would ask the Queen's pardon but refused and were both hanged, drawn, and quartered at Tyburn on August 30 when they refused to divulge the priest's hiding place. She was canonized as one of the Forty Martyrs of England and Wales in 1970 by Pope Paul VI.

WATSON, JOHN. *See* Ogilvie, John.

WEBSTER, AUGUSTINE (d. 1535). After studying at Cambridge, he became a Carthusian and then in 1531 prior of the charterhouse at Axholme, England. While on a visit to the London charterhouse, he accompanied St. John Houghton and St. Robert Lawrence to a meeting with Thomas Cromwell, who had the three arrested and imprisoned in the Tower. When they refused to accept the Act of Supremacy of Henry VIII, they were dragged through the streets of London, savagely treated, and executed at Tyburn on May 4. They were canonized as three of the Forty Martyrs of England and Wales by Pope Paul VI in 1970.

WELLS, SWITHUN (1536–91). Born at Bambridge, Hampshire, England, he lived the life of a country gentleman, founded a boys' school in Wiltshire, and was converted to Catholicism in 1583. He moved to London with his wife in 1585 and the following year was charged with being involved in the Babington plot but released. He went to Rome on a mission for the Earl of Southampton but then returned to England to work in the English Catholic underground. Though he was not at home when St. Edmund Gennings was saying Mass in his home, Swithun was later arrested, convicted of harboring a Catholic priest, and hanged near his own home at Gray's Inn Fields, London, on December 10 with Fr. Gennings. Swithun was canonized as one of the Forty Martyrs of England and Wales by Pope Paul VI in 1970. His name is sometimes spelled Swithin.

WENCESLAUS (c. 903–29). Also known by the Czech form of his name, Vaclav, he was born near Prague and was the son of Duke Wratislaw (or Ratislav) of Bohemia and Drahomira, daughter of the chieftain of a northern Slav tribe called the Veletians. He was raised a Christian and educated by his grandmother, St. Ludmila, and her chaplain, Paul. When Ratislav was killed fighting the Magyars in about 920,

Drahomira, with the anti-Christian faction who murdered
Ludmila, took over the government and instituted anti-Christian policies. She was deposed by an uprising, and Wenceslaus
became ruler in about 922. He encouraged Christianity, ruled
strictly but justly, and ruthlessly suppressed disorders and oppression by the nobles. In about 926 his acknowledgment of
King Henry the Fowler as his overlord, in keeping with his
policy of friendship with Germany, as well as his religion,
caused opposition among some of the nobles. When his wife
bore him a son, his brother Boleslaus, no longer successor to
the throne, joined the noble Czech dissenters. Boleslaus invited Wenceslaus to a religious festival at Boleslayvia, Bohemia, and while Wenceslaus was on his way to Mass on September 20 Boleslaus attacked him, and while they were
struggling, a group of Boleslaus' followers joined the fray and
Wenceslaus was murdered. He was at once venerated as a
martyr and is the patron of Bohemia. September 28.

WHITE, EUSTACE (d. 1591). Born at Louth, Lincolnshire, England, he was converted to Catholicism and went
to Rheims to study for the priesthood. He continued his studies at Rome and was ordained there in 1588. He was sent on
the English mission later the same year, worked in western
England, and was arrested three years later at Blandford.
Tortured for six weeks, he was convicted of being a priest,
then hanged, drawn, and quartered at Tyburn. He was canonized as one of the Forty Martyrs of England and Wales in
1970 by Pope Paul VI. December 10.

WILFRID (634–709). Perhaps born in Ripon, Northumbria, son of a thegn, he joined the court of King Oswy of
Northumbria when thirteen, and became a favorite of Queen
Eanfleda, who sent him to Lindisfarane for his education.
After a stay at Canterbury, where he studied under St. Honorius and became an adherent of Roman liturgical practices,
he left England for Rome in 654 in the company of St. Benet
Biscop. After a year at Lyons, where he refused an offer to
marry Bishop St. Annemund's niece, he arrived in Rome,
where he studied under Boniface, Pope St. Martin's secretary.
He then spent three years at Lyons, where he received the
tonsure, Roman instead of Celtic style, but escaped with his
life when Annemund was murdered, because he was a for-

eigner. He returned to England in about 660, was asked by King Alcfrid of Deira to instruct his people in the Roman rite, and when the monks at Ripon decided to return to their native Melrose rather than abandon their Celtic customs, Wilfrid was appointed abbot. He introduced the Roman usage and the rule of St. Benedict to the monastery, was ordained, and was a leader in replacing Celtic practices with Roman in northern England. When the Roman party triumphed at the council held in 664 at St. Hilda Monastery at St. Streaneschalch (Whitby) largely through his efforts, Alcfrid named him bishop of York, but since Wilfrid regarded the northern bishops who had refused to accept the decrees of Whitby as schismatic, he went to France to be ordained. Delayed until 666 in his return, he found that St. Chad had been appointed bishop of York by King Oswy of Northumbria; rather than contest the election of Chad, Wilfrid returned to Ripon. But in 669 the new archbishop of Canterbury, St. Theodore, ruled Chad's election irregular, removed him, and restored Wilfrid as bishop of York. He made a visitation of his entire diocese, restored his cathedral, and instituted Roman liturgical chant in all his churches. At the insistence of Oswy's successor, King Egfrid, whom Wilfrid had alienated by encouraging Egfrid's wife, Etheldreda, in refusing the King's marital rights and becoming a nun at Coldingham, Theodore in 678 as metropolitan, and encouraged by Egfrid, divided the see of York into four dioceses despite the objections of Wilfrid, who was deposed. He went to Rome to appeal the decision in 677, the first known appeal of an English bishop to Rome. He spent the winter in Friesland making converts, and when he arrived in Rome in 679 he was restored to his see by Pope St. Agatho. When Wilfrid returned to England in 680, Egfrid refused to accept the Pope's order and imprisoned Wilfrid for nine months. When freed he went to Sussex, converted practically all the inhabitants, and built a monastery at Selsey on land donated by King Ethelwalh. On the death of Egfrid in battle in 685, Wilfrid met with Theodore, who asked his forgiveness for his actions in deposing him and ordaining the bishops of the newly formed dioceses in Wilfrid's cathedral at York. In 686 Egfrid's successor, King Aldfrid, at Theodore's request, recalled Wilfrid and restored him to Ripon, but in 691 Aldfrid quarreled with Wilfrid and exiled him. Wilfrid went to Mercia, where at the request of King Ethelred he administered the vacant see of Litchfield. In 703 Theodore's successor, St. Berhtwald, at Aldfrid's instigation, called a synod that ordered Wilfrid to resign his bishopric and retire to Ripon. When he still refused to accept the division of his see, he again went to Rome, where Pope John VI upheld him and ordered Berhtwald to call a synod clearing Wilfrid. Only when Aldfrid died in 705, repenting of his actions against Wilfrid, was a compromise worked out by which Wilfrid was appointed bishop of Hexham while St. John of Beverly remained as bishop of York. Wilfrid died at St. Andrew's Monastery in Oundle, Northamptonshire, while on a visitation of monasteries he had founded in Mercia. October 12.

WILLEHAD (d. 789). Born in Northumbria, England, he was probably educated at York, became a friend of Alcuin, and was ordained. In about 766 he went to Friesland, preached at Dokkum and Overyssel, barely escaped with his life from Humsterland, where pagans wanted to put him to death, and then returned to the area around Utrecht, again escaping with his life when he and his comrades were attacked by a group of pagans whose pagan temples they had destroyed. In 780 Charlemagne sent him as a missionary to the Saxons, and in 782, when the Saxons rose against their Frankish conquerors, he fled to Friesland. After reporting on his missionary work to Pope Adrian I and spending two years at Echternach, where he reassembled his force of missionaries, he returned to the Weser-Elbe area, where Charlemagne had just finished ruthlessly suppressing the Saxons' revolt. In 787 Willehad was ordained bishop of the Saxons, with his see at newly founded Bremen. He founded numerous churches in his see, built a cathedral at Bremen, and died there on November 8.

WILLIAM ARNAUD (d. 1242). A Dominican, he and two other Dominicans were commissioned by Pope Gregory IX to combat Albigensianism in Languedoc. He and his companions were driven out of Toulouse, Narbonne, and several other towns by the Albigensians. After preaching a mission at Avignonet William and his group were given shelter for the night at the castle of Count Raymond VII of Toulouse there; all were murdered by a military patrol let into the castle. There were eleven martyrs in addition to William, among them two Franciscans: Stephen of Narbonne and Raymond. Miracles were soon reported at their graves, but their cult was not approved until 1856, as the Martyrs of Toulouse. May 29.

WILLIAM OF DIJON (962–1031). Also known as William of St. Benignus, he was the son of Count Robert of Volpiano. William was born in the family castle on San Giuglio Island in Lake Orta near Nocera while his father was defending the island against the attacking Emperor Otto, who became his sponsor when he captured the island. William was entered in the Benedictine abbey of Locadio when he was seven, became a monk there, and joined St. Majolus at Cluny in 987. He reorganized St. Sernin Abbey on the Rhone, was ordained in 990, named abbot of St. Benignus at Dijon, and built the abbey into a great center of spirituality, education, and culture, and the mother monastery of some forty monasteries in Burgundy, Lorraine, Normandy, and northern Italy. He traveled widely, spreading the Cluniac reform. He died at Fécamp Monastery in Normandy, which he had rebuilt, on January 1.

WILLIAM OF MONTE VERGINE. *See* William of Vercelli.

WILLIAM OF NORWICH (d. 1144). A twelve-year-old boy, an apprentice to a tanner in Norwich, England, he allegedly was kidnapped by two Jews and ritually tortured and crucified. There is no doubt that the boy was murdered, and the murderers may have been Jews, but there is no evidence that the boy was killed by Jews out of hatred of Christians, as was alleged at the time. (See also Simon of Trent.) March 24.

WILLIAM OF VERCELLI (1085–1142). Born at Vercelli, Italy, of noble parents, he was orphaned when an infant, was raised by relatives, and when fourteen went on a pilgrimage to Compostela. He was at Melfi in 1106 and then spent two years as a hermit on Monte Solicoli. After abandoning a pilgrimage to Jerusalem when attacked by robbers, he became a hermit on Monte Virgiliano (Vergine) and attracted so many disciples that he organized them into a community that by 1119 became known as the Hermits of Monte Vergine, and he built a monastery. When objections arose against the strictness of his rule, he and his friend St. John of Matera with five followers founded a community on Monte Laceno in Apulia. When fire destroyed their hermitages, William moved to Monte Cognato in the Basilicata. Again he left and founded monasteries at Conza, Guglietto, and Salerno opposite the palace where he became adviser to King Roger I of Naples. William died at Guglietto on June 25.

WILLIAM OF YORK (d. 1154). Also known as William of Thwayt, William Fitzherbert was the son of Count Herbert, treasurer to Henry I, and Emma, half sister of King Stephen. William became treasurer of the church of York when quite young and in 1140 was elected archbishop of York. Archdeacon Walter of York and several Cistercian abbots and Augustinian priors challenged his election, charging William with simony and unchastity, but eventually it was upheld by Rome and he was consecrated. When, through his procrastination, his pallium was sent back to Rome, he was obliged to go to Rome, where the new Pope, Eugene III, a Cistercian, suspended him. When his followers attacked Fountains Monastery in England where a colleague of Eugene's, Henry Murdac, was abbot, the Pope deposed William in 1147 and named Murdac archbishop of York. William retired to Winchester, led a penitential and austere life, and in 1153, when Eugene and Murdac died, was restored to his see by Pope Anastasius IV. William returned to York in 1154 but died there a month later on June 8, poisoned, some claim, by Osbert, the new archdeacon of York. William was canonized in 1227 by Pope Honorius III.

WILLIBALD (c. 700–86). Son of West Saxon Richard, often called the King, and brother of SS. Winebald and Walburga, he was born in Essex on October 21 and was educated at Waltham Monastery. He went on a pilgrimage to Rome with his father and brother in 721. When his father died on the way at Lucca, Italy, he continued on to Jerusalem in 724 after a time in Rome. He was captured and imprisoned by the Saracens as a spy at Emessa, but was released and continued his pilgrimage, visiting many monasteries, *lauras,* and hermitages. After spending some time in Constantinople, he returned to Italy in about 730 and spent the next ten years at Monte Cassino. While in Rome in 740 he met Pope St.

Gregory III, who sent him as a missionary to aid his cousin, St. Boniface. Willibald went to Thuringia, where Boniface ordained him in 741, and was most successful in missionary work around Eichstätt in Franconia; Boniface then consecrated him bishop of Eichstätt. With his brother Winebald, he founded a double monastery at Heidenheim, appointing Winebald abbot and his sister Walburga abbess; Heidenheim became the center of Willibald's missionary activities. He ruled for some forty-five years before his death at Eichstätt on July 7. Willibald was the first known Englishman to visit the Holy Land, and the account of his wanderings, *Hodoeporicon,* is the earliest known English travel book. He was canonized in 938 by Pope Leo VII. June 6.

WILLIBRORD (c. 658–739). Born in Northumbria, England, he was sent to Ripon Monastery under St. Wilfrid when seven and spent twelve years studying at Irish monasteries with SS. Egbert and Wigbert, beginning about 678. Willibrord was ordained when thirty and in 690 he and eleven English monks went to Friesland as missionaries. He received permission from Pope Sergius I in Rome to preach in Friesland, and encouraged by Pepin of Herstal, who had just wrested Lower Friesland from the pagan leader Radbod, Willibrord began to preach there. In 695 he was ordained bishop of the Frisians by Sergius, who gave him the name Clement, and established his see at Utrecht. He founded Echternach Monastery in Luxemburg, extended his missionary activities to Upper Friesland and Denmark, and escaped with his life when attacked by a pagan priest at Walcheren for destroying an idol. Willibrord baptized Charles Martel's son Pepin the Short in 714 and then saw most of his missionary work in Friesland undone when in 715 Radbod regained the territory Pepin of Herstal had conquered earlier. Radbod's death in 719 set off a new wave of missionary activity, aided by St. Boniface, who worked in Friesland for three years before proceeding to Germany. Willibrord was so successful that he became known as "the Apostle of the Frisians." He died while on a retreat at Echternach, Luxemburg, on November 7.

WINIFRED (d. c. 650). According to legend, she was the daughter of a wealthy resident of Tegeingl, Flintshire, Wales, and the sister of St. Beuno. She was most impressed by

Beuno, was supposedly beheaded on June 22 by one Caradog when she refused to submit to him, had her head restored by Beuno, and sometime later became a nun of the convent of a double monastery at Gwytherin in Denbigshire. She succeeded an Abbess Tenoi as abbess and died there fifteen years after her miraculous restoration to life. A spring supposedly springing up where Winifred's head fell is called Holywell or St. Winifred's Well and became a great pilgrimage center where many cures have been reported over the centuries. She is also known as Gwenfrewi. November 3.

WIRO (d. c. 739). A native of Northumbria (although perhaps of Ireland or Scotland), he was ordained, and with another priest, Plechelm (a fellow Northumbrian) and a deacon, Otger, went to Rome, where Wiro and Plechelm were consecrated regionary bishops. After doing missionary work in Northumbria, they went to the Netherlands, evangelized the inhabitants of the lower Meuse Valley, and built a church and cells at Odilienberg on land granted them by Pepin of Herstal. May 8.

WISDOM. *See* Charity.

WOLFGANG (c. 930–94). Of a Swabian family, he was educated at Reichinan Abbey and Wurzburg, joined his friend Henry in a school at Wurzburg, and went with him as a teacher in the cathedral school of Trier when Henry became archbishop there in 956. After Henry died in 964, Wolfgang became a Benedictine at Einsiedeln, was appointed director of the monastery school there, and was ordained in 971. He then went as a missionary to the Magyars in Pannonia and in 972 was appointed bishop of Regensburg by Emperor Otto II. Wolfgang at once instituted a reform of the clergy and monasteries in his see, preached widely and vigorously, and was known for his concern for the poor. He attempted to leave his see and live as a hermit at one time but was brought back. He accompanied the Emperor on a trip to France, surrendered part of his see in Bohemia for a new diocese, and was tutor of Duke Henry of Bavaria's son, who later became Emperor. Wolfgang died at Puppingen near Linz, Austria, and was canonized in 1052 by Pope Leo IX. October 31.

WOOLO. *See* Gundleus.

WOUTERS, ANDREW (d. 1572). *See* Pieck, Nicholas.

WULFSTAN (c. 1008–95). Also known as Wulstan, he was born at Long Itchington, Warwickshire, England, educated at Evesham and Peterborough monasteries, and then joined the staff of Bishop Brihtheah of Worcester, who ordained him. He entered the monastery at Worcester, became treasurer of the church and prior of the monastery, and in 1062 was named bishop of Worcester. A man of great simplicity, he was accused of being unfit to be a bishop at a synod at Westminster but eventually convinced all of his ability. He was the only bishop allowed to retain his see after William's conquest of England, and he tried to alleviate public unrest over the oppression of the Normans. He ended the practice in Bristol of kidnaping men into slavery, rebuilt his cathedral in about 1086, and ruled his see for more than thirty-two years. He was canonized in 1203. January 19.

WULSTAN. *See* Wulfstan.

X Y Z

XAINCTONGE, VEN. ANNE DE (1567–1621). Born at Dijon, France, on November 21, she was the daughter of a councilor and planned to found an order of nuns devoted to educating women. Despite strong opposition, she, Claudine de Boisset, and several other women founded the Sisters of St. Ursula of the Blessed Virgin at Dole, Franche-Comte, then ruled by the Spanish, in 1606, and the Order spread throughout France and Switzerland. She died at Dole on June 8, and was declared Venerable in 1900.

XANTIPPA (1st century). Though described in the Roman Martyrology, with Polyxena, as "disciples of the apostles" who died in Spain, nothing else is known of them. September 23.

XAVIER. *See* Francis Xavier.

XYSTUS. The spelling used for Sixtus in old documents.

YAXLEY, VEN. RICHARD (d. 1589). A native of Boston, Lincolnshire, England, he went to Rheims in 1582 to study for the priesthood and was ordained there three years later. He was sent on the English mission in 1586 and was captured at Oxford with Fr. George Nichols, Thomas Belson, and Humphrey Prichard. All four were tortured and then executed for their faith at Oxford on October 19.

YEMPO, BL. SIMON (d. 1623). A Japanese, he became a Buddhist monk but was converted to Christianity and became a lay catechist for the Jesuit missions. He was burned to death at Yeddo for his faith, and was beatified in 1867. December 4.

YOUVILLE, BL. MARGUERITE MARIE D' (1701-71). Born at Varennes, Quebec, on October 15, Marie Marguerite Dufrost de La Jemmerais studied under the Ursulines, married François D'Youville in 1722, and became a widow in 1730. She worked to support herself and her three children, devoted much of her time to the Confraternity of the Holy Family in charitable activities, and in 1737, with three companions, founded the Grey Nuns when they took their initial vows; a formal declaration took place in 1745. Two years later she was appointed directress of the General Hospital in Montreal, which was taken over by the Grey Nuns, and had the rule of the Grey Nuns, with Marguerite as superior, confirmed by Bishop Pontbriand of Quebec in 1755. She died in Montreal on December 23, and since her death the Grey Nuns have established schools, hospitals, and orphanages throughout Canada, the United States, Africa, and South America, and are especially known for their work among the Eskimos. She was beatified by Pope John XXIII in 1959.

ZACCARIA, ANTONY MARY (1502-39). Born in Cremona, Italy, he studied medicine at the University of Padua, practiced in his hometown after his graduation in 1524, but attracted by the religious life, began to study for the priesthood. He was ordained in 1528, moved to Metan, and in 1530, with Ven. Bartholomew Ferrari and Ven. James Morigia, founded the Clerks Regular of St. Paul (the Barnabites, named after St. Barnabas Church, which became their headquarters in Milan), dedicated to reviving spirituality in the Church. The congregation was approved by Pope Clement VI in 1533, with Antony its first provost general. He resigned in 1536, helped spread the community, and worked ceaselessly to reform the Church. He died at Cremona on July 15 when thirty-seven, and was canonized by Pope Leo XIII in 1897. July 5.

ZACHARY (1st century). A priest in the Temple in Jerusalem whose wife, Elizabeth, Mary's cousin, was beyond childbearing age, he was told by an angel in a vision that they would have a son and should name him John. When he doubted this he was struck dumb. Elizabeth was visited by Mary, at which time Mary spoke the hymn of praise now known as the Magnificat, and after John's birth Zachary's speech was restored. This is all that is known of Elizabeth and Zachary, and is found in Luke 1. An unverifiable tradition has Zachary murdered in the Temple when he refused to tell Herod where his son John was to be found. November 5.

ZACHARY (d. 752). Born at San Severino, Italy, of a Greek family, he became a deacon of the Church in Rome, was known for his learning and holiness, was elected Pope, succeeding St. Gregory III, and was consecrated on December 10, 741. He visited Liutprand, when Liutprand, King of the Lombards, was about to invade Roman lands at Terni, and made a treaty with him by which the King returned all prisoners of war and returned the Roman territory he had conquered; he then dissuaded Liutprand from attacking Ravenna. Zachary encouraged St. Boniface in his German mission and made him archbishop of Mainz, recognized Pepin the Short as King of the Franks in 751, and had Boniface, as papal legate, anoint Pepin King at Soissons. Zachary was known for his aid to the poor, provided shelter for nuns driven from Constantinople by the iconoclasts, ransomed slaves from the Venetians, and translated Gregory's *Dialogues*. He died in March. March 15.

ZENO (d. 250). *See* Ammon.

ZENO (d. c. 300). One of the more than ten thousand Christians condemned to work on the baths of Diocletian in Rome by that Emperor, Zeno was evidently their spokesman. All of them were slaughtered by Diocletian's orders. July 9.

ZEPHYRINUS (d. c. 217). A Roman of humble origins, he was elected Pope to succeed Pope St. Victor I in 199 and named Callistus his deacon and adviser. Though Zephyrinus excommunicated the two Theodati for their Monarchianism, he was denounced by Hippolytus, a severe critic who later became a schismatic, for failure to act decisively and authoritatively in repressing prevalent heresies and as a tool of Callistus in his *Philosophoumena*. Zephyrinus died on December 20, and though listed in the Roman Martyrology as a martyr, it is most doubtful that he suffered martyrdom. August 26.

ZITA (1218–78). Born at Monte Sagrati, Italy, she became a servant in the household of a wool dealer at nearby Lucca when she was twelve, was initially disliked by the other servants for her diligence, holiness, and austerities, but in time won them over. She was credited with many miracles, worked to alleviate the misery of the poor and criminals in prison, and died on April 27 after having been a servant in the Fatinelli family for some forty-eight years. She was canonized in 1696 and is the patroness of servants.

ZOSIMUS (d. c. 107). *See* Rufus.

ZOSIMUS (d. 418). Son of Abram, a presbyter, and a Greek, he was consecrated Pope on March 18, 417, succeeding Pope Innocent I. His pontificate was marred by two disputes that were not settled until after his death. The first involved his recognition of Bishop Patrocus as metropolitan of his area, which neighboring bishops opposed. In the other case he seems to have acted too hastily in accepting the appeal of Apiarius of Sicca from a condemnation by African bishops who objected to Zosimus' interference. He also formally and strongly denounced Pelagianism in *Epistola Tractoria* after being misled for a time by Pelagius and his supporter Caelestius. Zosimus died on December 27. December 26.

ZOSIMUS (5th century). *See* Mary of Egypt.

THE SAINTS

AS PATRONS AND INTERCESSORS
AS PATRONS OF COUNTRIES AND PLACES
THEIR SYMBOLS IN ART

THE SAINTS AS PATRONS AND INTERCESSORS

Abandoned children:
Jerome Emiliani
Accountants: Matthew
Actors: Genesius; Vitus
Advertising: Bernardine of
Siena
Air travelers: Joseph of
Cupertino
Altar boys: John Berchmans
Anesthetists: René Goupil
Angina sufferers: Swithbert
Archers: Sebastian
Architects: Barbara;
Thomas the Apostle
Art: Catherine of Bologna
Artists: Luke
Astronomers: Dominic
Athletes: Sebastian
Authors: Francis de Sales
Aviators: Joseph of Cuper-
tino; Thérèse of
Lisieux
Bakers: Elizabeth of Hun-
gary; Honoratus;
Nicholas
Bankers: Matthew
Barbers: Cosmas and
Damian; Louis
Barren women: Anthony of
Padua; Felicity
Beggars: Alexus; Giles
Blacksmiths: Dunstan

Blind: Odilia; Raphael
Blood banks: Januarius
Boatmen: Julian the Hos-
pitaler
Bookkeepers: Matthew
Boy Scouts: George
Brewers: Augustine; Luke;
Nicholas of Myra
Bricklayers: Stephen
Brides: Nicholas of Myra
Brushmakers: Anthony
Builders: Barbara; Vincent
Ferrer
Butchers: Adrian; Antony;
Luke
Cab drivers: Fiacre
Cabinetmakers: Anne
Cancer victims: Peregrine
Laziosi
Candlemakers: Bernard of
Clairvaux
Canonists: Raymond of
Peñafort
Carpenters: Joseph
Catechists: Charles Bor-
romeo; Robert Bellar-
mine
Catholic Action: Francis of
Assisi
Catholic press: Francis de
Sales

Charitable societies: Vincent de Paul
Childbirth: Gerard Majella
Children: Nicholas of Myra
Choirboys: Dominic Savio
* Church, the: Joseph
Clerics: Gabriel
Comedians: Vitus
Communications personnel: Bernardino of Siena
Confessors: Alphonsus Liguori; John Nepomucen
Convulsive children: Scholastica
Cooks: Lawrence; Martha
Coppersmiths: Maurus
Cripples: Giles
Dancers: Vitus
Deaf: Francis de Sales
Dentists: Apollonia
Desperate situations: Gregory of Neocaesarea; Jude; Rita of Cascia
Dietitians (in hospitals): Martha
Domestic animals: Antony
Druggists: Cosmas and Damian; James the Less
Dyers: Maurice and Lydia Purpuraria
* Dying: Barbara; Joseph
Dysentery sufferers: Matrona
Earthquakes: Emygdius
Ecologists: Francis of Assisi
Editors: John Bosco
Emigrants: Frances Xavier Cabrini
Engineers: Ferdinand III
Epileptics: Dymphna; Vitus
Eucharistic Congresses and Societies: Paschal Baylon
Expectant mothers: Gerard Majella
Eye trouble: Hervé; Lucy
Falsely accused: Raymond Nonnatus
Farmers: George; Isidore the Farmer
* Fathers of families: Joseph
Firemen: Florian
Fire prevention: Barbara; Catherine of Siena
First communicants: Tarcisius
Fishermen: Andrew
Florists: Thérèse of Lisieux
Foresters: John Gualbert
Founders: Barbara
Foundlings: Holy Innocents
Funeral directors: Joseph of Arimathea; Dismas
Gardeners: Adelard; Dorothy; Fiacre; Gertrude of Nivelles; Phocas; Tryphon
Girls: Agnes
Glassworkers: Luke
Goldsmiths: Dunstan; Anastasius
Gravediggers: Antony
Greetings: Valentine
Grocers: Michael
Hairdressers: Martin de Porres
Hatters: James the Less
Haymakers: Gervase and Protase
Headache sufferers: Aedh Mac Bricc; Teresa of Avila
Heart patients: John of God

Hospital administrators:
  Basil the Great; Frances
  Xavier Cabrini
Hospitals: Camillus de
  Lellis; John of God;
  Jude Thaddeus
Hotelkeepers: Amand; Julian
  the Hospitaler
Housewives: Anne
Hunters: Eustachius; Hubert
Infantrymen: Maurice
Interracial justice: Martin
  de Porres
Invalids: Roch
Jewelers: Dunstan; Eligius
Journalists: Francis de Sales
Jurists: John Capistran
Laborers: Isidore; James;
  John Bosco
Lawyers: Genesius; Ivo;
  Thomas More
Learning: Ambrose
Leatherworkers: Crispin and
  Crispinian
Librarians: Jerome
Lighthousekeepers: Dunstan
Locksmiths: Dunstan
Lost articles: Anthony of
  Padua
Lovers: Raphael; Valentine
Maidens: Catherine
Mariners: Michael; Nicholas
  of Tolentine
Married women: Monica
Medical technicians: Albert
  the Great
Mentally ill: Dymphna
Merchants: Francis of
  Assisi; Nicholas of
  Myra
Messengers: Gabriel
Metalworkers: Eligius

Midwives: Raymond Non-
  natus
Millers: Arnulph; Victor
Missions: Francis Xavier;
  Thérèse of Lisieux;
  Leonard of Port Mau-
  rice (parish)
Mothers: Monica
Motorists: Christopher;
  Frances of Rome
Mountaineers: Bernard of
  Montjoux
Musicians: Cecilia; Dunstan;
  Gregory the Great
Notaries: Luke; Mark
Nurses: Agatha; Camillus
  de Lellis; John of God;
  Raphael
Nursing service: Catherine
  of Siena; Elizabeth of
  Hungary
Orators: John Chrysostom
Orphans: Jerome Emiliani
Painters: Luke
Paratroopers: Michael
Parish priests: John Baptist
  Vianney
Pawnbrokers: Nicholas of
  Myra
Pharmacists: Cosmas and
  Damian; James the
  Greater
Pharmacists (in hospitals):
  Gemma Galgani
Philosophers: Catherine of
  Alexandria; Justin
Physicians: Cosmas and
  Damian; Luke; Panta-
  leon; Raphael
Pilgrims: James
Pilots: Joseph of Cupertino
Plague: Roch
Plasterers: Bartholomew

Poets: Cecilia; David

Poisoning: Benedict

Policemen: Michael

Poor: Anthony of Padua; Lawrence

Porters: Christopher

Postal workers: Gabriel

Preachers: Catherine of Alexandria; John Chrysostom

Pregnant women: Gerard Majella; Margaret; Raymond Nonnatus

Printers: Augustine; Genesius; John of God

Prisoners: Barbara; Dismas

Prisoners of war: Leonard

Prisons: Joseph Cafasso

Public relations: Bernardino of Siena

Public relations (for hospitals): Paul

Radiologists: Michael

Radio workers: Gabriel

Retreats: Ignatius Loyola

Rheumatism: James the Greater

Saddlers: Crispin and Crispinian

Sailors: Brendan; Christopher; Cuthbert; Elmo; Erasmus; Eulalia; Peter Gonzales; Nicholas

Scholars: Brigid

Scientists: Albert the Great

Sculptors: Claude

Secretaries: Genesius

Seminarians: Charles Borromeo

Servants: Martha; Zita

Shepherds: Drogo

Shoemakers: Crispin and Crispinian

Sick: John of God; Camillus de Lellis; Michael

Silversmiths: Andronicus; Dunstan

Singers: Cecilia; Gregory

Skaters: Lidwina

Skiers: Bernard

Skin diseases: Marculf

Social justice: Joseph

Social workers: Louise de Marillac

Soldiers: Adrian; George; Ignatius Loyola; Joan of Arc; Martin of Tours; Sebastian

Speleologists: Benedict

Stenographers: Cassian of Tangiers; Genesius

Stonecutters: Clement

Stonemasons: Barbara; Reinold; Stephen

Students: Catherine of Alexandria; Thomas Aquinas

Surgeons: Cosmas and Damian; Luke

Swordsmiths: Maurice

Tailors: Homobonus

Tanners: Crispin and Crispinian; Simon

Tax collectors: Matthew

Teachers: Gregory the Great; John Baptist de la Salle

Telecommunications workers: Gabriel

Television: Clare of Assisi

Television workers: Gabriel

Tertiaries: Elizabeth of Hungary; Louis

Theologians: Alphonsus Liguori; Augustine

Throat: Blaise

Travelers: Anthony of Padua; Christopher; Gertrude of Nivelles; Julian the Hospitaler; Nicholas of Myra; Raphael; Three Magi (Caspar, Melchior, and Balthasar)

Universities: Bl. Contardo Ferrini

Vocations: Alphonsus

Watchmen: Peter of Alcantara

Weavers: Anastasia; Anastasius; Paul the Hermit

Widows: Paula

Winegrowers: Morand; Vincent

Wine merchants: Amand

Women in difficult labor: John Thwing

Women in labor: Anne

✳ Workingmen: (Joseph)

Writers: Francis de Sales; Lucy

Yachtsmen: Adjutor

Youth: Aloysius Gonzaga; Gabriel Possenti; John Berchmans

AS PATRONS OF COUNTRIES AND PLACES

Alsace: Odilia

Americas: Rose of Lima

Aragon: George

Argentina: Our Lady of Lujan

Armenia: Gregory the Illuminator; Bartholomew

Asia Minor: John the Evangelist

Australia: Our Lady Help of Christians

Bavaria: Kilian

✳ Belgium: (Joseph)

Bohemia: Ludmilla; Wenceslaus

Brazil: Immaculate Conception; Peter of Alcántara

Canada: Anne; Joseph

Chile: Our Lady of Mount Carmel; James

China: Joseph

Colombia: Louis Bertrand; Peter Claver

Corsica: Immaculate Conception; Alexander Sauli; Julia of Corsica

Crete: Titus

Cyprus: Barnabas

Czechoslovakia: John Nepomucen; Procopius; Wenceslaus

Denmark: Ansgar; Canute

Dominican Republic: Our Lady of High Grace; Dominic

East Indies: Francis Xavier; Thomas

Ecuador: Sacred Heart

England: Augustine of
  Canterbury; George;
  Gregory the Great
Ethiopia: Frumentius
Europe: Benedict
Finland: Henry of Uppsala
France: Our Lady of the
  Assumption; Denis;
  Joan of Arc; Martin of
  Tours; Remigius;
  Thérèse of Lisieux
Genoa: George
Georgia (in U.S.S.R.): Nino
Germany: Boniface;
  Michael; Peter Canisius
Greece: Andrew; Nicholas
  of Myra
Holland: Plechelm; Willi-
  brord
Hungary: Bl. Astericus
  (Anastasius); Gerard;
  Stephen
India: Our Lady of the
  Assumption
Ireland: Brigid; Columba;
  Patrick
Italy: Bernardino of Siena;
  Catherine of Siena;
  Francis of Assisi
Japan: Francis Xavier;
  Peter Baptist
Lithuania: Casimir; Bl.
  Cunegund; John
  Cantius
Madrid: Isidore the Farmer
Mexico: Our Lady of
  Guadalupe
Monaco: Devota
Moravia: Cyril and Metho-
  dius
Moscow: Boris

New Zealand: Our Lady
  Help of Christians
North America: Isaac
  Jogues and companions
Norway: Olaf
Paraguay: Our Lady of the
  Assumption
Paris: Genevieve
Persia: Maruthas
Peru: Joseph
Philippines: Sacred Heart of
  Mary
Poland: Casimir; Cunegund;
  Hyacinth; John Cantius;
  Our Lady of Czesto-
  chowa; Stanislaus
Portugal: Francis Borgia;
  George; Immaculate
  Conception; Vincent
Prussia: Adalbert; Bruno of
  Querfurt
Romania: Nicetas
Rome: Philip Neri
Russia: Andrew; Nicholas
  of Myra; Thérèse of
  Lisieux; Vladimir I of
  Kiev
Ruthenia: Bruno
Saxony: Willehad
Scandinavia: Ansgar
Scotland: Andrew; Co-
  lumba; Margaret of
  Scotland; Palladius
Sicily: Nicholas of Myra
Silesia: Hedwig
Slovakia: Our Lady of the
  Assumption
South Africa: Our Lady of
  the Assumption
South America: Rose of
  Lima

Spain: Euphrasius; Felix; James; John of Avila; Teresa of Avila

Sri Lanka (Ceylon): Lawrence

Sweden: Ansgar; Bridget; Eric; Gall; Sigfrid

Switzerland: Gall

United States: Immaculate Conception

Uruguay: Our Lady of Lujan

Wales: David

West Indies: Gertrude

THEIR SYMBOLS IN ART

Agatha: tongs, veil

Agnes: lamb

Ambrose: bees, dove, ox, pen

Andrew: transverse cross

Angela Merici: ladder, cloak

Anne: door

Anthony of Padua: Christ Child, book, bread, lily

Antony: bell, hog

Augustine: child, dove, pen, shell

Barbara: cannon, chalice, palm, tower

Barnabas: ax, lance, stones

Bartholomew: flayed skin, knife

Benedict: bell, broken cup, bush, crozier, raven

Bernard: bees, pen

Bernardino of Siena: chrism, sun inscribed with IHS, tablet

Blaise: iron comb, wax candle

Bonaventure: cardinal's hat, ciborium

Boniface: ax, book, fox, fountain, oak, raven, scourge, sword

Bridget of Sweden: book, pilgrim's staff

Brigid: candle, cross, flame over her head

Bruno: chalice

Catherine of Alexandria: lamb, sword, wheel

Catherine di Ricci: crown, crucifix, ring

Catherine of Siena: cross, lily, ring, stigmata

Cecilia: organ

Charles Borromeo: Eucharist

Christopher: Christ Child, giant, torrent, tree

Clare: monstrance

Colette: birds, lamb

Cosmas and Damian: box of ointment, vial

Cyril of Alexandria: pen

Cyril of Jerusalem: book, purse

Dominic: rosary, star

Dorothy: flowers, fruit

Edmund: arrow, sword

Elizabeth of Hungary: bread, flowers, pitcher

Francis of Assisi: birds, deer, fish, skull, stigmata, wolf

Francis Xavier: bell, crucifix, ship

Genevieve: bread, candle, herd, keys

George: dragon

Gertrude: crown, lily, taper

Gervaise and Protase: club, scourge, sword

Giles: crozier, hermitage, hind

Gregory the Great: crozier, dove, tiara

Helena: cross

Hilary: child, pen, stick

Ignatius Loyola: book, chasuble, Eucharist

Isidore: bees, pen

James the Greater: key, pilgrim's staff, shell, sword

James the Less: club, halberd, square rule

Jerome: lion

John the Baptist: head on platter, lamb, skin of animal

John Berchmans: cross, rosary

John Chrysostom: bees, dove, pen

John Climacus: ladder

John the Evangelist: armor, chalice, eagle, kettle

John of God: alms, crown of thorns, heart

Josaphat: chalice, crown, winged deacon

Joseph: carpenter's square, Infant Jesus, lily, plane, rod

Jude: club, square rule

Justin Martyr: ax, sword

Lawrence: book of gospels, cross, gridiron

Leander: pen

Liborius: pebbles, peacock

Longinus: lance

Louis: crown of thorns, nails

Lucy: cord, eyes

Luke: book, bush, ox, palette

Margaret: dragon

Mark: book, lion

Martha: dragon, holy water sprinkler

Mary Magdalen: alabaster box of ointment

Matilda: alms, purse

Matthew: lance, purse, winged man

Matthias: lance

Maurus: crutch, scales, spade

Michael: banner, dragon, scales, sword

Monica: girdle, tears

Nicholas: anchor, boat, boy in boat, three purses

Patrick: baptismal font, cross, harp, serpent, shamrock

Paul: book, scroll, sword

Peter: boat, cock, keys

Philip: column

Philip Neri: altar, chasuble, vial

Rita: crucifix, rose, thorn

Roch: angel, bread, dog

Rose of Lima: anchor, city, crown of thorns

Sebastian: arrows, crown

Sergius and Bacchus: military uniform, palm
Simon: cross, saw
Simon Stock: scapular
Teresa of Avila: arrow, book, heart
Thérèse of Lisieux: roses entwining a crucifix
Thomas: ax, lance

Thomas Aquinas: chalice, dove, monstrance, ox
Ursula: arrow, clock, ship
Vincent: boat, gridiron
Vincent de Paul: children
Vincent Ferrer: captives, cardinal's hat, pulpit, trumpet